PLANETWISE

PLANETWISE

by Barbara Hill

W. Foulsham & Co. Ltd.
London • New York • Toronto • Cape Town • Sydney

W. Foulsham & Company Limited
Yeovil Road, Slough, Berkshire, SLI 4JH

ISBN 0-572-01475-9

Printed in Great Britain by Cox and Wyman Ltd,
Reading, Berkshire.

CONTENTS

INTRODUCTION

Nearly everybody knows his or her Sun sign, i.e. the zodiacal sign the Sun was present in at birth. Innumerable astrological books and magazines are to be found giving personality descriptions that are supposed to apply to each of these so-called birth signs. In many instances these all too familiar readings will seem more or less correct — but not in every case. This is not surprising, because the signs in which the *planets* happen to be in at birth have not been taken into consideration.

To give an example, someone born with the Sun sign Aries may show few of the typical Arien characteristics and may exhibit many Virgoan traits instead. Obviously the sign of Virgo plays an important part in this personality but popular books written for the non-astrologer have not been able to get round this problem.

The construction of a horoscope and its interpretation by an expert will give the full personality picture, but the drawing up of natal charts takes more time than many of us have and anyway is beyond a lot of people's ability. But the astrological system presented in this book will make it possible for *anyone* to ascertain a person's principal characteristics and his or her main interests and likely choice of career from planetary indications.

All you need to do is to look up your birthdate (or that of a friend or relative) in the tables, look at the numbers given for that date and then turn to the back of the book to find the readings corresponding to them.

It is not necessary for you to know the exact time and place of birth when using the system presented in this book; you would, of course, need to know these details to draw up a horoscope. Such factors as the Ascendant, Midheaven and planetary aspects are not used in my system. I do not regard them as totally irrelevant, but I find my system actually works very well without having to consider them. It has been the result of many years' scrutiny of the planets, the signs that they govern and their combined influence over people's pattern of behaviour.

In my system I take only the *dominant features* of each birth date and thereby reveal the *predominant characteristics* of the person born on that day. I have covered every birthday from 1st January 1930 to 31st December 1999. How I determine which features are dominant is described below in the outline of my method.

It must be stated that this system, by ignoring the time of birth, does throw up some discrepancies occasionally, in particular with the sign given for the Moon. This is because the Moon moves rather quickly and changes sign about every two days. Mercury is the next fastest planetary body and changes sign about every 20 days. A planet's daily motion through the zodiac is slower the further it is from the Sun. Pluto, the outermost planet, takes a number of years to go through a sign. Now it may happen that on your particular birthday the Moon (or, less likely, a planet) moved into a new sign on that day. In other words, during the course of that day the Moon was passing through two different signs. Only one of those signs can be allocated to the day in question and there is an even chance as to which one is correct for you, but do not worry. The overall picture given by the Sun and planets will not be affected to a very great extent.

Table 1 – The signs of the Zodiac

Sign	Element	Planetary ruler	Sign	Element	Planetary ruler
Aries ♈	Fire	Mars	Libra ♎	Air	Venus
Taurus ♉	Earth	Venus	Scorpio ♏	Water	Mars/Pluto
Gemini ♊	Air	Mercury	Sagittarius ♐	Fire	Jupiter
Cancer ♋	Water	Moon	Capricorn ♑	Earth	Saturn
Leo ♌	Fire	Sun	Aquarius ♒	Air	Uranus
Virgo ♍	Earth	Mercury	Pisces ♓	Water	Neptune

Theory and Method

If you do not particularly want to delve into how and why my system works, it is not essential to read the rest of this section (in fact it is somewhat complicated). For those who are interested, however, I will explain what I mean by *dominance* with regard to the planets (these are listed in Table 2) and to the signs.

Table 2 – The planets and what they represent

Sun ☉	Fundamental characteristics and abilities; the ego (*Those with a dominant Sun will have very strong characters*)	Jupiter ♃	The pattern of lifestyle (*Those with a dominant Jupiter will have strong beliefs, order or organisation in their lives*)
Moon ☽	Personality, outward behaviour (*Those with a dominant Moon will have a strong personality*)	Saturn ♄	Oppressive influences (*Those with a dominant Saturn are subject to frustration and restriction*)
Mercury ☿	The mind (*Those with a dominant Mercury will have a powerful thought process and be intelligent, eloquent communicators*)	Uranus ♅	Unpredictable, unconventional elements (*Those with a dominant Uranus will be eccentric, some to a greater degree than others*)
Venus ♀	Social attitudes and interests (*Those with a dominant Venus will give priority to relationships and possessions*)	Neptune ♆	Escapist qualities (*Those with a dominant Neptune will wish to have everything their own way*)
Mars ♂	Abilities to do with work, career (*Those with a dominant Mars will be active, enthusiastic and hard-working*)	Pluto ♇	Compulsions (*Those with a dominant Pluto are prone to obsessions*)

Table 3 is an example of the kind of worksheet that I use when working on my system (this one is for April 1940). It illustrates how I decide whether a planet is dominant or not.

If there are three of more planets in a sign, the planet ruling that sign is dominant. For example, taking 1st April, we see in the column D/S (which stands for *dominant sign*) that there are four planets in Taurus ♉ ; Venus ♀ rules Taurus, so Venus, in column D/P, is the *dominant planet.* Similarly, if there happened to be three or more planets in Leo ♌ , the Sun would be dominant; the Moon with three or more in Cancer ♋ and so on. *The dominant planet has power over whichever sign it happens to be in, i.e. its effects in that sign are strengthened.*

This is how I proceed, each step being in order of precedence. First of all I look for a dominant Sun or dominant Moon (see readings 145–156 and 157–168 respectively at the back of this book). Should both be dominant, I amalgamate them. If there is no dominant Sun or Moon, I make a Sun-Moon combination (1–144).

If Sun, Moon and Mercury are all in one sign, e.g. Gemini, I give a Sun/Gemini reading.

Next I look to see whether there is a *dominant element*, e.g. five or more planets in Earth signs, or similarly in Air, Fire or Water signs (see Table 1). If, for example, there is a dominant Water sign, then I look to see if one or more of the outermost planets is in a Water sign and if there is it is noted — Saturn (217–228), Uranus (229–240), Neptune (241–252) and Pluto (253–257).

There may be no cluster of five or more planets in either Leo or Cancer to make the Sun or Moon dominant, but nevertheless the Sun (or the Moon) will be dominant if it is in a dominant Water sign. Similarly, the Sun (or Moon) will be dominant if it happens to be in a dominant sign of any of the other elements.

If both Sun and Moon are in signs of the same element, e.g. Earth, then these signs are amalgamated to become a Sun/Moon reading.

If the signs of the dominant element contain seven or more planets, that is noted (276–279).

An absence of planets in any of the Earth, Air, Fire or Water signs respectively is also noted (260–263).

Dominant Earth/Water or Fire/Air combinations are noted (258 and 259).

Five or more planets in a sign is noted as a separate reading (264–275).

When there is no dominant Sun or Moon, no dominant Earth, Air, Fire or Water element and no dominant sign, I give a Sun/Moon reading, make Mercury dominant and make Jupiter dominant. I then take the Venus reading for social activities and the Mars reading for careers, according to their positions in the ephemeris (normally I treat Venus and Mars in an unconventional way, but this instance is an exception).

Venus and Mars

Anyone familiar with the use of an ephemeris is likely to be puzzled by the zodiacal signs ascribed to Venus (181–192) and Mars (193–204) in this book. You will notice that the sections concerned relate to careers and social activities.

Take a look at the worksheet for April 1940 (Table 3). From 5th April downwards, Venus (♀) and Mars (♂) are in the sign of Gemini

			♊	♉	♏												
	♌	♋	♍	♎	♈	♐	♑	♒	♓	♏						D/S	D/P
Apr 1940	☉	☽	☿	♀	♂	♃	♄	♅	♆	♇	E	W	F	A			
1	♈	♒	♓	♉	♉	♈	♉	♉	♍	♌	5	1	3	1	E	4/♉	♀
2	♈	♒	♓	♉	♊	♈	♉	♉	♍	♌	4	1	3	2		3/♉	♀
3																	
4		♓									4	2	3	1		3/♉	♀
5	♈	♓	♓	♊	♊	♈	♉	♉	♍	♌	3	2	3	2			
6		♈									3	1	4	2		3/♈	♂
7																	
8																	
9		♉									4	1	3	2		3/♉	♀
10																	
11		♊									3	1	3	3		3/♊	☿
12																	
13																	
14		♋									3	2	3	2			

		1	5																														
		1	6			♌										3	1	4	2														
		1	7		♈	♌	♈	♊	♊	♈	♉	♉	♍	♌		3	0	5	2		F					3/	♈						♂
		1	8			♍										4	0	4	2							3/	♈						♂
		1	9																														
		2	0		♉	♎										4	0	3	3							3/	♉						♀
		2	1																														
		2	2			♏										4	1	3	2							3/	♉						♀
		2	3																														
		2	4			♐										4	0	4	2							3/	♉						♀
		2	5																														
		2	6			♑										5	0	3	2		E					3/	♉						♀
		2	7																														
		2	8																														
		2	9			♒										4	0	3	3							3/	♉						♀
		3	0																														

(♊). You will see the columns headed D/S (*dominant sign*) and D/P (*dominant planet*). I have found that people with a dominant sign tend towards careers and social activities related to that sign rather than to the signs Venus and Mars happen to be in. Taking the birthdate 5th April 1940, this has no dominant sign or dominant planet; therefore careers and social activities will be found under ♀ ♊ (183a) and ♂ ♊ (195a). We see that 6th April, however, has a dominant sign — Aries (♈) — and a dominant planet — Mars (♂). This means that Mars dominates Gemini (♊), the reading for which will be found under No. 195. The dominant sign Aries is substituted for the Gemini signs under Venus and Mars, thus making the social activities and careers read ♀♈ (181a) and ♂ ♈(193a) and *not* ♀ ♊ or ♂ ♊.

When Venus and/or Mars is involved, it is possible to have two sets of dominant signs, such as four planets in Cancer and three in Gemini; these are amalgamated and given a reading under Gemini/Cancer (see Nos. 280a–345a). There can occasionally be cases where there are three sets of dominant signs; these, too, are amalgamated (see Nos. 346a–370a).

Using the system

In the pages which follow this introduction, for every day of the calendar for each year from 1930 to 1999 there is a series of numbers which correspond to the numbered information at the back of this book. Each piece of information has a note explaining the astrological influence behind it. Where later observations have caused me to make additions, these have a small letter 'i' after them, e.g. li; 64i; 180i.

Details appertaining to health are restricted to dates which have a dominant Sun reading (145–156) or dates which have five or more planets in one sign (264–275).

There are some dates, such as 24th February 1948 and 14th July 1949, which give seemingly conflicting, if not completely contradictory, readings. Such cases usually occur with strongly creative people who are deemed 'unusual' and who need truly to come to grips with an ideal objective in life to express fully their considerable talents.

My system is an effective means of discovering people's dominant characteristics concerning ability, intelligence, emotional volatility and physical vitality. People born on the same day in the same year share innate characteristics, but their individual upbringing, education and experiences determine whether those characteristics are developed or suppressed or whether they are used constructively or destructively.

Suggested uses for this book are as follows —

* For employers to check on characteristics, temperament, work qualities and the sort of career to which a person is ideally suited.

* For teachers to find avenues of interest for disruptive pupils.

* For parents to gain insight into the potential qualities, interests and careers of their children.

* For individuals to discover latent talents, and to compare characteristics and interests with those of another person.

The author invites any queries to be sent to her c/o W. Foulsham & Co. Ltd., Yeovil Road, Slough, SLI 4JH. *Please send a s.a.e.*.

DATES 1930–1999 WITH REFERENCE NUMBERS

1st January

1930 118,226,273,276,190a,202a
1931 111,226,190a,202a
1932 115,226,190a,202a
1933 120,177,186a,198a
1934 112,229,191a,203a
1935 116,227,190a,202a
1936 109,178,213,188a,203a
1937 114,228,259,262,190a,202a
1938 118,228,259,262,190a,202a
1939 110,177,216,263,188a,200a
1940 115,177,205,191a,204a
1941 154,189,273,182a,194a
1942 154,218,230,246,261,273,191a, 193a
1943 116,219,190a,202a
1944 120,178,183a,195a
1945 113,177,220,191a,201a
1946 117,177,211,190a,196a
1947 109,177,212,188a,202a
1948 114,178,213,261,191a,198a
1949 154,214,222,260,273,190a,202a
1950 159,247,191a,199a
1951 115,190,223,333a
1952 120,188,187a,199a
1953 112,177,206,191a,204a
1954 116,224,255,337a
1955 109,224,232,188a,240a
1956 154,255,273,320a
1957 118,225,190a,202a
1958 110,211,189a,201a
1959 114,256,259,263,190a,194a
1960 119,213,189a,201a
1961 154,226,273,190a,202a
1962 154,226,262,273,276,190a,202a
1963 120,178,188a,197a
1964 154,227,273,190a,202a
1965 154,177,206,259,263,273,327a
1966 109,177,207,191a,203a
1967 114,178,228,328a
1968 118,178,217,328a
1969 111,178,217,191a,200a
1970 154,218,259,262,273,190a,202a
1971 120,200,188a,200a
1972 112,213,189a,201a
1973 165,214,258,261,272,189a,201a
1974 109,178,220,191a,194a
1975 113,220,190a,202a
1976 118,217,190a,202a
1977 110,221,190a,202a
1978 114,177,236,190a,197a
1979 119,177,209,188a,202a
1980 111,177,186a,198a
1981 116,189,187a,199a
1982 120,191,187a,199a
1983 113,213,224,340
1984 165,213,272,189a,201a
1985 110,224,190a,202a
1986 114,215,225,340a
1987 119,225,190a,202a
1988 111,225,190a,202a
1989 154,226,273,190a,202a
1990 154,226,190a,202a
1991 154,226,259,263,273,190a,202a
1992 117,210,227,340a
1993 109,227,190a,202a
1994 154,227,273,190a,202a
1995 118,228,259,263,273,190a,202a
1996 110,228,273,190a,202a
1997 154,214,217,261,273,190a,202a
1998 167,239,258,261,274,191a,203a
1999 112,177,216,190a,199a

2nd January

1930 154,226,273,190a,202a
1931 111,326,190a,202a
1932 115,226,190a,202a
1933 120,177,186a,198a
1934 112,229,191a,203a
1935 117,227,190a,202a
1936 109,178,213,188a,203a
1937 114,230,246,259,262,191a,199a
1938 118,228,259,262,190a,202a
1939 110,177,216,263,188a,200a
1940 115,177,205,191a,204a
1941 154,189,259,263,273,182a,194a
1942 154,218,230,246,273,191a,193a
1943 116,219,190a,202a
1944 109,178,183a,195a
1945 113,177,220,191a,201a
1946 117,177,211,190a,196a
1947 110,177,212,188a,202a
1948 114,178,213,261,191a,198a
1949 154,214,222,260,273,190a,202a
1950 159,232,191a,203a
1951 115,190,223,333a
1952 120,188,187a,199a
1953 113,177,206,191a,204a
1954 117,224,190a,202a
1955 109,224,232,188a,204a
1956 114,200,188a,200a
1957 118,225,190a,202a
1958 110,211,189a,201a
1959 115,177,212,190a,194a
1960 120,,213,233,263,189a,201a
1961 154,226,273,190a,202a
1962 154,226,262,273,276,190a,202a
1963 109,179,216,188a,197a
1964 154,227,273,190a,202a
1965 118,177,259,263,186a,198a
1966 110,177,207,191a,203a
1967 114,178,228,328a
1968 154,178,273,186a,198a
1969 111,178,217,191a,200a
1970 154,218,259,262,273,190a,202a
1971 120,200,188a,200a
1972 161,213,258,261,189a,201a

1973 165,214,258,261,272,189a,201a
1974 109,178,220,191a,194a
1975 114,220,190a,202a
1976 118,217,190a,202a
1977 111,221,190a,202a
1978 115,177,236,190a,197a
1979 120,177,257,188a,202a
1980 154,178,273,186a,198a
1981 116,189,187a,199a
1982 109,191,187a,199a
1983 113,213,189a,201a
1984 118,213,224,340a
1985 110,224,190a,202a
1986 114,215,225,340a
1987 119,225,190a,202a
1988 111,225,190a,202a
1989 154,226,259,263,273,190a,202a
1990 154,226,190a,202a
1991 154,226,259,263,273,190a,202a
1992 117,210,227,340a
1993 109,227,190a,202a
1994 114,227,262,273,276,190a,202a
1995 118,228,259,263,273,190a,202a
1996 111,228,190a,202a
1997 154,214,217,261,273,190a,202a
1998 120,239,191a,203a
1999 112,177,216,190a,199a

3rd January

1930 154,226,273,190a,202a
1931 111,226,190a,202a
1932 116,226,190a,202a
1933 109,177,186a,198a
1934 113,229,191a,203a
1935 117,227,190a,202a
1936 110,230,246,188a,203a
1937 115,179,214,262,191a,199a
1938 154,228,259,262,273,190a,202a
1939 111,177,216,188a,200a
1940 115,177,205,191a,204a
1941 154,189,259,263,273,182a,194a
1942 154,218,230,246,273,191a,193a
1943 116,179,208,190a,201a
1944 109,178,261,183a,195a
1945 114,177,220,191a,202a
1946 118,220,190a,202a
1947 110,221,190a,202a
1948 115,178,213,261,191a,198a
1949 154,214,222,260,273,190a,202a
1950 112,232,247,191a,203a
1951 116,223,190a,202a
1952 157,189,187a,199a
1953 113,177,206,191a,204a
1954 117,224,190a,202a
1955 110,224,232,188a,204a
1956 114,200,188a,200a
1957 119,178,248,189a,193a
1958 111,211,189a,201a
1959 115,177,212,177,190a,194a
1960 120,213,233,263,189a,201a
1961 154,226,273,190a,202a
1962 154,226,273,276,190a,202a
1963 109,179,216,188a,197a
1964 114,178,227,328a
1965 118,177,259,263,186a,198a
1966 110,177,207,191a,203a
1967 154,228,273,190a,202a
1968 154,178,273,186a,198a
1969 112,178,217,191a,200a
1970 154,218,256,259,262,273,337a
1971 109,200,188a,200a
1972 161,213,258,261,189a,201a
1973 118,214,219,261,340a
1974 110,178,220,249,191a,194a
1975 114,220,190a,202a
1976 119,179,236,189a,195a
1977 111,221,190a,202a
1978 115,177,236,190a,197a
1979 120,177,257,188a,202a
1980 154,178,273,186a,198a
1981 117,189,211,332a
1982 109,191,187a,199a
1983 114,213,189a,201a
1984 118,213,224,340a
1985 110,224,190a,202a
1986 115,215,225,340a
1987 119,225,190a,202a
1988 112,225,190a,202a
1989 154,226,273,190a,202a
1990 154,226,190a,202a
1991 154,226,259,263,273,190a,202a
1992 117,210,227,340a
1993 110,227,259,262,190a,202a
1994 114,227,262,273,276,190a,202a
1995 154,228,273,190a,202a
1996 154,228,273,190a,202a
1997 115,217,261,190a,202a
1998 120,239,191a,203a
1999 113,177,216,190a,199a

4th January

1930 154,226,273,190a,202a
1931 160,226,263,315a
1932 116,226,190a,202a
1933 109,177,186a,198a
1934 113,229,191a,203a
1935 118,227,190a,202a
1936 110,230,246,188a,203a
1937 115,179,214,262,191a,199a
1938 154,228,259,262,273,190a,202a
1939 111,177,216,188a,200a
1940 116,193,217,255,181a,193a
1941 154,189,259,263,273,182a,194a
1942 154,218,230,246,261,273,191a, 193a
1943 117,179,208,190a,201a

1944 110,178,261,183a,195a
1945 114,277,220,191a,201a
1946 118,220,190a,202a
1947 111,221,190a,202a
1948 115,178,213,261,191a,198a
1949 154,222,273,190a,202a
1950 112,232,247,191a,203a
1951 116,223,190a,202a
1952 157,189,187a,199a
1953 114,177,206,191a,204a
1954 118,224,190a,202a
1955 110,224,232,188a,204a
1956 115,200,188a,200a
1957 199,178,248,189a,193a
1958 111,211,189a,201a
1959 116,194,263,188a,200a
1960 120,213,263,189a,201a
1961 154,226,273,190a,202a
1962 226,273,190a,202a
1963 110,179,216,188a,197a
1964 114,178,227,328a
1965 154,177,273,186a,198a
1966 111,177,207,191a,203a
1967 154,228,273,190a,202a
1968 154,178,273,186a,198a
1969 112,178,217,191a,200a
1970 154,218,256,259,262,273,337a
1971 109,200,188a,200a
1972 161,213,258,261,189a,201a
1973 118,214,219,261,340a
1974 110,178,220,249,191a,194a
1975 115,220,190a,202a
1976 119,179,236,189a,195a
1977 112,221,190a,202a
1978 116,177,207,190a,197a
1979 109,177,257,188a,202a
1980 154,178,273,186a,198a
1981 117,189,211,332a
1982 110,191,187a,199a
1983 114,213,189a,201a
1984 118,213,224,340a
1985 111,224,190a,202a
1986 115,215,225,340a
1987 168,225,250,259,263,344a
1988 122,225,190a,202a
1989 154,226,273,190a,202a
1990 154,226,190a,202a
1991 114,226,263,276,190a,202a
1992 118,210,227,340a
1993 110,227,259,262,190a,202a
1994 154,227,259,262,273,190a,202a
1995 154,228,273,190a,202a
1996 154,228,273,190a,202a
1997 116,217,190a,202a
1998 120,239,191a,203a
1999 113,177,216,190a,199a

5th January

1930 154,226,273,190a,202a
1931 160,226,263,315a
1932 117,226,190a,202a
1933 110,177,186a,198a
1934 114,229,191a,203a
1935 118,227,190a,202a
1936 111,178,213,189a,203a
1937 115,179,214,262,191a,199a
1938 154,228,259,262,273,190a,202a
1939 112,177,216,263,189a,200a
1940 116,193,217,255,181a,193a
1941 154,189,206,261,263,273,182a, 194a
1942 154,218,230,246,261,273,191a, 193a
1943 117,179,208,190a,201a
1944 110,178,261,183a,195a
1945 115,177,220,191a,201a
1946 119,177,211,190a,196a
1947 111,221,190a,202a
1948 116,178,213,191a,198a
1949 120,222,190a,202a
1950 112,232,247,191a,203a
1951 117,223,190a,202a
1952 157,189,187a,199a
1953 114,177,206,192a,204a
1954 118,224,190a,202a
1955 111,224,232,188a,204a
1956 115,200,188a,200a
1957 120,178,211,189a,193a
1958 112,211,189a,201a
1959 116,194,263,188a,200a
1960 157,213,226,263,340a
1961 154,226,259,263,273,190a,202a
1962 118,227,262,273,276,190a,202a
1963 110,179,216,188a,197a
1964 154,227,273,190a,202a
1965 154,177,273,186a,198a
1966 111,177,207,191a,203a
1967 154,228,273,190a,202a
1968 154,178,273,186a,198a
1969 113,179,211,192a,200a
1970 154,218,273,190a,202a
1971 110,200,188a,200a
1972 114,213,261,189a,201a
1973 118,214,219,261,340a
1974 159,235,257,191a,194a
1975 115,220,190a,202a
1976 120,179,205,189a,195a
1977 112,221,190a,202a
1978 116,177,207,190a,197a
1979 109,177,257,188a,202a
1980 154,178,273,186a,198a
1981 118,189,223,333a
1982 110,191,187a,199a
1983 115,213,189a,201a
1984 119,213,189a,201a
1985 111,224,190a,202a

1986 116,200,215,225,350a
1987 168,225,250,259,263,344a
1988 113,225,190a,202a
1989 154,226,273,190a,202a
1990 154,226,190a,202a
1991 114,226,190a,202a
1992 118,210,227,340a
1993 111,227,262,190a,202a
1994 154,227,259,262,273,190a,202a
1995 154,228,259,263,273,190a,202a
1996 154,228,273,190a,202a
1997 116,217,190a,202a
1998 109,239,261,191a,203a
1999 113,239,191a,203a

6th January

1930 154,226,273,190a,202a
1931 113,226,263,190a,202a
1932 117,226,190a,202a
1933 110,177,186a,198a
1934 114,229,191a,203a
1935 119,227,190a,202a
1936 111,179,213,189a,203a
1937 164,228,254,259,262,192a,200a
1938 154,228,246,259,262,273,344a
1939 112,177,216,263,189a,200a
1940 165,193,258,261,181a,193a
1941 154,189,206,261,263,273,182a, 194a
1942 154,218,230,246,261,273,191a, 193a
1943 118,179,219,190a,202a
1944 159,178,258,261,183a,195a
1945 115,177,210,192a,202a
1946 119,177,211,190a,196a
1947 112,221,190a,202a
1948 116,178,213,191a,198a
1949 109,179,214,261,189a,203a
1950 113,215,232,191a,203a
1951 117,223,190a,202a
1952 110,189,187a,199a
1953 114,117,206,192a,204a
1954 119,224,190a,202a
1955 111,178,208,189a,204a
1956 116,200,188a,200a
1957 120,178,211,189a,193a
1958 112,211,189a,201a
1959 154,226,259,263,273,190a,202a
1960 157,213,226,263,340a
1961 114,226,259,263,190a,202a
1962 118,227,262,273,276,190a,202a
1963 111,179,216,188a,197a
1964 154,227,273,190a,202a
1965 154,177,273,186a,198a
1966 112,177,207,191a,203a
1967 154,228,273,190a,202a
1968 154,178,273,186a,198a
1969 113,179,211,192a,200a
1970 154,218,273,190a,202a
1971 110,200,188a,200a
1972 114,213,261,189a,201a
1973 119,214,219,261,340a
1974 159,235,257,191a,194a
1975 116,178,216,191a,201a
1976 120,179,205,189a,195a
1977 112,221,190a,202a
1978 165,207,189a,201a
1979 109,177,257,188a,202a
1980 114,178,186a,198a
1981 118,189,223,333a
1982 110,191,223,257,187a,199a
1983 163,213,237,341a
1984 119,213,189a,201a
1985 160,224,259,263,190a,202a
1986 116,200,225,337a
1987 109,225,263,190a,202a
1988 113,225,190a,202a
1989 154,226,272,190a,202a
1990 110,226,190a,202a
1991 154,226,273,190a,202a
1992 119,210,227,340a
1993 111,227,262,190a,202a
1994 154,227,259,262,273,190a,202a
1995 154,228,259,263,273,190a,202a
1996 154,228,273,190a,202a
1997 117,214,217,261,340a
1998 109,239,261,191a,203a
1999 114,239,191a,203a

7th January

1930 154,226,273,190a,202a
1931 113,226,263,190a,202a
1932 118,226,190a,202a
1933 110,177,186a,198a,
1934 114,229,191a,203a
1935 119,227,190a,202a
1936 112,179,213,189a,203a
1937 164,228,254,259,262,192a,200a
1938 154,228,273,190a,202a
1939 161,217,255,263,189a,200a
1940 165,193,258,261,181a,193a
1941 110,189,206,263,276,182a,194a
1942 114,218,230,246,261,191a,193a
1943 167,219,231,247,190a,201a
1944 159,178,258,261,183a,195a
1945 115,177,210,192a,202a
1946 120,177,211,190a,196a
1947 112,221,190a,202a
1948 117,178,213,261,191a,198a
1949 109,179,214,261,189a,203a
1950 113,215,232,191a,203a
1951 118,223,190a,202a
1952 110,189,187a,199a
1953 115,192,187a,199a
1954 119,224,190a,202a
1955 160,208,224,232,184a,196a

1956 116,200,188a,200a
1957 120,178,211,189a,193a
1958 161,211,189a,201a
1959 117,177,212,191a,194a
1960 110,213,226,259,263,340a
1961 114,226,259,263,190a,202a
1962 118,227,262,273,276,190a,202a
1963 111,179,216,189a,197a
1964 154,227,273,190a,202a
1965 154,177,259,263,273,186a,198a
1966 112,177,207,191a,203a
1967 117,178,209,191a,199a
1968 154,178,273,186a,198a
1969 113,179,211,192a,200a
1970 118,218,190a,202a
1971 110,212,189a,201a
1972 163,191,213,258,261,332a
1973 119,214,219,261,340a
1974 112,178,249,191a,194a
1975 116,178,216,191a,201a
1976 120,179,205,189a,195a
1977 113,221,190a,202a
1978 165,207,189a,201a
1979 110,209,189a,201a
1980 114,178,186a,198a
1981 167,189,187a,199a
1982 159,191,187a,199a
1983 116,213,237,341a
1984 120,213,189a,201a
1985 160,224,259,263,190a,202a
1986 117,215,225,340a
1987 109,216,225,263,340a
1988 113,225,190a,202a
1989 118,226,273,190a,202a
1990 110,226,190a,202a
1991 154,226,273,190a,202a
1992 119,210,227,340a
1993 112,227,262,190a,202a
1994 154,227,259,262,273,190a,202a
1995 109,228,190a,202a
1996 154,228,273,190a,202a
1997 117,214,217,261,340a
1998 110,239,261,191a,203a
1999 114,239,191a,203a

8th January

1930 154,226,273,190a,202a
1931 114,226,259,263,190a,202a
1932 118,226,190a,202a
1933 154,178,273,186a,198a
1934 163,229,191a,203a
1935 120,227,190a,202a
1936 112,179,213,189a,203a
1937 117,179,214,192a,200
1938 109,177,215,192a,204a
1939 161,217,255,263,189a,200a
1940 154,193,217,261,273,288a
1941 110,189,206,261,263,276,182a, 194a
1942 114,218,230,246,261,191a,193a
1943 167,231,191a,203a
1944 159,178,258,261,183a,195a
1945 116,177,210,192a,202a
1946 120,177,211,190a,196a
1947 154,221,273,322a
1948 117,178,213,261,191a,198a
1949 109,179,214,261,189a,203a
1950 114,232,191a,203a
1951 118,223,190a,202a
1952 111,189,187a,199a
1953 115,192,187a,199a
1954 120,224,190a,202a
1955 160,208,224,232,184a,196a
1956 116,200,188a,200a
1957 157,178,225,233,189a,193a
1958 161,211,189a,201a
1959 118,226,190a,202a
1960 110,213,226,259,263,340a
1961 114,226,259,263,190a,202a
1962 119,234,259,262,191a,203a
1963 111,179,216,189a,197a
1964 154,227,273,190a,202a
1965 154,177,259,263,273,186a,198a
1966 113,178,207,191a,203a
1967 117,178,209,191a,199a
1968 154,178,273,186a,198a
1969 114,179,217,192a,200a
1970 118,218,190a,202a
1971 111,212,189a,201a
1972 163,191,213,258,261,332a
1973 120,214,219,340a
1974 112,219,235,257,191a,194a
1975 117,216,189a,201a
1976 157,221,249,189a,195a
1977 113,221,190a,202a
1978 118,221,190a,202a
1979 110,209,189a,201a
1980 114,178,186a,198a
1981 167,189,187a,199a
1982 159,191,187a,199a
1983 116,213,237,341a
1984 120,213,189a,201a
1985 113,224,263,190a,202a
1986 117,215,225,340a
1987 110,216,225,263,340a
1988 114,225,190a,202a
1989 118,226,273,190a,202a
1990 154,226,273,190a,202a
1991 154,226,273,190a,202a
1992 119,210,227,340a
1993 112,227,262,190a,202a
1994 154,227,273,190a,202a
1995 109,228,190a,202a
1996 113,228,238,343a
1997 118,214,217,261,273,190a,202a
1998 110,239,261,191a,203a
1999 163,239,191a,203a

9th January

1930 110,226,190a,202a
1931 114,226,259,263,190a,202a
1932 119,226,190a,202a
1933 154,178,273,186a,198a
1934 163,229,191a,203a
1935 120,178,229,191a,199a
1936 112,179,213,189a,203a
1937 117,179,214,192a,200a
1938 109,177,215,192a,204a
1939 114,177,216,263,189a,200a
1940 154,193,217,261,273,288a
1941 154,189,206,261,273,182a,194a
1942 154,218,230,246,261,273,191a, 193a
1943 167,231,191a,203a
1944 112,178,183a,195a
1945 116,177,210,192a,202a
1946 109,177,211,190a,196a
1947 154,221,273,322a
1948 117,178,213,261,191a,198a
1949 110,179,214,261,189a,203a
1950 114,232,191a,203a
1951 167,232,191a,203a
1952 111,189,187a,199a
1953 116,178,255,192a,204a
1954 120,224,190a,202a
1955 113,178,247,189a,204a
1956 117,200,188a,200a
1957 157,178,225,233,189a,193a
1958 114,211,189a,201a
1959 118,226,190a,202a
1960 110,213,226,259,263,340a
1961 154,226,273,190a,202a
1962 119,234,259,262,191a,203a
1963 112,179,216,189a,197a
1964 154,227,273,190a,202a
1965 154,177,259,263,273,186a,198a
1966 113,178,207,191a,203a
1967 118,228,190a,202a
1968 110,178,259,263,186a,198a
1969 114,179,217,192a,200a
1970 154,218,273,190a,202a
1971 111,212,189a,201a
1972 163,191,213,258,261,332a
1973 120,214,219,340a
1974 113,219,235,257,258,261,191a, 194a
1975 117,216,189a,201a
1976 157,221,249,189a,195a
1977 113,221,190a,202a
1978 118,221,190a,202a
1979 111,222,190a,202a
1980 154,178,273,186a,198a
1981 167,189,187a,199a
1982 112,191,223,257,187a,199a
1983 116,213,237,341a
1984 120,213,189a,201a
1985 113,224,263,190a,202a
1986 118,225,273,190a,202a
1987 110,216,225,263,340a
1988 114,205,225,304a
1989 154,226,273,190a,202a
1990 154,226,273,190a,202a
1991 154,226,273,190a,202a
1992 154,227,273,190a,202a
1993 113,227,190a,202a
1994 154,227,273,190a,202a
1995 109,228,190a,202a
1996 113,228,238,343a
1997 118,214,217,261,273,190a,202a
1998 159,239,258,261,191a,230a
1999 163,239,191a,203a

10th January

1930 110,226,190a,202a
1931 115,226,190a,202a
1932 119,226,190a,202a
1933 154,178,273,186a,198a
1934 116,229,191a,203a
1935 109,178,212,191a,199a
1936 113,179,213,189a,203a
1937 154,228,259,263,273,190a,202a
1938 110,230,246,192a,204a
1939 114,177,216,263,189a,200a
1940 154,193,217,261,273,288a
1941 154,189,206,261,273,182a,184a
1942 115,179,207,261,191a,193a
1943 120,219,231,247,191a,201a
1944 112,178,183a,195a
1945 117,177,210,192a,202a
1946 109,220,190a,202a
1947 114,221,190a,202a
1948 118,221,261,190a,202a
1949 110,179,214,261,189a,203a
1950 163,232,191a,203a
1951 167,232,191a,203a
1952 112,189,187a,199a
1953 116,178,255,192a,204a
1954 120,224,190a,202a
1955 113,178,247,189a,204a
1956 177,200,188a,200a
1957 110,178,148,189a,193a
1958 114,211,189a,201a
1959 119,177,212,191a,194a
1960 111,213,226,340a
1961 154,226,273,190a,202a
1962 120,227,233,343a
1963 112,179,216,189a,197a
1964 154,227,273,190a,202a
1965 154,177,259,263,273,186a,198a
1966 144,178,259,262,186a,198a
1967 118,228,190a,202a
1968 110,178,259,263,186a,198a
1969 115,192,187a,199a
1970 154,218,273,190a,202a
1971 112,212,189a,201a

1972 116,213,189a,201a
1973 120,214,219,340a
1974 113,219,257,258,261,191a,194a
1975 117,216,189a,201a
1976 157,221,249,189a,195a
1977 114,221,190a,202a
1978 119,177,236,190a,197a
1979 111,222,190a,202a
1980 154,178,273,186a,198a
1981 120,189,187a,199a
1982 112,191,223,257,187a,199a
1983 117,213,237,341a
1984 157,213,189a,201a
1985 114,224,263,190a,202a
1986 118,225,273,190a,202a
1987 110,216,225,263,340a
1988 114,205,189a,201a
1989 154,226,273,190a,202a
1990 154,226,273,190a,202a
1991 154,226,273,190a,202a
1992 154,227,273,190a,202a
1993 113,227,190a,202a
1994 118,227,262,273,276,190a,202a
1995 110,228,190a,202a
1996 114,228,238,343a
1997 154,214,217,261,273,190a,202a
1998 111,217,239,261,343a
1999 163,239,191a,203a

11th January

1930 154,226,273,190a,202a
1931 115,226,190a,202a
1932 120,226,190a,202a
1933 154,178,273,186a,198a
1934 116,229,191a,203a
1935 109,178,212,191a,199a
1936 113,179,213,189a,203a
1937 154,228,259,262,263,273,190a, 202a
1938 110,230,246,192a,204a
1939 115,177,216,189a,200a
1940 119,193,261,181a,193a
1941 154,189,206,261,273,182a,194a
1942 116,179,207,191a,193a
1943 120,219,231,247,191a,201a
1944 154,178,261,273,302a
1946 109,220,190a,202a
1947 114,221,190a,202a
1948 118,221,261,190a,202a
1949 159,231,247,258,261,189a,203a
1950 163,232,191a,203a
1951 120,178,255,191a,203a
1952 112,189,187a,199a
1953 116,178,255,192a,204a
1954 109,224,190a,202a
1955 113,179,208,189a,204a
1956 118,200,188a,200a
1957 110,178,248,189a,193a
1958 115,211,189a,201a
1959 154,226,273,190a,202a
1960 111,213,226,340a
1961 154,226,259,263,273,190a,202a
1962 120,227,233,343a
1963 113,179,216,189a,196a
1964 154,227,273,190a,202a
1965 154,177,259,263,273,186a,198a
1966 114,178,259,262,186a,198a
1967 118,228,190a,202a
1968 154,178,273,186a,198a
1969 115,192,187a,199a
1970 154,218,273,190a,202a
1971 112,212,189a,201a
1972 116,213,189a,201a
1973 109,214,219,261,340a
1974 114,219,235,257,258,261,191a, 194a
1975 118,179,216,191a,201a
1976 110,179,236,189a,195a
1977 114,221,190a,202a
1978 119,177,236,190a,197a
1979 112,222,190a,202a
1980 154,178,273,186a,198a
1981 120,190,223,333a
1982 113,191,223,257,187a,199a
1983 117,213,237,341a
1984 157,200,213,263,336a
1985 114,224,263,190a,202a
1986 119,225,190a,202a
1987 111,216,225,340a
1988 115,205,189a,201a
1989 154,226,273,190a,202a
1990 154,226,273,190a,202a
1991 154,226,273,190a,202a
1992 154,227,273,190a,202a
1993 144,227,259,262,190a,202a
1994 118,227,262,273,276,190a,202a
1995 110,228,190a,202a
1996 114,228,238,343a
1997 154,214,217,261,273,190a,202a
1998 112,217,239,343a
1999 116,239,191a,203a

12th January

1930 154,226,273,190a,202a
1931 116,226,263,190a,202a
1932 120,226,190a,202a
1933 154,178,273,186a,198a
1934 117,229,191a,203a
1935 109,178,212,191a,199a
1936 114,179,213,189a,203a
1937 154,228,259,262,263,273,190a, 202a
1938 110,230,246,192a,204a
1939 115,177,216,189a,200a
1940 119,193,261,181a,193a
1941 154,189,263,273,182a,194a

1942 154,191,273,182a,194a
1943 109,219,231,247,191a,201a
1944 154,178,261,273,302a
1945 118,220,190a,202a
1946 110,220,190a,202a
1947 115,221,190a,202a
1948 119,221,261,191a,198a
1949 159,231,247,258,261,189a,203a
1950 116,215,232,191a,203a
1951 120,178,255,191a,203a
1952 112,189,187a,199a
1953 117,178,206,192a,204a
1954 109,224,190a,202a
1955 114,179,208,189a,204a
1956 118,200,188a,200a
1957 111,178,248,189a,193a
1958 115,211,189a,201a
1959 154,226,273,190a,202a
1960 112,213,226,263,340a
1961 154,226,259,263,273,190a,202a
1962 109,227,233,343a
1963 113,179,216,189a,196a
1964 154,227,273,190a,202a
1965 110,177,263,276,186a,198a
1966 115,178,207,262,191a,203a
1967 119,178,209,191a,199a
1968 111,179,186a,198a
1969 116,200,188a,200a
1970 154,218,273,190a,202a
1971 113,212,189a,201a
1972 117,213,261,189a,201a
1973 109,219,261,190a,202a
1974 114,219,235,257,258,261,191a,
194a
1975 118,179,216,191a,201a
1976 110,179,236,189a,195a
1977 115,221,190a,202a
1978 120,177,207,190a,197a
1979 122,222,190a,202a
1980 154,178,273,186a,198a
1981 109,190,223,333a
1982 113,191,223,257,187a,199a
1983 118,213,237,340a
1984 110,200,213,263,336a
1985 115,224,190a,202a
1986 119,225,190a,202a
1987 111,216,225,340a
1988 115,205,189a,201a
1989 154,226,273,190a,202a
1990 154,226,273,190a,202a
1991 154,226,273,190a,202a
1992 154,227,273,190a,202a
1993 114,227,259,262,190a,202a
1994 118,227,262,273,276,190a,202a
1995 111,228,190a,202a
1996 163,228,239,343a
1997 154,217,273,190a,202a
1998 112,217,239,343a,i
1999 116,239,191a,203a

13th January

1930 154,226,273,190a,202a
1931 116,226,263,190a,202a
1932 120,226,190a,202a,
1933 154,178,273,186a,198a
1934 117,229,191a,203a
1935 110,229,191a,203a
1936 114,179,213,189a,203a
1937 154,228,259,262,273,190a,202a
1938 154,228,259,262,273,190a,202a
1939 116,177,216,263,189a,200a
1940 120,193,181a,193a
1941 154,189,263,273,182a,194a
1942 154,191,261,273,182a,194a
1943 109,219,231,247,191a,201a
1944 154,178,261,273,302a
1945 118,220,190a,202a
1946 110,220,190a,202a
1947 115,221,190a,202a
1948 119,221,261,191a,198a
1949 112,222,190a,202a
1950 116,215,232,191a,203a
1951 109,178,216,191a,203a
1952 113,189,187a,199a
1953 117,178,206,192a,204a
1954 110,224,190a,202a
1955 114,179,208,189a,204a
1956 118,179,210,191a,200a
1957 111,225,190a,202a
1958 116,211,189a,201a
1959 154,226,273,190a,202a
1960 112,213,226,263,340a
1961 154,226,259,263,273,190a,202a
1962 109,227,233,343a
1963 114,179,186a,198a
1964 118,227,234,343a
1965 110,178,228,262,263,276,328a
1966 115,178,207,262,191a,203a
1967 119,178,209,191a,199a
1968 111,179,186a,198a
1969 116,200,188a,200a
1970 154,218,273,190a,202a
1971 113,212,189a,201a
1972 117,213,261,189a,201a
1973 110,214,219,261,190a,202a
1974 163,191,258,261,187a,199a
1975 119,236,191a,203a
1976 111,179,236,189a,195a
1977 115,221,190a,202a
1978 120,177,207,190a,197a
1979 112,222,190a,202a
1980 154,178,273,186a,198a
1981 109,190,223,257,187a,199a
1982 114,191,223,257,187a,199a
1983 118,213,237,340a
1984 110,200,213,263,336a
1985 115,224,190a,202a
1986 120,225,190a,202a
1987 112,216,225,263,340a

1988 116,205,189a,201a
1989 154,226,273,190a,202a
1990 154,226,273,190a,202a
1991 154,226,273,190a,202a
1992 154,227,273,190a,202a
1993 115,227,262,190a,202a
1994 154,227,259,262,273,190a,202a
1995 111,228,190a,202a
1996 163,228,239,343a
1997 154,217,273,190a,202a
1998 113,217,239,261,343a
1999 117,239,191a,203a

14th January

1930 154,226,273,190a,202a
1931 117,226,263,190a,202a
1932 109,226,190a,202a
1933 154,178,227,273,328a
1934 118,229,191a,203a
1935 110,229,191a,203a
1936 114,179,213,189a,203a
1937 154,228,259,262,273,190a,203a
1938 154,217,273,190a,202a
1939 116,177,216,263,189a,200a
1940 120,193,181a,193a
1941 154,190,206,218,261,263,273, 298a
1942 154,191,261,273,182a,194a
1943 110,219,231,247,191a,201a
1944 114,178,261,183a,195a
1945 154,220,273,190a,202a
1946 111,220,190a,202a
1947 115,221,190a,202a
1948 167,231,258,261,191a,203a
1949 112,222,190a,202a
1950 117,215,232,191a,203a
1951 109,178,216,191a,203a
1952 113,189,187a,199a
1953 118,189,187a,199a
1954 110,224,190a,202a
1955 115,179,208,189a,204a
1956 119,233,191a,203a
1957 111,225,190a,202a
1958 116,201,188a,200a
1959 154,226,273,190a,202a
1960 154,226,259,263,273,190a,202a
1961 154,226,259,263,273,190a,202a
1962 110,227,233,343a
1963 114,179,186a,198a
1964 118,227,234,343a
1965 154,178,228,262,273,276,328a
1966 116,178,207,262,191a,203a
1967 120,178,209,191a,199a
1968 112,179,186a,198a
1969 117,179,211,192a,200a
1970 154,218,273,190a,202a
1971 113,213,189a,201a
1972 117,213,261,189a,201a
1973 110,214,219,261,190a,202a
1974 163,191,258,261,187a,199a
1975 119,236,191a,203a
1976 111,179,236,189a,195a
1977 116,221,190a,202a
1978 109,221,190a,202a
1979 113,222,190a,202a
1980 154,178,273,186a,198a
1981 110,190,223,257,187a,199a
1982 114,191,223,257,187a,199a
1983 118,213,237,340a
1984 110,200,213,263,336a
1985 164,204,224,259,263,337a
1986 120,225,190a,202a
1987 112,216,225,263,340a
1988 116,205,189a,201a
1989 154,226,273,190a,202a
1990 114,226,273,190a,202a
1991 118,226,273,276,190a,202a
1992 110,227,273,276,190a,202a
1993 115,227,262,190a,202a
1994 154,227,238,259,262,273,343a
1995 111,228,190a,202a
1996 116,228,239,343a
1997 154,214,217,261,273,190a,202a
1998 113,217,239,261,343a
1999 117,239,191a,203a

15th January

1930 154,226,273,190a,202a
1931 117,226,263,190a,202a
1932 154,226,273,190a,202a
1933 114,178,227,276,328a
1934 118,229,191a,203a
1935 159,229,191a,203a
1936 115,179,213,189a,204a
1937 154,228,259,262,273,190a,202a
1938 154,217,273,190a,202a
1939 116,177,216,263,189a,200a
1940 120,193,181a,193a
1941 154,190,206,218,261,263,273, 298a
1942 154,191,261,273,182a,194a
1943 110,219,231,247,191a,201a
1944 114,178,261,183a,195a
1945 119,220,190a,202a
1946 111,220,190a,202a
1947 116,221,190a,202a
1948 120,179,213,191a,198a
1949 113,222,261,190a,202a
1950 117,178,232,191a,199a
1951 109,178,216,191a,199a
1952 113,189,187a,199a
1953 118,223,190a,202a
1954 111,224,190a,202a
1955 115,179,208,189a,193a
1956 119,233,191a,203a
1957 112,225,190a,202a

1958 117,212,189a,201a
1959 154,226,273,190a,202a
1960 154,226,259,263,273,190a,202a
1961 118,226,190a,202a
1962 110,227,233,343a
1963 114,179,186a,198a
1964 119,234,191a,203a
1965 154,178,228,262,273,276,328a
1966 116,178,207,262,191a,203a
1967 120,178,209,191a,199a
1968 112,179,186a,198a
1969 117,179,211,192a,200a
1970 110,218,190a,202a
1971 154,213,273,189a,201a
1972 118,218,261,190a,202a
1973 111,219,261,190a,202a
1974 163,191,258,261,187a,199a
1975 119,236,191a,203a
1976 112,179,205,189a,195a
1977 116,221,190a,202a
1978 109,221,190a,202a
1979 113,222,190a,202a
1980 154,178,273,186a,198a
1981 110,190,223,257,187a,199a
1982 163,191,187a,199a
1983 119,213,237,341a
1984 111,200,213,336a
1985 164,204,224,259,263,337a
1986 120,225,190a,202a
1987 112,216,225,263,340a
1988 165,205,189a,201a
1989 110,226,273,276,190a,202a
1990 114,226,273,190a,202a
1991 118,226,273,276,190a,202a
1992 110,227,273,276,190a,202a
1993 115,227,262,190a,202a
1994 154,227,259,262,273,190a,202a
1995 112,228,190a,202a
1996 116,228,239,343a
1997 154,214,217,261,273,190a,202a
1998 113,217,239,261,343a
1999 117,239,191a,203a

16th January

1930 154,226,273,190a,202a
1931 117,226,263,190a,202a
1932 110,226,190a,202a
1933 114,178,227,276,328a
1934 167,229,191a,203a
1935 229,191a,203a
1936 115,179,213,189a,204a
1937 154,228,246,259,262,273,344a
1938 154,217,273,190a,202a
1939 117,177,216,263,189a,200a
1940 157,193,258,261,181a,193a
1941 114,190,206,218,261,263,198a
1942 154,191,261,273,182a,194a
1943 159,179,183a,195a
1944 163,178,259,261,183a,195a
1945 119,220,190a,202a
1946 160,220,315a
1947 116,221,190a,202a
1948 120,179,213,191a,198a
1949 113,222,261,190a,202a
1950 118,222,190a,202a
1951 110,178,255,191a,203a
1952 114,189,187a,199a
1953 119,178,255,192a,204a
1954 111,224,190a,202a
1955 116,179,208,189a,193a
1956 120,179,210,191a,201a
1957 112,225,190a,202a
1958 117,212,189a,201a
1959 154,226,273,190a,202a
1960 154,226,259,263,273,190a,202a
1961 118,226,190a,202a
1962 111,227,233,343a
1963 115,179,216,189a,197a
1964 119,234,191a,203a
1965 154,178,228,262,273,276,328a
1966 116,178,207,262,191a,203a
1967 109,178,208,191a,199a
1968 113,179,186a,198a
1969 118,179,217,192a,200a
1970 110,218,190a,202a
1971 154,213,272,189a,201a
1972 118,218,261,190a,202a
1973 111,219,261,190a,202a
1974 116,219,235,257,191a,203a
1975 120,179,216,191a,201a
1976 112,170,205,189a,195a
1977 117,221,190a,202a
1978 110,221,190a,202a
1979 114,222,190a,202a
1980 118,178,222,328a
1981 159,190,187a,199a
1982 163,191,187a,199a
1983 119,213,237,341a
1984 111,200,213,336a
1985 164,204,224,259,263,337a
1986 109,225,190a,202a
1987 113,216,225,263,340a
1988 165,205,189a,201a
1989 110,226,273,276,190a,202a
1990 114,226,273,190a,202a
1991 154,226,273,190a,202a
1992 154,227,273,276,190a,202a
1993 116,227,262,190a,202a
1994 154,227,259,262,273,190a,202a
1995 112,228,190a,202a
1996 116,228,239,343a
1997 110,214,217,261,273,190a,202a
1998 114,217,239,261,343a
1999 118,217,239,343a

17th January

1930 114,226,190a,202a
1931 118,226,259,263,190a,202a
1932 110,226,190a,202a
1933 154,178,227,273,328a
1934 167,229,191a,203a
1935 112,229,191a,203a
1936 116,179,213,189a,204a
1937 154,228,246,259,262,263,273, 344a
1938 154,217,273,190a,202a
1939 117,177,216,263,189a,200a
1940 157,193,258,261,181a,193a
1941 114,190,206,261,276,182a,194a
1942 154,191,230,261,273,299a
1943 159,179,183a,195a
1944 163,178,259,261,183a,195a
1945 120,220,190a,202a
1946 160,220,315a
1947 117,221,190a,202a
1948 109,179,213,261,191a,198a
1949 114,214,222,261,190a,202a
1950 118,222,190a,202a
1951 110,178,255,191a,203a
1952 114,189,187a,199a
1953 119,178,255,192a,204a
1954 112,224,190a,202a
1955 116,179,208,189a,193a
1956 120,179,210,191a,201a
1957 113,225,322a
1958 117,212,189a,201a
1959 110,226,190a,202a
1960 114,226,259,263,190a,202a
1961 119,226,190a,202a
1962 111,227,233,343a
1963 115,179,216,189a,197a
1964 119,234,191a,203a
1965 154,178,228,262,263,273,276, 328a
1966 117,178,207,191a,203a
1967 109,178,208,191a,199a
1968 113,179,186a,198a
1969 118,179,217,192a,200a
1970 154,218,273,190a,202a
1971 115,213,189a,201a
1972 119,178,213,192a,193a
1973 112,219,190a,202a
1974 116,219,235,257,191a,203a
1975 120,179,216,191a,201a
1976 113,179,205,189a,195a
1977 117,221,190a,202a
1978 110,221,190a,202a
1979 114,222,190a,202a
1980 118,178,222,328a
1981 159,190,182a,199a
1982 116,191,223,257,187a,199a
1983 120,213,189a,201a
1984 112,200,213,263,336a
1985 117,224,263,190a,202a
1986 109,225,190a,202a
1987 113,216,225,263,340a
1988 118,205,225,340a
1989 154,226,273,276,190a,202a
1990 154,226,273,190a,202a
1991 154,226,273,190a,202a
1992 154,227,273,276,190a,202a
1993 116,227,262,190a,202a
1994 154,227,273,190a,202a
1995 113,213,228,340a
1996 117,228,190a,202a
1997 110,214,217,261,273,190a,202a
1998 114,217,239,261,343a
1999 118,217,239,343a

18th January

1930 114,226,190a,202a
1931 118,226,259,263,190a,202a
1932 110,226,190a,202a
1933 154,178,227,273,328a
1934 120,229,191a,203a
1935 112,229,191a,203a
1936 116,179,213,189a,204a
1937 154,228,259,263,273,190a,202a
1938 154,217,273,190a,202a
1939 118,217,259,263,190a,202a
1940 110,193,261,181a,193a
1941 154,190,206,261,273,182a,194a
1942 154,191,230,261,273,299a
1943 159,179,183a,195a
1944 163,178,259,261,183a,195a
1945 120,220,190a,202a
1946 113,220,190a,202a
1947 117,221,190a,202a
1948 109,179,213,192a,198a
1949 114,214,222,261,190a,202a
1950 118,222,190a,202a
1951 159,223,247,191a,203a
1952 115,189,187a,199a
1953 120,247,192a,204a
1954 112,179,255,190a,200a
1955 116,179,208,189a,193a
1956 154,225,233,255,273,185a,197a
1957 113,225,322a
1958 118,225,190a,202a
1959 110,226,190a,202a
1960 114,226,259,263,190a,202a
1961 119,226,190a,202a
1962 112,227,233,191a,199a
1963 116,179,216,189a,197a
1964 120,178,205,192a,203a
1965 154,178,228,263,273,276,328a
1966 118,178,207,191a,203a
1967 109,178,208,191a,199a
1968 114,179,186a,198a
1969 119,179,217,192a,200a
1970 154,218,273,190a,202a
1971 115,213,189a,201a

1972 119,178,213,192a,193a
1973 112,219,190a,202a
1974 117,219,235,257,258,261,191a, 203a
1975 109,179,216,191a,201a
1976 113,179,205,189a,195a
1977 117,221,190a,202a
1978 110,221,190a,202a
1979 114,222,190a,202a
1980 154,178,273,186a,198a
1981 112,190,223,257,187a,199a
1982 116,191,223,257,187a,199a
1983 120,213,189a,201a
1984 112,200,213,263,336a
1985 117,224,263,190a,202a
1986 110,225,190a,202a
1987 114,216,189a,201a
1988 118,205,225,340a
1989 154,226,273,276,190a,202a
1990 154,226,273,190a,202a
1991 154,226,273,190a,202a
1992 154,227,273,276,190a,202a
1993 117,227,190a,202a
1994 154,227,273,190a,202a
1995 113,213,228,340a
1996 117,228,190a,202a
1997 154,214,217,261,273,190a,202a
1998 115,217,239,261,343a
1999 167,239,191a,203a

19th January

1930 154,226,273,190a,202a
1931 119,226,190a,202a
1932 111,226,190a,202a
1933 154,178,227,273,328a
1934 120,229,191a,203a
1935 112,229,191a,203a
1936 116,179,213,189a,204a
1937 154,228,259,263,273,190a,202a
1938 114,217,190a,202a
1939 118,217,259,263,190a,202a
1940 110,193,259,263,181a,193a
1941 154,190,206,261,273,182a,194a
1942 154,191,273,182a,194a
1943 112,219,231,247,191a,201a
1944 116,178,183a,195a
1945 109,220,190a,202a
1946 113,220,190a,202a
1947 117,221,190a,202a
1948 109,179,213,192a,198a
1949 163,222,258,190a,202a
1950 167,232,191a,203a
1951 159,223,247,191a,203a
1952 115,189,187a,199a
1953 120,247,192a,204a
1954 113,179,207,190a,200a
1955 117,179,208,189a,193a
1956 109,209,185a,197a
1957 114,225,190a,202a
1958 118,225,190a,202a
1959 110,226,190a,202a
1960 154,226,273,190a,202a
1961 120,226,190a,202a
1962 112,227,233,191a,199a
1963 116,179,216,189a,197a
1964 120,178,205,192a,203a
1965 154,178,263,273,276,328a
1966 118,228,259,262,190a,202a
1967 110,234,256,259,262,191a,199a
1968 114,179,186a,198a
1969 119,179,217,192a,200a
1970 154,218,273,190a,202a
1971 115,213,189a,201a
1972 120,178,213,192a,193a
1973 113,219,261,190a,202a
1974 117,219,235,257,258,261,191a, 203a
1975 109,179,216,191a,201a
1976 113,179,205,189a,195a
1977 118,221,190a,202a
1978 111,221,190a,202a
1979 115,222,190a,202a
1980 154,178,273,186a,198a
1981 112,190,223,257,187a,199a
1982 116,191,223,257,187a,199a
1983 120,213,189a,201a
1984 113,200,213,224,263,350a
1985 118,224,259,263,273,190a,202a
1986 110,225,190a,202a
1987 114,216,189a,201a
1988 119,205,189a,201a
1989 154,226,262,276,190a,202a
1990 154,226,259,263,273,190a,202a
1991 154,226,273,190a,202a
1992 154,227,273,276,190a,202a
1993 117,227,190a,202a
1994 154,227,273,190a,202a
1995 114,213,228,340a
1996 118,228,273,190a,202a
1997 154,214,217,261,273,190a,202a
1998 115,217,239,261,343a
1999 167,239,191a,203a

20th January

1930 154,226,273,190a,202a
1931 119,226,190a,202a
1932 111,226,190a,202a
1933 128,178,246,186a,198a
1934 109,227,229,191a,203a
1935 113,229,191a,203a
1936 117,213,189a,201a
1937 158,214,259,262,192a,200a
1938 114,217,190a,202a
1939 118,217,259,263,190a,202a
1940 111,193,181a,193a
1941 128,190,218,230,246,182a,194a

1942 154,191,273,182a,194a
1943 112,219,231,247,191a,201a
1944 116,178,183a,195a
1945 121,178,210,192a,202a
1946 114,220,190a,202a
1947 118,221,190a,202a
1948 110,179,213,192a,198a
1949 127,231,258,261,191a,203a
1950 167,232,191a,203a
1951 159,223,247,191a,203a
1952 116,178,205,189a,200a
1953 121,178,206,192a,204a
1954 113,179,207,190a,200a
1955 117,179,208,189a,193a
1956 109,209,185a,197a
1957 126,178,248,190a,193a
1958 119,178,212,191a,201a
1959 154,226,273,190a,202a
1960 154,226,273,190a,202a
1961 132,179,233,192a,196a
1962 112,227,233,191a,199a
1963 116,178,227,189a,197a
1964 109,178,205,192a,203a
1965 162,178,262,276,186a,198a
1966 118,228,259,262,190a,202a
1967 110,179,208,262,191a,199a
1968 114,179,186a,198a
1969 132,179,217,256,192a,200a
1970 124,178,249,290a,204a
1971 116,213,189a,201a
1972 120,178,213,192a,193a
1973 125,219,261,190a,202a
1974 155,235,261,274,279,191a,203a
1975 109,179,216,191a,201a
1976 114,179,205,189a,195a
1977 130,221,190a,202a
1978 123,178,236,190a,197a
1979 115,222,190a,202a
1980 154,178,273,186a,198a
1981 155,190,236,274,334a
1982 155,191,237,258,260,274,334a
1983 109,213,189a,201a
1984 113,200,224,263,337a
1985 130,224,190a,202a
1986 122,237,191a,203a
1987 115,216,189a,201a
1988 119,205,189a,201a
1989 124,226,238,250,259,262,190a, 202a
1990 128,226,238,250,273,190a,202a
1991 154,226,273,190a,202a
1992 154,227,273,276,190a,202a
1993 130,227,262,190a,202a
1994 122,227,238,262,343a
1995 114,213,228,340a
1996 118,228,273,190a,202a
1997 123,217,261,190a,202a
1998 127,217,239,258,261,343a
1999 120,239,191a,203a

21st January

1930 127,226,190a,202a
1931 132,178,208,189a,197a
1932 124,178,209,192a,203a
1933 129,178,246,186a,198a
1934 155,229,274,191a,203a
1935 155,229,274,191a,203a
1936 129,213,189a,201a
1937 158,214,259,262,192a,200a
1938 127,178,217,192a,204a
1939 131,178,216,189a,200a
1940 123,193,181a,193a
1941 128,190,218,230,246,182a,194a
1942 131,191,230,299a
1943 155,231,258,260,274,191a,203a
1944 155,178,258,261,274,183a,195a
1945 122,178,255,192a,202a
1946 126,178,255,190a,196a
1947 130,221,190a,202a
1948 122,179,213,192a,198a
1949 155,231,274,191a,203a
1950 155,232,274,191a,203a
1951 155,232,274,191a,203a
1952 128,178,205,189a,200a
1953 121,178,206,192a,204a
1954 125,179,207,190a,200a
1955 130,179,208,189a,193a
1956 155,225,233,245,274,185a,197a
1957 127,178,248,190a,193a
1958 131,233,191a,203a
1959 123,178,233,191a,194a
1960 127,226,190a,202a
1961 121,179,214,192a,196a
1962 125,233,191a,203a
1963 129,178,216,227,189a,197a
1964 121,234,191a,203a
1965 162,178,262,276,186a,198a
1966 130,234,262,191a,203a
1967 123,234,262,191a,203a
1968 127,179,186a,198a
1969 132,179,217,256,192a,200a
1970 124,178,249,191a,204a
1971 128,213,189a,201a
1972 121,178,213,192a,193a
1973 126,219,261,190a,202a
1974 155,235,261,274,279,191a,203a
1975 122,236,191a,203a
1976 126,179,205,189a,195a
1977 131,178,206,192a,202a
1978 124,178,207,236,191a,197a
1979 128,178,209,189a,203a
1980 132,179,186a,198a
1981 155,190,236,274,334a
1982 155,191,237,258,260,274,334a
1983 121,213,189a,201a
1984 126,200,224,337a
1985 131,224,190a,202a
1986 123,237,191a,203a
1987 127,216,189a,201a

1988 132,205,189a,201a
1989 124,226,238,250,259,190a,202a
1990 128,226,238,250,273,190a,202a
1991 121,226,190a,202a
1992 125,227,238,250,190a,202a
1993 130,227,238,262,343a
1994 122,227,238,262,343a
1995 126,213,189a,201a
1996 131,228,239,343a
1997 124,217,190a,202a
1998 128,217,239,343a
1999 155,239,274,191a,203a

22nd January

1930 128,226,190a,202a
1931 132,178,208,189a,197a
1932 124,178,209,192a,203a
1933 129,178,246,186a,198a
1934 155,229,274,191a,203a
1935 155,229,274,191a,203a
1936 130,179,213,189a,204a
1937 123,178,214,262,192a,200a
1938 127,178,217,192a,204a
1939 131,178,216,189a,200a
1940 123,193,181a,193a
1941 128,190,218,230,246,182a,194a
1942 121,191,230,261,299a
1943 155,231,258,260,274,191a,203a
1944 155,178,258,261,274,183a,195a
1945 122,178,255,192a,202a
1946 123,190,187a,199a
1947 155,231,274,191a,203a
1948 123,231,247,192a,198a
1949 155,231,274,191a,203a
1950 155,232,274,191a,203a
1951 155,232,274,191a,203a
1952 128,178,205,189a,200a
1953 122,178,255,192a,204a
1954 155,232,274,191a,203a
1955 130,179,208,189a,193a
1956 155,225,233,245,274,185a,197a
1957 127,178,248,190a,193a
1958 132,178,212,191a,201a
1959 124,178,233,191a,194a
1960 128,226,190a,202a
1961 121,179,214,192a,196a
1962 155,233,274,191a,203a
1963 129,178,216,227,189a,197a
1964 122,234,191a,203a
1965 127,178,234,256,259,262,186a, 198a
1966 131,207,234,262,191a,203a
1967 123,234,262,191a,203a
1968 127,179,186a,198a
1969 132,179,217,256,192a,200a
1970 125,178,212,191a,204a
1971 129,213,189a,201a
1972 121,178,213,192a,193a
1973 126,219,261,190a,202a
1974 155,235,261,274,279,191a,203a
1975 122,236,191a,203a
1976 127,257,258,260,189a,195a
1977 131,178,206,192a,202a
1978 124,178,207,236,191a,197a
1979 128,278,209,189a,203a
1980 121,179,186a,198a
1981 155,190,236,274,334a
1982 155,191,237,274,334a
1983 122,213,189a,201a
1984 126,200,224,337a
1985 131,224,190a,202a
1986 123,237,191a,203a
1987 127,216,189a,201a
1988 132,205,189a,201a
1989 125,226,238,250,190a,202a
1990 129,226,238,250,273,190a,202a
1991 121,226,190a,202a
1992 162,227,190a,202a
1993 130,227,238,262,343a
1994 123,227,238,262,343a
1995 127,213,189a,201a
1996 131,228,239,343a
1997 124,217,239,343a
1998 128,217,239,343a
1999 155,239,274,191a,203a

23rd January

1930 128,226,246,190a,202a
1931 132,178,208,189a,197a
1932 125,178,209,192a,203a
1933 128,178,246,186a,198a
1934 155,229,274,191a,203a
1935 155,229,274,191a,203a
1936 130,179,213,189a,204a
1937 123,178,214,262,192a,200a
1938 128,230,191a,203a
1939 132,178,216,189a,200a
1940 124,193,181a,193a
1941 129,190,206,218,230,246,261, 182a,194a
1942 121,191,230,261,299a
1943 155,231,258,260,274,191a,203a
1944 155,178,258,261,274,183a,195a
1945 123,178,255,192a,202a
1946 123,191,187a,199a
1947 155,231,274,191a,203a
1948 123,231,274,192a,198a
1949 155,231,274,191a,203a
1950 155,232,274,191a,203a
1951 155,178,216,274,191a,204a
1952 129,178,205,189a,200a
1953 122,178,255,192a,204a
1954 155,232,274,191a,203a
1955 130,179,208,189a,193a
1956 155,225,233,245,258,260,274, 185a,197a

1957 128,178,211,190a,193a
1958 132,178,212,191a,201a
1959 124,178,233,191a,194a
1960 128,179,213,189a,202a
1961 122,179,233,192a,196a
1962 155,233,274,191a,203a
1963 130,178,216,227,189a,197a
1964 122,234,191a,203a
1965 127,178,234,256,259,262,186a, 198a
1966 131,207,234,262,191a,203a
1967 123,234,262,191a,203a
1968 128,179,186a,198a
1969 121,179,256,192a,200a
1970 125,178,212,191a,204a
1971 165,213,258,261,272,189a,201a
1972 122,178,213,192a,193a
1973 127,190,219,258,261,333a
1974 131,235,261,274,279,191a,203a
1975 123,236,191a,203a
1976 127,257,258,260,189a,195a
1977 132,178,206,192a,202a
1978 124,178,207,236,191a,197a
1979 128,278,209,189a,203a
1980 121,179,186a,198a
1981 155,190,236,274,334
1982 155,191,274,187a,199a
1983 122,213,189a,201a
1984 127,200,224,337a
1985 168,224,250,344a
1986 124,237,191a,203a
1987 128,216,189a,201a
1988 157,205,189a,201a
1989 125,226,238,250,190a,202a
1990 129,226,238,250,273,190a,202a
1991 158,226,190a,202a
1992 162,227,190a,202a
1993 155,211,238,262,274,191a,203a
1994 123,227,238,262,343a
1995 127,213,189a,201a
1996 132,228,238,250,349a
1997 125,217,239,261,343a
1998 129,217,239,261,343a
1999 155,239,274,191a,203a

24th January

1930 129,226,190a,202a
1931 121,178,208,189a,197a
1932 125,178,209,192a,203a
1933 166,178,227,328a
1934 155,229,274,191a,203a
1935 155,229,274,191a,203a
1936 131,230,191a,203a
1937 160,228,254,259,262,192a,200a
1938 128,230,191a,203a
1939 132,178,216,189a,200a
1940 124,193,191a,193a
1941 129,190,206,218,230,246,261, 182a,194a
1942 158,191,230,299a
1943 155,231,274,191a,293a
1944 155,178,258,261,274,183a,195a
1945 123,178,255,192a,202a
1946 123,191,187a,199a
1947 155,231,274,919a,203a
1948 124,179,213,192a,198a
1949 155,231,258,261,191a,203a
1950 155,232,274,191a,203a
1951 155,178,216,174,191a,204a
1952 129,178.205,189a,200a
1953 123,178,255,192a,204a
1954 127,232,258,260,191a,203a
1955 131,232,191a,203a
1956 155,225,233,245,258,260,274, 185a,197a
1957 128,178,211,190a,193a
1958 132,178,212,191a,201a
1959 124,178,233,191a,194a
1960 129,213,189a,201a
1961 122,179,233,192a,196a
1962 155,233,274,191a,203a
1963 130,178,216,227,189a,197a
1964 123,234,191a,203a
1965 128,178,234,256,259,262,186a, 198a
1966 132,234,262,191a,203a
1967 124,234,262,191a,203a
1968 128,179,186a,198a
1969 121,179,256,192a,200a
1970 125,178,212,191a,204a
1971 130,213,261,189a,201a
1972 122,178,213,192a,193a
1973 127,190,258,261,187a,199a
1974 131,235,261,274,279,191a,203a
1975 123,236,191a,203a
1976 128,179,205,260,189a,195a
1977 132,178,206,192a,202a
1978 155,274,185a,197a
1979 129,209,189a,201a
1980 122,179,186a,198a
1981 155,190,236,274,334a
1982 155,191,274,187a,199a
1983 123,213,189a,201a
1984 127,200,224,337a
1985 168,224,250,344a
1986 124,237,191a,203a
1987 128,216,189a,201a
1988 157,205,189a,201a
1989 162,262,276,190a,202a
1990 166,226,273,190a,202a
1991 158,226,190a,202a
1992 127,227,238,250,190a,202a
1993 155,211,238,262,274,191a,203a
1994 123,227,238,262,343a
1995 128,213,189a,201a
1996 132,228,238,250,349a
1997 125,217,239,261,343a

1998 129,217,239,261,343a
1999 155,239,247,191a,203a

25th January

1930 129,226,190a,202a
1931 121,178,208,189a,197a
1932 125,178,209,192a,203a
1933 166,178,227,328a
1934 123,229,274,279,191a,203a
1935 127,229,191a,203a
1936 131,230,191a,203a
1937 160,228,254,259,262,191a.200a
1938 128,230,191a,203a
1939 132,178,216,189a,200a
1940 161,193,181a,193a
1941 166,190a,206,261,182a,194a
1942 158,191,230,299a
1943 155,231,274,191a,203a
1944 155,178,258,261,274,183a,195a
1945 124,178,255,192a,202a
1946 155,207,274,191a,196a
1947 155,231,258,260,274,191a,203a
1948 124,179,213,192a,198a
1949 155,231,258,261,274,191a,203a
1950 155,232,274,191a,203a
1951 126,178,255,191a,204a
1952 130,178,205,189a,200a
1953 123,178,255,192a,204a
1954 127,232,258,260,191a,203a
1955 131,232,191a,203a
1956 155,225,232,245,258,260,274, 185a,197a
1957 165,178,211,225,233,255,190a, 193a
1958 121,178,212,191a,210a
1959 125,178,212,191a,194a
1960 129,213,189a,201a
1961 122,179,233,192a,196a
1962 155,233,274,191a,203a
1963 131,234,191a,197a
1964 123,234,191a,203a
1965 128,178,234,256,259,262,186a, 198a
1966 132,234,262,191a,203a
1967 124,234,262,191a,203a
1968 129,179,186a,198a
1969 122,179,217,192a,200a
1970 126,178,212,191a,193a
1971 130,213,261,189a,201a
1972 123,178,213,192a,193a
1973 127,190,258,261,187a,199a
1974 131,235,261,274,279,191a,203a
1975 124,236,191a,203a
1976 128,178,205,189a,195a
1977 121,178,206,192a,202a
1978 155,274,185a,197a
1979 129,209,189a,201a
1980 122,179,186a,198a
1981 127,190,236,279,334a
1982 131,191,237,334a
1983 123,213,189a,201a
1984 128,200,224,337a
1985 168,224,250,344a
1986 124,237,191a,203a
1987 165,216,189a,201a
1988 157,205,189a,201a
1989 162,262,276,190a,202a
1990 166,226,273,191a,202a
1991 158,226,190a,202a
1992 127,227,238,250,259,262,273, 190a,202a
1993 132,238,262,191a,203a
1994 124,227,238,262,343a
1995 128,213,189a,201a
1996 121,228,239,343a
1997 125,217,239,261,343a
1998 129,217,239,343a
1999 155,239,274,203a

26th January

1930 166,226,190a,202a
1931 121,178,208,189a,197a
1932 126,178,209,192a,203a
1933 131,178,229,246,329a
1934 123,229,274,279,191a,203a
1935 127,229,191a,203a
1936 132,246,192a,204a
1937 125,178,214,192a,200a
1938 129,230,191a,203a
1939 121,178,216,189a,200a
1940 161,193,181a,193a
1941 166,190,206,261,182a,194a
1942 123,191,230,258,261,299a
1943 127,231,258,260,191a,203a
1944 155,178,258,261,274,183a,195a
1945 124,178,255,192a,202a
1946 155,207,274,191a,196a
1947 155,231,258,260,274,191a,203a
1948 155,274,185a,197a
1949 155,231,258,261,274,191a,203a
1950 155,232,274,191a,203a
1951 126,178,255,191a,204a
1952 130,178,205,189a,200a
1953 123,223,247,192a,204a
1954 127,232,258,260,191a,203a
1955 132,179,208,260,189a,193a
1956 155,225,233,245,258,260,274, 185a,197a
1957 165,178,211,225,233,255,190a, 193a
1958 121,178,212,191a,201a
1959 125,178,212,191a,194a
1960 130,226,190a,202a
1961 123,179,233,192a,196a
1962 127,233,274,191a,203a

1963 131,234,191a,197a
1964 124,234,191a,203a
1965 128,178,234,256,259,262,186a, 198a
1966 132,234,262,131a,203a
1967 125,234,191a,203a
1968 129,179,186a,198a
1969 122,179,217,192a,200a
1970 126,178,212,191a,193a
1971 130,213,261,189a,201a
1972 123,178,213,192a,193a
1973 155,219,235,257,274,190a,201a
1974 155,235,274,279,191a,203a
1975 124,236,191a,203a
1976 129,178,205,190a,195a
1977 121,178,206,192a,202a
1978 126,178,207,191a,196a
1979 130,178,236,189a,203a
1980 122,179,186a,198a
1981 127,190,236,279,334a
1982 131,191,237,334a
1983 124,213,189a,201a
1984 128,200,224,337a
1985 121,224,190a,202a
1986 125,237,191a,203a
1987 165,216,189a,201a
1988 122,205,189a,201a
1989 162,262,276,190a,202a
1990 131,226,238,250,273,190a,202a
1991 123,226,190a,202a
1992 128,227,238,250,259,262,273, 190a,202a
1993 132,238,262,191a,203a
1994 124,227,238,262,343a
1995 165,213,189a,201a
1996 121,228,239,343a
1997 126,217,239,261,343a
1998 130,217,239,343a
1999 155,239,274,191a,203a

27th January

1930 166,226,190a,202a
1931 122,178,208,189a,197a
1932 126,178,209,192a,203a
1933 131,178,229,246,329a
1934 155,229,274,191a,203a
1935 155,229,274,191a,203a
1936 132,246,192a,204a
1937 125,178,214,192a,200a
1938 129,230,191a,203a
1939 121,178,216,189a,200a
1940 126,193,181a,193a
1941 131,190,206,230,261,299a
1942 123,191,230,258,261,299a
1943 127,219,231,247,190a,201a
1944 155,178,274,183a,195a
1945 124,178,255,192a,202a
1946 155,207,274,191a,196a
1947 155,231,258,260,274,191a,203a
1948 155,274,185a,197a
1949 155,231,258,261,274,191a,203a
1950 155,232,274,191a,203a
1951 126,178,255,191a,204a
1952 131,178,205,189a,200a
1953 124,179,255,192a,204a
1954 155,232,255,258,260,274,338a
1955 132,179,208,260,189a,193a
1956 125,258,260,185a,197a
1957 130,225,190a,202a
1958 110,178,212,191a,201a
1959 162,226,256,191a,194a
1960 166,226,190a,202a
1961 123,179,233,192a,196a
1962 127,233,274,191a,203a
1963 132,178,216,227,189a,197a
1964 124,234,191a,203a
1965 129,178,234,256,186a,198a
1966 155,234,274,191a,203a
1967 125,234,191a,203a
1968 166,179,186a,198a
1969 123,179,235,192a,200a
1970 127,178,212,191a,193a
1971 131,213,261,189a,201a
1972 123,178,213,192a,193a
1973 155,219,235,257,274,190a,201a
1974 155,235,274,279,191a,203a
1975 125,236,191a,203a
1976 129,178,205,190a,195a
1977 121,178,206,192a,202a
1978 126,178,207,191a,196a
1979 130,178,236,189a,203a
1980 123,179,186a,198a
1981 155,190,236,274,334a
1982 155,191,274,187a,199a
1983 124,213,189a,201a
1984 129,200,224,337a
1985 121,224,190a,202a
1986 125,237,191a,203a
1987 130,216,189a,201a
1988 122,205,189a,201a
1989 127,226,259,262,190a,202a
1990 131,226,238,250,273,190a,202a
1991 123,226,190a,202a
1992 128,227,238,250,259,262,273, 190a,202a
1993 132,238,262,191a,203a
1994 125,227,238,343a
1995 165,213,189a,201a
1996 122,228,239,343a
1997 126,217,239,261,343a
1998 130,217,239,343a
1999 123,239,258,260,274,191a,203a

28th January

1930 166,226,190a,202a

1931 122,178,208,189a,197a
1932 127,178,209,192a,203a
1933 132,179,229,320a
1934 155,229,274,191a,203a
1935 155,2229,274,191a,203a
1936 121,179,213,189a,204a
1937 162,214,259,262,192a,200a
1938 130,230,191a,203a
1939 122,178,216,189a,200a
1940 126,193,181a,193a
1941 131,190,206,230,261,299a
1942 123,191,230,258,261,299a
1943 127,219,231,247,190a,201a
1944 155,178,274,183a,195a
1945 125,178,210,192a,202a
1946 155,207,274,191a,190a
1947 231,258,260,274,191a,203a
1948 126,179,213,192a,198a
1949 155,231,258,261,274,191a,203a
1950 123,232,191a,203a
1951 127,191,187a,199a
1952 131,178,205,190a,200a
1953 124,179,255,192a,204a
1954 155,232,255,258,260,274,338a
1955 121,179,208,260,189a,193a
1956 125,258,260,185a,197a
1957 130,225,190a,202a
1958 110,178,212,191a,201a
1959 162,226,256,191a,194a
1960 131,226,233,343a
1961 124,179,233,192a,196a
1962 155,233,274,191a,203a
1963 132,178,216,227,189a,197a
1964 125,234,191a,203a
1965 129,178,234,256,186a,198a
1966 155,234,274,191a,203a
1967 126,179,234,262,329a
1968 166,179,186a,198a
1969 123,179,235,192a,200a
1970 127,178,212,191a,193a
1971 131,213,261,189a,201a
1972 124,178,213,192a,193a
1973 155,214,258,261,274,189a,201a
1974 155,235,261,274,279,191a,203a
1975 125,236,191a,203a
1976 130,220,190a,202a
1977 122,178,206,192a,202a
1978 126,178,207,191a,196a
1979 131,236,191a,203a
1980 123,179,186a,198a
1981 155,190a,236,274,334a
1982 155,191,274,187a,199a
1983 125,213,189a,201a
1984 129,200,224,337a
1985 122,224,190a,202a
1986 126,237,191a,203a
1987 130,216,189a,201a
1988 123,205,189a,201a
1989 127,226,259,262,190a,202a
1990 131,226,238,250,273,190a,202a
1991 124,226,190a,202a
1992 128,227,238,250,259,262,273,
190a,202a
1993 121,238,191a,203a
1994 155,238,274,191a,203a
1995 130,213,228,340a
1996 122,228,239,343a
1997 127,217,239,258,261,343a
1998 131,217,239,343a
1999 123,239,258,260,274,191a,203a

29th January

1930 131,226,229,343a
1931 123,178,208,189a,197a
1932 127,178,209,192a,203a
1933 132,179,229,329a
1934 155,229,274,191a,203a
1935 155,229,274,191a,203a
1936 121,179,213,189a,204a
1937 162,214,259,262,192a,200a
1938 130,230,191a,203a
1939 122,178,216,189a,201a
1940 127,193,181a,193a
1941 132,190,206,218,230,182a,194a
1942 124,191a,230,299a
1943 128,178,208,190a,201a
1944 155,178,258,261,274,183a,195a
1945 125,178,210,192a,202a
1946 155,231,258,260,274,191a,203a
1947 155,231,274,191a,203a
1948 126,179,213,192a,198a
1949 155,231,258,261,274,191a,203a
1950 123,232,191a,203a
1951 127,191,187a,199a
1952 132,178,205,190a,200a
1953 125,179,206,192a,204a
1954 155,232,258,260,274,191a,203a
1955 121,179,208,260,189a,193a
1956 126,179,209,192a,201a
1957 130,225,190a,202a
1958 110.178.212.191a,201a
1959 127,178,233,191a,194a
1960 131,226,233,343a
1961 124,179,233,192a,196a
1962 155,233,274,191a,203a
1963 121,178,216,227,189a,197a
1964 125,234,191a,203a
1965 166,178,228,262,276,328a
1966 155,207,234,262,274,191a,203a
1967 126,179,234,262,329a
1968 131,179,234,329a
1969 123,179,235,192a,200a
1970 127,178,212,191a,193a
1971 132,213,189a,201a
1972 124,178,213,192a,193a
1973 155,214,258,261,274,189a,201a
1974 155,235,261,274,279,191a,203a
1975 126,236,191a,203a

1976 130,220,190a,202a
1977 122,178,206,192a,202a
1978 127,257,191a,196a
1979 155,236,274,191a,203a
1980 124,179,186a,198a
1981 155,190,236,274,334a
1982 155,191,187a,199a
1983 213,189a,201a
1984 129,200,224,337a
1985 122,224,190a,202a
1986 126,237,191a,203a
1987 131,216,237,341a
1988 123,205,189a,201a
1989 128,226,262,273,276,190a,202a
1990 132,226,238,250,273,190a,202a
1991 124,226,190a,202a
1992 129,227,238,250,273,190a,202a
1993 121,238,191a,203a
1994 126,238,262,191a,203a
1995 130,213,228,340a
1996 123,228,239,343a
1997 127,217,239,258,261,343a
1998 131,239,274,191a,203a
1999 124,239,260,191a,203a

30th January

1930 131,226,229,343a
1931 123,178,208,189a,197a
1932 128,278,209,192a,203a
1933 121,179,229,329a
1934 155,229,274,191a,203a
1935 155,229,274,191a,203a
1936 122,179,213,190a,204a
1937 162,214,259,262,192a,200a
1938 130,230,191a,203a
1939 123,178,216,189a,201a
1940 127,193,181a,193a
1941 132,190,206,218,182a,194a
1942 124,191,230,299a
1943 128,178,208,190a,201a
1944 155,178,258,261,274,183a,195a
1945 126,178,210,192a,202a
1946 155,231,274,191a,203a
1947 155,231,274,191a,203a
1948 127,231,247,192a,198a
1949 155,231,258,261,274,191a,203a
1950 123,232,191a,203a
1951 128,178,255,191a,204a
1952 132,178,205,190a,200a
1953 125,179,206,192a,204a
1954 155,232,258,260,274,191a,203a
1955 122,179,208,189a,193a
1956 126,179,209,192a,201a
1957 131,178,190a,194a
1958 111,178,212,191a,201a
1959 127,178,233,191a,194a
1960 132,226,190a,202a
1961 124,179,233,192a,196a
1962 155,233,274,191a,203a
1963 121,178,216,227,189a,197a
1964 125,234,191a,203a
1965 166,178,228,262,276,328a
1966 122,234,262,191a,203a
1967 127,234,262,191a,203a
1968 131,179,234,329a
1969 124,179,217,256,192a,200a
1970 128,178,212,191a,193a
1971 132,213,189a,201a
1972 125,178,213,192a,193a
1973 155,214,258,261,274,189a,201a
1974 155,235,258,261,274,191a,203a
1975 126,179,249,192a,202a
1976 131,178,205,190a,195a
1977 123,178,206,192a,202a
1978 127,257,191a,196a
1979 132,179,222,189a,203a
1980 124,179,186a,198a
1981 155,190,236,274,334a
1982 155,191,274,187a,199a
1983 126,213,189a,201a
1984 166,200,224,273,337a
1985 122,224,190a,202a
1986 127,237,191a,203a
1987 131,216,237,241a
1988 124,205,189a,201a
1989 128,226,262,273,276,190a,202a
1990 132,226,238,250,259,262,273,
190a,202a
1991 125,226,190a,202a
1992 129,227,238,250,343a
1993 122,238,262,191a,203a
1994 126,238,262,191a,203
1995 131,213,238,241a
1996 123,228,239,343a
1997 127,217,239,258,343a
1998 132,239,191a,203a
1999 124,239,260,191a,203a

31st January

1930 131,226,229,343a
1931 160,208,184a,196a
1932 128,178,209,192a,203a
1933 121,179,229,329a
1934 155,229,274,191a,203a
1935 155,229,274,191a,203a
1936 122,179,213,190a,204a
1937 127,178,214,262,19a,200a
1938 131,230,191a,203a
1939 123,178,216,189a,201a
1940 128,193,181a,193a
1941 132,190,206,218,230,182a,194a
1942 125,191,230,261,299a
1943 129,178,208,190a,201a
1944 155,178,258,261,274,183a,195a
1945 126,178,210,192a,202a
1946 155,231,274,191a,203a

1947 155,231,258,260,274,191a,203a
1948 127,231,247,192a,198a
1949 155,231,274,191a,203a
1950 155,232,274,191a,203a
1951 128,178,255,191a,204a
1952 121,178,205,190a,200a
1953 125,179,206,192a,204a
1954 155,232,274,191a,203a
1955 122,179,208,189a,193a
1956 127,179,209,260,191a,201a
1957 131,178,190a,194a
1958 111,178,212,191a,201a
1959 128,194,188a,200a
1960 132,226,190a,202a
1961 125,179,214,192a,196a
1962 155,233,274,191a,203a
1963 121,178,216,227,189a,197a
1964 126,234,191a,197a
1965 166,178,228,262,276,328a
1966 123,207,234,262,191a,203a
1967 127,208,262,192a,199a
1968 132,179,217,190a,204a
1969 124,179,217,256,192a,200a
1970 128,178,212,191a,193a
1971 157,213,258,261,189a,201a
1972 125,178,213,192a,193a
1973 155,219,258,261,274,190a,202a
1974 155,235,258,261,274,191a,203a
1975 127,179,249,192a,202a
1976 131,178,205,190a,195a
1977 123,178,206,192a,202a
1978 128,178,207,191a,196a
1979 132,179,222,189a,203a
1980 125,179,186a,198a
1981 155,190,236,274,334a
1982 155,191,274,187a,199a
1983 126,213,189a,201a
1984 166,200,224,273,337a
1985 123,224,190a,202a
1986 127,237,191a,203a
1987 132,216,189a,201a
1988 124,205,189a,201a
1989 128,226,262,273,276,190a,202a
1910 121,226,238,250,273,190a,202a
1991 125,226,190a,202a
1992 166,227,238,259,262,273,343a
1993 122,238,262,191a,203a
1994 127,238,262,191a,203a
1995 131,213,238,341a
1996 123,228,239,343a
1997 128,217,239,343a
1998 132,239,191a,203a
1999 125,239,260,191a,203a

1st February

1930 132,226,190a,202a
1931 160,208,184a,196a
1932 129,178,209,192a,203a
1933 158,179,229,329a
1934 155,229,274,191a,203a
1935 130,229,191a,203a
1936 123,179,213,190a,204a
1937 127,178,214,262,192a,200a
1938 131,230,191a,203a
1939 124,178,216,189a,201a
1940 128,193,181a,193a
1941 121,190,206,218,230,246,261, 182a,194a
1942 125,191,230,261,299a
1943 129,178,208,192a,202a
1944 155,178,258,261,274,183a,195a
1945 126,178,255,192a,202a
1946 155,231,260,274,279,191a,203a
1947 155,231,258,260,274,191a,203a
1948 128,179,213,192a,198a
1949 155,231,274,191a,203a
1950 155,232,274,191a,203a
1951 129,247,192a,204a
1952 121,178,205,190a,200a
1953 126,179,255,192a,204a
1954 155,232,274,191a,203a
1955 122,179,208,189a,193a
1956 127,179,209,260,192a,201a
1957 131,178,248,190a,194a
1958 124,178,212,191a,201a
1959 128,179,233,192a,194a
1960 121,179,190a,202a
1961 125,179,214,192a,196a
1962 155,233,274,191a,203a
1963 122,178,216,227,189a,197a
1964 126,178,234,329a
1965 131,178,234,256,259,262,186a, 198a
1966 123,207,234,262,191a,203a
1967 164,228,248,259,262,192a,199a
1968 132,179,186a,198a
1969 125,179,256,192a,200a
1970 129,178,212,192a,193a
1971 157,213,258,261,189a,201a
1972 126,179,213,192a,193a
1973 155,219,258,261,274,190a,202a
1974 155,235,258,261,274,191a,203a
1975 127,179,249,192a,202a
1976 131,178,205,190a,195a
1977 124,178,206,192a,202a
1978 128,178,207,191a,196a
1979 121,236,191a,203a
1980 125,179,186a,198a
1981 155,190,274,187a,199a
1982 155,190,274,187a,199a
1983 127,213,189a,201a
1984 131,200,224,337a
1985 123,179,224,237,192a,204a
1986 128,200,237,338a
1987 132,216,189a,201a
1988 124,205,189a,201a
1989 129,226,238,250,273,190a,202a
1990 121,226,238,250,273,190a,202a

1991 162,226,190a,202a
1992 166,227,238,259,262,343a
1993 123,211,238,262,191a,203a
1994 127,238,262,191a,203a
1995 132,213,189a,201a
1996 124,228,239,343a
1997 128,217,239,343a
1998 121,239,191a,203a
1999 125,239,260,191a,203a

2nd February

1930 132,226,190a,202a
1931 125,178,208,189a,197a
1932 129,178,209,192a,203a
1933 158,179,229,329a
1934 155,229,274,191a,203a
1935 130,180,229,192a,199a
1936 123,179,213,190a,204a
1937 128,178,214,181a,200a
1938 132,230,191a,203a
1939 124,179,216,189a,201a
1940 165,193,181a,193a
1941 121,190,206,218,230,246,261, 182a,194a
1942 125,191,230,261,299a
1943 130,219,190a,202a
1944 122,178,209,258,261,190a,195a
1945 127,178,220,181a,202a
1946 155,231,260,274,279,191a,203a
1947 155,231,258,260,274,191a,203a
1948 128,180,213,192a,198a
1949 155,231,258,261,274,191a,203a
1950 155,232,274,191a,203a
1951 129,247,192a,204a
1952 122,178,205,190a,200a
1953 126,179,206,181a,204a
1954 155,232,274,191a,203a
1955 123,179,208,224,260,189a,193a
1956 127,179,209,260,192a,201a
1957 132,178,211,190a,194a
1958 124,178,212,191a,201a
1959 129,179,212,192a,194a
1960 121,226,190a,202a
1961 126,180,214,181a,196a
1962 155,233,274,191a,203a
1963 122,178,216,227,189a,197a
1964 127,234,191a,203a
1965 131,178,234,256,259,262,186a, 198a
1966 123,207,234,262,191a,203a
1967 164,228,248,259,262,192a,199a
1968 132,179,248,330a
1969 125,179,256,181a,200a
1970 129,178,212,191a,193a
1971 122,213,261,189a,201a
1972 126,179,213,192a,193a
1973 155,235,258,261,274,191a,203a
1974 155,235,261,274,279,191a,203a
1975 164,220,236,192a,202a
1976 132,178,205,190a,195a
1977 124,178,206,181a,202a
1978 129,178,207,191a,196a
1979 121,236,191a,203a
1980 125,179,186a,198a
1981 155,190,274,187a,199a
1982 155,190,274,187a,199a
1983 127,213,189a,201a
1984 131,200,224,337a
1985 124,179,214,181a,204a
1986 128,215,237,341a
1987 157,216,189a,201a
1988 161,205,189a,201a
1989 129,226,238,250,273,190a,202a
1990 158,226,262,276,190a,202a
1991 162,226,190a,202a
1992 166,227,238,259,262,343a
1993 123,211,238,262,191a,203a
1994 164,203,238,259,262,338a
1995 132,213,189a,201a
1996 124,228,239,343a
1997 129,217,239,261,343a
1998 121,239,191a,203a
1999 126,239,191a,203a

3rd February

1930 121,226,190a,202a
1931 125,178,208,189a,197a
1932 130,226,190a,202a
1933 158,179,229,329a
1934 155,229,274,191a,203a
1935 131,229,191a,203a
1936 123,179,213,190a,204a
1937 128,178,214,181a,200a
1938 132,230,191a,203a
1939 161,217,255,189a,201a
1940 165,193,181a,193a
1941 158,190,206,261,182a,194a
1942 162,191,130,261,299a
1943 130,219,190a,202a
1944 123,178,258,261,183a,195a
1945 127,178,220,181a,202a
1946 155,231,260,274,191a,203a
1947 155,231,258,260,274,191a,203a
1948 129,180,213,192a,198a
1949 155,231,258,274,191a,203a
1950 155,232,274,191a,203a
1951 130,247,192a,204a
1952 122,179,205,190a,200a
1953 127,181,187a,199a
1954 155,232,258,260,274,191a,203a
1955 123,179,208,224,260,189a,193a
1956 128,178,209,192a,201a
1957 132,178,211,190a,194a
1958 125,178,212,191a,201a
1959 129,179,212,192a,194a
1960 158,226,190a,202a

1961 126,180,214,181a,196a
1962 155,233,274,191a,203a
1963 123,178,216,227,189a,197a
1964 127,234,191a,203a
1965 132,179,234,256,259,262,186a,
198a
1966 124,234,262,191a,203a
1967 129,179,208,192a,199a
1968 121,180,180i,186a,198a
1969 125,179,256,181a,200a
1970 130,178,212,191a,193a
1971 122,213,261,189a,201a
1972 127,192,178a,199a
1973 155,235,258,261,274,191a,203a
1974 155,219,235,257,274,190a,194a
1975 164,220,236,192a,202a
1976 132,178,205,190a,195a
1977 125,178,236,181a,202a
1978 129,178,207,191a,196a
1979 122,236,191a,203a
1980 126,179,186a,198a
1981 155,190,274,187a,199a
1982 123,190,187a,199a
1983 127,213,189a,201a
1984 132,200,224,337a
1985 124,179,214,181a,193a
1986 129,215,237,341a
1987 157,216,189a,201a
1988 161,205,189a,201a
1989 166,226,262,273,276,190a,202a
1990 158,226,262,276,190a,202a
1991 127,226,190a,202a
1992 131,227,238,250,259,262,343a
1993 123,238,191a,203a
1994 164,203,238,259,262,338a
1995 132,213,189a,201a
1996 125,228,239,343a
1997 155,239,258,261,274,191a,203a
1998 155,239,274,191a,203a
1999 126,239,191a,203a

4th February

1930 121,226,190a,202a
1931 126,178,208,189a,197a
1932 130,226,190a,202a
1933 123,179,229,329a
1934 127,229,191a,203a
1935 131,229,191a,203a
1936 179,213,190a,204a
1937 128,178,214,181a,200a
1938 121,193,230,289a
1939 161,217,255,189a,201a
1940 130,193,181a,193a
1941 158,190,182a,194a
1942 162,191,230,261,299a
1943 131,219,231,247,192a,202a
1944 123,178,258,261,183a,195a
1945 128,178,210,181a,202a
1946 155,231,260,274,191a,203a
1947 155,231,258,260,274,191a,203a
1948 129,180,213,182a,198a
1949 155,213,258,261,274,191a,203a
1950 155,232,274,191a,203a
1951 130,247,192a,204a
1952 123,223,247,190a,200a
1953 127,181,187a,199a
1954 155,232,258,260,274,191a,203a
1955 160,208,260,184a,196a
1956 128,178,209,192a,201a
1957 121,178,248,190a,194a
1958 125,178,212,191a,202a
1959 130,179,233,192a,194a
1960 158,226,190a,202a
1961 126,180,214,181a,196a
1962 155,233,274,279,191a,203a
1963 123,178,216,227,189a,197a
1964 128,234,191a,203a
1965 132,179,234,256,259,262,186a,
198a
1966 124,234,262,191a,203a
1967 129,179,208,192a,199a
1968 121,180,180i,186a,198a
1969 126,179,211,181a,200a
1970 130,178,212,191a,193a
1971 123,213,261,189a,201a
1972 127,192,187a,199a
1973 155,235,258,261,274,191a,203a
1974 155,219,235,257,274,190a,194a
1975 164,220,236,192a,202a
1976 121,178,205,190a,195a
1977 125,178,236,181a,202a
1978 130,178,207,191a,196a
1979 122,236,191a,203a
1980 126,179,186a,198a
1981 131,191,236,260,279,334a
1982 123,190,187a,199a
1983 128,213,189a,201a
1984 132,200,224,337a
1985 125,179,214,181a,193a
1986 129,215,237,341a
1987 122,216,189a,201a
1988 126,205,189a,201a
1989 166,226,273,276,190a,202a
1990 123,226,238,250,259,262,273,
190a,202a
1991 127,226,190a,202a
1992 131,227,238,250,259,262,343a
1993 124,238,191a,203a
1994 129,238,191a,203a
1995 157,213,189a,201a
1996 125,228,239,343a
1997 155,217,239,258,261,274,343a
1998 122,239,191a,203a
1999 127,239,258,191a,203a

5th February

1930 158,226,190a,202a
1931 126,178,208,189a,197a
1932 155,229,274,191a,203a
1933 123,179,229,329a
1934 127,229,191a,203a
1935 168,246,192a,204a
1936 124,179,213,190a,204a
1937 129,178,214,181a,200a
1938 121,193,230,289a
1939 126,179,216,189a,201a
1940 130,193,181a,193a
1941 158,190,182a,194a
1942 127,191,230,258,261,299a
1943 131,219,231,247,192a,202a
1944 155,178,274,183a,195a
1945 128,179,210,181a,202a
1946 155,231,260,274,191a,203a
1947 155,231,247,258,260,274,323a
1948 129,180,213,192a,198a
1949 155,231,258,261,274,191a,203a
1950 155,232,274,191a,203a
1951 131,274,192a,204a
1952 123,223,247,190a,200a
1953 127,181,187a,199a
1954 168,224,232,260,191a,200a
1955 160,208,260,184a,196a
1956 165,209,189a,201a
1957 121,178,248,190a,194a
1958 126,178,212,191a,202a
1959 130,179,233,192a,194a
1960 158,226,190a,202a
1961 127,180,214,181a,195a
1962 155,233,274,279,191a,203a
1963 124,178,216,227,189a,197a
1964 128,234,191a,203a
1965 132,179,234,262,329a
1966 125,234,191a,203a
1967 129,179,208,192a,199a
1968 158,180,180i,186a,198a
1969 126,179,211,181a,200a
1970 131,235,191a,203a
1971 123,213,261,189a,201a
1972 127,192,187a,199a
1973 155,235,274,191a,203a
1974 155,219,235,257,274,190a,194a
1975 129,179,216,192a,202a
1976 121,178,205,190a,195a
1977 126,178,236,181a,202a
1978 155,236,274,191a,203a
1979 123,236,191a,203a
1980 127,179,186a,198a
1981 131,191,236,260,279,334a
1982 155,190,274,187a,199a
1983 128,213,189a,201a
1984 132,200,224,337a
1985 125,179,214,181a,193a
1986 129,215,237,341a
1987 122,180,216,190a,193a
1988 126,205,189a,201a
1989 131,226,238,250,259,262,343a
1990 123,226,238,250,259,262,273, 190a,202a
1991 128,226,190a,202a
1992 132,227,238,250,259,262,343a
1993 124,238,191a,203a
1994 129,238,191a,203a
1995 121,228,190a,202a
1996 125,228,239,343a
1997 155,217,239,258,261,274,343a
1998 123,239,191a,203a
1999 127,239,258,260,191a,203a

6th February

1930 158,226,190a,202a
1931 127,178,208,189a,197a
1932 155,229,274,191a,203a
1933 124,179,229,329a
1934 155,229,274,191a,203a
1935 168,246,192a,204a
1936 125,179,213,190a,204a
1937 129,178,214,181a,200a
1938 121,193,230,289a
1939 126,179,216,190a,201a
1940 130,193,181a,193a
1941 123,190,218,230,246,182a,194a
1942 127,191,230,258,261,299a
1943 132,178,255,192a,202a
1944 155,178,274,183a,195a
1945 128,179,210,181a,202a
1946 155,231,258,260,274,191a,203a
1947 155,231,274,323a
1948 130,180,213,192a,198a
1949 155,231,258,261,274,191a,203a
1950 127,191,232,334a
1951 131,247,192a,204a
1952 123,223,247,190a,200a
1953 128,179,206,181a,204a
1954 168,224,232,260,191a,200a
1955 125,179,208,190a,193a
1956 165,209,189a,201a
1957 122,178,248,191a,194a
1958 126,178,212,191a,202a
1959 131,233,191a,203a
1960 123,226,190a,202a
1961 127,180,214,181a,195a
1962 155,233,274,191a,203a
1963 124,178,216,227,190a,197a
1964 128,234,191a,203a
1965 121,179,234,329a
1966 125,234,191a,203a
1967 130,228,248,259,262,192a,204a
1968 158,180,180i,186a,198a
1969 127,181,187a,199a
1970 131,235,191a,203a
1971 124,213,189a,201a
1972 128,179,218,192a,193a

1973 155,235,274,191a,203a
1974 155,219,235,257,274,190a,194a
1975 129,279,216,192a,202a
1976 121,178,205,190a,195a
1977 126,178,236,181a,202a
1978 155,236,258,260,274,191a,203a
1979 123,236,191a,203a
1980 127,179,186a,198a
1981 155,191,236,258,260,274,334a
1982 155,190,274,187a,199a
1983 129,213,189a,201a
1984 121,200,224,337a
1985 125,179,214,181a,193a
1986 130,215,237,341a
1987 122,180,216,190a,193a
1988 126,205,189a,201a
1989 131,226,238,250,259,262,343a
1990 124,226,238,250,259,262,273,
190a,202a
1991 128,226,190a,202a
1992 132,227,238,250,259,262,343a
1993 125,238,191a,203a
1994 129,238,191a,203a
1995 122,228,190a,202a
1996 126,228,239,343a
1997 131,239,258,261,274,191a,203a
1998 123,239,191a,203a
1999 127,239,258,260,191a,203a

7th February

1930 122,229,191a,203a
1931 127,226,190a,202a
1932 155,229,274,191a,203a
1933 124,179,229,329a
1934 128,229,191a,203a
1935 121,180,227,246,192a,199a
1936 125,179,213,190a,204a
1937 166,228,190a,202a
1938 122,230,191a,203a
1939 127,179,216,190a,201a
1940 155,193,230,274,289a
1941 123,191,261,182a,194a
1942 128,191a,230,299a
1943 132,178,255,192a,202a
1944 155,178,274,183a,195a
1945 129,179,220,181a,202a
1946 155,231,258,260,274,191a,203a
1947 155,231,274,191a,203a
1948 130,180,213,192a,198a
1949 123,231,261,179,191a,203a
1950 127,191,232,334a
1951 168,247,192a,202a
1952 124,179,205,190a,200a
1953 128,179,206,181a,204a
1954 121,180,207,260,191a,200a
1955 125,179,208,190a,193a
1956 165,209,189a,201a
1957 122,178,248,191a,194a
1958 127,233,191a,203a
1959 131,233,191a,203a
1960 123,226,190a,202a
1961 128,180,214,181a,196a
1962 155,233,274,191a,203a
1963 125,178,216,227,190a,197a
1964 129,234,191a,203a
1965 121,179,234,329a
1966 126,179,262,186a,198a
1967 130,228,248,259,262,192a,204a
1968 158,180,180i,186a,198a
1969 127,181,187a,199a
1970 132,178,212,191a,193a
1971 124,213,189a,201a
1972 128,179,214,192a,193a
1973 155,235,258,261,274,191a,203a
1974 155,219,235,257,274,190a,194a
1975 130,179,149,192a,202a
1976 122,178,205,190a,195a
1977 127,178,236,181a,202a
1978 155,236,258,260,274,191a,203a
1979 123,236,191a,203a
1980 127,180,186a,198a
1981 155,191,258,260,274,335a
1982 155,190,274,187a,199a
1983 129,213,189a,201a
1984 121,200,224,337a
1985 126,237,191a,203a
1986 130,215,237,341a
1987 123,180,216,190a,193a
1988 127,205,189a,201a
1989 132,226,238,250,259,262,190a,
202a
1990 124,226,238,250,259,262,273,
190a,202a
1991 128,238,191a,203a
1992 132,227,238,250,259,262,343a
1993 125,238,191a,203a
1994 130,228,238,262,343a
1995 122,228,190a,202a
1996 126,228,239,343a
1997 131,239,258,261,274,191a,203a
1998 124,239,191a,203a
1999 128,239,260,191a,203a

8th February

1930 123,229,191a,203a
1931 128,226,190a,202a
1932 132,229,191a,203a
1933 124,179,229,329a
1934 129,229,191a,203a
1935 121,180,246,192a,199a
1936 126,179,213,190a,204a
1937 166,228,190a,202a
1938 122,230,191a,203a
1939 127,179,216,190a,201a
1940 155,193,230,274,289a

1941 124,191,182a,194a
1942 128,191,230,299a
1943 121,178,208,192a,202a
1944 155,178,219,231,247,258,261, 274,302a
1945 129,179,220,181a,202a
1946 155,231,274,191a,203a
1947 126,180,212,190a,203a
1948 131,180,213,192a,198a
1949 123,231,261,279,191a,203a
1950 155,232,274,191a,203a
1951 168,247,192a,202a
1952 124,179,205,190a,200a
1953 129,179,232,181a,193a
1954 121,180,207,260,191a,200a
1955 126,179,208,190a,193a
1956 130,178,209,192a,201a
1957 122,178,248,191a,194a
1958 127,233,191a,203a
1959 131,233,191a,203a
1960 124,226,190a,202a
1961 128,180,214,181a,196a
1962 155,233,274,191a,203a
1963 125,178,216,227,190a,197a
1964 129,234,191a,203a
1965 158,179,234,259,262,329a
1966 126.179,262,186a,198a
1967 131,228,248,259,262,192a,204a
1968 123,180,180i,186a,198a
1969 128,200,188a,200a
1970 132,178,212,191a,193a
1971 124,213,189a,201a
1972 129,179,214,192a,193a
1973 155,235,258,261,274,191a,203a
1974 155,219,235,257,274,190a,194a
1975 130,179,249,192a,202a
1976 122,178,205,190a,195a
1977 127,178,236,181a,202a
1978 155,236,258,260,274,191a,203a
1979 124,236,191a,203a
1980 128,180,186a,198a
1981 155,191,258,260,274,335a
1982 155,190,274,187a,199a
1983 130,213,189a,201a
1984 121,200,224,337a
1985 126,237,191a,203a
1986 155,215,237,274,341a
1987 123,180,216,190a,193a
1988 127,205,189a,201a
1989 132,226,238,250,259,262,190a, 202a
1990 125,226,238,250,273,190a,202a
1991 129,238,191a,203a
1992 121,227,238,250,343a
1993 126,180,211,227,181a,196a
1994 130,228,238,262,343a
1995 122,228,190a,202a
1996 127,228,239,343a
1997 155,239,274,191a,203a
1998 124,239,191a,203a
1999 128,239,191a,203a.

9th February

1930 123,229,191a,203a
1931 128,226,190a,202a
1932 132,229,191a,203a
1933 125,179,229,329a
1934 129,229,191a,203a
1935 122,180,229,192a,199a
1936 126,179,213,190a,204a
1937 166,228,190a,202a
1938 123,230,191a,203a
1939 127,179,216,190a,201a
1940 132,193,181a,193a
1941 124,191,182a,194a
1942 129,230,261,299a
1943 121,178,208,192a,202a
1944 155,178,219,231,247,258,261, 274,302a
1945 130,179,220,181a,202a
1946 155,231,274,191a,203a
1947 127,231,247,190a,203a
1948 131,180,213,192a,198a
1949 123,231,261,279,191a,203a
1950 155,232,274,191a,203a
1951 121,247,192a,204a
1952 125,179,205,190a,200a
1953 129,179,232,181a,193a
1954 122,180,255,191a,200a
1955 126,179,208,190a,193a
1956 130,178,209,192a,201a
1957 123,178,248,191a,194a
1958 128,233,256,338a
1959 132,179,233,192a,194a
1960 124,226,190a,202a
1961 129,180,214,181a,196a
1962 155,233,274,191a,203a
1963 162,178,186a,198a
1964 130,234,191a,203a
1965 158,179,234,259,262,329a
1966 127,179,207,262,190a,204a
1967 131,228,248,259,262,192a,204a
1968 123,180,180i,186a,198a
1969 128,200,188a,200a
1970 121,178,212,191a,193a
1971 125,213,261,189a,201a
1972 129,179,214,192a,193a
1973 155,235,258,261,274,191a,203a
1974 155,219,235,257,274,190a,194a
1975 131,179,236,191a,203a
1976 123,178,205,190a,195a
1977 127,178,236,181a,203a
1978 155,236,258,260,174,191a,203a
1979 124,236,191a,203a
1980 128,180,186a,198a
1981 155,191,258,260,274,335a
1982 155,190,274,187a,199a

1983 130,213,189a,201a
1984 122,200,224,337a
1985 127,237,191a,203a
1986 155,215,237,274,341a
1987 124,180,216,190a,193a
1988 128,205,189a,201a
1989 121,226,190a,202a
1990 125,226,238,250,273,190a,202a
1991 129,238,191a,203a
1992 121,227,238,250,343a
1993 126,180,211,227,181a,196a
1994 131,238,262,191a,203a
1995 123,228,190a,202a
1996 127,228,239,343a
1997 155,239,274,191a,203a
1998 124,239,191a,203a
1999 129,239,260,191a,203a

10th February

1930 124,229,191a,203a
1931 129,226,190a,202a
1932 121,229,191a,203a
1933 125,179,229,329a
1934 130,229,191a,203a
1935 122,180,229,192a,199a
1936 126,179,213,190a,204a
1937 131,178,214,181a,200a
1938 123,230,191a,203a
1939 128,179,216,190a,201a
1940 132,193,181a,193a
1941 125,191,261,182a,194a
1942 129,191,230,261,299a
1943 122,178,255,192a,202a
1944 155,178,258,261,274,302a
1945 130,179,220,181a,202a
1946 123,231,260,279,191a,203a
1947 127,231,247,190a,203a
1948 131,180,213,192a,198a
1949 155,231,274,191a,203a
1950 155,232,274,191a,203a
1951 121,247,260,192a,204a
1952 125,179,205,190a,200a
1953 130,179,232,181a,193a
1954 122,180,207,191a,201a
1955 127,179,208,224,190a,193a
1956 131,178,209,192a,201a
1957 123,178,248,191a,194a
1958 128,233,256,338a
1959 132,179,233,192a,194a
1960 124,226,190a,202a
1961 129,180,214,181a,196a
1962 155,233,274,191a,203a
1963 162,178,186a,198a
1964 130,234,191a,203a
1965 123,179,234,262,329a
1966 127,179,207,262,190a,204a
1967 168,248,259,262,192a,204a
1968 124,180,180i,186a,198a
1969 128,200,188a,200a
1970 121,178,212,191a,193a
1971 125,213,261,189a,201a
1972 129,179,214,261,181a,193a
1973 122,180,214,191a,201a
1974 127,190,187a,199a
1975 131,179,236,191a,203a
1976 123,178,205,190a,195a
1977 128,178,206,181a,203a
1978 155,236,258,260,274,191a,203a
1979 125,236,191a,203a
1980 129,180,186a,198a
1981 155,191,274,187a,199a
1982 155,190,274,187a,199a
1983 130,213,189a,201a
1984 122,200,224,337a
1985 127,237,191a,203a
1986 132,215,237,341a
1987 124,180,216,190a,193a
1988 128,205,225,237,189a,201a
1989 121,226,190a,202a
1990 125,226,238,250,273,190a,202a
1991 130,227,238,343a
1992 158,227,259,262,343a
1993 127,180,211,227,181a,196a
1994 131,238,262,191a,203a
1995 123,228,190a,202a
1996 127,228,239,343a
1997 155,239,258,261,274,191a,203a
1998 125,239,191a,203a
1999 129,239,260,191a,203a

11th February

1930 124,229,191a,203a
1931 129,226,190a,202a
1932 121,229,191a,203a
1933 126,179,229,329a
1934 130,229,191a,203a
1935 123,180,229,246,192a,199a
1936 127,179,213,190a,204a
1937 131,178,214,181a,200a
1938 214,230,191a,203a
1939 128,179,216,190a,201a
1940 132,193,181a,193a
1941 125,191,261,182a,194a
1942 166,191,230,261,299a
1943 122,178,255,192a,202a
1944 155,178,258,261,274,302a
1945 155,231,274,191a,203a
1946 123,231,260,279,191a,203a
1947 128,180,212,190a,203a
1948 132,247,192a,204a
1949 155,231,274,191a,203a
1950 155,232,274,191a,203a
1951 121,247,260,192a,204a
1952 125,179,205,190a,200a
1953 130,179,232,181a,193a

1954 123,247,258,260,191a,201a
1955 127,179,208,224,190a,193a
1956 131,225,255,181a,201a
1957 124,178,211,191a,194a
1958 128,233,256,338a
1959 121,179,213,192a,195a
1960 125,226,190a,202a
1961 129,180,214,181a,196a
1962 155,233,274,191a,203a
1963 162,178,186a,198a
1964 130,234,191a,203a
1965 123,179,234,262,329a
1966 128,179,207,262,190a,204a
1967 168,248,259,262,192a,204a
1968 124,180,180i,186a,198a
1969 129,179,256,181a,200a
1970 122,178,212,191a,193a
1971 126,213,261,189a,201a
1972 130,179,214,261,181a,194a
1973 123,219,235,257,191a,201a
1974 127,190,187a,199a
1975 131,179,236,191a,203a
1976 123,178,205,190a,195a
1977 128,179,136,191a,203a
1978 155,236,258,260,274,191a,203a
1979 125,236,191a,203a
1980 129,180,186a,198a
1981 155,191,274,187a,199a
1982 127,190,187a,199a
1983 131,213,189a,201a
1984 123,200,224,337a
1985 128,193,237,338a
1986 132,215,237,341a
1987 124,180,216,190a,193a
1988 128,205,225,237,189a,201a
1989 158,191,226,262,276,298a
1990 162,226,262,273,276,190a,202a
1991 130,227,238,343a
1992 158,227,259,262,343a
1993 127,180,211,227,181a,196a
1994 168,238,250,259,262,345a
1995 124,228,190a,202a
1996 128,228,239,343a
1997 155,239,258,261,274,191a,203a
1998 125,239,191a,203a
1999 129,239,260,191a,203a

12th February

1930 125,229,191a,203a
1931 129,179,208,190a,197a
1932 121,229,191a,203a
1933 126,179,229,329a
1934 131,229,191a,203a
1935 123,180,229,246,192a,199a
1936 127,179,213,190a,204a
1937 132,178,214,181a,200a
1938 124,230,191a,203a
1939 129,179,216,190a,201a
1940 157,193,264,181a,193a
1941 125,261,182a,194a
1942 166,191,230,261,299a
1943 122,178,255,192a,202a
1944 155,178,258,261,274,302a
1945 155,231,274,191a,203a
1946 155,231,258,260,274,191a,203a
1947 128,180,212,190a,203a
1948 155,221,255,258,260,274,185a, 197a
1949 155,231,274,191a,203a
1950 155,232,274,191a,203a
1951 122,247,192a,204a
1952 126,179,205,190a,200a
1953 131,180,206,181a,193a
1954 123,247,258,260,191a,201a
1955 127,179,208,224,190a,193a
1956 131,225,255,181a,201a
1957 124,178,211,191a,194a
1958 129,233,191a,203a
1959 121,179,213,192a,195a
1960 125,226,190a,202a
1961 130,226,190a,202a
1962 123,233,274,279,191a,203a
1963 127,178,216,227,190a,197a
1964 155,234,274,191a,203a
1965 124,179,234,262,329a
1966 128,179,207,262,190a,204a
1967 168,248,259,192a,204a
1968 125,179,186a,198a
1969 129,179,256,181a,200a
1970 122,178,212,191a,193a
1971 126,213,261,189a,201a
1972 130,179,214,261,181a,194a
1973 123,219,235,257,190a,201a
1974 155,219,235,257,274,190a,194a
1975 168,249,192a,204a
1976 124,178,205,190a,195a
1977 129,179,236,191a,203a
1978 129,179,236,191a,203a
1979 125,236,191a,203a
1980 130,180,186a,198a
1981 123,191,258,260,187a,199a
1982 127,190,187a,199a
1983 131,213,189a,201a
1984 123,200,224,337a
1985 128,193,237,338a
1986 121,215,237,341a
1987 125,180,216,190a,193a
1988 165,205,189a,201a
1989 158,191,226,262,276,298a
1990 162,226,259,273,190a,202a
1991 130,227,238,343a
1992 123,227,238,250,259,262,343a
1993 128,180,211,227,181a,196a
1994 168,238,250,259,262,345a
1995 124,228,190a,202a
1996 128,228,239,343a
1997 155,239,258,261,274,191a,203a

1998 126,239,191a,203a
1999 130,239,191a,203a

13th February

1930 125,229,191a,203a
1931 130,226,190a,202a
1932 122,229,191a,203a
1933 127,179,229,329a
1934 131,229,191a,203a
1935 123,180,229,246,192a,199a
1936 127,179,213,190a,204a
1937 132,178,214,181a,200a
1938 125,230,191a,203a
1939 129,179,216,190a,201a
1940 157,193,264,181a,193a
1941 162,191,206,261,182a,194a
1942 166,191,230,261,299a
1943 123,178,183a,195a
1944 127,179,261,279,183a,195a
1945 132,179,210,181a,202a
1946 155,231,258,260,274,191a,203a
1947 129,180,212,190a,203a
1948 121,258,260,185a,197a
1949 155,231,274,191a,203a
1950 155,232,274,191a,203a
1951 122,247,192a,204a
1952 126,179,205,190a,200a
1953 131,180,206,181a,193a
1954 124,180,207,260,191a,201a
1955 128,179,208,190a,193a
1956 132,225,255,181a,201a
1957 155,233,274,323a
1958 129,233,191a,203a
1959 121,179,213,192a,195a
1960 162,226,190a,202a
1961 130,226,190a,202a
1962 123,233,274,179,191a,203a
1963 127,178,216,227,190a,197a
1964 155,234,274,191a,203a
1965 124,179,234,262,329a
1966 129,248,192a,204a
1967 121,228,248,192a,204a
1968 125,179,186a
1969 130,179,211,181a,200a
1970 122,178,212,191a,193a
1971 126,213,261,189a,201a
1972 155,235,258,261,274,191a,203a
1973 124,180,214,190a,201a
1974 155,219,235,257,274,190a,194a
1975 168,249,192a,204a
1976 124,178,205,190a,195a
1977 129,179,236,191a,203a
1978 155,236,258,260,274,191a,203a
1979 126,236,191a,203a
1980 130,180,186a,198a
1981 123,191,258,260,187a,199a
1982 127,190,187a,199a
1983 131,213,189a,201a
1984 124,200,224,337a
1985 129,237,191a,203a
1986 121,215,189a,201a
1987 125,180,216,190a,193a
1988 165,205,189a,201a
1989 123,226,238,250,259,262,190a, 202a
1990 127,226,238,250,259,262,273, 190a,202a
1991 155,238,274,191a,203a
1992 123,227,238,250,259,262,343a
1993 128,180,211,227,181a,196a
1994 168,250,259,262,192a,204a
1995 125,228,190a,202a
1996 129,228,239,343a
1997 155,239,258,261,274,191a,203a
1998 126,239,191a,203a
1999 130,239,191a,203a

14th February

1930 126,229,191a,203a
1931 130,226,190a,202a
1932 122,229,191a,203a
1933 127,180,180i,229,329a
1934 132,229,246,345a
1935 160,254,192a,199a
1936 128,179,213,190a,204a
1937 121,179,214,181a,200a
1938 125,230,191a,203a,
1939 130,179,216,190a,201a
1940 122,193,217,255,181a,193a
1941 162,191,206,261,182a,194a
1942 155,191,230,258,261,274,299a
1943 123,178,183a,195a
1944 127,179,261,279,183a,195a
1945 155,231,274,191a,203a
1946 155,231,258,260,274,191a,203a
1947 129,180,212,190a,203a
1948 121,258,260,185a,197a
1949 155,231,274,191a,203a
1950 155,232,274,191a.203a
1951 123,247,258,260,192a,204a
1952 127,190,187a,199a
1953 132,180,206,181a,193a
1954 124,180,207,260,191a,201a
1955 128,179,208,190a,193a
1956 132,225,255,181a,201a
1957 155,233,274,323a
1958 130,233,191a,203a
1959 122,179,213,192a,195a
1960 162,226,190a,202a
1961 131,180,214,181a,196a
1962 123,233,274,279,191a,203a
1963 128,178,216,227,190a,197a
1964 132,234,191a,203a
1965 125,179,234,329a
1966 129,248,192a,204a
1967 121,228,248,192a,204a

1968 125,179,186a,198a
1969 130,179,211,181a,200a
1970 123,179,212,192a,193a
1971 127,213,261,189a,201a
1972 155,235,258,261,274,191a,203a
1973 124,180,214,190a,201a
1974 155,219,235,257,274,190a,194a
1975 121,179,216,192a,202a
1976 125,178,190a,195a
1977 130,179,236,191a,203a
1978 122,179,207,192a,196a
1979 126,236,191a,203a
1980 130,180,186a,198a
1981 155,191,258,260,274,187a,199a
1982 155,190,274,187a,199a
1983 132,213,249,260,342a
1984 124,200,224,337a
1985 129,237,191a,203a
1986 122,215,189a,201a
1987 126,180,216,190a,193a
1988 130,226,190a,202a
1989 123,226,238,250,259,262,190a,202a
1990 127,226,238,250,259,262,273,190a,202a
1991 155,238,274,191a,203a
1992 124,227,238,250,259,262,343a
1993 129,180,211,227,181a,196a
1994 121,203,228,250,192a,204a
1995 125,228,190a,202a
1996 129,228,239,343a
1997 155,239,258,261,274,191a,203a
1998 126,239,191a,203a
1999 131,239,260,191a,203a

15th February

1930 126,229,191a,203a
1931 155,229,274,191a,203a
1932 123,229,191a,203a
1933 127,180,180i,229,329a
1934 132,229,246,345a
1935 160,228,254,192a,199a
1936 128,179,213,190a,204a
1937 121,179,214,181a,200a
1938 126,230,191a,203a
1939 130,179,216,190a,201a
1940 122,193,217,255,181a,193a
1941 127,191,261,182a,194a
1942 155,191,230,258,261,274,299a
1943 124,178,255,192a,202a
1944 155,179,274,183a,195a
1945 155,231,274,191a,203a
1946 155,231,258,260,274,191a,203a
1947 129,180,212,190a,203a
1948 121,258,260,185a,197a
1949 155,231,274,191a,203a
1950 155,232,274,279,191a,203a
1951 123,247,258,260,192a,204a
1952 127,190,187a,199a
1953 132,180,206,181a,193a
1954 160,224,232,260,192a,201a
1955 129,179,208,190a,193a
1956 157,225,255,258,260,181a,201a
1957 126,233,191a,203a
1958 130,233,191a,203a
1959 122,179,213,192a,195a
1960 162,226,190a,202a
1961 131,180,214,181a,196a
1962 155,233,274,191a,203a
1963 128,234,274,191a,203a
1964 132,234,191a,203a
1965 125,179,234,329a
1966 130,248,262,192a,204a
1967 122,228,248,259,262,192a,204a
1968 162,179,186a,198a
1969 155,235,274,191a,203a
1970 123,179,212,192a,193a
1971 127,213,261,189a,201a
1972 132,179,214,181a,194a
1973 125,180,214,181a,194a
1974 155,219,235,257,274,190a,194a
1975 121,179,216,192a,202a
1976 125,178,205,190a,195a
1977 130,179,236,191a,203a
1978 123,257,258,260,192a,196a
1979 127,180,209,190a,203a
1980 131,180,186,198a
1981 155,191,258,260,274,187a,199a
1982 155,190,274,187a,199a
1983 132,213,249,260,342a
1984 125,200,224,337a
1985 130,237,191a,203a
1986 122,215,189a,201a
1987 126,180,216,190a,193a
1988 130,226,190a,202a
1989 123,226,238,250,259,262,343a
1990 128,226,238,250,259,262,273,190a,202a
1991 132,238,191a,203a
1992 124,227,238,250,259,262,343a
1993 129,180,211,227,181a,196a
1994 121,203,228,250,192a,204a
1995 125,228,190a,202a
1996 130,228,239,343a
1997 123,239,261,274,279,191a,203a
1998 127,239,191a,203a
1999 131,239,260,191a,203a

16th February

1930 127,229,191a,203a
1931 155,229,274,191a,203a
1932 123,229,191a,203a
1933 128,180i,229,329a
1934 121,229,191a,203a
1935 125,179,246,192a,199a
1936 129,179,213,190a,204a

1937 122,179,213,181a,200a
1938 126,230,191a,203a
1939 130,179,216,190a,201a
1940 122,193,217,255,181a,193a
1941 127,191,261,182a,194a
1942 132,191,230,299a
1943 155,219,231,247,274,192a,202a
1944 155,179,274,183a,195a
1945 155,231,274,191a,203a
1946 126,180,255,192a,196a
1947 130,180,212,190a,203a
1948 155,221,255,185a,197a
1949 127,231,191a,203a
1950 155,232,274,279,191a,203a
1951 123,247,258,260,192a,204a
1952 127,190,187a,199a
1953 121,193,181a,193a
1954 125,180,207,260,192a,201a
1955 129,179,208,190a,193a
1956 157,225,255,258,250,181a,201a
1957 126,233,191a,203a
1958 131,233,191a,203a
1959 123,179,213,192a,195a
1960 127,226,190a,202a
1961 132,180,214,181a,196a
1962 155,233,274,191a,203a
1963 128,234,191a,203a
1964 121,203,234,289a
1965 162,179,234,259,262,329a
1966 130,248,262,192a,204a
1967 122,228,248,259,262,192a,204a
1968 162,179,186a,198a
1969 155,235,274,191a,203a
1970 124,179,212,192a,193a
1971 128,213,189a,201a
1972 132,179,214,181a,194a
1973 125,180,214,181a,194a
1974 155,219,235,257,274,190a,194a
1975 121,179,216,192a,202a
1976 126,179,205,190a,195a
1977 155,236,274,191a,203a
1978 123,257,258,260,192a,196a
1979 127,190,209,190a,203a
1980 131,180,186a,198a
1981 155,191,236,258,260,274,334a
1982 155,190,212,274,332a
1983 121,213,260,189a,201a
1984 125,200,224,337a
1985 130,237,191a,203a
1986 122,215,189a,201a
1987 126,180,216,190a,193a
1988 131,226,238,343a
1989 123,226,238,250,259,262,343a
1990 128,226,238,250,259,262,273, 190a,202a
1991 132,238,191a,203a
1992 125,227,238,250,190a,202a
1993 130,227,190a,202a
1994 122,203,228,250,259,262,192a, 204a
1995 126,228,190a,202a
1996 130,228,239,343a
1997 123,239,261,274,279,191a,203a
1998 127,239,191a,203a
1999 132,239,251,260,345a

17th February

1930 127,229,191a,203a
1931 155,229,274,316a
1932 123,229,191a,203a
1933 128,180,180i,229,329a
1934 121,229,191a,203a
1935 125,179,246,192a,199a
1936 129,179,213,190a,204a
1937 122,179,214,181a,200a
1938 127,230,191a,203a
1939 155,230,274,191a,203a
1940 123,194,182a,193a
1941 128,191,182a,194a
1942 132,191,230,299a
1943 155,219,231,247,274,192a,202a
1944 155,179,274,183a,195a
1945 155,231,274,191a,203a
1946 126,180,255,192a,196a
1947 130,180,212,190a,203a
1948 155,221,255,274,185a,197a
1949 127,231,191a,203a
1950 155,232,274,191a,203a
1951 160,216,247,260,192a,204a
1952 128,179,205,190a,200a
1953 121,193,181a,193a
1954 125,180,207,260,192a,201a
1955 129,179,208,190a,193a
1956 122,225,255,181a,201a
1957 127,233,191a,203a
1958 131,233,191a,203a
1959 123,180,213,192a,195a
1960 127,226,190a,202a
1961 132,180,204,181a,196a
1962 155,233,274,191a,203a
1963 129,234,191a,203a
1964 121,203,234,289a
1965 162,179,234,259,262,329a
1966 130,248,262,192a,204a
1967 122,228,248,259,262,192a,204a
1968 127,179,186a,198a
1969 132,179,256,181a,200a
1970 124,179,212,192a,193a
1971 128,213,189a,201a
1972 121,179,214,181a,194a
1973 125,180,214,190a,201a
1974 155,219,235,257,274,190a,194a
1975 121,179,249,192a,202a
1976 126,179,205,190a,195a
1977 155,236,274,191a,203a
1978 123,257,258,260,192a,196a
1979 127,180,209,190a,203a
1980 132,180,186a,198a

1981 155,191,236,258,260,274,334a
1982 155,190,212,274,332a
1983 121,213,260,189a,201a
1984 125,200,224,337a
1985 130,237,191a,203a
1986 123,215,189a,201a
1987 126,180,216,190a,193a
1988 131,226,238,343a
1989 123,226,238,250,259,262,343a
1990 128,226,238,250,259,262,273, 190a,202a
1991 121,238,191a,203a
1992 125,227,238,250,190a,202a
1993 130,227,190a,202a
1994 122,203,228,250,259,262,192a, 204a
1995 126,228,190a,202a
1996 131,239,191a,203a
1997 124,239,274,191a,203a
1998 128,239,191a,203a
1999 132,239,251,260,345a

18th February

1930 128,229,191a,203a
1931 168,208,184a,196a
1932 124,229,191a,203a
1933 129,180,180i,229,329a
1934 121,229,191a,203a
1935 125,179,246,192a,199a
1936 130,179,213,190a,204a
1937 123,179,214,181a,200a
1938 127,230,191a,203a
1939 155,230,274,191a,203a
1940 123,194,181a,193a
1941 128,191,218,230,246,182a,194a
1942 121,191,230,261,299a
1943 155,219,231,247,274,192a,202a
1944 155,179,258,261,274,183a,195a
1945 155,231,274,191a,203a
1946 126,180,255,192a,196a
1947 130,180,212,190a,203a
1948 155,221,255,258,260,274,185a, 197a
1949 155,231,274,191a,203a
1950 155,232,274,191a,203a
1951 160,216,247,260,192a,204a
1952 128,179,205,190a,200a
1953 122,180,206,181a,200a
1954 126,180,207,192a,201a
1955 130,179,208,190a,193a
1956 122,225,255,181a,201a
1957 127,233,191a,203a
1958 131,233,191a,203a
1959 123,180,213,192a,195a
1960 128,226,190a,202a
1961 121,180,214,181a,196a
1962 155,233,274,191a,203a
1963 129,234,191a,203a
1964 122,234,191a,203a
1965 127,179,234,262,329a
1966 131,248,262,192a,204a
1967 126,228,248,259,262,192a,204a
1968 127,179,186a,198a
1969 132,179,256,181a,200a
1970 124,179,212,192a,193a
1971 128,213,189a,201a
1972 121,179,214,261,181a,194a
1973 126,180,214,190a,194a
1974 155,219,235,257,274,190a,194a
1975 122,219,249,192a,202a
1976 127,257,190a,195a
1977 132,236,191a,203a
1978 124,179,207,260,192a,196a
1979 128,180,209,190a,203a
1980 132,180,186a,198a
1981 155,191,236,258,260,274,334a
1982 155,190,212,274,332a
1983 122,213,189a,201a
1984 126,200,224,337a
1985 131,237,191a,203a
1986 123,215,189a,201a
1987 127,180,216,190a,193a
1988 132,226,190a,202a
1989 125,226,238,250,343a
1990 129,226,238,250,273,190a,202a
1991 121,238,191a,203a
1992 126,227,238,259,262,343a
1993 130,227,190a,202a
1994 122,203,228,250,259,262,192a, 204a
1995 127,228,190a,202a
1996 131,239,191a,203a
1997 124,239,274,191a,203a
1998 128,239,191a,203a
1999 132,239,251,260,345a

19th February

1930 140,179,229,192a,203a
1931 168,208,184a,196a
1932 124,229,191a,203a
1933 141,180,180i,186a,198a
1934 134,246,192a,204a
1935 126,179,229,192a,199a
1936 130,179,213,190a,204a
1937 135,179,214,228,181a,200a
1938 164,179,215,192a,193a
1939 132,246,192a,204a
1940 124,194,181a,193a
1941 141,191,218,230,246,182a,194a
1942 133,191,182a,194a
1943 155,219,231,247,192a,202a
1944 155,179,258,261,274,183a,195a
1945 159,231,247,191a,202a
1946 156,192,247,260,275,335a
1947 143,180,212,190a,203a

1948 155,221,255,258,260,274,185a, 197a
1949 140,179,255,191a,204a
1950 144,232,247,191a,203a
1951 156,216,247,260,275,192a,204a
1952 129,179,205,190a,200a
1953 134,180,206,181a,193a
1954 156,247,275,192a,204a
1955 142,179,208,190a,193a
1956 123,225,255,258,260,181a,201a
1957 164,179,211,191a,194a
1958 144,179,212,191a,202a
1959 136,248,192a,204a
1960 128,226,190a,202a
1961 133,180,214,263,181a,196a
1962 137,233,191a,203a
1963 142,179,216,190a,197a
1964 122,234,191a,203a
1965 139,179,262,186a,198a
1966 156,248,259,262,275,192a,204a
1967 156,248,262,275,277,192a,204a
1968 128,179,186a,198a
1969 133,200,181a,193a
1970 137,179,212,192a,193a
1971 141,213,189a,201a
1972 122,181,182a,194a
1973 138,180,214,190a,201a
1974 167,219,235,257,190a,194a
1975 156,249,275,192a,204a
1976 127,257,190a,195a
1977 144,179,206,181a,203a
1978 136,236,260,192a,196a
1979 164,180,209,190a,203a
1980 133,180,180i,186a,198a
1981 138,191,223,257,187a,199a
1982 142,190,187a,199a
1983 134,213,249,342a
1984 139,200,188a,200a
1985 143,180,250,181a,193a
1986 135,215,250,342a
1987 140,250,259,263,192a,204a
1988 144,226,190a,202a
1989 137,226,238,250,190a,202a
1990 141,226,238,250,273,190a,202a
1991 133,179,209,192a,195a
1992 138,238,262,191a,203a
1993 148,180,211,181a,196a
1994 156,250,259,262,275,192a,204a
1995 139,228,190a,202a
1996 144,250,192a,204a
1997 136,239,191a,203a
1998 140,239,251,345a
1999 133,200,251,260,290a

20th February

1930 141,179,207,192a,203a
1931 157,208,184a,196a
1932 137,179,209,181a,203a
1933 142,180,180i,186a,198a
1934 134,246,192a,204a
1935 156,246,275,192a,204a
1936 142,246,192a,204a
1937 136,228,254,181a,200a
1938 164,179,215,192a,193a
1939 156,246,259,263,275,192a,204a
1940 136,194,263,181a,193a
1941 141,191,218,230,246,182a,194a
1942 158,191,182a,194a
1943 138,179,255,192a,202a
1944 142,179,219,231,247,183a,195a
1945 159,231,247,191a,202a
1946 156,192,247,260,275,335a
1947 143,180,212,190a,203a
1948 156,221,255,258,260,275,185a, 197a
1949 141,179,214,191a,204a
1950 133,232,247,191a,203a
1951 156,216,247,260,275,192a,204a
1952 141,179,205,190a,200a
1953 134,180,206,181a,193a
1954 156,247,260,275,192a,204a
1955 143,179,208,190a,193a
1956 135,225,255,258,260,181a,201a
1957 164,179,210,191a,194a
1958 144,179,212,191a,202a
1959 136,248,192a,204a
1960 141,226,263,190a,202a
1961 134,180,214,263,181a,196a
1962 138,233,191a,203a
1963 142,179,216,190a,197a
1964 135,179,205,181a,204a
1965 140,179,262,186a,198a
1966 156,248,259,262,275,192a,204a
1967 136,248,262,263,277,192a,204a
1968 140,179,186a,198a
1969 133,200,181a,193a
1970 137,179,212,192a,193a
1971 141,213,189a,201a
1972 134,181,182a,194a
1973 139,190,187a,199a
1974 167,219,235,257,190a,194a
1975 156,249,275,192a,204a
1976 164,179,205,260,191a,195a
1977 144,179,206,181a,203a
1978 137,179,207,260,192a,196a
1979 141,180,209,190a,203a
1980 133,180,180i,186a,198a
1981 138,191,223,257,187a,199a
1982 142,190,187a,199a
1983 134,213,249,342a
1984 139,200,188a,200a
1985 156,250,275,192a,204a
1986 136,215,250,342a
1987 140,250,259,263,192a,204a
1988 133,201,226,288a
1989 162,226,259,262,190a,202a
1990 166,226,259,262,273,190a,202a
1991 134,179,209,192a,195a

1992 139,238,262,191a,203a
1993 143,180,211,181a,196a
1994 156,250,259,262,275,192a,204a
1995 140,228,190a,202a
1996 144,250,192a,204a
1997 137,239,191a,203a
1998 141,251,192a,204a
1999 133,200,251,260,290a

21st February

1930 141,179,207,192a,203a
1931 157,208,184a,196a
1932 137,179,209,181a,203a
1933 142,180,180i,186a,198a
1934 135,246,192a,204a
1935 156,246,275,192a,204a
1936 143,246,192a,204a
1937 136,228,254,181a,200a
1938 164,179,215,192a,193a
1939 156,246,259,263,275,192a,204a
1940 161,194,205,263,181a,193a
1941 166,191,182a,194a
1942 158,191,182a,194a
1943 138,179,255,192a,202a
1944 142,179,219,231,247,183a,195a
1945 159,231,247,191a,202a
1946 140,247,260,192a,204a
1947 144,247,192a,204a
1948 156,221,255,258,260,275,185a, 197a
1949 141,179,214,191a,204a
1950 133,232,247,191a,203a
1951 156,216,247,260,275,192a,204a
1952 142,180,205,191a,200a
1953 135,180,206,181a,193a
1954 156,247,260,275,192a,204a
1955 143,179,208,190a,204a
1956 135,225,255,258,260,181a,201a
1957 141,179,210,191a,194a
1958 133,179,212,191a,202a
1959 137,248,192a,204a
1960 141,180,213,191a,202a
1961 134,180,214,263,181a,196a
1962 138,233,191a,203a
1963 142,179,216,190a,197a
1964 135,179,205,181a,204a
1965 140,180,180i,248,259,262,330a
1966 156,248,259,262,275,192a,204a
1967 136,248,262,263,277,192a,204a
1968 141,179,186a,198a
1969 134,179,211,181a,200a
1970 138,179,212,192a,193a
1971 142,213,189a,201a
1972 134,181,182a,194a
1973 139,190,187a,199a
1974 167,219,235,257,190a,194a
1975 156,249,275,192a,204a
1976 164,179,205,260,191a,195a
1977 133,179,206,181a,203a
1978 137,179,207,260,192a,196a
1979 141,180,209,190a,203a
1980 134,180,180i,186a,198a
1981 163,191,258,260,187a,199a
1982 167,190,187a,199a
1983 135,213,249,260,342a
1984 140,200,188a,200a
1985 156,250,275,192a,204a
1986 136,216,250,259,263,342a
1987 141,216,250,263,342a
1988 133,201,226,288a
1989 162,226,259,262,190a,202a
1990 166,226,259,262,273,190a,202a
1991 134,179,209,192a,195a
1992 139,238,262,191a,203a
1993 156,250,275,192a,204a
1994 136,250,262,277,192a,204a
1995 140,228,190a,202a
1996 133,214,250,342a
1997 137,239,191a,203a
1998 141,251,192a,204a
1999 134,251,192a,204a

22nd February

1930 141,179,207,192a,203a
1931 157,208,184a,196a
1932 138,179,209,181a,203a
1933 143,180,180i,229,329a
1934 135,246,192a,204a
1935 156,246,275,192a,204a
1936 143,230,191a,203a
1937 136,228,254,181a,200a
1938 141,179,215,192a,193a
1939 133,246,263,192a,204a
1940 161,194,205,263,181a,193a
1941 166,191,182a,194a
1942 158,191,182a,194a
1943 138,179,255,192a,202a
1944 167,179,231,260,279,308a
1945 136,179,255,191a,202a
1946 140,247,260,192a,204a
1947 144,247,192a,204a
1948 137,258,260,185a,197a
1949 142,179,255,191a,204a
1950 134,232,247,191a,203a
1951 156,247,275,192a,204a
1952 142,180,205,191a,200a
1953 135,180,206,181a,193a
1954 156,247,260,275,192a,204a
1955 144,224,232,190a,193a
1956 136,225,255,258,260,181a,201a
1957 141,179,210,191a,194a
1958 133,179,212,191a,202a
1959 137,248,192a,204a
1960 142,226,190a,202a
1961 135,180,214,181a,196a
1962 163,233,191a,203a

1963 143,234,191a,203a
1964 135,179,205,181a,204a
1965 140,180,180i,248,259,262,330a
1966 156,248,259,262,275,192a,204a
1967 156,248,262,275,277,192a,204a
1968 141,179,186a,198a
1969 134,179,211,181a,200a
1970 138,179,212,192a,193a
1971 142,213,189a,201a
1972 135,180,214,181a,194a
1973 164,180,214,190a,201a
1974 144,249,192a,204a
1975 136,249,192a,204a
1976 141,179,205,260,191a,195a
1977 133,179,206,181a,203a
1978 137,179,207,260,192a,196a
1979 142,180,209,190a,203a
1980 134,180,180i,186a,198a
1981 163,191,258,260,187a,199a
1982 167,190,187a,199a
1983 135,213,249,260,342a
1984 140,200,188a,200a
1985 133,193,181a,193a
1986 137,216,250,259,263,342a
1987 141,216,250,263,342a
1988 158,226,190a,202a
1989 162,226,259,262,190a,202a
1990 166,226,259,262,273,190a,202a
1991 135,179,209,181a,195a
1992 139,238,262,191a,203a
1993 156,250,275,192a,204a
1994 136,250,259,262,192a,204a
1995 141,213,228,340a
1996 133,214,250,342a
1997 138,239,191a,203a
1998 142,251,192a,204a
1999 134,200,181a,193a

23rd February

1930 142,179,229,192a,203a
1931 158,208,184a,196a
1932 138,180,209,181a,203a
1933 143,180,180i,229,329a
1934 135,246,192a,204a
1935 156,246,275,192a,204a
1936 144,249,192a,204a
1937 137,179,214,228,181a,200a
1938 141,179,215,192a,193a
1939 133,246,263,192a,204a
1940 138,194,263,181a,193a
1941 143,191,218,230,246,182a,194a
1942 135,191,182a,194a
1943 163,219,231,247,192a,202a
1944 167,179,231,260,279,308a
1945 136,180,255,191a,202a
1946 140,247,260,192a,204a
1947 133,180,212,190a,203a
1948 137,258,260,185a,197a
1949 142,179,255,191a,204a
1950 134,232,247,191a,203a
1951 156,247,275,192a,203a
1952 143,180,205,260,191a,200a
1953 136,180,206,181a,193a
1954 140,247,260,192a,204a
1955 144,224,232,190a,193a
1956 136,225,255,258,260,181a,201a
1957 141,179,212,191a,202a
1958 133,179,212,191a,202a
1959 138,248,192a,204a
1960 142,180,213,191a,203a
1961 135,180,214,181a,196a
1962 163,233,191a,203a
1963 143,234,191a,203a
1964 136,179,205,181a,204a
1965 141,180,180i,248,330
1966 156,248,275,192a,204a
1967 156,248,262,275,277,192a,204a
1968 142,179,186a,198a
1969 134,179,211,181a,200a
1970 138,179,212,192a,193a
1971 143,213,189a,201a
1972 135,180,214,181a,194a
1973 164,180,215,190a,201a
1974 144,249,192a,204a
1975 136,220,236,181a,202a
1976 141,179,205,260,191a,195a
1977 134,179,206,181a,203a
1978 156,249,275,192a,204a
1979 142,180,209,190a,203a
1980 135,180,180i,186a,198a
1981 163,191,258,260,187a,199a
1982 167,190,187a,199a
1983 136,213,260,189a,201a
1984 141,200,188a,200a
1985 133,193,181a,193a
1986 137,216,250,259,263,342a
1987 142,225,250,263,344a
1988 158,226,190a,202a
1989 139,226,238,250,258,262,190a,202a
1990 143,226,238,250,259,262,273,190a,202a
1991 135,179,209,181a,195a
1992 140,238,262,191a,203a
1993 156,250,275,192a,204a
1994 156,250,275,192a,204a
1995 141,213,228,340a
1996 134,250,192a,204a
1997 138,239,191a,203a
1998 142,251,192a,204a
1999 135,200,260,181a,193a

24th February

1930 142,179,229,192a,203a
1931 158,208,184a,196a
1932 139,180,209,181a,203a

1933 144,180,180i,246,330a
1934 136,246,192a,204a
1935 140,246,192a,204a
1936 144,246,192a,204a
1937 137,179,214,228,181a,200a
1938 142,179,215,182a,193a
1939 134,246,263,192a,204a
1940 138,194,263,181a,193a
1941 143,191,218,230,246,182a,194a
1942 135,191,182a,194a
1943 163,219,231,247,192a,202a
1944 144,179,258,260,183a,195a
1945 137,180,210,191a,202a
1946 156,247,260,275,192a,204a
1947 133,180,212,190a,203a
1948 156,221,255,275,185a,197a
1949 142,179,255,191a,204a
1950 134,232,247,191a,203a
1951 156,192,216,247,260,275,335a
1952 143,180,205,260,191a,200a
1953 136,180,206,181a,193a
1954 140,247,260,192a,204a
1955 133,179,208,190a,193a
1956 137,258,260,185a,197a
1957 142,179,210,191a,194a
1958 134,179,212,191a,202a
1959 138,180,213,181a,195a
1960 143,233,191a,203a
1961 135,180,214,181a,196a
1962 163,233,191a,203a
1963 144,248,192a,204a
1964 136,179,205,181a,204a
1965 141,180,180i,248,330a
1966 156,248,275,192a,204a
1967 156,180,180i,248,259,262,275,
330a
1968 143,179,186a,198a
1969 135,179,256,181a,200a
1970 139,179,212,192a,193a
1971 143,213,189a,201a
1972 136,180,214,181a,194a
1973 164,180,215,190a,201a
1974 133,180,215,190a,194a
1975 137,179,216,181a,202a
1976 142,179,205,191a,195a
1977 134,179,206,181a,203a
1978 156,249,275,192a,204a
1979 143,180,209,190a,203a
1980 135,180,180i,186a,198a
1981 140,191,223,257,258,260,187a,
199a
1982 144,190,187a,199a
1983 136,213,260,189a,201a
1984 141,200,188a,200a
1985 133,193,181a,193a
1986 138,216,250,259,263,342a
1987 142,225,250,263,344a
1988 135,226,190a,202a
1989 139,226,238,250,258,262,190a,
202a
1990 143,226,238,250,259,262,273,
190a,202a
1991 136,180,209,181a,195a
1992 140,238,262,191a,203a
1993 133,180,211,182a,196a
1994 156,250,275,192a,204a
1995 142,228,190a,202a
1996 134,250,192a,204a
1997 138,239,191a,203a
1998 143,239,251,345a
1999 135,200,260,181a,193a

25th February

1930 143,229,191a,203a
1931 159,208,184a,196a
1932 139,246,192a,204a
1933 144,180,180i,246,330a
1934 136,246,192a,204a
1935 140,246,192a,204a
1936 133,179,213,228,191a,193a
1937 138,179,214,228,181a,200a
1938 142,179,215,182a,193a
1939 134,246,263,192a,204a
1940 139,194,181a,193a
1941 143,191,218,230,246,182a,194a
1942 136,191,182a,194a
1943 164,179,208,181a,202a
1944 144,179,258,260,183a,195a
1945 137,180,210,191a,202a
1946 156,247,260,275,192a,204a
1947 133,180,212,190a,203a
1948 156,221,255,275,185a,197a
1949 167,231,191a,203a
1950 159,232,191a,203a
1951 139,181,247,260,335a
1952 144,247,260,192a,204a
1953 137,180,206,181a,193a
1954 156,247,260,275,192a,204a
1955 133,179,208,190a,193a
1956 137,258,260,185a,197a
1957 142,179,210,191a,194a
1958 134,180,212,191a,202a
1959 139,180,213,181a,195a
1960 143,233,191a,203a
1961 136,179,214,181a,196a
1962 140,233,191a,203a
1963 144,248,192a,204a
1964 137,179,205,181a,204a
1965 166,180,180i,248,259,262,330a
1966 156,248,259,262,275,192a,204a
1967 156,180,180i,248,259,262,275,
330a
1968 143,179,234,329a
1969 135,179,256,181a,201a
1970 139,179,212,192a,193a
1971 144,213,189a,201a
1972 136,180,214,181a,194a
1973 141,215,189a,201a

1974 133,180,215,190a,194a
1975 137,179,216,181a,202a
1976 142,179,205,191a,195a
1977 135,179,206,181a,203a
1978 156,236,249,260,275,192a,204a
1979 143,180,209,190a,203a
1980 136,180,180i,186a,198a
1981 140,191,223,257,258,260,187a, 199a
1982 144,190,187a,199a
1983 161,213,258,260,189a,201a
1984 141,200,188a,200a
1985 134,180,215,181a,193a
1986 138,216,250,259,263,342a
1987 143,250,192a,204a
1988 135,226,190a,202a
1989 139,226,238,250,258,262,190a, 202a
1990 144,226,238,250,259,262,273, 190a,202a
1991 136,180,209,181a,195a
1992 141,238,191a,203a
1993 133,180,211,181a,196a
1994 156,250,275,192a,204a
1995 142,228,190a,202a
1996 134,250,192a,204a
1997 163,239,191a,203a
1998 143,239,251,345a
1999 136,200,260,181a,193a

26th February

1930 143,229,191a,203a
1931 159,208,184a,196a
1932 140,246,192a,204a
1933 133,180,180i,186a,198a
1934 137,246,192a,204a
1935 141,179,228,246,181a,199a
1936 133,179,213,228,191a,193a
1937 138,179,214,228,181a,200a
1938 142,179,215,182a,193a
1939 134,246,263,192a,204a
1940 139,194,181a,193a
1941 144,191,218,230,246,182a,194a
1942 136,191,182a,194a
1943 164,179,208,181a,202a
1944 133,179,258,260,183a,195a
1945 138,180,255,191a,202a
1946 156,247,275,192a,204a
1947 134,180,212,190a,203a
1948 156,221,255,258,260,275,185a, 197a
1949 167,231,191a,203a
1950 159,232,191a,203a
1951 140,216,247,260,192a,204a
1952 144,247,260,192a,204a
1953 137,180,206,181a,193a
1954 156,247,260,275,192a,204a
1955 133,179,208,190a,194a
1956 138,225,255,181a,201a
1957 143,233,191a,203a
1958 135,180,212,191a,202a
1959 139,180,213,181a,195a
1960 144,248,192a,204a
1961 136,179,214,181a,196a
1962 140,233,191a,203a
1963 133,179,216,190a,197a
1964 137,179,205,181a,204a
1965 166,180,180i,248,259,262,330a
1966 156,248,259,262,275,192a,204a
1967 156,248,275,192a,204a
1968 143,179,234,329a
1969 136,179,256,181a,201a
1970 164,179,212,192a,193a
1971 144,213,342a
1972 137,180,214,181a,194a
1973 141,215,189a,201a
1974 133,180,215,190a,194a
1975 138,179,216,181a,202a
1976 142,179,205,191a,195a
1977 135,179,206,181a,203a
1978 156,236,249,260,175,192a,204a
1979 144,249,192a,204a
1980 136,180,180i,186a,198a
1981 141,191,211,223,257,258,260, 332a
1982 133,190,187a,199a
1983 161,213,258,260,189a,201a
1984 142,200,224,337a
1985 134,180,215,181a,193a
1986 156,216,250,275,342a
1987 143,250,192a,204a
1988 135,226,190a,202a
1989 140,226,238,250,259,262,190a, 202a
1990 144,226,238,250,259,262,273, 190a,202a
1991 137,180,209,181a,195a
1992 141,238,191a,203a
1993 134,180,211,181a,196a
1994 156,250,259,262,275,192a,204a
1995 142,228,190a,202a
1996 135,250,192a,204a
1997 163,239,191a,203a
1998 156,251,275,192a,204a
1999 136,200,260,181a,193a

27th February

1930 143,229,191a,203a
1931 136,208,184a,196a
1932 140,246,192a,204a
1933 133,180,180i,186a,198a
1934 137,246,192a,204a
1935 141,179,228,246,181a,197a
1936 134,179,213,228,191a,193a
1937 139,179,214,228,181a,200a
1938 143,246,192a,204a

1939 135,246,192a,204a
1940 140,194,263,181a,193a
1941 144,191,218,230,246,182a,194a
1942 136,191,182a,194a
1943 141,179,208,181a,202a
1944 133,179,258,260a,183a,195a
1945 138,180,255,191a,202a
1946 156,247,275,192a,204a
1947 137,180,212,190a,203a
1948 156,221,255,258,260,275,185a, 197a
1949 144,247,192a,204a
1950 159,232,191a,203a
1951 140,216,247,260,192a,204a
1952 133,180,205,260,191a,200a
1953 137,180,206,181a,193a
1954 156,247,260,275,192a,204a
1955 134,179,255,190a,194a
1956 138,225,255,181a,201a
1957 143,233,191a,203a
1958 135,180,212,191a,202a
1959 164,180,213,181a,195a
1960 144,248,192a,204a
1961 137,179,214,181a,196a
1962 141,233,191a,203a
1963 133,179,216,190a,197a
1964 138,179,186a,198a
1965 166,180,180i,248,259,262,330a
1966 156,248,259,262,275,192a,204a
1967 156,248,275,192a,204a
1968 143,234,191a,203a
1969 136,179,256,181a,201a
1970 164,179,212,192a,193a
1971 133,213,189a,201a
1972 137,180,214,181a,194a
1973 142,180,215,190a,201a
1974 134,219,235,257,190a,195a
1975 138,179,216,181a,202a
1976 167,236,260,191a,203a
1977 135,179,206,181a,203a
1978 140,236,249,260,192a,204a
1979 144,249,192a,204a
1980 137,180,180i,186a,198a
1981 141,191,211,223,257,258,260, 332a
1982 133,190,187a,199a
1983 138,213,237,249,189a,201a
1984 142,200,224,337a
1985 135,180,215,181a,193a
1986 156,216,250,275,342a
1987 156,250,259,263,275,192a,204a
1988 136,226,190a,202a
1989 140,226,238,250,259,262,190a, 202a
1990 133,226,238,250,273,190a,202a
1991 137,180,209,181a,195a
1992 142,238,262,191a,203a
1993 134,180,211,181a,196a
1994 156,250,259,262,275,192a,204a
1995 143,228,190a,202a
1996 135,250,192a,204a
1997 140,239,191a,203a
1998 156,251,275,192a,204a
1999 161,200,258,260,181a,193a

28th February

1930 144,246,192a,204a
1931 136,208,184a,196a
1932 141,246,192a,204a
1933 133,180,180i,186a,198a
1934 137,246,192a,204a
1935 142,179,212,228,181a,199a
1936 134,179,213,228,191a,193a
1937 139,179,214,228,181a,200a
1938 143,246,192a,204a
1939 135,246,192a,204a
1940 140,194,263,181a,193a
1941 133,191,218,230,246,182a,194a
1942 137,191,182a,194a
1943 141,179,208,181a,202a
1944 134,179,219,231,247,183a,195a
1945 138,180,255,191a,202a
1946 156,247,275,192a,204a
1947 135,180,212,190a,203a
1948 156,221,255,258,260,275,185a, 197a
1949 144,247,192a,204a
1950 159,232,191a,203a
1951 141,247,260,192a,204a
1952 133,180,205,260,191a,200a
1953 138,180,206,181a,193a
1954 156,247,275,192a,204a
1955 134,179,255,190a,194a
1956 139,225,255,258,260,181a,201a
1957 143,233,191a,203a
1958 135,180,212,191a,202a
1959 164,180,213,181a,195a
1960 133,180,213,191a,203a
1961 137,179,214,181a,196a
1962 141,233,191a,203a
1963 134,179,216,190a,197a
1964 138,179,186a,198a
1965 143,180,180i,248,262,330a
1966 156,248,259,262,275,192a,204a
1967 140,248,263,277,339a
1968 144,179,209,191a,193a
1969 136,179,256,181a,201a
1970 141,179,212,192a,193a
1971 133,213,189a,201a
1972 138,180,214,181a,194a
1973 142,180,215,190a,201a
1974 134,219,235,257,190a,195a
1975 139,179,216,181a,202a
1976 167,236,260,191a,203a
1977 136,179,206,181a,203a
1978 140,236,249,260,192a,204a
1979 133,249,192a,204a
1980 137,180,180i,186a,198a

1981 141,192,211,249,260,352a
1982 134,190,187a,199a
1983 138,213,237,249,189a,201a
1984 156,200,275,188a,200a
1985 135,180,215,181a,193a
1986 156,216,250,275,342a
1987 156,250,259,263,275,192a,204a
1988 136,226,190a,202a
1989 141,226,238,250,190a,202a
1990 133,226,238,250,273,190a,202a
1991 138,180,209,181a,195a
1992 142,238,262,191a,203a
1993 134,180,211,181a,196a
1994 156,250,259,262,275,192a,204a
1995 143,228,190a,202a
1996 136,250,192a,204a
1997 140,250,192a,204a
1998 133,192a,204a
1999 161,200,258,260,181a,193a

29th February

1932 141,246,192a,204a
1936 135,179,213,228,191a,193a
1940 165,194,205,263,181a,193a
1944 134,179,219,231,247,183a,195a
1948 156,221,255,258,260,275,185a, 197a
1952 134,180,205,191a,200a
1956 139,179,209,181a,202a
1960 133,180,213,191a,203a
1964 139,179,205,181a,204a
1968 144,179,209,191a,193a
1972 138,180,214,181a,194a
1976 144,179,205,260,191a,195a
1980 137,180,180i,186a,198a
1984 156,200,275,188a,200a
1988 137,226,190a,202a
1992 142,238,262,191a,203a
1996 136,250,192a,204a

1st March

1930 144,246,192a,204a
1931 136,208,184a,196a
1932 142,246,192a,196a
1933 134,180,180i,186a,198a
1934 138,246,192a,204a
1935 142,179,212,228,181a,199a
1936 135,179,213,228,191a,193a
1937 139,179,214,228,181a,200a
1938 156,246,275,192a,204a
1939 136,246,258,263,192a,204a
1940 165,194,205,263,181a,193a
1941 133,191,218,230,246,182a,194a
1942 137,191,182a,194a
1943 142,179,208,181a,202a
1944 159,179,260,279,183a,195a
1945 139,180,210,181a,203a
1946 156,247,260,275,192a,204a
1947 135,180,212,190a,203a
1948 156,221,255,258,260,275,185a, 197a
1949 144,247,192a,204a
1950 137,215,232,191a,203a
1951 156,216,247,260,275,192a,204a
1952 134,180,205,191a,200a
1953 138,180,206,181a,193a
1954 156,247,275,192a,204a
1955 135,179,255,190a,194a
1956 164,179,209,181a,202a
1957 164,179,210,191a,194a
1958 136,248,191a,202a
1959 141,180,213,181a,195a
1960 133,180,213,191a,203a
1961 137,179,213,181a,196a
1962 142,233,191a,203a
1963 134,179,216,190a,197a
1964 139,248,192a,204a
1965 156,180,180i,248,259,262,275, 330a
1966 156,248,259,262,275,192a,204a
1967 140,248,256,263,177,339a
1968 133,193,181a,193a
1969 137,179,256,181a,201a
1970 141,179,212,192a,193a
1971 134,213,189a,201a
1972 138,180,214,181a,194a
1973 142,249,192a,204a
1974 159,180,260,279,183a,195a
1975 139,216,181a,202a
1976 144,179,205,260,191a,195a
1977 136,179,206,181a,203a
1978 140,249,260,192a,204a
1979 133,249,192a,204a
1980 138,180,180i,186a,198a
1981 142,192,249,335a
1982 134,190,187a,199a
1983 139,213,237,249,258,260,189a, 201a
1984 156,200,275,188a,200a
1985 135,180,250,181a,193a
1986 140,216,250,259,263,342a
1987 156,250,259,263,275,192a,204a
1988 137,226,190a,202a
1989 141,226,238,250,190a,202a
1990 158,226,259,262,273,190a,202a
1991 138,180,209,181a,195a
1992 143,238,262,191a,203a,P
1993 135,180,211,181a,196a
1994 156,250,259,262,275,192a,204a
1995 144,228,250,344a
1996 136,250,192a,204a
1997 140,250,192a,204a
1998 133,251,192a,204a
1999 138,180,205,181a,200a

2nd March

1930 133,179,207,192a,203a
1931 161,208,184a,196a
1932 142,246,192a,204a
1933 134,180,180i,186a,198a
1934 138,246,192a,204a
1935 143,179,228,246,181a,199a
1936 136,179,213,228,191a,193a
1937 140,228,254,181a,200a
1938 156,246,275,192a,204a
1939 136,246,258,263,192a,204a,
1940 165,194,205,263,181a,193a
1941 133,191,218,230,246,182a,194a
1942 162,191,182a,194a
1943 142,179,208,181a,202a
1944 159,179,260,279,183a,195a
1945 139,180,210,181a,203a
1946 156,247,260,275,192a,204a
1947 136,180,212,190a,203a
1948 141,258,260,185a,197a,
1949 133,247,192a,204a
1950 137,215,232,191a,203a
1951 142,247,192a,204a
1952 134,180,205,191a,200a
1953 139,181,187a,199a
1954 156,247,260,275,192a,204a
1955 135,179,255,190a,194a
1956 164,179,209,181a,202a
1957 144,248,192a,204a
1958 136,248,191a,202a
1959 141,180,213,181a,195a
1960 134,180,233,191a,203a
1961 138,179,214,181a,196a
1962 142,233,191a,203a
1963 135,179,216,190a,197a
1964 139,248,192a,204a
1965 156,180,180i,248,259,262,275,
330a
1966 156,248,259,262,275,192a,204a
1967 156,248,259,263,275,192a,204a
1968 133,193,181a,193a
1969 137,179,256,181a,201a
1970 141,179,212,192a,193a
1971 134,213,189a,201a
1972 139,181,187a,199a
1973 167,249,192a,204a
1974 159,180,260,279,183a,195a
1975 140,220,236,181a,202a
1976 144,179,201,260,191a,195a
1977 137,180,206,181a,203a
1978 156,249,260,275,192a,204a
1979 134,249,192a,204a
1980 138,180,180i,186a,198a
1981 142,192,249,335a
1982 159,191,258,260,187a,199a
1983 139,213,237,249,258,260,189a,
201a,
1984 156,200,250,275,239a
1985 136,193,224,181a,193a
1986 140,216,250,259,263,342a
1987 133,250,263,192a,204a
1988 137,226,190a,202a
1989 166,226,259,262,190a,202a
1990 158,226,259,273,190a,202a
1991 139,180,209,181a,195a
1992 143,238,262,191a,203a
1993 135,180,211,181a,196a
1994 140,250,259,262,192a,204a
1995 144,228,250,344a
1996 137,250,192a,204a
1997 141,250,192a,204a
1998 134,251,192a,204a
1999 138,180,205,181a,200a

3rd March

1930 133,179,207,192a,203a
1931 137,259,263,184a,196a
1932 142,246,192a,204a,
1933 135,169,186a,198a
1934 139,246,192a,204a
1935 143,179,228,246,181a,199a
1936 179,213,228,191a,193a
1937 140,228,254,181a,200a
1938 156,246,275,192a,204a
1939 137,246,263,192a,204a
1940 142,194,263,181a,193a
1941 158,192,246,259,263,280a
1942 162,191,182a,194a
1943 167,219,231,247,181a,202a
1944 136,180,180i,219,231,247,258,
260,183a,195a
1945 164,180,210,181a,203a
1946 156,247,260,275,192a,204a,
1947 136,180,212,190a,203a
1948 141,258,260,185a,197a
1949 133,247,192a204a
1950 137,215,232,191a,203a
1951 142,247,192a,204a
1952 135,180,205,260,191a,200a
1953 139,181,193,285a
1954 156,247,260,275,192a,204a
1955 136,208,184a,196a
1956 165,225,255,181a,202a
1957 133,179,210,192a,194a
1958 137,180,212,191a,202a
1959 141,180,213,181a,195a
1960 134,180,233,191a,203a
1961 138,179,214,181a,196a
1962 167,233,274,191a,203a
1963 135,179,216,190a,197a,
1964 140,248,192a,204a,
1965 156,180,180i,248,259,262,263,
275,330a
1966 136,248,192a,204a
1967 156,248,259,263,275,192a,204a
1968 134,179,209,191a,193a
1969 138,179,211,181a,201a

1970 142,179,212,192a,193a
1971 135,213,189a,201a
1972 139,181,187a,199a
1973 167,249,192a,204a
1974 136,215,235,260,279,191a,203a
1975 140,216,220,236,260,181a,191a, 203a
1976 133,179,205,260,191a,195a
1977 137,180,206,181a,203a
1978 156,249,260,275,192a,204a
1979 134,249,192a,204a
1980 139,180,180i,186a,198a
1981 167,192,249,258,260,335a
1982 159,191,258,260,187a,199a
1983 140,213,237,249,258,260,189a, 201a
1984 156,200,250,275,339a
1985 136,193,224,181a,193a
1986 165,216,250,263.342a
1987 133,180,205,191a,194a
1988 162,226,190a,202a
1989 166,226,259,262,190a,202a
1990 135,226,259,262,273,190a,202a
1991 139,180,209,181a,195a
1992 144,238,250,262,345a
1993 136,180,211,181a,196a
1994 140,250,259,262,192a,204a
1995 133,179,213,228,191a,197a
1996 137,250.192a,204a
1997 141,250,192a,204a
1998 134,251,192a,204a
1999 138,200,181a,193a

4th March

1930 133,179,207,192a,203a,
1931 138,259,263,184a,196a
1932 143,246,192a,204a
1933 135,169,186a,198a
1934 139,249,192a,204a
1935 144,246,192a,204a
1936 137,179,213,228,191a,193a
1937 141,179,214,228,181a,200a
1938 133,193,246,290a
1939 137,246,263,192a,204a
1940 142,194,217,255,263,181a,193a
1941 158,192,246,259,263,280a
1942 139,191,182a,194a
1943 167,219,231,247,181a,202a
1944 136,180,180i,219,231,247,258, 260,183a,195a
1945 164,180,210,181a,203a
1946 156,247,260,275,192a,204a
1947 156,275,185a,197a
1948 156,212,275,185a,197a
1949 134,247,192a,204a
1950 138,215,232,191a,203a
1951 142,247,192a,204a
1952 135,180,205,260,191a,200a
1953 139,181,193,285a
1954 156,247,260,275,192a,204a
1955 136,208,184a,196a
1956 165,255,181a,202a
1957 156,248,259,263,273,19a,204a
1958 137,180,212,191a,202a
1959 142,180,213,181a,195a
1960 135,180,233,191a,203a
1961 139,179,214,191a,196a
1962 167,233,274,191a,203a
1963 136,234,191a,203a
1964 140,248,192a,204a
1965 156,180,180i,248,259,262,263, 275,330a
1966 137,248,192a,204a
1967 156,248,259,263,275,181a,200a
1968 134,179,209,191a,193a
1969 138,179,211,181a,201a
1970 142,179,212,197a,193a
1971 135,213,189a,201a
1972 164,180,214,181a,194a
1973 144,249,192a,204a
1974 136,215,235,260,279,191a,203a
1975 141,179,216,260,181a,203a
1976 133,179,205,260,191a,195a
1977 137,180,206,181a,203a
1978 156,249,275,192a,204a
1979 134,169,208,191a,204a
1980 139,180,180i,186a,198a
1981 167,192,249,258,260,335a
1982 136,191,223,257,258,260,187a, 199a
1983 140,213,237,249,258,260,189a, 201a
1984 156,200,275,188a,200a
1985 137,180,250,181a,193a
1986 165,216,250,263,342a
1987 134,180,205,191a,194a
1988 162,226,190a,202a
1989 166,226,259,262,190a,202a
1990 135,226,262,190a,202a
1991 139,180,209,181a,195a
1992 144,238,191a,203a
1993 136,180,211,181a,196a
1994 156,250,275,192a,204a
1995 133,179,213,228,191a,197a
1996 138,250,192a,204a
1997 142,250,182a,204a
1998 135,251,192a,204a
1999 139,200,181a,193a

5th March

1930 134,179,229,192a,203a
1931 138,259,263,184a,196a
1932 143,246,192a,204a
1933 135,169,186a,198a
1934 140,246,192a,204a
1935 144,246,192s,204a

1936 137,179,213,228,191a,193a
1937 141,179,214,228,181a,200a
1938 133,193,246,290a
1939 138,246,263,192a,204a
1940 143,194,217,255,181a,193a
1941 135,192,218,230,246,300a
1942 139,191,182a,194a
1943 144,179,208,181a,202a
1944 136,180,180i,219,231,247,258, 260,183a,195a
1945 164,180,210,181a,203a
1946 133,169,211,260,192a,196a
1947 156,247,260,275,324a
1948 156,212,275,185a,197a
1949 134,247,192a,204a
1950 138,215,232,191a,203a
1951 143,247,260,192a,204a
1952 136,232,260,191a,200a
1953 140,193,181a,193a
1954 156,247,260,275,192a,204a
1955 137,179,208,191a,194a
1956 165,255,181a,202a
1957 156,248,259,263,273,192a,204a
1958 138,180,212,191a,202a
1959 142,169,213,181a,195a
1960 135,180,233,191a,203a
1961 139,179,214,181a,196a
1962 144,233,248,345a
1963 136,234,191a,203a
1964 141,248,192a,204a
1965 156,180,180i,248,259,263,275, 330a
1966 137,248,192a,204a
1967 156,248,259,263,275,181a,200a
1968 134,179,209,191a,193a
1969 139,181,187a,199a
1970 143,179,212,192a,193a
1971 136,213,189a,201a
1972 164,180,214,181a,194a
1973 144,249,192a,204a
1974 137,215,235,260,279,191a,203a
1975 141,179,216,260,181a,203a
1976 134,179,205,191a,195a
1977 138,180,206,181a,203a
1978 156,249,275,192a,204a
1979 135,169,222,191a,204a
1980 139,180,180i,186a,198a
1981 144,192,249,260,335a
1982 136,191,223,257,258,260,187a, 199a
1983 165,213,258,260,189a,201a
1984 156,200,275,188a,200a
1985 137,180,250,181a,193a
1986 142,216,250,263,342a
1987 134,180,205,191a,194a
1988 139,226,190a,202a
1989 143,226,238,250,259,262,190a, 202a
1990 136,226,259,262,190a,202a
1991 164,180,209,181a,195a
1992 144,238,191a,203a
1993 137,180,211,181a,196a
1994 156,250,275,192a,204a
1995 134,179,213,228,191a,197a
1996 138,250,192a,204a
1997 142,250,192a,204a
1998 135,239,251,260,345a
1999 139,200,181a,193a

6th March

1930 134,179,229,192a,203a
1931 139,208,184a,196a
1932 156,246,275,192a,204a
1933 136,169,186a,198a
1934 140,246,192a,204a
1935 133,199,181a,193a
1936 137,179,213,228,191a,193a
1937 141,179,214,228,181a,200a
1938 134,246,263,192a,204a
1939 138,246,192a,204a
1940 143,194,217,255,181a,193a
1941 135,192,218,230,246,300a
1942 140,191,182a,194a
1943 144,179,208,181a,202a
1944 156,180,180i,219,231,247,258, 260,275,302a
1945 141,180,210,181a,203a
1946 133,169,211,260,192a,296a
1947 138,247,192a,204a
1948 156,212,275,185a,197a
1949 134,247,192a,204a
1950 163,191,189a,199a
1951 143,247,260,192a,204a
1952 136,232,260,191a,200a
1953 140,193,181a,193a
1954 156,247,260,275,192a,204a
1955 137,179,208,191a,194a
1956 142,179,209,181a,202a
1957 134,248,263,192a,204a
1958 138,180,212,191a,202a
1959 143,169,213,181a,195a
1960 135,180,233,191a,203a
1961 164,179,214,181a,196a
1962 144,233,248,345a
1963 137,234,191a,203a
1964 141,248,192a,204a
1965 156,180,180i,248,259,263,275, 330a
1966 138,169,248,330a
1967 156,248,259,263,275,181a,200a
1968 135,179,209,191,193a
1969 139,181,187a,199a
1970 143,249,192a,204a
1971 136,213,189a,201a
1972 140,169,214,181a,194a
1973 133,249,192a,204a
1974 137,215,235,260,279,191a,203a
1975 142,179,216,181a,203a

1976 134,179,205,191a,195a
1977 138,180,206,181a,203a
1978 156,249,260,275,192a,204a
1979 135,169,222,191a,204a
1980 140,180,180i,186a,198a
1981 144,192,249,260,335a
1982 137,191,223,257,258,260,187a, 199a
1983 165,213,258,260,189a,201a
1984 156,200,275,188a,200a
1985 138,180,215,250,181a,193a
1986 142,216,250,263,342a
1987 135,180,205,191a,194a
1988 139,226,238,250,190a,202a
1989 143,226,238,250,259,262,190a, 202a
1990 136,226,259,262,190a,202a
1991 164,180,209,181a,195a
1992 133,238,191a,203a
1993 137,180,211,181a,196a
1994 156,228,250,259,262,275,344a
1995 134,179,213,228,191a,197a
1996 138,250,192a,204a
1997 143,239,250,345a
1998 135,239,251,260,345a
1999 140,200,181a,193a

7th March

1930 135,179,229,192a,203a
1931 139,208,184a,196a
1932 156,246,275,192a,204a
1933 136,169,186a,198a
1934 141,246,192a,204a
1935 133,199,181a,193a
1936 138,179,213,228,191a,193a
1937 156,246,259,263,275,192a,204a
1938 134,246,263,192a,204a
1939 139,169,216,191a,201a
1940 143,194,217,255,181a,193a
1941 135,192,218,230,246,182a,194a
1942 164,179,255,191a,195a
1943 133,179,208,181a,202a
1944 156,180,180i,219,231,247,258, 260,275,302a
1945 141,180,210,181a,203a
1946 134,169,211,192a,196a
1947 138,247,192a,204a
1948 156,221,255,258,260,275,185a, 197a
1949 135,247,192a,204a
1950 163,191,187a,199a
1951 156,247,275,192a,204a
1952 136,232,260,191a,200a
1953 165,193,181a,193a
1954 156,247,260,275,192a,204a
1955 138,179,255,191a,194a
1956 142,179,209,181a,202a
1957 134,248,263,192a,204a
1958 139,180,212,191a,202a
1959 143,169,213,181a,195a
1960 136,180,233,191a,203a
1961 164,179,214,181a,196a
1962 133,233,191a,203a
1963 137,234,191a,203a
1964 141,248,192a,204a
1965 134,180,180i,248,259,262,263, 330a
1966 138,169,248,330a
1967 156,248,275,181a,200a
1968 135,179,209,191a,193a
1969 139,181,187a,199a
1970 156,249,275,192a,204a
1971 136,213,189a,201a
1972 141,169,214,182a,194a
1973 133,249,192a,204a
1974 138,215,235,279,191a,203a
1975 142,179,216,181a,203a
1976 134,179,205,191a,195a
1977 139,180,206,181a,203a
1978 156,249,260,275,192a,204a,P
1979 136,236,191a,204a
1980 140,180,180i,186a,198a
1981 133,192,249,260,335a
1982 137,191,223,257,258,260,187a, 199a
1983 165,213,258,260,189a,201a
1984 156,200,275,188a,200a
1985 138,193,181a,193a
1986 143,216,250,342a
1987 135,180,205,191a,194a
1988 139,226,238,250,190a,202a
1989 144,226,238,250,259,262,344a
1990 136,226,259,262,190a,202a
1991 141,180,209,181a,195a
1992 133,238,191a,203a
1993 138,180,211,181a,196a
1994 156,228,250,259,262,275,344a
1995 134,179,213,228,191a,197a
1996 139,250,192a,204a
1997 143,239,250,345a
1998 136,239,251,260,345a
1999 140,200,181a,193a

8th March

1930 135,179,229,192a,203a
1931 140,208,184a,196a
1932 133,204,246,290a
1933 137,169,228,186a,198a
1934 141,246,192a,204a
1935 134,179,212,181a,199a
1936 138,179,213,228,191a,193a
1937 156,246,259,263,275,192a,204a
1938 135,246,192a,204a
1939 139,169,216,191a,201a
1940 156,194,246,263,275,290a
1941 136,192,218,230,246,182a,194a

1942 164,179,255,191a,195a
1943 133,179,208,181a,202a
1944 138,180,180i,219,231,247,183a, 195a
1945 142,180,210,181a,203a
1946 134,169,211,192a,196a
1947 139,247,260,192a,204a
1948 156,275,185a,197a
1949 135,247,192a,204a
1950 164,180,222,255,191a,199a
1951 156,247,275,192a,204a
1952 137,169,205,260,191a,200a
1953 165,193,181a,193a
1954 156,247,275,192a,204a
1955 138,179,255,191a,194a
1956 143,179,209,182a,202a
1957 135,248,192a,204a
1958 139,180,212,191a,202a
1959 144,169,213,181a,195a
1960 136,180,233,191a,203a
1961 164,179,214,181a,196a
1962 133,233,191a,203a
1963 137,234,191a,203a
1964 142,248,192a,204a
1965 134,180,180i,248,259,262,263, 330a
1966 139,248,192a,204a
1967 156,248,275,181a,200a
1968 136,179,209,191a,193a
1969 164,179,256,181a,201a
1970 156,249,275,192a,204a
1971 137,213,189a,201a
1972 141,169,214,182a,194a
1973 134,249,192a,204a
1974 138,219,235,257,191a,195a
1975 142,179,216,181a,203a
1976 159,257,258,260,191a,195a
1977 139,180,206,181a,203a
1978 156,249,260,275,192a,204a
1979 136,236,191a,204a
1980 141,180,180i,186a,198a
1981 133,192,249,260,335a
1982 138,191,223,257,187a,199a
1983 142,213,237,249,189a,201a
1984 156,200,275,188a,200a
1985 139,193,181a,193a
1986 143,216,250,342a
1987 135,180,205,191a,194a
1988 140,226,238,250,190a,202a
1989 144,226,238,250,259,262,344a
1990 137,226,190a,202a
1991 141,180,209,181a,195a
1992 134,238,191a,203a
1993 138,180,211,181a,196a
1994 156,250,259,262,275,192a,204a
1995 135,179,213,228,191a,197a
1996 139,250,192a,204a
1997 144,250,192a,204a
1998 136,193,239,260,289a
1999 140,200,181a,193a

9th March

1930 136,179,229,192a,203a
1931 140,208,184a,196a
1932 133,246,192a,204a
1933 137,169,186a,198a
1934 141,246,192a,204a
1935 134,179,212,228,181a,199a
1936 139,179,213,228,191a,193a
1937 156,246,275,192a,204a
1938 135,246,192a,204a
1939 164,169,216,191a,201a
1940 156,182,246,263,275,300a
1941 136,218,230,246,182a,194a
1942 141,179,207,191a,195a
1943 133,219,231,247,258,260,181a, 203a
1944 138,180,180i,219,231,247,183a, 195a
1945 142,180,210,181a,203a
1946 135,169,211,260,192a,196a
1947 139,247,260,192a,204a
1948 156,275,185a,197a
1949 136,247,192a,204a
1950 164,180,222,255,191a,199a
1951 133,193,247,290a
1952 137,169,205,260,191a,200a
1953 165,193,181a,193a
1954 156,247,275,192a,204a
1955 138,179,255,191a,194a
1956 143,179,209,182a,202a
1957 135,248,192a,204a
1958 140,202,188a,200a
1959 144,169,213,181a,195a
1960 137,180,233,191a,203a
1961 141,179,214,181a,196a
1962 134,233,191a,203a
1963 138,180,248,330a
1964 142,248,192a,204a
1965 135,169,248,330a
1966 139,248,192a,204a
1967 156,248,275,181a,200a
1968 136,179,209,191a,193a
1969 164,179,256,181a,201a
1970 133,249,192a,204a
1971 137,213,189a,201a
1972 142,169,214,182a,194a
1973 134,249,192a,204a
1974 163,191,260,279,187a,199a
1975 143,236,260,191a,203a
1976 135,180,205,260,191a,195a
1977 164,180,206,181a,203a
1978 156,249,260,275,192a,204a
1979 137,169,222,191a,204a
1980 141,180,180i,186a,198a
1981 134,192,249,335a
1982 138,191,223,257,187a,199a
1983 142,213,237,249,189a,201a
1984 156,200,275,188a,200a
1985 139,193,181a,193a

1986 144,225,237,263,342a
1987 136,180,205,191a,194a
1988 140,226,238,250,259,252,190a, 202a
1989 133,226,238,250,190a,202a
1990 137,226,190a,202a
1991 141,180,209,181a,195a
1992 134,238,191a,203a
1993 139,180,211,181a,196a
1994 156,250,275,192a,204a
1995 135,179,213,228,191a,197a
1996 140,250,192a,204a
1997 144,250,192a,204a
1998 161,193,239,258,260,289a
1999 165,200,181a,193a

10th March

1930 136,246,192a,204a
1931 141,208,184a,196a
1932 133 204,181a,193a
1933 137,169,186a,198a
1934 142,246,192a,204a
1935 179,228,246,181a,199a
1936 139,179,213,228,191a,193a
1937 156,246,259,262,275,192a,204a
1938 136,246,192a,204a
1939 164,169,216,191a,201a
1940 133,182,194,263,280a
1941 137,192,218,230,246,182a,194a
1942 141,179,207,191a,195a
1943 134,219,231,247,181a,203a
1944 138,180,180i,219,231,247,183a, 195a
1945 142,180,210,181a,203a
1946 136,169,211,260,192a,196a
1947 140,212,247,260,192a,204a
1948 156,275,185a,197a
1949 136,247,192a,204a
1950 141,180,222,191a,199a
1951 133,193,247,290a
1952 138,169,205,191a,200a
1953 142,193,181a,193a
1954 156,247,260,275,192a,204a
1955 139,179,255,191a,194a
1956 143,179,209,182a,202a
1957 136,248,259,263,192a,204a
1958 140,202,188a,200a
1959 157,195,181a,193a
1960 137,180,233,191a,203a
1961 141,179,214,181a,196a
1962 134,233,191a,203a
1963 138,180,248,330a
1964 143,248,192a,204a
1965 135,169,248,330a
1966 164,169,207,228,191a,193a
1967 156,248,259,263,275,192a,204a
1968 136,179,209,191a,193a
1969 141,179,256,191a,201a
1970 133,180,235,181a,194a
1971 138,213,189a,201a
1972 142,169,214,182a,194a
1973 159,249,192a,204a
1974 163,191,260,279,187a,199a
1975 143,236,260,191a,203a
1976 136,220,236,260,191a,195a
1977 164,[illegible],206,181a,203a
1978 133,180,207,260,181a,196a
1979 137,169,222,191a,204a
1980 141,180,180i,186a,198a
1981 134,192,249,335a
1982 138,191,223,257,187a,199a
1983 143,213,237,249,258,260,189a, 201a,
1984 156,200,275,188a,200a
1985 140,193,286a
1986 144,225,237,263,342a
1987 136,180,205,191a,194a
1988 141,226,238,250,190a,202a
1989 133,226,238,250,190a,202a
1990 162,226,259,262,190a,202a
1991 142,227,190a,202a
1992 134,238,191a,203a
1993 139,180,211,181a,196a
1994 156,250,275,192a,204a
1995 136,179,213,228,191a,197a
1996 140,250,192a,204a
1997 133,250,192a,204a
1998 161,193,239,258,260,289a
1999 165,200,181a,193a

11th March

1930 137,180,207,192a,203a
1931 141,208,184a,196a
1932 134,169,227,182a,204a
1933 138,169,186a,198a
1934 142,246,192a,204a
1935 135,179,228,246,181a,199a
1936 139,179,213,228,191a,193a
1937 156,246,259,262,263,275,192a, 204a
1938 136,246,192a,204a
1939 141,169,216,191a,201a
1940 133,182,194,263,280a
1941 137,192,218,230,246,182a,194a
1942 142,179,255,191a,195a
1943 134,180,208,181a,203a
1944 163,180,180i,258,260,183a,195a
1945 143,169,210,182a,203a
1946 136,220,260,184a,196a
1947 140,212,247,260,192a,204a
1948 156,275,185a,197a
1949 137,247,192a,204a
1950 141,180,222,191a,199a
1951 134,247,192a,204a
1952 138,169,205,191a,200a
1953 142,193,181a,193a

1954 135,180,207,260,181a,201a
1955 139,179,255,191a,194a
1956 156,248,259,263,275,192a,204a
1957 136,248,259,263,192a,204a
1958 141,180,212,191a,202a
1959 157,195,181a,193a
1960 137,180,233,191a,203a
1961 142,226,190a,202a
1962 134,233,191a,203a
1963 139,248,192a,204a
1964 143,248,192a,204a
1965 136,169,248,259,263,330a
1966 164,169,207,228,191a,193a
1967 156,248,259,263,275,192a,204a
1968 137,179,209,191a,193a
1969 141,179,256,181a,201a
1970 134,181,182a,194a
1971 138,213,189a,201a
1972 142,169,214,182a,194a
1973 159,249,192a,204a
1974 140,219,235,257,258,260,191a, 195a
1975 144,216,249,260,192a,204a
1976 136,220,236,260,191a,195a
1977 141,180,206,181a,203a
1978 156,196,258,260,275,181a,193a
1979 137,169,222,191a,204a
1980 166,180,180i,186a,198a
1981 159,192,249,258,260,335a
1982 163,191,258,260,187a,199a
1983 143,213,237,249,258,260,189a, 201a
1984 136,200,188a,200a
1985 140,193,286a
1986 157,201,216,263,287a
1987 137,180,205,191a,194a
1988 141,226,238,250,190a,202a
1989 134,226,250,262,344a
1990 162,226,259,262,190a,202a
1991 142,227,190a,202a
1992 135,238,191a,203a
1993 140,196,181a,196a
1994 144,250,192a,204a
1995 136,179,213,228,191a,197a
1996 141,250,192a,204a
1997 133,250,192a,204a
1998 138,193,239,289a
1999 142,200,181a,193a

12th March

1930 137,180,207,192a,203a
1931 142,208,184a,196a
1932 134,169,227,182a,204a
1933 138,169,186a,198a
1934 143,229,246,345a
1935 135,179,228,246,181a,199a
1936 164,179,213,228,191a,193a
1937 156,246,259,262,263,275,192a, 204a
1938 137,180,215,181a,194a
1939 141,169,216,191a,201a
1940 133,182,194,263,280a
1941 162,192,182a,194a
1942 142,179,255,191a,195a
1943 159,180,180i,258,260,183a,195a
1944 163,180,180i,258,260,183a,195a
1945 143,169,210,182a,203a
1946 160,211,260,184a,196a
1947 140,212,247,260,192a,204a
1948 133,221,255,185a,197a
1949 137,247,192a,204a
1950 142,180,255,191a,199a
1951 134,247,192a,204a
1952 139,191,260,187a,199a
1953 143,193,181a,193a
1954 136,180,207,260,181a,201a
1955 140,224,232,191a,194a
1956 144,247,192a,204a
1957 156,248,263,275,324a
1958 141,180,212,191a,202a
1959 157,195,181a,193a
1960 138,180,233,191a,203a
1961 142,226,190a,202a
1962 135,233,191a,203a
1963 139,248,19a,204a
1964 156,248,275,192a,204a
1965 136,169,248,259,263,330a
1966 141,169,207,228,191a,193a
1967 156,200,259,263,275,181a,193a
1968 137,179,209,191a,193a
1969 142,179,211,181a,201a
1970 134,181,182a,194a
1971 162,180,180i,186a,198a
1972 143,169,214,182a,194a
1973 159,249,192a,204a
1974 140,219,235,257,258,260,191a, 195a
1975 144,216,249,260,192a,204a
1976 137,180,205,260,191a,195a
1977 141,180,206,181a,203a
1978 134,169,207,181a,196a
1979 138,169,208,191a,204a
1980 142,180,257,182a,197a
1981 159,192,249,258,1260,335a
1982 163,191,258,260,187a,199a
1983 143,213,237,249,258,260,189a, 201a
1984 136,200,188a,200a
1985 165,193,181a,193a
1986 157,216,250,263,342a
1987 137,179,205,191a,194a
1988 166,226,262,273,276,190a,202a
1989 134,226,250,262,344a
1990 139,226,262,190a,202a
1991 143,169,209,181a,195a
1992 135,238,191a,203a
1993 140,196,181a,196a

1994 144,250,192a,204a
1995 136,179,228,191a,197a
1996 141,250,192a,204a
1997 134,250,192a,204a
1998 138,193,239,289a
1999 142,200,181a,193a

13th March

1930 138,180,207,181a,203a
1931 142,208,184a,196a
1932 134,169,227,182a,204a
1933 139,169,186a,198a
1934 143,229,246,345a
1935 136,228,254,181a,199a
1936 140,246,192a,204a
1937 133,246,263,192a,204a
1938 137,180,215,181a,194a
1939 141,169,216,191a,201a
1940 158,182,259,262,182a,194a
1941 162,192,182a,194a
1942 167,230,191a,203a
1943 159,180,180i,258,260,183a,195a
1944 140,180,180i,219,231,247,258, 260,183a,195a
1945 144,169,210,182a,203a
1946 137,169,211,260,181a,196a
1947 141,247,260,192a,204a
1948 133,221,255,185a,197a
1949 138,247,192a,204a
1950 142,180,255,191a,199a
1951 134,247,192a,204a
1952 139,191,260,187a,199a
1953 143,193,181a,193a
1954 136,180,207,260,181a,201a
1955 140,224,232,191a,194a
1956 133,180,247,182a,202a
1957 156,248,275,324a
1958 142,169,212,191a,202a,
1959 134,169,213,181a,195a
1960 138,180,233,191a,203a
1961 143,179,214,181a,196a
1962 135,233,191a,203a
1963 139,248,192a,204a
1964 156,248,275,192a,204a
1965 136,248,259,263,330a
1966 141,169,207,228,191a,193a
1967 156,200,259,263,275,181a,193a
1968 138,179,186a,198a
1969 142,180,211,181a,201a
1970 135,180,212,181a,194a
1971 139,180.213,191a,202a
1972 143,169,214,182a,194a
1973 136,249,192a,204a
1974 140,219,235,257,258,260,191a, 195a
1975 144,216,249,260,192a,204a
1976 137,180,205,260,191a,195a
1977 142,180,206,181a,203a
1978 134,169,207,181a,196a
1979 138,169,208,191a,204a
1980 143,180,210,182a,197a
1981 159,192,249,258,260,335a
1982 140,191,258,260,187a,199a
1983 144,213,237,249,258,260,342a
1984 136,200,188a,200a
1985 165,193,181a,193a
1986 157,216,250,263,342a
1987 137,179,205,191a,194a
1988 166,226,262,273,276,190a,202a
1989 135,226,250,262,348a
1990 139,226,262,190a,202a
1991 143,169,209,181a,195a
1992 136,238,191a,203a
1993 141,180,211,181a,196a
1994 156,250,275,192a,204a
1995 137,179,213,228,191a,197a
1996 142,228,250,344a
1997 134,250,192a,204a
1998 138,193,239,289a
1999 142,200,181a,193a

14th March

1930 138,190,207,181a,203a
1931 143,208,184a,196a
1932 135,169,209,182a,204a
1933 139,169,186a,198a
1934 156,246,275,192a,204a
1935 136,228,254,181a,199a
1936 141,246,192a,204a
1937 133,246,263,192a,204a
1938 138,180,215,181a,194a
1939 142,169,216,191a,201a
1940 158,182,259,262,182a,194a
1941 139,192,218,230,246,182a,194a
1942 167,230,191a,203a
1943 136,180,208,260,181a,203a
1944 140,180,180i,219,231,258,260, 183a,195a
1945 144,169,210,182a,203a
1946 137,169,211,260,181a,196a
1947 141,247,260,192a,204a
1948 156,275,185a,197a
1949 138,247,192a,204a
1950 167,232,191a,203a
1951 135,247,192a,204a
1952 139,191,260,187a,199a,P
1953 144,193,181a,193a
1954 136,180,207,260,181a,201a
1955 140,224,232,191a,194a
1956 133,180,247,182a,202a
1957 138,248,263,192a,204a
1958 142,169,212,191a,202a
1959 134,169,213,181a,195a
1960 139,180,233,191a,203a
1961 143,179,214,181a,196a
1962 136,233,191a,203a

1963 140,248,192a,204a
1964 156,248,275,192a,204a
1965 137,169,248,263,330a
1966 141,169,207,228,191a,193a
1967 156,200,259,263,275,181a,193a
1968 138,179,186a,198a
1969 143,180,256,181a,201a
1970 135,180,212,181a,194a
1971 139,169,213,191a,202a
1972 144,169,214,182a,194a
1973 136,249,192a,204a
1974 141,219,235,257,258,260,191a, 195a
1975 133,179,216,260,181a,203a
1976 138,180,205,191a,195a
1977 142,180,206,181a,203a
1978 134,169,207,181a,196a
1979 139,169,208,191a,204a
1980 143,180,210,182a,192a
1981 136,192,249,260,335a
1982 140,191,260,187a,199a
1983 144,213,237,249,258,260,342a
1984 156,200,275,188a,200a
1985 142,193,181a,193a
1986 134,216,250,263,342a
1987 138,180,205,191a,194a
1988 143,226,262,276,190a,202a
1989 135,180,226,250,262,348a
1990 139,326,262,190a,202a
1991 144,169,209,181a,195a
1992 136,169,210,192a,203a
1993 141,180,211,181a,196a
1994 156,250,275,192a,204a
1995 137,179,213,228,191a,197a
1996 142,228,250,344a
1997 135,250,192a,204a
1998 139,193,239,260,289a
1999 143,200,239,289a

15th March

1930 139,180,207,181a,203a
1931 143,208,184a,196a
1932 135,169,209,182a,204a
1933 140,169,186a,198a
1934 156,246,275,192a,204a
1935 137,179,228,246,181a,199a
1936 141,246,192a,204a
1937 158,182,246,259,263,300a
1938 138,194,181a,193a
1939 142,169,216,191a,201a
1940 135,182,182a,194a
1941 139,192,218,230,246,182a,194a
1942 144,179,255,191a,195a
1943 136,180,208,260,181a,203a
1944 140,180,180i,219,231,247,260, 183a,195a
1945 133,169,210,182a,203a
1946 137,169,211,260,181a,196a
1947 142,247,192a,204a
1948 156,275,185a,197a
1949 139,247,192a,204a
1950 167,232,191a,203a
1951 135,247,192a,204a
1952 164,169,205,260,191a,200a
1953 144,169,206,182a,193a
1954 137,180,207,260,181a,201a
1955 141,179,208,191a,194a
1956 134,180,247,182a,202a
1957 138,248,263,192a,204a
1958 143,169,212,191a,202a
1959 135,169,213,181a,195a
1960 139,180,233,191a,203a
1961 144,179,215,181a,196a
1962 136,248,192a,204a
1963 140,248,192a,204a
1964 133,248,192a,204a
1965 137,169,248,263,330a
1966 142,169,207,228,191a,193a
1967 156,248,259,263,275,191a,200a
1968 139,179,209,191a,193a
1969 143,180,256,181a,201a
1970 136,180,235,181a,194a
1971 164,169,213,191a,202a
1972 144,169,214,182a,194a
1973 137,249,192a,204a
1974 141,219,235,257,258,260,191a, 195a
1975 133,179,216,260,181a,203a
1976 156,249,275,192a,204a
1977 143,180,206,181a,203a
1978 135,169,207,260,181a,196a
1979 139,169,208,191a,204a
1980 144,249,192a,204a
1981 136,192,249,260,335a
1982 141,191,212,260,332a
1983 133,193,213,258,260,287a
1984 156,200,259,263,275,188a,200a
1985 142,169,215,181a,194a
1986 134,216,250,263,342
1987 138,180,205,191a,194a
1988 143,226,262,276,190a,202a
1989 136,226,250,259,262,344a
1990 140,226,259,262,190a,202a
1991 144,169,209,181a,195a
1992 137,169,210,192a,203a
1993 141,180,211,181a,196a
1994 156,250,275,192a,204a
1995 138,250,192a,204a
1996 143,250,192a,204a
1997 135,250,192a,204a
1998 139,193,239,260,289a
1999 143,200,239,289a

16th March

1930 139,180,207,181a,203a
1931 143,208,184a,196a

1932 136,169,227,182a,204a
1933 140,169,186a,198a
1934 133,193,181a,193a
1935 137,179,228,246,181a,199a
1936 141,246,192a,204a
1937 158,182,246,259,263,300a
1938 138,193,181a,193a
1939 143,169,216,191a,201a
1940 135,182,182a,194a
1941 140,192,218,230,246,182a,194a
1942 144,179,255,191a,195a
1943 136,180,208,260,181a,203a
1944 141,180,180i,219,231,247,258, 260,183a,195a
1945 133,169,210,182a,203a
1946 138,169,211,181a,196a
1947 142,247,192a,204a
1948 156,275,185a,197a
1949 139,247,192a,204a
1950 144,247,192a,204a
1951 136,193,181a,193a
1952 164,169,205,260,191a,200a
1953 133,180,206,182a,193a
1954 137,180,207,260,181a,201a
1955 141,179,208,191a,194a
1956 134,180,247,182a,202a
1957 139,249,192a,204a
1958 143,169,212,191a,204a
1959 135,169,213,181a,195a
1960 140,248,192a,204a
1961 144,179,215,181a,196a
1962 137,248,192a,204a
1963 141,248,192a,204a
1964 133,248,259,263,330a
1965 162,169,248,259,263,330a
1966 142,169,207,228,191a,193a
1967 156,248,259,263,275,181a,200a
1968 139,179,209,192a,193a
1969 144,248,192a,204a
1970 136,180,235,181a,194a
1971 164,169,213,191a,202a
1972 133,169,214,182a,194a
1973 137,249,192a,204a
1974 142,219,235,257,191a,195a
1975 156,249,275,192a,204a
1976 156,249,260,275,192a,204a
1977 143,180,206,181a,203a
1978 135,169,207,260,181a,196a
1979 139,169,208,191a,204a
1980 144,249,192a,204a
1981 137,192,249,260,335a
1982 141,191,212,260,332a
1983 133,193,213,258,260,287a
1984 156,200,259,263,275,188a,200a
1985 142,169,215,181a,194a
1986 135,216,250,342a
1987 139,180,205,191a,194a
1988 144,226,238,250,259,262,263,344a
1989 136,226,250,259,262a,344a
1990 140,226,259,262,190a,202a
1991 144,169,209,181a,195a
1992 137,169,210,192a,203a
1993 142,227,190a,202a
1994 156,250,275,192a,204a
1995 138,250,192a,204a
1996 143,250,192a,204a
1997 136,169,215,192a,198a
1998 140,193,239,260,289a
1999 144,200,181a,193a

17th March

1930 140,246,192a,204a
1931 144,246,317a
1932 136,169,227,182a,204a
1933 141,169,186a,198a
1934 133,193,181a,193a
1935 137,179,228,246,181a,199a
1936 142,246,192a,204a
1937 135,246,192a,204a
1938 139,194,181a,193a
1939 143,169,216,191a,201a
1940 136,182,263,182a,194a
1941 140,192,218,230,246,259,263, 300a
1942 133,180,207,191a,195a
1943 137,180,208,260,181a,203a
1944 141,180,180i,247,260,309a
1945 134,169,210,182a,203a
1946 138,169,211,181a,196a
1947 142,247,192a,204a
1948 156,275,185a,197a
1949 140,247,192a,204a
1950 144,247,192a,204a
1951 136,193,181a,193a
1952 141,169,205,260,192a,200a
1953 133,180,206,182a,193a
1954 138,180,207,181a,201a
1955 142,179,255,191a,194a
1956 134,180,247,182a,202a
1957 139,248,192a,204a
1958 143,233,191a,203a
1959 135,169,213,181a,195a
1960 140,248,192a,204a
1961 133,179,215,181a,196a
1962 137,248,192a,204a
1963 141,248,192a,204a
1964 134,169,227,182a,204a
1965 162,169,248,259,263.330a
1966 143,169,207,228,191a,193a
1967 156,248,275,181a,200a
1968 164,179,209,192a,193a
1969 144,248,192a,204a
1970 136,180,235,181a,194a
1971 164,169,213,191a,202a
1972 133,169,214,182a,194a
1973 138,249,192a,204a
1974 142,219,235,257,191a,195a
1975 156,249,275,192a,204a

1976 156,249,260,275,192a,204a
1977 143,180,206,181a,203a
1978 136,169,207,260,181a,196a
1979 140,236,191a,204a
1980 133,180,257,182a,197a
1981 137,192,260,187a,199a
1982 114,191,212,260,332a
1983 133,193,213,258,260,287a
1984 156,200,259,263,275,188a,200a
1985 143,169,215,181a,194a
1986 135,216,250,342a
1987 139,180,205,191a,194a
1988 144,226,238,250,259,262,263, 344a
1989 137,226,250,344a
1990 141,226,190a,202a
1991 133,193,181a,193a
1992 138,169,210,192a,203a
1993 142,227,190a,202a
1994 156,250,275,192a,204a
1995 139,250,192a,204a
1996 156,250,275,192a,204a
1997 136,169,215,192a,198a
1998 140,193,239,260,289a
1999 144,200,181a,193a

18th March

1930 140,246,192a,204a
1931 144,246,317a
1932 137,169,227,182a,204a
1933 141,169,186a,198a
1934 134,180,211,191a,193a
1935 138,179,212,228,181a,199a
1936 156,246,259,263,275,192a,204a
1937 135,246,192a,204a
1938 139,194,181a,193a
1939 143,169,216,191a,201a
1940 136,182,263,182a,194a
1941 141,192,218,230,246,259,263, 300a
1942 133,180,207,191a,195a
1943 137,180,208,260,181a,203a
1944 142,180,180i,247,309a
1945 134,169,210,182a,203a
1946 139,181,260,187a,199a
1947 143,247,260,192a,204a
1948 156,275,185a,197a
1949 140,247,192a,204a
1950 144,247,192a,204a
1951 136,193,181a,193a
1952 141,169,205,260,192a,200a
1953 134,182,182a,193a
1954 138,180,207,181a,201a
1955 156,224,232,275,191a,194a
1956 135,180,209,182a,202a
1957 140,248,192a,204a
1958 144,169,256,191a,203a
1959 136,169,213,181a,195a
1960 141,248,192a,204a
1961 133,180,215,181a,196a
1962 137,248,192a,204a
1963 141,248,192a,204a
1964 134,169,227,182a,204a
1965 139,169,248,330a
1966 143,169,207,228,191a,193a
1967 156,248,275,181a,200a
1968 140,248,259,263,192a,204a
1969 133,201,181a,193a
1970 137,180,235,181a,194a
1971 141,213,189a,201a
1972 134,182,182a,194a
1973 138,249,192a,204a
1974 142,219,235,249,257,192a,204a
1975 156,249,275,192a,204a
1976 140,249,260,192a,204a
1977 144,249,192a,204a
1978 136,169,207,260,181a,196a
1979 140,236,191a,204a
1980 133,180,257,182a,197a
1981 138,192,249,335a
1982 142,191,187a,199a
1983 134,213,237,249,189a,201a
1984 156,200,275,188a,200a
1985 143,169,215,181a,194a
1986 135,216,250,342a
1987 164,180,205,191a,194a
1988 133,226,238,250,259,263,190a, 202a
1989 137,226,250,344a
1990 141,226,190a,202a
1991 133,193,181a,193a
1992 138,169,210,192a,203a
1993 143,180,211,181a,196a
1994 156,250,275,192a,204a
1995 139,250,192a,204a
1996 156,250,275,192a,204a
1997 136,169,215,192a,198a
1998 140,193,239,260,289a
1999 133,180,205,182a,200a

19th March

1930 140,246,192a,204a
1931 144,208,184a,196a
1932 137,169,227,182a,204a
1933 142,169,186a,198a
1934 134,180,211,191a,193a
1935 156,246,275,192a,204a
1936 156,246,275,192a,204a
1937 135,246,192a,204a
1938 140,194,181a,193a
1939 144,246,192a,204a
1940 136,182,263,182a,194a
1941 141,192,218,230,246,259,263, 300a
1942 133,180,207,191a,195a
1943 138,180,208,181a,203a

1944 142,169,183a,195a
1945 135,169,210,182a,203a
1946 139,181,260,187a,199a
1947 143,247,260,192a,204a
1948 156,275,185a,197a
1949 141,247,192a,204a
1950 133,180,222,191a,199a
1951 161,193,181a,193a
1952 142,169,205,192a,200a
1953 134,182,182a,193a
1954 138,180,207,181a,201a
1955 156,224,232,275,191a,194a
1956 135,180,209,182a,202a
1957 140,248,192a,204a
1958 144,169,256,191a,203
1959 136,169,213,181a,195a
1960 141,248,192a,204a
1961 134,180,215,181a,196a
1962 138,248,192a,204a
1963 142,248,192a,204a
1964 135,169,205,182a,204a
1965 139,169,248,330a
1966 143,169,207,228,191a,193a
1967 156,248,275,181a,200a
1968 141,248,263,192a,204a
1969 133,201,181a,193a
1970 137,180,235,181a,194a
1971 141,213,189a,201a
1972 134,182,182a,194a
1973 163,192,249,335a
1974 167,249,258,260,192a,204a
1975 135,180,205,260,181a,203a
1976 140,249,260,277,192a,204a
1977 144,249,192a,204a
1978 136,169,207,260,181a,196a
1979 141,169,222,191a,204a
1980 134,180,257,182a,197a
1981 138,192,249,335a
1982 142,191,187a,199a
1983 134,213,189a,201a
1984 156,200,275,188a,200a
1985 144,169,215,181a,194a
1986 136,216,250,259,263,342a
1987 164,205,191a,194a
1988 133,226,238,250,259,263,190a, 202a
1989 137,226,250,344a
1990 141,226,190a,202a
1991 134,169,209,182a,195a
1992 139,169,210,192a,203a
1993 143,180,211,181a,196a
1994 156,250,275,192a,204a
1995 140,250,192a,204a
1996 156,250,275,192a,204a
1997 137,169,215,192a,198a
1998 165,193,239,258,260,289a
1999 133,180,205,182a,200a

20th March

1930 141,246,192a,204a
1931 157,196,282a
1932 138,169,227,182a,204a
1933 142,169,186a,198a
1934 135,180,246,191a,193a
1935 156,246,275,192a,204a
1936 156,246,275,192a,204a
1937 136,246,259,263,192a,204a
1938 140,194,181a,193a
1939 144,246,192a,204a
1940 137,182,218,230,246,259,263, 182a,194a
1941 166,192,246,259,263,300a
1942 134,191,182a,194a
1943 138,180,208,181a,203a
1944 167,169,258,260,183a,195a
1945 135,169,210,182a,203a
1946 139,181,260,187a,199a
1947 156,212,247,260,275,192a,204a
1948 156,275,185a,197a
1949 141,247,192a,204a
1950 133,180,222,191a,199a
1951 161,193,181a,193a
1952 142,169,205,192a,200a
1953 135,182,182a,194a
1954 139,180,207,260,181a,201a
1955 156,224,232,275,191a,194a
1956 136,180,247,182a,202a
1957 140,248,192a,204a
1958 133,169,256,191a,203a
1959 161,233,181a,195a
1960 142,226,248,344a
1961 134,180,215,181a,196a
1962 138,248,192a,204a
1963 142,248,192a,204a
1964 135,169,205,182a,204a
1965 140,169,248,259,263,330a
1966 144,248,192a,204a
1967 136,248,259,263,182a,200a
1968 141,248,263,192a,204a
1969 133,201,181a,193a
1970 138,180,235,181a,194a
1971 166,218,246,256,191a,202a
1972 135,169,214,182a,194a
1973 163,192,249,335a
1974 167,249,258,260,192a,204a
1975 135,180,205,182a,203a
1976 9,220,236,249,260,192a,196a
1977 133,249,192a,204a
1978 161,221,249,258,260,181a,196a
1979 141,169,222,191a,204a
1980 2,180,257,182a,197a
1981 138,192,249,335a
1982 167,191,223,257,258,260,187a, 199a
1983 135,213,189a,201a
1984 164,200,259,263,188a,200a
1985 144,169,215,181a,194a

1986 136,216,250,259,263,342a
1987 141,205,189a,201a
1988 158,182,226,263,276,298a
1989 138,226,250,262,344a
1990 142,226,190a,202a
1991 134,169,209,182a,195a
1992 7,169,210,192a,203a
1993 143,180,211,181a,196a
1994 156,250,175,192a,204a
1995 140,250,192a,204a
1996 1,250,192a,204a
1997 137,169,215,192a,198a
1998 165,195,239,258,260,289a
1999 134,182,182a,194a

21st March

1930 9,204,181a,193a
1931 157,196,282a
1932 6,204,181a,193a
1933 143,169,198,284a
1934 3,193,181a,193a
1935 156,246,275,192a,204a
1936 168,246,259,263,192a,204a
1937 4,180,214,263,182a,201a
1938 9,194,181a,193a
1939 133,202,181a,193a
1940 5,182,218,230,246,259,263, 182a,194a
1941 166,192,259,263,182a,194a
1942 2,191,182a,194a
1943 6,180,208,181a,203a
1944 167,169,258,260,183a,195a
1945 4,169,210,182a,203a
1946 8,196,260,181a,193a
1947 12,247,260,192a,204a
1948 5,213,185a,197a
1949 9,247,192a,204a
1950 2,180,215,191a,199a
1951 6,193,181a,193a
1952 11,200,260,181a,193a
1953 3,182,182a,194a
1954 7,180,207,260,181a,201a
1955 11,180,208,191a,194a
1956 4,180,247,182a,202a
1957 9,225,233,255,192a,195a
1958 145,203,264,181a,193a
1959 5,233,182a,195a
1960 10,266,190a,202a
1961 3,180,215,181a,196a
1962 7,180,256,181a,204a
1963 11,234,191a,203a
1964 4,204,181a,193a
1965 8,169,263,186a,198a
1966 12,181a,193a
1967 4,248,259,263,182a,200a
1968 10,193,263,181a,193a
1969 2,201,181a,193a
1970 6,180,235,181a,194a
1971 166,218,246,256,261,191a,202a
1972 3,169,214,161,18a,194a
1973 8,180,215,192a,202a
1974 12,219,235,249,257,258,260, 192a,204a
1975 4,180,205,182a,203a
1976 9,220,236,249,260,192a,196a
1977 1,1i,204,181a,193a
1978 5,196,258,260,181a,193a
1979 10,169,208,191a,204a
1980 3,180,210,182a,197a
1981 7,192,260,187a,199a
1982 167,191,223,257,258,260,187a, 199a
1983 145,213,264,189a,201a
1984 164,200,259,263,188a,200a
1985 145,193,264,181a,193a
1986 5,216,263,189a,201a
1987 9,205,189a,201a
1988 158,182,226,263,276,298a
1989 6,226,190a,202a
1990 10,226,190a,202a
1991 3,169,195,182a,195a
1992 8,169,210,192a,203a
1993 12,180,211,181a,196a
1994 160,250,259,263,192a,204a
1995 8,180,213,191a,197a
1996 1,250,192a,204a
1997 6,198,181a,193a
1998 145,193,264,289a
1999 2,182,182a,194a

22nd March

1930 10,204,181a,193a
1931 158,196,282a
1932 7,204,181a,193a
1933 143,169,198,299,284a
1934 3,193,181a,193a
1935 7,180,212,182a,199a
1936 168,246,259,263,192a,204a
1937 5,180,214,263,182a,201a
1938 9,194,181a,193a
1939 145,202,264,181a,193a
1940 162,182,259,263,182a,194a
1941 11,192,218,230,246,182a,194a
1942 3,180,183a,195a
1943 163,219,231,247,182a,203a
1944 12,169,260,183a,195a
1945 4,169,210,182a,203a
1946 8,196,260,181a,193a
1947 12,247,260,192a,204a
1948 5,213,185a,197a
1949 10,180,214,192a,193a
1950 2,180,215,191a,199a
1951 6,193,181a,193a
1952 11,200,260,181a,193a
1953 4,182,182a,194a
1954 8,180,207,260,181a,201a

1955 168,247,192a,204a
1956 5,255,185a,197a
1957 9,225,233,255,192a,195a
1958 145,203,264,181a,193a
1959 5,233,182a,195a
1960 11,180,214,192a,203a
1961 3,180,215,181a,196a
1962 7,180,256,181a,204a
1963 11,234,191a,203a
1964 4,204,181a,193a
1965 9,169,263,186a,198a
1966 1,193,181a,193a
1967 5,180,208,217,263,182a,200a
1968 10,193,263,181a,193a
1969 2,201,181a,193a
1970 6,194,181a,193a
1971 11,169,213,261,191a,202a
1972 4,169,214,182a,194a
1973 8,180,215,192a,202a
1974 12,219,235,249,257,258,260, 192a,204a
1975 4,180,205,182a,203a
1976 9,220,236,249,260,192a,196a
1977 2,180,257,181a,204a
1978 145,196,264,181a,193a
1979 10,169,208,191a,204a
1980 3,180,210,182a,197a
1981 7,192,260,187a,199a
1982 167,191,233,257,258,260,287a, 199a
1983 145,213,264,189a,201a
1984 9,200,263,188a,200a
1985 145,193,264,181a,193a
1986 5,216,263,189a,201a
1987 9,205,189a,201a
1988 3,226,238,250,190a,202a
1989 7,266,190a,202a
1990 11,226,238,343a
1991 3,169,195,182a,195a
1992 8,169,210,192a,203a
1993 12,180,211,181a,196a
1994 160,250,259,263,192a,204a
1995 9,213,189a,201a
1996 2,250,192a,204a
1997 6,198,181a,193a
1998 145,193,264,289a
1999 3,180,205,182a,200a

23rd March

1930 10,204,181a,193a
1931 158,196,282a
1932 7,204,181a,193a
1933 144,169,198,284a
1934 4,193,181a,193a
1935 164,228,254,182a,199a
1936 1,193,246,263,290a
1937 5,179,214,263,182a,201a
1938 9,194,181a,193a
1939 2,202,181a,193a
1940 162,182,259,263,182a,194a
1941 11,192,218,230,246,182a,194a
1942 3,180,183a,195a
1943 163,219,231,247,182a,203a
1944 12,169,260,183a,195a
1945 5,169,220,182a,203a
1946 9,196,258,260,181a,193a
1947 1,180,212,260,191a,204a
1948 145,213,264,185a,197a
1949 10,180,214,192a,193a
1950 2,180,215,191a,199a
1951 7,193,181a,193a
1952 12,200,260,181a,193a
1953 4,182,182a,194a
1954 8,180,207,260,181a,201a
1955 168,247,192a,204a
1956 5,255,285a,197a
1957 10,180,210,192a,195a
1958 2,169,248,191a,203a
1959 6,169,248,182a,195a
1960 11,180,214,192a,203a
1961 3,180,215,181a,196a
1962 7,180,256,181a,204a
1963 12,248,192a,204a
1964 5,204,181a,193a
1965 9,169,263,186a,198a
1966 1,193,181a,193a
1967 5,180,208,217,263,182a,200a
1968 10,193,263,181a,193a
1969 3,201,181a,193a
1970 7,194,181a,193a
1971 11,169,213,261,191a,202a
1972 4,169,214,182a,194a
1973 8,180,215,192a,202a
1974 12,219,235,249,257,258,260, 192a,204a
1975 5,180,205,182a,203a
1976 10,220,236,192a,196a
1977 2,180,257,181a,204a
1978 145,196,264,181a,193a
1979 10,169,208,191a,204a
1980 4,180,257,182a,197a
1981 8,192,260,182a,199a
1982 12,191,260,187a,199a
1983 145,213,264,189a,201a
1984 9,200,263,188a,200a
1985 145,193,264,181a,193a
1986 5,216,263,289a,201a
1987 10,180,205,191a,194a
1988 3,226,238,250,190a,202a
1989 7,226,190a,202a
1990 11,226,238,343a
1991 4,169,209,182a,195a
1992 9,169,210,192a,203a
1993 1,196,181a,193a
1994 5,228,250,259,263,192a,204a
1995 9,213,189a,201a
1996 2,250,192a,204a
1997 145,198,258,261,264,181a,193a

1998 145,193,264,289a
1999 3,180,205,182a,200a

24th March

1930 10,204,181a,193a
1931 159,196,282a
1932 8,204,181a,193a
1933 144,169,198,284a
1934 4,193,181a,193a
1935 164,228,254,182a,199a
1936 1,193,246,263,290a
1937 162,230,246,259,263,182a,201a
1938 10,194,181a,193a
1939 2,202,181a,193a
1940 7,182,218,230,246,182a,194a
1941 11,192,218,230,246,182a,194a
1942 3,180,183a,195a
1943 8,180,208,182a,203a
1944 145,169,195,258,260,264,281a
1945 5,169,220,182a,203a
1946 9,196,258,260,181a,193a
1947 1,180,212,260,191a,204a
1948 145,213,264,185a,197a
1949 11,180,214,192a,193a
1950 159,247,191a,199a
1951 7,193,181a,193a
1952 12,200,260,181a,193a
1953 4,182,182a,194a
1954 8,180,207,260,181a,201a
1955 1,180,208,191a,194a
1956 6,180,247,182a,202a
1957 10,180,210,192a,195a
1958 2,169,248,191a,203a
1959 6,169,248,182a,195a
1960 11,180,214,192a,203a
1961 4,180,215,181a,196a
1962 8,180,256,181a,204a
1963 12,248,192a,204a
1964 5,204,263,181a,193a
1965 9,169,263,186a,198a
1966 1,193,181a,193a
1967 6,180,180i,263,186a,198a
1968 11,193,181a,193a
1969 3,201,181a,193a
1970 7,194,181a,193a
1971 12,169,213,191a,202a
1972 5,169,214,261,182a,194a
1973 9,180,215,192a,202a
1974 1,219,235,253,258,260,191a, 195a
1975 5,180,205,182a,203a
1976 10,220,236,192a,196a
1977 2,180,257,181a,204a
1978 145,196,258,260,264,181a,193a
1979 11,169,222,191a,204a
1980 4,180,257,182a,197a
1981 8,181,193,260,285a
1982 12,191,260,187a,199a
1983 5,193,213,278,287a
1984 10,200,224,263,337a
1985 2,193,181a,193a
1986 145,216,263,264,189a,201a
1987 10,180,205,191a,194a
1988 3,226,238,250,190a,202a
1989 7,226,190a,202a
1990 12,226,190a,202a
1991 4,169,209,182a,195a
1992 9,169,210,192a,203a
1993 1,196,181a,193a
1994 5,228,250,259,263,192a,204a
1995 10,228,190a,202a
1996 3,169,250,182a,204a
1997 145,198,258,261,264,181a,193a
1998 145,193,239,258,260,264,289a
1999 4,180,205,182a,200a

25th March

1930 11,204,181a,193a
1931 159,196,282a
1932 8,204,181a,193a
1933 144,169,198,284a
1934 5,193,181a,193a
1935 9,180,212,229,182a,199a
1936 2,246,263,192a,204a
1937 162,230,246,259,263,182a,201a
1938 10,194,181a,193a
1939 2,202,181a,193a
1940 7,182,218,230,246,182a,194a
1941 12,192,218,230,259,263,300a
1942 4,180,207,191a,195a
1943 8,180,208,182a,203a
1944 145,169,195,258,260,264,281a
1945 5,169,210,182a,204a
1946 9,196,258,260,181a,193a
1947 2,180,212,191a,204a
1948 145,213,264,185a,197a
1949 11,180,214,192a,193a
1950 159,247,191a,199a
1951 8,193,181a,193a
1952 145,200,258,260,264,181a,193a
1953 5,182,182a,194a
1954 9,255,258,260,181a,201a
1955 1,180,208,191a,194a
1956 6,180,247,182a,202a
1957 10,180,210,192a,195a
1958 2,169,248,191a,203a
1959 7,169,248,182a,195a
1960 12,248,192a,204a
1961 4,180,215,181a,196a
1962 8,180,256,181a,204a
1963 1,180,216,191a,197a
1964 6,169,204,263,284a
1965 166,169,198,259,263,284a
1966 2,180,207,191a,193a
1967 6,180,180i,263,186a,198a
1968 11,193,181a,193a

1969 3,201,181a,193a
1970 8,194,181a,193a
1971 12,169,213,191a,202a
1972 5,169,214,261,182a,194a
1973 9,180,215,181a,202a
1974 1,219,235,257,258,260,191a, 195a
1975 6,180,205,182a,203a
1976 11,220,236,260,192a,196a
1977 3,180,206,181a,204a
1978 145,196,258,260,264,181a,193a
1979 11,169,222,191a,204a
1980 4,180,257,182a,197a
1981 8,181,193,260,285a
1982 1,191,260,187a,199a
1983 5,193,213,278,287a
1984 10,200,224,263,337a
1985 22,193,181a,193a
1986 145,216,263,264,189a,201a
1987 11,180,205,191a,194a
1988 4,226,238,250,259,263,190a, 202a
1989 8,226,190a,202a
1990 12,226,190a,202a
1991 5,169,195,182a,195a
1992 9,169,210,192a,203a
1993 1,196,181a,193a
1994 6,228,250,259,263,192a,204a
1995 10,228,190a,202a
1996 3,193,181a,193a
1997 145,198,258,261,264,181a,193a
1998 145,193,239,258,260,264,289a
1999 4,180,205,182a,200a

26th March

1930 11,204,181a,193a
1931 159,196,282a
1932 9,204,181a,193a
1933 1,180,180i,198,284a
1934 5,193,181a,193a
1935 9,180,212,229,182a,199a
1936 2,246,263,192a,204a
1937 7,169,214,182a,201a
1938 11,194,181a,193a
1939 3,202,181a,193a
1940 8,182,218,230,246,259,263, 182a,194a
1941 12,192,218,230,246,259,263, 300a
1942 4,180,207,191a,195a
1943 9,180,208,182,203a
1944 2,169,183a,195a
1945 6,169,210,182a,204a
1946 10,196,181a,193a
1947 2,180,212,191a,204a
1948 145,213,264,185a,197a
1949 12,193,181a,193a
1950 4,169,222,191a,199a
1951 8,193,181a,193a
1952 145,200,258,260,264,181a,193a
1953 5,182,182a,194a
1954 9,255,258,260,181a,201a
1955 2,180,208,191a,194a
1956 7,180,209,182a,202a
1957 11,225,233,255,181a,195a
1958 3,169,248,256,191a,203a
1959 7,169,248,182a,195a
1960 12,248,192a,204a
1961 5,180,215,181a,196a
1962 9,248,192a,204a
1963 1,169,197,181a,193a
1964 6,169,204,263,284a
1965 166,169,198,259,263,284a
1966 2,180,207,191a,193a
1967 7,180,208,217,182a,200a
1968 12,193,248,263,290a
1969 4,201,181a,193a
1970 8,194,181a,193a
1971 145,202,258,261,264,181a,193a
1972 5,169,214,261,182a,194a
1973 10,180,215,181a,202a
1974 2,219,235,257,191a,195a
1975 6,180,205,182a,203a
1976 11,220,236,192a,196a
1977 3,180,206,181a,204a
1978 145,196,258,260,264,181a,193a
1979 12,169,222,191a,204a
1980 5,180,257,182a,197a
1981 9,181,193,258,260,285a
1982 1,191,260,187a,199a
1983 145,193,213,264,287a
1984 11,200,188a,200a
1985 2,193,181a,193a
1986 145,216,264,189a,201a
1987 11,180,205,191a,194a
1988 4,226,238,259,263,190a,202a
1989 8,226,190a,202a
1990 1,203,226,288a
1991 5,169,195,182a,195a
1992 10,227,190a,202a
1993 2,180,211,181a,196a
1994 6,228,250,259,263,192a,204a
1995 11,180,213,191a,197a
1996 3,193,181a,193a
1997 145,198,264,181a,193a
1998 145,193,239,258,260,264,289a
1999 5,180,205,182a,200a

27th March

1930 12,204,181a,193a
1931 160,196,282a
1932 9,204,181a,193a
1933 1,180,180i,198,284a
1934 5,193,181a,193a
1935 10,180,212,229,182a,199a
1936 3,246,192a,204a

1937 7,169,214,182a,201a
1938 11,194,181a,193a
1939 3,202,181a,193a
1940 8,182,218,230,246,259,263, 182a,194a
1941 1,181,202,218,230,246,259, 263,280a
1942 5,180,207,191a,195a
1943 9,180,208,182a,203a
1944 2,169,183a,195a
1945 6,169,210,182a,204a
1946 10,196,181a,193a
1947 3,180,212,260,191a,204a
1948 145,213,264,185a,197a
1949 12,193,181a,193a
1950 4,169,222,191a,199a
1951 8,193,181a,193a
1952 145,200,258,260,264,181a,193a
1953 6,182,182a,194a
1954 10,180,207,181a,201a
1955 2,180,208,191a,194a
1956 7,180,209,182a,202a
1957 11,225,233,255,181a,195a
1958 3,169,248,256,191a,203a
1959 8,169,213,182a,195a
1960 1,180,214,192a,203a
1961 5,180,215,181a,196a
1962 9,248,192a,204a
1963 2,169,216,191a,197a
1964 6,169,204,263,284a
1965 11,169,198,284a
1966 3,180,207,191a,193a
1967 7,180,208,217,182a,200a
1968 12,193,248,263,290a
1969 4,201,181a,193a
1970 8,194,181a,193a
1971 145,202,258,261,264,181a,193a
1972 6,169,214,261,182a,195a
1973 10,219,235,257,181a,203a
1974 2,219,235,257,191a,195a
1975 7,180,205,182a,203a
1976 168,220,236,192a,196a
1977 4,180,257,181a,204a
1978 145,196,158,260,264,181a,193a
1979 12,169,222,191a,204a
1980 5,180,257,18a,197a
1981 9,181,193,258,260,285a
1982 2,191,187a,199a
1983 145,193,213,264,287a
1984 11,200,188a,200a
1985 3,193,181a,193a
1986 145,216,264,189a,201a
1987 12,180,205,191a,194a
1988 5,226,238,250,259,263,190a, 202a
1989 9,226,190a,202a
1990 1,203,226,288a
1991 6,169,195,182a,195a
1992 10,227,190a,202a
1993 2,180,211,181a,196a
1994 7,228,250,192a,204a
1995 11,180,213,191a,197a
1996 4,193,181a,193a
1997 145,198,264,181a,193a
1998 145,193,239,258,260,264,289a
1999 5,180,205,182a,200a

28th March

1930 12,204,181a,193a
1931 160,196,282a
1932 9,204,181a,193a
1933 2,180,180i,198,284a
1934 6,193,181a,193a
1935 10,180,212,182a,199a
1936 3,246,192a,204a
1937 7,169,214,182a,201a
1938 11,194,181a,193a
1939 4,202,181a,193a
1940 9,182,218,230,246,259,263, 182a,194a
1941 1,181,202,218,230,246,259,263, 280a
1942 5,18,207,191a,195a
1943 9,169,208,182a,203a
1944 3,169,260,183a,195a
1945 7,169,210,182a,204a
1946 11,196,260,181a,193a
1947 3,180,212,260,191a,204a
1948 145,213,264,185a,197a
1949 12,193,181a,193a
1950 4,169,215,191a,198a
1951 9,193,181a,193a
1952 2,200,181a,193a
1953 6,182,182a,194a
1954 10,180,207,181a,201a
1955 3,180,208,191a,194a
1956 8,180,247,182a,202a
1957 12,225,233,255,181a,195a
1958 4,169,256,191a,203a
1959 8,169,213,182a,195a
1960 1,180,214,192a,203a
1961 5,180,215,181a,196a
1962 9,1248,192a,204a
1963 2,169,216,191a,197a
1964 7,204,181a,193a
1965 11,169,198,284a
1966 3,180,207,191a,193a
1967 164,200,259,263,188a,200a
1968 1,194,263,181a,193a
1969 5,201,181a,193a
1970 9,194,181a,193a
1971 158,218,246,256,261,191a,202a
1972 6,169,214,261,182a,195a
1973 10,219,235,257,181a,203a
1974 159,191a,258,260,183a,195a
1957 7,180,205,182a,203a
1976 168,220,236,192a,196a
1977 4,180,257,181a,204a

1978 145,196,258,260,264,181a,193a
1979 1,180,222,191a,204a
1980 6,180,180i,186a,198a
1981 10,181,193,285a
1982 2,191,187a,199a
1983 145,193,213,264,287a
1984 11,200,188a,200a
1985 3,193,181a,193a
1986 8,180,216,263,181a,202a
1987 12,180,205,191,194a
1988 5,226,238,250,259,263,190a, 202a
1989 9,195,226,288a
1990 2,226,190a,202a
1991 6,169,195,182a,195a
1992 11,169,210,192a,204a
1993 3,180,211,181a,196a
1994 7,228,250,192a,204a
1995 12,250,263,192a,204a
1996 4,193,181a,193a
1997 145,198,264,181a,193a
1998 145,193,239,258,260,264,289a
1999 5,180,205,182a,200a

29th March

1930 12,204,181a,193a
1931 161,196,282a
1932 10,204,181a,193a
1933 2,180,180i,198,284a
1934 6,193,181a,193a
1935 10,180,212,182a,199a
1936 160,246,259,263,192a,204a
1937 8,169,214,263,182a,201a
1938 12,194,181a,193a
1939 4,202,181a,193a
1940 9,182,218,230,246,259,263, 182a,194a
1941 1,181,202,218,230,246,259, 263,280a
1942 5,180,207,191a,195a
1943 10,169,208,182a,203a
1944 3,169,260,183a,195a
1945 7,169,210,182a,204a
1946 11,196,260,181a,193a
1947 4,180,212,260,191a,204a
1948 9,213,185a,197a
1949 1,1i,193,181a,193a
1950 5,169,232,191a,198a
1951 9,193,181a,193a
1952 2,200,181a,193a
1953 6,182,182a,194a
1954 11,180,207,260,181a,201a
1955 3,180,208,191a,194a
1956 145,225,255,264,182a,202a
1957 12,225,233,255,181a,195a
1958 4,169,256,191a,203a
1959 9,233,182a,195a
1960 2,180,214,192a,203a
1961 6,180,215,181a,196a
1962 10,248,192a,204a
1963 3,169,216,191a,197a
1964 7,193,181a,193a
1965 11,169,198,284a
1966 4,180,207,191a,193a
1967 164,200,259,263,188a,200a
1968 1,194,263,181a,193a
1969 5,201,181a,193a
1970 9,194,181a,193a
1971 158,218,246,256,261,191a,202a
1972 163,182,258,261,187a,199a
1973 167,235,258,260,191a,203a
1974 159,191,258,260,183a,195a
1975 8,180,205,182a,203a
1976 168,220,236,192a,196a
1977 4,180,257,181a,204a
1978 9,196,258,260,181a,196a
1979 1,236,249,192a,204a
1980 6,180,180i,186a,198a
1981 10,181,193,285a
1982 159,191,258,260,187a,199a
1983 145,193,213,264,287a
1984 168,200,259,263,188a,200a
1985 4,193,181a,193a
1986 8,180,216,263,181a,202a
1987 1,1i,194,263,181a,193a
1988 5,226,238,250,259,263,190a, 202a
1989 9,195,226,288a
1990 2,226,190a,202a
1991 6,169,195,182a,195a
1992 11,169,210,192a,204a
1993 3,180,211,181a,196a
1994 164,250,259,263,339a
1995 12,250,263,192a,204a
1996 5,193,181a,193a
1997 9,198,258,261,181a,193a
1998 145,193,239,258,260,264,289a
1999 6,180,205,182a,200a

30th March

1930 145,204,264,181a,193a
1931 5,197,181a,193a
1932 10,204,181a,193a
1933 2,180,180i,198,284a
1934 7,193,181a,193a
1935 11,180,212,182a,199a
1936 160,246,259,263,192a,204a
1937 8,169,214,263,182a,201a
1938 12,194,181a,193a
1939 5,202,181a,193a
1940 166,182,259,263,182a,194a
1941 158,181,259,263,182a,194a
1942 6,180,207,191a,195a
1943 10,169,208,182a,203a
1944 3,169,260,183a,195a
1945 7,169,210,182a,204a

1946 12,196,260,181a,193a
1947 4,180,212,260,191a,204a
1948 9,213,185a,197a
1949 1,1i,193,181a,193a
1950 5,169,232,191a,198a
1951 10,193,181a,193a
1952 3,200,260,181a,193a
1953 7,182,295a
1954 11,180,207,260,181a,201a
1955 160,208,184a,196a
1956 145,225,255,264,182a,202a
1957 12,225,233,255,181a,195a
1958 5,225,233,191a,203a
1959 9,233,182a,195a
1960 2,180,214,192a,203a
1961 6,180,215,181a,196a
1962 10,248,192a,204a
1963 3,169,216,192a,197a
1964 8,193,263,181a,193a
1965 12,169,198,263,284a
1966 4,180,207,191a,193a
1967 9,190,208,217,263,182a,200a
1968 1,194,263,181a,193a
1969 5,201,181a,193a
1970 10,194,181a,193a
1971 3,169,213,192a,202a
1972 163,182,258,261,187a,199a
1973 167,235,258,260,191a,203a
1974 4,219,235,257,258,260,191a, 195a
1975 8,180,205,182a,203a
1976 1,196,181a,193a
1977 5,221,249,181a,204a
1978 9,196,258,260,181a,196a
1979 2,236,249,192a,204a
1980 6,180,180i,196a,198a
1981 10,181,193,285a
1982 159,191,258,260,187a,199a
1983 145,193,213,264,287a
1984 160,200,259,263,188a,200a
1985 4,193,181a,193a
1986 9,216,263,189a,201a
1987 1,1i,194,263,181a,193a
1988 162,226,263,276,190a,202a
1989 10,195,226,288a
1990 3,226,190a,202a
1991 7,169,195,182a,195a
1992 11,169,210,192a,204a
1993 4,180,211,181a,196a
1994 164,250,259,263,339a
1995 1,1i,250,263,192a,204a
1996 5,193,181a,193a
1997 9,198,258,261,181a,193a
1998 145,193,239,264,289a
1999 6,180,205,182a,200a

31st March

1930 145,204,264,181a,193a
1931 6,197,181a,193a
1932 11,204,181a,193a
1933 3,180,180i,198,284a
1934 7,193,181a,193a
1935 11,180,212,182a,199a
1936 160,193,263,181a,193a
1937 9,169,214,163,182a,201a
1938 145,194,264,191a,193a
1939 5,202,263,181a,193a
1940 166,182,259,263,182a,194a
1941 158,181,259,263,182a,194a
1942 6,180,207,191a,195a
1943 167,219,231,247,182a,203a
1944 4,169,260,183a,195a
1945 8,169,210,182a,204a
1946 12,196,260,181a,193a
1947 145,247,260,264,324a
1948 145,213,264,185a,197a
1949 2,193,181a,193a
1950 6,169,186a,198a
1951 10,193,181a,193a
1952 3,200,260,181a,193a
1953 7,181,187a,199a
1954 11,180,207,260,181a,201a
1955 160,208,184a,196a
1956 9,225,255,182a,202a
1957 1,1i,195,181a,193a
1958 5,225,233,191a,203a
1959 10,169,248,192a,195a
1960 2,180,214,192a,203a
1961 7,180,215,181a,196a
1962 11,248,192a,204a
1963 4,169,227,192a,197a
1964 8,193,263,181a,193a
1965 12,169,198,263,284a
1966 5,180,207,191a,193a
1967 9,180,208,217,182a,199a
1968 2,180,209,217,263,192a,194a
1969 145,169,201,264,284a
1970 10,194,181a,193a
1971 3,169,213,192a,202a
1972 163,182,258,261,187a,199a
1973 12,219,235,257,258,260,181a, 203a
1974 4,219,235,257,258,260,191a, 195a
1975 9,180,205,182a,203a
1976 1,196,181a,193a
1977 5,221,249,181a,204a
1978 145,196,264,181a,193a
1979 2,236,249,192a,204a
1980 7,180,210,182a,197a
1981 11,181,193,260,285a
1982 4,191,260,187a,199a
1983 145,193,213,264,287a
1984 168,200,259,263,188a,200a
1985 5,193,181a,193a
1986 9,216,263,189a,201a
1987 2,180,205,263,192a,194a
1988 162,226,263,276,190a,202a

1989 10,195,226,288a
1990 3,226,190a,202a
1991 7,169,195,182a,195a
1992 12,250,192a,204a
1993 4,180,211,181a,196a
1994 9,228,250,259,263,192a,204a
1995 1,250,263,192a,204a
1996 5,193,181a,193a
1997 145,198,258,261,264,181a,193a
1998 145,193,239,264,189a
1999 7,180,205,182a,200a

1st April

1930 2,204,181a,193a
1931 6,197,263,181a,193a
1932 11,204,181a,193a
1933 3,180,180i,198,193a
1934 7,193,181a,193a
1935 168,246,192a,204a
1936 5,193,213,263,181a,193a
1937 9,169,214,263,182a,201a
1938 145,194,264,181a,201a
1939 6,202,263,181a,193a
1940 11,182,218,230,246,182a,194a
1941 3,181,218,230,246,182a,194a
1942 7,180,207,191a,195a
1943 167,219,231,247,182a,203a
1944 4,169,209,260,192a,196a
1945 8,169,210,182a,204a
1946 145,196,258,260,264,181a,193a
1947 145,247,260,264,324a
1948 145,264,185a,197a
1949 2,193,181a,193a
1950 6,169,186a,198a
1951 11,193,181a,193a
1952 4,200,260,181a,193a
1953 8,180,206,181a,194a
1954 12,180,207,260,181a,201a
1955 5,224,232,192a,194a
1956 9,225,255,182a,202a
1957 145,195,264,278,181a,193a
1958 6,169,248,191a,203a
1959 10,169,248,182a,195a
1960 3,180,214,192a,203a
1961 7,180,215,181a,196a
1962 11,248,192a,204a
1963 4,169,227,192a,197a
1964 9,193,205,263,181a,193a
1965 1,169,198,263,284a
1966 5,180,207,191a,193a
1967 10,180,208,217,182a,199a
1968 2,180,209,217,263,192a,194a
1969 145,169,201,264,284a
1970 11,194,181a,193a
1971 3,169,213,192a,202a
1972 8,169,214,182a,195a
1973 12,219,235,257,258,260,181a, 203a
1974 5,219,235,257,258,260,191a, 195a
1975 9,180,205,182a,203a
1976 2,169,257,192a,196a
1977 145,204,264,181a,193a
1978 145,196,264,181a,193a
1979 3,236,249,192a,204a
1980 7,180,210,182a,197a
1981 11,181,193,260,285a
1982 4,191,260,187a,199a
1983 145,193,213,264,287a
1984 1,200,263,188a,200a
1985 5,194,181a,193a
1986 10,225,263,190a,202a
1987 2,180,205,263,192a,194a
1988 7,226,238,250,190a,202a
1989 11,195,226,288a
1990 3,226,190a,202a
1991 8,209,182a,195a
1992 12,250,192a,204a
1993 4,180,211,181a,196a
1994 9,228,250,259,263,192a,204a
1995 1,1i,250,264,192a,204a
1996 6,193,181a,193a
1997 145,198,258,261,264,181a,193a
1998 145,193,239,258,260,264,289a
1999 7,180,205,182a,200a

2nd April

1930 2,204,181a,193a
1931 7,197,181a,193a
1932 12,204,181a,193a
1933 4,180,180i,198,284a
1934 8,193,181a,193a
1935 168,246,192a,193a
1936 5,169,213,263,192a,194a
1937 9,169,214,263,182a,201a
1938 158,181,194,280a
1939 6,202,263,181a,193a
1940 11,182,182a,194a
1941 3,181,182a,194a
1942 7,180,207,191a,195a
1943 12,169,208,182a,203a
1944 5,258,260,185a,197a
1945 9,169,210,182a,204a
1946 1,196,260,181a,193a
1947 6,247,192a,204a
1948 145,264,185a,197a
1949 145,193,258,261,264,181a,193a
1950 7,169,232,191a,198a
1951 11,170,216,182a,193a
1952 4,200,260,181a,193a
1953 8,180,206,181a,194a
1954 12,180,207,260,181a,201a
1955 5,224,232,192a,194a
1956 145,225,255,264,182a,202a
1957 145,195,264,181a,193a
1958 6,169,248,191a,203a

1959 11,169,248,182a,195a
1960 3,248,192a,204a
1961 7,180,215,181a,196a
1962 168,248,192a,204a
1963 4,169,227,192a,197a
1964 9,193,263,181a,193a
1965 1,169,198,263,284a
1966 6,180,180i,86a,198a
1967 10,180,208,217,182a,199a
1968 3,180,209,217,192a,194a
1969 145,201,164,181a,193a
1970 11,194,181a,193a
1971 4,170,235,192a,202a
1972 8,169,214,182a,195a
1973 12,129,235,257,258,260,181a, 203a
1974 5,219,235,257,258,260,191a, 195a
1975 10,180,205,182a,203a
1976 2,169,257,192a,196a
1977 145,204,264,181a,193a
1978 145,196,258,260,264,181a,193a
1979 3,236,249,192a,204a
1980 8,180,257,182a,197a
1981 12,181,193a,260,285a
1982 4,191,260,187a,199a
1983 9,193,213,1278,287a
1984 1,200,263,188a,200a
1985 6,194,181a,193a
1986 10,225,263,190a,202a
1987 2,180,205,263,192a,194a
1988 7,226,238,250,190a,202a
1989 11,195,226,288a
1990 4,226,190a,202a
1991 8,209,182a,195a
1992 145,204,164,181a,193a
1993 5,180,211,181a,196a
1994 10,228,250,259,263,192a,204a
1995 145,213,264,192a,197a
1996 6,193,181a,193a
1997 11,198,239,261,289a
1998 145,193,239,258,260,264,289a
1999 7,180,205,182a,200a

3rd April

1930 3,204,181a,193a
1931 7,197,181a,193a
1932 145,193,264,181a,193a
1933 4,180,180i,198,284a
1934 8,193,181a,193a
1935 1,180,212,182a,199a
1936 6,169,213,263,192a,194a
1937 166,230,246,259,263,182a,201a
1938 158,181,194,280a
1939 7,202,181a,193a
1940 11,182,182a,194a
1941 3,181,182a,194a
1942 8,180,207,191a,195a
1943 12,169,208,182a,203a
1944 5,258,260,185a,197a
1945 9,169,210,182a,204a
1946 2,180,211,181a,196a
1947 6,247,192a,204a
1948 145,264,185a,197a
1949 145,193,258,261,264,181a,193a
1950 7,169,232,191a,198a
1951 12,170,247,182a,193a
1952 4,200,260,181a,193a
1953 8,180,206,181a,194a
1954 1,1i,201,258,260,264,181a,193a
1955 5,224,232,192a,194a
1956 145,225,255,264,182a,202a
1957 145,195,264,181a,193a
1958 7,170,248,191a,203a
1959 11,169,248,182a,195a
1960 160,248,259,263,192a,204a
1961 8,180,215,181a,196a
1962 12,204,248,290a
1963 5,169,227,192a,197a
1964 9,193,263,181a,193a
1965 158,169,198,259,263,284a
1966 6,180,180i,186a,198a
1967 11,180,208,217,182a,199a
1968 3,180,209,217,192a,194a
1969 145,201,264,181a,193a
1970 12,182,182a,194a
1971 4,170,235,192a,202a
1972 9,169,214,261,182a,195a
1973 1,203,219,235,257,258,260, 181a,193a
1974 5,219,235,257,258,260,191a, 195a
1975 10,180,205,182a,203a
1976 2,169,257,192a,196a
1977 7,170,206,181a,204a
1978 11,169,207,182a,196a
1979 160,249,192a,204a
1980 8,180,257,182a,197a
1981 12,181,193,260,285a
1982 5,191,258,260,187a,199a
1983 9,193,213,278,287a
1984 2,200,263,188a,200a
1985 6,194,181a,193a
1986 11,180,216,182a,202a
1987 3,180,205,192a,194a
1988 7,226,238,250,190a,202a
1989 12,195,226,288a
1990 4,226,190a,202a
1991 9,227,182a,196a
1992 145,204,264,181a,193a
1993 5,180,211,181a,196a
1994 10,228,250,259,263,192a,204a
1995 145,213,264,192a,197a
1996 7,193,181a,193a
1997 11,198,239,261,289a
1998 145,193,239,258,260,264,289a
1999 8,180,205,182a,200a

4th April

1930 3,204,181a,193a
1931 8,170,208,229,263,192a,197a
1932 145,193,264,181a,193a
1933 4,180,180i,198,284a
1934 9,193,181a,193a
1935 1,180,212,182a,199a
1936 6,169,213,263,192a,194a
1937 166,230,246,259,263,182a,201a
1938 3,181,194,280a
1939 7,202,181a,193a
1940 12,18a,182a,194a
1941 4,181,182a,194a
1942 8,180,207,191a,195a
1943 145,203,264,181a,193a
1944 145,264,185a,197a
1945 9,169,210,182a,204a
1946 2,180,211,181a,196a
1947 6,247,192a,204a
1948 145,164,185a,197a
1949 145,193,258,261,264,181a,193a
1950 8,169,215,191a,198a
1951 12,170,247,182a,193a
1952 5,200,258,260,181a,193a
1953 9,180,206,181a,194a
1954 1,180,207,182a,201a
1955 6,224,232,192a,194a
1956 145,225,255,264,183a,202a
1957 145,195,264,181a,193a
1958 7,170,248,191a,203a
1959 12,169,213,182a,195a
1960 160,248,259,263,192a,204a
1961 8,180,215,181a,196a
1962 145,204,264,181a,193a
1963 5,197,181a,193a
1964 10,193,181a,193a
1965 158,169,198,259,263,284a
1966 7,180,207,191a,193a
1967 11,180,208,217,182a,199a
1968 3,180,209,217,192a,194a
1969 145,201,264,181a,193a
1970 12,182,182a,194a
1971 5,170,235,192a,202a
1972 9,169,219,235,257,258,261, 183a,195a
1973 1,203,219,235,257,258,260, 181a,193a
1974 6,219,235,257,191a,195a
1975 10,180,205,182a,203a
1976 3,169,206,192a,196a
1977 7,170,207,181a,204a
1978 12,169,207,182a,196a
1979 160,249,192a,204a
1980 8,180,210,183a,197a
1981 1,1i,181,193,258,260,285a
1982 5,191,258,260,187a,199a
1983 145,193,213,264,287a
1984 2,200,263,188a,200a
1985 7,194,181a,193a
1986 11,180,216,182a,202a
1987 3,180,205,192a,194a
1988 8,226,238,250,190a,202a
1989 12,195,226,288a
1990 5,226,190a,202a
1991 9,227,182a,196a
1992 2,250,192a,204a
1993 6,180,211,181a,196a
1994 11,228,250,259,263,192a,204a
1995 145,213,264,192a,197a
1996 7,169,228,183a,193a
1997 12,198,181a,193a
1998 145,193,239,258,260,264,289a
1999 8,180,205,182a,200a

5th April

1930 4,204,181a,193a
1931 8,170,208,229,192a,197a
1932 145,193,264,181a,193a
1933 5,180,180i,198,284a
1934 9,193,181a,193a
1935 2,182,182a,194a
1936 6,169,213,263,192a,194a
1937 11,169,214,182a,201a
1938 3,181,194,280a
1939 8,202,263,181a,193a
1940 12,180,205,183a,195a
1941 4,181,182a,194a
1942 9,169,207,261,191a,195a
1943 145,203,264,181a,193a
1944 6,170,209,192a,196a
1945 10,169,210,182a,204a
1946 3,180,211,182a,196a
1947 7,247,260,192a,204a
1948 145,258,260,264,185a,197a
1949 145,193,264,181a,193a
1950 8,169,215,191a,198a
1951 1,193,181a,193a
1952 5,200,258,260,181a,193a
1953 9,180,206,181a,194a
1954 2,180,207,182a,201a
1955 6,224,232,192a,194a
1956 145,225,255,264,183a,202a
1957 145,225,233,255,264,181a,195a
1958 8,170,211,191a,203a
1959 12,169,213,182a,195a
1960 160,248,259,263,192a,204a
1961 9,180,215,181a,196a
1962 145,204,264,181a,193a
1963 6,169,197,284a
1964 10,193,181a,193a
1965 158,169,198,259,263,284a
1966 7,180,207,191a,193a
1967 11,180,208,217,182a,199a
1968 4,180,209,263,192a,194a
1969 145,201,264,181a,193a
1970 145,182,194,264,280a
1971 5,170,235,192a,202a

1972 9,169,219,235,257,258,261,
183a,195a
1973 2,219,235,257,181a,203a
1974 6,219,235,257,191a,195a
1975 11,203,181a,193a
1976 3,169,206,192a,196a
1977 8,170,207,181a,204a
1978 12,169,207,182a,196a
1979 160,249,192a,204a
1980 9,180,210,183a,197a
1981 1,1i,193,258,260,285a
1982 6,191a,187a,199a
1983 145,213,264,189a,201a
1984 3,200,188a,200a
1985 7,194,181a,193a
1986 12,250,263,192a,204a
1987 4,180,205,263,192a,194a
1988 8,226,238,250,190a,202a
1989 145,195,226,264,288a
1990 5,226,190a,202a
1991 9,227,182a,196a
1992 2,250,192a,204a
1993 6,180,211,181a,196a
1994 11,228,250,259,263,192a,204a
1995 145,213,264,192a,197a
1996 8,193,181a,193a
1997 12,198,181a,193a
1998 5,193,239,258,260,289a
1999 9,180,205,182a,200a

6th April

1930 4,204,181a,193a
1931 9,170,208,299,263,192a,197a
1932 145,193,264,181a,193a
1933 5,180,180i,198,284a
1934 10,193,181a,193a
1935 2,182,182a,194a
1936 7,169,213,192a,194a
1937 11,169,214,182a,201a
1938 4,182,230,246,182a,194a
1939 8,202,263,181a,193a
1940 1,195,181a,193a
1941 5,181,182a,194a
1942 9,169,207,261,191a,195a
1943 2,169,208,182a,203a
1944 6,170,209,192a,203a
1945 10,169,210,182a,204a
1946 3,180,211,182a,196a
1947 7,247,260,192a,204a
1948 145,258,260,264,185a,197a
1949 145,193,264,181a,193a
1950 9,169,232,191a,198a
1951 1,193,181a,196a
1952 6,200,181a,193a
1953 10,180,206,181a,194a
1954 2,180,207,182a,201a
1955 7,224,232,192a,194a
1956 145,225,255,264,183a,202a
1957 145,225,233,255,264,181a,195a
1958 8,170,211,191a,203a
1959 12,169,213,182a,195a
1960 5,248,263,192a,204a
1961 9,180,215,181a,196a
1962 2,169,227,182a,204a
1963 6,169,197,284a
1964 11,193,181a,193a
1965 3,169,198,284a
1966 8,180,207,191a,193a
1967 12,180,208,217,182a,199a
1968 4,180,209,263,192a,194a
1969 9,201,181a,193a
1970 1,182,218,256,182a,194a
1971 5,170,235,192a,202a
1972 10,169,219,235,257,258,261,
183a,195a
1973 2,219,235,257,181a,203a
1974 163,191,258,260,187a,199a
1975 11,203,181a,193a
1976 160,220,236,184a,196a
1977 8,170,207,181a,204a
1978 145,196,264,181a,193a
1979 5,236,249,192a,204a
1980 9,180,210,183a,197a
1981 2,181,193,285a
1982 6,191,187a,199a
1983 145,213,264,189a,201a
1984 3,200,188a,200a
1985 8,194,286a
1986 12,250,263,192a,204a
1987 4,180,250,192a,195a
1988 9,226,238,250,190a,202a
1989 145,195,226,264,288a
1990 162,226,190a,202a
1991 10,227,190a,202a
1992 2,250,192a,204a
1993 7,180,211,181a,196a
1994 11,228,250,259,263,192a,204a
1995 145,213,264,192a,197a
1996 8,193,181a,193a
1997 1,1i,198,258,261,181a,193a
1998 5,193,258,260,181a,193a
1999 9,180,205,182a,200a

7th April

1930 5,204,181a,193a
1931 9,170,208,229,263,192a,197a
1932 145,193,264,181a,193a
1933 6,180,180i,198,284a
1934 10,193,181a,193a
1935 3,182,212,182a,199a
1936 7,169,213,192a,194a
1937 11,182,230,246,182a,194a
1938 4,182,230,246,182a,194a
1939 8,202,263,181a,193a
1940 1,195,181a,193a
1941 5,181,182a,194a

1942 10,169,207,192a,195a
1943 2,169,208,182a,203a
1944 7,170,209,192a,196a
1945 11,169,210,182a,204a
1946 3,180,211,182a,196a
1947 164,212,247,260,192a,204a
1948 145,258,260,264,185a,197a
1949 145,193,264,181a,193a
1950 9,169,215,192a,198a
1951 1,193,181a,193a
1952 6,200,181a,193a
1953 10,180,206,181a,194a
1954 3,180,207,182a,201a
1955 7,169,208a
1956 145,255,255,264,183a,202a
1957 145,225,233,255,264,181a,195a
1958 9,170,211,192a,203a
1959 145,195,264,181a,193a
1960 5,248,263,192a,204a
1961 10,180,215,181a,196a
1962 2,169,227,182a,204a
1963 7,197,181a,193a
1964 11,193,181a,193a
1965 3,169,198,284a
1966 164,248,192a,204a
1967 12,180,208,217,182a,199a
1968 5,194,209,263,181a,193a
1969 9,201,181a,193a
1970 158,182,265,182a,194a
1971 162,218,256,192a,202a
1972 10,169,219,235,257,258,261, 183a,95a
1973 159,215,258,260,181a,203a
1974 163,192,249,258,260,335a
1975 12,203,181a,193a
1976 160,220,236,184a,196a
1977 9,221,249,181a,204a
1978 145,196,264,181a,193a
1979 5,180,222,257,192a,193a
1980 10,180,210,183a,197a
1981 2,181,193,285a
1982 7,192,260,187a,199a
1983 145,213,264,189a,201a
1984 3,200,188a,200a
1985 8,194,286a
1986 12,250,263,192a,204a
1987 4,180,250,192a,195a
1988 9,226,190a,202a
1989 2,195,226,288a
1990 162,226,190a,202a
1991 10,227,190a,202a
1992 3,180,210,181a,204a
1993 7,180,211,181a,196a
1994 12,250,259,263,192a,204a
1995 145,213,264,192a,197a
1996 9,193,258,261,181a,193a
1997 1,1i,198,258,261,181a,193a
1998 5,193,258,260,181a,193a
1999 9,180,205,182a,200a

8th April

1930 5,204,181a,193a
1931 10,170,208,229,263,192a,197a
1932 145,193,264,181a,193a
1933 6,180,180i,198,284a
1934 11,193,181a,193a
1935 3,182,212,182a,199a
1936 8,169,213,263,192a,194a
1937 12,182,230,246,259,263,182a, 194a
1938 4,182,230,246,182a,194a
1939 9,202,263,181a,193a
1940 1,195,181a,193a
1941 162,181,182a,194a
1942 10,169,207,192a,195a
1943 159,169,183a,195a
1944 7,170,209,192a,196a
1945 11,204,181a,193a
1946 160,211,184a,196a
1947 164,212,247,260,192a,204a
1948 1,258,260,185a,197a
1949 5,193,261,278,283a
1950 10,170,215,192a,198a
1951 2,182,182a,194a
1952 6,200,181a,193a
1953 11,180,206,181a,194a
1954 3,180,207,182a,201a
1955 164,224,232,192a,194a
1956 145,225,255,264,183a,202a
1957 145,225,233,255,264,181a,195a
1958 9,170,211,192a,203a
1959 145,195,264,181a,193a
1960 6,248,263,192a,204a
1961 10,180,215,181a,196a
1962 3,169,216,182a,204a
1963 7,197,181a,193a
1964 11,193,181a,193a
1965 4,169,98,284a
1966 164,248,192a,204a
1967 1,199,181a,193a
1968 5,194,209,263,181a,193a
1969 145,201,264,181a,193a
1970 158,182,265,182a,194a
1971 162,218,256,192a,202a
1972 167,169,258,261,183a,195a
1973 159,215,258,260,181a,203a
1974 8,249,260,192a,204a
1975 12,203,181a,193a
1976 160,196,282a
1977 9,221,249,181a,204a
1978 145,196,264,181a,193a
1979 6,180,257,192a,193a
1980 10,180,210,183a,197a
1981 145,181,193,258,260,264,285a
1982 7,192,260,187a,199a
1983 11,182,213,297a
1984 4,200,263,188a,200a
1985 9,194,181a,193a
1986 1,180,216,263,182a,202a

1987 5,225,237,192a,195a
1988 166,226,190a,202a
1989 2,195,226,288a
1990 7,226,190a,202a
1991 11,209,182a,196a
1992 3,180,210,181a,204a
1993 8,180,211,181a,196a
1994 12,250,259,263,192a,204a
1995 145,213,264,192a,197a
1996 9,193,258,261,181a,193a
1997 2,198,261,181a,193a
1998 145,193,264,181a,193a
1999 10,180,205,182a,200a

9th April

1930 5,204,181a,193a
1931 10,170,208,299,263,192a,197a
1932 145,193,264,181a,193a
1933 7,180,180i,198,284a
1934 11,193,181a,193a
1935 4,169,212,182a,199a
1936 8,169,213,263,192a,194a
1937 12,182,230,246,259,263,182a, 194a
1938 5,182,230,246,182a,194a
1939 9,202,263,181a,193a
1940 2,183,182a,194a
1941 162,181,182a,194a
1942 11,169,207,192a,195a
1943 159,169,183a,195a
1944 7,170,209,192a,196a
1945 12,204,181a,193a
1946 160,211,184a,196a
1947 9,247,260,192a,204a
1948 1,197,260,261,278,283a
1949 5,193,261,278,283a
1950 10,170,215,192a,198a
1951 2,182,182a,194a
1952 7,192,200,260,285a
1953 11,180,206,181a,194a
1954 4,180,207,182a,201a
1955 164,224,232,192a,194a
1956 145,225,255,264,183a,202a
1957 5,210,185a,197a
1958 10,170,211,192a,203a
1959 2,169,248,182a,195a
1960 6,180,214,263,181a,204a
1961 11,180,215,181a,204a
1962 3,169,216,182a,204a
1963 7,197,181a,193a
1964 12,193,181a,193a
1965 4,169,198,284a
1966 9,248,192a,204a
1967 1,199,181a,193a
1968 5,194,209,263,181a,193a
1969 145,201,264,181a,193a
1970 3,182,218,256,182a,194a
1971 7,170,213,192a,202a
1972 167,169,258,261,183a,195a
1973 4,219,235,258,260,181a,203a
1974 8,249,260,192a,204a
1975 12,203,181a,193a
1976 5,196,181a,193a
1977 10,170,207,181a,204a
1978 2,169,207,182a,196a
1979 6,180,257,192a,193a
1980 11,180,210,183a,197a
1981 145,181,193,258,260,264,285a
1982 8,192,260,187a,199a
1983 12,182,213,297a
1984 4,200,263,188a,200a
1985 9,194,181a,193a
1986 1,180,216,263,182a,202a
1987 5,225,237,192a,195a
1988 166,226,190a,202a
1989 3,169,195,226,353a
1990 7,226,190a,202a
1991 11,209,182a,196a
1992 4,180,227,181a,204a
1993 8,180,211,181a,196a
1994 1,212,228,250,259,263,192a, 204a
1995 5,213,192a,197a
1996 10,193,217,261,288a
1997 2,198,261,181a,193a
1998 145,193,264,181a,193a
1999 10,180,205,182a,200a

10th April

1930 6,204,181a,193a
1931 10,170,208,299,263,192a,197a
1932 145,193,264,181a,193a
1933 7,180,180i,198,284a
1934 12,193,246,290a
1935 4,169,212,182a,199a
1936 8,169,213,263,192a,194a
1937 1,182,230,246,259,263,182a, 194a
1938 5,182,230,246,182a,194a
1939 10,202,263,181a,193a
1940 2,183,182a,194a
1941 7,181,182a,194a
1942 11,169,207,192a,195a
1943 159,169,183a,195a
1944 8,170,209,181a,196a
1945 12,204,181a,193a
1946 5,180,211,182a,196a
1947 9,247,260,192a,204a
1948 145,258,261,264,185a,197a
1949 145,193,258,261,264,181a,193a
1950 11,170,215,192a,198a
1951 3,182,182a,194a
1952 145,181,200,258,260,264,285a
1953 12,180,206,181a,194a
1954 4,180,207,182a,201a
1955 164,224,232,192a,194a

1956 145,202,264,181a,193a
1957 5,210,185a,197a
1958 10,170,211,192a,203a
1959 2,169,213,182a,196a
1960 7,180,214,181a,204a
1961 11,196,181a,193a
1962 4,169,227,182a,204a
1963 8,170,227,192a,197a
1964 12,193,181a,193a
1965 5,169,198,263,284a
1966 9,248,192a,204a
1967 1,199,181a,193a
1968 145,194,209,263,181a,193a
1969 145,201,264,193a
1970 3,182,218,256,182a,194a
1971 7,170,213,192a,202a
1972 12,169,219,235,257,183a,195a
1973 4,219,235,257,258,260,181a, 203a
1974 9,249,260,192a,204a
1975 145,203,264,181a,193a
1976 5,170,257,181a,196a
1977 10,170,207,181a,204a
1978 2,169,207,182a,196a
1979 6,180,257,192a,193a
1980 11,180,210,183a,197a
1981 145,181,193,258,260,264,285a
1982 8,192,260,187a,199a
1983 12,182,213,297a
1984 5,200,263,188a,200a
1985 9,194,181a,193a
1986 2,180,216,263,182a,202a
1987 6,180,205,192a,195a
1988 166,226,190a,202a
1989 3,169,195,226,353a
1990 7,226,190a,202a
1991 11,209,182a,196a
1992 4,180,227,181a,204a
1993 9,180,211,181a,196a
1994 145,204,263,264,181a,193a
1995 5,213,192a,197a
1996 10,193,217,261,288a
1997 3,198,261,181a,193a
1998 145,193,258,260,264,181a,193a
1999 11,239,191a,203a

11th April

1930 162,226,246,182a,204a
1931 11,170,208,229,192a,197a
1932 145,193,264,181a,193a
1933 8,180,180i,198,284a
1934 12,193,246,290a
1935 4,169,212,182a,199a
1936 9,194,213,263,181a,193a
1937 1,182,230,246,259,263,182a, 194a
1938 162,182,182a,194a
1939 10,202,263,181a,193a
1940 3,180,180i,183a,195a
1941 7,181,182a,194a
1942 12,169,207,192a,195a
1943 4,169,208,182a,203a
1944 8,170,209,181a,196a
1945 145,204,264,181a,193a
1946 5,180,211,182a,196a
1947 9,247,260,192a,204a
1948 145,258,261,264,185a,197a
1949 145,193,258,261,264,181a,193a
1950 11,170,215,192a,198a
1951 3,182,182a,194a
1952 145,200,258,260,264,181a,193a
1953 12,180,206,181a,194a
1954 5,180,207,182a,201a
1955 9,169,208,260,192a,195a
1956 145,202,264,181a,193a
1957 145,225,233,255,264,181a,195a
1958 145,225,233,255,264,192a,203a
1959 2,169,213,263,182a,196a
1960 7,180,214,181a,204a
1961 12,196,181a,193a
1962 4,169,227,182a,204a
1963 8,170,227,192a,197a
1964 1,193,181a,193a
1965 5,169,198,263,284a
1966 10,248,192a,204a
1967 2,180,208,217,182a,199a
1968 145,194,209,263,264,181a,193a
1969 145,201,264,181a,193a
1970 3,182,218,256,182a,194a
1971 7,170,213,192a,202a
1972 12,169,219,235,257,183a,195a
1973 5,219,235,258,260,181a,203a
1974 9,249,260,192a,204a
1975 145,203,264,181a,193a
1976 6,170,257,181a,193a
1977 11,170,207,181a,204a
1978 145,221,249,264,182a,197a
1979 7,180,222,192a,193a
1980 12,180,210,183a,197a
1981 145,181,193,258,260,264,285a
1982 8,192,260,187a,199a
1983 12,182,213,297a
1984 5,200,263,188a,200a
1985 10,194,182a,193a
1986 2,180,216,263,182a,202a
1987 6,180,205,192a,195a
1988 11,226,190a,202a
1989 4,195,226,288a
1990 8,226,190a,202a
1991 12,227,182a,196a
1992 5,180,227,181a,204a
1993 9,180,211,181a,196a
1994 145,204,263,264,181a,193a
1995 5,213,192a,197a
1996 10,193,217,261,288a
1997 3,198,261,181a,193a
1998 145,193,258,260,264,181a,193a
1999 11,239,191a,203a

12th April

1930 7,170,207,229,182a,204a
1931 11,170,208,229,192a,197a
1932 145,193,264,181a,193a
1933 8,180,180i,198,284a
1934 1,193,181a,193a
1935 5,169,212,182a,199a
1936 9,194,213,263,181a,193a
1937 2,182,259,263,182a,194a
1938 162,182,182a,194a
1939 11,202,181a,193a
1940 3,180,180i,183a,195a
1941 8,181,208,280a
1942 12,169,207,192a,195a
1943 4,170,208,182a,203a
1944 9,255,181a,196a
1945 145,204,264,181a,193a
1946 6,180,211,182a,196a
1947 10,180,212,192a,193a
1948 145,258,261,264,185a,197a
1949 145,193,258,261,264,181a,193a
1950 11,170,215,192a,198a
1951 3,182,182a,194a
1952 145,200,258,260,264,181a,193a
1953 1,194,181a,193a
1954 5,180,207,182a,201a
1955 9,169,208,260,192a,195a
1956 145,225,255,264,183a,202a
1957 145,225,233,255,264,181a,195a
1958 145,225,233,255,258,260,264, 192a,203a
1959 3,169,213,182a,196a
1960 8,180,214,163,181a,204a
1961 12,196,181a,193a
1962 4,169,227,182a,204a
1963 8,170,227,192a,197a
1964 1,193,181a,193a
1965 162,169,198,259,263,284a
1966 10,248,192a,204a
1967 2,180,208,217,182a,199a
1968 145,194,264,181a,193a
1969 145,201,264,181a,193a
1970 4,182,218,256,182a,194a
1971 8,170,235,192a,202a
1972 1,169,195,219,235,257,258,261, 281a
1973 5,219,235,257,258,260,181a,203a
1974 9,169,216,260,192a,195a
1975 2,204,181a,193a
1976 6,170,257,181a,196a
1977 11,170,207,181a,204a
1978 145,221,249,264,182a,197a
1979 7,180,222,192a,193a
1980 12,180,210,183a,197a
1981 5,181,193,258,260,285a
1982 9,192,212,258,260,332a
1983 1,1i,182,213,297a
1984 6,200,263,188a,200a
1985 10,194,181a,193a
1986 2,180,216,263,182a,202a
1987 7,180,205,192a,195a
1988 11,226,190a,202a
1989 4,226,190a,202a
1990 8,226,190a,202a
1991 12,227,182a,196a
1992 5,180,227,181a,204a
1993 10,227,190a,202a
1994 2,169,212,263,182a,204a
1995 145,213,264,192a,197a
1996 11,193,261,181a,193a
1997 3,198,261,181a,193a
1998 145,193,258,260,264,181a,193a
1999 12,180,205,182a,200a

13th April

1930 7,170,207,229,182a,204a
1931 12,170,208,229,263,192a,197a
1932 145,193,264,181a,193a
1933 9,180,180i,198,284a
1934 1,193,181a,193a
1935 5,169,212,182a,199a
1936 10,194,263,181a,193a
1937 2,182,259,263,182a,194a
1938 7,182,230,246,182a,194a
1939 11,202,181a,193a
1940 3,180,180i,183a,195a
1941 8,181,203,280a
1942 12,169,207,192a,195a
1943 5,170,208,182a,203a
1944 9,255,181a,196a
1945 2,204,181a,193a
1946 6,180,211,182a,196a
1947 10,180,212,192a,193a
1948 145,169,258,260,261,264,302a
1949 145,193,258,260,261,264,181a, 193a
1950 12,170,215,192a,198a
1951 4,182,182a,194a
1952 9,200,258,260,181a,193a
1953 1,194,181a,193a
1954 6,169,207,182a,202a
1955 10,169,208,192a,195a
1956 2,170,232,183a,202a
1957 145,225,233,255,264,181a,195a
1958 145,225,233,255,258,260,264, 192a,203a
1959 3,169,213,182a,196a
1960 8,180,214,263,181a,204a
1961 145,196,264,181a,193a
1962 5,169,227,182a,204a
1963 9,170,227,192a,197a
1964 158,183,182a,194a
1965 162,169,198,259,263,284a
1966 11,248,192a,204a
1967 3,180,208,217,182a,199a
1968 145,194,264,181a,193a

1969 145,201,264,181a,193a
1970 4,182,218,256,182a,194a
1971 8,170,235,192a,202a
1972 1,169,195,219,235,257,258, 261,281a
1973 6,219,235,257,181a,203a
1974 10,169,216,192a,195a
1975 2,204,181a,193a
1976 7,170,206,181a,196a
1977 11,170,207,181a,204a
1978 145,221,249,264,182a,197a
1979 164,248,192a,193a
1980 1,180,210,183a,197a
1981 5,181,193,258,260,285a
1982 9,192,212,258,260,332a
1983 1,1i,213,189a,201a
1984 6,200,263,188a,200a
1985 11,194,181a,193a
1986 3,180,216,182a,202a
1987 145,195,264,181a,193a
1988 12,226,190a,202a
1989 4,226,190a,202a
1990 9,226,190a,202a
1991 145,196,264,181a,193a
1992 6,180,227,181a,204a
1993 10,227,190a,202a
1994 2,169,212,263,182a,204a
1995 145,213,264,192a,197a
1996 11,193,261,181a,193a
1997 4,198,181a,193a
1998 8,194,181a,193a
1999 12,180,205,183a,200a

14th April

1930 8,170,207,229,182a,204a
1931 12,170,208,229,263,192a,197a
1932 145,193,264,181a,193a
1933 9,180,180i,198,284a
1934 2,193,181a,193a
1935 6,169,212,182a,199a
1936 10,194,263,181a,193a
1937 3,170,214,181a,201a
1938 7,182,230,246,182a,194a
1939 11,202,181a,193a
1940 4,180,205,183a,195a
1941 9,181,203,258,261,280a
1942 145,195,264,181a,193a
1943 5,170,208,182a,203a
1944 10,170,209,181a,196a
1945 2,204,181a,193a
1946 7,182,187a,199a
1947 11,180,212,260,192a,193a
1948 145,169,258,260,261,264,302a
1949 145,193,258,261,264,181a,193a
1950 12,170,215,192a,198a
1951 4,182,182a,194a
1952 9,200,258,260,181a,193a
1953 2,181,182a,194a
1954 6,169,207,182a,202a
1955 10,169,208,192a,195a
1956 3,170,232,183a,202a
1957 145,225,233,255,264,181a,195a
1958 145,225,233,255,258,260,264, 192a,203a
1959 4,169,213,263,182a,196a
1960 9,180,214,263,181a,204a
1961 145,196,264,181a,193a
1962 5,169,227,182a,204a
1963 9,170,227,192a,197a
1964 158,183,182a,194a
1965 7,169,198,284a
1966 11,248,192a,204a
1967 3,180,208,217,183a,199a
1968 145,194,209,263,264,181a,193a
1969 12,201,181a,196a
1970 5,182,218,256,182a,194a
1971 9,213,189a,201a
1972 2,169,219,235,257,258,261, 183a,195a
1973 6,219,235,257,181a,203a
1974 10,169,216,192a,195a
1975 2,204,181a,193a
1976 7,170,206,181a,196a
1977 12,170,207,181a,204a
1978 145,221,249,264,182a,197a
1979 164,248,192a,193a
1980 1,180,210,183a,197a
1981 145,181,193,264,285a
1982 10,192,187a,199a
1983 2,183,213,197a
1984 7,200,186a,200a
1985 11,194,181a,193a
1986 3,180,216,182a,202a
1987 145,195,264,181a,193a
1988 12,226,190a,202a
1989 5,226,190a,202a
1990 9,226,190a,202a
1991 145,196,264,181a,193a
1992 6,180,227,181a,204a
1993 11,180,211,181a,196a
1994 3,169,212,182a,204a
1995 145,213,264,192a,197a
1996 12,193,181a,193a
1997 4,198,181a,193a
1998 8,194,181a,193a
1999 1,180,205,183a,200a

15th April

1930 8,170,207,229,182a,204a
1931 12,170,208,229,263,192a,197a
1932 5,193,181a,193a
1933 10,180,180i,198,284a
1934 2,193,181a,193a
1935 6,169,212,182a,199a
1936 11,189,182a,194a
1937 3,170,214,181a,201a

1938 8,182,230,246,182a,194a
1939 12,202,246,263,290a
1940 4,180,205,183a,195a
1941 9,181,203,258,261,280a
1942 145,195,264,181a,193a
1943 5,170,208,182a,203a
1944 10,170,209,181a,196a
1945 3,204,181a,193a
1946 7,182,187a,199a
1947 11,180,212,260,192a,193a
1948 145,258,260,264,185a,197a
1949 145,193,258,261,264,181a,193a
1950 1,170,247,192a,198a
1951 5,170,216,183a,194a
1952 145,200,264,181a,193a
1953 2,181,182a,194a
1954 6,169,207,182a,202a
1955 10,169,208,192a,195a
1956 3,170,232,183a,203a
1957 145,225,233,255,264,181a,195a
1958 145,225,233,255,258,260,264, 192a,203a
1959 4,169,213,183a,196a
1960 9,180,214,263,181a,204a
1961 145,196,264,181a,193a
1962 6,169,227,182a,204a
1963 10,170,227,192a,197a
1964 3,170,206,183a,193a
1965 7,169,198,284a
1966 11,248,192a,204a
1967 3,199,181a,193a
1968 145,194,209,263,264,181a,193a
1969 1,1i,201,181a,193a
1970 5,182,218,256,182a,194a
1971 9,213,189a,201a
1972 2,169,219,235,257,258,261, 183a,195a
1973 163,181,258,260,187a,199a
1974 167,219,235,257,258,260,192a, 195a
1975 3,204,260,183a,204a
1976 8,170,257,181a,196a
1977 12,170,207,181a,204a
1978 145,221,249,264,182a,197a
1979 9,180,222,257,192a,193a
1980 2,169,248,183a,197a
1981 145,181,193a,264,285a
1982 10,192,187a,199a
1983 2,183,213,297a
1984 7,200,188a,200a
1985 12,194,181a,193a
1986 4,180,216,263,182a,202a
1987 145,195,264,181a,193a
1988 145,203,226,264,288a
1989 5,226,190a,202a
1990 9,226,290a,202a
1991 2,209,183a,196a
1992 7,204,181a,193a
1993 11,180,211,181a,196a
1994 3,193,181a,193a
1995 145,213,264,192a,197a
1996 12,193,181a,193a
1997 5,198,258,261,181a,193a
1998 9,194,181a,193a
1999 1,180,205,183a,200a

16th April

1930 9,170,207,229,182a,204a
1931 1,197,263,181a,193a
1932 5,193,181a,193a
1933 10,180,180i,198,284a
1934 2,193,181a,193a
1935 6,169,212,183a,199a
1936 11,181a,182a,194a
1937 4,182,214,263,181a,201a
1938 8,182,230,246,182a,194a
1939 12,202,246,263,290a
1940 5,180,205,183a,195a
1941 145,181,203,206,261,264,280a
1942 2,192,182a,194a
1943 6,170,219,231,247,183a,195a
1944 11,170,209,181a,196a
1945 3,204,181a,193a
1946 7,182,187a,199a
1947 145,193,258,260,264,181a,193a
1948 145,258,260,264,185a,197a
1949 9,193,260,261,278,181a,193a
1950 1,170,247,192a,198a
1951 5,170,216,183a,194a
1952 145,200,264,181a,193a
1953 3,180,206,181a,194a
1954 7,169,207,182a,202a
1955 11,169,208,260,192a,195a
1956 4,170,209,183a,203a
1957 145,225,233,255,264,181a,195a
1958 145,225,233,255,258,260,264, 192a,203a
1959 4,169,213,183a,196a
1960 9,204,263,181a,193a
1961 145,196,264,181a,193a
1962 6,169,227,182a,204a
1963 10,170,227,192a,197a
1964 3,170,206,183a,193a
1965 8,169,198,263,284a
1966 168,248,192a,204a
1967 4,199,181a,193a
1968 9,194,209,263,181a,193a
1969 1,1i,201,181a,193a
1970 5,182,218,256,182a,194a
1971 166,218,256,192a,202a
1972 159,169,258,261,183a,195a
1973 163,181,258,260,187a,199a
1974 167,219,235,257,258,260,192a, 195a
1975 3,204,260,183a,204a
1976 8,170,257,181a,196a
1977 1,1i,204,181a,193a
1978 5,197,185a,197a

1979 9,180,222,257,192a,193a
1980 2,169,248,183a,197a
1981 145,181,193,264,285a
1982 10,192,187a,199a
1983 3,213,189a,201a
1984 8,200,263,188a,200a
1985 12,194,181a,193a
1986 4,180,216,263,182a,202a
1987 145,195,264,181a,193a
1988 145,203,226,264,288a
1989 162,226,190a,202a
1990 166,226,190a,202a
1991 2,209,183a,196a
1992 7,204,181a,193a
1993 11,196,181a,193a
1994 3,193,181a,193a
1995 145,213,264,192a,197a
1996 1,193,258,261,181a,193a
1997 5,170,215,217,261,182a,198a
1998 9,194,181a,193a
1999 2,180,205,183a,200a

17th April

1930 9,170,207,229,182a,204a
1931 1,197,263,181a,193a
1932 145,193,264,181a,193a
1933 11,180,180i,198,284a
1934 2,193,181a,193a
1935 7,169,212,183a,199a
1936 12,181,263,182a,194a,
1937 4,182,214,263,181a,201a
1938 8,182,230,246,182a,194a
1939 1,202,263,181a,193a
1940 5,195,258,261,181a,193a
1941 145,181,203,206,261,264,280a
1942 2,192,182a,194a
1943 6,170,183a,195a
1944 11,170,209,181a,196a
1945 4,204,181a,193a
1946 8,169,211,182a,196a
1947 145,193,258,264,181a,193a
1948 5,260,261,278a
1949 9,193,258,261,181a,193a
1950 1,170,247,192a,198a
1951 6,170,216,183a,194a
1952 145,200,264,181a,193a
1953 3,180,206,181a,194a
1954 7,169,207,182a,202a
1955 11,169,208,260,192a,195a
1956 4,170.209,183a,203a
1957 9,225,233,255,181a,195a
1958 145,203,258,260,264,181a,193a
1959 5,233,183a,196a
1960 10,204,226,263,288a
1961 145,196,264,181a,193a
1962 6,169,227,182a,204a
1963 11,170,205,192a,197a
1964 4,170,206,183a,193a
1965 8,169,198,263,284a
1966 168,248,192a,204a
1967 4,199,181a,193a
1968 9,194,209,263,181a,193a
1969 2,201,181a,193a
1970 162,182,182a,194a
1971 166,218,256,192a,202a
1972 159,169,258,261,183a,195a
1973 163,181,203,258,260,261,285a
1974 167,219,235,257,258,260,192a, 195a
1975 4,204,260,181a,193a
1976 9,170,257,181a,196a,
1977 1,1i,204,181a,193a
1978 5,197,185a,197a
1979 9,180,222,257,192a,193a
1980 3,169,248,183a,197a
1981 7,182,193a,285a
1982 11,192,187a,199a
1983 3,213,189a,201a
1984 8,200,263,188a,200a
1985 12,194,181a,193a
1986 4,180,216,263,182a,202a
1987 9,195,205,287a
1988 158,226,190a,202a
1989 162,226,190a,202a
1990 166,226,190a,202a
1991 3,209,183a,196a
1992 8,204,181a,193a
1993 12,196,181a,193a
1994 4,193,263,181a,193a
1995 8,170,239,192a,197a
1996 1,193,258,261,181a,193a
1997 5,170,215,217,261,182a,198a
1998 9,194,181a,193a
1999 2,180,205,183a,200a

18th April

1930 166,170,207,182a,204a
1931 2,170,208,229,263,192a,197a
1932 145,193,264,181a,193a
1933 11,169,198,284a
1934 3,193,181a,193a
1935 7,169,212,183a,199a
1936 12,181,263,182a,194a
1937 5,182,214,263,181a,201a
1938 9,182,182a,194a
1939 1,202,263,181a,193a
1940 6,195,261,181a,193a
1941 145,181,203,206,261,264,280a
1942 3,169,183a,195a
1943 7,170,183a,195a
1944 11,170,209,181a,196a
1945 4,204,181a,193a
1946 8,169,211,182a,196a
1947 145,193,258,260,264,181a,193a
1948 5,260,261,278a
1949 145,193,258,261,264,181a,193a

1950 2,170,247,192a,198a
1951 6,170,216,183a,194a,
1952 145,200,258,260,264,181a,193a
1953 3,194,181a,193a
1954 8,169,207,182a,202a
1955 168,208,224,232,260,192a,195a
1956 5,209,185a,197a
1957 9,225,233,255,181a,195a
1958 145,203,258,260,264,181a,193a
1959 5,233,183a,196a
1960 10,204,226,263,288a
1961 3,196,181a,193a
1962 7,170,216,182a,204a
1963 11,170,205,192a,197a
1964 4,170,206,183a,193a
1965 8,169,198,263,284a
1966 145,194,264,181a,193a
1967 5,199,181a,193a
1968 145,194,209,263,264,181a,193a
1969 2,201,181a,193a
1970 162,182,182a,194a
1971 166,218,256,192a,202a
1972 4,169,183a,195a
1973 8,219,235,257,182a,203a
1973 12,1249,260,192a,204a
1974 12,249,260,192a,204a
1975 4,204,260,181a,193a
1976 9,170,257,181a,196a
1977 1,1i,204,181a,193a
1978 145,221,249,264,182a,197a
1979 10,193,181a,193a
1980 3,169,248,283a,197a
1981 7,182,193,285a
1982 11,192,187a,199a
1983 4,213,189a,201a
1984 9,200,263,188a,200a
1985 145,194,264,181a,193a
1986 5,225,237,263,182a,202a
1987 9,195,205,287a
1988 158,226,190a,202a
1989 162,226,190a,202a
1990 11,226,190a,202a
1991 3,209,183a,196a
1992 8,204,181a,193a
1993 12,196,181a,193a
1994 4,193,263,181a,193a
1995 9,213,189a,201a
1996 145,193,258,261,264,181a,193a
1997 162,250,261,182a,198a
1998 10,194,181a,193a
1999 3,200,181a,193a

19th April

1930 166,170,207,182a,204a
1931 2,170,208,229,263,192a,197a
1932 145,193,264,181a,193a
1933 11,169,198,284a
1934 4,193,181a,193a
1935 8,169,212,183a,199a
1936 1,181,194,263,280a
1937 5,182,214,263,181a,201a
1938 9,182,182a,194a,
1939 1,202,263,181a,193a
1940 6,195,261,181a,193a
1941 11,181,203,261,280a
1942 3,169,183a,195a
1943 7,170,183a,195a
1944 12,170,209,181a,196a
1945 5,204,181a,193a
1946 169,211,182a,196a
1947 145,193,258,260,264,181a,193a
1948 145,258,261,264,185a,197a
1949 145,193,258,261,264,181a,193a
1950 2,170,247,192a,198a
1951 6,170,216,183a,194a
1952 145,200,258,260,264,181a,193a
1953 4,194,181a,193a
1954 8,169,207,182a,202a
1955 168,208,224,232,260,192a,195a
1956 5,209,185a,197a
1957 10,170,248,182a,195a
1958 145,225,233,255,264,192a,203a
1959 6,169,213,183a,196a
1960 11,204,181a,193a
1961 3,196,181a,193a
1962 7,170,216,182a,204a
1963 11,170,205,192a,197a
1964 5,170,206,183a,193a
1965 9,169,234,256,259,263,186a, 198a
1966 145,194,264,181a,193a
1967 5,199,181a,193a
1968 145,194,209,263,264,181a,193a
1969 3,201,181a,193a
1970 7,182,182a,194a
1971 11,169,213,192a,202a
1972 4,169,183a,195a
1973 8,219,235,257,182a,203a
1974 12,249,260,192a,204a
1975 5,204,258,260,181a,193a
1976 10,170,257,181a,196a
1977 2,170,207,181a,204a
1978 145,221,249,264,182a,197a
1979 10,193,181a,193a
1980 3,169,248,183a,197a
1981 8,182,193,285a
1982 12,192,187a,199a
1983 4,213,189a,201a
1984 9,200,263,188a,200a
1985 145,194,264,181a,193a
1986 5,225,237,263,182a,202a
1987 145,195,264,181a,193a
1988 3,226,190a,202a
1989 7,226,238,250,190a,202a
1990 11,226,190a,202a
1991 4,209,183a,196a
1992 8,204,181a,193a
1993 145,196,264,181a,193a

1994 5,193,263,181a,193a
1995 9,213,189a,201a
1996 145,193,258,261,264,181a,193a
1997 162,250,261,182a,198a
1998 10,194,181a,193a
1999 3,200,181a,193a

20th April

1930 166,170,207,182a,204a
1931 2,170,208,229,263,192a,197a
1932 19,193,181a,193a
1933 12,169,198,284a
1934 4,193,181a,193a
1935 8,169,212,183a,199a
1936 146,181,259,263,265,182a,194a
1937 162,230,246,259,263,181a,201a
1938 166,182,182a,194a
1939 2,202,263,181a,193a
1940 19,183,261,182a,194a
1941 146,182,206,261,265,182a,194a
1942 3,169,183a,195a
1943 7,170,183a,195a
1944 24,170,209,181a,196a
1945 17,169,210,181a,204a
1946 9,169,210,181a,196a
1947 145,193,258,260,264,181a,193a
1948 146,221,255,258,261,265,185a, 197a
1949 23,182,261,182a,194a
1950 3,170,216,192a,198a
1951 7,170,216,183a,194a,
1952 24,200,181a,193a
1953 16,181,182a,194a
1954 8,169,207,182a,202a
1955 145,195,260,264,181a,193a
1956 18,170,232,183a,203a
1957 22,182,182a,194a
1958 145,225,233,255,264,192a,203a
1959 6,169,213,183a,196a
1960 23,169,214,181a,204a
1961 16,169,215,181a,196a
1962 8,170,227,182a,193a
1963 12,170,227,192a,197a
1964 146,183,265,182a,194a
1965 146,169,182,259,263,265,294a
1966 145,194,264,181a,193a
1967 6,169,199,284a
1968 23,194,181a,193a
1969 15,170,210,248,181a,201a
1970 7,182,182a,194a
1971 11,169,213,192a,202a
1972 17,169,261,183a,195a
1973 21,219,235,257,258,261,182a, 203a
1974 13,169,216,192a,196a
1975 5,170,205,183a,204a
1976 22,181,182a,194a
1977 146,181,265,182a,194a
1978 18,169,257,182a,197a
1979 145,264,193,181a,193a
1980 16,169,210,183a,197a
1981 20,182,187a,199a
1982 24,192,187a,199a
1983 5,213,189a,201a
1984 22,200,224,259,263,337a
1985 14,181,182a,194a
1986 18,250,259,263,182a,202a
1987 145,195,264,181a,193a
1988 146,183,226,259,262,265,298a
1989 146,182,226,259,262,265,298a
1990 146,226,259,262,265,190a,202a
1991 4,209,183a,196a
1992 21,169,227,181a,204a
1993 13,196,181a,193a
1994 17,169,212,263,182a,193a
1995 10,170,239,192a,197a,
1996 15,170,214,183a,193a
1997 146,182,261,265,182a,194a
1998 23,239,191a,203a
1999 4,200,181a,193a

21st April

1930 146,182,265,182a,194a
1931 15,170,208,192a,197
1932 20,193,181a,193a
1933 146,169,265,186a,198a
1934 16,193,181a,193a
1935 21,169,212,230,183a,199a
1936 146,181,259,263,265,182a,194a
1937 18,181,259,263,182a,194a
1938 22,182,265,276,182a,194a
1939 14,192,259,263,182a,194a
1940 19,183,261,182a,194a
1941 146,182,265,182a,194a
1942 146,192,265,182a,194a
1943 8,170,183a,195a
1944 13,170,209,181a,196a
1945 17,169,210,181a,204a
1946 21,169,211,182a,196a
1947 14,169,212,192a,193a
1948 146,221,255,258,261,265,185a, 197a
1949 23,182,261,182a,194a
1950 15,170,255,192a,198a
1951 19,183,182a,194a
1952 24,200,181a,193a
1953 17,181,182a,194a
1954 21,169,207,182a,202a
1955 13,169,208,192a,195a
1956 18,170,232,183a,203a
1957 22,182,182a,194a
1958 14,169,211,192a,203a
1959 19,169,213,183a,196a
1960 24,169,214,263,181a,204a
1961 16,169,215,181a,196a
1962 20,182,182a,194a

1963 24,170,227,192a,197a
1964 18,170,183,294a
1965 22,169,182,263,276,294a
1966 146,192,265,192a,194a
1967 18,169,186a,198a
1968 23,194,181a,193a
1969 15,170,248,181a,201a
1970 146,182,265,182a,194a
1971 24,169,218,235,192a,202a
1972 17,169,261,183a,195a
1973 21,219,235,257,258,261,182a, 203a
1974 13,169,216,192a,196a
1975 18,170,205,183a,204a
1976 23,181,182a,194a
1977 15,170,207,181a,204a
1978 19,169,208,182a,197a
1979 23,169,209,192a,193a
1980 16,169,210,183a,197a
1981 20,182,187a,199a
1982 24,192,187a,199a
1983 17,183,213,297a
1984 22,200,224,259,263,337a
1985 14,181,182a,194a
1986 18,250,259,263,182a,202a
1987 23,169,205,192a,195a
1988 146,226,259,262,265,190a,202a
1989 146,182,2261259,262,265,298a
1990 146,226,250,259,262,263,265, 344a,
1991 17,209,183a,196a,
1992 21,169,227,181a,204a
1993 13,196,181a,193a
1994 18,238,250,259,263a
1995 22,170,239,192a,197a
1996 15,170,214,183a,193a
1997 146,182,261,265,182a,194a
1998 23,239,191a,203a
1999 16,169,205,218,183a,200a

22nd April

1930 146,182,265,182a,194a
1931 15,170,208,192a,197a
1932 20,193,181a,193a
1933 146,169,198,265,284a,
1934 17,193,181a,193a
1935 21,169,212,230,183a,199a
1936 146,181,259,263,265,182a,194a
1937 18,181,259,263,182a,194a
1938 22,182,265,276,182a,194a
1939 15,169,216,230,192a,202a
1940 20,183,182a,194a
1941 146,182,265,182a,194a
1942 146,192,265,182a,194a
1943 8,170,183a,195a
1944 13,170,209,181a,196a
1945 18,169,210,181a,204a
1946 22,169,211,182a,196a
1947 14,169,212,192a,193a
1948 146,221,255,258,261,265,185a, 197a
1949 23,182,261,182a,194a
1950 15,170,255,192a,198a
1951 20,183,182a,194a
1952 157,200,181a,193a
1953 17,181,182a,194a
1954 21,169,207,182a,202a
1955 146,192,265,182a,194a
1956 19,170,232,183a,203a
1957 23,182,182a,194a
1958 15,169,211,192a,203a
1959 19,169,213,182a,196a
1960 24,169,214,263,181a,204a
1961 16,169,215,181a,196a
1962 21,182,182a,194a
1963 13,170,227,192a,197a
1964 18,170,183,294a
1965 22,169,182,263,276,294a
1966 146,192,265,182a,194a
1967 19,169,208,183a,199a
1968 24,194,263,181a,193a
1969 16,170,235,181a,201a
1970 146,182,265,182a,194a
1971 24,169,218,235,192a,202a
1972 17,169,261,183a,195a
1973 21,219,235,257,258,261,182a, 203a
1974 14,169,216,192a,196a
1975 18,170;205,183a,204a
1976 23,181,182a,194a
1977 15,170,207;181a,204a,
1978 19,169,208,182a,197a
1979 24,169,257,192a,193a
1980 17,169,248,183a,197a,
1981 21,182,187a,199a
1982 13,192,187a,199a
1983 17,183,213,297a
1984 22,200,224,259,263,337a
1985 14,181,182a,194a
1986 19,169,216,182a,202a
1987 23,169,205,192a,195a
1988 146,226,259,262,265,190a,202a
1989 146,182,226,259,262,265,298a
1990 146,226,250,259,262,263,265, 344a
1991 17,209,183a,196a
1992 22,227,190a,202a
1993 14,169,211,181a,196a
1994 18,238,250,259,263a
1995 23,170,213,181a,197a
1996 15,170,214,183a,193a
1997 146,182,261,265,182a,194a
1998 24,251,192a,204a
1999 16,169,205,218,183a,200a

23rd April

1930 146,182,265,182a,194a
1931 160,208,263,184a,196a
1932 165,193,181a,193a
1933 146,169,198,265,284a
1934 17,169,211,192a,194a
1935 21,169,212,230,183a,199a
1936 146,181,265,182a,194a
1937 146,181,265,182a,194a
1938 146,182,265,182a,194a
1939 15,169,216,230,192a,202a
1940 20,183,182a,194a
1941 146,182,265,182a,194a
1942 146,192,265,182a,194a
1943 9,170,183a,194a
1944 146,181,265,182a,194a
1945 18,169,210,181a,204a
1946 22,169,220,182a,197a
1947 15,169,212,192a,193a
1948 146,221,255,265,185a,197a
1949 24,182,182a,194a
1950 16,170,247,255,192a,198a
1951 20,183,182a,194a
1952 157,200,181a,193a
1953 18,181,182a,194a
1954 22,169,207,182a,202a
1955 146,192,265,182a,194a
1956 19,170,232,183a,203a
1957 23,182,182a,194a
1958 15,169,211,192a,203a
1959 20,169,213,183a,196a
1960 13,204,263,181a,204a
1961 17,169,215,181a,196a
1962 21,182,182a,194a
1963 13,170,227,192a,197a
1964 18,170,183,294a
1965 22,169,186a,198a
1966 15,169,207,192a,194a
1967 19,169,208,183a,199a
1968 146,181,259,263,265,182a,194a
1969 16,170,235,181a,201a
1970 146,182,265,182a,194a
1971 13,169,218,235,192a,202a
1972 18,169,261,183a,195a
1973 22,219,235,257,258,261,182a, 203a
1974 14,169,216,192a,196a
1975 19,170,205,183a,204a
1976 23,181,182a,194a
1977 15,170,207,181a,204a
1978 20,169,257,182a,197a
1979 24,193,249,181a,193a
1980 17,169,248,183a,197a
1981 21,182,187a,199a
1982 13,192,187a,199a
1983 18,183,213,297a
1984 23,200,188a,200a
1985 15,169,215,181a,194a
1986 19,169,216,182a,202a
1987 24,195,225,237,181a,193a
1988 146,226,259,262,265,190a,202a
1989 146,182,226,259,262,265,298a
1990 146,226,259,263,265,190a,202a
1991 17,209,183a,196a
1992 22,227,190a,202a
1993 14,169,211,181a,196a
1994 19,169,212,182a,193a
1995 23,170,213,181a,197a
1996 16,170,214,183a,193a
1997 146,182,265,182a,194a
1998 24,251,192a,204a
1999 17,169,205,218,183a,200a

24th April

1930 146,182,265,182a,194a
1931 160,208,263,184a,196a
1932 165,193,181a,193a
1933 14,169,182,294a
1934 18,169,211,192a,194a
1935 22,169,212,230,183a,199a
1936 146,181,265,182a,194a
1937 146,181,265,182a,194a
1938 23,182,182a,194a
1939 16,169,216,230,263,192a,202a
1940 21,183,261,182a,194a,
1941 146,182,206,261,265,182a,194a
1942 192,265,182a,194a
1943 19,170,183a,195a
1944 146,181,265,182a,194a
1945 19,169,210,181a,204a
1946 23,169,220,182a,197a
1947 15,169,212,192a,193a
1948 146,221,255,265,185a,197a
1949 24,182,182a,194a
1950 16,170,247,255,192a,198a
1951 21,183,182a,194a
1952 14,200,181a,193a
1953 18,181,182a,194a
1954 22,169,207,182a,202a
1955 15,170,255,192a,195a
1956 19,170,232,183a,203a
1957 24,182,182a,194a
1958 16,169,211,192a,203a
1959 20,169,213,183a,196a
1960 13,204,263,181a,204a
1961 17,169,215,181a,196a
1962 21,182,182a,194a
1963 146,181,265,182a,194a
1964 146,183,265,182a,194a
1965 146,169,265,186a,198a
1966 15,169,207,192a,194a
1967 20,169,208,183a,199a
1968 146,181,259,263,265,182a,194a
1969 17,170,235,248,181a,201a
1970 146,182,265,182a,194a
1971 157,202,258,261,181a,193a
1972 18,169,261,183a,195a

1973 22,219,235,258,261,182a,203a
1974 15,169,216,192a,196a
1975 19,170,205,183a,204a
1976 24,181,182a,194a
1977 16,170,207,181a,204a
1978 20,169,257,182a,197a
1979 157,193,181a,193a
1980 18,169,186a,198a
1981 22,182,295a
1982 146,192,265,295a
1983 18,183,213,297a,
1984 23,200,188a,200a
1985 i5,169,215,181a,194a
1986 20,169,216,263,182a,202a
1987 24,195,225,237,181a,193a
1988 146,183,226,265,298a
1989 146,182,226,265,298a
1990 146,226,259,263,265,190a,202a
1991 18,209,183a,196a
1992 23,169,210,181a,204a
1993 15,169,211,181a,196a
1994 19,169,212,182a,193a
1995 24,170,239,181a,197a
1996 16,170,214,183a,193a
1997 146,182,265,182a,194a
1998 13,194,181a,193a
1999 17,169,205,218,183a,200a

25th April

1930 146,182,265,182a,194a
1931 17,170,208,263,192a,197a
1932 22,193,181a,193a
1933 14,169,182,294a
1934 18,169,211,192a,194a
1935 22,183,259,262,182a,194a
1936 146,181,265,182a,194a
1937 146,181,259,263,265,182a,194a
1938 24,182,182a,194a
1939 16,169,216,230,263,192a,202a
1940 21,183,261,182a,194a
1941 146,182,206,261,265,182a,194a
1942 146,192,265,182a,194a
1943 10,170,183a,195a
1944 15,170,183a,195a
1945 19,169,210,181a,204a
1946 23,169,220,182a,197a
1947 16,193,221,255,181a,193a
1948 146,265,185a,197a
1949 13,182,261,182a,194a
1950 17,170,247,192a,198a
1951 21,183,182a,194a
1952 14,200,181a,193a
1953 18,181,182a,194a
1954 22,169,207,182a,202a
1955 15,170,208,181a,195a
1956 20,170,209,183a,203a
1957 24,182,182a,194a
1958 16,169,211,192a,203a
1959 21,169,212,183a,196a
1960 14,226,256,259,263,181a,204a
1961 18,169,215,181a,196a
1962 22,182,182a,194a
1963 146,181,265,182a,194a
1964 146,183,265,182a,194a
1965 146,169,265,186a,198a
1966 16,169,207,192a,194a
1967 20,169,208,183a,199a
1968 146,181,194,259,263,265,280a
1969 17,170,235,248,181a,201a
1970 146,182,265,182a,194a
1971 14,181,261,182a,194a
1972 163,169,258,261,183a,195a
1973 167,235,258,261,191a,203a
1974 15,169,216,192a,196a
1975 20,170,205,183a,204a
1976 24,181,182a,194a
1977 16,170,207,181a,204a
1978 165,221,249,182a,197a
1979 157,193,181a,193a
1980 18,169,186a,198a
1981 22,182,295a
1982 146,192,265,295a
1983 19,183,213,297a
1984 24,200,263,188a,200a
1985 16,169,215,181a,194a
1986 20,169,216,263,182a,202a
1987 157,195,181a,193a
1988 146,183,226,265,298a
1989 156,182,226,265,298a
1990 146,192,226,259,262,263,265, 298a
1991 18,209,183a,196a
1992 23,169,210,181a,204a
1993 15,169,211,181a,196a
1994 20,193,263,188a,200a
1995 24,170,239,181a,197a
1996 17,170,214,261,183a,193a
1997 146,182,261,265,182a,194a
1998 13,194,181a,193a
1999 18,169,205,218,183a,200a

26th April

1930 146,193,265,181a,193a
1931 17,170,208,263,192a,197a
1932 22,193,181a,193a
1933 14,169,182,294a
1934 18,169,211,192a,194a
1935 23,183,262,182a,194a
1936 146,181,259,263,265,182a,194a
1937 146,181,259,263,265,182a,194a
1938 24,182,182a,194a
1939 17,202,263,181a,193a
1940 22,483,261,182a,194a
1941 14,182,261,265,276,182a,194a
1942 18,192,182a,194a

1943 10,170,183a,195a
1944 15,170,183a,195a
1945 19,169,210,181a,204a
1946 23,169,220,182a,197a
1947 16,193,221,255,181a,193a
1948 21,258,261,185a,197a
1949 13,182,261,182a,194a
1950 17,170,247,192a,198a
1951 22,183,182a,194a
1952 15,200,181a,193a
1953 19,181,295a
1954 23,169,207,182a,202a
1955 160,208,184a,196a
1956 20,170,209,183a,203a
1957 24,182,182a,194a
1958 17,185a,197a
1959 21,169,212,183a,196a
1960 14,226,256,259,263,181a,204a
1961 18,169,215,181a,196a
1962 22,182,182a,194a
1963 15,170,248,181a,197a
1964 146,183,265,182a,194a
1965 146,169,265,186a,198a
1966 16,169,207,192a,194a
1967 21,169,208,183a,199a
1968 146,181,194,259,263,265,280a
1969 17,170,235,248,181a,201a
1970 22,182,182a,194a
1971 14,181,261,182a,194a
1972 163,169,258,261,183a,195a
1973 167,235,258,261,191a,203a
1974 15,169,216,192a,196a
1975 20,170,205,183a,204a
1976 13,181,182a,194a
1977 17,170,207,181a,204a
1978 165,221,249,182a,197a
1979 14,193,249,181a,193a
1980 18,169,186a,198a
1981 22,182,295a
1982 15,192,187a,199a
1983 19,183,213,297a
1984 24,200,263,188a,200a
1985 16,169,215,181a,195a
1986 21,216,263,189a,201a
1987 157,195,181a,193a
1988 18,183,226,262,276,298a
1989 22,182,226,262,276,298a
1990 146,192,226,259,262,263,265, 298a
1991 19,209,183a,196a
1992 23,169,210,181a,204a
1993 15,169,211,181a,196a
1994 20,193,188a,200a
1995 24,170,239,181a,197a
1996 17,170,214,261,183a,193a
1997 146,182,261,265,182a,194a
1998 14,192,182a,194a
1999 18,169,205,218,183a,200a

27th April

1930 146,193,265,181a,193a
1931 18,226,246,259,263,181a,197a
1932 23,193,181a,193a
1933 146,169,265,186a,198a
1934 19,169,211,192a,194a
1935 23,183,262,182a,194a
1936 146,181,259,263,265,182a,194a
1937 146,181,259,263,265,182a,194a
1938 13,182,195,280a
1939 17,202,263,181a,193a
1940 22,183,261,182a,194a
1941 14,182,261,265,276,182a,197a
1942 18,192,182a,194a,
1943 23,170,183a,195a
1944 16,170,209,181a,196a
1945 20,169,210,181a,204a
1946 24,169,211,182a,197a
1947 17,193,283a
1948 21,258,261,185a,197a
1949 13,182,261,182a,194a
1950 18,170,186a,198a
1951 22,183,182a,194a
1952 15,200,181a,193a
1953 19,181,295a
1954 23,169,207,182a,202a
1955 160,208,184a,196a
1956 21,170,232,183a,203a
1957 13,182,182a,194a
1958 17,185a,197a
1959 22,169,212,183a,196a
1960 14,226,256,259,263,181a,204a
1961 18,226,256,181a,196a
1962 23,182,182a,194a
1963 15,170,248,181a,197a
1964 146,183,265,182a,194a
1965 146,169,265,186a,198a
1966 16,169,207,192a,194a
1967 21,169,208,183a,199a
1968 146,181,259,263,265,182a,194a
1969 18,170,186a,198a
1970 22,182,182a,194a
1971 15,169,213,218,261,181a,202a
1972 163,169,258,261,183a,195a
1973 167,235,258,261,191a,203a
1974 160,216,183a,196a
1975 20,170,205,183a,204a
1976 13,181,182a,194a
1977 17,170,207,181a,204a
1978 22,169,208,183a,197a
1979 14,193,249,181a,193a
1980 19,169,248,183a,197a
1981 23,182,295a
1982 15,192,187a,199a
1983 20,183,213,197a
1984 24,200,263,188a,200a
1985 16,169,215,181a,195a
1986 21,169,216,183a,202a
1987 157,195,181a,193a

1988 18,183,226,262,276,298a
1989 22,182,226,262,276,298a
1990 146,226,259,262,265,202a
1991 19,209,183a,196a
1992 24,169,227,181a,204a
1993 16,169,211,181a,196a
1994 21,170,212,183a,193a
1995 13,170,239,181a,197a
1996 17,170,214,261,183a,193a
1997 22,182,261,182a,194a
1998 14,192,182a,194a
1999 19,169,205,218,183a,200a

28th April

1930 146,182,265,182a,194a
1931 18,226,246,259,263,181a,197a
1932 23,193,181a,193a
1933 146,169,265,186a
1934 19,169,211,192a,194a
1935 24,183,262,182a,194a
1936 146,181,259,263,265,182a,194a
1937 146,181,259,263,265,182a,194a
1938 13,182,195,280a
1939 18,202,259,263,181a,193a
1940 22,183,261,182a,194a
1941 14,182,261,265,276,182a,194a
1942 146,192,265,182a,194a
1943 23,170,183a,195a
1944 16,170,209,181a,196a
1945 20,169,210,181a,204a
1946 24,169,211,182a,197a
1947 17,193,283a
1948 146,261,265,185a,197a
1949 146,182,261,265,182a,194a
1950 18,170,186a,198a
1951 23,183,182a,194a
1952 15,200,181a,193a
1953 20,181,182a,194a
1954 24,169,207,182a,202a
1955 160,208,184a,196a
1956 21,170,232,183a,203a
1957 13,182,182a,194a
1958 17,185a,197a
1959 22,169,212,183a,196a
1960 15,169,214,181a,204a
1961 19,170,215,181a,196a
1962 23,170,216,183a,193a
1963 16,170,227,181a,197a
1964 146,183,265,182a,194a
1965 146,169,265,186a,198a
1966 17,169,207,192a,194a
1967 22,169,208,183a,199a
1968 146,181,259,263,265,182a,194a
1969 18,170,186a,198a
1970 23,183,182a,194a
1971 15,169,213,218,261,181a,202a
1972 20,169,183a,195a
1973 24,219,235,257,182a,203a
1974 160,216,184a,196a
1975 21,170,205,183a,204a
1976 13,181,182a,194a
1977 18,170,236,181a,193a
1978 22,169,208,183a,197a
1979 15,193,249,181a,193a
1980 19.169,248,183a,197a
1981 23,182,295a
1982 16,192,187a,199a
1983 20,183,213,297a
1984 13,200,263,286a
1985 17,169,215,181a,195a
1986 22,225,190a,202a
1987 14,195,225,237,181a,193a
1988 18,183,226,262,276,298a
1989 146,182,226,259,262,265,298a
1990 146,226,259,262,265,190a,202a
1991 20,209,183a,196a
1992 24,169,227,181a,204a
1993 16,169,211,181a,197a
1994 21,170,212,183a,193a
1995 13,170,239,181a,197a
1996 18,214,217,261,183a,193a
1997 22,182,261,182a,194a
1998 15,169,216,192a,194a
1999 19,169,205,218,183a,200a

29th April

1930 146,182,265,182a,194a
1931 19,170,208,181a,197a
1932 24,193,181a,193a
1933 146,169,265,186a,198a
1934 20,169,211,192a,194a
1935 24,183,262,182a,194a
1936 146,181,259,263,265,182a,194a
1937 146,181,259,263,265,182a,194a
1938 13,182,195,280a
1939 18,202,259,263,181a,193a
1940 23,183,261,182a,194a,
1941 146,182,261,265,176,182a,194a,
1942 146,192,265,182a,194a
1943 24,170,183a,195a
1944 146,265,185a,197a
1945 21,169,210,181a,204a
1946 13,169,220,183a,197a
1947 17,193,283a
1948 146,261,265,185a,197a
1949 146,182,261,265,182a,194a
1950 19,170,255,192a,198a
1951 23,183,182a,194a
1952 16,169,206,181a,200a
1953 20,181,182a,194a
1954 24,169,207,183a,202a
1955 17,170,208,181a,195a
1956 21,170,232,183a,203a
1957 146,182,265,182a,194a
1958 18,169,211,192a,204a
1959 23,169,212,183a,196a

1960 15,169,214,181a,204a
1961 19,170,215,181a,196a
1962 24,170,216,183a,193a
1963 16,170,227,181a,197a
1964 146,183,265,182a,194a
1965 146,169,265,186a,198a
1966 17,169,207,192a,194a
1967 22,169,208,183a,199a
1968 146,181,259,263,265,182a,194a
1969 19,170,248,181a,201a
1970 23,183,182a,194a
1971 16,169,218,235,181a,202a
1972 20,169,183a,195a
1973 24,219,235,257,182a,203a
1974 17,170,216,192a,196a
1975 21,170,205,183a,204a
1976 146,181,265,182a,194a
1977 18,170,236,181a,193a
1978 23,169,208,183a,197a
1979 15,193,249,181a,193a
1980 20,169,210,183a,197a
1981 24,182,295a
1982 16,192,187a,199a
1983 21,183,213,297a
1984 13,200,263,286a
1985 17,169,215,181a,195a
1986 22,225,190a,202a
1987 14,195,225,237,181a,193a
1988 146,183,226,259,262,263,298a
1989 146,182,226,259,262,265,298a
1990 146,226,259,262,263,265,190a, 202a
1991 20,209,183a,196a
1992 13,204,181a,193a
1993 17,169,197,181a,197a
1994 21,170,212,183a,193a
1995 146,181,265,182a,194a
1996 18,214,217,261,183a,193a
1997 146,182,239,261,265,299a
1998 15,169,216,192a,194a
1999 19,169,205,218,183a,200a

30th April

1930 146,182,265,182a,194a
1931 19,170,208,181a,197a
1932 24,193,181a,193a
1933 146,169,265,186a,198a
1934 20,169,211,192a,194a
1935 13,183,182a,194a
1936 18,181,259,263,182a,194a
1937 22,181,259,263,182a,194a
1938 14,183a,182a,194a
1939 18,202,259,263,181a,193a
1940 23,183,261,182a,194a
1941 146,182,261,265,276,182a,194a
1942 146,192,265,182a,194a
1943 24,170,183a,195a
1944 146,265,185a,197a
1945 21,169,210,181a,204a
1946 13,169,220,183a,197a
1947 18,193,221,255,181a,193a
1948 146,261,265,185a,187a
1949 15,182,261,182a,194a
1950 19,170,255,192a,198a
1951 24,183,182a,194a
1952 16,169,206,181a,200a
1953 20,181,182a,194a
1954 13,170,207,183a,202a
1955 17,170,208,181a,195a
1956 22,171,232a
1957 146,182,265,182a,194a
1958 18,169,211,192a,204a
1959 23,169,222,183a,196a
1960 16,169,214,263,181a,204a
1961 20,170,215,181a,196a
1962 24,170,216,183a,193a
1963 17,170,227,248,181a,197a
1964 146,183,265,182a,194a
1965 146,169,265,185a,198a
1966 18,169,186a,198a
1967 22,169,208,183a,199a
1968 146,181,265,182a,194a
1969 146,181,265,182a,194a
1970 24,183,182a,184a
1971 16,169,218,235,181a,202a
1972 21,169,261,183a,195a
1973 13,169,215,258,261,182a,203a
1974 17,170,216,192a,196a
1975 22,170,205,183a,204a
1976 14,181,182a,194a
1977 18,170,236,181a,193a
1978 23,169,208,183a,197a
1979 15,193,249,181a,193a
1980 20,169,210,183a,197a
1981 24,182,295a
1982 17,192,187a,199a
1983 21,183,213,297a
1984 14,200,263,188a,200a
1985 18,169,215,181a,195a
1986 23,169,216,183a,202a
1987 15,170,205,181a,195a
1988 146,183,226,259,262,263,298a
1989 146,225,259,262,265,190a,202a
1990 146,226,259,262,263,265,190a, 202a
1991 20,209,183a,196a
1992 13,204,181a,193a
1993 17,169,197,181a,197a
1994 22,228,190a,202a
1995 146,181,265,182a,194a
1996 19,170,214,261,183a,193a
1997 146,182,239,261,265,299a
1998 16,169,216,192a,194a
1999 20,169,205,218,183a,200a

1st May

1930 15,171,183a,195a
1931 20,170,208,263,181a,197a
1932 24,193,181a,193a
1933 146,169,265,186a,198a
1934 21,169,211,192a,194a
1935 13,183,182a,194a
1936 18,181,182a,194a
1937 22,181,259,263,182a,194a
1938 14,183,182a,194a
1939 19,202,181a,193a
1940 24,183,182a,194a
1941 146,182,265,276,182a,194a
1942 146,192,265,182a,194a
1943 13,171,183a,195a
1944 146,265,185a,197a
1945 21,169,210,181a,204a
1946 14,169,220,183a,197a
1947 18,193,221,255,181a,193a
1948 146,261,265,185a,197a
1949 15,182,261,182a,194a
1950 20,170,247,255,192a,198a
1951 24,183,182a,194a
1952 17,169,206,181a,200a
1953 21,169,232,181a,195a
1954 13,170,207,183a,202a
1955 18,170,208,181a,195a
1956 22,171,232,183a,203a
1957 146,182,265,182a,194a
1958 19,169,211,192a,204a
1959 24,169,212,183a,196a
1960 16,169,214,263,181a,204a
1961 20,170,215,181a,196a
1962 13,170,216,183a,193a
1963 17,170,227,248,181a,197a
1964 22,183,182a,194a
1965 146,169,182,265,294a
1966 18,169,186a,198a
1967 23,169,208,183a,199a
1968 146,181,265,182a,194a
1969 20,171,200,218,181a,201a
1970 24,183,182a,194a
1971 161,249,258,261,181a,202a
1972 21,169,261,183a,195a
1973 13,219,235,257,258,261,182a, 203a
1974 18,170,249,192a,196a
1975 22,170,205,183a,204a
1976 15,171,206,181a,196a
1977 19,170,236,181a,193a
1978 24,169,208,183a,197a
1979 16,193,249,181a,193a
1980 20,169,210,183a,197a
1981 13,182,295a
1982 17,192,187a,199a
1983 22,183,213,297a
1984 14,200,263,188a,200a
1985 18,169,215,181a,195a
1986 23,169,216,183a,202a
1987 15,170,195,181a,195a
1988 146,183,226,259,262,265,298a
1989 146,226,259,262,265,190a,202a
1990 17,226,259,263,190a,202a
1991 21,169,209,183a,196a
1992 13,204,181a,193a
1993 18,169,197,181a,197a
1994 22,228,190a,202a
1995 15,170,213,181a,197a
1996 19,170,214,261,183a,193a
1997 146,182,239,261,265,299a
1998 16,169,216,192a,194a
1999 20,169,205,218,183a,200a

2nd May

1930 15,171,183a,195a
1931 21,170,208,263,181a,197a
1932 157,193,181a,193a
1933 146,169,265,186a,198a
1934 21,169,211,192a,194a
1935 146,183,259,262,265,182a,194a
1936 18,181,182a,194a
1937 22,181,259,263,182a,194a
1938 15,169,183a,195a
1939 19,202,181a,193a
1940 24,183,182a,194a
1941 146,182,265,276,182a,194a
1942 146,192,265,182a,194a
1943 13,171,183a,195a
1944 18,170,209,181a,196a
1945 22,169,210,181a,204a
1946 14,169,220,183a,197a
1947 19,193,221,255,181a,193a
1948 146,261,265,185a,197a
1949 15,171,182,258,261,291a
1950 20,170,247,255,192a,198a
1951 13,194,181a,193a
1952 17,169,206,181a,200a
1953 21,169,232,181a,195a
1954 146,183,265,182a,194a
1955 18,170,208,181a,195a
1956 167,247,183a,203a
1957 15,182,182a,194a
1958 19,169,211,192a,204a
1959 24,169,212,183a,196a
1960 16,169,214,263,181a,204a
1961 21,170,215,181a,196a
1962 13,170,216,183a,193a
1963 18,170,186a,198a
1964 22,183,182a,194a
1965 146,169,182,265,294a
1966 19,169,207,192a,194a
1967 23,170,217,183a,199a
1968 146,181,259,263,265,182a,194a
1969 20,171,210,218,181a,201a
1970 13,183,261,182a,194a
1971 161,249,258,261,181a,202a
1972 21,169,261,183a,195a

1973 14,182,219,235,257,258,261, 182a,194a
1974 18,170,249,192a,196a
1975 23,170,205,183a,204a
1976 15,171,206,181a,196a
1977 19,170,236,181a,193a
1978 24,208,183a,197a
1979 16,193,249,181a,193a
1980 21,170,236,183a,197a
1981 13,182,295a
1982 18,192,187a,199a
1983 22,183,213,297a
1984 146,182,200,259,263,265,296a
1985 19,169,215,181a,195a
1986 23,169,216,183a,202a
1987 16,170,205,181a,195a
1988 146,183,226,259,262,265,298a
1989 146,226,265,190a,202a
1990 17,226,259,263,190a,202a
1991 21,169,209,183a,196a
1992 14,182,182a,194a
1993 18,169,197,181a,197a
1994 23,170,212,183a,193a
1995 15,170,213,181a,197a
1996 19,170,214,261,183a,193a
1997 146,182,265,182a,194a
1998 17,169,216,192a,194a
1999 21,169,205,218,183a,200a

3rd May

1930 16,171,183a,195a
1931 20,170,208,181a,197a
1932 157,193,181a,193a
1933 146,169,265,186a,198a
1934 22,192,182a,194a
1935 146,183,259,262,265,182a,194a
1936 19,181,182a,194a
1937 146,181,265,182a,194a
1938 15,169,183a,195a
1939 20,202,263,181a,193a
1940 24,183,182a,194a
1941 146,182,261,265,276,182a,194a
1942 146,192,265,182a,194a
1943 14,171,183a,195a
1944 18,170,209,181a,196a
1945 22,193,181a,193a
1946 159,169,183a,195a
1947 19,193,221,255,181a,193a
1948 146,265,185a,197a
1949 16,182,182a,194a
1950 21,170,247,192a,198a
1951 13,194,181a,193a
1952 17,169,206,181a,200a
1953 22,169,232,181a,195a
1954 146,169,265,182a,194a
1955 19,170,208,181a,195a
1956 167,247,183a,203a
1957 15,182,182a,194a
1958 20,169,211,192a,204a
1959 24,169,212,183a,196a
1960 17,169,214,263,181a,204a
1961 21,170,215,181a,196a
1962 14,171,216,183a,193a
1963 18,170,186a,198a
1964 22,183,182a,194a
1965 146,169,265,186a,198a
1966 19,169,207,192a,194a
1967 24,170,217,183a,199a
1968 146,182,259,263,265,182a,194a
1969 21,171,218,248,181a,201a
1970 13,183,182a,194a
1971 161,249,258,261,181a,202a
1972 22,169,261,183a,195a
1973 14,182,219,235,257,258,261, 182a,194a
1974 19,192,187a,199a
1975 23,170,205,183a,204a
1976 15,182,182a,194a
1977 20,170,207,181a,193a
1978 24,169,208,183a,197a
1979 161,193,181a,193a
1980 21,170,236,183a,197a
1981 146,182,265,295a
1982 18,192,187a,199a
1983 22,183,213,297a
1984 15,200,188a,200a
1985 19,169,215,181a,195a
1986 24,169,216,183a,202a
1987 16,170,205,181a,195a
1988 146,183,226,265,298a
1989 146,226,265,190a,202a
1990 18,226,259,262,263,190a,202a
1991 22,227,190a,202a
1992 14,182,182a,194a
1993 19,169,197a,181a,197a
1994 23,170,212,183a,193a
1995 15,171,213,181a,197a
1996 146,183,265,182a,194a
1997 146,182,265,182a,194a
1998 17,169,216,192a,194a
1999 21,169,205,218,183a,200a

4th May

1930 16,171,183a,195a
1931 21,170,208,263,181a,197a
1932 14,193,181a,193a
1933 18,169,186a,198a
1934 22,192,182a,194a
1935 15,183,262,182a,194a
1936 19,181,182a,194a
1937 146,181,265,182a,194a
1938 16,169,215,230,183a,195a
1939 20,202,263,181a,193a
1940 13,183,195,261,280a
1941 146,182,261,265,276,182a,194a
1942 22,192,182a,194a

1943 14,171,183a,195a
1944 19,170,209,181a,196a
1945 23,193,181a,193a
1946 159,169,183a,195a
1947 20,170,212,181a,193a
1948 146,265,185a,197a
1949 16,182,182a,194a
1950 21,170,247,192a,198a
1951 13,194,181a,193a
1952 18,182,182a,194a
1953 22,169,232,181a,195a
1954 15,170,183a,195a
1955 19,170,208,181a,195a
1956 167,247,183a,203a
1957 16,182,182a,194a
1958 20,169,211,192a,204a
1959 13,169,212,183a,196a
1960 17,226,256,259,263,182a,204a
1961 22,226,256,181a,196a
1962 14,171,216,183a,193a
1963 18,170,186a,198a
1964 146,183,265,182a,194a
1965 146,169,265,186a,198a
1966 20,169,207,192a,194a
1967 24,170,217,183a,199a
1968 146,182,259,263,265,182a,194a
1969 21,171,218,248,181a,201a
1970 13,183,182a,194a
1971 18,169,213,218,261,181a,203a
1972 22,169,261,183a,195a
1973 159,219,235,257,258,261,182a, 203a
1974 19,192,187a,199a
1975 167,235,257,183a,204a
1976 16,182,292a
1977 20,170,207,181a,193a
1978 13,257,183a,197a
1979 161,193,181a,193a
1980 22,170,186a,198a
1981 146,182,265,295a
1982 163,192,187a,199a
1983 23,183,213,297a
1984 15,200,188a,200a
1985 20,195,188a,200a
1986 24,169,216,183a,202a
1987 16,170,205,181a,195a
1988 146,183,226,265,298a
1989 14,182,226,259,262,298a
1990 18,226,259,263,190a,202a
1991 22,227,190a,202a
1992 146,238,250,265,182a,204a
1993 19,170,197,181a,197a
1994 24,170,212,183a,193a
1995 16,171,213,181a,197a
1996 146,183,265,182a,194a
1997 146,182,261,265,182a,194a
1998 161,194,181a,193a
1999 21,169,205,218,183a,200a

5th May

1930 17,171,183a,195a
1931 21,170,208,263,181a,197a
1932 14,193,181a,193a
1933 18,169,186a,198a
1934 23,192,182a,194a
1935 15,183,262,182a,194a
1936 146,182,265,182a,194a
1937 146,181,259,263,265,182a,194a
1938 16,169,215,230,183a,195a
1939 21,202,263,181a,193a
1940 13,183,195,261,280a
1941 146,182,261,265,276,182a,194a
1942 22,192,182a,194a
1943 14,171,183a,195a
1944 19,182,182a,194a
1945 23,193,181a,193a
1946 16,169,211,183a,197a
1947 20,170,212,181a,193a
1948 13,258,261,185a,197a
1949 146,182,261,265,293a
1950 22,222,192a,198a
1951 14,183,182a,194a
1952 18,182,182a,194a
1953 23,169,232,181a,195a
1954 15,170,183a,195a
1955 19,170,208,181a,195a
1956 24,171,209,183a,203a
1957 16,182,263,182a,194a
1958 165,225,233,255,181a,204a
1959 13,169,212,183a,196a
1960 18,182,263,276,182a,194a
1961 22,226,256,181a,196a
1962 15,171,183a,195a
1963 19,171,248,181a,197a
1964 146,183,265,182a,194a
1965 146,169,265,186a,198a
1966 20,169,207,181a,194a
1967 24,170,217,183a,199a
1968 146,182,259,263,265,182a,194a
1969 22,218,256,181a,201a
1970 146,183,259,262,265,182a,194a
1971 18,169,213,218,261,181a,203a
1972 167,169,258,261,183a,195a
1973 219,235,257,261,182a,203a
1974 20,170,216,181a,196a
1975 24,171,205,183a,204a
1976 160,182,292a
1977 165,221,249,181a,193a
1978 13,257,183a,197a
1979 161,193,181a,193a
1980 22,170,186a,198a
1981 15,182,295a
1982 163,181,187a,199a
1983 23,183,213,297a
1984 16,200,263,188a,200a
1985 20,195,188a,200a
1986 13,169,216,183a,202a
1987 161,225,237,181a,195a

1988 146,226,265,190a,202a
1989 14,182,226,259,262,298a
1990 18,226,259,263,190a,202a
1991 22,227,190a,202a
1992 146,238,250,265,182a,204a
1993 20,170,211,181a,197a
1994 24,170,212,183a,193a
1995 16,171,213,181a,197a
1996 146,183,214,261,265,182a,194a
1997 13,198,261,181a,193a
1998 18,194,181a,193a
1999 22,169,205,218,183a,200a

6th May

1930 17,171,183a,195a
1931 22,226,246,259,263,181a,197a
1932 14,193,181a,193a
1933 18,169,186a,198a
1934 23,181,182a,194a
1935 16,183,262,182a,194a
1936 146,182,265,182a,194a
1937 146,181,259,263,265,182a,194a
1938 17,169,230,254,183a,195a
1939 21,202,263,181a,193a
1940 14,183,261,182a,194a
1941 18,182,261,265,276,182a,194a
1942 23,181,182a,194a
1943 159,171,266,183a,195a
1944 19,182,182a,194a
1945 24,193,181a,193a
1946 16,169,211,183a,197a
1947 20,170,212,181a,193a
1948 13,258,261,185a,197a
1949 146,182,261,265,293a
1950 22,222,192a,198a
1951 14,183,182a,194a
1952 19,182,295a
1953 23,169,232,181a,195a
1954 16,170,255,183a,202a
1955 20,170,209,181a,195a
1956 24,171,209,183a,203a
1957 146,182,263,265,293a
1958 165,225,233,255,181a,204a
1959 14,169,212,183a,196a
1960 18,182,263,276,182a,194a
1961 146,170,248,256,181a,197a
1962 15,171,183a,195a
1963 19,171,248,181a,197a
1964 146,183,265,182a,194a
1965 146,169,265,186a,198a
1966 21,169,207,181a,194a
1967 13,170,208,183a,199a
1968 146,182,259,263,265,182a,194a
1969 22,218,256,181a,201a
1970 146,183,259,262,265,182a,194a
1971 19,169,213,218,261,181a,203a
1972 167,169,258,261,183a,195a
1973 16,182,219,235,257,182a,194a
1974 20,170,216,181a,196a
1975 24,171,205,183a,204a
1976 17,182,182a,194a
1977 165,221,249,181a,193a
1978 14,169,208,183a,197a
1979 18,193,249,181a,193a
1980 22,170,186a,198a
1981 158,182,295a
1982 163,181,187a,199a
1983 24,183,213,297a
1984 16,200,263,188a,200a
1985 21,169,215,181a,195a
1986 13,169,216,183a,202a
1987 161,225,237,181a,195a
1988 22,226,259,262,190a,202a
1989 14,182,226,259,262,298a
1990 146,226,265,190a,202a
1991 23,169,209,193a,196a
1992 146,238,250,265,182a,193a
1993 20,170,211,181a,197a
1994 24,170,212,183a,193a
1995 16,171,213,181a,197a,P
1996 146,183,214,261,265,182a,194a
1997 14,182,261,182a,194a
1998 18,194,181a,193a
1999 22,169,205,218,261,183a,199a

7th May

1930 18,171,183a,195a
1931 22,226,246,259,263,181a,197a
1932 15,193,181a,193a
1933 146,169,265,186a,198a
1934 24,181,182a,194a
1935 16,183,262,182a,194a
1936 146,182,265,182a,194a
1937 146,181,201,259,263,265,280a
1938 17,169,230,254,183a,195a
1939 22,202,259,263,181a,193a
1940 146,184,265,182a,194a
1941 18,182,261,265,276,182a,194a
1942 23,181,182a,194a
1943 159,171,266,183a,195a
1944 20,182,182a,194a
1945 24,193,181a,193a
1946 265,185a,197a
1947 165,221,255,181a,193a
1948 13,221,255,185a,197a
1949 18,182,261,182a,194a
1950 22,222,192a,198a
1951 15,183,183a,194a
1952 19,182,295a
1953 23,169,232,181a,195a
1954 16,170,255,183a,202a
1955 20,171,208,181a,193a
1956 13,171,232,183a,203a
1957 146,182,263,265,293a
1958 22,225,233,255,181a,204a
1959 14,169,212,183a,196a

1960 18,182,263,276,182a,194a
1961 146,170,248,256,181a,197a
1962 15,171,183a,195a
1963 20,171,205,181a,197a
1964 146,183,265,182a,194a
1965 146,169,265,186a,198a
1966 21,169,207,181a,194a
1967 13,170,208,183a,199a
1968 18,171,182,294a
1969 22,218,256,181a,201a
1970 159,170,183,211,235,262,291a
1971 19,169,213,218,261,181a,203a
1972 167.169,258,261,183a,195a
1973 16,182,219,235,257,182a,194a
1974 20,170,216,181a,196a
1975 13,171,205,183a,204a
1976 17,182,182a,194a
1977 22,170,236,181a,193a
1978 14,169,208,183a,197a
1979 18,193,249,181a,193a
1980 146,170,265,186a,198a
1981 16,182,295a
1982 20,181,187a,199a
1983 24,183,213,297a
1984 17,200,263,188a,200a
1985 21,169,215,181a,195a
1986 14,169,216,183a,202a
1987 18,170,195,181a,195a
1988 22,226,259,262,190a,202a
1989 146,171,226,259,265,307a
1990 146,226,265,190a,202a
1991 23,169,209,193a,196a
1992 146,238,250,265,182a,193a
1993 21,170,211,181a,197a,
1994 13,170,212,183a,193a
1995 17,171,213,181a,197a
1996 22,214,217,261,190a,202a
1997 14,182,261,182a,194a
1998 19,194,181a,193a
1999 167,239,251,258,261,183a,199a

8th May

1930 18,171,183a,195a
1931 23,170,208,181a,197a
1932 15,193,181a,193a
1933 146,169,265,186a,198a
1934 24,181,182a,194a
1935 16,183,262,182a,194a
1936 146,182,265,182a,194a
1937 146,181,201,259,263,265,280a
1938 18,169,230,254,183a,195a
1939 22,202,259,263,181a,193a
1940 146,184,265,182a,194a,
1941 146,182,261,265,276,182a,194a
1942 23,181,182a,194a
1943 16,171,183a,195a
1944 20,182,182a,194a
1945 13,193,181a,193a
1946 146,265,185a,197a
1947 165,221,255,181a,193a
1948 146,184,265,193a
1949 18,182,261,182a,194a
1950 23,170,216,181a,198a
1951 15,183,183a,194a
1952 20,182,182a,194a
1953 24,181,182a,194a
1954 17,170,207,183a,202a
1955 21,171,208,181a,195a
1956 13,171,209,184a,203a
1957 18,182,259,263,182a,194a
1958 22,225,233,255,181a,204a
1959 14,169,212,183a,196a
1960 146,182,265,182a,194a
1961 146,170,248,256,181a,197a
1962 16,171,216,183a,193a
1963 20,171,205,181a,197a
1964 146,183,265,182a,194a
1965 146,169,265,186a,198a
1966 22,234,256,259,265,181a,194a
1967 146,170,265,112a,194a
1968 18,171,182,294a
1969 23,171,218,248,181a,201a
1970 159,170,183,211,235,262,291a
1971 19,169,213,218,261,181a,203a
1972 24,169,183a,195a
1973 17,182,182a,194a
1974 21,170,216,181a,196a
1975 13,171,205,183a,204a
1976 18,182,182a,194a
1977 22,170,236,181a,193a
1978 15,169,208,183a,197a
1979 19,193,249,181a,193a
1980 146,170,265,186a,198a
1981 16,182,295a
1982 20,181,187a,199a
1983 24,183,213,297a
1984 17,200,263,188a,200a
1985 22,169,215,181a,195a
1986 146,183,265,182a,194a
1987 18,170,195,181a,195a
1988 146,226,259,262,265,190a,202a
1989 146,171,226,259,265,207,a
1990 146,226,259,263,265,190a,202a
1991 24,169,209,183a,196a
1992 146,238,250,265,182a,193a
1993 21,170,211,181a,197a
1994 13,170,212,183a,193a
1995 17,171,213,181a,197a
1996 22,214,217,261,190a,202a
1997 15,169,215,261,182a,198a
1998 19,194,181a,193a
1999 167,239,251,258,261,183a,199a

9th May

1930 19,171,183a,195a
1931 23,170,208,181a,197a

1932 160,193,282a
1933 146,169,265,186a,198a
1934 24,181,182a,194a
1935 17,171,212,230,183a,199a
1936 146,182,265,182a,194a
1937 146,181,259,263,265,182a,194a
1938 18,169,230,254,183a,195a
1939 22,202,259,263,181a,193a
1940 146,184,265,182a,194a
1941 146,182,261,265,276,182a,194a
1942 24,171,183a,195a
1943 16,171,183a,195a
1944 21,182,182a,194a
1945 13,193,181a,193a
1946 18,169,220,183a,197a
1947 22,170,212,181a,193a
1948 146,265,185a,197a
1949 163,182,258,261,182a,194a
1950 23,170,216,181a,198a
1951 15,183,183a,194a
1952 20,182,182a,194a
1953 24,181,182a,194a
1954 17,170,207,183a,202a
1955 21,171,208,181a,195a
1956 14,171,209,184a,203a
1957 18,182,259,263,182a,194a
1958 23,225,223,255,181a,204a
1959 15,169,212,183a,196a
1960 146,182,265,182a,194a
1961 24,170,215,181a,197a
1962 16,171,216,183a,193a
1963 20,171,205,181a,197a
1964 146,184,259,263,265,182a,194a
1965 18,169,186a,198a
1966 22,234,256,259,263,181a,194a
1967 146,170,265,192a,194a
1968 19,171,248,182a,195a
1969 23,171,218,248,181a,201a
1970 16,183,262,182a,194a
1971 20,169,213,218,181a,203a
1972 24,169,183a,195a
1973 17,182,182a,194a
1974 21,170,216,181a,196a
1975 13,171,205,183a,204a
1976 18,182,182a,194a
1977 23,170,236,181a,193a
1978 15,169,208,183a,197a
1979 19,193,249,181a,193a
1980 146,170,265,186a,198a
1981 17,182,295a
1982 21,181,212,332a
1983 13,184,213,297a
1984 18,200,259,263,188a,200a
1985 22,169,215,181a,195a
1986 146,183,265,182a,194a
1987 18,170,195,181a,195a
1988 146,226,259,262,265,190a,202a
1989 146,226,259,265,190a,202a
1990 146,226,259,263,265,190a,202a
1991 24,169,227,184a,196a
1992 146,238,250,265,182a,193a
1993 22,227,190a,202a
1994 146,183,265,182a,194a
1995 18,171,213,181a,197a,
1996 146,183,214,265,182a,194a
1997 15,169,215,261,182a,198a
1998 19,194,181a,193a
1999 23,184,239,299a

10th May

1930 19,171,183a,195a
1931 23,170,208,181a,197a
1932 160,193,282a
1933 146,170,182,265,294a
1934 13,181,194,280a
1935 17,171,212,230,183a,199a
1936 22,182,182a,194a
1937 146,181,259,263,265,182a,194a
1938 19,169,230,254,183a,195a
1939 23,202,181a,193a
1940 146,184,265,182a,194a
1941 146,182,265,276,182a,194a
1942 24,171,183a,195a
1943 16,171,183a,195a
1944 21,182,182a,194a
1945 14,193,181a,193a
1946 18,169,220,183a,197a
1947 22,170,212,181a,193a
1948 146,171,265,302a
1949 163,182,258,261,182a,194a
1950 24,170,247,181a,198a
1951 16,183,183a,194a
1952 20,182,182a,194a
1953 13,170,232,181a,195a
1954 17,170,207,183a,202a
1955 21,171,208,181a,195a
1956 14,171,209,184a,203a
1957 19,182,182a,194a
1958 23,225,233,255,181a,204a
1959 15,169,212,183a,196a
1960 146,182,259,263,265,182a,194a
1961 24,170,215,181a,197a
1962 17,171,216,183a,193a
1963 21,171,248,181a,197a
1964 146,184,262,263,265,276,182a, 194a
1965 18,169,186a,198a
1966 22,181,234,259,263,182a,194a
1967 146,170,265,182a,194a
1968 19,171,248,182a,195a
1969 24,171,210,218,181a,201a
1970 16,183,262,182a,194a
1971 20,169,213,218,181a,203a
1972 13,169,261,183a,195a
1973 18,182,182a,194a
1974 22,170,216,181a,196a
1975 14,171,205,184a,204a
1976 19,182,182a,194a

1977 23,170,236,181a,193a
1978 15,169,208,183a,197a
1979 19,193,249,181a,193a
1980 146,170,265,186a,198a
1981 17,182,295a
1982 21,181,212,332a
1983 13,184,213,297a
1984 18,200,259,263,188a,200a
1985 23,169,215,181a,195a
1986 15,170,216,183a,202a
1987 19,170,195,181a,195a
1988 146,226,259,262,265,190a,202a
1989 146,226,259,265,190a,202a
1990 146,226,259,263,265,190a,202a
1991 13,169,227,184a,196a
1992 18,238,250,182a,193a
1993 22,227,190a,202a
1994 14,171,212,183a,193a
1995 18,171,213,181a,197a
1996 146,183,214,265,182a,194a
1997 16,169,215,182a,198a
1998 20,194,181a,193a
1999 24,184,182a,194a

11th May

1930 20,171,183a,195a
1931 24,170,208,263,181a,197a
1932 160,193,282a
1933 146,170,182,265,294a
1934 13,181,194,280a
1935 18,171,212,230,262,183a,199a
1936 22,182,182a,194a
1937 146,181,265,182a,194a
1938 19,169,230,254,183a,195a
1939 23,202,181a,193a
1940 146,184,265,182a,194a
1941 146,182,265,276,182a,194a
1942 13,171,183a,195a
1943 17,171,183a,195a
1944 21,182,182a,194a
1945 14,193,181a,193a
1946 18,169,220,183a,197a
1947 22,170,212,181a,193a
1948 146,171,265,302a
1949 20,182,182a,194a
1950 24,170,247,181a,198a
1951 160,205,184a,196a
1952 21,182,182a,194a
1953 13,170,232,181a,195a
1954 18,170,255,183a,202a
1955 22,171,208,181a,195a
1956 15,171,209,184a,203a
1957 19,182,182a,194a
1958 24,225,233,255,181a,204a
1959 160,248,259,263,184a,196a
1960 146,182,259,263,265,18a,194a
1961 13,171,248,181a,197a
1962 17,171,216,183a,193a
1963 21,170,227,248,181a,197a
1964 146,184,262,263,265,276,182a, 194a
1965 18,169,186a,198a
1966 146,181,265,182a,194a
1967 15,170,217,184a,199a
1968 20,171,209,182a,195a
1969 24,171,210,218,181a,201a
1970 16,183,262,182a,194a
1971 165,213,258,261,189a,201a
1972 13,169,214,184a,195a
1973 18,182,182a,194a
1974 22,170,216,181a,196a
1975 14,171,205,184a,204a
1976 19,182,182a,194a
1977 24,170,207,181a,193a
1978 16,169,208,183a,197a
1979 20,170,257,181a,193a
1980 146,170,265,186a,198a
1981 17,182,295a
1982 21,181,212,332a
1983 146,184,213,265,297a
1984 19,200,188a,200a
1985 23,169,215,181a,195a
1986 15,170,216,183a,203a
1987 19,170,195,181a,195a
1988 146,226,259,262,265,190a,202a
1989 17,171,226,307a
1990 146,226,259,263,265,190a,202a
1991 13,169,227,184a,196a
1992 18,182,276,182a,194a
1993 22,227,190a,202a
1994 14,171,212,183a,193a
1995 19,171,213,181a,197a
1996 146,183,265,182a,194a
1997 16,169,215,183a,198a
1998 20,194,181a,193a
1999 24,184,182a,194a

12th May

1930 20,171,183a,195a
1931 24,170,208,263,181a,197a
1932 17,169,227,184a,194a
1933 146,170,182,265,294a
1934 146,181,265,182a,194a
1935 18,171,212,230,262,184a,199a
1936 22,182,182a,194a
1937 146,181,265,182a,194a
1938 19,169,230,254,183a,195a
1939 24,202,263,181a,193a
1940 146,184,265,182a,194a
1941 146,182,261,265,276,182a,194a
1942 13,171,183a,195a
1943 17,171,183a,195a
1944 22,182,182a,194a
1945 15,193,181a,193a
1946 163,183,187a,199a
1947 23,170,212,181a,193a

1948 146,265,185a,197a
1949 20,182,182a,194a
1950 13,170,247,181a,198a
1951 17,169,247,184a,194a
1952 21,182,182a,194a
1953 146,181,265,182a,194a
1954 18,170,255,183a,202a
1955 22,171,208,181a,195a
1956 15,171,209,184a,203a
1957 20,182,263,182a,194a
1958 24,225,233,255,181a,204a
1959 160,248,259,263,184a,196a
1960 146,182,259,263,265,182a,194a
1961 13,171,248,181a,197a
1962 18,171,216,183a,193a
1963 22,234,256,181a,197a
1964 146,184,259,262,265,182a,194a
1965 18,169,186a,198a
1966 146,181,265,182a,194a
1967 15,170,217,184a,199a
1968 20,171,209,182a,195a
1969 171,248,181a,201a
1970 17,183,182a,194a
1971 165,213,258,261,189a,201a
1972 14,169,214,184a,195a
1973 18,219,235,257,183a,204a
1974 23,171,216,181a,196a
1975 15,171,205,184a,204a
1976 20,182,182a,194a
1977 24,170,207,181a,193a
1978 16,169,208,183a,197a
1979 20,170,257,181a,193a
1980 146,170,265,186a,198a
1981 18,183,223,257,187a,199a
1982 22,181,187a,199a
1983 146,184,213,265,297a
1984 19,200,188a,200a
1985 24,169,215,181a,195a
1986 16,170,216,183a,202a
1987 20,170,195,181a,195a
1988 146,226,265,190a,202a
1989 17,171,226,307a
1990 146,226,259,263,265,190a,202a
1991 13,169,227,184a,196a
1992 18,182,276,182a,194a
1993 23,170,197,181a,197a
1994 15,171,183a,195a
1995 19,171,213,181a,197a
1996 146,183,265,182a,194a
1997 17,170,215,261,183a,198a
1998 165,194,181a,193a
1999 13,184,182a,194a

13th May

1930 21,171,183a,195a
1931 13,197,263,181a,193a
1932 17,169,227,184a,194a
1933 22,170,182,276,294a
1934 146,181,265,182a,194a
1935 18,171,212,230,262,184a,199a
1936 23,182,182a,194a
1937 146,181,259,263,265,182a,194a
1938 20,169,215,230,183a,195a
1939 24,202,263,181a,193a
1940 146,184,182a,194a
1941 146,182,206,261,265,182a,194a
1942 14,171,181,291a
1943 18,171,183a,195a
1944 22,182,182a,194a
1945 15,193,181a,193a
1946 163,183,187a,199a
1947 23,170,212,181a,193a
1948 146,265,185a,197a
1949 21,182,261,182a,194a
1950 13,170,247,181a,198a
1951 17,169,247,184a,194a
1952 22,182,182a,194a
1953 146,181,265,182a,194a
1954 19,170,255,183a,202a
1955 23,171,208,181a,195a
1956 160,209,184a,196a
1957 20,170,210,183a,196a
1958 24,225,233,255,181a,204a
1959 160,248,259,263,184a,196a
1960 146,182,259,263,265,182a,194a
1961 14,171,248,181a,197a
1962 18,171,216,183a,193a
1963 22,234,256,181a,197a
1964 146,184,259,262,265,182a,194a
1965 19,169,186a,198a
1966 146,181,259,263,265,182a,194a
1967 160,208,184a,196a
1968 21,171,248,182a,195a
1969 13,171,248,181a,201a
1970 17,183,182a,194a
1971 165,213,258,261,189a,201a
1972 146,184,265,182a,194a
1973 163,183,187a,199a
1974 23,171,216,181a,196a
1975 15,171,205,184a,204a
1976 20,182,182a,194a
1977 157,193,181a,193a
1978 146,257,265,185a,197a
1979 165,249,181a,193a
1980 146,170,184,265,294a
1981 18,183,223,257,187a,199a
1982 22,181,187a,199a
1983 15,184,213,297a
1984 20,200,263,188a,200a
1985 24,169,215,181a,195a
1986 16,170,216,183a,202a
1987 20,170,195,181a,195a
1988 146,226,265,190a,202a
1989 18,171,226,259,262,307a
1990 22,226,259,263,190a,202a
1991 14,169,227,184a,196a
1992 146,182,265,182a,194a
1993 23,170,197,181a,197a

1994 15,171,183a,195a
1995 20,171,213,181a,197a
1996 146,183,214,261,265,182a,194a
1997 17,170,215,261,183a,198a
1998 165,194,181a,193a
1999 13,184,182a,194a

14th May

1930 21,171,183a,195a
1931 13,197,263,181a,193a
1932 18,169,227,184a,194a
1933 22,170,182,276,294a
1934 15,181,182a,194a
1935 19,171,212,230,262,184a,199a
1936 23,182,182a,194a
1937 146,181,259,263,265,182a,194a
1938 20,169,216,230,183a,195a
1939 24,202,263,181a,193a
1940 146,184,182a,194a
1941 22,182,261,265,276,182a,194a
1942 14,171,181,291a
1943 18,171,183a,195a
1944 23,182,182a,194a
1945 15,193,181a,193a
1946 20,170,211,183a,197a
1947 24,170,212,181a,193a
1948 17,221,255,185a,197a
1949 21,171,231,247,258,261,183a, 195a
1950 13,170,247,181a,198a
1951 17,169,247,184a,194a
1952 22,182,182a,194a
1953 159,170,183a,195a
1954 19,170,255,183a,202a
1955 23,171,208,181a,195a
1956 160,209,184a,196a
1957 21,170,210,183a,196a
1958 157,204,181a,193a
1959 17,170,212,263,184a,196a
1960 22,182,226,263,276,298a
1961 14,171,248,181a,197a
1962 18,171,216,183a,193a
1963 22,234,256,181a,197a
1964 146,184,259,262,263,265,182a, 194a
1965 20,169,186a,198a
1966 146,181,259,263,265,182a,194a
1967 160,208,184a,196a
1968 21,171,248,182a,195a
1969 14,181,182a,194a
1970 18,183,259,262,182a,194a
1971 22,169,218,261,181a,203a
1972 15,170,249,184a,196a
1973 163,183,187a,199a
1974 23,171,216,181a,196a
1975 160,205,184a,196a
1976 21,182,182a,194a
1977 157,193,181a,193a
1978 146,257,265,185a,197a
1979 165,249,181a,193a
1980 146,170,184,265,294a
1981 163,183,187a,199a
1982 167,181,187a,199a
1983 15,184,213,297a
1984 20,200,263,188a,200a
1985 24,170,215,181a,195a
1986 16,170,216,183a,202a
1987 165,205,189a,201a
1988 14,183,226,259,262,298a
1989 18,171,226,259,262,307a
1990 22,226,259,263,190a,202a
1991 14,169,227,184a,196a
1992 146,182,265,182a,194a
1993 24,170,211,181a,197a
1994 16,171,212,183a,193a
1995 20,171,213,181a,197a
1996 146,183,214,261,265,182a,194a
1997 17,170,215,261,183a,198a
1998 165,194,181a,193a
1999 146,184,265,182a,194a

15th May

1930 21,171,183a,195a
1931 13,197,263,181a,193a
1932 18,169,227,184a,194a
1933 146,170,265,186a,198a
1934 15,181,182a,194a
1935 19,171,212,230,262,184a,199a
1936 24,182,182a,194a
1937 146,181,259,263,265,182a,194a
1938 21,169,216,230,183a,195a
1939 146,181,202,259,263,265,280a
1940 18,184,182a,194a
1941 22,183,206,261,182a,194a
1942 14,171,183a,195a
1943 18,171,183a,195a
1944 23,182,182a,194a
1945 16,193,181a,193a
1946 20,170,211,183a,197a
1947 24,170,212,181a,193a
1948 17,221,255,185a,197a
1949 22,171,231,247,258,261,183a, 195a
1950 146,181,265,182a,194a
1951 18,184,182a,194a
1952 23,182,182a,194a
1953 159,170,183a,195a
1954 163,171,183a,195a
1955 23,171,208,181a,195a
1956 146,265,185a,197a
1957 21,170,210,183a,196a
1958 157,204,181a,193a
1959 17,170,212,263,184a,196a
1960 22,182,226,263,276,298a
1961 15,171,248,181a,197a
1962 19,171,216,183a,193a

1963 23,170,248,181a,197a
1964 146,184,259,262,263,265,182a, 194a
1965 20,169,186a,198a
1966 146,181,259,263,265,182a,194a
1967 17,170,208,184a,199a
1968 22,234,256,182a,195a
1969 14,181,182a,194a
1970 18,183,259,262,182a,194a
1971 22,169,218,261,181a,203a
1972 15,170,249,184a,196a
1973 20,219,235,257,183a,204a
1974 24,171,216,181a,196a
1975 160,205,184a,196a
1976 21,182,182a,194a
1977 157,193,181a,193a
1978 146,257,265,185a,197a
1979 22,170,236,257,181a,193a
1980 146,170,265,186a,198a
1981 163,183,187a,199a
1982 167,181,187a,199a
1983 15,184,213,297a
1984 20,200,263,188a,200a
1985 13,170,215,181a,195a
1986 17,170,216,183a,202a
1987 165,205,189a,201a
1988 14,183,226,259,262,298a
1989 18,171,226,259,262,307a
1990 22,226,259,263,190a,202a
1991 15,169,209,184a,196a
1992 146,182,265,182a,194a
1993 24,170,211,181a,197a
1994 16,171,212,183a,193a
1995 21,171,213,181a,197a
1996 146,183,214,261,265,182a,194a
1997 18,250,261,183a,198a
1998 22,181,182a,194a
1999 146,184,265,182a,194a

16th May

1930 22,171,183a,195a
1931 146,181,259,263,265,182a,194a
1932 19,184,182a,194a
1933 146,170,265,186a,198a
1934 15,181,182a,194a
1935 164,228,254,259,262,184a,199a
1936 24,182,182a,194a
1937 146,181,259,263,265,182a,194a
1938 21,169,216,230,183a,195a
1939 146,181,202,259,263,265,280a
1940 18,184,265,276,182a,194a
1941 146,183,265,182a,194a
1942 159,171,266,183a,195a
1943 19,171,183a,195a
1944 24,182,182a,194a
1945 16,193,181a,193a
1946 20,170,211,183a,197a
1947 157,193,181a,193a
1948 146,265,185a,197a
1949 22,171,231,247,258,261,183a, 195a
1950 146,181,265,182a,194a
1951 18,184,182a,194a
1952 23,182,182a,194a
1953 16,170,207,181a,195a
1954 20,171,183a,195a
1955 24,171,208,181a,195a
1956 146,265,185a,197a
1957 21,170,210,183a,196a
1958 157,204,181a,193a
1959 18,226,256,259,263,184a,196a
1960 146,182,265,182a,194a
1961 15,171,248,181a,197a
1962 19,171,216,183a,193a
1963 23,170,248,181a,197a
1964 146,184,259,262,263,265,182a, 194a
1965 146,170,265,186a,198a
1966 146,181,259,263,265,182a,194a
1967 17,171,208,184a,199a
1968 22,234,256,182a,195a
1969 14,181,182a,194a
1970 18,183,259,262,182a,194a
1971 23,169,213,218,261,181a,203a
1972 160,214,184a,196a
1973 20,219,235,257,183a,204a
1974 24,171,216,181a,204a
1975 160,205,184a,196a
1976 22,182,182a,194a
1977 146,181,265,182a,194a
1978 18,170,208,183a,197a
1979 22,181,182a,194a
1980 146,170,265,186a,198a
1981 163,183,187a,199a
1982 167,181,187a,199a
1983 16,184,213,297a
1984 146,182,200,259,263,265,296a
1985 13,170,215,181a,195a
1986 17,170,216,183a,202a
1987 22,171,195,181a,195a
1988 146,171,226,259,262,265,307a
1989 19,171,226,262,307a
1990 146,226,265,190a,202a
1991 15,169,209,184a,196a
1992 146,182,265,182a,194a
1993 24,170,211,181a,197a
1994 17,171,212,183a,193a
1995 21,171,213,181a,197a
1996 146,183,214,261,265,182a,194a
1997 18,250,261,183a,198a
1998 22,181,182a,194a
1999 15,184,182a,194a

17th May

1930 22,226,246,183a,193a
1931 146,181,259,263,265,182a,194a

1932 19,184,182a,194a
1933 146,170,265,186a,198a
1934 16,171,211,181a,194a
1935 164,228,254,1259,262,184a,199a
1936 13,182,182a,194a
1937 146,181,259,263,265,182a,194a
1938 22,183,182a,194a
1939 14,181,202,259,263,280a
1940 146,184,265,182a,194a
1941 146,183,265,182a,194a
1942 159,171,266,183a,195a
1943 19,171,183a,195a
1944 24,182,182a,194a
1945 17,170,220,181a,193a
1946 21,170,220,183a,197a
1947 157,193,181a,193a
1948 146,265,185a,197a
1949 22,171,231,247,258,261,183a, 195a
1950 15,170,216,181a,198a
1951 19,184,182a,194a
1952 24,182,182a,194a
1953 16,170,207,181a,195a
1954 20,171,183a,195a
1955 24,171,208,181a,195a
1956 18,171,209,184a,203a
1957 22,170,210,183a,196a
1958 146,181,265,182a,194a
1959 18,226,256,259,263,184a,196a
1960 146,182,265,182a,194a
1961 15,171,248,181a,197a
1962 20,171,216,183a,193a
1963 24,170,227,181a,197a
1964 146,184,259,263,265,182a,194a
1965 146,170,265,186a,198a
1966 146,181,259,263,265,182a,194a
1967 17,171,208,184a,199a
1968 23,171,248,182a,195a
1969 15,171,218,248,181a,201a
1970 163,183,211,235,262,295a
1971 23,181,261,182a,194a
1972 160,214,184a,196a
1973 20,219,235,257,183a,204a
1974 13,171,216,181a,196a
1975 17,171,205,184a,204a
1976 22,182,182a,194a
1977 146,181,265,182a,194a
1978 18,170,208,183a,197a
1979 23,181,182a,194a
1980 16,171,186a,198a
1981 20,183,223,257,287a,199a
1982 24,181,187a,199a
1983 16,213,189a,201a
1984 146,182,200,259,263,265,296a
1985 146,181,265,182a,194a
1986 18,250,183a,202a
1987 22,171,195,182a,195a
1988 146,171,226,259,262,265,307a
1989 19,171,226,262,307a
1990 146,226,265,190a,202a
1991 160,209,184a,196a
1992 146,182,265,182a,194a
1993 13,170,197,181a,197a
1994 17,171,212,183a,193a
1995 22,171,213,182a,197a
1996 146,183,214,261,265,182a,194a
1997 18,250,261,183a,198a
1998 23,181,182a,194a
1999 15,184,182a,194a

18th May

1930 23,170,254,183a,193a
1931 15,170,208,181a,197a
1932 20,184,182a,184a
1933 146,170,265,186a,198a
1934 16,171,211,181a,194a
1935 164,228,254,259,262,184a,199a
1936 13,182,182a,194a
1937 18,181,259,263,182a,194a
1938 22,183,182a,194a
1939 14,181,202,259,263,280a
1940 146,184,265,182a,194a
1941 146,183,265,182a,194a
1942 16,171,183a,195a
1943 20,171,183a,195a
1944 13,182,182a,194a
1945 17,170,220,181a,193a
1946 21,170,220,183a,197a
1947 157,193,181a,193a
1948 146,265,185a,197a
1949 167,171,258,261,183a,195a
1950 15,170,216,181a,198a
1951 19,184,182a,194a
1952 24,182,182a,194a
1953 17,170,232,181a,195a
1954 21,171,183a,195a
1955 13,171,208,181a,195a
1956 18,171,209,184a,203a
1957 22,170,210,183a,196a
1958 146,181,265,182a,194a
1959 19,170,233,184a,196a
1960 146,182,259,263,265,182a,194a
1961 16,171,215,181a,197a
1962 20,171,216,183a,193a
1963 24,170,227,181a,197a
1964 146,184,259,263,265,182a,194a
1965 22,170,259,262,186a,198a
1966 146,181,259,263,265,182a,194a
1967 18,171,186a,198a
1968 23,171,248,182a,195a
1969 15,171,218,248,181a,201a
1970 163,183,211,235,262,295a
1971 24,181,182a,194a
1972 17,170,214,184a,196a
1973 21,219,235,257,183a,204a
1974 13,171,216,181a,196a
1975 17,171,205,184a,204a
1976 22,182,182a,194a

1977 15,170,236,181a,193a
1978 19,170,208,183a,197a
1979 146,182,265,182a,194a
1980 16,171,186a,198a
1981 20,183,223,257,187a,199a
1982 24,181,187a,199a
1983 17,213,189a,201a
1984 22,182,224,298a
1985 146,181,265,182a,194a
1986 18,250,183a,202a
1987 23,171,195,182a,195a
1988 146,226,259,262,265,190a,202a
1989 20,171,226,262,307a
1990 146,226,259,263,265,190a,202a
1991 160,209,184a,196a
1992 146,182,265,182a,194a
1993 13,171,197,181a,197a
1994 17,171,212,183a,193a
1995 22,171,213,182a,197a
1996 146,183,214,261,265,182a,194a
1997 19,170,215,261,183a,198a
1998 23,181,182a,194a
1999 16,184,182a,194a

19th May

1930 23,170,254,183a,193a
1931 15,170,208,181a,197a
1932 20,184,182a,194a
1933 146,170,186a,198a
1934 17,171,254,181a,194a
1935 21,171,212,230,184a,199a
1936 14,182,182a,194a
1937 18,181,259,263,182a,194a
1938 22,183,182a,194a
1939 146,181202,265,280a
1940 146,184,259,263,265,182a,194a
1941 146,183,1265,182a,194a
1942 16,171,183a,195a
1943 20,171,183a,195a
1944 13,182,182a,194a
1945 18,170,220,181a,193a
1946 22,170,220,183a,197a
1947 14,171,212,181a,193a
1948 19,171,213,184a,198a
1949 167,171,258,261,183a,195a
1950 15,170,216,181a,198a
1951 20,184,182a,194a
1952 13,182,182a,194a
1953 17,170,232,181a,195a
1954 21,171,183a,195a
1955 13,171,208,181a,195a
1956 18,171,209,184a,203a
1957 23,170,210,183a,196a
1958 15,170,211,181a,204a
1959 19,170,233,184a,196a
1960 146,226,256,265,182a,193a
1961 16,171,215,181a,197a
1962 20,171,216,183a,193a
1963 146,182,265,182a,194a
1964 18,170,184,262,263,276,294a
1965 22,170,259,262,186a,198a
1966 146,181,259,263,265,182a,194a
1967 18,171,186a,198a
1968 24,171,248,182a,195a
1969 16,171,210,218,181a,201a
1970 20,183,262,182a,194a
1971 146,182,265,182a,194a
1972 17,170,214,184a,196a
1973 21,219,235,257,183a,204a
1974 13,171,216,181a,196a
1975 18,171,205,184a,204a
1976 23,182,182a,194a
1977 15,170,236,181a,193a
1978 19,170,208,183a,197a
1979 24,182,182a,194a
1980 17,171,186a,198a
1981 21,183,223,257,187a,199a
1982 13,181,187a,199a
1983 17,213,189a,201a
1984 22,182,224,298a
1985 146,181,265,182a,194a
1986 18,250,183a,202a
1987 23,171,195,182a,195a
1988 146,226,259,262,265,190a,202a
1989 20,171,226,262,307a
1990 146,226,259,263,265,190a,202a
1991 17,170,227,184a,196a
1992 22,182,227,276,298a
1993 14,171,197,181a,197a
1994 18,171,212,183a,193a
1995 23,171,213,182a,197a
1996 146,183,214,261,265,182a,194a
1997 19,170,215,261,183a,198a
1998 24,181,182a,194a
1999 16,184,182a,194a

20th May

1930 23,170,254,183a,193a
1931 160,208,263,184a,196a
1932 21,184,182a,194a
1933 146,170,186a,198a
1934 17,171,254,181a,194a
1935 21,171,212,230,184a,199a
1936 14,182,182a,194a
1937 146,181,265,182a,194a
1938 23,183,182a,194a
1939 146,181,202,265,280a
1940 146,184,259,263,265,182a,194a
1941 146,183,265,182a,194a
1942 16,171,183a,195a
1943 21,171,183a,195a
1944 146,182,265,182a,194a
1945 18,170,220,181a,193a
1946 22,170,220,183a,197a
1947 14,182,182a,194a
1948 19,171,213,184a,198a

1949 24,171,231,247,183a,195a
1950 16,170,247,181a,198a
1951 20,184,182a,194a
1952 13,182,182a,194a
1953 17,170,232,181a,195a
1954 21,171,183a,195a
1955 14,182,182a,194a
1956 19,171,209,184a,230a
1957 23,170,210,183a,196a
1958 15,170,211,181a,204a
1959 19,170,233,184a,196a
1960 146,226,256,265,182a,193a
1961 146,265,185a,197a
1962 21,171,216,183a,193a
1963 146,182,265,182a,194a
1964 18,170,184,262,263,276,294a
1965 22,170,259,262,186a,198a
1966 146,181,265,182a,194a
1967 19,171,217,184a,199a
1968 24,171,248,182a,195a
1969 16,171,210,218,181a,201a
1970 20,183,262,182a,194a
1971 146,182,218,256,261,265,182a, 194a
1972 18,256,184a,196a
1973 22,219,235,257,183a,204a
1974 14,171,216,181a,196a
1975 18,171,205,184a,204a
1976 23,182,182a,194a
1977 15,170,236,181a,193a
1978 20,170,208,183a,197a
1979 24,182,182a,194a
1980 17,171,186a,198a
1981 21,183,223,257,187a,199a
1982 13,181,187a,199a
1983 18,213,189a,201a
1984 146,182,265,182a,194a
1985 15,170,215,181a,195a
1986 19,170,216,183a,202a
1987 24,171,205,182a,195a
1988 146,226,259,262,265,190a,202a
1989 20,171,226,262,307a
1990 146,226,259,263,265,190a,202a
1991 17,170,227,184a,196a
1992 22,182,227,276,298a
1993 14,171,197,181a,197a
1994 18,171,212,183a,193a
1995 23,171,213,182a,197a
1996 146,183,265,182a,194a
1997 20,170,215,183a,198a
1998 24,181,182a,194a
1999 17,184,182a,194a

21st May

1930 24,170,207,183a,193a
1931 16,182,259,263,292a
1932 33,170,209,184a,194a
1933 146,170,186a,198a
1934 17,171,254,181a,194a
1935 22,171,212,230,262,184a,199a
1936 147,171,266,183a,195a
1937 31,170,214,181a,200a
1938 23,183,182a,194a
1939 146,182,265,182a,194a
1940 32,184,218,230,246,182a,194a
1941 25,171,183,291a
1942 17,171,183a,193a
1943 21,171,183a,195a
1944 26,170,182,291a
1945 30,170,220,181a,193a
1946 22,170,220,183a,197a
1947 15,171,182,291a
1948 32,171,183a,195a
1949 147,171,266,183a,195a
1950 16,170,247,181a,198a
1951 21,184,182a,194a
1952 26,182,182a,194a
1953 147,170,266,183a,195a
1954 22,171,183a,195a
1955 14,182,182a,194a
1956 31,247,258,260,184a,203a
1957 35,170,210,183a,196a
1958 16,170,211,181a,204a
1959 164,256,259,263,188a,200a
1960 25,171,248,182a,193a
1961 147,266,185a,197a
1962 21,171,216,183a,193a
1963 146,182,265,182a,194a
1964 31,184,234,256,259,262,182a, 194a
1965 35,170,262,303a
1966 146,181,265,182a,194a
1967 19,171,217,184a,199a
1968 36,171,183a,195a
1969 28,171,186a,198a
1970 147,170,266,183a,195a
1971 146,182,218,256,261,265,182a, 194a
1972 30,170,219,249,184a,196a
1973 147,171,266,279,183a,195a
1974 26,171,216,181a,196a
1975 19,184,187a,199a
1976 36,182,182a,194a
1977 28,170,207,181a,193a
1978 32,170,208,183a,197a
1979 146,182,265,182a,194a
1980 29,171,186a,198a
1981 147,171,183,266,304a
1982 147,181,266,187a,199a
1983 18,213,189a,201a
1984 35,170,237,182a,200a
1985 27,170,183a,195a
1986 31,170,216,183a,202a
1987 24,171,205,182a,196a
1988 29,226,190a,202a
1989 33,171,226,307a
1990 25,226,190a,202a
1991 18,238,250,184a,196a

1992 166,227,190a,202a
1993 26,171,211,181a,197a
1994 31,171,212,184a,193a
1995 24,171,213,182a,197a
1996 28,170,214,183a,194a
1997 32,170,215,183a,198a
1998 25,194,181a,193a
1999 29,170,205,184a,199a

22nd May

1930 36,170,183a,195a
1931 29,170,208,182a,197a
1932 34,170,209,184a,194a
1933 158,170,186a,198a
1934 30,171,254,181a,194a
1935 34,171,212,262,184a,199a
1936 147,171,266,183a,195a
1937 32,170,214,181a,200a
1938 36,170,183a,195a
1939 28,182,230,246,182a,194a
1940 33,184,182a,194a
1941 25,171,183,291a
1942 147,171,266,183a,195a
1943 34,171,133a,195a
1944 27,170,183a,195a
1945 31,170,220,181a,193a
1946 35,170,183a,195a
1947 147,171,266,183a,195a
1948 32,171,183a,195a
1949 147,171,258,261,266,183a,195a
1950 29,170,216,181a,198a
1951 33,170,205,184a,195a
1952 26,182,182a,194a
1953 147,171,266,183a,195a
1954 147,171,266,183a,195a
1955 147,171,266,183a,195a
1956 32,171,209,260,184a,203a
1957 36,170,210,183a,196a
1958 28,170,211,181a,204a
1959 33,170,212,184a,196a
1960 25,171,248,182a,193a
1961 147,266,185a,197a
1962 34,171,183a,195a
1963 158,182,182a,194a
1964 31,184,234,256,259,262,182a,
194a
1965 35,170,262,303a
1966 27,170,208,181a,194a
1967 32,171,217,184a,199a
1968 25,171,183a,195a
1969 29,171,186a,198a
1970 147,170,266,183a,195a
1971 158,182,218,256,261,182a,194a
1972 30,170,219,249,184a,196a
1973 147,171,266,279,183a,195a
1974 147,171,258,260,266,183a,195a
1975 31,184,258,260,187a,199a
1976 36,182,182a,194a
1977 28,170,207,181a,193a
1978 33,170,208,184a,197a
1979 25,182,182a,194a
1980 30,171,186a,198a
1981 147,171,183a,266,304a
1982 147,181,266,187a,199a
1983 31,184,213,332a
1984 35,170,237,182a,200a
1985 28,170,215,181a,195a
1986 32,171,216,184a,202a
1987 25,171,205,182a,196a
1988 29,226,190a,202a
1989 33,171,226,307a
1990 158,226,190a,202a
1991 30,170,209,184a,196a
1992 35,238,250,182a,193a
1993 147,171,266,183a,195a
1994 31,171,212,184a,193a
1995 36,171,213,182a,197a
1996 28,170,214,183a,194a
1997 33,170,215,261,183a,198a
1998 25,194,181a,193a
1999 30,170,205,184a,199a

23rd May

1930 25,170,193,281a
1931 29,170,208,182a,197a
1932 34,170,209,184a,194a
1933 158,170,186a,198a
1934 30,171,254,181a,194a
1935 35,171,212,262,184a,199a
1936 28,171,183a,195a
1937 32,170,214,181a,200a
1938 36,170,183a,195a
1939 28,182,230,246,182a,194a
1940 33,184,182a,194a
1941 158,171,183,291a
1942 147,171,266,183a,195a
1943 34,171,183a,195a
1944 147,170,258,261,266,302a
1945 31,170,220,181a,193a
1946 35,170,183a,195a
1947 28,171,183a,195a
1948 33,171,183a,195a
1949 147,171,258,261,266,183a,195a
1950 29,170,216,181a,198a
1951 34,170,205,184a,195a
1952 26,182,182a,194a
1953 31,171,181,260,279,304a
1954 35,171,183a,195a
1955 147,171,266,183a,195a
1956 32,171,209,260,184a,203a
1957 36,170,210,183a,196a
1958 28,170,211,181a,204a
1959 33,170,212,184a,196a
1960 158,226,256,182a,193a
1961 30,171,248,181a,197a
1962 34,171,216,184a,193a

1963 27,170,248,182a,197a
1964 32,184,234,256,259,262,182a, 194a
1965 36,170,262,303a
1966 28,170,208,181a,194a
1967 32,171,209,184a,199a
1968 25,171,183a,195a
1969 29,171,186a,198a
1970 34,170,211,262,184a,195a
1971 158,182,218,256,261,182a,194a
1972 31,170,219,249,184a,196a
1973 35,171,260,279,183a,195a
1974 147,171,258,260,266,183a,195a
1975 32,171,205,260,184a,193a
1976 25,182,182a,194a
1977 161,221,249,181a,193a
1978 33,170,208,184a,197a
1979 158,182,182a,194a
1980 30,171,186a,198a
1981 147,171,183,266,304a
1982 147,171,181,258,260,266,304a
1983 31,184,213,332a
1984 36,170,237,182a,200a
1985 28,170,215,181a,195a
1986 32,171,216,184a,202a
1987 25,171,205,182a,196a
1988 162,226,259,262,190a,202a
1989 34,171,226,262,307a
1990 158,226,190a,202a
1991 31,170,209,184a,196a
1992 35,238,250,182a,193a
1993 147,171,266,183a,195a
1994 164,193,188a,200a
1995 36,171,213,182a,197a
1996 29,170,214,261,183a,194a
1997 33,170,215,261,183a,198a
1998 25,194,181a,193a
1999 30,170,205,184a,199a

24th May

1930 25,170,193a,281a
1931 29,170,208,182a,197a
1932 35,170,209,184a,194a
1933 27,170,303a
1934 31,227,181a,194a
1935 35,171,212,262,184a,199a
1936 28,171,183a,195a
1937 32,214,181a,200a
1938 36,170,183a,195a
1939 29,182,230,246,182a,194a
1940 166,184,182a,194a
1941 158,171,183,291a
1942 147,171,266,183a,195a
1943 35,171,183a,195a
1944 147,170,266,302a
1945 32,170,210,231,181a,193a
1946 36,170,211,231,184a,197a
1947 28,171,183a,195a
1948 33,171,183a,195a
1949 147,171,258,261,266,183a,195a
1950 29,170,216,181a,198a
1951 34,170,205,184a,195a
1952 27,182,182a,194a
1953 31,171,181,260,279,304a
1954 167,208,184a,196a
1955 160,171,301a
1956 33,171,209,260,184a,203a
1957 25,170,210,183a,196a
1958 29,225,233,255,185a,197a
1959 34,170,233,184a,196a
1960 158,226,256,182a,193a
1961 30,171,248,181a,197a
1962 35,171,216,184a,193a
1963 27,170,248,182a,197a
1964 32,184,234,256,259,262,182a, 194a
1965 36,170,262,303a
1966 28,170,208,181a,194a
1967 33,171,209,184a,199a
1968 26,171,183a,195a
1969 162,171,186a,198a
1970 34,170,211,262,184a,195a
1971 27,182,261,182a,194a
1972 31,170,219,249,184a,196a
1973 35,171,260,279,183a,195a
1974 160,216,260,184a,196a
1975 32,171,205,260,184a,193a
1976 25,182,182a,194a
1977 161,221,249,181a,193a
1978 34,170,208,184a,197a
1979 158,182,182a,194a
1980 31,171,186a,198a
1981 35,171,183,304a
1982 147,171,181,258,260,266,304a
1983 32,213,189a,201a
1984 36,170,237,182a,200a
1985 28,170,215,181a,195a
1986 33,216,189a,201a
1987 25,171,205,182a,196a
1988 162,226,259,262,190a,202a
1989 34,171,226,262,307a
1990 27,226,190a,202a
1991 31,170,209,184a,196a
1992 36,238,250,182a,193a
1993 28,171,211,181a,197a
1994 164,194,259,262,188a,200a
1995 25,171,213,182a,197a
1996 29,170,214,261,183a,194a
1997 34,170,215,261,183a,198a
1998 26,170,216,181a,195a
1999 147,239,251,266,184a,199a

25th May

1930 25,193,181a,193a
1931 162,226,246,182a,197a
1932 35,170,209,184a,194a

1933 27,170,303a
1934 31,227,181a,194a
1935 168,228,254,259,262,184a,199a
1936 29,171,183a,195a
1937 33,170,214,181a,200a
1938 25,170,216,184a,195a
1939 29,182,182a,194a
1940 166,184,182a,194a
1941 158,171,183,291a
1942 147,171,266,183a,195a
1943 35,171,183a,195a
1944 147,170,266,302a
1945 32,170,210,231,181a,193a
1946 36,170,211,231,184a,197a
1947 147,171,266,302a
1948 34,171,183a,195a
1949 147,171,258,261,266,183a,195a
1950 30,170,186a,198a
1951 35,170,205,184a,195a
1952 27,182,182a,194a
1953 31,171,181,260,279,304a
1954 168,208,184a,196a
1955 160,171,301a
1956 33,171,209,260,184a,203a
1957 25,170,210,183a,196a
1958 29,225,233,255,185a,197a
1959 34,170,233,184a,196a
1960 147,171,266,183a,195a
1961 31,171,248,181a,197a
1962 35,171,216,184a,193a
1963 28,170,205,182a,197a
1964 32,184,234,256,259,262,182a, 194a
1965 36,170,262,303a
1966 29,171,208,181a,194a
1967 33,171,209,184a,199a
1968 26,171,183a,195a
1969 162,171,186a,198a
1970 35,211,235,262,184a,195a
1971 27,182,261,182a,194a
1972 32,170,219,249,184a,196a
1973 147,171,260,266,279,183a,195a
1974 160,216,260,184a,196a
1975 33,171,205,260,184a,193a
1976 25,182,182a,194a
1977 161,221,249,181a,193a
1978 34,170,208,184a,197a
1979 158,182,182a,194a
1980 31,171,186a,198a
1981 35,171,183,304a
1982 147,181,258,260,266,187a,199a
1983 32,213,189a,201a
1984 25,170,214,182a,200a
1985 29,170,215,181a,195a
1986 33,216,189a,201a
1987 26,171,205,182a,196a
1988 162,226,259,262,190a,202a
1989 35,171,207,226,262,307a
1990 27,226,190a,202a
1991 32,170,209,184a,196a
1992 36,238,250,182a,193a
1993 28,171,211,181a,197a
1994 33,171,212,184a,194a
1995 25,171,213,182a,197a
1996 162,214,250,261,183a,194a
1997 34,170,215,261,183a,198a
1998 26,170,216,181a,195a
1999 31,239,251,184a,199a

26th May

1930 26,170,207,184a,193a
1931 162,226,246,182a,197a
1932 35,170,209,184a,194a
1933 147,171,266,303a
1934 32,171,211,181a,194a
1935 168,228,254,259,262,184a,199a
1936 29,171,183a,195a
1937 33,170,214,181a,200a
1938 25,170,216,184a,195a
1939 162,182,182a,194a
1940 35,184,182,194a
1941 147,171,266,183a,195a
1942 31,171,266,183a,195a
1943 36,170,183a,195a
1944 147,170,266,302a
1945 32,170,210,231,181a,193a
1946 25,170,211,231,184a,197a
1947 147,171,266,302a
1948 34,171,183a,195a
1949 147,171,258,261,266,183a,195a
1950 30,170,186a,198a
1951 35,170,205,184a,195a
1952 28,182,182a,194a
1953 147,171,258,260,266,183a,195a
1954 168,208,184a,196a
1955 161,208,184a,196a
1956 33,171,209,260,184a,203a
1957 25,170,210,183a,196a
1958 30,170,211,181a,204a
1959 34,170,233,184a,196a
1960 147,171,266,183a,195a
1961 31,171,248,181a,197a
1962 36,171,216,184a,193a
1963 28,170,205,182a,197a
1964 33,184,234,256,182a,194a
1965 25,170,303a
1966 29,171,208,181a,194a
1967 34,171,209,184a,199a
1968 26,171,183a,195a
1969 162,171,186a,198a
1970 35,211,235,262,184a,195a
1971 28,182,182a,194a
1972 32,170,219,249,184a,196a
1973 147,171,260,266,279,183a,195a
1974 29,171,216,260,181a,196a
1975 33,171,205,260,184a,193a
1976 26,182,182a,194a
1977 30,170,236,181a,193a

1978 34,170,208,184a,197a
1979 147,171,266,183a,195a
1980 31,171,186a,198a
1981 147,171,183,266,304a
1982 147,181,258,260,266,187a,199a
1983 33,213,189a,201a
1984 25,170,214,182a,200a
1985 29,170,215,181a,195a
1986 34,225,190a,202a
1987 26,171,205,182a,196a
1988 31,226,262,190a,202a
1989 35,171,207,226,262,307a
1990 28,226,190a,202a
1991 32,170,209,184a,196a
1992 36,170,210,183a,193a
1993 29,171,211,181a,197a
1994 33,171,212,184a,194a
1995 26,171,213,182a,198a
1996 162,214,250,261,183a,194a
1997 34,170,215,261,183a,198a
1998 27,170,183a,195a
1999 31,239,251,184a,199a

27th May

1930 26,170,207,184a,193a
1931 31,170,208,182a,197a
1932 36,170,209,184a,194a
1933 28,171,303a
1934 32,171,211,181a,194a
1935 25,171,212,184a,199a
1936 29,171,183a,195a
1937 33,170,214,181a,200a
1938 26,184,182a,194a
1939 162,182,182a,194a
1940 35,184,182a,194a
1941 147,171,266,183a,195a
1942 31,171,266,183a,195a
1943 26,170,183a,195a
1944 147,170,261,266,302a
1945 33,170,220,181a,193a
1946 147,171,258,260,266,183a,195a
1947 30,171,183a,195a
1948 34,171,183a,195a
1949 147,171,261,266,279,183a,195a
1950 31,170,216,181a,198a
1951 36,170,205,184a,195a
1952 28,182,182a,194a
1953 147,171,258,260,266,183a,195a
1954 157,208,184a,196a
1955 161,208,184a,196a
1956 34,171,209,184a,203a
1957 26,170,210,183a,196a
1958 30,170,211,181a,204a
1959 35,170,233,184a,196a
1960 147,171,266,183a,195a
1961 32,171,215,181a,197a
1962 36,171,216,184a,193a
1963 29,170,248,182a,197a
1964 33,184,234,256,182a,194a
1965 25,170,303a
1966 30,171,186a,198a
1967 34,171,209,184a,199a
1968 147,171,248,266,182a,195a
1969 31,171,186a,198a
1970 36,170,211,262,184a,195a
1971 28,182,182a,194a
1972 32,170,219,249,184a,196a
1973 147,171,260,266,1279,183a,195a
1974 29,171,216,260,181a,196a
1975 34,171,205,184a,193a
1976 26,183,182a,194a
1977 30,170,236,181a,193a
1978 35,170,208,184a,197a
1979 147,171,266,183a,195a
1980 32,171,186a,198a
1981 147,171,183,266,304a
1982 147,181,258,260,266,187a,199a
1983 33,213,189a,201a
1984 25,170,214,183a,200a
1985 30,170,215,181a,195a
1986 34,225,190a,202a
1987 147,171,266,183a,195a
1988 31,171,183a,195a
1989 35,171,207,226,262,307a
1990 28,226,190a,202a
1991 32,170,209,185a,196a
1992 25,171,183a,195a
1993 29,171,181a,197a
1994 34,228,262,190a,202a
1995 26,171,213,182a,198a
1996 162,214,250,261,183a,194a
1997 35,239,258,261,191a,203a
1998 27,170,183a,195a
1999 147,239,251,266,184a,199a

28th May

1930 27,170,183a,195a
1931 31,170,208,182a,197a
1932 36,170,209,184a,194a
1933 28,171,303a
1934 33,171,254,181a,194a
1935 25,171,212,184a,199a
1936 30,171,183a,195a
1937 166,230,246,181a,200a
1938 26,184,182a,194a
1939 31,182,182a,194a
1940 36,184,182a,194a
1941 28,171,183a,195a
1942 147,171,266,183a,195a
1943 25,170,183a,195a
1944 147,170,261,266,302a
1945 33,170,220,181a,193a
1946 147,171,266,183a,195a
1947 30,171,183a,195a
1948 35,172,213,231,184a,198a
1949 147,171,261,266,279,183a,195a

1950 31,170,216,181a,198a
1951 36,170,205,184a,195a
1952 29,182,182a,194a
1953 147,171,259,260,266,183a,195a
1954 157,208,184a,196a
1955 162,208,184a,196a
1956 34,171,209,184a,203a
1957 26,170,210,183a,196a
1958 31,170,211,181a,204a
1959 35,170,233,184a,196a
1960 28,171,183a,195a
1961 32,171,215,181a,197a
1962 36,171,216,184a,193a
1963 29,170,248,182a,197a
1964 33,184,234,256,182a,194a
1965 158,170,259,262,303a
1966 30,171,186a,198a
1967 35,171,209,184a,199a
1968 147,171,266,183a,195a
1969 31,171,186a,198a
1970 36,170,211,262,184a,195a
1971 28,182,182a,194a
1972 33,170,214,184a,196a
1973 147,171,260,266,279,183a,195a
1974 30,171,216,181a,196a
1975 34,171,205,184a,193a
1976 27,170,183a,195a
1977 31,170,236,181a,193a
1978 35,170,208,184a,197a
1979 28,171,209,182a,194a
1980 32,171,186a,198a
1981 147,171,183,266,304a
1982 147,181,258,266,187a,199a
1983 33,213,189a,201a
1984 26,170,237,183a,200a
1985 30,170,215,181a,195a
1986 35,171,216,183a,202a
1987 147,171,266,183a,195a
1988 32,171,183a,195a
1989 36,171,226,262,307a
1990 29,226,190a,202a
1991 33,170,209,185a,196a
1992 25,171,183a,195a
1993 30,171,211,181a,197a
1994 34,228,262,190a,202a
1995 26,171,213,182a,198a
1996 31,170,214,261,183a,194a
1997 35,239,258,261,191a,203a
1998 28,170,216,181a,195a
1999 147,239,251,266,184a,199a

29th May

1930 27,170,183a,195a
1931 32,170,208,182a,197a
1932 25,170,209,184a,194a
1933 29,171,303a
1934 33,171,254,181a,194a
1935 26,171,212,262,184a,199a
1936 30,171,183a,195a
1937 166,230,246,181a,200a
1938 27,170,183a,195a
1939 31,182,182a,194a
1940 36,184,182a,194a
1941 28,171,183a,195a
1942 147,171,266,183a,195a
1943 25,170,183a,195a
1944 147,170,258,261,266,302a
1945 34,170,220,181a,193a
1946 147,171,266,183a,195a
1947 31,171,183a,195a
1948 35,172,213,231,184a,198a
1949 147,171,261,266,279,183a,195a
1950 32,170,216,181a,198a
1951 36,170,205,184a,195a
1952 29,170,206,183a,200a
1953 147,171,258,260,266,183a,195a
1954 158,208,184a,196a
1955 162,208,184a,196a
1956 35,224,247,258,260,183a,203a
1957 27,170,183a,195a
1958 31,170,211,181a,204a
1959 168,248,184a,196a
1960 28,171,183a,195a
1961 32,172,172i,215,181a,197a
1962 25,171,216,184a,194a
1963 29,170,248,182a,197a
1964 166,184,259,262,182a,194a
1965 158,170,259,262,303a
1966 31,171,183a,195a
1967 35,171,209,184a,199a
1968 28,171,183a,195a
1969 32,171,186a,198a
1970 36,170,211,262,184a,195a
1971 29,182,261,182a,194a
1972 33,171,183a,195a
1973 147,171,266,279,183a,195a
1974 162,216,184a,196a
1975 34,1711205,184a,193a
1976 27,170,183a,195a
1977 31,170,236,181a,193a
1978 36,170,208,184a,197a
1979 28,171,209,182a,194a
1980 33,171,186a,198a
1981 147,183,266,187a,199a
1982 147,181,266,187a,199a
1983 34,213,189a,201a
1984 26,170,237,183a,200a
1985 31,170,215,181a,195a
1986 35,171,216,184a,202a
1987 147,171,266,183a,195a
1988 32,171,183a,195a
1989 36,170,226,262,307a
1990 29,226,190a,202a
1991 33,170,209,185a,196a
1992 26,171,183a,195a
1993 30,171,211,181a,197a
1994 35,194,228,259,262,184a,194a
1995 147,171,266,183a,195a

1996 31,170,214,261,183a,194a
1997 36,170,215,183a,198a
1998 28,170,216,181a,195a
1999 147,239,251,266,184a,199a

30th May

1930 160,207,184a,196a
1931 32,170,208,182a,197a
1932 25,170,209,184a,194a
1933 29,171,303a
1934 34,171,254,181a,194a
1935 158,228,254,259,262,184a,196a
1936 31,171,183a,195a
1937 35,170,214,181a,200a
1938 27,170,183a,195a
1939 32,182,182a,194a
1940 36,184,182a,194a
1941 28,172,183a,195a
1942 147,171,266,183a,195a
1943 25,170,183a,195a
1944 147,170,258,261,266,302a
1945 34,170,220,181a,193a
1946 147,171,258,260,266,183a,193a
1947 31,171,183a,195a
1948 36,172,213,231,184a,198a
1949 147,171,266,183a,195a
1950 32,170,216,181a,198a
1951 25,170,205,184a,195a
1952 29,170,206,183a,200a
1953 147,171,266,183a,195a
1954 158,208,184a,196a
1955 163,208,184a,196a
1956 35,224,247,258,260,184a,203a
1957 27,1701183a,195a
1958 32,170,211,181a,204a
1959 168,248,184a,196a
1960 29,171,183a,195a
1961 33,172,172i,215,181a,197a
1962 25,171,216,184a,194a
1963 162,170,186a,198a
1964 166,184,259,262,182a,194a
1965 27,170,262,303a
1966 31,171,183a,195a
1967 36,171,209,184a,199a
1968 28,172,183a,195a
1969 32,171,186a,198a
1970 25,170,211,184a,195a
1971 29,182,261,182a,194a
1972 34,171,183a,195a
1973 147,171,266,279,183a,195a
1974 163,181,260,312a
1975 35,235,257,258,260,184a,193a
1976 27,170,183a,195a
1977 32,170,207,181a,193a
1978 36,170,208,184a,197a
1979 28,171,236,182a,194a
1980 33,171,186a,198a
1981 147,183,266,187a,199a
1982 147,181,266,187a,199a
1983 34,213,189a,201a
1984 27,170,183a,195a
1985 31,170,215,181a,195a
1986 36,171,216,184a,202a
1987 160,205,184a,196a
1988 32,171,183a,195a
1989 25,170,226,307a
1990 29,226,238,250,190a,202a
1991 34,227,190a,202a
1992 26,171,183a,195a
1993 31,171,211,181a,197a
1994 35,194,228,259,262,184a,194a
1995 147,171,266,183a,195a
1996 32,170,214,183a,194a
1997 36,170,215,183a,198a
1998 29,170,216,182a,195a
1999 147,239,251,266,184a,199a

31st May

1930 160,207,184a,196a
1931 33,170,208,182a,197a
1932 25,170,209,184a,194a
1933 29,171,303a
1934 34,171,254,181a,194a
1935 158,228,254,259,262,184a,196a
1936 31,171,183a,195a
1937 35,170,214,181a,200a
1938 160,216,184a,196a
1939 32,171,205,182a,203a
1940 25,184,182a,194a
1941 29,172,183a,195a
1942 147,171,266,183a,195a
1943 26,170,183a,195a
1944 147,170,258,261,266,302a
1945 35,170,220,181a,193a
1946 147,171,258,260,266,183a,193a
1947 32,171,183a,195a
1948 36,172,213,231,184a,198a
1949 147,171,266,183a,195a
1950 33,170,216,181a,198a
1951 25,170,205,184a,195a
1952 30,170,255,183a,200a
1953 147,171,266,183a,195a
1954 159,224,232,184a,196a
1955 163,208,184a,196a
1956 35,224,247,258,260,184a,203a
1957 28,170,210,183a,196a
1958 32,170,211,181a,204a
1959 25,171,212,184a,196a
1960 29,171,183a,195a
1961 33,172,172i,215,181a,197a
1962 26,171,233,184a,194a
1963 162,170,186a,198a
1964 35,184,234,256,259,262,186a, 194a
1965 27,170,262,303a
1966 32,171,183a,195a

1967 36,171,209,184a,199a
1968 28,172,183a,195a
1969 33,171,186a,198a
1970 25,170,211,184a,195a
1971 162,182,218,256,261,182a,194a
1972 34,171,183a,195a
1973 147,171,260,266,279,183a,195a
1974 163,182,312a
1975 35,235,257,258,260,184a,193a
1976 28,170,206,183a,197a
1977 32,170,207,181a,193a
1978 25,170,208,184a,197a
1979 29,171,236,182a,194a
1980 33,171,186a,198a
1981 147,183,266,187a,199a
1982 147,182,266,187a,199a
1983 35,213,189a,201a
1984 27,170,183a,195a
1985 32,171,195,305a
1986 36,171,216,184a,202a
1987 160,205,184a,196a
1988 33,171,183a,195a
1989 25,170,226,307a
1990 162,226,190a,202a
1991 34,227,190a,202a
1992 147,171,266,183a,195a
1993 31,171,211,181a,197a
1994 168,259,262,184a,194a
1995 28,171,213,182a,198a
1996 32,170,214,183a,194a
1997 25,170,215,261,183a,198a
1998 29,170,216,182a,195a
1999 147,239,251,266,184a,199a

1st June

1930 29,170,207,184a,193a
1931 33,170,208,182a,197a
1932 26,184,182a,194a
1933 30,171,303a
1934 35,172,172i,211,181a,194a
1935 159,228,254,259,262,184a,196a
1936 31,171,183a,195a
1937 36,170,214,181a,200a
1938 160,216,184a,196a
1939 33,171,254,182a,203a
1940 25,184,182a,194a
1941 29,172,172i,183a,195a
1942 147,171,266,183a,195a
1943 26,170,183a,195a
1944 31,170,258,261,302a
1945 35,170,220,231,181a,193a
1946 28,171,258,260,301a
1947 32,171,183a,195a
1948 36,172,172i,213,231,184a,198a
1949 147,171,258,261,266,183a,195a
1950 33,170,216,181a,198a
1951 26,170,205,184a,195a
1952 147,171,266,183a,195a
1953 147,171,266,183a,195a
1954 159,208,184a,196a
1955 163,208,184a,196a
1956 36,171,209,260,184a,203a
1957 28,170,210,183a,196a
1958 33,170,211,182a,204a
1959 25,171,212,184a,197a
1960 29,171,183a,195a
1961 34,172,172i,215,181a,197a
1962 26,171,233,184a,194a
1963 31,170,248,182a,197a
1964 35,184,234,256,259,262,182a,
194a
1965 28,170,262,303a
1966 32,171,262,183a,195a
1967 36,172,172i,209,184a,199a
1968 29,172,172i,183a,195a
1969 33,171,186a,198a
1970 26,184,262,182a,194a
1971 162,182,261,182a,194a
1972 34,171,183a,195a
1973 147,171,260,266,279,183a,195a
1974 164,216,184a,196a
1975 36,171,205,260,184a,193a
1976 28,170,206,183a,197a
1977 165,221,249,181a,193a
1978 25,170,208,184a,197a
1979 29,171,236,182a,194a
1980 34,172,172i,186a,198a
1981 147,183,266,187a,199a
1982 31,182,187a,199a
1983 167,213,189a,201a
1984 28,170,237,183a,200a
1985 32,195,188a,200a
1986 25,171,216,184a,202a
1987 29,172,172i,205,182a,196a
1988 33,171,183a,195a
1989 158,170,226,259,262,307a
1990 162,226,190a,202a
1991 34,227,190a,202a
1992 147,171,266,183a,195a
1993 32,171,211,181a,197a
1994 168,228,259,262,184a,194a
1995 28,171,213,182a,198a
1996 33,170,214,261,183a,194a
1997 25,170,215,261,183a,198a
1998 147,171,266,183a,195a
1999 147,239,251,266,184a,199a

2nd June

1930 29,170,207,184a,193a
1931 166,226,246,182a,197a
1932 26,184,182a,194a
1933 30,171,303a
1934 35,172,172i,229,182a,194a
1935 159,228,254,259,262,184a,196a
1936 32,171,183a,195a
1937 36,170,214,181a,200a

1938 29,170,216,184a,195a
1939 33,171,254,182a,203a
1940 158,184,182a,194a
1941 30,172,172i,183a,195a
1942 147,171,266,183a,195a
1943 27,170,183a,195a
1944 31,170,258,261,302a
1945 35,170,220,231,181a,193a
1946 28,171,258,260,301a
1947 32,171,183a,195a
1948 25,172,172i,213,231,184a,198a
1949 147,171,258,261,266,183a,195a
1950 166,170,222,255,182a,198a
1951 26,170,205,184a,195a
1952 147,171,266,183a,195a
1953 147,171,260,266,279,183a,195a
1954 159,208,184a,196a
1955 164,224,232,184a,196a
1956 36,171,209,260,184a,203a
1957 147,266,185a,197a
1958 33,170,211,182a,204a
1959 25,171,212,184a,197a
1960 30,171,183a,195a
1961 34,172,172i,215,181a,197a
1962 147,171,266,183a,195a
1963 31,170,248,182a,197a
1964 36,184,234,256,259,262,182a, 194a
1965 28,171,262,303a
1966 33,171,183a,195a
1967 25,172,172i,209,184a,199a
1968 29,172,172i,183a,195a
1969 166,171,186a,198a
1970 26,184,262,182a,194a
1971 162,182,261,182a,194a
1972 35,171,183a,195a
1973 147,171,260,266,279,183a,195a
1974 164,216,184a,196a
1975 36,171,205,260,184a,193a
1976 29,170,206,183a,197a
1977 165,221,249,181a,193a
1978 26,170,208,184a,197a
1979 30,171,236,182a,194a
1980 34,172,172i,186a,198a
1981 27,172,172i,183,304a
1982 31,182,187a,199a
1983 167,213,189a,201a
1984 28,170,237,183a,200a
1985 33,171,183a,195a
1986 25,171,216,184a,202a
1987 29,172,172i,205,182a,196a
1988 34,171,226,307a
1989 158,170,226,259,262,307a
1990 31,226,238,250,190a,202a
1991 35,170,209,184a,197a
1992 28,171,183a,195a
1993 32,172,172i,211,181a,197a
1994 168,228,259,262,184a,194a
1995 28,171,203,182a,198a
1996 33,170,214,261,183a,194a
1997 26,170,215,261,183a,198a
1998 147,171,266,183a,195a
1999 147,239,251,266,184a,199a

3rd June

1930 162,226,246,184a,194a
1931 166,226,246,182a,197a
1932 147,171,266,183a,195a
1933 31,171,303a
1934 35,227,182a,195a
1935 160,212,228,259,262,194a,196a
1936 32,171,183a,195a
1937 36,170,214,181a,200a
1938 29,170,216,184a,195a
1939 33,171,254,182a,203a
1940 158,184,182a,194a
1941 30,172,172i,183a,195a
1942 35,171,266,183a,195a
1943 27,170,183a,195a
1944 147,170,266,302a
1945 36,170,210,231,181a,193a
1946 147,171,258,260,266,302a
1947 33,172,172i,212,231,182a,194a
1948 25,172,172i,213,231,184a,198a
1949 147,171,258,261,266,183a,195a
1950 166,170,222,255,182a,198a
1951 26,170,205,184a,195a
1952 31,171,183,304a
1953 147,171,260,266,279,183a,195a
1954 160,224,232,267,184a,196a
1955 164,224,232,184a,196a
1956 25,171,209,260,184a,204a
1957 147,266,185a,197a
1958 34,170,211,182a,204a
1959 26,171,212,184a,197a
1960 30,172,172i,214,183a,193a
1961 35,172,172i,215,181a,197a
1962 147,171,266,183a,195a
1963 31,170,234,256,186a,198a
1964 36,184,234,256,259,262,182a, 194a
1965 29,171,303a
1966 33,171,183a,195a
1967 25,172,172i,209,184a,199a
1968 30,172,172i,303a
1969 166,171,186a,198a
1970 27,170,211,262,184a,196a
1971 31,182,261,182a,194a
1972 35,171,183a,195a
1973 147,171,260,266,279,183a,195a
1974 164,216,184,196a
1975 36,171,205,260,184a,193a
1976 29,170,206,183a,197a
1977 34,170,236,181a,193a
1978 26,170,208,184a,197a
1979 30,171,236,182a,194a
1980 35,172,172i,186a,198a
1981 27,172,172i,183,304a

1982 147,182,266,187a,199a
1983 36,213,189a,201a
1984 29,170,214,183a,200a
1985 33,171,183a,195a
1986 25,171,216,184a,202a
1987 29,172,172i,205,182a,196a
1988 34,171,226,307a
1989 27,170,226,262,307a
1990 31,226,238,250,190a,202a
1991 35,170,209,184a,197a
1992 28,171,183a,195a
1993 32,172,172i,211,181a,197a
1994 25,228,184a,194a
1995 29,171,213,182a,198a
1996 166,214,217,261,190a,202a
1997 26,170,215,261,183a,198a
1998 147,171,266,183a,195a
1999 147,239,251,266,184a,199a

4th June

1930 162,226,246,184a,194a
1931 35,170,208,182a,197a
1932 147,171,266,183a,195a
1933 31,171,303a
1934 36,172172i,229,182a,195a
1935 160,212,228,259,262,184a,196a
1936 33,171,183a,195a
1937 25,182,230,246,182a,194a
1938 30,170,217,184a,195a
1939 34,171,254,182a,203a
1940 158,184,182a,194a
1941 31,172,172i,183a,195a
1942 35,171,266,183a,195a
1943 160,170,301a
1944 147,170,266,302a
1945 36,171,183a,195a
1946 147,171,258,260,266,302a
1947 33,172,172i,212,231,182a,194a
1948 26,172,172i,213,231,184a,198a
1949 147,171,258,261,266,183a,195a
1950 35,170,255,182a,198a
1951 27,170,183a,195a
1952 31,171,183,304a
1953 147,171,258,260,266,183a,195a
1954 160,224,232,267,184a,196a
1955 165,208,184a,196a
1956 25,171,209,260,184a,204a
1957 30,170,210,183a,196a
1958 34,170,211,182a,204a
1959 26,171,212,184a,197a
1960 31,172,172i,214,183a,193a
1961 35,172,172i,215,181a,197a
1962 28,171,233,184a,194a
1963 32,170,234,256,186a,198a
1964 36,184,234,256,259,262,182a, 194a
1965 29,171,303a
1966 33,171,183a,195a
1967 26,172,172i,209,184a,199a
1968 30,172,172i,303a
1969 35,171,186a,198a
1970 27,170,211,262,184a,196a
1971 31,182,182a,194a
1972 36,171,183a,195a
1973 147,172,258,260,266,183a,195a
1974 165,216,184a,196a
1975 25,193,260,181a,193a
1976 30,170,206,183a,197a
1977 34,170,236,181a,193a
1978 26,171,208,184a,197a
1979 31,171,236,182a,194a
1980 35,172,172i,186a,198a
1981 147,183,266,187a,199a
1982 147,182,266,187a,199a
1983 36,213,189a,201a
1984 29,170,214,183a,200a
1985 34,171,183a,195a
1986 26,171,216,184a,202a
1987 30,172,162i,205,182a,196a
1988 35,171,183a,195a
1989 27,170,226,262,307a
1990 32,226,238,250,190a,202a
1991 36,170,209,184a,197a
1992 28,171,183a,195a
1993 33,172,172i,211,181a,197a
1994 25,228,184,194a
1995 29,171,213,182a,198a
1996 166,214,217,261,190a,202a
1997 27,170,215,184a,198a
1998 31,171,183a,195a
1999 35,239,191a,203a

5th June

1930 31,170,229,184a,192a
1931 35,170,208,182a,197a
1932 147,171,266,183a,195a
1933 32,171,303a
1934 36,172,172i,229,182a,195a
1935 161,212,184a,196a
1936 33,171,183a,195a
1937 25,182,230,246,182a,194a
1938 30,170,217,184a,195a
1939 34,171,254,182a,203a
1940 159,184,292a
1941 31,172,172i,183,195a
1942 147,171,266,183a,195a
1943 160,170,301a
1944 147,170,266,302a
1945 25,171,183a,195a
1946 147,171,266,183a,195a
1947 34,172,172i,212,231,182a,194a
1948 26,172,172i,213,231,184a,198a
1949 31,171,261,279,183a,195a
1950 35,170,255,182a,198a
1951 27,170,183a,195a
1952 147,171,266,183a,195a

1953 147,171,266,183a,195a
1954 161,208,184a,196a
1955 165,208,184a,196a
1956 25,171,209,260,184a,204a
1957 30,170,210,183a,196a
1958 35,170,211,182a,204a
1959 147,171,266,183a,195a
1960 31,172,172i,214,183a,193a
1961 36,172,172i,215,181a,197a
1962 28,171,233,184a,194a
1963 32,170,234,256,186a,198a
1964 25,184,234,256,182a,194a
1965 30,171,262,303a
1966 34,171,262,183a,195a
1967 26,172,172i,209,184a,199a
1968 31,172,172i,183a,195a
1969 35,171,186a,198a
1970 160,211,262,184a,196a
1971 32,182,182a,194a
1972 36,171,183a,195a
1973 147,172,172i,258,260,266,183a,195a
1974 165,216,184a,196a
1975 25,193,260,181a,193a
1976 30,170,236,183a,197a
1977 35,170,236,181a,193a
1978 147,171,260,266,183a,195a
1979 31,171,236,182a,194a
1980 36,172,172i,186a,198a
1981 28,184,258,260,312a
1982 147,182,212,266,332a
1983 25,213,189a,201a
1984 29,170,214,183a,200a
1985 34,171,183a,195a
1986 26,171,216,184a,202a
1987 30,172,172i,205,182a,196a
1988 35,171,183a,195a
1989 160,226,262,315a
1990 32,226,238,250,190a,202a
1991 36,171,209,184a,197a
1992 29,171,183a,195a
1993 33,172,172i,211,181a,197a
1994 26,228,259,262,184a,194a
1995 30,171,213,182a,198a
1996 35,170,214,261,183a,194a
1997 27,170,215,184a,198a
1998 31,171,183a,195a
1999 35,239,191a,203a

6th June

1930 31,170,229,184a,192a
1931 35,170,208,182a,197a
1932 160,209,184a,196a
1933 32,171,303a
1934 25,172,172i,211,182a,195a
1935 161,212,184a,196a
1936 34,171,183a,195a
1937 158,182,182a,194a
1938 31,170,217,184a,195a
1939 35,171,254,182a,203a
1940 159,184,292a
1941 32,172,172i,183a,195a
1942 147,171,266,183a,195a
1943 160,170,301a
1944 147,170,258,261,266,302a
1945 25,171,183a,195a
1946 147,171,266,183a,195a
1947 34,172,172i,212,231,182a,194a
1948 27,172,172i,183a,195a
1949 31,171,261,279,183a,195a
1950 36,170,255,182a,198a
1951 160,205,184a,196a
1952 147,171,266,183a,195a
1953 147,172,172i,266,183a,195a
1954 161,208,184a,196a
1955 165,208,184a,196a
1956 26,171,209,184a,204a
1957 31,170,210,183a,196a
1958 35,171,211,182a,204a
1959 147,171,266,183a,195a
1960 32,172,172i,214,183a,193a
1961 36,172,172i,215,182a,197a
1962 29,171,216,184a,194a
1963 33,170,234,256,186a,198a
1964 25,184,234,256,182a,194a
1965 30,171,262,303a
1966 34,171,262,183a,195a
1967 26,172,172i,209,184a,199a
1968 31,172,172i,183a,195a
1969 36,171,218,234,256,186a,198a
1970 160,211,262,184a,196a
1971 32,182,182a,194a
1972 25,171,183a,195a
1973 147,219,235,257,258,260,266, 184a,204a
1974 166,216,184a,196a
1975 26,171,220,185a,193a
1976 30,170,236,183a,197a
1977 35,182,182a,194a
1978 147,171,260,266,183a,195a
1979 31,171,236,182a,194a
1980 36,172,172i,186a,198a
1981 147,184,258,260,266,187a,199a
1982 147,182,212,266,332a
1983 157,213,258,261,189a,201a
1984 30,170,237,183a,200a
1985 35,171,183a,195a
1986 27,172,172i,216,184a,202a
1987 31,172,172i,205,182a,196a
1988 36,171,183a,195a
1989 160,226,262,315a
1990 32,226,238,250,190a,202a
1991 147,266,185a,197a
1992 29,171,183a,195a
1993 34,228,190a,202a
1994 26,228,259,262,184a,194a
1995 30,171,213,182a,198a
1996 35,170,214,261,183a,194a
1997 28,170,215,184a,198a

1998 147,171,266,183a,195a
1999 147,239,251,266,185a,199a

7th June

1930 32,170,229,184a,192a
1931 36,170,208,182a,197a
1932 160,209,184a,196a
1933 33,171,303a
1934 25,172,172i,211,182a,195a
1935 161,212,184a,196a
1936 34,171,183a,195a
1937 158,182,182a,194a
1938 163,216,184a,196a
1939 35,171,254,182a,203a
1940 160,184,292a
1941 32,172,172i,183a,195a
1942 147,171,266,183a,195a
1943 29,170,183a,195a
1944 147,170,258,261,266,302a
1945 26,171,183a,195a
1946 147,171,266,183a,195a
1947 34,172,172i,212,231,182a,194a
1948 27,172,172i,183a,195a
1949 147,171,266,183a,195a
1950 36,170,255,182a,198a
1951 28,170,205,185a,195a
1952 147,171,266,183a,195a
1953 147,172,172i,266,183a,195a
1954 162,208,184a,196a
1955 166,208,184a,196a
1956 26,171,209,184a,204a
1957 31,170,210,184a,196a
1958 35,171,248,182a,193a
1959 147,171,266,302a
1960 32,172,172i,214,183a,193a
1961 25,172,172i,215,182a,197a
1962 29,171,216,184a,194a
1963 33,170,234,256,186a,198a
1964 158,184,259,262,182a,194a
1965 30,171,262,303a
1966 35,171,262,183a,195a
1967 27,172,172i,209,185a,199a
1968 31,172,172i,183a,195a
1969 36,171,218,234,256,186a,198a
1970 160,211,262,184a,196a
1971 32,171,249,182a,203a
1972 25,171,183a,195a
1973 147,219,235,257,266,184a,204a
1974 166,216,183a,196a
1975 26,171,220,195a,193a
1976 31,170,236,183a,197a
1977 36,182,182a,194a
1978 160,208,260,184a,196a
1979 32,171,209,182a,194a
1980 25,172,172i,186a,198a
1981 147,184,258,260,266,187a,199a
1982 147,182,212,266,332a
1983 157,213,258,261,189a,201a
1984 30,170,237,183a,200a
1985 35,171,183a,195a
1986 27,172,172i,216,184a,202a
1987 31,172,172i,205,182a,196a
1988 36,171,183a,195a
1989 29,226,190a,202a
1990 33,226,190a,202a
1991 147,266,185a,197a
1992 30,171,210,183a,193a
1993 34,228,190a,202a
1994 26,228,259,262,184a,194a
1995 30,171,213,182a,198a
1996 36,170,214,183a,194a
1997 28,170,215,184a,198a
1998 147,171,266,183a,195a
1999 36,172,172i,218,185a,199a

8th June

1930 32,170,229,184a,192a
1931 36,170,208,182a,197a
1932 29,171,209,184a,194a
1933 33,171,303a
1934 26,182,262,182a,194a
1935 30,172,172i,212,185a,199a
1936 34,171,183a,195a
1937 27,182,230,246,182a,194a
1938 163,216,184a,196a
1939 35,171,254,182a,203a
1940 160,184,292a
1941 33,172,172i,207,184a,204a
1942 147,171,266,183a,195a
1943 147,170,266,302a
1944 147,170,258,261,266,302a
1945 26,171,183a,195a
1946 31,171,184,258,260,304a
1947 35,172,172i,231,182a,194a
1948 160,213,184a,196a
1949 147,171,266,183a,195a
1950 36,170,255,182a,198a
1951 28,170,205,185a,195a
1952 147,171,266,183a,195a
1953 147,172,172i,266,183a,195a
1954 162,208,184a,196a
1955 166,208,184a,196a
1956 147,171,260,266,183a,195a
1957 31,170,210,184a,196a
1958 36,171,211,182a,193a
1959 147,266,185a,197a
1960 33,172,172i,214,183a,193a
1961 25,172,172i,215,182a,197a
1962 29,171,216,184a,194a
1963 33,170,234,256,186a,198a
1964 158,184,259,262,182a,194a
1965 31,171,262,303a
1966 35,172,172i,208,262,182a,195a
1967 27,172,172i,209,185a,199a
1968 32,172,172i,183a,195a
1969 25,171,186a,198a

1970 29,170,211,184a,196a
1971 33,171,212,182a,203a
1972 26,171,183a,195a
1973 147,219,235,257,266,184a,204a
1974 166,216,184a,196a
1975 147,171,258,260,266,183a,195a
1976 31,170,236,183a,197a
1977 36,182,182a,194a
1978 160,208,260,184a,196a
1979 32,171,209,182a,194a
1980 25,172,172i,186a,198a
1981 147,184,266,187a,199a
1982 147,182,266,187a,199a
1983 26,213,261,189a,201a
1984 31,171,183a,195a
1985 35,171,183a,195a
1986 27,172,172i,216,184a,202a
1987 32,172,172i,205,182a,196a
1988 25,171,183a,195a
1989 29,226,190a,202a
1990 33,226,190a,202a
1991 147,266,185a,197a
1992 30,171,210,183a,193a
1993 35,172,172i,211,182a,197a
1994 27,228,259,262,184a,194a
1995 31,171,213,182a,198a
1996 36,170,214,183a,194a
1997 28,170,215,184a,198a
1998 147,171,266,183a,195a
1999 25,172,172i,218,185a,199a

9th June

1930 32,170,229,184a,192a
1931 25,170,208,182a,197a
1932 29,171,209,184a,194a
1933 166,172,172i,311a
1934 26,182,262,182a,194a
1935 30,172,172i,212,185a,199a
1936 35,171,183a,195a
1937 27,182,230,246,182a,196a
1938 164,216,184a,196a
1939 171,205,182a,203a
1940 161,184a,292a
1941 33,172,172i,207,184a,204a
1942 147,171,266,183a,195a
1943 147,170,266,302a
1944 147,170,258,261,266,302a
1945 147,171,266,183a,195a
1946 31,171,184,258,260,304a
1947 35,172,172i,212,231,182a,194a
1948 160,213,184a,196a
1949 147,171,266,183a,195a
1950 25,170,216,182a,198a
1951 147,171,266,302a
1952 147,171,266,183a,195a
1953 147,172,172i,266,183a,195a
1954 163,208,184a,196a
1955 167,208,184a,196a
1956 147,171,260,266,183a,195a
1957 32,170,210,184a,196a
1958 36,171,211,182a,193a
1959 147,266,185a,197a
1960 33,172,172i,214,183a,193a
1961 26,172,172i,215,182a,197a
1962 30,171,233,184a,194a
1963 166,170,186a,198a
1964 27,184,234,256,259,262,182a, 194a
1965 31,171,262,303a
1966 35,172,172i,208,262,182a,195a
1967 28,172,172i,209,185a,199a
1968 32,172,172i,183a,195a
1969 25,171,186a,198a
1970 29,170,211,284a,196a
1971 33,171,212,182a,203a
1972 26,171,183a,195a
1973 31,184,258,260,187a,199a
1974 35,172,172i,216,182a,197a
1975 147,171,258,260,266,183a,195a
1976 32,170,236,183a,197a
1977 36,182,182a,194a
1978 160,208,260,184a,196a
1979 33,172,172i,209,182a,194a
1980 26,172,172i,186a,198a
1981 147,184,266,187a,199a
1982 147,182,266,187a,199a
1983 26,213,261,189a,201a
1984 31,171,183a,195a
1985 36,171,237,182a,196a
1986 160,216,184a,196a
1987 32,172,172i,205,182a,196a
1988 25,171,183a,195a
1989 29,226,190a,202a
1990 33,226,190a,202a
1991 147,266,185a,197a
1992 31,171,183a,195a
1993 35,172,172i,182a,197a
1994 27,228,259,262,184a,194a
1995 31,171,213,182a,198a
1996 25,170,214,261,183a,194a
1997 29,171,215,184a,198a
1998 147,171,266,183a,195a
1999 25,172,172i,218,185a,199a

10th June

1930 33,170,207,184a,194a
1931 25,170,208,182a,197a
1932 30,171,209,184a,194a
1933 166,172,172i,311a
1934 27,172,172i,211,262,183a,195a
1935 31,172,172i,212,185a,199a
1936 35,171,183a,195a
1937 28,182,230,246,182a,194a
1938 164,216,184a,196a
1939 36,171,205,182a,203a
1940 161,184,292a

1941 34,172,172i,255,184a,204a
1942 26,171,183a,195a
1943 30,170,183a,195a
1944 35,170,258,261,302a
1945 147,171,266,183a,195a
1946 164,211,260,184a,196a
1947 36,172,172i,212,231,182a,194a
1948 160,213,184a,196a
1949 147,171,266,183a,195a
1950 25,170,216,182a,198a
1951 147,171,266,302a
1952 147,171,266,183a,195a
1953 27,172,172i,183a,195a
1954 163,208,184a,196a
1955 167,208,184a,196a
1956 147,260,266,185a,197a
1957 32,170,210,184a,196a
1958 157,225,233,255,182a,193a
1959 147,266,185a,197a
1960 34,172,172i,213,183a,193a
1961 26,172,172i,215,182a,197a
1962 30,171,233,183a,194a
1963 166,170,186a,198a
1964 147,171,262,266,183a,195a
1965 32,171,262,303a
1966 168,228,248,259,262,182a,195a
1967 28,172,172i,209,185a,199a
1968 33,172,172i,209,183a,195a
1969 25,171,186a,198a
1970 30,170,211,262,184a,196a
1971 34,171,249,182a,203a
1972 147,171,266,183a,195a
1973 31,184,258,260,187a,199a
1974 35,172,172i,216,182a,197a
1975 147,171,258,260,266,183a,195a
1976 32,170,236,183a,197a
1977 25,182,182a,194a
1978 147,260,266,185a,197a
1979 33,172,172i,209,182a,194a
1980 26,172,172i,186a,198a
1981 31,184,258,260,187a,199a
1982 35,182,197a,199a
1983 27,170,213,258,261,306a
1984 32,171,257,305a
1985 36,171,237,182a,196a
1986 160,216,184a,196a
1987 33,205,189a,201a
1988 26,171,183a,195a
1989 30,226,259,262,190a,202a
1990 34,226,190a,202a
1991 147,266,185a,197a
1992 31,172,172i,210,183a,193a
1993 36,172,172i,211,182a,197a
1994 160,212,259,262,184a,196a
1995 32,171,213,182a,198a
1996 25,170,214,261,183a,194a
1997 29,171,215,184a,198a
1998 147,171,266,183a,195a
1999 26,172,172i,205,185a,199a

11th June

1930 33,170,207,184a,194a
1931 25,171,208,182a,198a
1932 30,171,209,184a,194a
1933 167,172,172i,311a
1934 27,172,172i,211,262,183a,195a
1935 31,172,172i,212,185a,199a
1936 36,171,183a,195a
1937 28,182,230,246,182a,194a
1938 165,216,184a,196a
1939 25,203,181a,193a
1940 161,184,292a
1941 34,172,172i,255,184a,204a
1942 26,171,183a,195a
1943 30,170,183a,195a
1944 35,171,260,261,266,279,302a
1945 28,171,183a,195a
1946 164,211,260,184a,196a
1947 36,172,172i,212,231,182a,194a
1948 147,266,185a,197a
1949 147,171,266,183a,195a
1950 158,182,182a,194a
1951 30,171,183a,195a
1952 35,171,183a,195a
1953 27,172,172i,183a,195a
1954 163,208,184a,196a
1955 167,208,184a,196a
1956 147,260,266,185a,197a
1957 33,170,210,184a,196a
1958 25,171,248,182a,193a
1959 147,266,185a,197a
1960 34,172,172i,213,183a,193a
1961 27,172,172i,215,182a,197a
1962 31,171,233,184a,194a
1963 35,170,234,248,186a,198a
1964 28,171,206,262,184a,194a
1965 32,171,262,303a
1966 168,288,248,259,262,182a,195a
1967 28,172,172i,209,185a,199a
1968 33,172,172i,209,183a,195a
1969 158,171,182,294a
1970 30,170,211,262,184a,196a
1971 34,171,249,182a,203a
1972 147,171,266,183a,195a
1973 147,219,235,257,258,260,266,
184a,204a
1974 36,172,172i,216,182a,197a
1975 28,171,205,260,185a,193a
1976 33,170,236,183a,197a
1977 25,171,183a,195a
1978 147,260,266,185a,197a
1979 34,172,172i,209,182a,194a
1980 27,172,172i,303a
1981 31,184,258,260,187a,199a
1982 35,182,187a,199a
1983 27,170,213,258,261,306a
1984 32,171,257,305a
1985 25,171,215,182a,196a
1986 29,172,172i,216,184a,202a

1987 33,205,189a,201a
1988 26,171,183a,195a
1989 30,226,259,262,190a,202a
1990 34,226,190a,202a
1991 147,171,266,302a
1992 32,172,172i,210,183a,193a
1993 36,172,172i,211,182a,197a
1994 160,212,259,262,184a,196a
1995 32,171,183a,195a
1996 25,170,214,261,183a,194a
1997 30,171,215,184a,198a
1998 147,171,266,183a,195a
1999 26,172,172i,205,185a,199a

12th June

1930 166,226,246,184a,194a
1931 158,226,246,182a,198a
1932 30,171,209,184a,194a
1933 167,172,172i,311a
1934 27,172,172i,211,262,183a,195a
1935 31,172,172i,212,185a,199a
1936 36,171,183a,195a
1937 29,182,230,246,182a,194a
1938 165,216,184a,196a
1939 25,203,181a,193a
1940 162,184a,292a
1941 35,172,172i,255,184a,204a
1942 147,171,266,183a,195a
1943 31,170,183a,195a
1944 147,171,258,260,266,302a
1945 28,171,183a,195a
1946 164,211,260,184a,196a
1947 36,172,172i,212,231,182a,194a
1948 147,266,185a,197a
1949 147,171,266,183a,195a
1950 26,182,182a,194a
1951 30,171,183a,195a
1992 35,171,183a,195a
1953 28,172,172a,301a
1954 164,224,232,184a,196a
1955 168,224,232,184a,196a
1956 147,260,266,185a,197a
1957 33,170,210,184a,196a
1958 25,171,248,182a,193a
1959 147,266,185a,197a
1960 35,172,172i,213,183a,193a
1961 27,172,172i,215,182a,197a
1962 31,171,233,184a,194a
1963 35,170,234,248,186a,198a
1964 28,171,206,262,184a,194a
1965 33,171,303a
1966 25,172,172i,208,182a,195a
1967 147,266,185a,197a
1968 34,172,172i,209,183a,195a
1969 158,171,182,294a
1970 30,170,211,262,184a,196a
1971 35,171,183a,195a
1972 160,172,172i,301a
1973 147,219,235,257,258,260,266, 184a,204a
1974 36,172,172i,216,182a,197a
1975 28,171,205,260,185a,193a
1976 33,170,236,183a,197a
1977 26,171,291a
1978 30,171,208,184a,197a
1979 34,172,172i
1980 27,172,172i,303a
1981 31,184,258,260,187a,199a
1982 35,182,187a,199a
1983 28,213,189a,201a
1984 33,171,183a,195a
1985 25,171,215,182a,196a
1986 29,172,172i,216,184a,201a
1987 33,205,189a,201a
1988 26,171,183a,195a
1989 31,171,226,262,307a
1990 35,226,190a,202a
1991 147,171,266,302a
1992 32,172,162i,210,183a,193a
1993 36,172,172i,211,182a,197a
1994 160,212,259,262,184a,196a
1995 33,171,183a,195a
1996 158,183,250,261,182a,194a
1997 30,171,215,184a,198a
1998 147,171,266,183a,195a
1999 27,239,251,185a,199a

13th June

1930 166,226,246,184a,194a
1931 158,226,246,182a,198a
1932 31,171,209,184a,194a
1933 168,172,172i,311a
1934 28,211,262,184a,196a
1935 164,128,154,185a,199a
1936 25,171,183a,195a
1937 29,182,230,246,182a,194a
1938 165,216,184a,196a
1939 25,203,181a,193a
1940 162,184,292a
1941 35,172,172i,255,184a,204a
1942 147,171,266,183a,195a
1943 31,170,183a,195a
1944 147,171,258,260,266,302a
1945 29,171,183a,195a
1946 165,211,260,184a,196a
1947 25,172,172i,212,231,182a,194a
1948 30,172,172i,213,231,184a,198a
1949 147,171,266,183a,195a
1950 26,182,182a,194a
1951 31,171,183a,195a
1952 36,171,183a,195a
1953 28,172,172i,301a
1954 164,224,232,184a,196a
1955 36,171,260,183a,195a
1956 147,260,266,185a,197a
1957 34,171,210,184a,196a

1958 26,171,248,182a,193a
1959 147,266,185a,197a
1960 35,172,172i,213,183a,193a
1961 27,172,172i,215,182a,197a
1962 31,171,233,184a,194a
1963 36,170,186a,198a
1964 29,171,206,184a,194a
1965 33,171,303a
1966 25,172,172i,208,182a,195a
1967 147,266,185a,197a
1968 34,172,172i,209,183a,195a
1969 147,171,218,234,256,266,303a
1970 31,184,262,187a,199a
1971 35,171,183a,195a
1972 160,172,172i,301a
1973 147,219,235,257,258,260,266, 184a,204a
1974 36,172,172i,216,182a,197a
1975 161,249,258,260,185a,193a
1976 34,170,236,183a,197a
1977 36,171,291a
1978 30,171,208,184a,197a
1979 35,172,172i,209,183a,194a
1980 28,172,172i,186a,198a
1981 147,184,258,260,266,187a,199a
1982 147,182,266,187a,199a
1983 28,213,189a,201a
1984 33,171,183a,195a
1985 25,171,215,182a,196a
1986 29,172,172i,216,184a,202a
1987 34,172,172i,205,183a,196a
1988 147,171,266,183a,195a
1989 31,171,226,262,307a
1990 35,226,190a,202a
1991 147,266,185a,197a
1992 33,172,172i,210,183a,193a
1993 25,172,172i,211,182a,197a
1994 29,228,184a,194a
1995 33,171,183a,195a
1996 26,170,261,183a,195a
1997 30,171,215,184a,198a
1998 35,171,239,308a
1999 27,239,251,185a,199a

14th June

1930 166,226,246,184a,194a
1931 147,171,266,183a,195a
1932 31,171,209,184a,194a
1933 168,172,172i,311a
1934 28,211,262,184a,196a
1935 164,228,254,185a,199a
1936 25,171,183a,195a
1937 162,230,246,182a,200a
1938 166,216,184a,196a
1939 26,172,172i,205,183a,203a
1940 163,184,292a
1941 35,172,172i,255,184a,204a
1942 147,171,266,183a,195a
1943 32,171,183a,195a
1944 147,171,258,260,261,266,302a
1945 29,171,183a,195a
1946 165,211,260,184a,196a
1947 25,172,172i,183a,195a
1948 30,172,172i,213,231,184a,198a
1949 35,171,183a,195a
1950 27,170,255,182a,199a
1951 31,171,183a,195a
1952 36,171,183a,195a
1953 160,207,184a,196a
1954 165,224,232,184a,196a
1955 25,171,260,183a,195a
1956 147,266,185a,197a
1957 34,171,210,184a,196a
1958 26,171,248,182a,193a
1959 147,266,185a,197a
1960 36,172,172i,213,183a,193a
1961 28,172,172i,215,182a,197a
1962 32,171,233,184a,194a
1963 36,170,186a,198a
1964 29,171,206,184a,194a
1965 33,171,303a
1966 25,172,172i,208,182a,195a
1967 30,172,172i,186a,198a
1968 35,171,183a,195a
1969 147,171,218,234,256,266,303a
1970 31,184,211,262,187a,199a
1971 147,171,266,183a,195a
1972 29,172,172i,183a,195a
1973 147,219,235,257,258,260,266, 184a,204a
1974 25,172,172i,216,182a,197a
1975 161,249,258,260,185a,193a
1976 34,171,183a,195a
1977 26,171,291a
1978 30,171,208,184a,198a
1979 35,172,172i,209,183a,194a
1980 28,172,172i,186a,198a
1981 147,184,258,260,266,187a,199a
1982 147,182,266,187a,199a
1983 29,171,213,260,261,306a
1984 34,171,224,307a
1985 26,172,172i,237,182a,196a
1986 30,172,172i,216,184a,202a
1987 35,172,172i,250,183a,196a
1988 147,171,266,183a,195a
1989 31,171,226,262,307a
1990 36,226,190a,202a
1991 147,266,185a,197a
1992 33,172,172i,210,183a,193a
1993 25,172,172i,211,182a,197a
1994 29,228,184a,194a
1995 34,171,228,307a
1996 147,171,258,261,266,183a,195a
1997 31,171,239,184a,198a
1998 35,171,239,308a
1999 28,172,218,185a,199a

15th June

1930 35,171,182a,195a
1931 147,171,266,183a,195a
1932 32,171,209,184a,194a
1933 157,172,172i,311a
1934 29,172,172i,211,82a,195a
1935 33,172,172i,212,185a,199a
1936 26,171,183a,195a
1937 162,230,246,182a,200a
1938 166,216,184a,196a
1939 26,172,172i,205,183a,203a
1940 163,184,292a
1941 36,172,172i,255,184a,204a
1942 28,171,183a,195a
1943 32,171,183a,195a
1944 147,171,258,260,261,266,302a
1945 30,171,183a,195a
1946 166,211,184a,196a
1947 26,172,172i,183a,195a
1948 31,172,172i,213,231,184a,198a
1949 35,171,183a,195a
1950 147,171,266,183a,195a
1951 31,171,183a,195a
1952 25,172,172i,206,183a,200a
1953 161,207,184a,196a
1954 165,224,232,184a,196a
1955 25,171,260,183a,195a
1956 147,266,185a,197a
1957 34,171,210,184a,196a
1958 147,171,266,183a,195a
1959 147,266,185a,197a
1960 36,172,172i,213,183a,193a
1961 28,172,172i,215,182a,197a
1962 32,171,233,184a,194a
1963 25,171,303a
1964 162,171,259,262,186a,198a
1965 34,171,262,303a
1966 26,172,172i,209,262,182a,195a
1967 30,172,172i,186a,198a
1968 35,171,183a,195a
1969 28,171,218,234,256,186a,198a
1970 32,171,211,262,184a,196a
1971 147,171,266,183a,195a
1972 29,172,172i,183a,195a
1973 147,219,235,257,258,260,266,
184a,204a
1974 24,172,172i,216,182a,197a
1975 30,171,220,185a,193a
1976 35,171,183a,195a
1977 147,171,266,183a,195a
1978 31,171,208,184a,198a
1979 36,172,172i,209,183a,194a
1980 28,171,172i,186a,198a
1981 147,184,258,260,266,187a,199a
1982 147,182,266,187a,199a
1983 29,171,213,260,261,306a
1984 34,171,224,307a
1985 26,172,172i,237,182a,196a
1986 30,172,172i,216,184a,202a
1987 35,172,172i,250,183a,196a
1988 28,171,183a,195a
1989 32,171,226,262,307a
1990 36,226,190a,202a
1991 147,266,185a,197a
1992 33,172,172i,210,183a,194a
1993 26,172,172i,211,182a,197a
1994 30,172,172i,212,185a,194a
1995 34,171,228,307a
1996 147,171,258,261,266,183a,195a
1997 31,171,239,184a,198a
1998 35,239,191a,203a
1999 28,172,218,185a,199a

16th June

1930 35,171,183a,195a
1931 147,171,266,183a,195a
1932 32,171,209,184a,194a
1933 157,172,172i,311a
1934 29,172,172i,211,182a,195a
1935 33,172,172i,212,185a,199a
1936 26,171,183a,195a
1937 31,171,217,182a,200a
1938 167,216,184a,196a
1939 27,172,172i,183a,195a
1940 164,184,292a
1941 36,172,172i,255,184a,204a
1942 28,171,183a,195a
1943 33,171,183a,195a
1944 147,171,258,261,266,302a
1945 30,171,183a,195a
1946 166,211,184a,196a
1947 26,172,172i,183a,195a
1948 31,172,172i,213,184a,198a
1949 147,171,266,183a,195a
1950 28,171,255,182a,199a
1951 32,171,183a,195a
1952 25,172,172i,206,183a,200a
1953 161,207,184a,196a
1954 165,224,232,184a,196a
1955 26,171,183a,195a
1956 147,260,266,185a,197a
1957 35,171,210,184a,196a
1958 147,171,266,183a,195a
1959 147,266,185a,197a
1960 36,172,172i,213,183a,193a
1961 147,266,185a,197a
1962 33,171,216,184a,194a
1963 25,171,303a
1964 162,171,259,262,186a,198a
1965 34,172,172i,262,186a,198a
1966 26,172,172i,208,262,182a,195a
1967 31,172,172i,209,185a,199a
1968 36,171,303a
1969 28,171,218,234,256,186a,198a
1970 32,171,211,262,184a,196a
1971 147,171,266,183a,195a
1972 30,172,172i,183a,195a

1973 147,219,235,257,266,184a,204a
1974 26,172,172i,216,182a,197a
1975 30,171,220,185a,193a
1976 25,171,183a,195a
1977 147,171,266,183a,195a
1978 31,171,208,184a,198a
1979 36,172,172i,209,183a,194a
1980 29,172,172i,186a,198a
1981 147,184,258,260,266,187a,199a
1982 147,182,266,187a,199a
1983 147,171,213,258,261,266,306a
1984 35,171,183a,195a
1985 27,172,172i,237,182a,196a
1986 31,172,172i,216,185a,202a
1987 35,172,172i,250,183a,196a
1988 28,171,183a,195a
1989 32,171,226,262,307a
1990 36,226,190a,202a
1991 147,266,185a,197a
1992 166,227,259,262,190a,202a
1993 26,172,172i,211,182a,197a
1994 30,172,172i,212,185a,194a
1995 35,171,183a,195a
1996 147,171,266,183a,195a
1997 32,171,215,184a,198a
1998 36,172,172i,216,182a,195a
1999 29,172,172i,218,185a,199a

17th June

1930 36,171,183a,195a
1931 160,171,301a
1932 165,209,184a,196a
1933 157,172,172i,311a
1934 29,172,172i,211,182a,195a
1935 34,172,172i,212,185a,199a
1936 147,171,266,183a,195a
1937 31,171,217,182a,200a
1938 167,216,184a,196a
1939 27,172,172i,183a,195a
1940 164,184,292a
1941 25,172,172i,207,184a,204a
1942 147,171,266,302a
1943 33,171,183a,195a
1944 147,171,258,261,266,302a
1945 30,171,183a,195a
1946 166,211,184a,196a
1947 27,172,172i,183a,195a
1948 32,172,172i,213,231,184a,198a
1949 147,171,266,183a,195a
1950 28,171,255,182a,199a
1951 32,171,183a,195a
1952 25,172,172i,206,183a,200a
1953 162,207,184a,196a
1954 166,224,232,184a,196a
1955 26,171,183a,195a
1956 147,260,266,185a,197a
1957 35,171,210,184a,196a
1958 147,171,266,183a,195a
1959 147,256,266,320a
1960 25,172,172i,213,183a,193a
1961 147,266,185a,197a
1962 33,171,216,185a,194a
1963 26,171,303a
1964 31,171,262,183a,195a
1965 35,172,172i,262,186a,198a
1966 27,172,172i,162,183a,195a
1967 31,172,172i,209,185a,199a
1968 36,171,303a
1969 28,171,218,234,256,186a,198a
1970 32,171,211,185a,196a
1971 147,171,266,183a,195a
1972 30,172,172i,183a,195a
1973 147,219,235,257,266,184a,204a
1974 26,172,172i,216,182a,197a
1975 31,185,258,260,187a,199a
1976 36,171,183a,195a
1977 28,171,183a,195a
1978 32,171,208,185a,198a
1979 36,172,172i,209,183a,194a
1980 29,172,172i,186a,198a
1981 147,184,258,260,266,187a,199a
1982 147,182,266,187a,199a
1983 147,171,213,2581261,266,306a
1984 35,171,183a,195a
1985 27,172,172i,237,182a,196a
1986 31,172,172i,216,185a,202a
1987 36,172,172i,250,183a,196a
1988 29,171,183a,195a
1989 33,171,226,307a
1990 25,226,190a,202a
1991 147,266,185a,197a
1992 166,227,259,262,190a,202a
1993 26,172,172i,211,182a,197a
1994 31,172,172i,212,185a,194a
1995 35,171,183a,195a
1996 147,171,166,183a,195a
1997 32,171,215,184a,198a
1998 36,172,172i,216,182a,195a
1999 29,172,172i,218,185a,199a

18th June

1930 36,171,183a,195a
1931 160,171,301a
1932 165,309,184a,196a
1933 158,172,172i,311a
1934 30,172,172i,211,262,182a,195a
1935 34,172,172i,212,185a,199a
1936 147,171,266,183a,195a
1937 31,171,217,182a,200a
1938 167,216,184a,196a
1939 28,172,172i,205,183a,203a
1940 165,184,292a
1941 25,172,172i,207,184a,204a
1942 147,171,266,302a
1943 34,171,183a,195a

1944 147,171,258,261,266,302a
1945 31,171,183a,195a
1946 35,258,260,185a,197a
1947 27,172,172i,183a,195a
1948 32,172,172i,213,231,184a,198a
1949 147,171,266,183a,195a
1950 28,171,255,182a,199a
1951 33,171,183a,195a
1952 26,172,172i,255,183a,200a
1953 162,207,184a,196a
1954 166,208,184a,196a
1955 147,171,258,260,266,183a,195a
1956 147,260,266,185a,197a
1957 36,171,210,184a,196a
1958 28,171,211,182a,193a
1959 147,256,266,320a
1960 25,172,172i,213,183a,193a
1961 147,266,185a,197a
1962 34,171,216,185a,194a
1963 26,171,303a
1964 31,171,262,183a,195a
1965 35,172,172i,262,186a,198a
1966 27,172,172i,262,183a,195a
1967 32,172,172i,209,185a,199a
1968 25,171,303a
1969 29,171,218,234,256,186a,198a
1970 33,171,211,185a,196a
1971 147,171,266,183,195a
1972 30,172,172i,183a,195a
1973 147,219,235,257,266,184a,204a
1974 27,172,172i,216,182a,197a
1975 31,185,258,260,187a,199a
1976 36,171,183a,195a
1977 28,171,183a,195a
1978 32,172,172i,208,185a,198a
1979 25,172,172i,209,183a,194a
1980 30,172,172i,186a,198a
1981 147,184,266,187a,199a
1982 147,182,266,187a,199a
1983 31,171,185,213,258,260,261, 356a
1984 36,171,183a,195a
1985 27,172,172i,237,182a,196a
1986 32,172,172i,216,185a,202a
1987 36,172,172i,250,183a,196a
1988 29,171,183a,195a
1989 33,171,226,307a
1990 25,226,190a,202a
1991 147,266,185a,197a
1992 35,172,210,162,183a,194a
1993 27,172,172i,211,182a,197a
1994 31,172,172i,212,185a,194a
1995 36,171,183a,195a
1996 147,171,266,183a,195a
1997 32,171,215,184a,198a
1998 25,172,216,182a,195a
1999 29,172,172i,218,185a,199a

19th June

1930 36,171,183a,195a
1931 29,171,183a,195a
1932 166,209,184a,196a
1933 158,172,172i,311a
1934 30,172,172i,211,162,182a,195a
1935 35,172,172i,212,185a,199a
1936 28,171,183a,195a
1937 32,171,217,182a,200a
1938 36,171,216,185a,196a
1939 28,172,172i,205,183a,203a
1940 165,184,292a
1941 25,172,172i,207,184a,204a
1942 147,171,266,302a
1943 34,171,183a,195a
1944 147,171,258,260,261,266,302a
1945 31,172,172i,231,255,182a,194a
1946 35,258,260,185a,197a
1947 28,172,172i,183a,195a
1948 33,172,172i,213,231,184a,198a
1949 147,171,266,183a,195a
1950 29,171,216,182a,199a
1951 33,171,183a,195a
1952 26,172,172i,255,183a,200a
1953 162,207,184a,196a
1954 167,208,184a,196a
1955 147,171,258,260,266,183a,195a
1956 147,260,266,185a,197a
1957 36,171,210,184a,196a
1958 28,171,211,182a,193a
1959 147,266,185a,197a
1960 26,172,172i,213,183a,193a
1961 30,172,172i,215,182a,197a
1962 34,171,216,185,194a
1963 147,171,266,303a
1964 31,171,262,183a,195a
1965 35,172,172i,262,186a,198a
1966 168,208,259,262,184a,196a
1967 32,172,172i,209,185a,199a
1968 25,171,303a
1969 29,171,218,234,256,186a,198a
1970 33,171,211,185a,196a
1971 147,171,266,183a,195a
1972 31,172,172i,183a,195a
1973 35,219,235,257,258,260,184a, 204a
1974 27,172,172i,216,182,197a
1975 32,171,205,260,185a,193a
1976 36,171,183a,195a
1977 28,171,183a,195a
1978 33,172,172i,208,185a,198a
1979 25,172,172i,209,183a,194a
1980 30,172,172i,186a,198a
1981 147,184,266,187a,199a
1982 147,182,266,187a,199a
1983 31,171,185,213,258,260,261, 356a
1984 36,171,183a,195a
1985 160,196,224,184a,196a

1986 32,172,172i,216,185a,202a
1987 25,172,172i,250,183a,196a
1988 29,171,183a,195a
1989 34,171,226,307a
1990 26,226,190a,202a
1991 147,266,185a,197a
1992 35,172,210,262,184a,194a
1993 27,172,172i,211,182a,197a
1994 164,182,188,200a
1995 36,171,183a,195a
1996 147,171,258,261,266,183a,195a
1997 147,239,266,184a,199a
1998 25,172,216,182a,195a
1999 30,172,172i,205,185a,199a

20th June

1930 25,171,183a,195a
1931 29,171,183a,195a
1932 166,209,184a,196a
1933 159,172,172i,311a
1934 31,211,227,262,182a,195a
1935 35,172,172i,212,185a,199a
1936 28,171,183a,195a
1937 32,171,217,182a,200a
1938 36,171,216,185a,196a
1939 29,172,172i,205,183a,203a
1940 166,184,292a
1941 26,184,182a,194a
1942 30,171,183a,195a
1943 35,171,183a,195a
1944 147,171,258,260,266,302a
1945 32,172,172i,231,255,182a,194a
1946 36,172,172i,211,231,185a,198a
1947 28,172.172i,183a,195a
1948 33,172,172i,213,231,184a,198a
1949 147,171,266,183a,195a
1950 29,171,216,182a,199a
1951 34,171,183a,195a
1952 27,172,172i,183a,195a
1953 31,182,312a
1954 167,208,184a,196a
1955 160,171,260,301a
1956 147,260,266,185a,197a
1957 36,171,210,184a,196a
1958 29,172,172i,211,182a,193a
1959 147,266,185a,197a
1960 26,172,172i,213,182a,194a
1961 30,172,172i,215,182a,197a
1962 34,171,216,185a,194a
1963 147,171,266,303a
1964 32,171,262,183a,195a
1965 168,172,172i,259,262,186a,198a
1966 160,208,259,262,184a,196a
1967 33,172,172i,209,185a,199a
1968 25,171,303a
1969 29,171,218,234,256,186a,198a
1970 34,171,211,185a,196a
1971 147,171,266,183a,195a
1972 31,172,172i,183a,195a
1973 35,219,235,257,258,260,184a, 204a
1974 160,216,184a,196a
1975 32,171,205,260,185a,193a
1976 25,171,183a,195a
1977 29,171,183a,195a
1978 33,172,172i,208,185a,198a
1979 26,172,172i,209,183a,194a
1980 30,172,172i,186a,198a
1981 35,184,258,260,187a,199a
1982 147,171,182,266,304a
1983 147,171,213,258,260,266,306a
1984 36,171,237,184a,200a
1985 160,196,224,184a,196a
1986 33,216,189a,201a
1987 25,172,172i,250,183a,196a
1988 30,171,183a,195a
1989 34,171,226,307a
1990 26,226,190a,202a
1991 147,266,185a,197a
1992 35,172,210,262,184a,194a
1993 28,172,172i,211,182a,197a
1994 164,182,188a,200a
1995 25,171,183a,195a
1996 147,171,258,261,266,182a,195a
1997 147,239,266,184a,199a
1998 26,182,182a,194a
1999 30,172,172i,205,185a,199a

21st June

1930 25,171,183a,195a
1931 30,171,303a
1932 167,209,184a,196a
1933 159,172,172i,311a
1934 31,211,227,262,182a,195a
1935 36,171,212,185a,199a
1936 28,171,183a,195a
1937 33,171,214,182a,200a
1938 25,171,216,185a,196a
1939 29,172,172i,205,183a,203a
1940 166,184,292a
1941 26,184,182a,194a
1942 30,171,183a,195a
1943 35,171,183a,195a
1944 147,171,258,260,266,302a
1945 32,172,172i,231,255,182a,194a
1946 36,172,172i,211,231,185a,198a
1947 147,172,172i,266,302a
1948 33,172,172i,213,231,184a,198a
1949 147,171,266,183a,195a
1950 30,171,216,182a,199a
1951 34,171,183a,195a
1952 159,206,184a,196a
1953 31,182,321a
1954 167,208,184a,196a
1955 160,171,260,301a
1956 148,260,267,185a,197a

1957 25,171,210,184a,196a
1958 29,172,172i,211,182a,193a
1959 147,266,185a,197a
1960 39,172,213,183a,194a
1961 31,172,172i,215,182a,197a
1962 35,171,216,185a,194a
1963 147,171,266,303a
1964 44,171,262,183a,195a
1965 168,172,172i,259,262,186a,198a
1966 29,172,172i,208,182a,195a
1967 33,172,172i,209,185a,199a
1968 158,171,311a
1969 162,171,186a,198a
1970 34,171,211,185a,196a
1971 147,171,266,279,183a,195a
1972 164,214,184a,196a
1973 147,219,235,257,258,260,266,
184a,193a
1974 160,216,184a,196a
1975 165,249,258,260,185a,193a
1976 37,171,206,184a,197a
1977 29,171,183a,195a
1978 34,172,172i,208,185a,198a
1979 26,172,172i,209,182a,194a
1980 43,172,186a,198a
1981 167,184,258,260,312a
1982 147,171,182,266,304a
1983 147,171,213,258,260,266,306a
1984 37,171,214,184a,200a
1985 41,196,224,184a,196a
1986 33,216,189a,201a
1987 26,172,172i,250,183a,196a
1988 42,171,206,183a,204a
1989 46,226,190a,202a
1990 147,171,226,266,307a
1991 147,266,185a,197a
1992 48,210,259,262,184a,196a
1993 148,267,184a,196a
1994 33,172,212,185a,194a
1995 25,171,183a,195a
1996 41,171,183a,195a
1997 46,171,215,184a,199a
1998 26,182,182a,194a
1999 31,239,251,185a,199a

22nd June

1930 38,171,207,254,185a,194a
1931 162,171,311a
1932 167,209,184a,196a
1933 159,172 311a
1934 163,211,262,184a,196a
1935 48,228,254,185a,199a
1936 41,171,183a,195a
1937 45,171,214,254,182a,200a
1938 157,216,184a,196a
1939 42,172,205,183a,203a
1940 167,184,292a
1941 159,207,184a,196a
1942 43,171,183a,195a
1943 47,171,183a,195a
1944 40,171,260,354a
1945 164,210,184a,196a
1946 168,211,184a,196a
1947 148,267,185a,197a
1948 166,213,184a,196a
1949 158,215,184a,196a
1950 42,171,216,232,182a,199a
1951 47,171,222,232,185a,195a
1952 148,267,184a,196a
1953 44,232,184a,196a
1954 48,208,184a,196a
1955 41,209,260,310a
1956 148,260,267,185a,197a
1957 37,233,255,185a,197a
1958 42,172,211,182a,193a
1959 148,263,267,185a,197a
1960 159,213,184a,196a
1961 43,172,215,182a,197a
1962 47,171,216,185a,194a
1963 40,171,186a,198a
1964 45,171,183a,195a
1965 37,172,311a
1966 148,228,248,267,182a,195a
1967 46,172,209,185a,199a
1968 158,171,311a
1969 162,171,186a,198a
1970 47,171,211,185a,196a
1971 159,172,183a,195a
1972 164,214,184a,196a
1973 168,215,260,184a,196a
1974 161,216,184a,196a
1975 165,249,258,260,185a,193a
1976 38,171,206,184a,197a
1977 42,171,207,182a,194a
1978 166,208,184a,196a
1979 39,172,209,183a,194a
1980 43,172,186a,198a
1981 167,184,258,260,312a
1982 40,182,187a,199a
1983 44,213,260,189a,201a
1984 37,224,184a,196a
1985 41,196,224,184a,196a
1986 46,225,263,190a,202a
1987 158,205,184a,196a
1988 43,171,206,183a,204a
1989 47,226,190a,202a
1990 39,226,190a,202a
1991 148,267,185a,197a
1992 48,210,259,262,184a,196a
1993 41,172,211,182a,197a
1994 148,228,259,263,267,185a,193a
1995 38,171,213,183a,198a
1996 42,171,183a,195a
1997 46,171,215,184a,199a
1998 39,172,216,182a,195a
1999 43,172,218,185a,199a

23rd June

1930 38,171,207,254,185a,194a
1931 163,208,184a,196a
1932 48,209,184a,196a
1933 40,172,267,311a
1934 164,211,262,184a,196a
1935 48,228,254,185a,199a
1936 161,213,184a,196a
1937 45,171,214,254,182a,200a
1938 38,259,263,184a,196a
1939 42,172,205,183a,203a
1940 167,184,292a
1941 159,207,184a,196a
1942 43,171,183a,195a
1943 48,171,183a,195a
1944 41,260,310a
1945 165,210,184a,196a
1946 157,211,184a,196a
1947 42,172,212,183a,194a
1948 166,213,184a,196a
1949 158,215,184a,196a
1950 43,182,187a,199a
1951 47,171,222,232,185a,195a
1952 148,267,184a,196a
1953 44,232,184a,196a
1954 48,208,184a,196a
1955 41,209,260,310a
1956 148,267,185a,197a
1957 148,267,185a,197a
1958 42,172,211,182a,193a
1959 148,267,185a,197a
1960 159,213,184a,196a
1961 43,172,215,182a,197a
1962 48,171,216,185a,194a
1963 40,171,186a,198a
1964 45,171,183a,195a
1965 37,172,311a
1966 162,172,259,262,311a
1967 46,172,209,185a,199a
1968 159,171,311a
1969 43,171,218,234,256,186a,198a
1970 47,171,211,185a,196a
1971 160,212,184a,196a
1972 164,214,184a,196a
1973 168,215,260,184a,196a
1974 161,216,184a,196a
1975 165,249,258,260,185a,193a
1976 38,171,206,184a,197a
1977 42,171,207,182a,194a
1978 167,208,184a,196a
1979 39,172,209,183a,194a
1980 44,172,186a,198a
1981 48,184,223,257,258,260,187a, 199a
1982 41,182,187a,199a
1983 165,213,258,260,189a,201a
1984 37,224,184a,196a
1985 42,196,224,184a,196a
1986 46,225,262,190a,202a
1987 159,205,184a,196a
1988 43,171,206,183a,204a
1989 47,226,190a,202a
1990 160,226,315a
1991 148,267,185a,197a
1992 157,210,184a,196a
1993 41,172,211,182a,198a
1994 148,228,259,263,267,190a,202a
1995 38,171,213,183a,198a
1996 42,171,183a,195a
1997 167,239,181a,203a
1998 39,172,216,182a,195a
1999 44,172,218,185a,199a

24th June

1930 39,171,183a,195a
1931 163,208,184a,196a
1932 48,209,184a,196a
1933 40,172,267,311a
1934 164,211,262,184a,196a
1935 37,171,212,254,185a,199a
1936 162,213,184a,196a
1937 166,230,246,182a,200a
1938 38,259,263,184a,196a
1939 43,172,205,183a,203a
1940 167,184,292a
1941 159,207,183a,196a
1942 44,171,183a,195a
1943 48,171,183a,195a
1944 41,260,310a
1945 165,210,184a,196a
1946 157,211,184a,196a
1947 42,172,212,183a,194a
1948 167,213,184a,196a
1949 159,171,301a
1950 43,182,187a,199a
1951 168,205,184a,196a
1952 148,267,184a,196a
1953 44,232,184a,196a
1954 37,208,184a,196a
1955 162,209,184a,196a
1956 148,267,185a,197a
1957 148,267,185a,197a
1958 43,172,211,182a,193a
1959 148,267,185a,197a
1960 148,248,259,263,267,184a,196a
1961 44,172,215,182a,197a
1962 48,171,216,185a,194a
1963 41,171,186a,198a
1964 45,171,183a,195a
1965 37,172,311a
1966 162,172,259,262,311a
1967 47,172,209,185a,199a
1968 159,171,311a
1969 43,171,210,182a,201a
1970 48,171,211,185a,196a
1971 160,212,184a,196a
1972 165,214,184a,196a

1973 157,215,260,184a,196a
1974 162,216,184a,196a
1975 46,171,205,220,185a,193a
1976 38,171,206,184a,197a
1977 43,171,207,182a,194a
1978 167,208,184a,196a
1979 160,209,184a,196a
1980 44,172,186a,198a
1981 48,184,223,257,258,260,187a, 199a
1982 41,182,187,199a
1983 165,213,258,260,189a,201a
1984 38,224,184a,196a
1985 42,196,224,184a,196a
1986 47,172,216,185a,202a
1987 159,205,184a,196a
1988 43,171,206,183a,204a
1989 48,226,190a,202a
1990 160,226,315a
1991 148,267,185a,197a
1992 157,210,184a,196a
1993 162,238,250,259,262,182a,198a
1994 148,228,259,263,267,190a,202a
1995 38,171,213,183a,198a
1996 163,171,183a,195a
1997 167,239,316a
1998 160,216,184a,196a
1999 44,172,218,185a,199a

25th June

1930 39,171,183a,195a
1931 164,208,184a,196a
1932 48,209,184a,196a
1933 161,172,311a
1934 165,211,262,184a,196a
1935 37,171,212,254,185a,199a
1936 162,213,184a,196a
1937 166,230,246,182a,200a
1938 38,259,263,184a,196a
1939 43,172,205,183a,203a
1940 48,184,259,263,292a
1941 148,267,184a,196a
1942 44,171,183a,195a
1943 37,171,183a,195a
1944 41,260,310a
1945 166,210,184a,196a
1946 158,211,184a,196a
1947 43,172,212,183a,194a
1948 167,213,184a,196a
1949 159,171,301a
1950 44,171,232,255,182a,199a
1951 168,205,184a,196a
1952 41,232,184a,196a
1953 165,207,184a,196a
1954 37,208,184a,196a
1955 162,209,184a,196a
1956 148,267,185a,197a
1957 148,267,185a,197a
1958 43,172,211,182a,193a
1959 48,248,259,263,185a,197a
1960 148,248,259,263,267,184a,196a
1961 44,172,215,182a,197a
1962 37,171,216,185a,194a
1963 41,171,186a,198a
1964 46,172,206,262,183a,195a
1965 38,172,259,262,311a
1966 43,208,259,262,184a,196a
1967 47,172,209,185a,199a
1968 159,171,311a
1969 44,171,210,182a,201a
1970 48,171,211,185a,196a
1971 41,172,256,183a,203a
1972 165,214,184a,196a
1973 157,215,260,184a,196a
1974 162,216,184a,196a
1975 46,171,205,220,185a,193a
1976 39,171,206,184a,197a
1977 43,171,207,182a,194a
1978 48,208,184a,196a
1979 160,209,184a,196a
1980 44,172,186a,198a
1981 37,184,223,257,258,260,187a, 199a
1982 41,182,187,199a
1983 46,213,189a,201a
1984 38,224,184a,196a
1985 43,196,224,184a,196a
1986 47,172,216,185a,202a
1987 159,205,184a,196a
1988 44,171,206,183a,204a
1989 48,226,190a,202a
1990 41,226,190a,202a
1991 148,267,185a,197a
1992 157,210,184a,196a
1993 162,238,250,259,262,182a,198a
1994 148,228,267,185a,194a
1995 39,171,183a,195a
1996 163,171,183a,195a
1997 168,215,184a,196a
1998 160,216,184a,196a
1999 44,172,218,185a,199a

26th June

1930 160,207,184a,196a
1931 164,208,184a,196a
1932 157,209,184a,196a
1933 161,172,311a
1934 165,211,262,184a,196a
1935 38,171,212,254,185a,199a
1936 43,254,184a,196a
1937 47,171,217,254,182a,200a
1938 39,216,184a,196a
1939 44,172,205,183a,203a
1940 48,184,259,263,292a
1941 148,267,184a,196a

1942 45,171,183a,195a
1943 37,171,183a,195a
1944 42,209,310a
1945 166,210,184a,196a
1946 158,211,184a,196a
1947 43,172,212,183a,194a
1948 168,213,184a,196a
1949 160,215,184a,196a
1950 44,171,232,255,182a,199a
1951 157,205,184a,196a
1952 41,232,184a,196a
1953 165,207,184a,196a
1954 38,208,184a,196a
1955 162,209,184a,196a
1956 148,160,267,185a,197a
1957 148,267,185a,197a
1958 44,172,211,182a,193a
1959 48,248,259,263,185a,197a
1960 161,213,263,184a,196a
1961 45,172,215,182a,197a
1962 37,171,216,185a,194a
1963 42,171,186a,198a
1964 46,172,206,262,183a,195a
1965 38,172,259,262,311a
1966 43,208,259,262,184a,196a
1967 47,172,209,185a,199a
1968 40,171,311a
1969 44,171,210,182a,201a
1970 37,171,211,185a,196a
1971 41,172,256,183a,203a
1972 166,214,184a,196a
1973 158,215,184a,196a
1974 163,183,260,312a
1975 47,171,205,220,260,185a,193a
1976 39,171,206,184a,197a
1977 44,172,207,182a,194a
1978 48,208,184a,196a
1979 160,209,184a,196a
1980 45,172,186a,198a
1981 37,184,223,257,258,260,187a, 199a
1982 42,183,223,257,187a,199a
1983 46,213,189a,201a
1984 39,224,184a,196a
1985 43,196,224,284a,196a
1986 48,216,259,263,185a,202a
1987 148,267,184a,196a
1988 44,171,206,183a,204a
1989 37,226,190a,202a
1990 41,226,190a,202a
1991 148,267,185a,197a
1992 158,210,259,184a,196a
1993 162,238,250,259,262,182a,198a
1994 148,228,267,185a,194a
1995 39,171,183a,195a
1996 44,171,183a,195a
1997 168,215,184a,196a
1998 41,172,216,183a,195a
1999 45,172,218,185a,199a

27th June

1930 160,208,184a,196a
1931 165,208,184a,196a
1932 157,209,184a,196a
1933 161,173,311a
1934 165,211,262,184a,196a
1935 38,171,212,254,185a,199a
1936 43,254,184a,196a
1937 47,171,254,182a,200a
1938 39,216,184a,196a
1939 44,172,205,183a,203a
1940 157,184,263,292a
1941 161,207,184a,196a
1942 45,171,183a,195a
1943 38,171,183a,195a
1944 42,209,310a
1945 166,210,184a,196a
1946 159,211,184a,196a
1947 43,172,212,183a,194a
1948 168,213,184a,196a
1949 160,215,184a,196a
1950 45,171,222,232,183a,199a
1951 157,205,184a,196a
1952 41,232,184a,196a
1953 166,207,184a,196a
1954 38,208,184a,196a
1955 163,209,260,184a,196a
1956 148,160,267,185a,197a
1957 40,210,310a
1958 44,172,256,183a,193a
1959 148,263,267,185a,197a
1960 161,213,263,184a,196a
1961 45,172,215,182a,197a
1962 38,171,216,185a,194a
1963 42,171,186a,198a
1964 47,172,206,262,183a,195a
1965 39,172,259,262,311a
1966 44,208,183a,195a
1967 48,172,209,185a,199a
1968 40,171,311a
1969 45,171,210,182a,201a
1970 37,171,211,185a,196a
1971 41,172,256,183a,203a
1972 166,214,184a,196a
1973 38,173,215,184a,193a
1974 163,183,260,312a
1975 47,171,205,220,260,185a,193a
1976 160,206,184a,196a
1977 44,172,207,182a,194a
1978 157,208,184a,196a
1979 148,267,185a,197a
1980 45,172,186a,198a
1981 38,184,223,258,187a,199a
1982 42,183,223,257,187a,199a
1983 46,213,189a,201a
1984 39,224,184a,196a
1985 43,196,224,284a,196a
1986 48,173,216,263,185a,202a
1987 148,267,184a,196a

1988 45,206,189a,201a
1989 37,226,190a,202a
1990 42,226,190a,202a
1991 148,227,267,322a
1992 158,238,250,184a,196a
1993 43,172,211,262,182a,198a
1994 148,228,267,185a,194a
1995 39,171,183a,195a
1996 44,171,183a,195a
1997 157,215,184a,196a
1998 41,172,216,183a,195a
1999 165,205,185a,199a

28th June

1930 161,208,184a,196a
1931 165,208,184a,196a
1932 158,209,184a,196a
1933 162,173,311a
1934 166,211,262,184a,196a
1935 39,171,212,254,185a,199a
1936 43,254,184a,196a
1937 47,171,217,254,182a,200a
1938 148,259,263,184a,196a
1939 44,172,205,183a,203a
1940 157,184,263,292a
1941 161,207,184a,196a
1942 46,171,183a,195a
1943 38,171,183a,195a
1944 43,260,310a
1945 167,210,184a,196a
1946 148,267,185a,197a
1947 44,172,212,183a,194a
1948 168,213,184a,196a
1949 161,214,184a,196a
1950 45,171,222,232,184a,199a
1951 158,205,184a,196a
1952 42,232,184a,196a
1953 166,207,184a,196a
1954 39,208,184a,196a
1955 163,209,260,184a,196a
1956 148,260,267,185a,197a
1957 40,210,310a
1958 45,172,256,183a,193a
1959 148,263,185a,197a
1960 161,213,263,184a,196a
1961 46,172,215,182a,197a
1962 38,171,216,185a,194a
1963 43,171,186a,198a
1964 47,172,206,262,183a,195a
1965 39,172,259,262,311a
1966 44,208,183a,195a
1967 48,172,209,185a,199a
1968 161,171,311a
1969 45,171,210,182a,201a
1970 38,171,211,185a,196a
1971 42,172,249,183a,203a
1972 166,214,186a,196a
1973 159,219,235,257,258,260,184a, 193a
1974 163,183,260,312a
1975 48,171,205,220,260,185a,193a
1976 160,206,184a,196a
1977 44,172,207,182a,194a
1978 157,208,184a,196a
1979 148,267,185a,197a
1980 46,172,186a,198a
1981 38,184,223,257,187a,199a
1982 163,183,258,260,187a,199a
1983 167,213,258,260,189a,201a
1984 39,224,184a,196a
1985 44,196,244,313a
1986 157,217,237,263,185a,202a
1987 161,205,184a,196a
1988 45,206,189a,201a
1989 38,226,190a,202a
1990 162,226,315a
1991 148,227,267,322a
1992 39,173,210,184a,194a
1993 43,172,211,262,182a,198a
1994 48,228,259,263,185a,194a
1995 40,171,213,183a,198a
1996 44,171,183a,195a
1997 157,215,184a,196a
1998 42,172,216,183a,195a
1999 46,173,206,185a,199a

29th June

1930 161,208,184a,196a
1931 166,208,184a,196a
1932 158,209,184a,196a
1933 162,173,311a
1934 167,211,227,262,183a,195a
1935 39,171,212,254,185a,199a
1936 44,254,184a,196a
1937 48,171,217,254,182a,200a
1938 41,259,263,184a,196a
1939 45,172,205,183a,205a
1940 157,184,263,292a
1941 162,207,184a,196a
1942 46,171,183a,195a
1943 39,171,183a,195a
1944 43,260,310a
1945 167,210,184a,196a
1946 40,211,310a
1947 44,172,212,183a,194a
1948 37,171,183a,195a
1949 161,214,184a,196a
1950 46,171,232,255,183a,199a
1951 158,205,184a,196a
1952 42,232,184a,196a
1953 167,207,184a,196a
1954 39,208,184a,196a
1955 44,209,260,184a,196a
1956 148,260,267,185a,197a
1957 148,267,310a

1958 45,172,256,183a,193a
1959 37,233,263,185a,197a
1960 162,213,263,184a,196a
1961 166,226,256,182a,198a
1962 39,171,216,185a,194a
1963 43,171,186a,198a
1964 47,172,206,262,183a,195a
1965 160,259,262,184a,196a
1966 44,208,183a,195a
1967 37,172,209,185a,199a
1968 161,171,311a
1969 166,171,218,256,182a,201a
1970 38,171,211,185a,196a
1971 42,172,249,183a,203a
1972 47,173,214,183a,197a
1973 159,219,235,257,258,260,183a, 193a
1974 44,216,260,184a,196a
1975 48,171,205,220,260,185a,193a
1976 148,267,185a,197a
1977 45,172,207,182a,194a
1978 158,208,184a,196a
1979 42,173,209,183a,195a
1980 46,172,186a,198a
1981 159,171,184,258,260,304a
1982 163,183,258,260,187a,199a
1983 47,213,260,189a,201a
1984 160,224,184a,196a
1985 44,196,224,313a
1986 157,217,237,263,185a,202a
1987 161,205,184a,196a
1988 46,171,206,183a,204a
1989 38,226,190a,202a
1990 163,226,315a
1991 148,267,185a,197a
1992 39,173,210,184a,194a
1993 45,228,259,262,182a,198a
1994 48,228,259,263,185a,194a
1995 40,171,213,183a,198a
1996 45,171,183a,195a
1997 38,172,215,185a,199a
1998 42,172,216,183a,195a
1999 46,173,206,185a,199a

30th June

1930 162,208,184a,196a
1931 166,208,184a,196a
1932 158,209,184a,196a
1933 163,173,311a
1934 167,211,227,262,183a,195a
1935 40,212,184a,196a
1936 44,254,184a,196a
1937 48,171,217,254,182a,200a
1938 41,259,263,184a,196a
1939 165,217,255,183a,203a
1940 158,184,259,263,292a
1941 162,207,184a,196a
1942 167,171,183a,195a
1943 39,171,183a,195a
1944 43,260,310a
1945 168,210,184a,196a
1946 40,211,310a
1947 45,172,212,183a,194a
1948 37,171,183a,195a
1949 162,214,184a,196a
1950 46,171,232,255,183a,199a
1951 158,205,184a,196a
1952 163,184,312a
1953 167,207,184a,196a
1954 148,267,184a,196a
1955 44,209,260,184a,196a
1956 148,260,267,185a,197a
1957 41,233,255,310a
1958 45,172,256,183a,193a
1959 148,263,267,185a,197a
1960 162,213,263,184a,196a
1961 47,172,233,182a,198a
1962 39,171,216,185a,194a
1963 43,171,186a,198a
1964 48,228,248,259,262,183a,195a
1965 160,259,262,184a,196a
1966 45,173,208,183a,195a
1967 37,172,209,185a,199a
1968 162,171,311a
1969 166,171,218,256,182a,201a
1970 159,211,184a,196a
1971 163,219,235,183a,203a
1972 47,173,214,183a,197a
1973 40,173,215,260,185a,193a
1974 44,216,260,184a,196a
1975 48,171,205,220,260,185a,193a
1976 148,267,197a
1977 45,172,207,182a,194a
1978 158,208,184a,196a
1979 42,173,209,195a
1980 47,172,186a,198a
1981 159,171,185,258,260,304a
1982 44,183,258,260,187a,199a
1983 48,213,260,189a,201a
1984 160,224,184a,196a
1985 45,173,215,182a,196a
1986 157,217,237,263,185a,202a
1987 161,205,184a,196a
1988 46,171,206,183a,204a
1989 39,171,226,307a
1990 163,226,315a
1991 148,267,185a,197a
1992 160,210,184a,196a
1993 44,172,211,262,182a,198a
1994 148,228,259,263,267,185a,194a
1995 41,171,213,183a,198a
1996 45,171,183a,195a
1997 38,172,215,185a,199a
1998 42,172,216,183a,195a
1999 46,173,206,185a,199a

1st July

1930 162,208,184a,196a
1931 166,208,184a,196a
1932 159,209,184a,196a
1933 163,173,311a
1934 168,211,262,184a,196a
1935 40,212,184a,196a
1936 45,213,184a,196a
1937 157,263,184a,196a
1938 41,259,263,184a,196a
1939 46,173,205,183a,203a
1940 158,184,218,230,246,259,263, 292a
1941 163,207,184a,196a
1942 167,171,183a,195a
1943 148,171,267,302a
1944 44,220,260,310a
1945 168,210,184a,196a
1946 148,267,185a,197a
1947 45,172,260,183a,195a
1948 38,171,183a,195a
1949 162,214,184a,196a
1950 167,247,183a,199a
1951 159,205,184a,196a
1952 163,184,312a
1953 168,207,184a,196a
1954 148,267,184a,196a
1955 44,209,260,184a,196a
1956 148,260,267,185a,197a
1957 41,268,185a,197a
1958 46,172,211,183a,193a
1959 148,263,267,185a,197a
1960 43,173,213,184a,194a
1961 47,172,233,182a,198a
1962 40,171,216,185a,194a
1963 44,171,186a,198a
1964 48,228,248,259,262,183a,195a
1965 41,172,207,185a,199a
1966 45,173,208,183a,195a
1967 37,172,209,185a,199a
1968 162,171,311a
1969 47,171,210,182a,201a
1970 159,211,184a,196a
1971 163,219,235,183a,203a
1972 48,173,214,183a,197a
1973 40,173,215,260,185a,193a
1974 165,216,260,184a,196a
1975 37,171,205,185a,194a
1976 148,267,185a,197a
1977 46,172,207,182a,194a
1978 158,208,184a,196a
1979 42,173,209,183a,195a
1980 47,172,186a,198a
1981 40,185,223,257,258,260,187a, 199a
1982 44,183a,223,257,260,187a,199a
1983 48,213,260,189a,201a
1984 41,214,184a,196a
1985 45,173,215,182a,196a
1986 38,173,216,263,185a,202a
1987 162,205,184a,196a
1988 47,171,206,183a,204a
1989 39,171,226,307a
1990 163,226,315a
1991 148,267,185a,197a
1992 160,210,184a,196a
1993 45,172,211,182a,198a
1994 148,228,259,263,267,185a,194a
1995 41,171,213,183a,198a
1996 46,171,217,307a
1997 39,172,250,185a,199a
1998 163,239,251,183a,195a
1999 47,239,191a,203a

2nd July

1930 163,208,184a,196a
1931 167,208,184a,196a
1932 159,209,184a,196a
1933 164,173,311a
1934 168,211,262,184a,196a
1935 40,212,184a,196a
1936 45,213,184a,196a
1937 157,263,184a,196a
1938 42,259,263,184a,196a
1939 46,173,205,183a,203a
1940 159,184,292a
1941 163,207,184a,196a
1942 48,171,183a,195a
1943 148,171,267,302a
1944 44,220,260,310a
1945 157,201,184a,196a
1946 148,267,185a,197a
1947 45,172,260,183a,195a
1948 38,171,183a,195a
1949 42,171,214,232,185a,195a
1950 167,247,183a,199a
1951 159,205,184a,196a
1952 44,206,184a,196a
1953 168,207,184a,196a
1954 41,224,232,267,310a
1955 165,209,260,184a,196a
1956 148,260,267,185a,197a
1957 148,225,233,255,267,185a,197a
1958 46,172,211,183a,193a
1959 148,263,267,185a,197a
1960 43,173,213,184a,194a
1961 48,172,233,182a,198a
1962 40,171,216,185a,194a
1963 44,171,186a,198a
1964 37,172,206,183a,195a
1965 148,267,185a,197a
1966 46,173,208,183a,195a
1967 38,172,209,185a,199a
1968 162,171,311a
1969 47,171,210,182a,201a
1970 159,211,184a,196a
1971 163,219,235,183a,203a

1972 48,173,214,183a,197a
1973 41,215,258,260,185a,197a
1974 165,216,260,184a,196a
1975 37,171,205,185a,194a
1976 42,171,206,184a,197a
1977 46,172,207,182a,194a
1978 159,208,184a,196a
1979 43,173,222,183a,195a
1980 48,172,186a,198a
1981 40,185,223,257,258,260,187a, 199a
1982 44,183,223,257,258,260,187a, 199a
1983 168,213,260,314a
1984 41,214,184a,196a
1985 46,173,215,182a,196a
1986 38,173,216,263,185a,202a
1987 162,205,184a,196a
1988 47,171,206,183a,204a
1989 40,226,190a,202a
1990 164,226,315a
1991 148,267,285a,197a
1992 41,173,227,184a,194a
1993 45,172,211,182a,198a
1994 148,228,259,263,267,185a,194a
1995 42,171,213,183a,198a
1996 46,217,190a,202a
1997 39,172,250,185a,199a
1998 163,239,251,183a,195a
1999 47,239,191a,203a

3rd July

1930 163,208,184a,196a
1931 167,208,184a,196a
1932 160,209,184a,196a
1933 44,173,186a,198a
1934 157,211,184a,196a
1935 41,171,212,254,185a,199a
1936 45,213,184a,196a
1937 158,182,230,246,259,263,292a
1938 42,259,263,184a,196a
1939 47,173,205,183a,203a
1940 148,184,267,292a
1941 43,172,207,185a,193a
1942 48,171,183a,195a
1943 148,171,267,292a
1944 45,260,310a
1945 157,210,184a,196a
1946 148,267,185a,197a
1947 46,172,183a,195a
1948 38,171,183a,195a
1949 43,171,214,232,185a,195a
1950 167,216,184a,196a
1951 160,205,184a,196a
1952 44,206,184a,196a
1953 157,207,184a,196a
1954 41,225,232,267,310a
1955 165,209,260,184a,196a
1956 148,267,185a,197a
1957 148,225,233,255,267,185a,197a
1958 47,172,256,183a,193a
1959 148,267,185a,197a
1960 43,173,213,184a,194a
1961 48,172,233,182a,198a
1962 40,171,216,185a,194a
1963 45,171,186a,198a
1964 37,172,206,183a,195a
1965 42,173,186a,198a
1966 46,173,208,183a,195a
1967 38,172,209,185a,199a
1968 163,171,311a
1969 48,171,210,182a,201a
1970 148,267,184a,196a
1971 44,172,249,256,183a,203a
1972 37,173,214,183a,197a
1973 41,215,258,260,185a,197a
1974 165,216,260,184a,196a
1975 38,171,205,185a,194a
1976 42,171,206,184a,197a
1977 47,172,207,182a,194a
1978 148,267,185a,197a
1979 43,173,222,183a,195a
1980 48,172,186a,198a
1981 41,185,223,257,258,260,187a, 199a
1982 45,183,212,223,257,258,260, 332a
1983 157,213,237,249,258,260,314a
1984 42,214,184a,196a
1985 46,173,215,182a,196a
1986 39,173,216,185a,202a
1987 163,205,184a,196a
1988 48,171,206,183a,204a
1989 40,226,190a,202a
1990 164,226,315a
1991 148,267,185a,197a
1992 41,173,227,184a,194a
1993 166,227,259,262,190a,202a
1994 38,171,212,185a,194a
1995 42,171,213,183a,198a
1996 47,172,214,183a,195a
1997 39,172,250,185a,199a
1998 44,173,218,183a,195a
1999 48,173,206,185a,199a

4th July

1930 163,208,184a,196a
1931 48,208,184a,196a
1932 160,209,184a,196a
1933 44,173,186a,198a
1934 157,211,184a,196a
1935 41,171,212,254,185a,199a
1936 46,213,184a,196a
1937 158,182,230,246,259,263,292a
1938 43,216,184a,196a
1939 47,173,205,183a,203a

1940 148,184,267,292a
1941 44,172,207,185a,193a
1942 37,171,183a,195a
1943 41,171,302a
1944 45,260,310a
1945 38,182,182a,194a
1946 148,267,185a,197a
1947 46,172,183a,195a
1948 159,171,183a,195a
1949 43,171,214,232,185a,195a
1950 48,216,247,184a,196a
1951 148,267,184a,196a
1952 165,206,184a,196a
1953 157,207,184a,196a
1954 42,208,184a,196a
1955 166,209,184a,196a
1956 148,267,185a,197a
1957 148,225,233,255,267,185a,197a
1958 47,172,256,183a,193a
1959 148,267,185a,197a
1960 44,173,213,263,184a,194a
1961 37,172,215,182a,198a
1962 148,267,185a,197a
1963 45,172,186a,198a
1964 38,172,206,262,183a,195a
1965 42,173,186a,198a
1966 47,173,208,183a,195a
1967 39,172,209,185a,199a
1968 163,171,311a
1969 48,171,210,182a,201a
1970 148,267,184a,196a
1971 44,172,249,256,183a,203a
1972 37,173,214,183a,197a
1973 42,173,215,185a,193a
1974 166,216,184a,196a
1975 38,171,205,185a,194a
1976 43,171,206,184a,196a
1977 47,172,207,182a,194a
1978 40,208,310a
1979 44,173,222,183a,195a
1980 37,172,186a,198a
1981 41,185,223,257,258,260,187a, 199a
1982 45,183,212,223,257,258,260, 332a
1983 157,213,237,249,258,260,314a
1984 42,214,184a,196a
1985 47,173,215,182a,196a
1986 39,173,216,185a,202a
1987 163,205,184a,196a
1988 48,171,206,183a,204a
1989 40,226,190a,202a
1990 165,226,315a
1991 37,209,185a,197a
1992 162,238,250,184a,194a
1993 166,227,259,262,190a,202a
1994 38,171,212,185a,195a
1995 42,171,213,183a,198a
1996 47,172,214,183a,195
1997 160,215,184a,196a
1998 44,173,218,183a,195a
1999 48,173,206,185a,199a

5th July

1930 44,259,263,184a,196a
1931 48,208,184a,196a
1932 41,209,310a
1933 45,173,186a,198a
1934 158,211,262,184a,196a
1935 42,171,212,254,1865a,199a
1936 46,213,184a,196a
1937 159,214,184a,196a
1938 43,216,184a,196a
1939 47,173,205,183a,203a
1940 40,184,263,358a
1941 44,172,207,185a,193a
1942 37,171,183a,195a
1943 41,171,302a
1944 46,209,310a
1945 38,182,182a,194a
1946 148,185,267,319a
1947 167,172,260,183a,195a
1948 159,171,183a,195a
1949 44,171,214,232,185a,195a
1950 48,216,247,184a,196a
1951 148,267,184a,196a
1952 165,206,184a,196a
1953 158,207,184a,196a
1954 42,208,184a,196a
1955 166,209,184a,196a
1956 148,171,260,267,302a
1957 1248,225,233,255,267,185a,197a
1958 48,173,256,183a,193a
1959 148,263,267,185a,197a
1960 44,173,213,263,184a,194a
1961 37,172,215,182a,198a
1962 148,267,185a,197a
1963 45,172,186a,198a
1964 38,172,206,262,183a,195a
1965 43,173,207,185a,199a
1966 47,173,208,183a,195a
1967 39,172,209,185a,199a
1968 44,171,311a
1969 37,171,210,182a,201a
1970 161,211,184a,196a
1971 45,172,256,183a,203a
1972 38,173,214,183a,197a
1973 42,173,215,185a,193a
1974 166,216,184a,196a
1975 38,171,205,185a,194a
1976 163,206,184a,196a
1977 48,172,207,182a,194a
1978 40,208,310a
1979 44,173,222,183a,195a
1980 37,172,186a,198a
1981 42,185,223,257,187a,199a
1982 46,183,223,257,187a,199a
1983 158,213,314a

1984 43,214,184a,196a
1985 47,173,215,182a,196a
1986 39,173,216,185a,202a
1987 163,205,184a,196a
1988 37,171,206,183a,204a
1989 148,226,267,322a
1990 165,226,315a
1991 37,209,185a,197a
1992 162,238,250,184a,194a
1993 47,172,211,262,182a,198a
1994 39,171,183a,195a
1995 43,171,213,184a,198a
1996 48,172,214,183a,195a
1997 160,215,184a,196a
1998 45,173,218,183a,196a
1999 37,173,206,185a,200a

6th July

1930 44,259,263,184a,196a
1931 48,208,184a,196a
1932 41,209,310a
1933 45,173,186a,198a
1934 158,211,262,184a,196a
1935 42,171,212,254,185a,196a
1936 47,213,184a,196a
1937 159,214,184a,196a
1938 44,216,259,263,184a,196a
1939 48,173,205,183a,203a
1940 148,183,267,293a
1941 45,172,207,185a,193a
1942 37,171,183a,195a
1943 41,209,185a,197a
1944 46,209,310a
1945 39,173,210,220,182a,194a
1946 148,185,267,319a
1947 167,172,260,183a,195a
1948 40,171,183a,195a
1949 44,171,214,232,185a,195a
1950 157,216,184a,196a
1951 41,205,310a
1952 165,206,184a,196a
1953 158,207,184a,196a
1954 42,208,184a,196a
1955 166,209,184a,196a
1956 148,171,260,267,302a
1957 148,225,233,255,267,185a,197a
1958 48,173,256,183a,193a
1959 148,263,267,185a,197a
1960 165,213,263,184a,196a
1961 158,226,256,182a,198a
1962 42,171,216,185a,194a
1963 46,172,186a,198a
1964 39,172,262,183a,195a
1965 43,173,207,185a,199a
1966 47,173,208,183a,195a
1967 39,172,209,185a,201a
1968 44,171,311a
1969 37,171,210,182a,201a
1970 161,211,184a,196a
1971 45,173,256,183a,203a
1972 38,173,214,183a,197a
1973 163,185,258,260,187a,199a
1974 167,216,260,184a,196a
1975 39,171,205,184a,196a
1976 44,206,184a,196a
1977 48,172,207,182a,194a
1978 40,208,310a
1979 4,173,222,184a,195a
1980 38,172,186a,198a
1981 42,185,223,257,187a,199a
1982 46,183,223,257,187a,199a
1983 158,213,314a
1984 43,214,184a,196a
1985 48,196,224,183a,196a
1986 40,173,216,263,185a,202a
1987 44,205,259,263,184a,296a
1988 37,171,206,183a,204a
1989 148,226,267,322a
1990 165,226,315a
1991 148,267,185a,197a
1992 43,173,210,184a,194a
1993 47,172,211,262,183a,198a
1994 39,171,183a,198a
1995 43,171,213,184a,198a
1996 48,172,214,183a,195a
1997 41,172,250,185a,199a
1998 45,173,218,183a,196a
1999 37,173,206,185a,200a

7th July

1930 165,263,184a,196a
1931 157,208,184a,196a
1932 41,209,310a
1933 46,173,210,254,185a,199a
1934 158,211,262,184a,196a
1935 42,171,212,254,185a,199a
1936 47,213,184a,196a
1937 148,259,263,267,184a,196a
1938 44,216,259,263,184a,196a
1939 48,173,205,183a,203a
1940 148,183,267,293a
1941 45,172,207,185a,193a
1942 38,171,183a,195a
1943 148,267,185a,197a
1944 47,260,310a
1945 39,173,210,220,182a,194a
1946 148,185,267,319a
1947 167,172,260,183a,195a
1948 40,171,183a,195a
1949 45,171,214,232,185a,195a
1950 157,216,184a,196a
1951 41,205,310a
1952 166,206,184a,196a
1953 159,173,223,247,258,260,301a
1954 43,208,184a,196a
1955 167,209,260,184a,196a

1956 148,260,267,310a
1957 148,225,233,255,267,185a,197a
1958 48,173,256,183a,193a
1959 41,263,268,185a,197a
1960 165,213,263,184a,196a
1961 38,172,233,183a,198a
1962 42,171,216,185a,194a
1963 166,172,311a
1964 39,172,262,183a,195a
1965 44,173,207,185a,199a
1966 48,228,248,183a,194a
1967 160,209,184a,196a
1968 165,171,311a
1969 37,171,210,183a,195a
1970 161,211,184a,196a
1971 46,173,212,184a,203a
1972 39,173,183a,195a
1973 163,185,258,260,187a,199a
1974 167,216,260,184a,196a
1975 39,171,205,185a,194a
1976 44,206,184a,196a
1977 37,172,207,183a,194a
1978 41,208,185a,197a
1979 45,173,222,184a,195a
1980 38,172,186a,198a
1981 42,185,223,257,187a,199a
1982 46,183,223,257,187a,199a
1983 159,213,260,314a
1984 44,257,188a,200a
1985 48,196,224,183a,196a
1986 40,173,216,263,185a,202a
1987 164,205,259,263,184a,196a
1988 37,171,206,183a,204a
1989 42,226,190a,202a
1990 166,226,315a
1991 148,267,185a,197a
1992 43,173,210,184a,194a
1993 47,172,211,262,183a,198a
1994 39,171,183a,195a
1995 44,228,184a,198a
1996 37,172,214,183a,195a
1997 41,172,250,185a,199a
1998 45,173,218,183a,196a
1999 37,173,206,185a,200a

8th July

1930 165,263,184a,196a
1931 157,208,184a,196a
1932 162,209,184a,196a
1933 46,173,210,254,185a,199a
1934 159,172,211,227,262,301a
1935 43,171,212,254,262,186a,199a
1936 48,213,184a,196a
1937 148,267,184a,196a
1938 165,263,184a,196a
1939 37,173,205,183a,203a
1940 148,183,267,293a
1941 46,172,207,185a,193a
1942 38,171,183a,195a
1943 42,172,186a,198a
1944 47,260,310a
1945 160,210,184a,196a
1946 148,267,185a,197a
1947 48,172,260,183a,195a
1948 148,171,267,302a
1949 45,171,214,232,185a,195a
1950 158,216,184a,196a
1951 162,172,311a
1952 167,206,184a,196a
1953 159,173,223,247,258,260,301a
1954 43,208,184a,196a
1955 47,209,260,184a,196a
1956 148,267,184a,196a
1957 45,210,185a,197a
1958 37,225,233,183a,193a
1959 41,263,268,185a,197a
1960 166,213,263,184a,196a
1961 38,172,233,183a,198a
1962 42,171,216,185a,194a
1963 167,172,311a
1964 148,259,262,267,184a,196a
1965 44,173,207,185a,199a
1966 48,228,248,183a,195a
1967 160,209,184a,196a
1968 165,171,311a
1969 38,172,210,183a,201a
1970 162,211,184a,196a
1971 46,173,212,184a,203a
1972 39,173,183a,195a
1973 163,185,258,260,187a,199a
1974 167,216,260,184a,196a
1975 160,205,184a,196a
1976 165,206,184a,196a
1977 37,172,207,183a,194a
1978 41,208,195a,197a
1979 45,173,222,184a,195a
1980 38,172,186,198a
1981 163,185,258,260,187a,199a
1982 167,183,258,260,187a,199a
1983 159,213,260,314a
1984 44,257,188a,200a
1985 48,196,224,183a,196a
1986 41,216,263,185a,197a
1987 165,205,225,237,259,263,314a
1988 38,171,206,183a,204a
1989 42,226,190a,202a
1990 166,226,315a
1991 148,267,185a,197a
1992 44,173,227,184a,194a
1993 48,172,211,262,183a,198a
1994 40,228,185a,195a
1995 44,228,184a,198a
1996 37,172,214,183a,197a
1997 41,215,185a,197a
1998 46,173,216,183a,196a
1999 38,185,182a,194a

9th July

1930 166,263,184a,196a
1931 158,208,184a,196a
1932 162,209,196a
1933 47,173,210,254,185a,199a
1934 159,172,211,227,262,301a
1935 43,171,212,254,262,186a,199a
1936 48,213,263,267,277,184a,196a
1937 161,214,184a,203a
1938 165,253,184a,203a
1939 37,173,205,184a,203a
1940 42,183,293a
1941 46,172,207,185a,193a
1942 159,171,266,183a,195a
1943 43,172,209,186a,194a
1944 48,220,260,310a
1945 160,210,184a,196a
1946 148,267,185a,197a
1947 48,212,260,184a,196a
1948 148,171,267,302a
1949 46,171,214,232,185a,195a
1950 158,216,184a,196a
1951 162,173,311a
1952 167,206,184a,196a
1953 159,173,223,247,258,260,301a
1954 44,208,184a,196a
1955 48,209,260,184a,196a
1956 148,267,185a,197a
1957 45,210,185a,197a
1958 37,225,233,183a,193a
1959 148,263,267,185a,197a
1960 166,213,263,184a,196a
1961 39,172,233,183a,198a
1962 43,171,256,185a,195a
1963 167,172,311a
1964 40,173,206,183a,195a
1965 45,173,207,185a,199a
1966 37,173,208,183a,195a
1967 41,172,186a,198a
1968 166,211,184a,196a
1969 38,172,210,183a,201a
1970 162,211,184a,203a
1971 47,173,256,184a,203a
1972 39,173,183a,193a
1973 44,173,215,260,185a,193a
1974 48,216,260,184a,196a
1975 160,205,184a,196a
1976 165,206,184a,196a
1977 38,172,207,183a,194a
1978 148,267,185a,197a
1979 46,173,209,184a,196a
1980 39,172,186a,198a
1981 163,185,258,260,187a,199a
1982 167,183,258,260,187a,199a
1983 160,213,260,314a
1984 45,214,189a,201a
1985 37,173,250,183a,196a
1986 41,216,263,185a,197a
1987 165,205,225,237,259,263,314a
1988 38,171,206,183a,204a
1989 43,226,190a,202a
1990 167,226,315a
1991 148,267,185a,197a
1992 44,173,227,184a,194a
1993 48,172,211,262,183a,198a
1994 40,228,185a,195a
1995 45,171,213,184a,198a
1996 38,172,214,183a,195a
1997 42,173,215,185a,199a
1998 46,173,216,183a,196a
1999 38,185,182a,194a

10th July

1930 166,263,184a,196a
1931 38,259,263,267,184a,196a
1932 163,209,184a,196a
1933 47,173,210,254,185a,199a
1934 160,211,262,184a,196a
1935 44,228,254,259,262,186a,199a
1936 37,259,263,267,184a,196a
1937 161,214,184a,196a
1938 165,263,184a,196a
1939 37,173,205,184a,196a
1940 42,183a,293a
1941 47,172,207,185a,193a
1942 159,171,266,183a,195a
1943 43,172,209,186a,194a
1944 48,220,260,310a
1945 160,210,184a,196a
1946 148,267,185a,197a
1947 157,212,260,184a,196a
1948 42,171,183a,195a
1949 166,214,184a,196a
1950 158,216,184a,196a
1951 162,173,311a
1952 48,206,184a,196a
1953 160,207,260,184a,196a
1954 44,208,184a,196a
1955 48,209,260,184a,196a
1956 148,267,185a,197a
1957 148,225,233,255,267,185a,197a
1958 38,173,211,183a,193a
1959 148,263,267,185a,197a
1960 167,213,184a,196a
1961 39,172,233,183a,198a
1962 43,171,256,185a,195a
1963 48,172,311a
1964 41,173,206,183a,195a
1965 45,173,207,185a,199a
1966 37,173,208,183a,195a
1967 41,172,186a,198a
1968 166,171,311a
1969 39,172,210,183a,201a
1970 163,185,312a
1971 47,173,256,184a,201a
1972 40,173,214,183a,197a
1973 44,173,215,260,185a,193a

1974 48,216,260,184a,196a
1975 41,171,205,220,186a,194a
1976 16,206,184a,196a
1977 38,173,207,183a,194a
1978 148,213,267,314a
1979 46,173,184a,195a
1980 39,172,186a,198a
1981 44,185,223,257,258,260,187a, 199a
1982 48,183,260,187a,199a
1983 148,213,267,314a
1984 45,214,189a,201a
1985 37,173,250,183a,196a
1986 41,216,263,185a,197a
1987 166,205,263,184a,196a
1988 39,171,183a,195a
1989 43,226,190a,202a
1990 167,226,315a
1991 148,267,185a,197a
1992 44,173,227,184a,194a
1993 37,172,211,183a,198a
1994 41,171,212,185a,195a
1995 455,171,213,184a,198a
1996 38,172,214,183a,195a
1997 42,173,215,185a,199a
1998 46,173,216,183a,196a
1999 39,173,206,185a,200a

11th July

1930 166,263,184a,196a
1931 158,208,263,184a,196a
1932 163,209,184a,196a
1933 48,173,210,254,185a,199a
1934 160,211,262,184a,196a
1935 44,228,254,259,262,186a,199a
1936 37,259,263,267,184a,196a
1937 162,214,184a,196a
1938 166,263,184a,196a
1939 38,184,182a,194a
1940 148,183,267,293a
1941 47,172,207,185a,193a
1942 159,171,266,183a,195a
1943 43,172,209,186a,194a
1944 37,255,258,260,310a
1945 148,267,185a,197a
1946 148,267,185a,197a
1947 157,212,260,184a,196a
1948 42,171,183a,195a
1949 167,214,184a,196a
1950 159,216,184a,196a
1951 163,205,184a,196a
1952 48,206,184a,196a
1953 160,207,260,184a,196a
1954 44,208,184a,196a
1955 37,209,260,310a
1956 42,172,210,183a,204a
1957 148,225,233,255,267,185a,197a
1958 38,173,211,183a,193a
1959 148,263,267,185a,197a
1960 167,213,184a,196a
1961 160,215,184a,196a
1962 44,172,256,185a,195a
1963 48,172,311a
1964 41,173,206,183a,195a
1965 45,173,207,185a,199a
1966 37,208,184a,196a
1967 42,172,186a,198a
1968 167,171,311a
1969 39,172,210,183a,201a
1970 163,185,312a
1971 47,173,256,184a,203a
1972 40,173,214,183a,197a
1973 165,249,258,260,185a,193a
1974 157,216,260,184a,196a
1975 41,171,205,220,186a,194a
1976 166,206,184a,196a
1977 38,173,207,183a,194a
1978 148,267,185a,197a
1979 47,173,222,184a,195a
1980 148,267,184a,196a
1981 44,185,223,257,258,260,187a,199a
1982 48,183,260,187a,199a
1983 161,213,314a
1984 46,173,257,184a,200a
1985 38,173,215,183a,196a
1986 42,173,216,263,185a,202a
1987 166,205,263,184a,196a
1988 39,171,183a,195a
1989 43,226,190a,202a
1990 167,226,315a
1991 148,267,185a,197a
1992 45,173,227,184a,194a
1993 37,172,211,183a,198a
1994 148,228,267,186a,195a
1995 46,228,259,263,315a
1996 39,172,183a,195a
1997 43,173,250,185a,199a
1998 47,239,191a,203a
1999 39,173,206,185a,200a

12th July

1930 167,208,184a,196a
1931 159,208,184a,196a
1932 164,209,184a,196a
1933 48,173,210,254,185a,199a
1934 160,211,262,184a,196a
1935 45,171,212,254,186a,199a
1936 38,259,267,184a,196a
1937 162,214,184a,196a
1938 166,263,184a,196a
1939 38,184,182a,194a
1940 148,183,267,293a
1941 48,172,207,185a,193a
1942 160,171,301a
1943 44,172,209,186a,194a

1944 37,209,310a
1945 148,267,185a,197a
1946 148,267,185a,197a
1947 158,212,184a,196a
1948 43,172,213,183a,198a
1949 167,214,184a,196a
1950 159,216,184a,196a
1951 163,205,184a,196a
1952 48,206,184a,196a
1953 41,207,260,310a
1954 45,208,184a,196a
1955 37,209,260,310a
1956 42,172,210,183a,204a
1957 148,225,233,255,267,185a,197a
1958 38,173,211,267,193a
1959 !48,267,185a,197a
1960 48,213,259,263,184a,196a
1961 160,215,184a,196a
1962 44,172,256,185a,195a
1963 48,172,311a
1964 42,173,186a,198a
1965 46,173,207,185a,199a
1966 38,208,184a,196a
1967 42,172,186a,198a
1968 167,171,311a
1969 39,172,210,183a,201a
1970 163,185,312a
1971 48,173,256,184a,203a
1972 148,267,185a,197a
1973 165,249,258,260,185a,193a
1974 157,216,260,184a,196a
1975 162,205,184a,196a
1976 167,206,184a,196a
1977 39,173,183a,195a
1978 43,173,20-8,186a,198a
1979 47,173,222,184a,195a
1980 148,267,184a,196a
1981 44,185,223,257,258,260,187a, 199a
1982 48,183,260,187a,199a
1983 161,213,314a
1984 46,173,257,184a,200a
1985 38,173,215,183a,196a
1986 42,173,216,263,186a,202a
1987 167,205,184a,196a
1988 148,267,184a,196a
1989 44,226,190a,202a
1990 40a,226,190a,202a
1991 148,267,185a,197a
1992 45,173,227,184a,194a
1993 37,172,211,183a,198a
1994 148,22a,259,263,267,186a,195a
1995 46,228,259,263,315a
1996 172,183a,195a
1997 43,173,250,185a,199a
1998 47,239,191a,203a
1999 40,173,206,185a,200a

13th July

1930 167,208,184a,196a
1931 159,208,184a,196a
1932 44,173,246,254,183a,195a
1933 37,173,210,254,185a,199a
1934 161,211,184a,196a
1935 45,171,212,254,186a,199a
1936 38,259,263,267,148a,196a
1937 162,214,184a,196a
1938 166,263,184a,196a
1939 39,173,205,184a,203a
1940 148,183,267,293a
1941 48,172,207,185a,193a
1942 148,172,267,301a
1943 44,172,209,186a,194a
1944 37,209,310a
1945 42,173,210,220,183a
1946 148,267,185a,197a
1947 158,212,184a,196a
1948 43,172,213,183a,198a
1949 167,214,184a,196a
1950 160,216,184a,196a
1951 164,205,184a,196a
1952 157,206,184a,196a
1953 41,207,260,310a
1954 45,208,184a,196a
1955 37,209,260,310a
1956 43,172,210,183a,204a
1957 148,225,233,255,267,185a
1958 39,173,256,183a,193a
1959 148,267,185a,197a
1960 48,213,259,263,184a,196a
1961 160,215,184a,196a
1962 45,172,216,186a,195a
1963 157,172,311a
1964 42,173,186a,198a
1965 46,173,207,185a,199a
1966 38,208,184a,196a
1967 43,172,186a,198a
1968 48,172,259,263,311a
1969 160,210,184a,196a
1970 44,259,262,184a,196a
1971 48,173,256,184a,203a
1972 148,267,185a,197a
1973 165,249,258,260,185a,193a
1974 158,216,184a,196a
1975 162,205,184a,196a
1976 167,206,184a,196a
1977 39,173,183a,195a
1978 43,173,208,186a,198a
1979 48,173,222,184a,195a
1980 41,172,210,183a,199a
1981 45,185,260,187a,199a
1982 37,183,260,187a,199a
1983 162,213,314a
1984 46,173,257,184a,200a
1985 38,173,215,183a,196a
1986 43,173,216,186a,202a
1987 167,205,184a,196a

1988 148,267,184a,196a
1989 44,226,190a,202a
1990 48,226,190a,202a
1991 148,267,185a,197a
1992 166,227,190a,202a
1993 38,172,211,262,183a,198a
1994 148,228,259,263,186a,195a
1995 47,213,184a,196a
1996 39,172,183a,195a
1997 43,173,250,185a,199a
1998 48,173,218,183a,196a
1999 40,173,206,186a,200a

14th July

1930 48,259,263,184a,196a
1931 160,208,259,263,267,184a,196a
1932 47,173,246,254,183a,195a
1933 37,173,210,254,185a,199a
1934 161,211,184a,196a
1935 45,212,184a,196a
1936 38,259,263,267,184a,196a
1937 163,214,184a,196a
1938 167,216,184a,196a
1939 39,173,205,184a,203a
1940 148,83,267,293a
1941 37,172,207,185a,193a
1942 41,172,354a
1943 45,172,209,186a,194a
1944 38,209,310
1945 42,173,210,220,183a,194a
1946 46,173,211,220,186a,198a
1947 158,212,184a,196a
1948 44,172,213,183a,198a
1949 168,214,184a,196a
1950 160,216,184a,196a
1951 164,205,184a,196a
1952 157,206,184a,196a
1953 162,207,184a,196a
1954 46,208,184a,196a
1955 38,224,232,259,263,310a
1956 43,172,210,183a,204a
1957 148,225,233,255,267,185a,197a
1958 39,173,256,183aq,193a
1959 148,256,263,267,320a
1960 157,213,263,184a,196a
1961 41,172,215,183a,198a
1962 45,172,216,186a,195a
1963 157,172,311a
1964 42,173,186a,198a
1965 47,173,207,185a,199a
1966 39,208,184a,196a
1967 43,172,186a,198a
1968 48,172,259,263,311a
1969 160,210,184a,196a
1970 44,173,211,186a,196a
1971 37,173,256,184a,203a
1972 12,173,214,183a,197a
1973 46,173,215,185a,193a
1974 158,216,184a,196a
1975 163,186,312a
1976 167,206,184a,196a
1977 40,173,207,183a,194a
1978 44,173,257,186a,198a
1979 48,173,222,184a,195a
1980 41,172,210,183a,199a
1981 45,185,260,187a,199a
1982 37,183,260,187a,199a
1983 162,213,314a
1984 47,173,214,185a,200a
1985 39,173,250,183a,196a
1986 43,173,216,186a,202a
1987 48,205,259,263,184a,196a
1988 148,267,184a,196a
1989 45,226,190a,202a
1990 37,226,190a,202a
1991 148,267,185a,197a
1992 166,227,190a,202a
1993 38,172,211,262,183a,198a
1994 148,228,259,267,186a,195a
1995 47,213,194a,196a
1996 160,214,184a,196a
1997 44,173,218,183a,199a
1998 48,173,218,183a,196a
1999 41,173,206,186a,200a

15th July

1930 48,208,184a,196a
1931 160,208,259,263,267,184a,196a
1932 45,173,246,254,183a,195a
1933 38,173,210,254,185a,199a
1934 162,211,262,184a,196a
1935 46,212,259,184a,196a
1936 39,267,184a,196a
1937 43,173,214,254,183a,200a
1938 167,216,184a,196a
1939 160,205,184a,196a
1940 148,183,267,293a
1941 37,172,207,185a,193a
1942 41,172,354a
1943 45,172,209,186a,194a
1944 38,209,310a
1945 43,173,210,220,183a,194a
1946 47,173,211,220,186a,198a
1947 159,172,260,301a
1948 44,172,213,183a,198a
1949 168,214,184a,196a
1950 160,216,184a,196a
1951 165,205,184a,196a
1952 158,206,184a,196a
1953 162,207,184a,196a
1954 48,204,184a,196a
1955 38,224,232,259,263,310a
1956 44,224,183a,204a
1957 148,225,233,255,267,185a,197a
1958 40,173,256,183a,193a
1959 148,256,263,267,320a

1960 157,213,263,184a,196a
1961 41,172,215,183a,198a
1962 42,172,216,186a,195a
1963 158,172,311a
1964 43,173,206,183a,195a
1965 47,173,207,185a,195a
1966 39,208,184a,196a
1967 44,172,186a,198a
1968 37,172,259,263,311a
1969 41,172,210,183a,210a
1970 45,173,211,186a,196a
1971 37,173,256,184a,203a
1972 42,173,214,183a,197a
1973 46,173,215,185a,193a
1974 158,216,184a,196a
1975 163,186,312a
1976 48,172,257,185a,198a
1977 40,173,207,183a,194a
1978 44,173,257,186a,198a
1979 37,173,222,184a,195a
1980 42,172,210,186a,198a
1981 46,185,187a,199a
1982 38,183,187a,199a
1983 163,186,213,359a
1984 47,173,214,185a,200a
1985 39,173,214,185a,200a
1986 44,173,216,263,186a,202a
1987 48,205,259,263,184a,196a
1988 41,172,206,183a,193a
1989 45,226,190a,202a
1990 37,226,190a,202a
1991 148,267,185a,197a
1992 47,173,210,185a,194a
1993 39,172,211,262,183a,198a
1994 148,228,259,262,267,186a,195a
1995 48,213,259,263,184a,196a
1996 160,214,184a,196a
1997 44,173,250,185a,199a
1998 37,173,218,183a,196a
1999 41,173,206,186a,200a

16th July

1930 48,208,184a,196a
1931 161,208,263,184a,196a
1932 46,173,209,254,183a,195a
1933 38,173,210,254,185a,199a
1934 162,211,262,184a,196a
1935 46,212,259,262,184a,196a
1936 39,267,184a,196a
1937 44,173,214,254,183a,200a
1938 48,259,263,184a,196a
1939 160,205,184a,196a
1940 148,183,267,293a
1941 37,172,207,185a,193a
1942 41,172,254a
1943 46,172,209,186a,194a
1944 39,209,310a
1945 43,173,210,220,183a,194a
1946 47,173,211,220,186a,194a
1947 159,172,260,301a
1948 45,172,213,183qa,198a
1949 157,214,184a,196a
1950 161,216,184a,196a
1951 165,205,184a,196a
1952 158,206,184a,196a
1953 167,207,184a,196a
1954 46,208,184a,196a
1955 39,224,232,260,310a
1956 44,224,183a,204a
1957 143,225,233,255,267,185a,197a
1958 40,173,256,183a,193a
1959 148,263,267,185a,197a
1960 38,172,213,185a,194a
1961 42,172,186a,198a
1962 46,172,233,186a,195a
1963 158,172,311a
1964 43,173,206,183a,195a
1965 47,173,207,185a,199a
1966 40,208,184a,196a
1967 44,172,186a,198a
1968 157,172,263,311a
1969 41,172,211,183a,201a
1970 45,173,211,186a,196a
1971 38,173,212,184a,203a
1972 43,173,214,183a,197a
1973 167,219,235,257,258,260,185a, 193a
1974 159,216,184a,196a
1975 164,205,184a,196a
1976 48,172,257,185a,198a
1977 40,173,257,186a,198a
1978 45,173,257,186a,198a
1979 37,173,222,184a,195a
1980 42,172,210,186a,198a
1981 46,185,87a,199a
1982 38,183,187a,199a
1983 43,186,87a,199a
1984 48,173,257,185a,200a
1985 40,215,184a,196a
1986 44,173,216,263,186a,202a
1987 157,205,225,237,263,184a,196a
1988 41,172,206,183a,193a
1989 45,226,190a,202a
1990 158,226,190a,202
1991 162,173,186a,198a
1992 47,173,210,185a,194a
1993 39,172,211,262,183a,198a
1994 148,228,259,262,267,186a,195a
1995 48,213,259,263,184a,196a
1996 41,173,214,183a,195a
1997 165,217,185a,199a
1998 37,173,218,183a,196a
1999 42,173,206,186a,200a

17th July

1930 157,208,184a,196a

1931 41,209,263,310a
1932 46,173,209,254,183a,195a
1933 38,173,210,254,185a,199a
1934 162,211,262,184a,196a
1935 47,212,259,262,184a,196a
1936 148,263,267,277,184a,196a
1937 44,173,214,254,183a,200a
1938 48,259,263,184a,196a
1939 148,267,285a,197a
1940 46,183,293a
1941 38,185,182a,194a
1942 42,172,208,183a,197a
1943 46,172,209,186a,194a
1944 148,267,185a,197a
1945 43,173,210,220,183a,194a
1946 48,173,211,220,186a,198a
1947 148,212,260,267,184a,196a
1948 45,172,213,260,183a,199a
1949 157,214,184a,196a
1950 148,267,185a,197a
1951 166,205,185a,197a
1952 148,267,185a,197a
1953 163,183,223,247,258,260,312
1954 47,208,184a,196a
1955 39,224,232,260,310a
1956 44,224,183a,204a
1957 148,225,233,255,267,18a,197a
1958 41,211,185a,197a
1959 148,263,267,185a,197a
1960 38,172,213,263,185a,194a
1961 42,172,186a,198a
1962 46,172,233,186a,195a
1963 159,172,311a
1964 44,173,206,183a,195a
1965 48,173,207,185a,199a
1966 40,208,184a,199a
1967 45,172,186a,198a
1968 157,172,263,311a
1969 41,172,211,183,201a
1970 46,173,211,186a,196a
1971 38,173,212,184a,203a
1972 43,173,214,183a,197a
1973 167,219,235,257,258,260,185a,
193a
1974 159,216,184a,196a
1975 164,205,184a,196a
1976 37,172,257,185a,198a
1977 148,267,185a,197a
1978 45,173,257,186a,198a
1979 38,173,209,184a,195a
1980 42,172,210,186a,198a
1981 46,185,187a,199a
1982 159,183,258,260,187a,199a
1983 43,186,187a,199a
1984 48,173,257,183a,200a
1985 40,215,184a,196a
1986 44,173,216,263,186a,202a
1987 157,205,225,237,263,184a,196a
1988 42,172,206,183a,193a
1989 46,226,190a,202a
1990 158,226,190a,202a
1991 43,173,209,186a,198a
1992 47,173,210,185a,194a
1993 39,172,211,262,183a,198a
1994 44,195,259,262,188a,200a
1995 37,213,259,263,184a,196a
1996 41,173,214,183a,195a
1997 165,217,185a,199a
1998 38,173,216,183a,196a
1999 42,173,206,186a,200a

18th July

1930 157,208,184a,196a
1931 162,173,263,311a
1932 47,173,246,254,183a,195a
1933 39,173,210,254,185a,199a
1934 163,211,262,184a,196a
1935 47,212,259,262,184a,196a
1936 148,259,163,267,184a,196a
1937 44,173,214,254,183a,200a
1938 157,263,184a,196a
1939 148,267,185a,197a
1940 46,183,293a
1941 38,185,182a,194a
1942 42,172,208,183a,197a
1943 47,172,209,186a,194a
1944 40,209,310a
1945 44,173,210,220,183a,194a
1946 48,173,211,220,186a,198a
1947 148,212,260,267,184a,196a
1948 45,172,213,260,183a,199a
1949 157,214,184a,196a
1950 42,173,216,232,183a,199a
1951 166,205,184a,196a
1952 148,267,185a,197a
1953 163,183,223,247,258,260,312a
1954 47,208,184a,196a
1955 148,260,267,310a
1956 45,172,210,183a,204a
1957 37,210,268,278,185a,197a
1958 41,211,185a,197a
1959 148,263,267,285a,197a
1960 38,172,213,263,185a,194a
1961 42,172,186a,198a
1962 47,172,233,186a,195a
1963 39,173,186a,198a
1964 44,173,206,183a,195a
1965 48,173,207,185a,199a
1966 40,208,184a,196a
1967 45,172,186a,198a
1968 158,172,263,311a
1969 42,172,211,183a,201a
1970 46,173,211,186a,197a
1971 39,173,256,184a,203a
1972 43,173,214,183a,197a
1973 167,219,235,257,258,260,185a,
193a
1974 148,216,260,267,184a,196a

1975 164,205,184a,196a
1976 37,172,257,185a,198a
1977 148,173,260,267,302a
1978 46,173,257,186a,198a
1979 38,173,209,184a,195a
1980 43,183,187a,199a
1981 167,185,260,312a
1982 159,183,258,260,187a,199a
1983 44,213,189a,201a
1984 48,173,257,185a,200a
1985 41,173,250,183a,196a
1986 45,216,263,189a,210a
1987 158,205,263,184a,196a
1988 42,172,206,183a,193a
1989 46,226,190a,202a
1990 39,226,190a,202a
1991 43,173,209,186a,198a
1992 48,173,227,185a,194a
1993 160,211,262,184a,196a
1994 44,195,259,262,188a,200a
1995 37,213,259,263,184a,196a
1996 41,173,214,183a,195a
1998 38,173,216,183a,196a
1999 43,173,206,186a,200a

19th July

1930 158,208,184a,196a
1931 162,173,263,311a
1932 47,173,246,254,183a,195a
1933 39,173,210,254,185a,199a
1934 163,211,262,184a,196a
1935 48,212,259,262,184a,196a
1936 41,259,263,184a,196a
1937 45,173,214,254,183a,200a
1938 157,263,184a,196a
1939 42,173,205,184a,203a
1940 46,183,293a
1941 39,172,207,185a,193a
1942 163,172,209,186a,194a
1943 47,172,209,186a,194a
1944 40,209,310a
1945 44,173,210,220,183a,194a
1946 48,173,211,220,186a,198a
1947 41,212,260,310a
1948 46,172,213,183a,199a
1949 158,214,184a,196a
1950 42,173,216,232,183a,199a
1951 167,205,184a,196a
1952 148,267,185a,197a
1953 163,183,223,247,258,260,312a
1954 48,208,184a,196a
1955 148,260,267,310a
1956 45,172,210,183a,204a
1957 210,268,278,185a,197a
1958 42,173,211,183a,193a
1959 148,263,267,185a,197a
1960 39,172,213,185a,194a
1961 43,172,233,183a,198a
1962 47,172,233,186a,195a
1963 160,173,311a
1964 45,173,206,183a,195a
1965 37,173,207,185a,199a
1966 41,208,184a,196a
1967 45,172,186a,198a
1968 158,172,263,311a
1969 42,172,211,183a,201a
1970 47,173,211,186a,197a
1971 39,173,256,184a,203a
1972 44,173,214,183a,197a
1973 48,172,215,260,185a,193a
1974 148,216,260,267,184a,196a
1975 165,205,184a,196a
1976 37,206,185a,197a
1977 42,173,183a,195a
1978 46,173,257,186a,198a
1979 39,173,222,184a,195a
1980 43,183,187a,199a
1981 167,185,260,312a
1982 160,183,260,312a
1983 44,213,189a,201a
1984 157,237,249,185a,200a
1985 41,173,250,183a,196a
1986 45,216,263,189a,201a
1987 158,205,263,184a,196a
1988 42,172,206,183a,193a
1989 47,226,190a,202a
1990 39,226,190a,202a
1991 44,173,227,186a,198a
1992 48,173,185a,194a
1993 160,211,262,184a,196a
1994 148,228,267,186a,195a
1995 37,228,267,186a,195a
1996 42,173,214,183a,195a
1997 46,173,215,185a,199a
1998 39,173,218,183a,196a
1999 43,173,206,186a,200a

20th July

1930 158,208,184a,196a
1931 163,209,184a,196a
1932 48,173,246,254,183a,195a
1933 160,210,184a,196a
1934 44,211,259,262,184a,196a
1935 48,212,259,262,184a,196a
1936 41,259,263,184a,196a
1937 45,173,214,254,183,200a
1938 157,263,184a,196a
1939 42,173,205,184a,203a
1940 148,183,267,293a
1941 39,172,207,185a,193a
1942 163,172,301a
1943 48,172,209,186a,194a
1944 41,268,185a,197a
1945 45,173,210,220,183a,194a
1946 37,173,211,220,186a,198a
1947 41,212,260,310a

1948 46,172,213,183a,199a
1949 158,214,184a,196a
1950 43,183,187a,199a
1951 167,205,184a,196a
1952 40,206,310a
1953 164,207,260,184a,196a
1954 48,208,184a,196a
1955 41,224,232,260,310a
1956 46,172,210,183a,204a
1957 38,210,268,185a,197a
1958 42,173,211,183a,193a
1959 47,173,186a,198a
1960 39,172,213,185a,194a
1961 43,172,233,183a,198a
1962 48,172,233,186a,195a
1963 160,173,311a
1964 45,173,206,183a,195a
1965 37,173,207,185a,199a
1966 41,208,184a,196a
1967 46,172,263,186a,198a
1968 159,172,311a
1969 43,183,187a,199a
1970 47,173,211,186a,197a
1971 160,212,184a,196a
1972 44,173,214,183a,197a
1973 48,172,215,260,185a,193a
1974 161,260,184a,196a
1975 165,205,184a,196a
1976 148,267,185a,197a
1977 42,173,183a,195a
1978 47,173,208,186a,198a
1979 39,173,222,184a,195a
1980 44,172,249,183a,199a
1981 48,185,260,312a
1982 160,183,260,312a
1983 165,213,189a,210a
1984 157,237,249,185a,200a
1985 41,173,250,183a,196a
1986 46,225,263,190a,202a
1987 158,205,263,184a,196a
1988 43,206,172,183a,193a
1989 148,226,267,322a
1990 42,226,259,263,315a
1991 44,173,227,186a,198a
1992 37,173,227,185a,194a
1993 41,172,211,183a,198a
1994 148,228,267,186a,195a
1995 38,213,259,263,184a,196a
1996 42,173,214,183a,195a
1997 47,239,191a,203a
1998 159,216,184a,196a
1999 43,173,206,186a,200a

21st July

1930 158,208,184a,196a
1931 163,209,184a,196a
1932 48,173,246,254,183a,195a
1933 160,210,184a,196a
1934 44,211,259,262,184a,196a
1935 37,212,184a,196a
1936 42,259,263,184a,196a
1937 46,173,214,254,183a,200a
1938 158,263,184a,196a
1939 43,173,205,184a,203a
1940 47,183,182a,194a
1941 39,172,207,185a,193a
1942 164,172,301a
1943 148,267,185a,197a
1944 41,268,185a,197a
1945 45,173,210,220,183a,194a
1946 37,173,211,220,186a,198a
1947 162,212,184a,196a
1948 167,231,247,258,260,183a,199a
1949 159,214,184a,196a
1950 43,183,187a,199a
1951 168,205,184a,196a
1952 40,206,310a
1953 164,207,260,184a,196a
1954 37,208,184a,196a
1955 41,224,232,260,310a
1956 148,267,185a,197a
1957 38,210,268,185a,197a
1958 43,173,211,183a,194a
1959 47,173,186a,198a
1960 160,213,263,184a,196a
1961 44,172,233,183a,198a
1962 48,172,233,186a,195a
1963 41,173,186a,198a
1964 45,173,206,183a,193a
1965 37,173,207,185a,199a
1966 42,173,311a
1967 46,172,263,186a,198a
1968 159,172,311a
1969 43,183,187a,199a
1970 48,183,211,186a,197a
1971 160,212,184a,196a
1972 45,173,214,183a,197a
1973 37,172,215,260,185a,193a
1974 41,216,260,184a,196a
1975 166,205,184a,196a
1976 148,267,185a,197a
1977 42,173,183a,195a
1978 47,173,208,186a,198a
1979 39,173,222,184a,195a
1980 44,172,249,183a,199a
1981 48,185,260,312a
1982 161,184,260,312a
1983 165,213,189a,210a
1984 38,173,257,185a,200a
1985 42,173,215,183a,196a
1986 46,225,263,190a,202a
1987 159,205,184a,196a
1988 43,206,172,183a,193a
1989 148,226,267,322a
1990 40,226,259,263,315a
1991 45,173,227,186a,198a
1992 37,173,227,185a,194a
1993 41,172,211,183a,198a

1994 148,228,259,262,267,190a,202a
1995 38,213,184a,196a
1996 43,173,214,183a,195a
1997 47,239,191a,203a
1998 40,216,184a,196a
1999 44,173,206,186a,200a

22nd July

1930 159,208,184a,196a
1931 164,209,263,184a,196a
1932 48,173,246,254,183a,195a
1933 160,210,184a,196a
1934 165,211,184a,196a
1935 37,212,184a,196a
1936 42,259,263,184a,196a
1937 46,173,254,183a,200a
1938 158,263,184a,196a
1939 43,173,205,184a,202a
1940 48,183,182a,194a
1941 160,207,184a,196a
1942 164,172,301a
1943 148,262,185a,197a
1944 41,268,185a,197a
1945 45,173,210,220,183,194a
1946 38,173,211,220,186a,198a
1947 162,212,184a,196a
1948 167,231,247,258,260,183a,199a
1949 159,214,184a,196a
1950 43,183,187a,199a
1951 168,205,184a,196a
1952 148,267,184a,196a
1953 165,207,260,184a,196a
1954 37,208,184a,196a
1955 42,224,232,310a
1956 148,267,185a,197a
1957 38,210,268,185a,197a
1958 43,173,211,184a,194a
1959 47,173,186a,198a
1960 160,213,263,184a,196a
1961 44,172,233,183a,198a
1962 37,172,216,186a,195a
1963 41,173,186a,198a
1964 46,173,206,183a,195a
1965 38,173,207,185a,199a
1966 42,173,259,263,311a
1967 47,172,186a,198a
1968 159,172,311a
1969 43,183,187a,199a
1970 48,173,211,186a,197a
1971 41,173,256,184a,203a
1972 45,173,214,183a,197a
1973 37,172,215,260,185a,193a
1974 42,216,184a,196a
1975 166,205,184a,196a
1976 148,267,185a,197a
1977 163,173,258,260,183a,195a
1978 48,173,257,186a,197a
1979 160,209,184a,196a
1980 44,172,249,183a,199a
1981 157,185,260,312a
1982 161,184,260,312a
1983 46,213,189a,201a
1984 38,173,257,185a,200a
1985 42,173,215,183a,196a
1986 47,173,216,186a,202a
1987 159,205,184a,196a
1988 44,172,250,183a,193a
1989 148,226,267,322a
1990 161,226,263,315a
1991 45,173,227,186a,198a
1992 37,173,227,185a,194a
1993 42,172,211,183a,198a
1994 148,228,259,262,267,190a,202a
1995 39,213,184a,196a
1996 43,173,214,183a,195a
1997 48,173,250,185a,199a
1998 40,216,184a,196a
1999 44,173,206,186a,200a

23rd July

1930 159,208,184a,196a
1931 164,209,263,184a,196a
1932 49,209,185a,197a
1933 53,210,185a,197a
1934 165,211,184a,196a
1935 38,212,259,262,184a,196a
1936 162,263,184a,196a
1937 149,268,185a,197a
1938 58,173,214,183a,200a
1939 39,173,216,186a,197a
1940 43,173,205,184a,202a
1941 149,268,185a,197a
1942 57,208,310a
1943 148m267,185a,197a
1944 149,255,268,185a,197a
1945 149,173,268,302a
1946 149,268,185a,197a
1947 163,212,260,184a,196a
1948 59,258,260,185a,197a
1949 52,214,310a
1950 149,268,185a,197a
1951 157,205,184a,196a
1952 149,268,185a,197a
1953 149,260,268,185a,197a
1954 158,208,184a,196a
1955 42,224,232,310a
1956 149,268,185a,197a
1957 149,225,233,255,261,268,278, 197a
1958 149,268,185a,197a
1959 48,173,263,186a,198a
1960 149,263,268,185a,197a
1961 57,263,215,233,183a,198a
1962 49,172,216,233,186a,195a
1963 42,173,186a,198a
1964 58,173,206,183a,195a

1965 149,268,185a,197a
1966 163,228,248,184a,196a
1967 47,172,186a,198a
1968 160,172,263,311a
1969 56,173,211,183a,201a
1970 149,268,185a,197a
1971 41,173,256,184a,203a
1972 57,268,261,185a,197a
1973 50,172,215,185a,193a
1974 162,216,184a,196a
1975 59,172,205,186a,194a
1976 149,217,249,268,185a,197a
1977 55,173,258,260,302a
1978 149,268,185a,197a
1979 149,268,185a,197a
1980 57,172,210,183a,199a
1981 49,185,260,187a,199a
1982 54,172,212,184a,199a
1983 149,213,268,189a,201a
1984 149,237,249,268,185a,197a
1985 55,173,250,283a,196a
1986 59,173,216,186a,202a
1987 52,205,263,184a,196a
1988 56,172,250,183a,193a
1989 49,226,322a
1990 149,226,263,268,322a
1991 149,268,185a,197a
1992 50,210,185a,197a
1993 54,172,211,183a,198a
1994 59,172,228,186a,195a
1995 51,172,213,184a,199a
1996 55,173,214,261,183a,195a
1997 149,217,268,185a,197a
1998 160,216,184a,196a
1999 57,173,206,186a,200a

24th July

1930 160,208,184a,196a
1931 149,263,268,185a,197a
1932 49,209,185a,197a
1933 53,210,185a,197a
1934 166,211,184a,196a
1935 50,172,212,186a,199a
1936 149,268,185a,197a
1937 59,173,214,183a,200a
1938 149,268,185a,197a
1939 149,263,268,185a,197a
1940 149,183,268,293a
1941 53,207,185a,197a
1942 57,208,310a
1943 149,261,268,185a,197a
1944 149,255,268,185a,197a
1945 149,173,268,302a
1946 149,268,185a,197a
1947 149,260,268,185a,197a
1948 149,260,268,197a
1949 52,214,310a
1950 149,268,185a,197a
1951 49,205,185a,197a
1952 149,268,185a,197a
1953 149,268,185a,197a
1954 158,208,184a,196a
1955 55,209,260,310a
1956 149,268,185a,197a
1957 149,225,233,255,261,268,278,
185a,197a
1958 149,268,185a,197a
1959 149,173,263,268,318a
1960 53,213,263,185a,197a
1961 57,172,215,233,183a,198a
1962 50,172,227,186a,195a
1963 54,173,186a,198a
1964 58,173,206,183a,195a
1965 149,268,185a,197a
1966 163,228,248,184a,196a
1967 60,172,263,186a,198a
1968 160,172,263,311a
1969 56,173,211,183a,201a
1970 149,268,185a,197a
1971 149,268,185a,197a
1972 149,261,268,185a,197a
1973 50,172,215,185a,193a
1974 163,184,260,312a
1975 59,172,205,186a,194a
1976 149,217,249,268,185a,197a
1977 149,173,260,268,302a
1978 49,208,185a,197a
1979 149,268,185a,197a
1980 57,172,210,183a,199a
1981 50,185a,187a,199a
1982 54,184,187a,199a
1983 149,213,268,189a,201a
1984 149,237,249,268,185a,197a
1985 55,173,250,183a,196a
1986 60,172,216,263,186a,202a
1987 52,205,263,184a,196a
1988 57,207,189a,201a
1989 149,226,322a
1990 54,226,259,263,190a,202a
1991 58,227,322a
1992 50,210,185a,197a
1993 55,172,211,183a,198a
1994 59,172,228,186a,195a
1995 51,172,213,184a,199a
1996 56,173,214,183a,195a
1997 49,217,258,261,186a,199a
1998 149,268,185a,197a
1999 57,173,206,186a,200a

25th July

1930 160,208,184a,196a
1931 149,209,263,268,185a,197a
1932 149,268,185a,197a
1933 149,173,268,318a
1934 166,211,184a,196a
1935 51,172,212,186a,199a

1936 149,263,268,185a,197a
1937 59,173,214,183a,200a
1938 149,263,268,185a,197a
1939 149,263,268,185a,197a
1940 149,183,268,293a
1941 53,207,185a,197a
1942 57,208,310a
1943 149,261,268,185a,197a
1944 149,255,268,185a,196a
1945 59,173,302a
1946 149,268,185a,197a
1947 149,260,268,185a,197a
1948 149,260,268,185a,197a
1949 52,214,310a
1950 149,268,185a,197a
1951 49,205,185a,197a
1952 149,268,185a,197a
1953 149,268,185a,197a
1954 159,208,184a,196a
1955 55,209,260,310a
1956 149,268,185a,197a
1957 149,225,233,255,268,278,185a, 197a
1958 149,268,185a,197a
1959 149,173,263,268,316a
1960 53,213,263,185a,197a
1961 57,172,215,233,183a,198a
1962 50,172,227,186a,195a
1963 54,173,186a,198a
1964 59,173,206,183a,195a
1965 149,268,185a,197a
1966 164,226,248,259,263,184a,196a
1967 60,172,263,186a,198a
1968 149,172,263,268,318a
1969 57,173,248,183a,201a
1970 149,268,185a,197a
1971 54,173,212,184a,203a
1972 149,249,258,261,268,185a,197a
1973 159,219,235,257,186a,193a
1974 163,184,260,312a
1975 59,172,205,186a,194a
1976 149,217,249,268,185a,197a
1977 149,173,260,268,302a
1978 49,208,185a,197a
1979 149,269,185a,197a
1980 58,172,210,183a,199a
1981 50,186,187a,199a
1982 55,184,260,187a,199a
1983 149,213,268,189a,201a
1984 149,237,249,268,185a,197a
1985 149,197,268,320a
1986 60,172,216,263,186a,202a
1987 52,205,263,184a,196a
1988 57,207,189a,201a
1989 50,226,322a
1990 54,226,259,263,190a,202a
1991 58,227,322a
1992 149,268,185a,197a
1993 55,172,211,183a,198a
1994 168,228,186a,195a
1995 160,228,184a,196a
1996 56,173,214,183a,195a
1997 49,217,258,261,186a,199a
1998 149,268,185a,197a
1999 57,173,206a,186a,200a

26th July

1930 149,268,185a,197a
1931 149,209,263,268,185a,197a
1932 149,268,185a,197a
1933 149,173,268,318a
1934 167,211,184a,196a
1935 51,172,212,186a,199a
1936 149,263,268,185a,197a
1937 60,173,214,184a,200a
1938 149,263,268,185a,197a
1939 57,205,263,185a,197a
1940 149,183,268,293a
1941 53,207,185a,197a
1942 58,208,310a
1943 149,261,268,185a,197a
1944 149,268,185a,197a
1945 59,173,302a
1946 149,268,185a,197a
1947 149,260,268,185a,197a
1948 49,258,260,185a,197a
1949 149,268,185a,197a
1950 149,268,185a,197a
1951 149,268,185a,197a
1952 149,268,185a,197a
1953 59,207,258,260,185a,197a
1954 159,208,184a,196a
1955 56,224,232,260,310a
1956 149,268,185a,197a
1957 149,225,233,255,268,185a,197a
1958 57,174,211,233,184a,194a
1959 149,173,263,268,318a
1960 149,263,268,185a,187a
1961 58,172,215,233,183a,198a
1962 51,172,216,233,186a,195a
1963 55,173,186a,198a
1964 59,173,206,183a,195a
1965 52,173,186a,198a
1966 164,228,248,259,263,184a,196a
1967 60,172,263,186a,198a
1968 149,172,263,268,318a
1969 57,173,248,183a,201a
1970 149,268,185a,197a
1971 54,173,212,184a,203a
1972 149,249,258,261,268,185a,197a
1973 159,219,235,257,186a,193a
1974 164,216,220,260,184a,196a
1975 60,172,205,186a,194a
1976 149,217,249,268,185a,197a
1977 149,173,258,260,268,302a
1978 49,173,257,186a,198a
1979 149,268,185a,197a
1980 58,172,210,183a,199a

1981 51,186,187a,199a
1982 55,184,260,187a,199a
1983 149,213,268,189a,201a
1984 52,174,257,185a,200a
1985 149,197,268,320a
1986 49,172,216,263,186a,202a
1987 53,205,263,185a,197a
1988 57,207,189a,201a
1989 50,226,322a
1990 54,226,259,263,190a,202a
1991 149,268,185a,197a
1992 149,268,185a,197a
1993 56,172,211,183a,198a
1994 168,228,186a,195a
1995 52,173,213,184a,199a
1996 57,217,183a,196a
1997 50,173,215,261,186a,199a
1998 54,173,216,184a,196a
1999 58,173,206,186a,200a

27th July

1930 149,268,185a,197a
1931 149,263,268,185a,197a
1932 149,268,185a,197a
1933 149,268,185a,197a
1934 167,211,184a,196a
1935 160,228,254,184a,196a
1936 149,263,268,185a,197a
1937 60,173,214,183a,200a
1938 149,174,263,268,318a
1939 57,205,263,185a,197a
1940 50,183,293a
1941 162,172,186a,198a
1942 58,208,310a
1943 149,173,261,268,302a
1944 149,268,185a,197a
1945 60,174,183a,197a
1946 149,268,185a,197a
1947 149,260,268,185a,197a
1948 49,258,260,185a,197a
1949 149,268,185a,197a
1950 149,268,185a,197a
1951 149,268,185a,197a
1952 149,185,268,319a
1953 59,207,258,260,185a,197a
1954 160,208,224,232,184a,196a
1955 56,224,232,260,310a
1956 149,268,185a,197a
1957 149,261,268,278,185a,197a
1958 57,174,211,233,184a,194a
1959 50,173,259,263,318a
1960 149,263,268,185a,197a
1961 58,172,215,233,183a,198a
1962 149,268,185a,197a
1963 55,173,205,184a,199a
1964 60,174,186a,198a
1965 52,173,186a,198a
1966 165,228,248,259,263,184a,196a
1967 49,172,263,186a,198a
1968 149,172,263,268,318a
1969 58,173,248,183a,201a
1970 149,268,185a,197a
1971 55,174,212,184a,203a
1972 149,249,258,261,268,185a,197a
1973 160,172,215,186a,193a
1974 164,216,220,260,184a,196a
1975 60,172,205,186a,194a
1976 149,268,185a,197a
1977 149,173,258,260,268,302a
1978 158,174,186a,198a
1979 149,268,185a,197a
1980 59,172,210,183a,199a
1981 51,186,187a,199a
1982 56,184,260,187a,199a
1983 149,213,268,198a,201a
1984 52,174,257,185a,200a
1985 57,215,185a,197a
1986 49,172,216,263,186a,202a
1987 53,205,263,185a,197a
1988 58,172,207,183a,193a
1989 50,226,322a
1990 55,226,190a,202a
1991 59,174,238,250,186a,198a
1992 149,268,185a,197a
1993 56,172,211,183a,198a
1994 49,172,212,186a,195a
1995 149,268,185a,197a
1996 57,217,183a,196a
1997 50,174,215,261,186a,199a
1998 54,173,216,184a,196a
1999 58,173,206,186a,200a

28th July

1930 54,173,186a,198a
1931 149,263,185a,197a
1932 51,174,183a,195a
1933 55,173,186a,198a
1934 168,211,254,184a,196a
1935 160,228,254,184a,196a
1936 149,263,268,185a,197a
1937 49,173,214,183a,200a
1938 149,174,263,268,318a
1939 58,259,263,185a,197a
1940 50,183,293a
1941 162,172,186a,198a
1942 59,208,310a
1943 149,173,261,268,302a
1944 149,268,185a,197a
1945 60,174,183a,195a
1946 149,268,185a,197a
1947 149,260,268,185a,197a
1948 49,258,260,185a,197a
1949 149,173,268,318a
1950 149,268,185a,197a
1951 51,174,186a,198a
1952 149,185,268,319a

1953 149,260,268,185a,197a
1954 160,208,224,232,184a,196a
1955 56,224,232,260,310a
1956 49,210,185a,197a
1957 149,261,268,278,185a,197a
1958 58,174,211,233,184a,194a
1959 50,173,259,263,318a
1960 149,263,268,185a,197a
1961 59,172,215,233,183a,198a
1962 149,268,185a,197a
1963 56,173,205,184a,199a
1964 60,174,186a
1965 149,173,268,318a
1966 165,228,248,259,263,184a,196a
1967 49,172,263,186a,198a
1968 54,172,263,186a,198a
1969 58,173,248,183a,201a
1970 149,268,185a,197a
1971 55,174,212,184a,203a
1972 149,249,268,185a,197a
1973 160,172,215,186a,193a
1974 165,216,184a,196a
1975 49,173,220,186a,194a
1976 149,268,185a,197a
1977 58,174,183a,195a
1978 158,174,186a,198a
1979 149,268,185a,197a
1980 59,172,210,183a,199a
1981 160,186,312a
1982 56,184,260,187a,199a
1983 149,213,268,189a,201a
1984 53,214,185a,197a
1985 57,215,185a,197a
1986 50,172,216,263,186a,202a
1987 149,205,225,237,263,268,184a,197a
1988 58,172,207,183a,193a
1989 149,226,268,322a
1990 55,226,190a,202a
1991 59,174,238,250,186a,198a
1992 149,268,185a,197a
1993 57,172,211,183a,198a
1994 49,172,212,186a,195a
1995 149,268,185a,197a
1996 58,217,190a,202a
1997 50,174,215,261,186a,199a
1998 55,173,218,184a,196a
1999 59,239,191a,203a

29th July

1930 54,173,186a,198a
1931 59,174,186a,198a
1932 51,174,209,184a,195a
1933 55,173,186a,198a
1934 168,211,254,184a,196a
1935 160,228,254,184a,196a
1936 57,213,263,185a,197a
1937 49,173,214,183a,200a
1938 162,174,259,263,186a,198a
1939 58,259,263,185a,197a
1940 50,183a,293a
1941 55,172,207,186a,193a
1942 149,268,185a,197a
1943 149,268,185a,197a
1944 149,174,268,318a
1945 49,173,183a,195a
1946 149,173,183a,195a
1947 149,260,268,185a,197a
1948 149,268,185a,197a
1949 149,173,268,318a
1950 149,268,185a,197a
1951 51,174,186a,198a
1952 149,185,268,319a
1953 168,207,260,184a,196a
1954 53,208,310a
1955 57,255,258,260,310a
1956 49,210,185a,197a
1957 149,173,225,233,255,258,261,268,318a
1958 58,174,211,233,184a,194a
1959 50,173,259,263,318a
1960 149,268,185a,197a
1961 59,172,215,233,183a,198a
1962 149,268,185a,197a
1963 56,173,205,184a,199a
1964 49,174,186a,198a
1965 149,173,268,318a
1966 166,228,248,259,263,184a,196a
1967 50,172,263,186a,198a
1968 54,172,263,186a,198a
1969 59,173,248,183a,201a
1970 149,268,185a,197a
1971 55,174,212,184a,203a
1972 149,249,268,185a,197a
1973 53,172,215,186a,193a
1974 165,216,184a,196a
1975 49,173,220,186a,194a
1976 149,221,249,268,185a,197a
1977 58,174,183a,195a
1978 51,174,186a,198a
1979 149,268,185a,197a
1980 59,172,210,183a,199a
1981 160,186,312a
1982 56,184,260,187a,199a
1983 149,213,268,189a,201a
1984 53,214,185a,197a
1985 149,268,185a,197a
1986 50,172,216,263,186a,202a
1987 149,205,225,237,263,268,184a,197a
1988 149,249,250,268,183a,193a
1989 149,226,268,322a
1990 56,226,238,249,259,263,190a,202a
1991 60,174,238,250,186a,198a
1992 149,268,185a,197a
1993 57,172,211,183a,198a
1994 49,172,212,186a,195a
1995 149,268,185a,197a

1996 58,217,190a,202a
1997 51,174,215,261,186a,199a
1998 55,173,218,184a,196a
1999 59,239,191a,203a

30th July

1930 55,173,208,186a,195a
1931 59,174,186a,198a
1932 160,209,184a,196a
1933 56,173,186a,198a
1934 157,211,184a,196a
1935 53,228,254,259,263a,186a,200a
1936 57,213,263,185a,197a
1937 50,173,214,183a,200a
1938 162,174,186a,198a
1939 58,259,263,185a,197a
1940 149,183,268,293a
1941 55,172,207,186a,193a
1942 149,268,185a,197a
1943 149,268,185a,197a
1944 149,174,268,318a
1945 49,174,183a,195a
1946 149,173,268,318a
1947 149,268,185a,197a
1948 149,268,185a,197a
1949 149,268,185a,197a
1950 149,268,185a,197a
1951 51,174,186a,198a
1952 149,268,185a,197a
1953 149,260,268,185a,197a
1954 53,208,310a
1955 57,255,258,260,310a
1956 149,268,185a,197a
1957 149,174,225,233,255,258,261,
268,318a
1958 59,174,211,233,184a,194a
1959 149,173,268,318a
1960 149,258,185a,197a
1961 60,172,215,233,183a,198a
1962 149,268,185a,197a
1963 56,173,205,184a,199a
1964 49,174,186a,198a
1965 54,173,186a,198a
1966 166,228,248,259,263,184a,196a
1967 50,172,263,186a,198a
1968 55,172,186a,198a
1969 59,173,248,183a,201a
1970 149,268,185a,197a
1971 56,174,212,184a,203a
1972 49,258,260,261,185a,197a
1973 53,172,215,186a,193a
1974 165,216,184a,196a
1975 49,173,220,186a,194a
1976 149,221,249,268,185a,197a
1977 167,174,183a,195a
1978 51,174,186a,198a
1979 149,268,185a,197a
1980 60,172,210,183a,199a
1981 160,186,312a
1982 57,184,212,258,260,332a
1983 49,213,189a,201a
1984 54,174,257,185a,200a
1985 149,268,185a,197a
1986 50,172,216,263,186a,202a
1987 149,205,225,237,263,268,185a,
197a
1988 149,249,250,268,183a,193a
1989 149,226,268,322a
1990 56,226,238,249,259,263,190a,
202a
1991 60,174,238,250,186a,198a
1992 149,268,185a,197a
1993 58,227,190a,202a
1994 50,172,212,186a,195a
1995 149,268,185a,197a
1996 59,173,214,183a,196a
1997 51,174,215,261,186a,199a
1998 55,173,218,184a,196a
1999 60,173,206,186a,200a

31st July

1930 55,173,208,186a,195a
1931 59,174,186a,198a
1932 160,209,184a,196a
1933 56,173,186a,198a
1934 157,211,184a,196a
1935 53,228,254,259,263,186a,200a
1936 149,263,268,185a,197a
1937 50,173,214,183a,200a
1938 55,174,186a,198a
1939 149,268,185a,197a
1940 149,183,268,293a
1941 56,172,207,186a,193a
1942 149,268,185a,197a
1943 149,268,261,268,185a,197a
1944 149,174,268,318a
1945 50,174,183a,195a
1946 149,173,268,318a
1947 149,268,185a,197a
1948 51,172,258,260,302a
1949 149,268,185a,197a
1950 149,268,185a,197a
1951 160,174,311a
1952 149,268,185a,197a
1953 149,260,268,185a,197a
1954 53,208,310a
1955 149,255,268,185a,197a
1956 149,268,185a,197a
1957 149,174,225,233,255,258,261,
268,318a
1958 59,174,211,233,184a,194a
1959 149,173,268,318a
1960 149,263,268,185a,197a
1961 60,172,215,233,183a,198a
1962 149,268,185a,197a
1963 57,173,205,184a,199a

1964 49,174,186a,198a
1965 162,174,269,186a,198a
1966 166,228,248,259,263,184a,196a
1967 50,172,263,186a,198a
1967 149,173,268,318a
1969 60,173,211,183a,201a
1970 52,174,186a,198a
1971 56,174,212,185a,203a
1972 49,258,260,261,185a,197a
1973 54,172,215,186a,193a
1974 166,216,18a,196a
1975 50,173,220,186a,194a
1976 149,221,249,268,185a,197a
1977 167,174,183a,195a
1978 51,174,186a,198a
1979 149,249,268,185a,197a
1980 60,172,210,183a,199a
1981 53,186,187a,199a
1982 57,184,212,258,260,332a
1983 49,213,189a,210a
1984 54,174,257,185a,200a
1985 149,268,185a,197a
1986 51,172,216,186a,202a
1987 149,225,237,268,185a,197a
1988 149,249,250,268,183a,193a
1989 149,226,268,322a
1990 56,226,238,249,259,263,190a, 202a
1991 49,174,238,250,186a,198a
1992 149,268,185a,197a
1993 58,227,190a,202a
1994 50,172,212,186a,195a
1995 149,268,185a,197a
1996 59,173,214,183a,196a
1997 52,174,215,186a,199a
1998 56,173,218,184a,196a
1999 60,173,206,186a,200a

1st August

1930 56,173,208,186a,195a
1931 60,174,263,186a,198a
1932 160,209,184a,196a
1933 57,173,186a,198a
1934 157,211,184a,196a
1935 54,172,228,254,259,263,186a, 198a
1936 149,263,268,185a,197a
1937 51,174,214,183a,200a
1938 55,174,186a,198a
1939 149,268,185a,197a
1940 52,184,263,358a
1941 56,172,207,186a,193a
1942 149,268,185a,197a
1943 149,258,261,268,185a,197a
1944 149,174,268,318a
1945 50,174,183a,195a
1946 149,173,268,318a
1947 149,260,268,185a,197a
1948 51,172,258,260,302a
1949 149,268,185a,197a
1950 149,268,185a,197a
1951 52,174,186a,198a
1952 57,206,185a,197a
1953 149,268,185a,197a
1954 162,208,184a,196a
1955 149,255,268,185a,197a
1956 149,268,185a,197a
1957 149,174,225,233,255,258,261, 268,318a
1958 59,174,211,233,184a,194a
1959 149,173,263,268,318a
1960 149,263,268,185a,197a
1961 49,172,215,233,183a,198a
1962 149,268,185a,197a
1963 57,205,185a,197a
1964 158,174,186a,198a
1965 55,174,186a,198a
1966 167,228,248,184a,196a
1967 51,172,186a,198a
1968 149,173,263,268,318a
1969 60,173,211,183a,201a
1970 149,174,268,318a
1971 57,174,212,185a,203a
1972 49,258,260,261,185a,197a
1973 54,172,215,186a,193a
1974 166,216,184a,196a
1975 50,173,220,186a,194a
1976 149,223,249,268,185a,197a
1977 60,174,173a,195a
1978 52,174,186a,198a
1979 149,249,268,185a,197a
1980 49,172,210,183a,199a
1981 53,186,187a,199a
1982 58,184,187a,199a
1983 50,213,189a,201a
1984 55,174,214,185a,200a
1985 149,268,185a,197a
1986 51,172,216,186a,202a
1987 149,225,237,268,185a,197a
1988 149,225,237,268,183a,193a
1989 149,226,268,322a
1990 57,226,238,250,259,263,190a, 202a
1991 49,174,238,250,186a,198a
1992 149,268,185a,197a
1993 58,227,190a,202a
1994 51,172,212,186a,195a
1995 149,268,185a,197a
1996 60,173,214,183a,196a
1997 52,174,215,186a,199a
1998 56,173,218,184a,196a
1999 60,172,206,186a,200a

2nd August

1930 56,173,208,186a,195a
1931 60,174,209,184a,199a

1932 149,268,185a,197a
1933 57,173,186a,198a
1934 158,211,184a,196a
1935 54,173,263,186a,198a
1936 149,268,185a,197a
1937 51,174,214,183a,200a
1938 56,174,186a,198a
1939 149,263,268,185a,197a
1940 52,184,263,358a
1941 57,172,207,186a,193a
1942 149,268,185a,197a
1943 149,258,261,268,185a,197a
1944 149,174,268,318a
1945 159,174,183a,195a
1946 149,186,3268,319a
1947 149,260,268,185a,197a
1948 149,260,268,185a,197a
1949 149,268,185a,197a
1950 49,174,216,255,184a,199a
1951 149,174,268,318a
1952 57,206,185a,197a
1953 149,268,185a,197a
1954 162,208,184a,196a
1955 149,255,268,185a,197a
1956 149,268,185a,197a
1957 149,174,225,233,255,268,318a
1958 60,174,211,233,184a,194a
1959 149,173,263,268,318a
1960 57,213,185a,197a
1961 49,172,215,233,183a,198a
1962 149,173,268,318a
1963 149,268,185a,197a
1964 158,174,186a,198a
1965 55,174,186a,198a
1966 167,228,248,184a,196a
1967 51,172,186a,198a
1968 149,173a,263,268,318a
1969 49,173,248,183a,201a
1970 149,174,268,318a
1971 57,174,212,185a,203a
1972 149,249,268,261,268,185a,197a
1973 54,172,215,186a,193a
1974 167,216,184a,196a
1975 51,173,220,186a,194a
1976 149,223,249,268,185a,197a
1977 60,174,183a,195a
1978 52,174,186a,198a
1979 149,249,268,185a,197a
1980 49,172,210,183a,199a
1981 54,186,187a,199a
1982 58,184,187a,199a
1983 50,213,189a,201a
1984 55,174,214,185a,200a
1985 149,268,185a,197a
1986 52,172,216,263,186a,202a
1987 56,205,225,237,263,185a,197a
1988 49,225,237,183a,193a
1989 149,226,268,322a
1990 57,226,238,250,259,263,190a, 202a
1991 49,174,238,250,186a,198a
1992 149,268,185a,197a
1993 59,172,211,184a,198a
1994 51,172,212,186a,195a
1995 149,268,185a,197a
1996 60,174,214,183a,196a
1997 53,174,215,261,186a,199a
1998 57,173,218,184a,196a
1999 49,172,206,186a,200a

3rd August

1930 57,173,208,186a,195a
1931 49,209,185a,197a
1932 149,268,185a,197a
1933 58,173,186a,198a
1934 158,211,184a,196a
1935 54,173,263,186a,198a
1936 149,268,185a,197a
1937 52,174,214,183a,200a
1938 56,174,186a,198a
1939 149,205,255,263,268,185a,197a
1940 149,184,263,268,293a
1941 57,172,207,186a,193a
1942 149,268,185a,197a
1943 149,261,268,185a,197a
1944 149,174,268,318a
1945 159,174,183a,195a
1946 149,173,261,268,318a
1947 149,260,268,185a,197a
1948 149,221,255,260,268,185a,197a
1949 149,268,185a,197a
1950 49,174,216,255,184a,199a
1951 149,174,268,318a
1952 149,268,185a,197a
1953 149,268,185a,197a
1954 163,208,184a,196a
1955 149,255,258,260,268,185a,197a
1956 149,268,185a,197a
1957 149,174,225,233,255,268,318a
1958 60,174,211,233,184a,194a
1959 149,173,263,268,318a
1960 57,213,185a,197a
1961 50,172,215,233,183a,198a
1962 149,173,268,318a
1963 58,174,186a,198a
1964 51,174,186a,198a
1965 56,173,186a,198a
1966 168,228,248,259,263,184a,196a
1967 52,172,263,186a,198a
1968 57,173,263,318a
1969 49,173,211,184a,201a
1970 149,174,268,318a
1971 57,174,212,185a,203a
1972 149,249,258,261,268,185a,197a
1973 55,186,187a,199a
1974 167,216,184a,196a
1975 51,173,220,186a,194a
1976 149,223,249,268,185a,197a

1977 49,174,207,221,184a,195a
1978 53,174,186a,198a
1979 57,209,185a,197a
1980 50,172,210,183a,199a
1981 54,186,187a,199a
1982 58,173,212,184a,200a
1983 50,213,189a,201a
1984 56,257,188a,200a
1985 149,268,185a,197a
1986 52,172,216,263,186a,202a
1987 56,205,225,237,263,185a,197a
1988 49,225,237,183a,193a
1989 54,226,259,263,322a
1990 166,226,259,263,190a,202a
1991 50,174,186a,198a
1992 149,268,185a,197a
1993 59,172,,211,184a,198a
1994 51,173,212,186a,195a,
1995 149,268,185a,197a,
1996 49,174,214,183a,196a,
1997 53,174,215,261,186a,199a
1998 57,173,218,184a,196a,
1999 49,172,206,186a,200a

4th August

1930 57,174,186a,198a
1931 49,209,185a,197a
1932 54,174,186a,198a
1933 58,173,186a,198a
1934 159,211,184a,196a
1935 55,173,212,186a,200a
1936 149,268,185a,197a
1937 52,174,214,183a,200a
1938 149,174,263,268,318a
1939 149,205,255,263,268,185a,197a
1940 149,184,263,268,293a
1941 166,218,230,246,186a,193a
1942 149,268,185a,197a
1943 149,261,268,185a,197a
1944 149,174,268,318a
1945 51,174,183a,195a
1946 149,268,185a,197a
1947 149,260,268,185a,197a
1948 149,258,260,185a,197a
1949 149,268,185a,197a
1950 49,174,216,255,184a,199a
1951 149,174,268,318a
1952 149,268,185a,197a
1953 51,207,260,310a
1954 163,208,184a,196a
1955 149,255,258,260,268,185a,197a
1956 149,268,185a,197a
1957 57,174,268,261,318a
1958 49,174,211,233,184a,194a
1959 149,173,263,268,318a
1960 149,268,185a,197a
1961 149,268,185a,197a
1962 149,173,268,318a
1963 59,174,186a,198a
1964 51,174,186a,198a
1965 56,173,186a,198a
1966 168,228,248,259,263,184a,196a
1967 52,172,263,186a,198a
1968 57,173,263,318a
1969 50,173,211,184a,201a
1970 162,174,186a,198a
1971 58,174,212,185a,203a
1972 51,173,258,260,261,302a
1973 55,186a,197a,199a
1974 167,216,184a,196a
1975 52,173,205,186a,194a
1976 57,206,185a,197a
1977 49,174,207,221,184a,195a
1978 53,174,186a,198a
1979 57,209,185a,197a
1980 50,172,210,183a,199a
1981 55,186,187a,199a
1982 59,173,212,260,184a,200a
1983 51,213,189a,201a
1984 56,257,188a,200a
1985 149,268,185a,197a
1986 52,172,216,263,186a,202a
1987 57,205,263,278,321a
1988 149,225,237,268,183a,193a
1989 162,173,226,259,263,328a
1990 162,174,226,263,279,328a
1991 166,226,259,263,190a,202a
1992 50,174,186a,198a
1993 149,268,185a,197a
1994 60,172,211,184a,198a
1995 52,173,212,186a,195a
1996 149,268,185a,197a
1997 49,174,214,183a,196a
1998 57,173,218,184a,196a
1999 50,186,182a,194a

5th August

1930 57,174,186a,198a
1931 49,209,185a,197a
1932 162,174,311a
1933 59,173,186a,198a
1934 159,211,184a,196a
1935 55,173,212,186a,200a
1936 149,263,268,185a,197a
1937 160,214,263,184a,196a
1938 57,174,258,261,318a
1939 49,205,261,263,185a,197a
1940 54,184,259,263,293a
1941 166,218,230,246,186a,193a
1942 149,268,185a,197a
1943 149,174,261,268,318a
1944 149,174,268,318a
1945 160,210,184a,196a
1946 149,268,185a,197a
1947 149,260,268,185a,197a
1948 149,258,260,268,185a,197a

1949 149,268,185a,197a
1950 50,174,216,255,184a,199a
1951 54,174,186a,198a
1952 149,268,185a,197a
1953 51,207,260,310a
1954 163,208,184a,196a
1955 149,255,258,260,268,185a,197a
1956 149,268,185a,197a
1957 57,174,258,261,318a
1958 49,174,211,233,184a,194a
1959 149,173,263,268,318a
1960 149,268,185a,197a
1961 149,268,185a,197a
1962 149,268,185a,197a
1963 59,174,186a,198a
1964 160,174,228,248,259,263,311a
1965 56,173,186a,198a
1966 168,228,248,259,263,184a,196a
1967 149,172,263,268,318a
1968 149,173,263,318a
1969 50,173,211,184a,201a
1970 162,174,186a,198a
1971 58,174,212,185a,203a
1972 51,173,260,261,302a
1973 56,172,215,186a,193a
1974 60,173,216,184a,198a
1975 52,173,205,186a,194a
1976 57,206,185a,197a
1977 49,174,207,221,184a,195a
1978 53,174,186a,198a
1979 149,249,268,185a,197a
1980 51,172,210,183a,199a
1981 55,186,187a,199a
1982 59,173,212,260,184a,200a
1983 51,213,189a,201a
1984 57,214,189a,201a
1985 49,215,185a,197a
1986 53,172,216,263,186a,202a
1987 57,205,263,278,321a
1988 149,225,237,268,183a,193a
1989 55,174,226,238,250,328a
1990 166,226,259,263,190a,202a
1991 51,174,238,250,186a,198a
1992 149,268,185a,197a
1993 60,172,211,184a,198a
1994 52,173,212,186a,195a
1995 57,213,185a,197a
1996 50,174,214,183a,196a
1997 54,174,261,186a,199a
1998 58,173,216,184a,196a
1999 50,186,182a,194a

6th August

1930 166,174,186a,198a
1931 149,268,185a,197a
1932 163,209,184a,196a
1933 59,173,186a,198a
1934 160,211,254,267,184a,196a
1935 164,254,259,263,188a,200a
1936 149,263,268,185a,197a
1937 53,174,214,263,184a,200a
1938 57,174,258,261,318a
1939 49,205,261,263,185a,197a
1940 54,184,259,263,293a
1941 149,261,268,185a,197a
1942 149,173,268,302a
1943 149,261,268,185a,197a
1944 149,174,268,318a
1945 160,210,184a,196a
1946 57,258,261,185a,197a
1947 49,212,258,260,185a,197a
1948 149,221,255,268,185a,197a
1949 149,268,185a,197a
1950 50,174,216,255,184a,199a
1951 54,174,186a,198a
1952 149,268,185a,197a
1953 52,207,260,310a
1954 164,208,224,232,184a,196a
1955 149,255,258,260,268,185a,197a
1956 149,268,185a,197a
1957 57,174,263,318a
1958 49,174,211,233,184a,194a
1959 54,173,259,263,318a
1960 149,268,185a,197a
1961 149,268,185a,197a
1962 149,268,185a,197a
1963 59,174,186a,198a
1964 160,174,228,248,259,263,311a
1965 57,173,186a,198a
1966 157,228,248,259,263,184a,196a
1967 149,172,263,268,318a
1968 149,173,263,268,318a
1969 51,173,211,184a,201a
1970 162,174,186a,198a
1971 59,174,212,185a,203a
1972 149,258,260,268,185a,197a
1973 56,172,215,186a,193a
1974 60,173,216,184a,198a
1975 52,173,205,186a,194a
1976 149,268,185a,197a
1977 50,174,207,221,184a,195a
1978 54,174,186a,198a
1979 149,249,268,185a,197a
1980 51,172,210,183a,199a
1981 55,186,187a,199a
1982 60,173,212,260,184a,200a
1983 52,213,189a,201a
1984 57,214,189a,201a
1985 49,215,185a,197a
1986 53,172,216,263,186a,202a
1987 149,205,225,237,263,268,185a, 197a
1988 149,173,268,183a,195a
1989 55,174,226,238,250,328a
1990 59,226,238,250,190a,202a
1991 51,174,238,250,186a,198a
1992 149,268,185a,197a
1993 60,172,211,184a,198a

1994 149,268,185a,197a
1995 57,213,185a,197a
1996 50,174,214,183a,196a
1997 54,174,261,186a,199a
1998 58,173,216,184a,196a
1999 51,172,206,186a,200a

7th August

1930 166,174,186a,198a
1931 149,268,185a,197a
1932 163,209,184a,196a
1933 60,173,186a,198a
1934 160,211,254,267,184a,196a
1935 164,254,259,263,188a,200a
1936 49,213,263,185a,197a
1937 53,174,214,263,184a,200a
1938 58,174,261,318a
1939 50,185,205,255,261,263,293a
1940 149,184,268,293a
1941 149,261,268,185a,197a
1942 149,173,268,302a
1943 149,261,268,185a,197a
1944 149,174,268,318a
1945 149,268,185a,197a
1946 57,258,261,185a,197a
1947 49,212,258,260,185a,197a
1948 149,221,255,268,185a,197a
1949 149,268,185a,197a
1950 51,174,216,255,184a,199a
1951 55,174,186a,198a
1952 149,268.185a,197a
1953 52,207,260,310a
1954 164,208,224,232,184a,196a
1955 149,255,258,260,268,185a,197a
1956 149,268,185a,197a
1957 149,225,233,255,268,185a,197a
1958 50,174,211,233,184a,194a
1959 54,173,259,263,318a
1960 149,268,185a,197a
1961 149,268,185a,197a
1962 149,268,185a,197a
1963 60,174,186a,198a
1964 53,174,263,186a,198a
1965 57,173,186a,198a
1966 157,228,248,258,263,184a,196a
1967 54,172,263,186a,198a
1968 149,173,268,318a
1969 51,174,211,184a,201a
1970 55,174,186,325a
1971 59,174,212,185a,203a
1972 149,258,260,268,185a,197a
1973 57,172,215,186a,193a
1974 49,173,216,184a,198a
1975 149,268,185a,197a
1976 149,268,185a,197a
1977 50,174,207,221,184a,195a
1978 54,174,186a,198a
1979 149,249,268,185a,197a
1980 160,211,184a,196a
1981 56,186,187a,199a
1982 60,173,212,260,184a,200a
1983 52,213,189a,201a
1984 57,214,189a,201a
1985 149,268,185a,197a
1986 54,172,216,263,186a,202a
1987 149,225,237,263,268,278,185a,197a
1988 149,225,237,268,184a,193a
1989 55,174,226,238,250,328a
1990 59,226,238,250,190a,202a
1991 52,174,238,250,186a,198a
1992 57,173,210,186a,195a
1993 49,172,211,184a,198a
1994 149,268,185a,197a
1995 57,213,185a,197a
1996 51,174,214,184a,196a
1997 55,174,215,261,186a,199a
1998 59,239,191a,203a
1999 51,172,206,186a,200a

8th August

1930 59,174,186a,198a
1931 149,268,185a,197a
1932 164,209,184a,196a
1933 60,173,186a,198a
1934 160,211,254,267,184a,196a
1935 164,254,259,263,188a,200a
1936 49,174,213,263,185a,196a
1937 162,174,259,263,186a,198a
1938 58,174,261,318a
1939 50,185,205,255,261,263,293a
1940 149,184,268,293a
1941 149,268,185a,197a
1942 52,208,310a
1943 149,268,185a,197a
1944 149,174,268,318a
1945 149,268,185a,197a
1946 57,258,261,185a,197a
1947 49,212,258,260,185a,197a
1948 149,184,221,255,260,268,319a
1949 149,268,185a,197a
1950 51,174,216,255,184a,199a
1951 55,174,186a,198a
1952 149,268,185a,197a
1953 53,207,260,310a
1954 57,208,185a,197a
1955 49,209,260,278,185a,197a
1956 149,174,268,318a
1957 149,174,268,318a
1958 50,174,211,233,184a,194a
1959 149,173,268,318a
1960 149,268,185a,197a
1961 149,268,185a,197a
1962 149,268,185a,197a
1963 60,174,186a,198a
1964 53,174,263,186a,198a

1965 58,173,186a,198a
1966 158,228,248,259,263,184a,196a
1967 54,172,263,186a,198a
1968 149,173,268,318a
1969 51,174,211,184a,201a
1970 55,187,187a,199a
1971 60,174,212,185a,203a
1972 149,258,260,268,185a,197a
1973 57,172,215,186a,193a
1974 49,173,216,184a,198a
1975 149,268,185a,197a
1976 166,174,186a,198a
1977 51,174,183a,195a
1978 55,187,187a,199a
1979 149,249,268,185a,197a
1980 160,211,184a,196a
1981 56,186,187a,199a
1982 60,173,212,260,184a,200a
1983 53,213,189a,201a
1984 58,174,257,186a,200a
1985 149,268,185a,197a
1986 54,172,216,187a,202a
1987 149,225,237,268,278,185a,197a
1988 149,225,237,268,184a,193a
1989 56,174,226,238,250,259,263, 328a
1990 60,226,238,250,259,263,190a, 202a
1991 52,174,238,250,186a,198a
1992 57,173,210,186a,195a
1993 49,172,211,184a,198a
1994 54,173,212,187a,195a
1995 149,228,268,322a
1996 51,174,214,184a,196a
1997 55,174,215,261,186a,199a
1998 59,239,191a,203a
1999 52,172,206,186a,200a

9th August

1930 59,174,186a,198a
1931 149,268,185a,197a
1932 164,209,184a,196a
1933 49,173,186a,198a
1934 161,211,184a,196a
1935 57,173,212,263,186a,200a
1936 50,174,213,263,185a,196a
1937 162,174,259,263,186a,198a
1938 58,174,261,318a
1939 50,185,205,255,261,263,293a
1940 149,184,263,268,293a
1941 149,268,185a,197a
1942 52,208,310a
1943 149,268,185a,197a
1944 149,174,268,318a
1945 54,174,186a,198a
1946 149,187,261,268,319a
1947 149,268,185a,197a
1948 149,184,221,255,258,260,268, 319a
1949 59,174,186a,198a
1950 51,174,216,255,184a,199a
1951 56,174,186a,198a
1952 49,206,185a,197a
1953 53,207,260,310a
1954 57,208,258,260,185a,197a
1955 49,209,260,268,278,185a,197a
1956 149,174,268,318a
1957 149,174,268,318a
1958 51,174,211,233,184a,194a
1959 149,173,268,318a
1960 60,172,213,233,186a,195a
1961 149,268,185a,197a
1962 149,268,185a,197a
1963 49,174,186a,198a
1964 162,174,259,263,186a,198a
1965 58,173,186a,198a
1966 158,228,248,259,263,184a,196a
1967 149,173,268,318a
1968 149,173,263,268,318a
1969 52,174,211,184a,201a
1970 56,187,187a,199a
1971 60,174,212,185a,203a
1972 149,258,260,268,185a,197a
1973 57,172,215,186a,193a
1974 49,173,216,184a,198a
1975 54,173,220,186a,194a
1976 59,174,186a,198a
1977 51,174,183a,195a
1978 55,187,187a,199a
1979 149,249,268,185a,197a
1980 149,268,185a,197a
1981 57,186,187a,199a
1982 49,174,212,184a,200a
1983 53,213,189a,201a
1984 58,174,257,186a,200a
1985 149,268,185a,197a
1986 55,172,216,187a,202a
1987 149,225,237,268,278,185a,197a
1988 149,225,237,268,184a,193a
1989 56,174,226,238,250,259,263, 328a
1990 60,226,238,250,259,263,190a, 202a
1991 149,174,238,250,268,318a
1992 166,227,190a,202a
1993 50,172,211,184a,198a
1994 54,173,212,187a,195a
1995 149,228,268,322a
1996 51,174,214,184a,196a
1997 55,174,215,261,186a,199a
1998 60,173218,184a,196a
1999 52,172,206,186a,200a

10th August

1930 59,174,208,187a,195a
1931 149,268,185a,197a
1932 57,209,310a
1933 49,173,186a,198a
1934 149,268,310a
1935 57,173,212,263,186a,200a
1936 149,263,268,185a,197a
1937 55,174,214,184a,201a
1938 149,261,268,185a,197a
1939 149,255,258,261,268,185a,197a
1940 149,184,263,268,293a
1941 149,268,185a,197a
1942 52,208,310a
1943 149,261,268,185a,197a
1944 149,174,268,318a
1945 54,174,186a,198a
1946 149,187,219,247,258,261,268, 319a
1947 149,268,185a,197a
1948 149,221,255,258,260,268,185a, 197a
1949 60,174,186a,198a
1950 160,216,184a,196a
1951 56,174,186a,198a
1952 149,268,185a,197a
1953 53,207,260,310a
1954 57,208,258,260,185a,197a
1955 149,255,268,185a,197a
1956 149,268,185a,197a
1957 149,174,268,318a
1958 51,174,211,233,184a,194a
1959 149,173,256,263,268,361a
1960 49,172,213,233,186a,195a
1961 149,268,185a,197a
1962 57,173,216,187a,195a
1963 49,174,186a,198a
1964 162,174,259,263,186a,195a
1965 58,173,186a,198a
1966 158,228,248,259,263,184a,196a
1967 149,173,268,318a
1968 149,173,263,268,318a
1969 52,174,211,184a,201a
1970 56,187,187a,199a
1971 49,174,212,185a,203a
1972 149,249,268,185a,197a
1973 58,172,215,186a,193a
1974 50,173,216,184a,198a
1975 54,173,220,186a,194a
1976 59,174,186a,198a
1977 51,174,183a,195a
1978 56,187,187a,199a
1979 149,249,268,185a,197a
1980 149,268,185a,197a
1981 57,186,187a,199a
1982 49,174,212,184a,200a
1983 54,174,213,327a
1984 59,174,214,186a,200a
1985 149,268,185a,197a
1986 55,172,216,187a,202a
1987 149,225,237,263,268,278,185a, 197a
1988 149,225,237,268,184a,193a
1989 56,174,226,238,250,259,263, 328a
1990 49,226,238,250,259,263,190a, 202a
1991 149,174,238,250,268,318a
1992 166,227,190a,202a
1993 50,173,211,184a,198a
1994 54,173,212,187a,195a
1995 59,174,213,185a,199a
1996 160,214,184a,196a
1997 56,174,215,186a,199a
1998 60,173,218,184a,196a
1999 53,172,206,186a,200a

11th August

1930 60,174,208,187a,195a
1931 149,268,185a,197a
1932 165,210,184a,196a
1933 49,173,186a,198a
1934 162,211,184a,196a
1935 58,173,212,263,186a,200a
1936 51,174,186a,198a
1937 55,174,214,184a,201a
1938 149,261,268,185a,197a
1939 149,255,258,261,268,185a,197a
1940 149,184,263,268,293a
1941 49,258,261,185a,197a
1942 149,268,185a,197a
1943 149,261,268,185a,197a
1944 158,174,186a,198a
1945 54,174,186a,198a
1946 59,187,258,260,261,319a
1947 149,221,245,255,258,260,268, 185a,197a
1948 149,221,255,258,260,268,185a, 197a
1949 60,174,186a,198a
1950 160,216,232,184a,196a
1951 57,174,186a,198a
1952 149,268,185a,197a
1953 54,207,310a
1954 149,268,185a,197a
1955 149,255,268,185a,19a
1956 149,268,185a,197a
1957 149,174,268,318a
1958 52,174,211,233,184a,194a
1959 149,173,256,263,268,361a
1960 49,213,185a,197a
1961 149,268,185a,197a
1962 57,174,186a,198a
1963 50,174,186a,198a
1964 55,174,186a,198a
1965 59,173,186a,198a
1966 159,228,248,184a,196a

1967 149,173,256,263,268,361a
1968 149,173,263,268,318a
1969 52,174,211,184a,201a
1970 57,187,187a,199a
1971 49,174,212,185a,203a
1972 149,249,268,185a,197a
1973 58,172,215,186a,193a
1974 50,173,216,184a,198a
1975 55,186,187a,199a
1976 60,174,186a,198a
1977 52,174,207,221,184a,195a
1978 56,187,187a,199a
1979 49,209,185a,197a
1980 149,268,185a,197a
1981 57,186,187a,199a
1982 50,174,212,184a,200a
1983 54,174,213,327a
1984 59,174,214,186a,200a
1985 149,268,185a,197a
1986 55,172,216,187a,202a
1987 149,225,237,263,268,278,185a, 197a
1988 149,225,237,268,185a,197a
1989 57,174,226,238,250,259,263, 328a
1990 49,226,238,250,259,263,190a, 202a
1991 162,174,186a,198a
1992 166,227,190a,202a
1993 50,173,211,184a,198a
1994 55,173,212,187a,195a
1995 59,174,213,185a,199a
1996 160,214,184a,196a
1997 56,174,215,186a,199a
1998 49,173,218,184a,196a
1999 149,268,185a,197a

12th August

1930 60,174,208,187a,195a
1931 53,209,185a,197a
1932 166,210,184a,196a
1933 50,173,186a,198a
1934 162,211,184a,196a
1935 58,173,212,263,186a,200a
1936 51,174,186a,198a
1937 56,174,214,263,184a,201a
1938 149,268,185a,197a
1939 149,205,255,263,268,185a,197a
1940 57,184,263,293a
1941 49,258,261,185a,197a
1942 149,268,185a,197a
1943 149,261,268,185a,197a
1944 51,174,186a,198a
1945 55,174,210,255,184a,195a
1946 59,187,258,260,261,319a
1947 149,221,245,255,258,260,268, 188a,197a
1948 149,221,255,258,260,268,185a, 197a
1949 49,174,186a,198a
1950 149,268,185a,197a
1951 57,174,186a,198a
1952 149,268,185a,197a
1953 149,268,185a,197a
1954 149,268,185a,197a
1955 149,255,258,260,268,185a,197a
1956 149,268,185a,197a
1957 149,174,268,318a
1958 52,174,211,233,184a,194a
1959 149,173,256,263,268,361a
1960 49,213,185a,197a
1961 54,173,259,263,318a
1962 58,174,186a,198a
1963 50,174,186a,198a
1964 55,174,186a,198a
1965 59,173,186a,198a
1966 159,228,248,184a,196a
1967 149,173,256,263,268,361a
1968 49,173,263,318a
1969 53,174,211,184a,201a
1970 57,187,187a,199a
1971 50,174,212,185a,203a
1972 149,249,268,185a,197a
1973 59,173,220,186a,193a
1974 51,173,216,184a,198a
1975 55,186,187a,199a
1976 60,174,186a,198a
1977 52,174,207,221,184a,195a
1978 56,187,187a,199a
1979 49,209,185a2197a
1980 54,173,186a,198a
1981 58,186,187a,199a
1982 50,174,212,184a,200a
1983 55,186,213,332a
1984 59,174,214,186a,200a
1985 149,268,185a,197a
1986 56,173,216,187a,202a
1987 149,263,268,278,185a,197a
1988 149,225,237,268,185a,197a
1989 57,174,226,238,250,259,263, 328a
1990 50,226,259,263,190a,202a
1991 162,174,186a,198a
1992 59,173,210,186a,195a
1993 51,173,211,184a,199a
1994 55,173,212,187a,195a
1995 60,174,213,185a,199a
1996 53,174,239,184a,196a
1997 57,174,215,261,186a,199a
1998 49,173,218,184a,196a
1999 54,173,206,186a,200a

13th August

1930 49,174,208,187a,195a
1931 53,209,185a,197a

1932 166,210,263,184a,196a
1933 50,173,186a,198a
1934 162,211,184a,196a
1935 59,173,212,186a,200a
1936 52,174,263,186a,198a
1937 56,174,214,263,184a,201a
1938 149,268,185a,197a
1939 149,205,255,263,268,185a,197a
1940 57,184,263,293a
1941 149,261,268,185a,197a
1942 54,174,186a,198a
1943 149,261,268,185a,197a
1944 51,174,186a,198a
1945 55,174,210,255,184a,195a
1946 59,187,258,260,261,319a
1947 149,221,245,255,258,260,268,
185a,197a
1948 57,213,258,260,185a,197a
1949 49,174,186a,198a
1950 149,268,185a,197a
1951 57,174,186a,198a
1952 149,268,185a,197a
1953 149,184,268,319a
1954 149,260,268,185a,197a
1955 149,255,258,260,268,185a,197a
1956 149,268,185a,197a
1957 149,174,268,318a
1958 52,174,211,233,184a,194a
1959 149,173,263,268,318a
1960 149,268,185a,197a
1961 54,173,259,263,318a
1962 58,174,186a,198a
1963 51,174,186a.198a
1964 164,174,259,263,186a,198a
1965 60,173,186a,198a
1966 160,228,248,259,263,184a,196a
1967 149,173,256,263,268,361a
1968 49,173,263,318a
1969 53,174,211,184a,201a
1970 57,187a,199a
1971 50,174,212,185a,203a
1972 149,184,249,258,260,268,319a
1973 59,173,220,186a,193a
1974 51,173,216,184a,198a
1975 56,174,205,186a,194a
1976 49,174,186a,198a
1977 149,268,185a,197a
1978 57,187,187a,199a
1979 149,268,185a,197a
1980 54,173,186a,198a
1981 58,186,187a,199a
1982 51,174,212,184a,200a
1983 55,186,213,332a
1984 60,174,257,186a,200a
1985 149,268,185a,197a
1986 56,173,216,187a,202a
1987 149,263,268,278,185a,197a
1988 54,174,186a,198a
1989 166,174,226,263,276,328a
1990 50,226,259,263,190a,202a
1991 55,174,238,250,186a,198a
1992 59,173,210,186a,195a
1993 51,173,211,184a,199a
1994 56,195,188a,200a
1995 60,174,213,185a,199a
1996 53,174,239,184a,196a
1997 57,174,215,261,186a,199a
1998 149,268,185a,197a
1999 54,173,206,186a,200a

14th August

1930 49,174,208,187a,195a
1931 53,209,185a,197a
1932 166,210,263,184a,196a
1933 51,173,186a,198a
1934 163,211,184a,196a
1935 59,173,212,186a,200a
1936 52,174,263,186a,198a
1937 56,174,214,263,184a,201a
1938 149,268,185a,197a
1939 53,205,261,263,268,185a,197a
1940 58,184,259,263,293a
1941 149,260,268,185a,197a
1942 54,174,186a,198a
1943 149,161,168,185a,197a
1944 52,174,186a,198a
1945 56,174,210,255,184a,195a
1946 149,187,219,247,258,260,268,
319a
1947 149,221,245,255,258,260,268,
185a,197a
1948 57,213,258,260,185a,197a
1949 49,174,186a,198a
1950 54,174,186a,198a
1951 58,174,205,255,186a,196a
1952 149,268,185a,197a
1953 149,184,268,319a
1954 149,260,268,185a,197a
1955 149,255,258,260,268,185a,197a
1956 149,268,185a,197a
1957 49,174,318a
1958 149,268,185a,197a
1959 149,173,263,268,318a
1960 149,268,185a,197a
1961 54,173,259,263,318a
1962 59,174,186a,198a
1963 51,174,186a,198a
1964 164,174,259,263,186a,198a
1965 60,173,186a,198a
1966 160,228,248,258,263,184a,196a
1967 57,173,209,263,318a
1968 50,173,259,263,318a
1969 54,174,186a,198a
1970 58,187,187a,199a
1971 51,174,212,185a,203a
1972 149,184,249,258,260,268,319a
1973 59,173,220,186a,193a
1974 160,216,184a,196a

1975 56,174,205,186a,194a
1976 49,174,186a,198a
1977 149,268,185a,197a
1978 57,187,187a,199a
1979 149,268,185a,197a
1980 55,184,187a,199a
1981 59,186,187a,199a
1982 51,174,212,185a,200a
1983 149,213,268,189a,201a
1984 60,174,257,186a,200a
1985 149,268,185a,197a
1986 57,216,189a,201a
1987 149,263,268,278,185a,197a
1988 54,174,186a,198a
1989 166,174,226,263,276,328a
1990 51,226,238,250,190a,202a
1991 55,174,238,250,186a,198a
1992 60,173210,186a,195a
1993 52,173,211,184a,199a
1994 56,195,188a,200a
1995 49,174,213,185a,199a
1996 53,174,239,184a,196a
1997 57,174,215,186a,200a
1998 149,268,185a,197a
1999 54,173,206,186a,200a

15th August

1930 49,174,208,187a,195a
1931 149,174,268,318a
1932 167,210,184a,196a
1933 51,173,186a,199a
1934 163,211,184a,196a
1935 168,228,254,259,263,186a,200a
1936 149,174,263,268,318a
1937 57,174,214,263,184a,201a
1938 49,258,261,185a,197a
1939 53,205,261,263,268,185a,197a
1940 58,184,259,263,293a
1941 149,261,268,185a,197a
1942 55,174,186a,198a
1943 149,161,168,185a,197a
1944 52,174,186a,198a
1945 56,174,210,255,184a,195a
1946 149,187,219,247,258,260,268, 319a
1947 149,260,268,278,185a,197a
1948 149,221,255,268,185a,197a
1949 158,174,186a,198a
1950 54,174,186a,198a
1951 58,174,205,255,186a,196a
1952 149,268,185a,197a
1953 149,184,268,319a
1954 149,260,268,185a,197a
1955 149,255,268,185a,197a
1956 149,268,185a,197a
1957 49,174,318a
1958 149,268,185a,197a
1959 147,173,259,263,268,318a
1960 149,268,185a,197a
1961 149,268,185a,197a
1962 59,174,186a,198a
1963 52,174,186a,198a
1964 164,174,259,263,186a,198a
1965 60,173,186a,198a
1966 149,259,263,268,310a
1967 57,173,209,263,318a
1968 158,174,259,263,269,186a,198a
1969 54,174,186a,198a
1970 58,187,187a,199a
1971 51,174,212,185a,203a
1972 56,173,213,184a,198a
1973 60,173,215,186a,198a
1974 149,268,185a,197a
1975 57,174,220,186a,195a
1976 49,174,186a,198a
1977 149,268,185a,197a
1978 58,187,187a,199a
1979 149,249,268,185a,197a
1980 55,184,187a,199a
1981 56,186,187a,199a
1982 52,174,212,185a,200a
1983 149,213,268,189a,201a
1984 49,174,257,186a,200a
1985 149,268,185a,197a
1986 57,216,189a,201a
1987 149,225,237,263,268,278,185a, 197a
1988 54,174,186a,198a
1989 59,174,226,328a
1990 51,226,238,250,190a,202a
1991 56,174,186a,198a
1992 60,173,210,186a,195a
1993 52,173,211,184a,199a
1994 57,173,212,187a,195a
1995 49,174,213,185a,199a
1996 54,174,239,184a,196a
1997 58,174,215,186a,200a
1998 149,268,185a,197a
1999 55,173,206,186a,200a

16th August

1930 50,174,208,187a,195a
1931 149,174,268,318a
1932 167,210,184a,196a
1933 51,173,186a,198a
1934 164,211,184a,196a
1935 169,228,254,259,263,186a,200a
1936 149,174,263,268,318a
1937 57,174,214,263,184a,201a
1938 49,258,261,185a,197a
1939 54,205,255,261,263,185a,197a
1940 149,184,268,293a
1941 149,173,261,268,302a
1942 55,174,186a,198a
1943 149,268,185a,197a
1944 52,174,186a,198a

1945 56,174,210,255,184a,195a
1946 49,187,219,247,258,260,319a
1947 149,260,268,278,185a,197a
1948 149,221,255,268,185a,197a
1949 158,174,186a,198a
1950 54,174,186a,198a
1951 59,174,205,225,186a,196a
1952 149,268,185a,197a
1953 149,260,268,185a,197a
1954 149,260,268,185a,197a
1955 53,209,268,185a,197a
1956 149,268,185a,197a
1957 49,174,318a
1958 149,174,268,318a
1959 149,173,259,263,268,318a
1960 149,268,185a,197a
1961 149,268,185a,197a
1962 60,174,186a,198a
1963 52,174,186a,198a
1964 57,174,263,186a,198a
1965 49,173,186a,198a
1966 149,263,268,185a,197a
1967 149,173,263,268,318a
1968 158,174,259,263,269,186a,198a
1969 55,184,187a,199a
1970 59,174,212,187a,197a
1971 52,174,212,185a,203a
1972 56,173,213,184a,198a
1973 60,173,215,186a,194a
1974 149,268,249,185a,197a
1975 57,174,220,186a,195a
1976 158,174,186a,198a
1977 54,174,207,221,184a,195a
1978 58,187,187a,199a
1979 149,249,268,185a,197a
1980 55,184,187a,199a
1981 60,186,187a,199a
1982 52,174,212,185a,200a
1983 57,213,258,261,189a,201a
1984 49,174,257,186a,200a
1985 149,268,185a,197a
1986 58,225,190a,202a
1987 149,225,237,263,268,278,185a,197a
1988 55,174,207,184a,193a
1989 59,174,226,328a
1990 52,226,238,250,259,263,190a,202a
1991 56,174,186a,198a
1992 60,173,210,186a,195a
1993 149,268,185a,197a
1994 57,173,212,187a,195a
1995 50,174,213,185a,199a
1996 54,174,239,184a,196a
1997 58,174,215,186a,200a
1998 149,268,185a,197a
1999 149,268,185a,197a

17th August

1930 50,174,208,187a,195a
1931 149,209,268,185a,197a
1932 169,210,263,184a,196a
1933 52,173,186a,198a
1934 164,211,184a,196a
1935 49,174,263,186a,198a
1936 149,174,263,268,318a
1937 166,230,246,259,263,184a,201a
1938 149,261,268,185a,197a
1939 54,205,255,261,263,185a,197a
1940 149,184,268,293a
1941 149,173,261,268,302a
1942 149,174,268,318a
1943 149,268,185a,197a
1944 149,174,268,318a
1945 149,268,185a,197a
1946 49,187,219,247,258,260,319a
1947 149,221,245,255,268,185a,197a
1948 149,268,185a,197a
1949 51,174,185a,198a
1950 149,268,185a,197a
1951 59,174,205,255,186a,196a
1952 149,268,185a,197a
1953 149,260,268,185a,197a
1954 49,208,258,260,185a,197a
1955 53,209,268,185a,197a
1956 149,268,185a,197a
1957 149,174,268,318a
1958 149,174,268,318a
1959 149,173,268,318a
1960 149,268,185a,197a
1961 149,268,185a,197a
1962 60,174,186a,198a
1963 149,174,268,318a
1964 57,174,263,186a,198a
1965 49,173,186a,198a
1966 149,173,263,268,318a
1967 149,173,263,268,318a
1968 51,174,234,256,269,186a,198a
1969 55,184,187a,199a
1970 59,174,212,187a,197a
1971 52,174,212,185a,203a
1972 56,173,213,184a,198a
1973 49,173,220,186a,194a
1974 149,268,249,185a,197a
1975 58,174,220,186a,195a
1976 158,174,186a,198a
1977 54,174,207,221,184a,195a
1978 59,187,187a,199a
1979 149,249,268,185a,197a
1980 56,173,210,184a,199a
1981 60,186,187a,199a
1982 53,212,185a,197a
1983 57,213,258,261,189a,201a
1984 49,174,257,186a,200a
1985 149,268,185a,197a
1986 58,225,190a,202a
1987 149,225,237,268,278,185a,197a

1988 55,174,207,184a,193a
1989 59,174,226,328a
1990 52,226,238,250,259,263,190a, 202a
1991 56,174,186a,198a
1992 49,173,210,186a,195a
1993 149,268,185a,197a
1994 58,228,190a,202a
1995 50,174,213,185a,199a
1996 55,174,214,184a,196a
1997 59,239,191a,203a
1998 149,268,185a,197a
1999 149,268,185a,197a

18th August

1930 51,174,208,187a,195a
1931 149,209,268,185a,197a
1932 168,210,263,184a,196a
1933 52,173,186a,198a
1934 149,268,185a,197a
1935 49,174,263,186a,198a
1936 162,174,259,263,186a,198a
1937 166,230,246,259,263,184a,201a
1938 149,261,268,185a,197a
1939 149,255,258,261,268,281a,197a
1940 149,184,263,268,293a
1941 149,268,185a,197a
1942 149,174,268,318a
1943 149,261,268,185a,197a
1944 149,174,268,318a
1945 149,268,185,197a
1946 149,187,219,247,258,261,268, 319a
1947 149,221,245,245,255,268,185a, 197a
1948 149,268,185a,197a
1949 51,174,186a,198a
1950 149,268,185a,197a
1951 149,268,185a,197a
1952 149,268,185a,197a
1953 57,207,258,260,185a,197a
1954 49,208,258,260,185a,197a
1955 149,255,268,185a,197a
1956 149,268,185a,197a
1957 149,174,268,318a
1958 149,268,185a,197a
1959 149,173,268,318a
1960 149,268,185a,197a
1961 149,268,185a,197a
1962 49,174,186a,198a
1963 149,174,268,318a
1964 166,174,259,263,186a,198a
1965 50,173,186a,198a
1966 149,173,263,268,318a
1967 149,173,268,318a
1968 51,174,234,256,269,186a,198a
1969 55,184,187a,199a
1970 60,174,212,187a,197a
1971 52,174,212,185a,203a
1972 57,213,189a,201a
1973 49,173,220,186a,194a
1974 149,268,185a,197a
1975 58,174,220,186a,195a
1976 51,174,186a,198a
1977 55,174,207,221,184a,195a
1978 59,187,187a,199a
1979 149,249,268,185a,197a
1980 56,173,210,184a,199a
1981 49,186,187a,199a
1982 53,212,185a,197a
1983 57,213,258,261,189a,201a
1984 50,214,189a,201a
1985 149,268,185a,197a
1986 59,173,216,187a,202a
1987 149,225,237,268,278,185a,197a
1988 56,207,174,263,184a,193a
1989 60,226,238,250,190a,202a
1990 149,226,238,250,259,263,268, 322a
1991 57,174,186a,198a
1992 49,173,210,186a,195a
1993 54,173,211,184a,199a
1994 58,228,190a,202a
1995 50,174,213,185a,199a
1996 55,174,214,184a,196a
1997 59,239,191a,203a
1998 149,268,185a,197a
1999 149,268,185a,197a

19th August

1930 51,174,208,187a,195a
1931 149,209,268,185a,197a
1932 157,210,263,184a,196a
1933 149,173,268,318a
1934 149,268,185a,197a
1935 158,174,259,263,186a,198a
1936 162,174,259,263,186a,198a
1937 166,230,246,259,263,184a,201a
1938 149,261,268,185a,197a
1939 149,255,258,261,268,185a,197a
1940 149,184,263,268,293a
1941 149,268,185a,197a
1942 149,174,268,318a
1943 149,261,268,185a,197a
1944 162,174,269,186a,198a
1945 149,268,185a,197a
1946 149,187,219,247,258,261,268, 319a
1947 149,221,245,255,258,260,268, 185a,197a
1948 149,268,185a,197a
1949 51,174,186a,198a
1950 149,268,185a,197a
1951 149,268,185a,197a
1952 149,268,185a,197a
1953 57,207,258,260,185a,197a

1954 149,268,185a,197a
1955 149,255,268,185a,197a
1956 149,268,185a,197a
1957 51,174,186a,198a
1958 149,268,185a,197a
1959 149,173,263,268,318a
1960 149,268,185a,197a
1961 56,174,214,223,184a,199a
1962 49,174,186a,198a
1963 149,174,268,318a
1964 166,174,259,263,186a,198a
1965 50,173,186a,198a
1966 149,268,185a,197a
1967 149,173,268,318a
1968 52,174,234,256,259,263,269, 186a,198a
1969 56,174,211,184a,201a
1970 60,174,212,187a,197a
1971 149,268,185a,197a
1972 57,213,189a,201a
1973 50,187,187a,199a
1974 149,268,185a,197a
1975 58,174,220,186a,195a
1976 51,174,186a,198a
1977 55,174,207,221,184a,195a
1978 60,187,187a,199a
1979 149,249,268,185a,197a
1980 57,173,210,184a,199a
1981 49,187,187a,199a
1982 54,174,21,185a,200a
1983 149,213,258,261,268,189a,201a
1984 50,214,189a,201a
1985 149,268,185a,197a
1986 59,173,216,187a,202a
1987 149,225,237,263,268,278,185a, 197a
1988 56,207,174,263,184a,193a
1989 60,226,238,250,190a,202a
1990 149,226,238,250,259,263,268, 322a
1991 57,174,186a,198a
1992 158,238,250,186a,195a
1993 54,173,211,184a,199a
1994 59,174,212,187a,196a
1995 51,174,213,185a,199a
1996 55,174,214,184a,196a
1997 60,174,215,187a,200a
1998 149,268,185a,197a
1999 57,206,185a,197a

20th August

1930 160,208,184a,196a
1931 149,209,268,185a,197a
1932 157,210,263,184a,196a
1933 149,173,268,318a
1934 149,268,185a,197a
1935 158,174,259,263,186a,198a
1936 55,174,186a,198a
1937 59,174,214,184a,201a
1938 149,261,268,185a,197a
1939 149,205,255,263,268,185a,197a
1940 149,184,218,230,246,263,268, 293a
1941 149,268,185a,197a
1942 149,174,268,318a
1943 149,261,268,185a,197a
1944 162,174,269,286a,198a
1945 149,268,185a,197a
1946 51,187,219,247,258,260,319a
1947 149,221,245,255,258,260,268, 185a,197a
1948 149,268,185a,197a
1949 160,174,311a
1950 149,268,185a,197a
1951 49,205,185a,197a
1952 149,268,185a,197a
1953 57,207,258,260,185a,197a
1954 149,268,185a,197a
1955 149,255,268,185a,197a
1956 149,268,185a,197a
1957 51,174,186a,198a
1958 149,268,185a,197a
1959 149,173,263,268,318a
1960 149,268,185a,197a
1961 57,174,214,233,184a,199a
1962 50,174,186a,198a
1963 54,174,186a,198a,
1964 166,174,269,263,186a,198a
1965 51,173,207,187a,199a
1966 149,268,185a,197a
1967 149,173,263,268,318a
1968 52,174,234,256,259,263,269, 186a,198a
1969 56,174,211,184a,201a
1970 49,174,212,187a,197a
1971 149,268,185a,197a
1972 58,173,213,184a,198a
1973 50,187,187a,199a
1974 55,185,187a,199a
1975 59,174,220,186a,195a
1976 51,174,186a,198a
1977 56,174,207,221,184a,195a
1978 60,187,187a,199a
1979 149,249,268,185a,197a
1980 57,173,210,184a,199a
1981 49,187,187a,199a
1982 54,174,212,185a,200a
1983 149,213,258,261,268,189a,201a
1984 51,214,189a,201a
1985 149,268,185a,197a
1986 60,73,216,187a,202a
1987 149,225,237,263,268,278,185a, 197a
1988 56,207,174,263,184a,193a
1989 49,226,238,250,190a,202a
1990 149,226,238,250,259,263,258, 322a
1991 149,227,322a

1992 158,238,250,186a,195a
1993 55,184,187a,199a
1994 59,174,212,187a,196a
1995 51,174,213,185a,199a
1996 56,174,239,184a,196a
1997 60,174,215,187a,200a
1998 149,268,185a,197a
1999 57,206,185a,197a

21st August

1930 160,208,184a,196a
1931 57,209,185a,197a
1932 157,210,263,184a,196a
1933 54,173,186a,198a
1934 149,268,185a,197a
1935 51,174,186a,198a
1936 55,174,186a,198a
1937 59,174,214,184a,201a
1938 149,268,261,185a,197a
1939 149,205,255,263,268,185a,197a
1940 149,184,218,230,246,263,268, 293a
1941 149,261,268,185a,197a
1942 149,174,268,318a
1943 149,261,268,185a,197a
1944 162,174,269,186a,198a
1945 149,268,185a,197a
1946 51,187,219,247,258,260,319a
1947 149,221,245,255,258,260,268, 185a,197a
1948 149,268,185a,197a
1949 160,214,184a,196a
1950 149,268,185a,197a
1951 49,205,185a,197a
1952 149,268,185a,197a
1953 149,268,185a,197a
1954 149,260,268,185a,197a
1955 149,255,268,185a,197a
1956 149,268,185a,197a
1957 52,174,186a,198a
1958 149,268,185a,197a
1959 149,173,263,268,318a
1960 149,268,185a,197a
1961 57,174,214,233,184a,199a
1962 50,174,186a,198a
1963 54,174,186a,198a
1964 59,174,186a,198a
1965 51,173,207,187a,200a
1966 56,208,259,263,185a,197a
1967 149,173,263,268,318a
1968 52,174,234,256,259,263,269, 186a,198a
1969 57,174,211,184a,201a
1970 49,174,212,187a,197a
1971 54,174,186a,198a
1972 58,173,213,184a,198a
1973 50,187,187a,199a
1974 55,185,187a,199a
1975 59,174,220,186a,195a
1976 52,174,186a,198a
1977 56,174,208,221,184a,195a
1978 49,187,187a,199a
1979 149,249,268,185a,197a
1980 57,173,210,184a,199a
1981 50,187,187a,199a
1982 54,174,212,185a,200a
1983 149,213,258,261,268,189a,201a
1984 51,214,189a,201a
1985 149,197,268,320a
1986 60,173,216,187a,202a
1987 149,225,238,263,268,278,185a, 197a
1988 57,207,189a,201a
1989 49,226,238,250,190a,202a
1990 54,226,259,263,322a
1991 149,227,322a
1992 158,238,250,186a,195a
1993 55,184,187a,199a
1994 168,228,187a,196a
1995 52,174,213,185a,199a
1996 56,174,239,184a,196a
1997 49,174,215,187a,200a
1998 149,268,185a,197a
1999 57,206,185a,197a

22nd August

1930 53,174,208,187a,195a
1931 57,209,185a,197a
1932 158,210,263,184a,196a
1933 54,173,186a,198a
1934 149,268,185a,197a
1935 51,174,186a,198a
1936 55,174,186a,198a
1937 60,174,214,263,184a,201a
1938 149,268,261,185a,197a
1939 57,205,261,263,185a,197a
1940 149,184,208,230,246,263,268, 293a
1941 149,261,268,185a,197a
1942 149,174,268,318a
1943 149,261,268,185a,197a
1944 55,174,186a,198a
1945 149,268,185a,197a
1946 149,187,219,247,258,260,268, 319a
1947 149,221,245,255,258,260,268, 185a,197a
1948 149,268,185a,197a
1949 149,268,185a,197a
1950 149,268,185a,197a
1951 149,268,185a,197a
1952 149,268,185a,197a
1953 149,268,185a,197a
1954 149,260,268,185a,197a
1955 149,255,268,185a,197a
1956 149,268,185a,197a

1957 52,174,186a,198a
1958 57,211,185a,197a
1959 149,173,263,268,318a
1960 149,173,268,318a
1961 166,226,190a,202a
1962 50,174,186a,198a
1963 55,174,186a,198a
1964 59,174,186a,198a
1965 51,173,207,187a,200a
1966 56,208,259,263,185a,197a
1967 149,173,263,268,318a
1968 149,174,234,256,259,263,268,269,318a
1969 57,174,211,184a,201a
1970 50,174,212,187a,197a
1971 54,174,186a,198a
1972 59,173,213,184a,198a
1973 159,187,187a,199a
1974 56,174,216,185a,198a
1975 60,174,205,186a,195a
1976 52,174,186a,198a
1977 57,174,208,221,184a,195a
1978 49,187,187a,199a
1979 149,249,268,185a,197a
1980 58,173,210,184a,199a
1981 50,187,187a,199a
1982 55,185,187a,199a
1983 149,213,258,261,268,189a,201a
1984 52,214,189a,201a
1985 149,197,268,320a
1986 49,225,237,187a,202a
1987 53,263,278,185a,197a
1988 57,207,189a,201a
1989 158,226,190a,202a
1990 54,226,259,263,322a
1991 149,227,268,322a
1992 51,173,210,186a,195a
1993 56,173,211,184a,199a
1994 168,228,187a,196a
1995 52,174,213,185a,199a
1996 57,174,239,184a,196a
1997 49,174,215,187a,200a
1998 149,268,185a,197a
1999 149,268,185a,197a

23rd August

1930 53,174,208,187a,195a
1931 149,268,185a,197a
1932 62,173,259,263,311a
1933 54,173,186a,198a
1934 149,268,185a,197a
1935 51,174,186a,198a
1936 150,174,259,263,269,186a,198a
1937 60,174,214,263,184a,201a
1938 53,258,261,185a,197a
1939 57,205,261,263,185a,197a
1940 62,173,184,263,276,294a
1941 54,174,261,186a,198a
1942 149,174,268,318a
1943 149,174,261,268,302a
1944 150,174,269,186a,198a
1945 149,268,185a,197a
1946 149,187,219,247,258,260,268,319a
1947 149,221,245,255,258,260,268,185a,197a
1948 61,174,213,184a,199a
1949 65,174,186a,198a
1950 149,268,185a,197a
1951 149,268,185a,197a
1952 67,186,187a,199a
1953 150,269,185a,197a
1954 51,174,208,255,187a,201a
1955 149,255,268,185a,197a
1956 72,174,186a,198a
1957 65,174,186a,198a
1958 57,211,185a,197a
1959 149,173,263,268,318a
1960 66,173,186a,198a
1961 58,174,186a,198a
1962 51,174,186a,198a
1963 55,174,186a,198a
1964 72,174,259,262,263,186a,198a
1965 64,64i,173,186a,198a
1966 149,263,268,185a,197a
1967 49,173,209,263,318a
1968 150,174,259,263,269,186a,198a
1969 70,174,186a,198a
1970 50,174,212,187a,197a
1971 54,174,186a,198a
1972 71,173,213,184a,198a
1973 159,187,187a,199a
1974 56,174,216,185a,198a
1975 60,174,205,186a,195a
1976 65,174,186a,198a
1977 69,174,208,184a,195a
1978 62,187,187a,199a
1979 149,249,268,185a,197a
1980 70,173,186a,198a
1981 159,187,187a,199a
1982 185,187a,199
1983 149,213,258,261,268,189a,201a
1984 64,64i,174,214,327a
1985 69,173,215,184a,197a
1986 61,173,216,187a,202a
1987 53,205,263,185a,197a
1988 70,174,186a,198a
1989 62,174,226,262,276,328a
1990 150,226,269,190a,202a
1991 149,268,185a,197a
1992 150,173,269,186a,198a
1993 68,173,211,184a,199a
1994 168,228,259,262,187a,196a
1995 52,174,213,186a,199a
1996 69,174,239,184a,196a
1997 62,174,215,187a,202a
1998 150,269,185a,197a
1999 149,268,185a,197a

24th August

1930 150,174,269,186a,198a
1931 70,174,186a,198a
1932 159,173,311a
1933 67,173,187,325a
1934 71,173,211,246,185a,196a
1935 64,64i,174,259,262,263,186a, 198a
1936 150,174,259,263,269,186a,198a
1937 150,174,259,263,269,186a,198a
1938 150,174,261,269,318a
1939 70,205,261,263,185a,202a
1940 62,173,184,263,276,294a
1941 150,174,261,269,186a,198a
1942 71,174,186a,198a
1943 159,174,258,261,303a
1944 150,174,269,186a,198a
1945 72,173,210,184a,195a
1946 150,187,219,247,269,319a
1947 69,212,268,185a,197a
1948 61,174,213,184a,199a
1949 150,174,269,186a,198a
1950 70,174,186a,198a
1951 63,174,186a,198a
1952 67,186,187a,199a
1953 150,269,185a,197a
1954 160,208,184a,196a
1955 150,269,185a,197a
1956 61,174,186,198a
1957 65,174,186a,198a
1958 150,269,185a,197a
1959 62,173,259,263,186a,198a
1960 66,173,186a,198a
1961 150,74,269,186a,198a
1962 63,174,262,186a,198a
1963 68,174,186a,198a
1964 72,174,259,262,263,186a,198a
1965 64,64i,173,186a,198a
1966 69,173,263,186a,198a
1967 150,174,259,263,269,186a,198a
1968 150,174,263,269,276,186a,198a
1969 70,174,186a,198a
1970 63,174,186a,198a
1971 67,174,186a,198a
1972 71,173,213,184a,198a
1973 64,187,187a,199a
1974 68,174,186a,198a
1975 72,174,186a,198a
1976 65,174,186a,198a
1977 70,174,208,184a,195a
1978 62,187,187a,199a
1979 66,173,186a,198a
1980 71,173,186a,198a
1981 159,187,187a,199a
1982 68,257,188a,200a
1983 72,174,213,327a
1984 64,64i,174,214,327a
1985 69,173,215,184a,197a
1986 61,173,216,187a,202a
1987 150,174,259,263,186a,198a
1988 70,174,186a,198a
1989 150,226,259,262,269,328a
1990 150,226,269,190a,202a
1991 150,269,185a,197a
1992 150,173,269,186a,198a
1993 69,173,211,184a,199a
1994 61,174,212,187a,196a
1995 150,174,269,186a,198a
1996 70,217,190a,202a
1997 62,174,215,187a,200a
1998 150,269,185a,197a
1999 71,239,191a,203a

25th August

1930 150,174,269,186a,198a
1931 71,174,186a,198a
1932 159,173,311a
1933 67,173,187,325a
1934 72,174,186a,198a
1935 64,64i,174,269,262,263,186a, 198a
1936 150,174,259,263,269,186a,198a
1937 150,174,259,263,269,186a,198a
1938 150,174,261,269,186a,198a
1939 70,205,261,263,185a,202a
1940 62,173,184,263,276,294a
1941 67,174,261,186a,198a
1942 71,174,186a,198a
1943 64,64i,174,303a
1944 150,174,269,186a,198a
1945 72,173,211,184a,195a
1946 150,187,219,247,258,261, 269,319a
1947 69,212,268,185a,197a
1948 62,174,213,184a,199a
1949 150,174,269,186a,198a
1950 71,174,186a,198a
1951 63,174,186a,198a
1952 67,186a,187a,199a
1953 150,269,185a,197a
1954 160,208,184a,196a
1955 69,209,268,185a,197a
1956 61,174,186a,198a
1957 150,174,269,186a,198a
1958 150,269,185a,197a
1959 62,173,259,263,186a,198a
1960 67,173,186a,198a
1961 150,174,209,186a,198a
1962 64,64i,174,262,186a,198a
1963 150,174,269,186a,198a
1964 72,174,259,262,263,186a,198a
1965 65,173,186a,198a
1966 70,173,263,186a,198a
1967 62,174,259,263,269,186a,198a
1968 150,174,263,269,276,186a,198a

1969 71,174,186a,198a
1970 63,174,186a,198a
1971 67,174,186a,198a
1972 72,173,213,184a,198a
1973 64,187,187a,199a
1974 69,174,186a,198a
1975 61,174,186a,198a
1976 150,174,269,186a,198a
1977 70,174,208,184a,195a
1978 63,187,187a,199a
1979 67,173,186a,198a
1980 71,174,186a,198a
1981 64,187,187a,199a
1982 68,257,188a,200a
1983 72,174,213,327a
1984 65,174,214,327a
1985 70,173,215,184a,197a
1986 62,173,216,187a,202a
1987 150,174,259,263,269,186a,198a
1988 71,174,186a,198a
1989 150,226,259,262,269,328a
1990 150,226,259,263,269,190a,202a
1991 150,269,185a,197a
1992 150,173,269,186a,198a
1996 69,173,211,184a,199a
1994 61,174,212,187a,196a
1995 150,174,269,186a,198a
1996 70,217,190a,202a
1997 63174,215,187a,200a
1998 150,269,185a,197a
1999 71,239,191a,203a

26th August

1930 67,174,186a,198a
1931 71,174,186a,198a
1932 159,173,311a
1933 68,173,186a,198a
1934 72,174,186a,198a
1935 150,174,259,263,269,186a,198a
1936 150,174,259,263,269,186a,198a
1937 62,184,259,263,186a,198a
1938 150,174,261,269,186a,198a
1939 70,205,261,263,185a,202a
1940 150,173,184,269,294a
1941 67,174,261,186a,198a
1942 72,174,186a,198a
1943 64,64i,174,303a
1944 150,174,269,186a,198a
1945 61,173,211,184a,195a
1946 150,187,219,247,258,261,269, 319a
1947 150,269,185a,197a
1948 62,174,213,184a,199a
1949 67,174,187,325a
1950 71,174,186a,198a
1951 63,174,186a,198a
1952 68,173,206,186a,200a
1953 150,269,185a,197a
1954 65,174,208,187a,202a
1955 69,174,209,318a
1956 62,174,186a,198a
1957 150,174,269,186a,198a
1958 150,269,185a,197a
1959 150,173,269,186a,198a
1960 67,173,186a,198a
1961 150,174,269,186a,198a
1962 64,64i,174,262,186a,198a
1963 150,174,269,186a,198a
1964 150,259,263,269,86a,198a
1965 150,259,263,269,186a,198a
1966 65,173,186a,198a
1967 62,174,259,263,269,186a,198a
1968 150,174,269,186a,198a
1969 71,174,186a,198a
1970 64,64i,174,186a,198a
1971 68,174,186a,198a
1972 72,173,213,184a,198a
1973 65,187,187a,199a
1974 69,174,186a,198a
1975 61,174,186a,198a
1976 66,175,186,325a
1977 71,174,208,184a,195a
1978 63,187,187a,199a
1979 67,173,186a,198a
1980 72,174,186a,198a
1981 64,187,187a,199a
1982 69,212,189a,201a
1983 157,174,213,327a
1984 65,174,214,327a
1985 70,173,215,184a,197a
1986 62,173,216,187a,202a
1987 150,174,259,263,269,186a,198a
1988 71,174,186a,198a
1989 150,226,259,262,269,190a,202a
1990 150,226,259,263,269,190a,202a
1991 150,269,185a,197a
1992 150,173,269,186a,198a
1993 69,174,211,184a,199a
1994 62,238,250,259,262,187a,196a
1995 150,174,269,186a,198a
1996 71,175,214,184a,196a
1997 63,174,215,187a,200a
1998 150,269,185a,197a
1999 71,239,191a,203a

27th August

1930 67,187,187a,199a
1931 150,174,269,186a,198a
1932 160,173,263,311a
1933 68,173,186a,198a
1934 61,174,186a,198a
1935 150,174,259,263,269,186a,198a
1936 150,174,259,263,269,186a,198a
1937 62,174,259,263,186a,198a
1938 67,174,261,186a,198a
1939 150,173,261,269,186a,198a

1940 150,173,184,269,294a
1941 68,174,186a,198a
1942 72,174,186a,198a
1943 64,64i,175,219,231,247,183a, 195a
1944 150,174,269,186a,198a
1945 61,173,211,184a,195a
1946 150,187,219,247,258,261,269, 319a
1947 150,174,269,318a
1948 63,174,213,184a,199a
1949 67,174,187,325a
1950 72,174,186a,198a
1951 64,64i,174,186a,198a
1952 68,173,206,186a,200a
1953 150,269,185a,197a
1954 65,174,208,187a,202a
1955 150,174,269,318a
1956 62,176,210,184a,204a
1957 67,187,325a
1958 150,269,185a,197a
1959 150,173,269,186a,198a
1960 150,174,269,186a,198a
1961 150,174,269,186a,198a
1962 65,174,186a,198a
1963 69,175,205,186a,198a
1964 150,259,263,269,186a,198a
1965 66,173,186a,198a
1966 150,173,263,269,318a
1967 62,174,259,263,269,186a,198a
1968 150,174,269,186a,198a
1969 72,184,187a,199a
1970 64,64i,174,186a,198a
1971 68,174,186a,198a
1972 61,173,213,184a,198a
1973 65,187,187a,199a
1974 70,174,186a,198a
1975 62,174,186a,198a
1976 163,186,187a,199a
1977 71,174,208,184a,195a
1978 63,187,187a,199a
1979 67,173,186a,198a
1980 72,174,186a,198a
1981 65,187,187a,199a
1982 69,212,184a,201a
1983 157,213,189a,201a
1984 150,174,214,269,327a
1985 70,173,215,184a,197a
1986 63,173,216,187a,202a
1987 150,174,269,186a,198a
1988 72,174,186a,198a
1989 150,226,259,262,269,190a,202a
1990 150,226,259,263,269,190a,202a
1991 150,269,185a,197a
1992 150,173,269,186a,198a
1993 70,227,190a,202a
1994 62,238,250,259,262,187a,196a
1995 150,174,269,186a,198a
1996 71,175,214,184a,196a
1997 64,174,215,187a,200a
1998 150,269,185a,197a
1999 72,173,206,185a,200a

28th August

1930 164,208,184a,196a
1931 72,174,186a,198a
1932 160,173,263,311a
1933 69,173,186a,198a
1934 61,174,186a,198a
1935 150,174,259,263,269,186a,198a
1936 70,175,186a,198a
1937 62,174,259,263,186a,198a
1938 67,174,261,186a,198a
1939 150,173,261,269,186a,198a
1940 150,173,184,259,263,269,294a
1941 68,174,186a,198a
1942 61,174,186a,198a
1943 150,175,219,231,247,258,261, 269,302a
1944 150,174,269,186a,198a
1945 62,173,211,184a,195a
1946 150,187,219,247,258,261,269, 19a
1947 150,174,269,318a
1948 63,174,213,184a,199a
1949 68,174,186a,198a
1950 72,175,216,222,185a,200a
1951 64,64i,174,186a,198a
1952 69,173,232,186a,201a
1953 150,269,185a,197a
1954 150,174,269,186a,198a
1955 150,173,269,318a
1956 62,175,210,184a,204a
1957 67,187,325a
1958 150,269,185a,197a
1959 150,173,269,186a,198a
1960 150,174,269,186a,198a
1961 150,174,269,186a,198a
1962 65,174,186a,198a
1963 69,175,205,186a,198a
1964 62,174,259,262,263,186a,198a
1965 66,173,186a,198a
1966 150,173,269,318a
1967 150,174,269,186a,198a
1968 150,174,259,263,269,186a,198a
1969 72,184,187a,199a
1970 64,64i,174,186a,198a
1971 68,174,186a,198a
1972 61,173,213,184a,198a
1973 66,187,187a,199a
1974 70,174,186a,198a
1975 62,174,186a,198a
1976 163,186,187a,199a
1977 72,174,208,184a,195a
1978 64,187,187a,199a
1979 68,173,186a,198a
1980 61,174,186a,198a
1981 65,187,187a,199a

1982 69,185,212,332a
1983 157,213,189a,201a
1984 150,174,214,259,263,268,327a
1985 150,269,185a,197a
1986 63,173,216,187a,202a
1987 150,174,269,186a,198a
1988 72,174,186a,198a
1989 150,226,269,190a,202a
1990 150,226,259,263,269,190a,202a
1991 150,269,185a,197a
1992 150,173,269,186a,198a
1993 70,227,190a,202a
1994 62,238,250,259,262,187a,196a
1995 150,174,269,186a,198a
1996 72,175,214,184a,196a
1997 64,174,215,187a,200a
1998 150,269,185a,197a
1999 72,173,206,185a,200a

29th August

1930 164,208,184a,196a
1931 72,174,186a,198a
1932 161,173,263,311a
1933 69,173,186a,198a
1934 62,174,186a,198a
1935 150,174,259,262,263,269,186a, 198a
1936 70,175,186a,198a
1937 150,174,269,186a,198a
1938 67,174,261,186a,198a
1939 150,173,259,263,269,186a,198a
1940 150,174,184,263,269,276,294a
1941 69,174,261,186a,198a
1942 61,174,186a,198a
1943 150,175,219,231,247,258,261, 269,302a
1944 70,174,186a,198a
1945 62,173,211,184a,195a
1946 67,187,219,247,258,261,319a
1947 150,174,269,318a
1948 63,174,213,184a,199a
1949 68,187,187a,199a
1950 72,175,216,222,185a,200a
1951 150,174,269,318a
1952 69,173,232,186a,201a
1953 150,269,185a,197a
1954 150,174,269,186a,198a
1955 150,174,269,318a
1956 63,175,210,184a,204a
1957 68,174,186a,198a
1958 150,269,185a,197a
1959 150,173,259,263,269,186a,198a
1960 69,174,186a,198a
1961 150,174,269,186a,198a
1962 65,174,186a,198a
1963 70,175,186a,198a
1964 62,174,259,262,263,186a,198a
1965 67,173,186a,198a
1966 150,173,269,318a
1967 150,174,269,186a,198a
1968 150,174,259,263,269,186a,198a
1969 61,185,187a,199a
1970 65,174,186a,198a
1971 69,174,186a,198a
1972 62,173,213,184a,198a
1973 150,174,187,269,325a
1974 70,174,186a,198a
1975 63,174,186a,198a
1976 68,186,187a,199a
1977 72,174,208,185a,195a
1978 64,187,197a,199a
1979 68,173,186a,198a
1980 61,174,186a,198a
1981 66,174,187,325a
1982 70,185,187a,199a
1983 62,213,237,249,189a,201a
1984 67,174,214,327a
1985 150,269,185a,197a
1986 63,173,216,187a,202a
1987 150,174,259,263,269,186a,198a
1988 61,174,186a,198a
1989 150,226,269,190a,202a
1990 150,226,259,263,269,190a,202a
1991 150,269,185a,197a
1992 150,173,269,186a,198a
1993 71,174,211,185a,199a
1994 63,174,212,262,187a,196a
1995 67,186,187a,199a
1996 72,175,214,184a,196a
1997 64,174,215,187a,200a
1998 150,269,185a,197a
1999 61,173,206,185a,200a

30th August

1930 165,208,184a,196a
1931 150,174,269,186a,199a
1932 161,173,263,311a
1933 70,173,186a,198a
1934 62,174,186,198a
1935 150,174,259,262,263,269,186a, 198a
1936 71,175,186a,198a
1937 150,174,269,186a,198a
1938 68,174,186a,198a
1939 150,173,259,263,269,186a,198a
1940 150,174,184,263,269,276,294a
1941 69,174,261,186a,198a
1942 62,174,186a,198a
1943 66,175,219,231,247
1944 70,174,186a,198a
1945 159,173,183a,195a
1946 67,187,219,247,258,261,319a
1947 150,174,269,318a
1948 64,174,213,184a,199a
1949 69,187,187a,199a
1950 49,175,216,222,185a,200a

1951 150,174,269,318a
1952 70,173,232,186a,201a
1953 150,269,185a,197a
1954 67,187,187a,199a
1955 150,174,269,318a
1956 63,175,210,184a,204a
1957 68,174,186a,198a
1958 150,269,185a,197a
1959 150,173,259,263,269,186a,198a
1960 69,174,186a,198a
1961 62,174,186a,198a
1962 66,174,262,186a,198a
1963 70,175,186a,198a
1964 150,174,259,262,269,186a,198a
1965 67,173,186a,198a
1966 150,173,263,269,318a
1967 150,174,259,263,269,186a,198a
1968 150,174,259,263,269,186a,198a
1969 61,185,187a,199a
1970 65,174,186a,198a
1971 69,173,186a,198a
1972 62,173,213,184a,198a
1973 163,187,187a,199a
1974 71,174,186a,198a
1975 63,174,186a,198a
1976 68,186,187a,199a
1977 72,174,208,185a,195a
1978 65,187,187a,199a
1979 69,173,186a,198a
1980 62,174,186a,198a
1981 66,174,187,325a
1982 70,185,187a,199a
1983 62,213,237,249,189a,201a
1984 67,174,214,327a
1985 150,269,185a,197a
1986 64,174,216,187a,202a
1987 150,174,259,263,269,186a,198a
1988 61,174,186a,198a
1989 150,226,269,190a,202a
1990 70,226,263,276,190a,202a
1991 62,209,185a,197a
1992 150,173,269,186a,198a
1993 71,174,211,185a,199a
1994 63,174,212,262,187a,196a
1995 67,186,187a,199a
1996 61,175,214,184a,196a
1997 65,174,215,187a,200a
1998 69,216,185a,197a
1999 61,173,206,185a,200a

31st August

1930 165,208,184a,196a
1931 150,174,269,186a,199a
1932 66,173,259,263,311a
1933 70,173,186a,198a
1934 63,174,186a,198a
1935 150,174,259,262,269,156a,198a
1936 71,175,186a,198a
1937 150,174,259,263,269,186a,198a
1938 68,174,186a,198a
1939 150,173,259,263,269,186a,198a
1940 150,174,184,263,269,276,294a
1941 70,174,261,186a,198a
1942 62,175,186a,198a
1943 66,175,219,231,247,258,261,
303a
1944 71,174,186a,198a
1945 63,173,302a
1946 150,187,219,247,269,319a
1947 150,174,269,318a
1948 160,213,184a,196a
1949 69,187,187a,199a
1950 49,175,216,222,185a,200a
1951 150,174,269,318a
1952 70,173,232,186a,201a
1953 150,269,185a,197a
1954 67,187,187a,199a
1955 150,174,269,318a
1956 64,175,210,184a,204a
1957 68,174,186a,198a
1958 61,211,185a,197a
1959 150,173,226,256,259,263,269,
318a
1960 70,174,186a,198a
1961 62,174,186a,198a
1962 66,174,262,186a,198a
1963 70,175,186a,198a
1964 150,174,259,262,269,186a,198a
1965 68,173,256,326a
1966 150,173,263,269,318a
1967 150,174,259,263,269,186a,198a
1968 150,174,259,263,269,186a,198a
1969 62,185,187a,199a
1970 150,174,269,186a,198a
1971 70,173,186a,198a
1972 63,173,213,184a,198a
1973 163,187,187a,199a
1974 71,174,208,185a,195a
1978 65,187,187a,199a
1979 69,173,186a,198a
1980 62,174,186a,198a
1981 163,187,270,187a,199a
1982 71,185,187a,199a
1983 63,213,237,249,189a,201a
1984 68,174,201,214,263,368a
1985 150,269,185a,197a
1986 64,174,216,187a,202a
1987 150,174,259,263,269,186a,198a
1988 62,175,207,184a,193a
1989 66,175,226,259,262,328a
1990 70,226,190a,202a
1991 62,209,185a,197a
1992 150,173,269,186a,198a
1993 72,174,211,185a,199a
1994 160,228,259,262,187a,196a
1995 68,175,186a,199a
1996 61,175,214,184a,196a
1997 65,174,215,187a,200a

1998 69,216,185a,197a
1999 62,185,182a,194a

1st September

1930 165,208,184a,196a
1931 150,174,269,186a,198a
1932 66,173,259,263,311a
1933 71,173,186a,198a
1934 63,174,186a,198a
1935 150,174,259,262,269,186a,198a
1936 72,175,186a,198a
1937 150,174,259,263,269,186a,198a
1938 69,174,261,186a,198a
1939 150,173,261,263,269,186a,198a
1940 150,174,184,263,269,276,294a
1941 150,174,261,269,186a,198a
1942 62,175,186a,198a
1943 66,175,259,261,303a
1944 71,174,186a,198a
1945 150,269,185a,197a
1946 150,187,231,247,269,319a
1947 72,174,186a,198a
1948 150,269,185a,197a
1949 69,187,187a,199a
1950 62,175,216,222,185a,200a
1951 150,174,269,186a,198a
1952 71,173,232,186a,201a
1953 150,269,185a,197a
1954 67,187,187a,199a
1955 150,175,269,318a
1956 175,210,184a,204a
1957 69,174,186a,198a
1958 61,211,185a,197a
1959 150,173,226,256,259,263,269, 318a
1960 70,174,186a,198a
1961 150,174,269,186a,198a
1962 67,175,187,262,325a
1963 71,175,186a,198a
1964 64,64i,174,228,248,259,262, 263,311a
1965 68,173,256,326a
1966 72,174,263,186a,198a
1967 150,174,259,263,269,186a,198a
1968 150,174,259,263,269,186a,198a
1969 62,185,187a,199a
1970 150,174,269,186a,198a
1971 70,173,186a,198a
1972 63,173,213,184a,198a
1973 68,187,187a,199a
1974 72,174,186a,198a
1975 64,186,187a,199a
1976 69,186,187a,199a
1977 61,174,257,185a,196a
1978 65,187,187a,199a
1979 70,173,186a,198a
1980 63,174,186a,198a
1981 163,187,270,187a,199a
1982 71,185,187a,199a
1983 63,213,237,249,189a,201a
1984 68,201,214,336a
1985 61,215,185a,197a
1986 65,174,216,187a,202a
1987 150,174,205,259,263,269,327a
1988 62,175,207,184a,193a
1989 66,175,226,259,262,328a
1990 70,226,190a,202a
1991 150,269,185a,197a
1992 68,173,210,187a,195a
1993 72,174,211,185a,199a
1994 160,228,258,262,187a,196a
1995 68,175,186a,199a
1996 61,175,214,184a,196a
1997 150,174,269,186a,198a
1998 150,269,185a,197a
1999 62,185,182a,194a

2nd September

1930 166,208,184a,196a
1931 150,174,269,186a,198a
1932 163,173,311a
1933 71,174,186a,198a
1934 63,174,186a,198a
1935 150,174,259,262,269,186a,198a
1936 72,175,186a,198a
1937 150,174,259,263,269,186a,198a
1938 69,174,261,186a,198a
1939 150,173,261,263,269,186a,198a
1940 150,174,184,263,269,276,294a
1941 71,174,261,186a,198a
1942 63,175,303a
1943 163,175,186,258,261,304a
1944 72,174,186,a198a
1945 150,269,185a,197a
1946 150,187,231,247,269,319a
1947 72,174,186a,198a
1948 150,269,185a,197a
1949 70,187,187a,199a
1950 62,175,216,222,185a,200a
1951 150,174,269,186a,198a
1952 71,173,232,186a,201a
1953 150,269,185a,197a
1954 68,174,255,187a,202a
1955 150,175,269,318a
1956 150,269,185a,197a
1957 69,174,186a,198a
1958 61,211,175a,197a
1959 66,173,259,263,269,186a,198a
1960 70,174,186a,198a
1961 150,174,269,186a,198a
1962 67,175,187,262,325a
1963 71,175,186a,198a
1964 64,64i,174,228,248,259,262, 263,311a
1965 69,173,186a,198a
1966 61,174,263,186a,198a

1967 150,174,259,263,269,186a,198a
1968 70,175,186a,198a
1969 62,185,187a,199a
1970 150,174,269,186a,198a
1971 71,173,186a,198a
1972 64,173,213,184a,198a
1973 68,187,187a,199a
1974 72,174,186a,198a
1975 64,186,187a,199a
1976 69,186,257,187a,199a
1977 62,174,257,185a,196a
1978 66,173,187,325a
1979 70,173,186a,198a
1980 63,174,186a,198a
1981 163,187,270,187a,199a
1982 71,185,187a,199a
1983 64,213,237,249,189a,201a
1984 69,214,189a,201a
1985 61,215,185a,197a
1986 65,174,216,187a,202a
1987 150,174,205,259,263,269,327a
1988 63,175,207,184a,193a
1989 1550,187,226,259,262,269,333a
1990 150,226,269,190a,202a
1991 150,269,185a,197a
1992 68,173,210,187a,195a
1993 72,174,211,185a,199a
1994 160,228,258,262,187a,196a
1995 69,175,213,186a,199a
1996 62,175,214,184a,196a
1997 150,174,269,186a,198a
1998 150,269,185a,197a
1999 63,174,206,185a,200a

3rd September

1930 166,208,184a,196a
1931 150,174,269,186a,198a
1932 163,173,311a
1933 72,174,186a,198a
1934 64,174,186a,198a
1935 164,175,254,259,262,326a
1936 61,175,186a,198a
1937 150,174,259,263,269,186a,198a
1938 150,258,261,269,185a,197a
1939 62,173,286,261,263,276,294a
1940 150,174,184,263,269,276,294a
1941 71,174,261,186a,198a
1942 63,175,303a
1943 163,175,186,258,261,304a
1944 72,174,186a,198a
1945 150,269,185a,197a
1946 150,187,231,247,258,261,269,
319a
1947 61,174,186a,198a
1948 150,174,269,186a,198a
1949 70,187,187a,199a
1950 62,175,216,222,185a,200a
1951 67,174,186,325a
1952 72,187,187a,199a
1953 150,269,185a,197a
1954 68,174,255,187a,202a
1955 150,175,269,318a
1956 150,269,185a,197a
1957 70,174,186a,198a
1958 150,269,185a,197a
1959 66,173,259,263,269,186a,198a
1960 71,174,186a,198a
1961 150,174,269,186a,198a
1962 67,175,187,262,325a
1963 72,175,186a,198a
1964 150,174,259,263,269,186a,198a
1965 69,173,186a,198a
1966 61,174,263,186a,198a
1967 150,174,259,263,269,186a,198a
1968 70,175,186a,198a
1969 63,185,187a,199a
1970 150,174,187,259,262,269,325a
1971 71,173,186a,198a
1972 64,173,213,184a,198a
1973 68,187,187a,199a
1974 72,174,186a,198a
1975 65,185,197a,199a
1976 70,186,257,187a,199a
1977 62,174,257,185a,196a
1978 66,173,187,325a
1979 70,174,186a,198a
1980 64,174,186a,198a
1981 68,187,223,257,270,187a,199a
1982 72,185,187a,199a
1983 64,213,237,249,189a,201a
1984 69,214,189a,201a
1985 61,215,185a,197a
1986 150,174,269,186a,198a
1987 70,174,259,263,186a,198a
1988 63,175,207,184a,193a
1989 150,187,226,259,262,269,333a
1990 150,226,269,190a,202a
1991 150,269,185a,197a
1992 150,174,269,186a,198a
1993 61,174,211,185a,199a
1994 65,174,212,187a,196a
1995 69,175,213,186a,199a
1996 62,175,214,184a,196a
1997 150,174,269,186a,198a
1998 150,269,185a,197a
1999 63,174,206,261,185a,201a

4th September

1930 167,208,184a,196a
1931 150,174,269,186a,198a
1932 164,173,263,311a
1933 72,174,186a,198a
1934 64,174,186a,198a
1935 164,175,254,259,262,326a
1936 61,175,213,246,187a,197a
1937 150,174,259,263,269,186a,198a

1938 150,261,269,185a,197a
1939 62,173,186a,261,263,276,294a
1940 150,174,184,269,276,294a
1941 71,174,261,186a,198a
1942 64,175,186a,198a
1943 68,175,219,231,247,183a,195a
1944 61,174,187,325a
1945 150,269,185a,197a
1946 69,187,231,247,258,261,187a, 199a
1947 61,174,186a,198a
1948 66,175,213,184a,200a
1949 71,187,187a,199a
1950 63,175,216,222,185a,200a
1951 67,174,186a,325a
1952 72,187,187a,199a
1953 150,269,185a,197a
1954 69,174,208,187a,202a
1955 150,175,269,318a
1956 66,175,186a,198a
1957 70,174,186a,198a
1958 150,269,185a,197a
1959 66,173,259,263,269,186a,198a
1960 71,174,186a,198a
1961 150,174,269,186a,198a
1962 68,175,262,186a,198a
1963 72,175,186a,198a
1964 150,174,259,263,269,186a,198a
1965 70,173,186a,198a
1966 62,174,259,263,186a,198a
1967 150,174,259,263,269,186a,198a
1968 71,175,186a,198a
1969 63,185,187a,199a
1970 150,174,187,259,262,269,325a
1971 72,173,186a,198a
1972 65,173,213,184a,198a
1973 69,187,187a,199a
1974 61,174,186a,198a
1975 65,185,187a,199a
1976 70,186,257,187a,199a
1977 62,174,257,185a,196a
1978 67,187,187a,199a
1979 71,174,186a,198a
1980 64,174,186a,198a
1981 68,187,223,257,270,187a,199a
1982 72,185,187a,199a
1983 150,213,269,321a
1984 70,214,198a,201a
1985 150,215,269,185a,197a
1986 150,174,269,186a,198a
1987 70,174,259,263,186a,198a
1988 63,175,207,184a,193a
1989 150,187,226,259,262,269,333a
1990 150,226,269,190a,202a
1991 150,269,185a,197a
1992 150,174,269,186a,198a
1993 61,174,211,185a,199a
1994 65,175,212,187a,196a
1995 70,228,190a,202a
1996 63,175,214,184a,196a
1997 67,174,215,187a,200a
1998 150,269,185a,197a
1999 64,174,206,185a,201a

5th September

1930 167,208,184a,196a
1931 150,174,269,186a,198a
1932 164,173,263,311a
1933 72,174,186a,198a
1934 150,174,269,318a
1935 69,175,186a,198a
1936 62,175,213,246,187a,195a
1937 150,174,259,263,269,186a,198a
1938 150,261,269,185a,197a
1939 62,173,186,261,263,276,294a
1940 150,174,184,269,276,294a
1941 72,174,186a,198a
1942 64,175,186a,198a
1943 68,175,219,231,247,183a,195a
1944 61,174,187,325a
1945 150,269,185a,197a
1946 70,187,231,247,258,261,187a, 199a
1947 62,174,186a,198a
1948 67,184,187a,199a
1949 71,187,187a,199a
1950 63,175,216,222,185a,200a
1951 68,174,186,186a,198a
1952 61,187,187a,199a
1953 150,269,185a,197a
1954 69,174,208,187a,202a
1955 150,175,269,318a
1956 66,175,186a,198a
1957 71,174,186a,198a
1958 150,269,185a,197a
1959 150,174,269,186a,198a
1960 72,174,186a,198a
1961 64,175,214,256,185a,199a
1962 68,175,262,196a,198a
1963 61,175,186a,198a
1964 150,174,259,262,263,269,186a, 198a
1965 70,173,186a,198a
1966 62,174,259,263,186a,198a
1967 150,174,259,263,269,186a,198a
1968 71,175,186a,198a
1969 64,185,187a,199a
1970 150,174,256,259,262,269,326a
1971 72,173,186a,198a
1972 65,174,186a,198a
1973 69,187,187a,199a
1974 61,174,186a,198a
1975 66,185,187a,199a
1976 167,187,187a,199a
1977 63,174,208,185a,196a
1978 67,187,187a,199a
1979 71,174,186a,198a
1980 64,174,186a,198a

1981 69,187,223,257,270,187a,199a
1982 61,185,197a,199a
1983 150,213,269,321a
1984 70,214,189a,201a
1985 150,215,269,185a,197a
1986 150,174,269,186a,198a
1987 150,174,269,186a,198a
1988 64,175,207,184a,193a
1989 150,226,259,262,269,190a,202a
1990 150,226,269,190a,202a
1991 150,269,185a,197a
1992 70,174,227,259,262,328a
1993 62,238,250,185a,199a
1994 66,175,212,262,187a,196a
1995 70,228,190a,202a
1996 63,175,214,184a,196a
1997 67,174,215,187a,200a
1998 150,269,185a,197a
1999 64,174,206,185a,201a

6th September

1930 167,208,184a,196a
1931 150,174,269,186a,198a
1932 165,173,263,311a
1933 61,174,186a,198a
1934 150,174,269,318a
1935 69,175,186a,198a
1936 62,175,213,246,187a,195a
1937 150,174,269,186a,198a
1938 150,261,269,185a,197a
1939 150,173,261,269,186a,198a
1940 150,174,184,263,269,276,294a
1941 72,174,186a,198a
1942 64,175,186a,198a
1943 69,175,219,231,247,258,261, 183a,195a
1944 62,174,187,325a
1945 150,269,185a,197a
1946 70,187,231,247,258,261,187a, 199a
1947 62,174,186a,198a
1948 67,184,187a,199a
1949 72,187,187a,199a
1950 64,175,216,222,185a,200a
1951 68,174,186,186a,198a
1952 61,187,187a,199a
1953 150,269,185a,197a
1954 69,174,208,187a,202a
1955 151,175,269,318a
1956 67,184,187a,199a
1957 71,174,186a,198a
1958 150,269,185a,197a
1959 150,174,269,186a,198a
1960 72,174,186a,198a
1961 150,269,185a,197a
1962 69,175,186a,198a
1963 61,175,186a,198a,
1964 150,174,259,262,263,269,186a, 198a
1965 70,173,186a,198a
1966 62,174,259,263,186a,198a
1967 150,174,269,186a,198a
1968 72,175,186a,198a
1969 64,185,187a,199a
1970 150,174,256,259,262,269,326a
1971 61,173,186a,198a
1972 65,174,186a,198a
1973 70,187,187a,199a
1974 62,185,187a,199a
1975 66,185,187a,199a
1976 167,187,187a,199a
1977 63,174,208,185a,196a
1978 67,187,187a,199a
1979 72,174,186a,198a
1980 65,174,186a,198a
1981 69,187,223,257,270,187a,199a
1982 61,185,197a,199a
1983 150,174,213,237,249,269,327a
1984 71,214,189a,201a
1985 150,215,269,185a,197a
1986 67,174,216,187a,202a
1987 150,174,269,186a,198a
1988 64,175,207,184a,193a
1989 150,226,258,262,269,190a,202a
1990 150,226,269,190a,202a
1991 150,269,185a,197a
1992 70,174,227,259,262,328a
1993 62,238,250,185a,199a
1994 66,175,212,262,187a,196a
1995 71,175,213,186a,199a
1996 160,214,184a,196a
1997 68,174,215,187a,200a
1998 150,269,185a,197a
1999 65,174,206,261,185a,201a

7th September

1930 168,208,254,184a
1931 150,174,269,186a,198a
1932 165,173,263,311a
1933 61,174,186a,198a
1934 150,174,269,318a
1935 70,175,259,262,186a,198a
1936 63,175,213,246,187a,197a
1937 150,174,269,186a,198a
1938 150,269,185a,197a
1939 150,174,261,269,276,186a,198a
1940 150,174,184,263,269,276,294a
1941 61,175,207,246,261,187a,193a
1942 150,175,269,318a
1943 69,175,219,231,247,258,261, 183a,195a
1944 62,174,187,325a
1945 150,269,185a,197a
1946 70,188,187a,199a
1947 63,174,186a,198a

1948 68,175,184a,200a
1949 72,187,187a,199a
1950 64,175,216,222,185a,200a
1951 68,174,186,186a,198a
1952 62,187,187a,199a
1953 150,174,269,318a
1954 70,174,247,255,188a,202a
1955 150,175,269,318a
1956 67,184,187a,199a
1957 71,174,186a,198a
1958 150,269,185a,197a
1959 150,174,256,269,326a
1960 61,174,186a,198a
1961 150,269,185a,197a
1962 69,175,186a,198a
1963 62,175,186a,198a
1964 150,174,259,262,269,186a,198a
1965 173,186a,198a
1966 63,174,186a,198a
1967 150,174,269,186a,198a
1968 72,175,186a,198a
1969 64,185,187a,199a
1970 150,174,256,259,262,269,326a
1971 61,173,186a,198a
1972 150,174,269,186a,198a
1973 70,187,187a,199a
1974 62,185,187a,199a
1975 163,185,187a,199a
1976 76,187,187a,199a
1977 160,208,184a,196a
1978 68,257,188a,200a
1979 72,174,186a,198a
1980 65,174,186a,198a
1981 69,187,223,257,270,187a,199a
1982 62,185,187a,199a
1983 150,174,213,237,249,269,327a
1984 71,214,189a,201a
1985 63,174,215,185a,197a
1986 67,174,216,188a,202a
1987 150,174,259,263,269,186a,198a
1988 65,225,237,185a,193a
1989 150,226,269,190a,202a
1990 150,174,226,269,328a
1991 150,269,185a,197a
1992 70,174,227,259,262,328a
1993 62,238,250,185a,199a
1994 67,187,262,187a,199a
1995 71,175,213,186a,200a
1996 64,175,214,185a,196a
1997 68,174,215,187a,200a
1998 72,173,239,186a,197a
1999 65,174,206,261,185a,201a

8th September

1930 168,208,254,184a,196a
1931 150,174,269,186a,198a
1932 165,173,263,311a
1933 62,174,186a,198a
1934 150,174,269,186a,198a
1935 70,175,259,262,186a,198a
1936 63,175,213,246,187a,197a
1937 150,174,269,186a,198a
1938 71,173,186a,198a
1939 150,174,263,269,276,186a,198a
1940 150,174,184,263,269,276,294a
1941 61,175,207,246,261,187a,193a
1942 150,175,269,318a
1943 69,175,219,231,247,258,261, 183a,195a
1944 159,174,187,325a
1945 150,185,269,319a
1946 167,188,187a,199a
1947 63,174,186a,198a
1948 63,174,186a,198a
1948 68,175,184a,200a
1949 72,187,187a,199a
1950 64,175,216,222,185a,200a
1951 69,174,186a,198a
1952 62,187,187a,199a
1953 150,174,269,318a
1954 70,174,255,188a,202a
1955 150,175,269,318a
1956 158,269,185a,197a
1957 72,174,186a,198a
1958 150,263,269,185a,197a
1959 150,174,256,269,326a
1960 61,174,186a,198a
1961 150,269,185a,197a
1962 69,175,186a,198a
1963 62,175,186a,198a
1964 150,174,269,186a,198a
1965 71,173,186a,198a
1966 63,174,186a,198a
1967 150,174,256,259,263,269,325a
1968 61,175,186a,198a
1969 65,185,187a,199a
1970 150,174,256,259,326a
1971 62,173,186a,198a
1972 150,174,261,269,186a,198a
1973 70,187,187a,199a
1974 63,175,186,325a
1975 67,185,187a,199a
1976 76,187,187a,199a
1977 160,208,184a,196a
1978 68,257,188a,200a
1979 61,174,186a,198a
1980 150,174,269,186a,198a
1981 70,187,223,257,270,187a,199a
1982 62,186,187a,199a
1983 67,213,237,249,189a,201a
1984 71,214,189a,201a
1985 63,174,215,185a,197a
1986 68,202,263,188a,200a
1987 72,175,186a,198a
1988 62,225,237,185a,193a
1989 150,226,269,190a,202a
1990 150,174,226,269,276,328a
1991 150,269,185a,197a

1992 150,174,259,262,269,186a,198a
1993 63,174,211,185a,199a
1994 67,196,228,259,262,188a,200a
1995 72,175,213,186a,200a
1996 64,175,214,185a,196a
1997 68,174,215,187a,200a
1998 150,174,269,186a,198a
1999 65,174,206,261,185a,201a

9th September

1930 157,208,184a,196a
1931 150,174,269,186a,198a
1932 70,174,259,263,186a,198a
1933 62,174,186a,198a
1934 150,174,269,186a,198a
1935 70,175,259,262,186a,198a
1936 64,175,213,246,187a,197a
1937 150,174,259,263,269,186a,198a
1938 72,173,186a,198a
1939 150,174,263,269,276,186a,198a
1940 150,174,185,261,263,269,276 ,294a
1941 61,175,207,246,261,187a,193a
1942 66,175,186a,198a
1943 70,175,219,231,247,258,261, 183a,195a
1944 159,174,187,325a
1945 150,185,269,319a
1946 167,188,187a,199a
1947 64,64i,174,186a,198a
1948 69,213,185a,197a
1949 61,187,187a,199a
1950 150,269,185a,197a
1951 69,174,186a,198a
1952 62,187,187a,199a
1953 151,174,269,318a
1954 71,175,255,188a,202a
1955 150,175,269,318a
1956 150,269,185a,197a
1957 72,174,186a,198a
1958 150,263,269,185a,197a
1959 150,174,269,186a,198a
1960 62,174,186a,198a
1961 66,175,186a,198a
1962 70,175,262,186a,198a
1963 63,175,186a,198a
1964 150,174,269,186a,198a
1965 72,174,262,186a,198a
1966 150,174,259,263,269,186a,198a
1967 68,174,256,263,326a
1968 61,175,186a,198a
1969 65,185,187a,199a
1970 150,174,256,259,326a
1971 62,173,186a,198a
1972 67,174,185,261,325a
1973 167,187,187a,199a
1974 63,175,186,325a
1975 68,175,205,185a,195a
1976 76,187,187a,199a
1977 160,208,184a,196a
1978 69,173,209,188a,199a
1979 61,174,186a,198a
1980 150,174,269,186a,198a
1981 70,187,223,257,270,187a,199a
1982 63,186,187a,199a
1983 67,213,237,249,189a,201a
1984 72,214,189a,201a
1985 64,174,215,185a,197a
1986 68,202,263,188a,200a
1987 61,175,186a,198a
1988 65,225,237,185a,193a
1989 150,226,269,190a,202a
1990 150,174,226,269,276,328a
1991 150,269,185a,197a
1992 150,174,259,262,269,186a,198a
1993 63,174,211,185a,199a
1994 164,196,259,262,188a,200a
1995 72,175,213,186a,200a
1996 65,175,214,185a,196a
1997 69,174,215,187a,200a
1998 150,174,269,186a,198a
1999 150,174,206,261,269,186a,198a

10th September

1930 157,208,184a,196a
1931 150,174,269,186a,198a
1932 70,174,259,263,186a,198a
1933 63,174,186a,198a
1934 67,185,187a,199a
1935 71,175,262,186a,198a
1936 64,175,213,246,187a,197a
1937 150,174,259,263,269,186a,198a
1938 72,173,186a,198a
1939 150,174,261,263,269,276,186a, 198a
1940 70,174,185,261,263,276,294a
1941 62,175,207,246,261,187a,193a
1942 66,175,186a,198a
1943 70,175,219,231,247,258,261, 183a,195a
1944 159,174,187,325a
1945 68,174,211,185a,196a
1946 72,188,187a,199a
1947 64,64i,174,186a,198a
1948 69,213,185a,197a
1949 61,187,187a,199a
1950 65,175,186a,198a
1951 70,174,186a,198a
1952 63,187,187a,199a
1953 150,185,269,319a
1954 71,175,255,188a,202a
1955 150,175,269,318a
1956 150,269,185a,197a
1957 61,174,186a,198a
1958 150,173,263,269,318a
1959 150,174,269,186a,198a

1960 62,174,186a,198a
1961 66,175,186a,198a
1962 70,175,262,186a,198a
1963 63,175,186a,198a
1964 150,174,259,263,269,186a,198a
1965 72,174,262,186a,198a
1966 150,174,259,263,269,186a,198a
1967 165,175,186a,198a
1968 61,175,186a,198a
1969 66,175,185,325a
1970 70,174,256,259,262,326a
1971 63,173,186a,198a
1972 67,174,185,261,325a
1973 167,187,187a,199a
1974 64,64i,175,186,325a
1975 68,175,205,185a,195a
1976 61,187,257,187a,199a
1977 150,269,185a,197a
1978 69,174,186a,198a
1979 62,174,186a,198a
1980 66,175,186a,198a
1981 167,187,270,187a,199a
1982 63,186,187a,199a
1983 68,213,237,249,189a,201a
1984 72,214,189a,201a
1985 64,174,186a,198a
1986 69,216,263,189a,201a
1987 61,175,186a,198a
1988 66,175,207,185a,193a
1989 70,226,259,262,190a,202a
1990 150,174,226,269,328a
1991 150,269,185a,197a
1992 150,174,259,262,269,186a,198a
1993 64,174,211,185a,199a
1994 164,196,259,262,188a,200a
1995 61,175,213,186a,200a
1996 65,214,258,261,185a,197a
1997 69,174,215,187a,200a
1998 62,174,186a,198a
1999 150,174,206,261,269,186a,198a

11th September

1930 157,208,184a,196a
1931 66,174,269,186a,198a
1932 150,174,269,186a,198a
1933 63,174,186a,198a
1934 67,175,185,325a
1935 71,175,262,186a,198a
1936 64,175,213,246,187a,197a
1937 150,174,259,263,269,186a,198a
1938 150,174,269,186a,198a
1939 150,174,261,263,269,276,186a, 198a
1940 70,174,185,261,263,276,294a
1941 62,175,207,246,261,187a,193a
1942 66,175,269,186a,198a
1943 167,175,258,261,183a,195a
1944 64,64i,174,187,325a
1945 68,174,211,185a,196a
1946 72,188,187a,199a
1947 150,174,269,318a
1948 150,269,185a,197a
1949 62,187,187a,199a
1950 150,174,269,186a,198a
1951 70,174,186a,198a
1952 63,187,187a,199a
1953 150,185,269,319a
1954 168,224,232,188a,202a
1955 150,175,269,318a
1956 150,269,185a,197a
1957 61,174,186a,198a
1958 150,173,259,263,269,186a,198a
1959 70,174,186a,198a
1960 63,174,186a,198a
1961 67,185,187a,199a
1962 71,175,262,186a,198a
1963 64,64i,175,186a,198a
1964 150,174,259,263,269,186a,198a
1965 72,174,262,186a,198a
1966 150,174,259,263,269,186a,198a
1967 165,175,186a,198a
1968 175,186a,198a
1969 66,175,185,325a
1970 70,174,256,259,262,326a
1971 63,174,186a,198a
1972 68,174,186a,198a
1973 168,187,187a,199a
1974 64,64i,175,186,325a
1975 69,175,205,185a,195a
1976 61,187,257,187a,199a
1977 150,269,185a,197a
1978 70,174,186a,198a
1979 62,174,186a,198a
1980 67,175,185,325a
1981 167,187,270,187a,199a
1982 63,186,187a,199a
1983 68,213,237,249,189a,201a
1984 61,214,189a,201a
1985 65,174,186a,198a
1986 69,216,263,189a,201a
1987 62,175,186a,198a
1988 66,175,207,185a,193a
1989 70,226,259,262,190a,202a
1990 150,174,226,269,328a
1991 67,174,209,185a,199a
1992 150,174,259,262,269,186a,198a
1993 64,185,187a,199a
1994 69,196,228,188a,200a
1995 61,175,213,186a,200a
1996 66,175,261,185a,197a
1997 70,174,215,187a,200a
1998 62,174,186a,198a
1999 67,174,206,261,185a,201a

12th September

1930 158,208,184a,196a

1931 66,174,269,186a,198a
1932 150,174,269,186a,198a
1933 63,174,186a,198a
1934 67,175,185,325a
1935 168,175,259,262,186a,198a
1936 65,175,213,246,187a,197a
1937 150,174,259,263,269,186a,198a
1938 150,174,269,186a,198a
1939 150,174,261,263,269,276,186a, 198a
1940 150,174,185,261,269,276,294a
1941 159,175,258,261,183a,195a
1942 67,175,186a,198a
1943 167,175,258,261,183a,195a
1944 64,64i,174,187,325a
1945 68,174,211,185a,196a
1946 61,188,187a,199a
1947 150,269,185a,197a
1948 150,269,185a,197a
1949 62,187,187a,199a
1950 150,174,269,186a,198a
1951 71,174,186a,198a
1952 64,187,187a,199a
1953 150,269,185a,197a
1954 168,224,232,188a,202a
1955 150,175,269,318a
1956 150,269,185a,197a
1957 61,174,186a,198a
1958 150,174,259,263,269,186a,198a
1959 70,174,186a,198a
1960 63,175,248,256,187a,195a
1961 67,185,187a,199a
1962 71,175,262,186a,198a
1963 64,64i,175,186a,198a
1964 150,174,259,263,269,186a,198a
1965 61,174,186a,198a
1966 150,174,259,263,269,186a,198a
1967 70,175,186a,198a
1968 62,175,186a,198a
1969 66,175,185,325a
1970 150,174,256,259,262,269,326a
1971 63,174,261,186a,198a
1972 68,174,186a,198a
1973 168,187,187a,199a
1974 64,64i,175,186,325a
1975 69,175,205,185a,195a
1976 62,187,257,187a,199a
1977 150,174,269,186a,198a
1978 70,174,186a,198a
1979 63,174,186a,198a
1980 67,175,185a,325a
1981 167,187,270,187a,199a
1982 64,186,187a,199a
1983 165,213,189a,201a
1984 61,214,189a,201a
1985 65,174,186a,198a
1986 70,250,259,263,188a,202a
1987 62,175,186a,198a
1988 67,175,207,185a,193a
1989 150,226,259,262,269,190a,202a
1990 150,174,226,269,328a
1991 150,174,269,186a,198a
1992 150,174,259,262,269,186a,198a
1993 64,185,187a,199a
1994 69,196,228,188a,200a
1995 62,238,250,186a,200a
1996 150,174,214,261,269,186a,198a
1997 70,174,215,188a,200a
1998 150,174,269,186a,198a
1999 67,174,206,261,185a,201a

13th September

1930 158,208,184a,196a
1931 150,174,269,186a,198a
1932 150,174,259,263,269,186a,198a
1933 64,174,186a,198a
1934 68,175,186a,198a
1935 168,175,259,262,186a,198a
1936 65,175,213,246,187a,197a
1937 150,174,259,263,269,186a,198a
1938 62,174,186a,198a
1939 150,174,261,263,269,273,186a, 198a
1940 150,174,185,261,269,276,294a
1941 159,175,258,261,183a,195a
1942 67,175,186a,198a
1943 72,175,219,231,247,183a,195a
1944 64,174,187a,325a
1945 69,174,211,185a,196a
1946 61,188,187a,199a
1947 66,175,186a,199a
1948 150,269,185a,197a
1949 62,187,187a,199a
1950 67,174,186a,198a
1951 71,174,186a,198a
1952 64,187,187a,199a
1953 150,269,185a,197a
1954 168,224,232,188a,202a
1955 150,175,269,318a
1956 150,269,185a,197a
1957 62,174,186a,198a
1958 150,174,259,263,269,186a,198a
1959 150,174,269,186a,198a
1960 63,175,249,256,187a,195a
1961 67,185,187a,199a
1962 168,175,259,262,186a,198a
1963 64,64i,175,186a,198a
1964 150,174,259,263,269,186a,198a
1965 61,174,186a,198a
1966 150,174,259,263,269,186a,198a
1967 70,175,186a,198a
1968 63,175,186a,198a
1969 67,185,187a,199a
1970 150,174,256,259,262,269,326a
1971 64,64i,174,186a,198a
1972 68,174,186a,198a
1973 61,174,215,188a,194a
1974 65,186,187a,199a

1975 70,175,205,185a,195a
1976 62,187,257,187a,199a
1977 150,174,269,186a,198a
1978 71,174,186a,198a
1979 63,174,186a,198a
1980 68,175,257,326a
1981 72,188,187a,199a
1982 64,186,187a,199a
1983 165,213,189a,201a
1984 61,214,189a,201a
1985 150,174,269,186a,198a
1986 70,250,259,263,188a,202a
1987 63,175,186a,198a
1988 67,175,207,185a,193a
1989 150,226,259,262,269,190a,202a
1990 150,174,226,269,328a
1991 150,174,269,186a,198a
1992 150,174,269,186a,198a
1993 65,185,187a,199a
1994 70,196,228,259,262,337a
1995 62,238,250,186a,200a
1996 150,174,214,261,269,186a,198a
1997 71,239,191a,203a
1998 150,174,269,186a,198a
1999 68,174,206,185a,201a

14th September

1930 159,208,184a,196a
1931 150,174,269,186a,198a
1932 150,174,259,263,269,186a,198a
1933 64,174,186,198a
1934 68,175,186a,198a
1935 61,175,186a,198a
1936 66,175,186a,198a
1937 70,174,259,263,186a,198a
1938 62,174,186a,198a
1939 150,174,261,269,276,186a,198a
1940 150,175,185,206,261,269,294a
1941 159,175,258,261,183a,195a
1942 68,175,186a,198a
1943 72,175,219,231,247,183a,195a
1944 65,174,187,325a
1945 69,174,211,185a,196a
1946 62,188,187a,199a
1947 66,175,186a,199a
1948 150,269,185a,197a
1949 63,187,187a,199a
1950 67,174,186a,198a
1951 72,174,186a,198a
1952 64,187,187a,199a
1953 150,269,185a,197a
1954 61,175,208,188a,202a
1955 150,175,269,318a
1956 150,269,185a,197a
1957 62,174,186a,198a
1958 150,174,269,186a,198a
1959 150,174,269,186a,198a
1960 64,175,213,256,187a,195a
1961 68,175,214,256,185a,199a
1962 168,175,259,262,186a,198a
1963 65,175,186a,198a
1964 150,174,259,263,269,186a,198a
1965 62,174,256,259,262,326a
1966 150,174,259,263,269,186a,198a
1967 71,175,186a,198a
1968 63,175,186a,198a
1969 63,185,187a,199a
1970 150,174,256,259,262,269,326a
1971 64,64i,174,186a,198a
1972 69,174,213,327a
1973 61,188,187a,199a
1974 65,186,187a,199a
1975 70,175,205,185a,195a
1976 62,187,257,187a,197a
1977 67,174,208,185a,196a
1978 71,174,186a,198a
1979 64,64i,174,186a,198a
1980 68,175,257,326a
1981 72,188,187a,199a
1982 65,186,187a,199a
1983 165,213,189a,201a
1984 62,214,189a,201a
1985 150,174,269,186a,198a
1986 71,174,216,188a,202a
1987 63,175,186a,198a
1988 67,175,207,185a,193a
1989 150,226,259,262,269,190a,202a
1990 150,174,226,269,328a
1991 150,174,269,186a,198a
1992 150,174,269,186a,198a
1993 65,185,187a,199a
1994 70,196,228,259,262,337a
1995 62,238,250,186a,200a
1996 67,174,214,261,185a,197a
1997 71,239,191a,203a
1998 150,174,269,186a,198a
1999 68,174,206,185a,201a

15th September

1930 159,208,184a,196a
1931 150,174,269,186a,198a
1932 150,174,259,263,269,186a,198a
1933 65,174,186a,198a
1934 69,175,186a,198a
1935 61,175,186a,198a
1936 66,175,186a,198a
1937 70,174,259,263,186a,198a
1938 150,174,269,186a,198a
1939 150,174,261,269,276,186a,198a
1940 150,175,185,269,294a
1941 64,175,207,246,188a,193a
1942 68,175,186a,198a
1943 61,175,219,231,247,258,261, 183a,195a
1944 150,174,187,269,325a
1945 70,174,211,185a,196a

1946 62,188,187a,199a
1947 67,186,187a,199a
1948 150,269,185a,197a
1949 63,175,214,222,188a,197a
1950 68,174,186a,198a
1951 72,174,186a,198a
1952 65,187,187a,199a
1953 69,174,186a,198a
1954 61,175,208,188a,202a
1955 150,175,269,318a
1956 150,269,185a,197a
1957 63,174,186a,198a
1958 150,174,269,186a,198a
1959 150,174,269,186a,198a
1960 65,175,213,256,187a,195a
1961 68,175,214,256,185a,199a
1962 61,175,186a,198a
1963 65,175,186a,198a
1964 70,174,259,263,186a,198a
1965 62,174,256,259,262,326a
1966 150,174,269,186a,198a
1967 71,175,186a,198a
1968 63,175,186a,198a
1969 68,185,187a,199a
1970 150,174,256,259,262,269,326a
1971 65,174,261,186a,198a
1972 69,174,213,327a
1973 61,188,187a,199a
1974 66,175,186a,325a
1975 70,175,205,185a,195a
1976 159,187,187a,199a
1977 67,174,208,185a,196a
1978 72,174,186a,198a
1979 64,64i,174,186a,198a
1980 68,175,257,326a
1981 61,188,187a,199a
1982 65,186,187a,199a
1983 70,213,237,249,189a,201a
1984 62,214,189a,201a
1985 67,174,186a,198a
1986 71,175,216,188a,202a
1987 63,175,186a,198a
1988 68,175,207,185a,193a
1989 150,226,259,262,269,190a,202a
1990 150,174,226,269,328a
1991 150,174,269,186a,198a
1992 62,174,259,262,186a,198a
1993 66,185,187a,199a
1994 71,196,228,259,262,188a,200a
1995 63,175,213,186a,200a
1996 67,174,214,261,185a,197a
1997 72,174,215,188a,200a
1998 150,174,269,186a,198a
1999 68,174,206,185a,201a

16th September

1930 160,208,254,184a,196a
1931 150,174,269,186a,198a
1932 150,174,259,263,269,186a,198a
1933 65,174,186a,198a
1934 69,175,186a,198a
1935 62,178,259,262,186a,198a
1936 67,187,187a,199a
1937 150,174,269,186a,198a
1938 150,174,269,186a,198a
1939 150,174,263,269,276,186a,198a
1940 150,175,185,269,294a
1941 64,175,207,246,188a,193a
1942 69,175,186a,198a
1943 61,175,219,231,247,258,261,
183a,195a
1944 150,174,187,269,325a
1945 70,174,211,185a,196a
1946 62,188,187a,199a
1947 67,186,187a,199a
1948 150,269,185a,197a
1949 64,175,214,222,188a,197a
1950 68,174,186a,198a
1951 61,174,186a,198a
1952 65,187,187a,199a
1953 69,185,187a,199a
1954 62,175,255,188a,202a
1955 150,175,269,318a
1956 150,269,185a,197a
1957 63,174,186a,198a
1958 150,174,256,259,263,269,326a
1959 150,174,269,186a,198a
1960 65,175,248,256,187a,195a
1961 69,175,248,185a,199a
1962 61,175,186a,198a
1963 66,175,269,186a,198a
1964 70,174,259,263,186a,198a
1965 62,174,256,259,262,326a
1966 150,174,269,186a,198a
1967 71,175,186a,198a
1968 64,64i,175,186a,198a
1969 68,185,187a,199a
1970 150,174,256,269,326a
1971 64,174,261,186a,198a
1972 70,174,261,186a,198a
1973 62,188,187a,199a
1974 66,175,186,325a
1975 71,175,205,185a,195a
1976 159,187,187a,199a
1977 68,174,257,185a,196a
1978 72,174,186a,198a
1979 64,64i,174,186a,198a
1980 69,175,186a,198a
1981 61,188,187a,199a
1982 66,175,186,325a
1983 70,213,237,249,189a,201a
1984 63,214,189a,201a
1985 67,174,186a,198a
1986 72,175,216,188a,202a
1987 64,64i,175,186a,198a
1988 68,175,207,185a,193a
1989 150,226,269,190a,202a
1990 150,174,226,269,328a

1991 150,174,269,186a,198a
1992 62,174,259,262,186a,198a
1993 66,185,187a,199a
1994 71,196,228,259,262,188a,200a
1995 63,175,213,187a,200a
1996 68,174,214,239,185a,197a
1997 72,174,215,188a,200a
1998 150,174,269,186a,198a
1999 69,206,261,189a,201a

17th September

1930 160,208,254,184a,196a
1931 150,174,259,263,269,186a,198a
1932 150,174,259,263,269,186a,198a
1933 65,174,186a,198a
1934 70,175,186a,198a
1935 62,175,259,262,186a,198a
1936 67,187,187a,199a
1937 150,174,269,186a,198a
1938 150,174,269,186a,198a
1939 150,174,263,269,276,186a,198a
1940 150,175,185,206,261,269,294a
1941 65,175,207,246,188a,193a
1942 69,175,186a,198a
1943 62,175,219,231,247,258,261, 183a,195a
1944 150,174,187,269,325a
1945 70,174,211,185a,196a
1946 159,188,187a,199a
1947 67,186,187a,199a
1948 150,269,185a,197a
1949 64,175,214,222,188a,197a
1950 69,174,186a,198a
1951 61,174,186a,198a
1952 150,174,269,325a
1953 70,185,187a,199a
1954 62,175,255,188a,202a
1955 150,175,186,269,363a
1956 150,269,185a,197a
1957 63,174,186a,198a
1958 150,174,256,259,263,269,326a
1959 150,174,269,186a,198a,
1960 65,175,248,256,187a,195a
1961 69,175,248,185a,199a
1962 62,175,262,186a,198a
1963 150,174,269,186a,198a
1964 150,174,269,186a,198a
1965 63,174,256,262,326a
1966 68,175,186a,198a
1967 72,175,186a,198a
1968 64,64i,175,186a,198a
1969 69,185,197a,199a
1970 150,174,256,269,326a
1971 150,174,261,269,186a,198a
1972 70,174,261,186a,198a
1973 62,188,187a,199a
1974 163,186,270,187a,199a
1975 71,175,236,185a,195a
1976 160,187,257,187a,199a
1977 68,174,257,185a,196a
1978 61,174,186a,198a
1979 65,174,186a,198a
1980 69,175,186a,198a
1981 62,188,187a,199a
1982 66,175,186a,325a
1983 71,213,237,249,189a,201a
1984 63,214,189a,201a
1985 68,174,198,326a
1986 72,175,216,188a,202a
1987 64,175,205,187a,198a
1988 165,207,189a,201a
1989 150,226,269,190a,202a
1990 150,174,226,269,276,328a
1991 70,174,227,328a
1992 62,174,259,262,186a,198a
1993 163,185,187a,199a
1994 71,196,228,259,262,188a,200a
1995 64,175,213,187a,200a
1996 68,174,214,239,185a,197a
1997 61,174,215,188a,200a
1998 150,174,269,186a,198a
1999 69,206,261,189a,201a

18th September

1930 160,208,254,184a,196a
1931 150,174,259,263,269,186a,198a
1932 62,174,259,263,186a,198a
1933 66,175,186a,198a
1934 70,175,186a,198a
1935 63,175,186a,198a
1936 67,187,187a,199a
1937 150,174,269,186a,198a
1938 150,174,269,186a,198a
1939 150,174,261,263,276,186a,198a
1940 150,175,185,206,261,269,294a
1941 65,175,207,246,188a,193a
1942 70,175,186a,198a
1943 62,175,219,231,247,258,261, 183a,195a
1944 67,174,187,325a
1945 71,174,211,185a,196a
1946 159,188,187a,199a
1947 68,175,212,186a,196a
1948 150,269,185a,197a
1949 150,269,185a,197a
1950 69,174,186a,198a
1951 62,174,186a,198a
1952 150,174,269,325a
1953 70,185,187a,199a
1954 63,175,255,188a,202a
1955 150,175,186,269,363a
1956 150,269,185a,197a
1957 64,174,186a,198a
1958 150,174,259,263,269,186a,198a
1959 150,174,269,186a,198a
1960 65,175,248,256,187a,195a

1961 70,226,190a,202a
1962 62,175,262,186a,198a
1963 67,174,186a,198a
1964 150,174,269,186a,198a
1965 63,174,256,262,326a
1966 68,175,186a,198a
1967 72,175,186a,198a
1968 65,175,186a,198a
1969 69,185,187a,199a
1970 150,174,256,259,262,269,326a
1971 150,174,261,269,186a,198a
1972 70,174,261,186a,198a
1973 159,188,187a,199a
1974 163,186,270,187a,199a
1975 72,175,205,185a,195a
1976 160,187,257,187a,199a
1977 69,174,257,185a,196a
1978 61,174,186a,198a
1979 65,174,186a,198a
1980 70,175,186a,198a
1981 62,188,187a,199a
1982 67,186,187a,199a
1983 71,213,237,249,189a,201a
1984 63,214,189a,201a
1985 68,174,198,326a
1986 72,175,216,188a,202a
1987 65,175,205,187a,198a
1988 165,207,189a,201a
1989 62,226,259,262,190a,202a
1990 150,174,226,269,276,328a
1991 70,174,227,328a
1992 150,174,259,262,269,186a,198a
1993 163,185,182a,199a
1994 168,196,259,262,188a,200a
1995 64,175,213,187a,200a
1996 165,217,258,261,185a,197a
1997 61,174,215,188a,200a
1998 150,174,269,186a,198a
1999 70,175,206,261,185a,201a

19th September

1930 161,208,184a,196a
1931 70,174,259,263,186a,198a
1932 62,174,259,263,186a,198a
1933 66,175,186a,198a
1934 71,175,186a,198a
1935 63,175,186a,198a
1936 68,175,187a,197a
1937 150,174,259,263,269,186a,198a
1938 150,174,269,186a,198a
1939 150,174,261,263,269,276,186a,198a
1940 150,175,185,206,261,269,294a
1941 66,175,186a,198a
1942 70,175,186a,198a
1943 159,175,258,261,183a,195a
1944 67,174,187,325a
1945 71,174,211,185a,196a
1946 64,188,187a,199a
1947 68,187,187a,199a
1948 61,175,213,222,185a,200a
1949 150,269,185a,197a
1950 70,174,186a,198a
1951 62,174,186a,198a
1952 150,174,269,325a
1953 167,185,187a,199a
1954 63,175,255,188a,202a
1955 150,187,269,319a
1956 150,269,185a,197a
1957 64,174,186a,198a
1958 150,174,259,263,269,186a,198a
1959 150,174,269,186a,198a
1960 66,175,186a,198a
1961 70,226,190a,202a
1962 63,175,262,186a,198a
1963 174,186a,198a
1964 150,174,269,186a,198a
1965 160,174,256,262,326a
1966 69,175,186a,198a
1967 61,175,186a,198a
1968 65,175,186a,198a
1969 70,185,187a,199a
1970 150,174,256,259,262,269,326a
1971 150,174,261,269,186a,198a
1972 71,174,261,186a,198a
1973 159,188,187a,199a
1974 68,186,187a,199a
1975 72,175,205,185a,195a
1976 160,187,257,187a,199a
1977 69,174,257,185a,196a
1978 62,174,186a,198a
1979 66,175,184,325a
1980 70,175,186a,198a
1981 159,188,187a,199a
1982 67,186,187a,199a
1983 71,213,237,249,189a,201a
1984 64,214,189a,201a
1985 69,174,186a,198a
1986 61,175,216,188a,202a
1987 65,175,205,187a,198a
1988 70,175,207,185a,193a
1989 62,226,259,262,190a,202a
1990 150,174,226,269,328a
1991 150,174,269,186a,198a
1992 63,175,210,262,187a,196a
1993 68,185,187a,199a
1994 169,196,259,262,188a,200a
1995 64,175,213,187a,200a
1996 165,217,259,261,185a,197a
1997 62,174,215,188a,200a
1998 150,174,269,186a,198a
1999 70,175,206,261,185a,201a

20th September

1930 161,174,263,311a
1931 70,174,259,263,186a,198a

1932 62,174,259,263,186a,198a
1933 67,188,87a,199a
1934 71,175,186a,198a
1935 64,54i,175,186a,198a
1936 68,175,187a,197a
1937 150,174,259,263,269,186a,198a
1938 150,174,269,186a,198a
1939 150,174,261,269,186a,198a
1940 62,175,185,261,276,294a
1941 66,175,186a,198a
1942 167,175,186a,198a
1943 159,175,258,261,173a,195a
1944 67,174,187a,325a
1945 72,174,211,185a,196a
1946 64,188,231,247,187a,199a
1947 69,187,187a,199a
1948 61,175,213,222,185a,200a
1949 150,269,185a,197a
1950 70,174,186a,198a
1951 62,174,186a,198a
1952 67,187,187a,199a
1953 167,185,187a,199a
1954 160,224,232,184a,196a
1955 150,187,269,319a
1956 150,269,185a,197a
1957 65,174,186a,198a
1958 70,174,259,263,186a,198a
1959 62,174,186a,198a
1960 66,175,186a,198a
1961 71,175,248,256,185a,199a
1962 63,175,262,186a,198a
1963 67,174,186a,198a
1964 150,174,269,186a,198a
1965 160,,74,256,259,262,326a
1966 69,175,186a,198a
1967 175,186a,198a
1968 66,175,269,186a,198a
1969 70,185,187a,199a
1970 150,174,256,259,262,269,326a
1971 163,174,187,258,261,325a
1972 71,174,261,186a,198a
1973 64,188,187a,199a
1974 68,186,187a,199a
1975 72,175,205,185a,195a
1976 65,187,257,187a,199a
1977 70,174,257,185a,196a
1978 62,174,257,326a
1979 66,175,187,325a
1980 71,175,186a,198a
1981 159,188,187a,199a
1982 68,186,212,332a
1983 72,213,237,249,189a,201a
1984 64,214,189a,201a
1985 69,174,186a,198a
1986 61,175,216,188a,202a
1987 65,175,205,187a,198a
1988 70,175,207,185a,193a
1989 150,226,238,250,262,269,188a, 199a
1990 150,174,226,269,328a
1991 150,174,269,186a,198a
1992 64,175,210,262,187a,196a
1993 68,185,187a,199a
1994 61,196,228,188a,200a
1995 65,175,213,187a,200a
1996 165,217,258,261,185a,197a
1997 62,174,215,188a,200a
1998 150,174,269,186a,198a
1999 70,175,206,261,185a,201a

21st September

1930 150,174,259,263,269,311a
1931 70,174,186a,198a
1932 150,174,269,186a,198a
1933 67,188,187a,199a
1934 72,175,186a,198a
1935 64,64i,175,186a,198a
1936 69,175,213,246,187a,195a
1937 150,174,259,263,269,186a,198a
1938 150,174,269,186a,198a
1939 70,174,261,276,186a,198a
1940 62,175,185,261,276,294a
1941 67,175,207,246,188a,193a
1942 167,175,186a,198a
1943 159,175,259,261,183a,195a
1944 68,174,187,325a
1945 72,174,211,185a,196a
1946 150,188,231,247,269,319a
1947 69,187,187a,199a
1948 62,175,213,222,185a,200a
1949 66,175,186a,198a
1950 71,174,186a,198a
1951 63,174,186a,198a
1952 67,187,187a,199a
1953 168,185,187a,199a
1954 160,224,232,184a,196a
1955 150,187,269,319a
1956 150,269,185a,197a
1957 65,174,186a,198a
1958 70,174,186a,198a
1959 62,175,212,256,185a,199a
1960 67,187,187a,199a
1961 71,175,248,256,185a,199a
1962 160,175,259,262,186a,198a
1963 68,174,256,326a
1964 150,174,269,186a,198a
1965 65,174,228,248,256,262,326a
1966 69,175,186a,198a
1967 61,175,186a,198a
1968 66,175,269,186a,198a
1969 71,185,187a,199a
1970 150,174,256,259,262,269,326a
1971 163,174,187,258,261,325a
1972 72,174,186a,198a
1973 64,188,187a,199a
1974 69,186,187a,199a
1975 157,221,249,185a,195a
1976 65,187,187a,199a

1977 70,174,257,185a,196a
1978 62,174,257,326a
1979 66,175,187,325a
1980 71,185,187a,199a
1981 64,188,187a,199a
1982 68,186,212,332a
1983 72,213,237,249,189a,201a
1984 65,214,189a,201a
1985 69,174,186a,198a
1986 62,175,216,188a,202a
1987 66,175,186a,198a
1988 70,175,207,185a,193a
1989 150,226,238,250,262,269,188a, 199a
1990 150,174,226,269,328a
1991 150,174,269,186a,198a
1992 64,175,210,262,187a,196a
1993 69,185,187a,199a
1994 61,196,228,188a,200a
1995 65,175,213,187a,200a
1996 70,214,217,261,190a,202a
1997 63,174,215,188a,200a
1998 150,174,269,186a,198a
1999 71,239,261,191a,203a

22nd September

1930 150,174,259,263,269,311a
1931 71,174,186a,198a
1932 150,174,269,186a,198a
1933 68,254,188a,200a
1934 72,175,186a,198a
1935 65,175,186a,198a
1936 69,175,213,246,187a,195a
1937 150,174,259,263,269,186a,198a
1938 150,174,269,186a,198a
1939 70,174,230,246,261,187a,202a
1940 150,175,185,206,261,269,294a
1941 67,175,207,246,188a,193a
1942 168,175,186a,198a
1943 64,64i,175,219,231,247,183a, 195a
1944 68,174,187,325a
1945 61,174,211,185a,196a
1946 150,188,231,247,269,319a
1947 70,187,187a,199a
1948 62,175,213,222,185a,200a
1949 66,175,186a,198a
1950 71,174,186a,198a
1951 63,174,186a,198a
1952 68,187,187a,199a
1953 168,185,187a,199a
1954 65,175,208,188a,202a
1955 150,187,269,319a
1956 150,269,185a,197a
1957 150,174,269,186a,198a
1958 70,174,186a,198a
1959 63,175,212,256,185a,199a
1960 67,187,187a,199a
1961 72,175,214,185a,199a
1962 160,175,259,262,186a,198a
1963 68,174,256,326a
1964 150,174,269,186a,198a
1965 65,174,228,248,256,259,262, 326a
1966 70,175,186a,198a
1967 62,175,186a,197a
1968 66,175,269,186a,198a
1969 71,185,187a,199a
1970 150,174,256,259,262,269,326a
1971 68,174,186a,198a
1972 72,175,187a,199a
1973 65,188,187a,199a
1974 69,186,187a,199a
1975 157,221,249,185a,195a
1976 150,174,187,269,325a
1977 70,174,257,185a,196a
1978 63,174,257,326a
1979 67,187,187a,199a
1980 72,185,187a,199a
1981 64,188,187a,199a
1982 68,186,212,332a
1983 157,213,189a,201
1984 65,214,189a,201a
1985 70,174,186a,198a
1986 62,175,216,188a,202a
1987 66,175,186a,198a
1988 71,175,207,185a,193a
1989 64,226,262,190a,202a
1990 150,174,226,269,328a
1991 150,174,269,186a,198a
1992 65,175,210,187a,196a
1993 69,186,187a,199a
1994 61,196,228,188a,200a
1995 66,175,213,187a,200a
1996 70,214,217,261,190a,202a
1997 63,174,215,188a,200a
1998 150,174,269,186a,198a
1999 71 239,261,191,203a

23rd September

1930 163,174,311a
1931 71,174,186a,198a
1932 76,174,186a,198a
1933 80,188,254,331a
1934 61,175,186a,198a
1935 65,175,186a,198a
1936 81,187,187a,199a
1937 158,230,246,185a,201a
1938 150,174,269,186a,198a
1939 71,157,175,246,261,187a,202a
1940 75,185,206,261,182a,194a
1941 80,175,207,188a,193a
1942 168,175,186a,198a
1943 64,64i,175,219,231,247,183a, 195a
1944 151,187,270,187a,199a

1945 73,185,187a,199a
1946 66,188,231,247,187a,199a
1947 70,187,187a,199a
1948 74,185,187a,199a
1949 151,188,270,187a,199a
1950 71,174,186a,198a
1951 64,174,186a,198a
1952 80,187,187a,199a
1953 151,185,270,187a,199a
1954 65,175,208,188a,202a
1955 150,187,269,319a
1956 151,185,270,319a
1957 78,174,186a,198a
1958 71,174,186a,198a
1959 63,175,212,256,185a,199a
1960 80,187,187a,199a
1961 84,185,187a,199a
1962 65,175,186a,198a
1963 69,174,186a,198a
1964 73,174,186a,198a
1965 78,174,228,248,256,259,262, 326a
1966 82,175,186a,198a
1967 62,175,186,197a
1968 79,175,187,325a
1969 83,186,211,262,187a,199a
1970 76,174,256,262,326a
1971 68,174,186a,198a
1972 151,185,258,261,270,187a,199a
1973 151,188,270,187a,199a
1974 151,186,270,187a,199a
1975 62,175,236,185a,195a
1976 151,187,270,187a,199a
1977 83,174,208,186a,196a
1978 75,257,188a,200a
1979 67,187,187a,199a
1980 84,185,187a,199a
1981 151,188,258,260,270,187a,199a
1982 81,186,212,332a
1983 157,213,189a,201a
1984 78,214,189a,201a
1985 82,175,237,186a,198a
1986 75,175,216,188a,202a
1987 67,187,187a,199a
1988 83,175,250,185a,193a
1989 76,188,226,262,333a
1990 80,226,238,250,190a,202a
1991 150,174,269,186a,198a
1992 77,187,187a,199a
1993 151,186,211,227,262,270,333a
1994 74,196,228,259,262,188a,200a
1995 66,175,213,187a,200a
1996 83,174,214,261,185a,197a
1997 75,174,215,188a,200a
1998 80,174,216,186a,197a
1999 84,175,206,185a,201a

24th September

1930 163,208,184a,196a
1931 84,174,209,187a,200a
1932 76,174,186a,198a
1933 81,188,187a,199a
1934 73,186,187a,199a
1935 77,175,212,186a,201a
1936 82,187,187a,199a
1937 158,230,246,185a,201a
1938 79,174,186a,198a
1939 83,187,258,261,187a,199a
1940 75,185,206,261,182a,194a
1941 80,175,207,188a,193a
1942 151,186,270,187a,199a
1943 151,175,186,258,261,270,362a
1944 151,187,270,187a,199a
1945 74,185,187a,199a
1945 74,185,187a,199a
1946 151,188,270,187a,199a
1947 151,187,270,187a,199a
1948 75,185,187a,199a
1949 151,188,270,187a,199a
1950 84,174,186a,198a
1951 76,186,187a,199a
1952 151,187,270,187a,199a
1953 151,186,270,187a,199a
1954 78,188,187a,199a
1955 151,187,270,319a
1956 151,185,270,319a
1957 79,188,187a,199a
1958 83,174,186a,198a
1959 75,185,187a,199a
1960 80,187,187a,199a
1961 73,186,187a,199a
1962 77,175,216,188a,196a
1963 81,174,186a,198a
1964 158,174,186a,198a
1965 78,174,228,248,256,259,262, 326a
1966 83,175,186a,198a
1967 75,175,248,185a,201a
1968 79,175,187,325a
1969 84,186,262,187a,199a
1970 76,174,256,262,326a
1971 515,187,270,187a,199a
1972 151,185,258,261,270,187a,199a
1973 151,188,270,187a,199a
1974 151,186,270,187a,199a
1975 74,185,187a,199a
1976 79,187,270,187a,199a
1977 83,174,208,186a,196a
1978 76,257,188a,200a
1979 80,187,187a,199a
1980 73,185,187a,199a
1981 151,188,258,260,270,187a,199a
1982 81,186,212,332a
1983 157,213,189a,201a
1984 78,214,189a,201a
1985 83,175,237,186a,198a

1986 75,175,216,188a,202a
1987 151,187,270,187a,199a
1988 84,175,250,185a,193a
1989 77,188,226,333a
1990 81,226,238,250,190a,202a
1991 73,174,210,185a,199a
1992 78,187,262,187a,199a
1993 151,186,211,227,262,270,333a
1994 74,196,228,259,262,188a,200a
1995 78,187,187a,199a
1996 83,174,214,261,185a,197a
1997 76,174,215,188a,200a
1998 80,175,216,186a,197a
1999 84,175,206,185a,201a

25th September

1930 164,208,254,184a,196a
1931 84,174,209,187a,200a
1932 151,174,270,318a
1933 81,188,187a,199a
1934 74,186,187a,199a
1935 78,175,186a,198a
1936 82,187,187a,199a
1937 75,174,230,246,186a,198a
1938 79,174,186a,198a
1939 83,187,258,261,187a,199a
1940 76,185,218,230,246,182a,194a
1941 81,175,207,188a,193a
1942 151,186,270,187a,199a
1943 151,175,258,261,270,302a
1944 151,187,270,187a,199a
1945 74,186,187a,199a
1946 151,188,200,258,260,270,331a
1947 83,187,258,260,187a,199a
1948 75,185,187a,199a
1949 80,188,187a,199a
1950 84,174,186a,198a
1951 76,186,187a,199a
1952 151,187,270,187a,199a
1953 151,186,270,187a,199a
1954 78,188,187a,199a
1955 151,187,270,319a
1956 151,185,270,319a
1957 79,188,187a,199a
1958 84,174,186a,198a
1959 76,186,187a,199a
1960 80,187,187a,199a
1961 73,186,187a,199a
1962 77,175,216,188a,196a
1963 81,174,186a,198a
1964 158,174,186a,198a
1965 151,188,228,248,256,259,262, 270,331a
1966 83,175,186a,198a
1967 75,175,248,185a,201a
1968 80,175,187,325a
1969 84,186,262,187a,199a
1970 77,174,256,326a
1971 151,187,213,258,261,270,332a
1972 151,185,258,261,270,187a,199a
1973 151,188,270,187a,199a
1974 151,186,270,187a,199a
1975 74,185,187a,199a
1976 79,187,187a,199a
1977 84,174,208,186a,196a
1978 76,257,188a,200a
1979 80,187,187a,199a
1980 73,185,187a,199a
1981 151,188,270,187a,199a
1982 82,186,212,332a
1983 74,213,237,249,189a,201a
1984 79,187,214,332a
1985 83,175,237,186a,198a
1986 75,175,216,188a,202a
1987 151,187,270,187a,199a
1988 84,175,250,185a,193a
1989 77,188,226,333a
1990 81,226,238,250,190a,202a
1991 73,174,210,185a,199a
1992 78,187,210,262,188a,196a
1993 83,186,211,262,187a,199a
1994 75,196,228,259,262,188a,200a
1995 151,187,270,187a,199a
1996 84,174,214,185a,197a
1997 76,174,215,188a,200a
1998 80,175,216,186a,197a
1999 73,175,206,261,185a,201a

26th September

1930 164,208,254,184a,196a
1931 84,174,209,187a,200a
1932 151,270,185a,197a
1933 82,188,187a,199a
1934 74,186,187a,199a
1935 78,175,186a,198a
1936 83,187,187a,199a
1937 75,174,230,246,186a,198a
1938 80,174,186a,198a
1939 84,187,187a,199a
1940 76,185,218,230,246,182a,194a
1941 81,175,207,188a,193a
1942 151,186,270,187a,199a
1943 151,175,258,261,270,302a
1944 151,187,270,187a,199a
1945 75,186,187a,199a
1946 151,188,200,258,260,270,331a
1947 83,187,258,260,187a,199a
1948 76,185,187a,199a
1949 80,188,187a,199a
1950 73,174,186a,198a
1951 151,186,270,319a
1952 151,187,270,187a,199a
1953 151,186,270,187a,199a
1954 78,188,187a,199a
1955 151,187,270,319a
1956 151,185,270,319a

1957 80,188,256,331a
1958 84,174,186a,198a
1959 76,186,187a,199a
1960 81,187,187a,199a
1961 158,186,187a,199a
1962 78,175,262,186a,198a
1963 82,174,186a,198a
1964 75,174,186a,198a
1965 151,188,228,248,256,259,262,
270,331a
1966 83,175,186a,198a
1967 75,175,248,185a,201a
1968 80,175,187a,325a
1969 73,186,187a,199a
1970 77,174,256,326a
1971 151,187,213,258,261,270,332a
1972 151,185,258,261,270,187a,199a
1973 151,188,270,187a,199a
1974 83,186,270,187a,199a
1975 75,185,258,260,187a,199a
1976 80,188,257,331a
1977 84,174,208,186a,196a
1978 76,257,188a,200a
1979 81,187,187a,199a
1980 74,185,187a,199a
1981 151,188,270,187a,199a
1982 82,186,212,332a
1983 74,213,237,249,189a,201a
1984 79,201,214,336a
1985 84,175,237,186a,198a
1986 76,175,216,188a,202a
1987 80,187,187a,199a
1988 157,225,237,185a,193a
1989 77,188,226,333a
1990 81,226,238,250,190a,202a
1991 158,238,250,185a,199a
1992 151,188,262,270,187a,199a
1993 83,186,211,262,187a,199a
1994 75,196,228,259,262,188a,200a
1995 151,187,270,187a,199a
1996 84,174,214,185a,197a
1997 77,174,215,188a,200a
1998 81,175,216,186a,197a
1999 73,175,206,261,185a,201a

27th September

1930 165,208,184a,196a
1931 73,174,209,187a,200a
1932 151,270,185a,197a
1933 82,188,187a,199a
1934 186,187a,199a
1935 151,186,270,187a,199a
1936 83,187,187a,199a
1937 76,174,246,186a,198a
1938 80,174,186a,198a
1939 84,187,187a,199a
1940 151,185,206,218,246,261,270,
293a
1941 81,175,207,188a,193a
1942 151,186,270,187a,199a
1943 151,175,258,261,270,303a
1944 151,187,270,187a,199a
1945 75,186,187a,199a
1946 151,188,200,258,260,270,331a
1947 151,187,258,260,270,187a,199a
1948 76,186,222,247,185a,200a
1949 81,188,187a,199a
1950 73,174,186a,198a
1951 151,186,270,319a
1952 151,187,270,187a,199a
1953 75,186,187a,199a
1954 151,188,270,187a,199a
1955 83,187,319a
1956 151,185,270,319a
1957 80,188,256,331a
1958 84,174,186a,198a
1959 77,186,187a,199a
1960 81,175,213,188a,196a
1961 158,186,187a,199a
1962 78,175,262,186a,198a
1963 82,174,186a,198a
1964 75,174,186a,198a
1965 164,256,259,262,188a,200a
1966 84,175,186a,198a
1967 76,175,209,185a,201a
1968 81,175,186a,198a
1969 73,186,187a,199a
1970 162,174,256,259,262,326a
1971 151,187,258,261,270,187a,199a
1972 75,185,258,261,187a,199a
1973 151,188,270,187a,199a
1974 83,186,270,187a,199a
1975 75,185,258,260,187a,199a
1976 80,188,257,331a
1977 73,174,208,186a,196a
1978 77,188,257,331a
1979 81,187,187a,199a
1980 74,185,187a,199a
1981 78,188,257,331a
1982 82,186,212,332a
1983 75,213,237,249,189a,201a
1984 80,201,214,336a
1985 84,175,237,186a,198a
1986 76,175,216,188a,202a
1987 80,187,187a,199a
1988 157,225,237,185a,193a
1989 162,226,259,262,190a,202a
1990 166,226,190a,202a
1991 158,238,250,185a,199a
1992 151,188,262,270,187a,199a
1993 83,186,211,262,187a,199a
1994 75,196,228,259,262,188a,200a
1995 80,187,200,331a
1996 73,217,258,261,185a,197a
1997 77,174,215,188a,200a
1998 81,175,216,186a,197a
1999 74,185,182a,194a

28th September

1930 165,208,184a,196a
1931 73,174,209,187a,200a
1932 78,175,186a,198a
1933 82,188,187a,199a
1934 75,186,187a,199a
1935 151,186,270,187a,199a
1936 84,187,187a,199a
1937 76,174,246,186a,198a
1938 81,174,186a,198a
1939 73,187,203,261,285a
1940 151,185,206,218,246,261,270, 293a
1941 82,176,207,188a,193a
1942 151,186,270,187a,199a
1943 151,175,258,261,270,303a
1944 83,188,187a,199a
1945 76,186,312a
1946 80,188,200,260,331a
1947 151,187,258,260,270,187a,199a
1948 151,270,185a,197a
1949 81,188,187a,199a
1950 74,174,186a,198a
1951 78,174,186,325a
1952 82,188,187a,199a
1953 75,186,187a,199a
1954 151,188,270,187a,199a
1955 83,187,319a
1956 151,185,270,319a
1957 81,188,187a,199a
1958 73,174,186a,198a
1959 77,186,187a,199a
1960 82,175,213,188a,196a
1961 158,226,256,186a,199a
1962 151,188,262,270,187a,199a
1963 83,174,186a,198a
1964 76,174,186a,198a
1965 164,256,259,262,188a,200a
1966 84,175,186a,198a
1967 76,175,209,185a,201a
1968 81,175,186a,198a
1969 158,186,259,262,187a,199a
1970 162,174,256,259,262,326a
1971 151,187,258,261,270,187a,199a
1972 75,185,258,261,187a,199a
1973 151,188,270,187a,199a
1974 84,186,187a,199a
1975 76,185,260,187a,199a
1976 81,188,187a,199a
1977 73,174,208,186a,196a
1978 77,188,257,331a
1979 81,187,187a,199a
1980 75,185,187a,199a
1981 79,188,257,258,260,270,331a
1982 83,186,212,332a
1983 75,213,237,249,189a,201a
1984 80,201,214,336a
1985 84,175,237,186a,198a
1986 77,175,216,188a,202a
1987 81,187,205,332a
1988 74,175,207,185a,193a
1989 162,226,259,262,190a,202a
1990 166,226,190a,202a
1991 75,185,187a,199a
1992 80,196,262,188a,200a
1993 84,186,262,187a,199a
1994 160,196,228,262,277,188a,200a
1995 80,187,200,331a
1996 73,217,258,261,185a,197a
1997 78,174,215,188a,200a
1998 82,175,216,186a,197a
1999 74,185,182a,194a

29th September

1930 166,208,184a,196a
1931 74,174,209,187a,200a
1932 78,175,186a,198a
1933 83,188,187a,199a
1934 75,186,187a,199a
1935 79,176,212,186a,201a
1936 84,175,213,188a,198a
1937 77,74,230,246,186a,198a
1938 81,174,186a,198a
1939 73,187,203,261,285a
1940 162,175,185,206,261,294a
1941 82,176,207,188a,193a
1942 75,175,186,304a
1943 79,174,186,258,261,304a
1944 83,188,187a,199a
1945 76,186,312a
1946 80,188,200,260,331a
1947 151,187,258,260,270,187a,199a
1948 151,270,185a,197a
1949 82,188,187a,199a
1950 74,174,186a,198a
1951 78,174,186,325a
1952 83,188,187a,199a
1953 151,186,270,187a,199a
1954 164,255,188a,200a
1955 151,187,270,319a
1956 151,185,270,319a
1957 81,188,187a,199a
1958 73,175,212,186a,195a
1959 77,186,187a,199a
1960 82,175,213,188a,196a
1961 75,176,233,186a,199a
1962 151,188,262,270,187a,199a
1963 83,174,186a,198a
1964 76,174,186a,198a
1965 81,228,248,256,188a,200a
1966 73,175,186a,198a
1967 77,209,185a,197a
1968 82,176,256,326a
1969 158,186,259,262,187a,199a
1970 162,174,256,259,262,326a
1971 151,187,258,261,270,187a,199a
1972 151,185,270,187a,199a

1973 151,188,270,187a,199a
1974 84,186,187a,199a
1975 76,185,260,187a,199a
1976 81,188,187a,199a
1977 74,174,208,186a,196a
1978 78,188,257,331a
1979 82,187,187a,199a
1980 75,185,187a,199a
1981 79,188,257,258,260,270,331a
1982 83,186,212,332a
1983 76,237,249,189a,201a
1984 81,201,214,336a
1985 73,175,215,186a,198a
1986 73,175,216,188a,202a
1987 81,205,189a,201a
1988 74,175,207,185a,193a
1989 79,188,226,262,333a
1990 83,226,238,250,190a,202a
1991 75,185,187a,199a
1992 80,196,262,188a,200a
1993 84,186,262,187a,199a
1994 160,196,228,262,277,188a,200a
1995 81,187,187a,199a
1996 74,174,214,261,185a,197a
1997 78,174,215,188a,201a
1998 82,175,216,186a,197a
1999 75,239,251,258,261,185a,201a

30th September

1930 166,208,184a,196a
1931 74,174,209,187a,200a
1932 151,185,270,187a,199a
1933 83,188,187a,199a
1934 76,186,187a,199a
1935 164,254,188a,200a
1936 73,175,213,188a,198a
1937 77,174,230,246,186a,198a
1938 81,174,186a,198a
1939 73,187,203,261,285a
1940 162,175,185,206,261,294a
1941 83,176,207,188a,193a
1942 75,175,186,304a
1943 79,174,186,258,261,304a
1944 84,188,187a,199a
1945 77,186,187a,199a
1946 81,188,200,260,331a
1947 151,187,258,260,270,187a,199a
1948 78,176,213,247,247i,185a,200a
1949 82,188,187a,199a
1950 74,174,186a,198a
1951 78,174,186a,325a
1952 83,188,187a,199a
1953 151,186,270,187a,199a
1954 164,255,188a,200a
1955 151,187,270,319a
1956 151,270,185a,197a
1957 82,188,187a,199a
1958 74,175,212,186a,195a
1959 78,175,186,325a
1960 83,175,213,188a,196a
1961 75,176,233,186a,199a
1962 151,188,262,270,187a,199a
1963 84,174,186a,198a
1964 151,174,270,318a
1965 81,228,248,256,188a,200a
1966 73,175,186a,198a
1967 77,209,185a,197a
1968 82,176,256,326a
1969 75,186,211,262,187a,199a
1970 79,174,188,256,262,364a
1971 83,187,261,279,187a,199a
1972 151,185,270,187a,199a
1973 151,188,270,187a,199a
1974 84,186,187a,199a
1975 77,185,258,260,319a
1976 82,188,187a,199a
1977 74,174,208,186a,196a
1978 78,188,257,331a
1979 82,187,187a,199a
1980 75,257,331a
1981 80,257,260,331a
1982 84,186,212,332a
1983 76,213,189a,201a
1984 81,201,214,336a
1985 73,175,215,186a,198a
1986 73,175,216,188a,202a
1987 82,176,205,187a,198a
1988 75,175,250,185a,193a
1989 79,188,226,262,333a
1990 83,226,238,250,190a,202a
1991 76,185,187a,199a
1992 81,175,210,188a,196a
1993 73,186,187a,199a
1994 77,196,228,188a,200a
1995 81,187,187a,199a
1996 74,174,214,261,185a,197a
1997 78,174,215,188a,201a
1998 82,175,216,186a,197a
1999 75,239,251,258,261,185a,201a

1st October

1930 166,208,184a,196a
1931 74,174,209,187a,200a
1932 151,185,270,187a,199a
1933 84,188,187a,199a
1934 76,176,211,186a,197a
1935 164,254,188a,200a
1936 73,175,213,188a,198a
1937 162,174,276,186a,198a
1938 82,175,215,188a,198a
1939 74,187,261,187a,199a
1940 79,185,206,218,230,246,261, 295a
1941 83,176,207,188a,193a
1942 75,175,186,304a
1943 151,174,270,183a,195a

1944 84,188,187a,199a
1945 151,186,270,187a,199a
1946 81,188,255,260,331a
1947 151,187,231,247,247i,258,260,
270,319a
1948 78,176,213,247,247i,185a,200a
1949 83,188,187a,199a
1950 75,174,186a,198a
1951 79,186,187a,199a
1952 84,188,187a,199a
1953 151,186,270,187a,199a
1954 164,255,188a,200a
1955 151,187,270,319a
1956 151,174,270,318a
1957 82,188,187a,199a
1958 74,175,212,186a,195a
1959 78,186,325a
1960 83,175,213,188a,196a
1961 76,176,233,186a,199a
1962 164,256,259,262,188a,200a
1963 84,174,186a,198a
1964 151,174,270,318a
1965 81,228,248,256,188a,200a
1966 73,175,186a,198a
1967 78,176,186a,198a
1968 83,176,256,326a
1969 75,186,211,262,187a,199a
1970 79,174,188,256,262,364a
1971 83,187,261,279,187a,199a
1972 151,185,270,187a,199a
1973 151,188,270,187a,199a
1974 73,186,187a,199a
1975 77,185,258,260,319a
1976 82,188,187a,199a
1977 74,174,208,257,186a,196a
1978 78,188,257,331a
1979 83,187,187a,199a
1980 76,185,257,331a
1981 80,188,257,260,331a
1982 84,186,212,332a
1983 76,213,189a,201a
1984 82,201,214,336a
1985 74,175,237,186a,198a
1986 78,175,216,188a,202a
1987 82,176,205,187a,198a
1988 75,175,250,185a,193a
1989 79,188,226,262,333a
1990 83,226,190a,202a
1991 76,185,187a,199a
1992 81,175,210,188a,196a
1993 73,200,188a,200a
1994 77,196,228,188a,200a
1995 82,187,228,333a
1996 75,174,214,261,185a,197a
1997 79,174,215,188a,201a
1998 83,187,187a,199a
1999 75,239,251,258,261,185a,201a

2nd October

1930 167,208,184a,196a
1931 75,174,209,187a,200a
1932 80,175,210,185a,197a
1933 84,188,187a,199a
1934 77,176,211,186a,197a
1935 81,176,212,186a,201a
1936 74,175,213,188a,198a
1937 162,174,276,186a,198a
1938 82,175,215,188a,198a
1939 74,187,261,187a,199a
1940 79,185,206,218,230,246,261,
295a
1941 84,176,207,188a,193a
1942 76,186,187a,199a
1943 151,174,270,183a,195a
1944 73,188,187a,199a
1945 151,186,270,187a,199a
1946 81,188,255,260,331a
1947 151,187,270,319a
1948 79,185,187a,199a
1949 83,188,187a,199a
1950 75,174,186a,198a
1951 79,186,187a,199a
1952 84,188,187a,199a
1953 151,186,270,187a,199a
1954 81,224,232,255,188a,200a
1955 151,187,270,319a
1956 151,174,270,318a
1957 82,188,187a,199a
1958 74,175,212,186a,195a
1959 151,186,270,187,199a
1960 168,256,188a,200a
1961 76,256,188a,200a
1962 164,256,259,262,188a,200a
1963 84,174,186a,198a
1964 151,174,270,318a
1965 82,228,248,256,259,262,188a,
200a
1966 74,175,186a,198a
1967 78,176,186a,198a
1968 83,176,256,326a
1969 75,186,211,262,187a,199a
1970 80,174,256,262,326a
1971 151,187,270,187a,199a
1972 151,185,258,261,270,187a,199a
1973 151,188,270,187a,199a
1974 73,186,187a,199a
1975 78,185,187a,199a
1976 83,188,187a,199a
1977 75,174,208,257,186a,196a
1978 151,188,257,270,331a
1979 83,187,187a,199a
1980 76,185,257,331a
1981 80,188,257,260,331a
1982 515 187,212,258,260,270,332a
1983 161,213,189a,201a
1984 82,201,214,336a
1985 74,175,237,186a,198a

1986 78,175,216,188a,202a
1987 83,176,205,187a,198a
1988 76,175,250,185a,193a
1989 80,199,226,262,337a
1990 84,226,190a,202a
1991 76,185,187a,199a
1992 81,175,210,188a,196a
1993 73,200,188a,200a
1994 78,196,228,259,262,188a,200a
1995 82,187,228,333a
1996 75,174,214,261,185a,197a
1997 151,188,270,187a,199a
1998 83,187,187a,199a
1999 76,175,206,185a,201a

3rd October

1930 167,208,184a,196a
1931 75,174,209,187a,200a
1932 80,175,210,185a,197a
1933 73,188,185a,197a
1934 77,176,211,186a,197a
1935 81,176,212,186a,201a
1936 74,175,213,188a,198a
1937 162,174,276,186a,198a
1938 175,215,188a,198a
1939 159,187,258,261,187a,199a
1940 80,185,218,230,246,182a,194a
1941 84,176,207,188a,193a
1942 76,186,187a,199a
1943 151,174,270,183a,195a
1944 73,188,187a,199a
1945 151,186,270,187a,199a
1946 82,188,255,331a
1947 151,187,270,319a
1948 79,185,187a,199a
1949 84,188,187a,199a
1950 76,174,186a,198a
1951 80,186,187a,199a
1952 73,188,187a,199a
1953 151,186,270,187a,199a
1954 81,224,232,255,188a,200a
1955 151,187,270,319a
1956 151,185,270,319a
1957 83,188,187a,199a
1958 75,175,212,186a,195a
1959 151,186,270,187a,199a
1960 168,256,188a,200a
1961 77,256,188a,200a
1962 81,175,216,188a,196a
1963 73,174,186a,198a
1964 78,175,186a,198a
1965 82,228,248,256,259,262,188a, 200a
1966 74,187,187a,199a
1967 76,176,186a,198a
1968 84,176,256,326a
1969 76,186,262,187a,199a
1970 80,174,256,262,326a
1971 151,187,270,187a,199a
1972 151,185,258,261,270,187a,199a
1973 81,188,187a,199a
1974 151,187,270,187a,199a
1975 78,185,187a,199a
1976 83,188,187a,199a
1977 75,174,208,257,186a,196a
1978 151,188,257,270,331a
1979 84,187,187a,199a
1980 77,185,257,331a
1981 81,188,257,260,331a
1982 151,187,212,258,260,270,332a
1983 161,213,189a,201a
1984 82,201,214,336a
1985 74,175,237,186a,198a
1986 79,188,187a,199a
1987 83,176,205,187a,198a
1988 76,175,250,185a,193a
1989 80,199,226,262,337a
1990 84,226,190a,202a
1991 77,185,187a,199a
1992 82,227,262,190a,202a
1993 74,200,262,188a,200a
1994 78,196,228,259,262,188a,200a
1995 83,187,187a,199a
1996 75,174,214,261,185a,197a
1997 80,175,250,188a,201a
1998 84,187,187a,199a
1999 76,175,206,185a,201a

4th October

1930 168,208,254,184a,196a
1931 76,174,209,187a,200a
1932 81,175,254,185a,197a
1933 73,188,185a,197a
1934 77,176,211,186a,197a
1935 81,176,212,186a,201a
1936 75,175,213,188a,198a
1937 79,174,230,246,186a,198a
1938 83,175,215,188a,198a
1939 159,187,258,261,187a,199a
1940 80,185,218,230,246,182a,194a
1941 73,176,207,188a,193a
1942 151,186,270,187a,199a
1943 151,174,258,261,270,183a,195a
1944 74,188,187a,199a
1945 151,186,270,187a,199a
1946 82,188,255,331a
1947 75,187,258,260,319a
1948 80,255,188a,200a
1949 84,188,187a,199a
1950 76,187,187a,199a
1951 80,186,187a,199a
1952 73,188,187a,199a
1953 151,175,186,270,325a
1954 82,224,232,255,188a,200a
1955 151,187,270,319a
1956 151,185,270,319a

1957 83,188,187a,199a
1958 75,187,187a,199a
1959 80,186,256,331a
1960 73,256,188a,200a
1961 77,256,188a,200a
1962 81,175,216,188a,196a
1963 73,174,186a,198a
1964 78,175,186a,198a
1965 83,175,208,188a,201a
1966 75,187,187a,199a
1967 79,176,186a,198a
1968 84,176,256,326a
1969 76,186,262,187a,199a
1970 80,174,256,262,326a
1971 151,187,258,261,270,187a,199a
1972 151,185,258,261,270,187a,199a
1973 82,188,187a,199a
1974 151,187,270,187a,199a
1975 151,186,270,187a,199a
1976 83,188,187a,199a
1977 160,186,312a
1978 80,188,257,331a
1979 84,187,187a,199a
1980 77,185,257,331a
1981 81,188,257,260,331a
1982 151,187,212,258,260,270,332a
1983 78,174,213,327a
1984 83,201,214,336a
1985 75,175,237,186a,198a
1986 79,202,188a,200a
1987 84,176,205,187a,198a
1988 161,225,237,185a,193a
1989 81,226,190a,202a
1990 73,226,190a,202a
1991 77,185,187a,199a
1992 82,227,262,190a,202a
1993 74,200,262,188a,200a
1994 79,196,228,259,262,188a,200a
1995 83,187,187a,199a
1996 76,174,214,186a,197a
1997 80,175,250,188a,201a
1998 84,187,187a,199a
1999 77,175,206,261,201a

5th October

1930 168,208,254,184a,196a
1931 76,187,187a,199a
1932 81,175,254,185a,197a
1933 74,188,187a,199a
1934 78,187,187a,199a
1935 82,176,212,186a,201a
1936 75,175,213,188a,198a
1937 79,174,230,246,186a,198a
1938 83,175,215,188a,198a
1939 76,187,187a,199a
1940 81,185,218,230,246,182a,194a
1941 73,176,207,188a,193a
1942 151,187,260,270,279,187a,199a
1943 151,174,258,261,270,183a,195a
1944 151,188,270,187a,199a
1945 151,186,270,187a,199a
1946 83,188,255,258,260,331a
1947 75,187,258,260,319a
1948 80,255,188a,200a
1949 84,188,187a,199a
1950 76,187,187a,199a
1951 81,186,187a,199a
1952 74,188,187a,199a
1953 78,176,325a
1954 82,224,232,255,188a,200a
1955 75,187,319a
1956 151,185,270,319a
1957 84,188,187a,199a
1958 76,187,187a,199a
1959 80,186,256,331a
1960 73,256,188a,200a
1961 77,256,188a,200a
1962 81,175,216,188a,196a
1963 74,174,186a,198a
1964 151,185,270,187a,199a
1965 83,175,208,188a,201a
1966 75,187,187a,199a
1967 80,176,256,326a
1968 73,176,256,326a
1969 77,186,187a,199a
1970 81,174,256,326a
1971 151,187,260,26o,270,279,187a,199a
1972 151,186,258,261,270,187a,199a
1973 82,188,187a,199a
1974 151,187,270,187a,199a
1975 151,186,270,187a,199a
1976 84,188,187a,199a
1977 160,186,312a
1978 80,188,257,331a
1979 73,187,187a,199a
1980 78,176,186,257,364a
1981 82,188,257,331a
1982 151,187,212,270,332a
1983 78,174,213,327a
1984 83,202,188a,200a
1985 75,175,237,186a,198a
1986 164,202,188a,200a
1987 84,176,205,187a,198a
1988 77,175,207,186a,193a
1989 81,226,190a,202a
1990 73,226,190a,202a
1991 78,185,187a,199a
1992 83,175,210,262,188a,196a
1993 75,200,262,188a,200a
1994 79,196,228,188a,200a
1995 84,187,187a,199a
1996 76,174,214,186a,197a
1997 80,175,250,188a,201a
1998 73,187,187a,199a
1999 77,176,206,185a,201a

6th October

1930 168,208,254,184a,196a
1931 77,187,187a,199a
1932 82,175,254,185a,197a
1933 74,188,187a,199a
1934 78,187,187a,199a
1935 82,176,212,186a,201a
1936 76,175,213,188a,198a
1937 80,174,230,246,186a,198a
1938 84,175,215,188a,198a
1939 76,187,187a,199a
1940 81,185,182a,194a
1941 73,176,207,188a,193a
1942 151,187,260,270,279,187a,199a
1943 151,174,258,261,270,183a,195a
1944 75,188,187a,199a
1945 151,186,270,187a,199a
1946 83,188,255,258,260,331a
1947 151,187,260,270,319a
1948 81,176,222,247,247i,185a,200a
1949 73,188,187a,199a
1950 77,187,187a,199a
1951 81,186,187a,199a
1952 74,188,187a,199a
1953 78,176,325a
1954 82,224,232,255,188a,200a
1955 75,187,319a
1956 80,174,186a,198a
1957 84,188,197a,199a
1958 76,187,187a,199a
1959 81,186,187a,199a
1960 74,256,188a,200a
1961 162,176,256,326a
1962 82,175,262,188a,196a
1963 74,174,186a,198a
1964 151,185,186,270,325a
1965 83,175,208,188a,201a
1966 75,176,209,187a,197a
1967 80,176,256,326a
1968 73,176,256,326a
1969 77,186,187a,199a
1970 81,174,256,326a
1971 151,187,261,270,279,187a,199a
1972 151,186,261,270,279,187a,199a
1973 83,188,187a,199a
1974 75,187,258,260,270,187a,199a
1975 80,186,187a,199a
1976 84,188,187a,199a
1977 160,186,312a
1978 81,188,257,331a
1979 73,187,187a,199a
1980 78,176,186,257,364a
1981 82,188,257,331a
1982 151,187,212,270,332a
1983 79,174,186,213,367a
1984 84,202,188a,200a
1985 76,175,237,186a,198a
1986 164,202,188a,200a
1987 73,176,205,187a,198a
1988 77,175,207,186a,193a
1989 81,226,190a,202a
1990 74,187,226,333a
1991 78,185,187a,199a
1992 83,175,210,262,188a,196a
1993 75,200,262,188a,200a
1994 164,197,188a,200a
1995 84,187,187a,199a
1996 77,174,214,261,186a,197a
1997 81,215,189a,201a
1998 73,187,187a,199a
1999 78,176,206,185a,201a

7th October

1930 157,208,184a,196a
1931 77,187,187a,199a
1932 166,226,246,186a,197a
1933 74,254,188a,200a
1934 79,187,187a,199a
1935 83,176,186a,201a
1936 76,175,213,188a,198a
1937 80,174,230,246,186a,198a
1938 84,175,215,188a,198a
1939 76,187,187a,199a
1940 166,186,182a,194a
1941 74,188,182a,194a
1942 151,187,270,179,187a,199a
1943 151,174,258,261,270,183a,195a
1944 75,188,187a,199a
1945 151,186,270,187a,199a
1946 84,188,255,260,331a
1947 151,187,260,270,319a
1948 81,176,213,247,247i,186a,200a
1949 73,188,187a,199a
1950 77,187,187a,199a
1951 82,186,187a,199a
1952 75,188,187a,199a
1953 79,186,187a,199a
1954 83,224,232,255,188a,200a
1955 75,187,319a
1956 80,174,186a,198a
1957 84,188,197a,199a
1958 77,187,187a,199a
1959 81,186,187a,199a
1960 74,256,188a,200a
1961 162,176,256,326a
1962 82,175,262,188a,196a
1963 75,174,186a,198a
1964 80,175,186a,198a
1965 84,228,248,188a,201a
1966 76,176,209,187a,197a
1967 81,176,186a,198a
1968 73,176,256,326a
1969 77,174,186,218,256,325a
1970 166,174,256,259,262,326a
1971 151,187,261,270,279,187a,199a
1972 151,186,261,270,279,187a,199a
1973 83,188,187a,199a

1974 75,187,258,260,270,187a,199a
1975 80,186,187a,199a
1976 73,188,187a,199a
1977 77,186,187a,199a
1978 81,188,257,331a
1979 74,187,187a,199a
1980 78,176,186,257,364a
1981 82,188,257,331a
1982 75,187,212,258,260,332a
1983 79,174,186,213,357a
1984 84,202,188a,200a
1985 76,175,237,186a,198a
1986 81,202,216,336a
1987 73,177,205,187a,198a
1988 78,175,207,186a,193a
1989 166,226,259,262,190a,202a
1990 74,187,226,333a
1991 151,186,262,270,187a,199a
1992 83,196,262,188a,200a
1993 75,200,262,188a,200a
1994 164,197,188a,200a
1995 84,187,187a,199a
1996 77,174,214,261,186a,197a
1997 81,215,189a,201a
1998 74,187,187a,199a
1999 78,176,206,185a,201a

8th October

1930 157,208,184a,196a
1931 78,187,187a,199a
1932 83,175,186a,198a
1933 75,254,188a,200a
1934 79,187,187a,199a
1935 83,176,212,186a,201a
1936 76,175,213,188a,198a
1937 80,174,230,186a,202a
1938 73,175,215,188a,198a
1939 77,187,261,187a,199a
1940 166,186,182a,194a
1941 74,188,182a,194a
1942 151,187,270,279,187a,199a
1943 83,174,258,261,183a,195a
1944 151,188,270,187a,199a
1945 151,186,270,187a,199a
1946 168,212,255,260,188a,200a
1947 151,187,260,270,319a
1948 81,176,213,247,247i,186a,200a
1949 73,188,187a,199a
1950 78,174,187,325a
1951 82,186,187a,199a
1952 75,188,187a,199a
1953 79,186,187a,199a
1954 83,224,232,255,188a,200a
1955 151,187,270,319a
1956 81,174,186a,198a
1957 73,188,187a,199a
1958 77,187,187a,199a
1959 82,186,187a,199a
1960 74,256,188a,200a
1961 79,256,188a,200a
1962 83,175,262,188a,196a
1963 75,174,186a,198a
1964 80,175,186a,198a
1965 84,228,248,188a,201a
1966 76,176,209,187a,197a
1967 81,176,186a,198a
1968 74,175,188,325a
1969 162,174,186,259,262,325a
1970 82,188,256,262,331a
1971 75,187,260,261,279,187a,199a
1972 151,186,261,270,279,187a,199a
1973 84,188,187a,199a
1974 151,187,258,260,270,187a,199a
1975 81,186,187a,199a
1976 73,188,187a,199a
1977 77,186,187a,199a
1978 82,188,257,331a
1979 74,187,187a,199a
1980 79,186,257,331a
1981 83,188,257,258,260,331a
1982 75,187,212,258,260,332a
1983 80,174,213,327a
1984 84,202,188a,200a
1985 77,175,215,186a,198a
1986 81,202,216,336a
1987 74,176,205,187a,198a
1988 78,175,207,186a,193a
1989 166,226,259,262,190a,202a
1990 75,187,226,333a
1991 151,186,262,270,187a,199a
1992 168,196,259,262,188a,200a
1993 76,200,262,188a,200a
1994 81,197,228,188a,200a
1995 73,187,187a,199a
1996 77,174,214,261,186a,197a
1997 82,215,261,189a,201a
1998 74,187,187a,199a
1999 79,176,206,186a,201a

9th October

1930 158,208,184a,196a
1931 78,187,187a,199a
1932 83,175,186a,198a
1933 75,176,246,188a,201a
1934 79,187,187a,199a
1935 168,228,254,186a,201a
1936 77,175,213,188a,198a
1937 81,174,214,230,261,186a,202a
1938 73,175,215,188a,198a
1939 77,187,261,187a,199a
1940 83,186,218,230,246,182a,194a
1941 75,176,207,188a,193a
1942 151,187,260,270,279,187a,199a
1943 83,174,258,261,183a,195a
1944 151,188,270,187a,199a
1945 151,186,270,187a,199a

1946 168,212,255,260,188a,200a
1947 151,187,260,270,319a
1948 82,176,213,247,247i,186a,200a
1949 74,188,187a,199a
1950 78,174,187,325a
1951 83,186,187a,199a
1952 76,188,187a,199a
1953 80,186,187a,199a
1954 168,255,188a,200a
1955 151,187,270,319a
1956 81,174,186a,198a
1957 73,188,187a,199a
1958 77,187,187a,199a
1959 82,176,213,186a,199a
1960 75,256,188a,200a
1961 79,256,188a,200a
1962 83,175,262,188a,196a
1963 76,174,186a,198a
1964 81,175,186a,198a
1965 73,175,208,188a,201a
1966 151,270,185a,197a
1967 82,176,186a,198a
1968 74,175,188,325a
1969 162,174,186,259,262,325a
1970 83,188,256,262,331a
1971 75,187,260,261,279,187a,199a
1972 151,186,270,187a,199a
1973 84,189,187a,199a
1974 151,187,258,260,270,187a,199a
1975 81,186,187a,199a
1976 74,257,188a,200a
1977 78,186,187a,199a
1978 82,188,257,331a
1979 75,187,187a,199a
1980 79,186,257,331a
1981 83,189,258,260,187a,199a
1982 151,187,212,258,260,270,332a
1983 80,186,213,332a
1984 73,202,188a,200a
1985 77,175,215,186a,198a
1986 82,203,188a,200a
1987 74,187,187a,199a
1988 151,186,270,187a,199a
1989 83,226,190a,202a
1990 75,187,226,333a
1991 80,186,262,187a,199a
1992 168,196,259,262,188a,200a
1993 76,200,262,188a,200a
1994 81,197,228,188a,200a
1995 73,187,187a,199a
1996 78,175,214,261,186a,197a
1997 82,215,261,189a,201a
1998 75,187,187a,199a
1999 79,176,206,186a,201a

10th October

1930 158,208,184a,196a
1931 151,187,270,187a,199a
1932 84,175,186a,198a
1933 76,176,246,188a,201a
1934 80,187,187a,199a
1935 168,228,254,186a,201a
1936 77,175,213,188a,198a
1937 81,174,214,230,261,186a,202a
1938 74,175,215,188a,198a
1939 78,187,261,187a,199a
1940 83,186,218,230,246,182a,194a
1941 75,176,207,188a,193a
1942 151,187,260,270,279,187a,199a
1943 151,174,270,183a,195a
1944 151,188,270,187a,199
1945 151,186,270,187a,199a
1946 73,255,260,188a,200a
1947 151,187,260,270,319a
1948 82,176,213,247,247i,186a,200a
1949 74,189,187a,199a
1950 151,187,270,187a,199a
1951 83,186,187a,199a
1952 76,188,187a,199a
1953 80,186,187a,199a
1954 168,255,188a,200a
1955 151,187,270,319a
1956 82,174,186a,198a
1957 74,189,187a,199a
1958 78,187,187a,199a
1959 83,176,213,186a,199a
1960 75,256,188a,199a
1961 79,256,188a,200a
1962 168,248,259,262,188a,196a
1963 76,174,186a,198a
1964 81,175,186a,198a
1965 73,175,208,189a,201a
1966 151,270,185a,197a
1967 82,176,186a,198a
1968 75,175,188,325a
1969 151,186,211,262,270,187a,199a
1970 83,188,256,262,331a
1971 75,187,260,279,187a,199a
1972 151,186,270,187a,199a
1973 84,189,187a,199a
1974 151,187,258,260,270,187a,199a
1975 81,186,187a,199a
1976 74,257,188a,200a
1977 78,186,187a199a
1978 83,188,257,331a
1979 75,187,187a,199a
1980 80,186,257,331a
1981 84,189,260,187a,199a
1982 151,187,212,258,260,270,332a
1983 81,186,213,332a
1984 73,202,188a,200a
1985 77,175,215,186a,198a
1986 82,203,188a,200a
1987 74,187,187a,199a
1988 151,186,270,187a,199a
1989 83,226,190a,202a
1990 76,187,226,333a
1991 80,186,262,187a,199a

1992 73,196,188a,200a
1993 77,200,188a,200a
1994 82,197,228,337a
1995 74,200,188a,200a
1996 78,175,214,261,186a,197a
1997 82,215,261,189a,201a
1998 75,187,187a,199a
1999 79,176,206,186a,201a

11th October

1930 159,208,184a,196a
1931 151,187,270,187a,199a
1932 84,175,186a,198a
1933 76,176,246,189a,201a
1934 80,154,188a,200a
1935 73,176,212,186a,201a
1936 78,175,186a,198a
1937 166,214,217,261,190a,202a
1938 74,175,215,188a,198a
1939 78,176,205,187a,203a
1940 83,186,218,230,246,182a,194a
1941 75,176,207,189a,193a
1942 151,187,260,270,279,187a,199a
1943 151,174,270,183a,195a
1944 151,188,270,187a,199a
1945 151,186,270,187a,199a
1946 73,255,260,188a,200a
1947 151,187,270,319a
1948 83,176,213,247,247i,186a,200a
1949 75,189,187a,199a
1950 151,187,270,187a,199a
1951 84,186,187a,199a
1952 76,188,187a,199a
1953 80,186,187a,199a
1954 73,224,232,255,188a,200a
1955 151,187,270,319a
1956 82,186,187a,199a
1957 74,189,187a,199a
1958 78,187,187a,199a
1959 83,176,213,186a,199a
1960 160,256,188a,200a
1961 80,256,188a,200a
1962 168,248,259,262,188a,196a
1963 77,187,187a,199a
1964 81,175,186a,198a
1965 73,175,208,189a,201a
1966 78,176,186a,198a
1967 82,176,186a,198a
1968 75,175,188,325a
1969 151,186,211,262,270,187a,199a
1970 84,188,256,262,331a
1971 75,187,260,279,187a,199a
1972 151,186,270,187a,199a
1973 73,189,187a,199a
1974 151,187,258,260,270,187a,199a
1975 82,186,187a,199a
1976 74,188,257,331a
1977 151,186,270,187a,199a
1978 83,188,257,331a
1979 76,257,188a,200a
1980 80,186,257,331a
1981 84,189,260,187a,199a
1982 151,187,212,258,260,270,332a
1983 81,186,213,332a
1984 74,202,188a,200a
1985 78,176,198,326a
1986 83,203,188a,200a
1987 75,199,188a,200a
1988 151,186,270,187a,199a
1989 84,189,226,333a
1990 76,187,226,333a
1991 81,186,187a,199a
1992 73,196,188a,200a
1993 77,200,188a,200a
1994 82,197,228,337a
1995 74,200,188a,200a
1996 79,186,261,187a,199a
1997 83,215,239,258,261,341a
1998 76,187,187a,199a
1999 80,176,206,186a,201a

12th October

1930 159,208,184a,196a
1931 80,187,187a,200a
1932 84,175,186a,198a
1933 76,176,246,189a,201a
1934 81,176,246,187a,197a
1935 73,176,212,186a,201a
1936 78,175,186a,198a
1937 166,214,217,261,190a,202a
1938 74,175,215,188a,198a
1939 79,187,187a,199a
1940 84,186,218,230,246,182a,194a
1941 76,176,207,189a,193a
1942 151,187,260,270,187a,199a
1943 151,175,186,258,261,270,304a
1944 151,188,270,187a,199a
1945 151,186,270,187a,199a
1946 74,255,188a,200a
1947 151,187,270,319a
1948 83,176,213,247,247i,186a,200a
1949 75,189,187a,199a
1950 151,187,270,187a,199a
1951 84,186,187a,199a
1952 77,188,187a,199a
1953 81,186,187a,199a
1954 73,224,232,255,188a,200a
1955 151,187,270,319a
1956 82,186,187a,199a
1957 74,189,187a,199a
1958 151,187,270,187a,199a
1959 83,176,213,186a,199a
1960 160,256,188a,200a
1961 80,256,188a,200a
1962 73,175,216,188a,197a
1963 77,256,188a,200a

1964 166,175,186a,198a
1965 74,175,208,189a,201a
1966 78,176,186a,198a
1967 83,176,186a,198a
1968 75,175,188a,325a
1969 80,186,262,187a,199a
1970 84,188,256,262,331a
1971 151,188,258,260,270,187a,199a
1972 151,186,270,187a,199a
1973 73,189,187a,199a
1974 151,187,270,187a,199a
1975 82,186,187a,199a
1976 75,188,257,258,260,331a
1977 151,186,270,187a,199a
1978 83,188,257,331a
1979 76,257,188a,200a
1980 80,186,257,331a
1981 73,189,260,187a,199a
1982 151,187,212,258,260,270,332a
1983 82,186,213,332a
1984 74,202,188a,200a
1985 78,176,198,326a
1986 83,203,188a,200a
1987 75,199,188a,200a
1988 80,175,207,186a,193a
1989 84,189,226,333a
1990 77,187,226,333a
1991 81,186,187a,199a
1992 73,196,188a,200a
1993 78,200,262,188a,200a
1994 82,197,228,337a
1995 75,200,188a,200a
1996 79,186,261187a,199a
1997 83,215,239,258,261,341a
1998 76,176,216,187a,198a
1999 80,176,206,186a,201a

13th October

1930 159,208,184a,196a
1931 80,187,187a,200a
1932 73,175,186a,198a
1933 77,176,246,189a,201a
1934 81,176,246,187a,197a
1935 74,175,212,186a,201a
1936 78,175,186a,198a
1937 166,214,217,261,190a,202a
1938 75,175,215,188a,198a
1939 79,187,187a,199a
1940 84,186,218,230,246,182a,194a
1941 76,176,207,189a,193a
1942 151,187,260,270,187a,199a
1943 151,175,186,258,261,270,304a
1944 78,188,187a,199a
1945 151,186,270,187a,199a
1946 74,255,188a,200a
1947 79,187,258,260,319a
1948 83,176,213,247,247i,186a,200a
1949 76,189,187a,199a
1950 151,187,270,187a,199a
1951 73,186,187a,199a
1952 77,188,187a,199a
1953 81,186,187a,199a
1954 74,224,232,255,188a,200a
1955 151,188,270,319a
1956 83,186,187a,199a
1957 75,189,187a,199a
1958 151,187,270,187a,199a
1959 84,176,213,186a,199a
1960 160,256,188a,200a
1961 81,256,188a,200a
1962 73,175,216,188a,197a
1963 78,175,256,326a
1964 166,175,186a,198a
1965 74,176,208,189a,201a
1966 79,176,187,325a
1967 83,176,186a,198a
1968 76,175,188a,325a
1969 80,186,262,187a,199a
1970 73,188,256,331a
1971 151,188,258,260,270,187a,199a
1972 151,186,270,187a,199a
1973 74,189,187a,199a
1974 151,187,270,187a,199a
1975 83,186,187a,199a
1976 75,188,257,258,260,331a
1977 151,186,270,187a,199a
1978 84,188,257,331a
1979 76,257,188a,200a
1980 81,186,210,332a
1981 73,189,260,187a,199a
1982 151,187,212,270,332a
1983 82,186,213,332a
1984 74,202,188a,200a
1985 79,198,188a,200a
1986 83,203,188a,200a
1987 76,199,188a,200a
1988 80,175,207,186a,193a
1989 73,189,226,333a
1990 77,187,226,333a
1991 81,186,187a,199a
1992 74,196,262,188a,200a
1993 78,200,262,188a,200a
1994 83,228,188a,197a
1995 75,200,188a,200a
1996 80,175,214,186a,197a
1997 84,215,189a,201a
1998 77,176,216,187a,198a
1999 81,206,189a,201a

14th October

1930 160,208,184a,196a
1931 81,187,187a,199a
1932 73,176,186a,198a
1933 77,176,246,189a,201a
1934 82,176,212,187a,197a
1935 74,175,212,186a,201a

1936 151,188,270,187a,199a
1937 83,214,230,246,261,186a,202a
1938 75,175,215,261,186a,198a
1939 80,255,188a,200a
1940 73,186,218,230,246,182a,194a
1941 77,176,207,189a,193a
1942 151,187,260,270,279,187a,199a
1943 151,175,186,258,261,270,304a
1944 78,188,187a,199a
1945 151,186,270,187a,199a
1946 75,255,260,188a,200a
1947 151,188,255,260,270,365a
1948 84,176,213,247,247i,186a,200a
1949 76,189,187a,199a
1950 151,187,270,187a,199a
1951 73,186,187a,199a
1952 78,188,187a,199a
1953 82,186,187a,199a
1954 74,224,232,255,188a,200a
1955 151,188,258,260,270,319a
1956 83,186,187a,199a
1957 75,189,187a,199a
1958 80,187,256,331a
1959 84,176,213,186a,199a
1960 77,256,188a,200a
1961 81,256,188a,200a
1962 74,175,216,188a,197a
1963 78,175,256,326a
1964 166,175,186a,198a
1965 75,176,208,189a,201a
1966 79,176,187,325a
1967 84,176,186a,198a
1968 76,175,188,325a
1969 81,186,187a,199a
1970 73,188,256,331a
1971 151,188,258,260,270,187a,199a
1972 151,186,270,187a,199a
1973 74,189,187a,199a
1974 79,187,258,260,270,187a,199a
1975 83,186,187a,199a
1976 75,188,257,258,260,331a
1977 80,186,187a,199a
1978 168,257,188a,200a
1979 77,257,188a,200a
1980 81,186,210,332a
1981 151,189,270,187a,199a
1982 151,187,212,270,332a
1983 82,186,213,332a
1984 75,202,188a,200a
1985 79,198,188a,200a
1986 168,203,188a,200a
1987 76,199,188a,200a
1988 165,207,189a,201a
1989 73,189,226,333a
1990 78,187,226,333a
1991 166,186,227,259,262,333a
1992 74,196,262,188a,200a
1993 79,186,200,262,331a
1994 83,228,188a,197a
1995 75,200,188a,200a
1996 80,175,214,186a,197a
1997 84,215,189a,201a
1998 77,176,216,187a,198a
1999 81,206,189a,201a

15th October

1930 160,208,184a,196a
1931 81,175,208,188a,200a
1932 158,176,186a,198a
1933 78,176,211,189a,201a
1934 82,176,212,187a,197a
1935 75,175,212,186a,201a
1936 151,188,270,187a,199a
1937 83,214,230,246,261,186a,202a
1938 76,175,215,189a,198a
1939 80,255,188a,200a
1940 73,186,218,230,246,182a,194a
1941 77,176,207,189a,193a
1942 151,187,270,279,187a,199a
1943 151,175,186,258,261,270,304a
1944 151,188,270,187a,199a
1945 83,186,187a,199a
1946 75,255,260,188a,200a
1947 151,255,260,270,320a
1948 84,176,213,247,247i,186a,200a
1949 76,189,187a,199a
1950 151,187,270,187a,199a
1951 73,186,187a,199a
1952 78,188,187a,199a
1953 82,186,187a,199a
1954 75,224,232,255,188a,200a
1955 151,188,258,260,270,319a
1956 84,186,187a,199a
1957 76,189,187a,199a
1958 80,187,256,331a
1959 73,176,213,186a,199a
1960 77,256,188a,200a
1961 166,226,256,337a
1962 74,175,216,188a,197a
1963 78,175,256,326a
1964 83,175,186a,198a
1965 75,176,208,189a,201a
1966 80,176,256,326a
1967 84,176,186a,198a
1968 77,175,188,325a
1969 81,186,187a,199a
1970 74,188,256,262,331a
1971 151,188,270,187a,199a
1972 151,186,270,187a,199a
1973 75,189,187a,199a
1974 79,187,258,260,270,187a,199a
1975 84,186,187a,199a
1976 76,188,257,260,331a
1977 80,186,187a,199a
1978 73,257,188a,200a
1979 77,257,188a,200a
1980 82,186,187a,199a
1981 151,189,270,187a,199a

1982 151,187,212,258,260,270,332a
1983 83,186,213,332a
1984 75,202,188a,200a
1985 80,198,188a,200a
1986 168,203,188a,200a
1987 76,199,188a,200a
1988 165,207,189a,201a
1989 74,189,226,333a
1990 78,187,226,333a
1991 166,186,227,259,262,333a
1992 75,196,262,188a,200a
1993 79,186,200,262,331a
1994 168,197,188a,200a
1995 160,200,188a,200a
1996 80,175,214,186a,197a
1997 157,215,258,261,189a,201a
1998 77,176,216,187a,198a
1999 81,206,189a,201a

16th October

1930 161,208,184a,196a
1931 81,175,208,188a,200a
1932 158,176,186a,198a
1933 78,176,211,189a,201a
1934 83,176,246,187a,197a
1935 75,175,212,186a,201a
1936 80,175,213,188a,198a
1937 84,230,246,186a,202a
1938 76,175,215,189a,198a
1939 81,176,205,188a,203a
1940 73,186,218,230,246,182a,194a
1941 77,176,207,189a,193a
1942 151,187,270,279,187a,199a
1943 151,175,186,258,261,270,304a
1944 151,188,270,187a,199a
1945 83,186,187a,199a
1946 76,255,260,188a,200a
1947 151,255,260,270,320a
1948 73,176,213,247,247i,186a,200a
1949 151,189,270,319a
1950 151,187,270,187a,199a
1951 74,186,187a,199a
1952 78,188,187a,199a
1953 83,186,187a,199a
1954 75,224,232,255,188a,200a
1955 151,188,255,258,260,270,365a
1956 84,186,187a,199a
1957 76,189,187a,199a
1958 81,256,188a,200a
1959 73,176,213,186a,199a
1960 78,256,188a,200a
1961 166,226,256,337a
1962 75,175,216,188a,197a
1963 151,188,256,270,331a
1964 83,175,186a,198a
1965 160,228,248,189a,201a
1966 80,176,256,326a
1967 73,176,186a,198a
1968 77,175,188,325a
1969 81,186,187a,199a
1970 74,188,256,262,331a
1971 151,188,270,187a,199a
1972 83,186,187a,199a
1973 75,189,197a,199a
1974 151,187,258,260,270,187a,199a
1975 84,186,187a,199a
1976 76,188,257,260,331a
1977 81,186,187a,199a
1978 73,257,188a,200a
1979 78,176,257,326a
1980 82,186,187a,199a
1981 75,189,258,260,187a,199a
1982 151,187,212,258,260,270,332a
1983 83,186,213,332a
1984 76,202,188a,200a
1985 80,198,188a,200a
1986 73,203,188a,200a
1987 77,199,188a,200a
1988 165,207,189a,201a
1989 74,189,226,333a
1990 78,187,226,333a
1991 83,176,210,262,186a,199a
1992 75,196,262,188a,200a
1993 80,187,200,331a
1994 168,197,188a,200a
1995 160,200,188a,200a
1996 81,175,214,261,186a,197a
1997 157,215,258,261,189a,201a
1998 78,176,216,187a,198a
1999 82,176,206,186a,201a

17th October

1930 161,208,184a,196a
1931 82,175,209,188a,200a
1932 158,176,186a,198a
1933 79,189,187a,199a
1934 83,176,246,187a,197a
1935 76,175,212,186a,201a
1936 80,175,213,188a,198a
1937 84,230,246,186a,202a
1938 77,175,215,261,189a,198a
1939 81,176,205,188a,203a
1940 158,186,182a,194a
1941 78,176,207,189a,193a
1942 83,187,260,279,187a,199a
1943 75,175,186,261,279,304a
1944 151,188,270,187a,199a
1945 84,186,187a,199a
1946 76,255,260,188a,200a
1947 151,255,260,270,320a
1948 73,186,187a,199a
1949 151,189,270,319a
1950 151,187,270,187a,199a
1951 74,186,187a,199a
1952 79,188,187a,199a
1953 83,186,187a,199a

1954 160,224,232,255,313a
1955 151,188,255,258,260,270,365a
1956 84,186,187a,199a
1957 77,189,187a,199a
1958 81,256,188a,200a
1959 74,176,213,186a,199a
1960 78,256,188a,200a
1961 166,226,256,337a
1962 75,175,216,188a,197a
1963 151,188,256,270,331a
1964 84,175,186a,198a
1965 160,228,248,189a,201a
1966 81,176,186a,198a
1967 73,176,186a,198a
1968 77,175,188,325a
1969 166,186,259,262,187a,199a
1970 74,188,256,262,187a,199a
1971 151,188,260,270,279,187a,199a
1972 83,186,187a,199a
1973 76,189,187a,199a
1974 151,187,258,260,270,187a,199a
1975 84,186,187a,199a
1976 77,188,257,331a
1977 81,187,260,187a,199a
1978 74,257,188a,200a
1979 78,176,257,326a
1980 82,186,187a,199a
1981 75,189,258,260,187a,199a
1982 151,187,212,258,260,270,332a
1983 84,186,213,332a
1984 76,202,188a,200a
1985 81,198,188a,200a
1986 73,203,188a,200a
1987 77,199,188a,200a
1988 82,175,207,186a,193a
1989 75,189,226,333a
1990 151,187,226,270,333a
1991 83,200,262,188a,200a
1992 160,196,259,262,188a,200a
1993 80,187,200,331a
1994 73,197,228,188a,200a
1995 77,200,188a,200a
1996 81,175,214,261,186a,197a
1997 74,215,261,189a,201a
1998 78,176,187a,198a
1999 166,218,186a,202a

18th October

1930 162,208,184a,196a
1931 82,175,209,188a,200a
1932 75,176,186a,198a
1933 79,189,187a,199a
1934 83,176,229,187a,198a
1935 76,175,212,186a,201a
1936 80,175,213,188a,198a
1937 73,230,246,186a,202a
1938 77,175,215,261,189a,198a
1939 82,176,205,188a,203a
1940 158,186,182a,194a
1941 78,176,207,189a,193a
1942 83,187,260,279,187a,199a
1943 75,175,186,261,279,304a
1944 80,188,255,331a
1945 84,186,187a,199a
1946 151,255,260,270,320a
1947 151,255,260,270,320a
1948 73,186,187a,199a
1949 78,189,187a,199a
1950 151,187,270,187a,199a
1951 75,186,187a,199a
1952 79,188,187a,199a
1953 83,186,187a,199a
1954 160,224,232,255,313a
1955 151,188,255,258,260,270,365a
1956 73,186,187a,199a
1957 77,189,187a,199a
1958 82,256,188a,200a
1959 74,176,213,186a,199a
1960 79,256,188a,200a
1961 83,256,188a,200a
1962 76,175,216,188a,197a
1963 80,256,188a,200a
1964 84,175,186a,198a
1965 77,176,208,189a,201a
1966 81,176,186a,198a
1967 73,176,186a,198a
1968 78,175,188,325a
1969 151,187,211,262,270,187a,199a
1970 75,188,256,262,331a
1971 79,188,258,260,187a,199a
1972 151,186,270,187a,199a
1973 76,189,187a,199a
1974 151,187,258,260,270,187a,199a
1975 73,186,187a,199a
1976 77,188,257,331a
1977 82,187,187a,199a
1978 74,257,188a,200a
1979 78,176,257,326a
1980 83,186,187a,199a
1981 151,189,258,260,270,187a,199a
1982 151,187,212,258,260,270,332a
1983 84,186,213,332a
1984 77,202,188a,200a
1985 81,198,188a,200a
1986 74,203,188a,200a
1987 78,199,188a,200a
1988 82,175,207,186a,193a
1989 75,189,226,333a
1990 151,187,226,270,333a
1991 83,200,262,188a,200a
1992 160,196,259,262,188a,200a
1993 81,187,200,331a
1994 73,197,228,188a,200a
1995 77,200,188a,200a
1996 82,217,261,190a,202a
1997 74,215,261,189a,201a
1998 79,187,187a,199a
1999 83,239,191a,203a

19th October

1930 162,208,184a,196a
1931 83,175,209,188a,200a
1932 75,176,186a,198a
1933 79,189,187a,199a
1934 84,176,229,187a,198a
1935 76,175,212,186a,201a
1936 81,175,213,188a,198a
1937 73,230,246,186a,202a
1938 78,176,186a,198a
1939 82,176,205,188a,203a
1940 75,186,218,230,246,182a,194a
1941 79,176,207,189a,193a
1942 83,187,260,279,187a,199a
1943 151,175,186,270,304a
1944 80,188,255,331a
1945 151,187,258,260,270,187a,199a
1946 151,255,260,270,320a
1947 151,255,260,270,320a
1948 74,186,187a,199a
1949 78,189,187a,199a
1950 83,187,187a,199a
1951 75,186,187a,199a
1952 80,188,255,331a
1953 151,187,270,187a,199a
1954 77,224,232,255,188a,200a
1955 151,188,260,270,319a
1956 73,175,210,186a,204a
1957 78,189,187a,199a
1958 82,256,188a,200a
1959 74,176,213,186a,199a
1960 79,256,188a,200a
1961 83,256,188a,200a
1962 76,175,216,188a,197a
1963 80,256,188a,200a
1964 73,175,186a,198a
1965 77,176,208,189a,201a
1966 82,176,186a,198a
1967 158,176,186a,198a
1968 78,175,188,325a
1969 83,187,211,262,270,187a,199a
1970 75,188,256,262,331a
1971 79,188,258,260,187a,199a
1972 151,186,270,187a,199a
1973 77,189,187a,199a
1974 151,187,258,260,270,187a,199a
1975 73,186,187a,199a
1976 78,188,257,331a
1977 82,187,187a,199a
1978 75,257,188a,200a
1979 79,188,257,331a
1980 83,186,187a,199a
1981 151,189,258,260,270,187a,199a
1982 151,187,212,258,260,270,332a
1983 84,186,213,332a
1984 77,202,188a,200a
1985 82,198,188a,200a
1986 74,203,188a,200a
1987 78,199,188a,200a
1988 83,175,207,186a,193a
1989 76,189,226,333a
1990 80,187,226,333a
1991 84,200,262,188a,200a
1992 77,196,188a,200a
1993 81,187,200,331a
1994 73,197,188a,200a
1995 77,200,188a,200a
1996 82,217,261,190a,202a
1997 75,215,189a,201a
1998 79,187,187a,199a
1999 83,239,191a,203a

20th October

1930 151,189,270,312a
1931 83,175,209,188a,200a
1932 76,176,186a,198a
1933 80,189,246,189a,201a
1934 84,176,229,187a,198a
1935 77,175,212,186a,201a
1936 81,175,213,188a,198a
1937 158,187,187a,199a
1938 78,176,186a,198a
1939 83,176,205,188a,203a
1940 75,186,218,230,246,182a,194a
1941 79,176,207,189a,193a
1942 151,187,260,270,279,187a,199a
1943 151,175,186,270,304a
1944 81,188,187a,199a
1945 151,187,258,260,270,187a,199a
1946 78,255,188a,200a
1947 151,255,270,320a
1948 74,186,187a,199a
1949 151,189,270,187a,199a
1950 83,187,187a,199a
1951 75,186,187a,199a
1952 80,188,255,331a
1953 151,187,270,187a,199a
1954 77,224,232,255,188a,200a
1955 151,188,260,270,319a
1956 74,175,186a,198a
1957 78,189,187a,199a
1958 83,256,188a,200a
1959 75,176,213,186a,199a
1960 79,256,188a,200a
1961 84,256,188a,200a
1962 76,175,216,188a,197a
1963 80,256,188a,200a
1964 73,175,186a,198a
1965 78,176,186a,198a
1966 82,176,186a,198a
1967 158,176,186a,198a
1968 151,175,188,270,325a
1969 83,187,211,262,270,187a,199a
1970 76,188,256,262,331a
1971 151,188,257,258,260,270,331a

1972 151,186,270,187a,199a
1973 77,189,187a,199a
1974 151,187,258,260,270,187a,199a
1975 73,186,187a,199a
1976 78,188,257,331a
1977 83,187,258,260,187a,199a
1978 75,257,188a,200a
1979 79,188,257,331a
1980 84,186,187a,199a
1981 151,189,258,260,270,187a,199a
1982 151,187,212,258,260,270,332a
1983 73,186,213,332a
1984 78,202,214,336a
1985 82,198,188a,200a
1986 74,203,188a,200a
1987 79,188,199,331a
1988 83,175,207,186a,193a
1989 76,189,226,333a
1990 80,187,226,333a
1991 84,200,262,188a,200a
1992 77,176,211,189a,196a
1993 82,187,200,227,262,369a
1994 74,197,188a,200a
1995 78,200,188a,200a
1996 83,175,214,261,186a,197a
1997 75,215,189a,201a
1998 79,187,187a,199a
1999 83,239,191a,203a

21st October

1930 151,189,270,187a,199a
1931 84,175,209,188a,200a
1932 76,176,186a,198a
1933 80,189,246,189a,201a
1934 73,176,212,187a,198a
1935 77,175,212,186a,201a
1936 82,175,213,188a,198a
1937 158,187,187a,199a
1938 79,176,215,189a,198a
1939 83,176,205,188a,203a
1940 75,186,218,230,246,182a,194a
1941 80,176,207,189a,193a
1942 151,187,260,270,279,187a,199a
1943 151,175,186,219,231,247,258,
261,270,362a
1944 81,188,187a,199a
1945 151,187,270,187a,199a
1946 78,255,188a,200a
1947 151,255,270,320a
1948 75,186,187a,199a
1949 151,189,270,187a,199a
1950 151,187,270,187a,199a
1951 76,186,187a,199a
1952 80,188,255,331a
1953 151,187,270,187a,199a
1954 77,208,224,232,255,260,188a,
200a
1955 151,188,270,319a
1956 74,175,186a,198a
1957 151,189,270,187a,199a
1958 83,256,188a,200a
1959 75,256,188a,200a
1960 80,256,188a,200a
1961 84,256,188a,200a
1962 77,175,216,188a,197a
1963 81,256,188a,200a
1964 158,176,186a,198a
1965 78,176,186a,198a
1966 83,176,186a,198a
1967 75,176,186a,198a
1968 151,175,189,270,325a
1969 151,187,211,262,270,187a,199a
1970 76,188,256,262,331a
1971 151,188,257,258,260,270,331a
1972 151,186,270,187a,199a
1973 78,189,187a,199a
1974 151,187,270,187a,199a
1975 74,186,187a,199a
1976 151,189,270,199a
1977 83,187,258,260,187a,199a
1978 160,257,188a,200a
1979 80,257,188a,200a
1980 84,186,187a,199a
1981 151,189,270,187a,199a
1982 151,187,212,258,260,270,332a
1983 73,186,213,332a
1984 78,202,214,336a
1985 83,198,188a,200a
1986 75,203,188a,200a
1987 79,188,199,331a
1988 84,175,207,186a,193a
1989 76,189,226,333a
1990 80,187,226,333a
1991 73,200,188a,200a
1992 77,176,211,189a,196a
1993 82,187,200,227,262,369a
1994 74,197,188a,200a
1995 78,175,213,188a,201a
1996 83,175,214,261,186a,197a
1997 76,215,189a,201a
1998 80,176,216,187a,198a
1999 84,176,206,186a,202a

22nd October

1930 80,175,208,189a,197a
1931 168,254,188a,200a
1932 76,176,186a,198a
1933 81,211,189a,201a
1934 73,176,212,187a,198a
1935 78,175,186a,198a
1936 82,175,213,188a,198a
1937 75,187,182a,199a
1938 79,176,215,189a,198a
1939 83,176,205,188a,203a
1940 76,186,218,230,246,182a,194a
1941 80,176,207,189a,193a

1942 151,187,260,270,279,187a,199a
1943 151,175,186,219,231,247,258, 261,270,362a
1944 81,255,188a,200a
1945 151,187,270,187a,199a
1946 78,255,188a,200a
1947 151,255,260,270,320a
1948 75,186,187a,199a
1949 80,189,187a,199a
1950 151,187,270,187a,199a
1951 76,186,187a,199a
1952 81,189,187a,199a
1953 151,187,270,187a,199a
1954 78,224,232,255,188a,200a
1955 151,188,270,319a
1956 75,175,186a,198a
1957 151,189,270,187a,199a
1958 84,256,188a,200a
1959 76,256,188a,200a
1960 80,256,188a,200a
1961 73,187,187a,199a
1962 77,175,216,188a,197a
1963 81,256,188a,200a
1964 158,176,186a,198a
1965 79,176,208,189a,201a
1966 83,176,186a,198a
1967 75,176,186a,198a
1968 80,175,189,325a
1969 151,187,211,262,270,187a,199a
1970 77,188,256,331a
1971 151,188,213,258,260,270,332a
1972 151,186,270,187a,199a
1973 78,189,187a,199a
1974 151,187,270,187a,199a
1975 74,186,187a,199a
1976 151,189,270,187a,199a
1977 151,187,208,260,270,187a,199a
1978 160,257,188a,200a
1979 80,257,188a,200a
1980 73,186,187a,199a
1981 151,189,270,187a,199a
1982 151,187,212,270,332a
1983 74,186,213,332a
1984 79,202,214,336a
1985 83,198,188a,200a
1986 75,203,188a,200a
1987 79,188,199,331a
1988 84,175,207,186a,193a
1989 77,189,226,333a
1990 81,187,226,333a
1991 73,200,188a,200a
1992 78,176,211,189a,196a
1993 83,187,200,211,262,331a
1994 75,197,188a,200a
1995 79,188,187a,199a
1996 84,175,214,186a,197a
1997 76,215,189a,201a
1998 80,176,216,187a,198a
1999 84,176,206,186a,202a

23rd October

1930 80,175,208,189a,197a
1931 168,254,188a,200a
1932 77,176,186a,198a
1933 81,211,189a,201a
1934 74,176,229,187a,198a
1935 78,175,186a,198a
1936 82,175,213,189a,198a
1937 75,187,187a,199a
1938 80,176,215,189a,198a
1939 84,176,205,188a,203a
1940 76,186,218,230,246,182a,194a
1941 81,176,207,189a,193a
1942 151,187,260,270,279,187a,199a
1943 151,175,186,219,231,247,258, 261,270,362a
1944 82,176,210,247,247i,189a,200a
1945 75,187,258,260,187a,199a
1946 79,189,255,331a
1947 151,255,260,270,320a
1948 76,186,187a,199a
1949 80,189,187a,199a
1950 151,187,270,187a,199a
1951 77,186,187a,199a
1952 93,176,176i,206,189a,202a
1953 74,187,187a,199a
1954 78,224,232,255,188a,200a
1955 151,188,270,319a
1956 87,175,186a,198a
1957 80,189,187a,199a
1958 84,256,188a,200a
1959 76,256,188a,200a
1960 93,213,256,263,336a
1961 73,187,187a,199a
1962 78,175,186a,198a
1963 82,256,188a,200a
1964 87,176,256,326a
1965 79,176,208,189a,201a
1966 83,176,186a,198a
1967 75,176,234,256,186a,198a
1968 92,175,256,326a
1969 151,187,270,187a,199a
1970 77,188,256,331a
1971 151,188,213,258,260,270,332a
1972 86,186,187a,199a
1973 78,189,187a,199a
1974 83,187,258,260,270,187a,199a
1975 75,186,187a,199a
1976 92,1257,188a,200a
1977 151,187,208,260,270,187a,199a
1978 160,257,188a,200a
1979 80,257,188a,200a
1980 85,257,188a,200a
1981 151,189,270,187a,199a
1982 151,187,212,270,332a
1983 74,186,213,332a
1984 91,202,214,336a
1985 84,198,188a,200a
1986 160,203,188a,200a

1987 80,199,188a,200a
1988 85,175,207,186a,193a
1989 89,226,190a,202a
1990 81,226,190a,202a
1991 158,200,259,262,188a,200a
1992 90,196,188a,200a
1993 95,200,262,188a,200a
1994 75,197,188a,200a
1995 79,188,187a,199a
1996 96,175,214,186a,197a
1997 161,215,189a,201a
1998 81,176,216,187a,198a
1999 73,176,203,186a,202a

24th October

1930 93,175,208.189a,197a
1931 152,254,259,263,271,188a,200a
1932 89,176,263,186a,198a
1933 94,176,211,189a,201a
1934 86,254,188a,200a
1935 90,175,186a,198a
1936 95,175,213,189a,198a
1937 88,175,255,187a,202a
1938 152,255,271,188a,200a
1939 96,255,188a,200a
1940 77,186,218,230,246,182a,194a
1941 93,176,207,189a,193a
1942 86,187,219,231,247,187a,199a
1943 90,175,219,231,247,183a,195a
1944 94,255,188a,200a
1945 159,187,258,260,187a,199a
1946 91,255,260,188a,200a
1947 152,255,260,271,320a
1948 88,175,213,186a,201a
1949 93,175,214,189a,197a
1950 85,187,187a,199a
1951 89,176,176i,205,186a,198a
1952 94,176,176i,206,189a,202a
1953 86,255,188a,200a
1954 152,208,255,260,271,188a,200a
1955 152,188,255,260,271,365a
1956 88,175,186a,198a
1957 152,256,271,188a,200a
1958 96,256,188a,200a
1959 88,256,259,263,188a,200a
1960 93,213,256,263,336a
1961 86,256,188a,200a
1962 90,175,256,326a
1963 94,256,188a,200a
1964 87,176,256,326a
1965 152,256,271,188a,200a
1966 96,176,256,326a
1967 88,176,256,234,326a
1968 93,175,186a,198a
1969 85,187,187a,199a
1970 89,188,256,331a
1971 93,213,257,260,336a
1972 86,186,187a,199a
1973 91,189,197a,199a
1974 167,187,258,260,187a,199a
1975 87,175,205,236,186a,196a
1976 92,257,188a,200a
1977 85,208,257,260,188a,200a
1978 152,257,271,188a,200a
1979 93,257,188a,200a
1980 86,257,188a,200a
1981 90,189,187a,199a
1982 94,187a,212,332a
1983 87,213,189a,201a
1984 152,202,214,263,271,336a
1985 84,198,188a,200a
1986 88,203,188a,200a
1987 152,199,271,188a,200a
1988 85,175,207,186a,204a
1989 90,226,190a,202a
1990 94,195,226,337a
1991 158,200,259,262,188a,200a
1992 91,196,188a,200a
1993 95,200,262,188a,200a
1994 152,197,271,188a,200a
1995 92,201,188a,200a
1996 85,175,214,186a,197a
1997 161,215,189a,201a
1998 93,176,216,187a,198a
1999 85,176,205,186a,202a

25th October

1930 93,175,208,189a,197a
1931 152,254,259,263,271,188a,200a
1932 162,176,259,263,186a,198a
1933 94,176,211,189a,201a
1934 87,254,188a,200a
1935 91,175,212,186a,201a
1936 95,175,213,189a,198a
1937 88,175,255,187a,202a
1938 152,255,271,188a,200a
1939 96,255,188a,200a
1940 77,186,218,230,246,182a,194a
1941 94,176,207,189a,193a
1942 86,187,219,231,247,187a,199a
1943 90,175,219,231,247,183a,195a
1944 95,255,188a,200a
1945 88,187,260,312a
1946 152,212,255,260,271,188a,200a
1947 152,255,260,271,320a
1948 89,175,213,186a,201a
1949 93,175,214,189a,197a
1950 85,187,187a,199a
1951 89,176,176i,205,186a,198a
1952 94,176,176i,206,189a,202a
1953 87,176,224,255,187a,198a
1954 152,208,255,260,271,188a,200a
1955 152,188,255,260,271,365a
1956 88,175,186a,198a
1957 93,211,256,336a
1958 85,256,188a,200a

1959 89,256,263,188a,200a
1960 94,256,263,188a,200a
1961 86,256,188a,200a
1962 90,175,256,326a
1963 94,256,188a,200a
1964 88,176,256,326a
1965 152,256,259,263,271,188a,200a
1966 96,176,256,326a
1967 88,176,256,234,326a
1968 93,175,186a,198a
1969 86,187,262,187a,199a
1970 152,256,259,262,271,188a,200a
1971 94,257,188a,200a
1972 159,186,187a,199a
1973 91,189,187a,199a
1974 167,187,258,260,187a,199a
1975 88,175,205,236,186a,196a
1976 93,206,257,336a
1977 85,208,257,260,188a,200a
1978 152,257,271,188a,200a
1979 93,257,188a,200a
1980 86,257,188a,200a
1981 163,189,187a,199a
1982 167,187,212,258,260,332a
1983 87,213,189a,201a
1984 152,202,214,263,271,336a
1985 84,198,188a,200a
1986 88,203,188a,200a
1987 93,188,205,336a
1988 86,175,207,186a,204a
1989 90,226,190a,202a
1990 94,195,226,337a
1991 158,200,259,262,188a,200a
1992 91,186,188a,200a
1993 961200,259,262,188a,200a
1994 88,197,188a,200a
1995 92,201,188a,200a
1996 85,175,214,186a,197a
1997 161,215,189a,201a
1998 93,198,188a,200a
1999 86,176,205,186a,202a

26th October

1930 93,175,208,189a,197a
1931 152,254,259,263,271,188a,200a
1932 162,176,259,263,186a,198a
1933 95,176,246,189a,201a
1934 87,254,188a,200a
1935 91,175,212,186a,201a
1936 96,175,213,189a,198a
1937 89,176,176i,214,187a,202a
1938 93,176,215,189a,199a
1939 85,203,255,286a
1940 162,176,176i,186,294a
1941 94,176,207,189a,193a
1942 86,187,219,231,147,187a,199a
1943 163,175,186,304a
1944 95,255,188a,200a
1945 88,187,260,312a
1946 152,212,255,260,271,188a,200a
1947 152,255,260,271,320a
1948 89,175,213,186a,201a
1949 94,175,214,189a,197a
1950 86,187,187a,199a
1951 90,176,186a,198a
1952 95,176,176i,206,189a,202a
1953 87,176,224,255,187a,198a
1954 152,208,255,260,271,188a,200a
1955 152,188,255,260,271,365a
1956 88,175,186,198a
1957 93,211,256,336a
1958 85,256,188a,200a
1959 89,256,263,188a,200a
1960 94,226,256,263,337a
1961 87,256,188a,200a
1962 91,256,188a,200a
1963 95,256,188a,200a
1964 88,176,256,326a
1965 152,256,259,263,271,188a,200a
1966 85,176,256,326a
1967 89,176,234,256,259,263,326a
1968 94,175,186a,198a
1969 86,187,262,187a,199a
1970 152,256,259,262,271,188a,200a
1971 94,257,188a,200a
1972 159,186,187a,199a
1973 152,257,271,188a,200a
1974 96,187,216,260,187a,199a
1975 88,175,205,236,186a,196a
1976 93,206,257,336a
1977 85,208,257,260,188a,200a
1978 155,257,271,188a,200a
1979 94,257,188a,200a
1980 87,257,188a,200a
1981 163,189,187a,199a
1982 95,188,212,257,260,366a
1983 87,213,189a,201a
1984 93,202,214,263,336a
1985 85,198,188a,200a
1986 152,203,271,188a,200a
1987 93,199,205,336a
1988 86,175,207,186a,204a
1989 90,226,190a,202a
1990 94,195,226,337a
1991 87,200,262,188a,200a
1992 152,196,271,188a,200a
1993 96,200,259,262,188a,200a
1994 88,197,188a,200a
1995 93,201,213,336a
1996 86,175,214,186a,197a
1997 90,215,189a,201a
1998 94,198,188a,200a
1999 86,176,205,186a,202a

27th October

1930 94,175,208,189a,197a

1931 152,254,259,263,271,188a,200a
1932 91,176,186a,198a
1933 95,176,246,189a,201a
1934 88,254,188a,200a
1935 92,254,188a,200a
1936 96,175,213,189a,198a
1937 89,176,176i,214,187a,202a
1938 93,176,215,189a,199a
1939 85,203,255,286a
1940 162,176,176i,186,294a
1941 95,176,207,189a,193a
1942 159,175,187,260,279,304a
1943 163,175,186,304a
1944 96,255,188a,200a
1945 88,187,260,312a
1946 93,255,260,188a,200a
1947 85,255,258,260,320a
1948 89,175,213,186a,201a
1949 94,175,214,189a,198a
1950 86,176,176i,215,187a,201a
1951 90,176,186a,198a
1952 95,176,176i,206,189a,202a
1953 88,255,188a,200a
1954 152,255,260,271,277,188a,200a
1955 152,188,255,260,271,365a
1956 89,175,186a,198a
1957 93,211,256,336a
1958 86,256,188a,200a
1959 90,176,256,263,326a
1960 95,256,188a,200a
1961 87,256,188a,200a
1962 91,256,188a,200a
1963 95,256,188a,200a
1964 88,176,256,326a
1965 152,208,256,259,263,271,336a
1966 152,176,256,259,263,271,326a
1967 89,176,234,256,259,263,326a
1968 94,175,186a,198a
1969 86,187,262,187a,199a
1970 152,188,256,259,262,271,331a
1971 167,257,258,260,188a,200a
1972 88,186,187a,199a
1973 152,257,271,188a,200a
1974 96,188,216,260,187a,199a
1975 88,175,205,236,186a,196a
1976 94,257,188a,200a
1977 86,257,188a,200a
1978 152,257,271,188a,200a
1979 94,257,188a,200a
1980 87,186,257,331a
1981 92,189,257,331a
1982 96,188,212,257,260,366a
1983 88,213,257,336a
1984 93,202,214,263,336a
1985 85,198,188a,200a
1986 152,203,271,188a,200a
1987 94,199,188a,200a
1988 87,175,207,186a,204a
1989 91,189,226,333a
1990 95,195,226,337a
1991 87,200,262,188a,200a
1992 152,196,271,188a,200a
1993 85,200,188a,200a
1994 152,197,271,188a,200a
1995 93,201,213,336a
1996 86,176,176i,239,186a,197a
1997 90,215,189a,201a
1998 94,198,188a,200a
1999 87,176,205,186a,202a

28th October

1930 94,175,208,189a,197a
1931 152,254,259,263,271,188a,200a
1932 91,176,186a,198a
1933 96,176,246,189a,201a
1934 88,254,188a,200a
1935 92,254,188a,200a
1936 85,175,213,189a,198a
1937 89,176,176i,214,187a,202a
1938 94,176,215,189a,199a
1939 86,255,188a,200a
1940 91,186,218,230,246,182a,194a
1941 95,176,207,189a,193a
1942 159,175,187,260,279,304a
1943 163,175,186,304a
1944 96,255,188a,200a
1945 89,187,260,187a,199a
1946 255,260,188a,200a
1947 85,255,258,260,320a
1948 90,175,186a,198a
1949 95,175,214,189a,198a
1950 87,255,188a,200a
1951 91,186,187a,199a
1952 96,176,176i,206,189a,202a
1953 88,255,188a,200a
1954 152,255,260,271,277,188a,200a
1955 152,188,255,260,271,365a
1956 89,175,186a,198a
1957 94,256,188a,200a
1958 152,256,271,188a,200a
1959 90,176,256,263,326a
1960 95,256,188a,200a
1961 88,256,188a,200a
1962 92,256,188a,200a
1963 96,256,188a,200a
1964 89,176,256,326a
1965 152,208,256,259,263,271,336a
1966 152,176,256,259,263,271,326a
1967 89,176,234,256,259,263,326a
1968 95,175,186a,198a
1969 159,187,211,262,187a,199a
1970 152,188,256,259,262,271,331a
1971 167,257,258,260,188a,200a
1972 88,186,187a,199a
1973 93,215,189a,201a
1974 151,188,216,257,260,270,331a
1975 89,175,205,236,186a,196a
1976 94,257,188a,200a

1977 86,257,188a,200a
1978 152,257,271,188a,200a
1979 95,257,188a,200a
1980 88,186,257,331a
1981 92,189,257,331a
1982 96,188,212,257,260,366a
1983 88,213,257,336a
1984 93,202,214,263,336a
1985 86,199,188a,200a
1986 152,203,271,188a,200a
1987 94,199,188a,200a
1988 87,175,207,186a,204a
1989 91,189,226,333a
1990 95,185,226,337a
1991 88,200,259,262,188a,200a
1992 93,196,188a,200a
1993 85,200,188a,200a
1994 152,197,271,188a,200a
1995 94,201,228,337a
1996 86,176,176i,239,186a,197a
1997 91,215,189a,201a
1998 95,198,188a,200a
1999 87,176,205,186a,202a

29th October

1930 95,175,208,189a,197a
1931 152,254,271,188a,200a
1932 152,176,254,263,271,326a
1933 96,176,246,189a,201a
1934 88,254,188a,200a
1935 92,254,259,262,188a,200a
1936 85,175,213,189a,198a
1937 162,230,246,187a,202a
1938 94,176,215,189a,199a
1939 86,255,188a,200a
1940 91,186,218,230,246,182a,194a
1941 96,176,207,189a,193a
1942 88,188,219,231,247,258,260, 187a,199a
1943 92,175,219,231,247,183a,195a
1944 85,255,188a,200a
1945 89,187,260,187a,199a
1946 93,255,260,188a,200a
1947 152,255,271,320a
1948 90,175,186a,198a
1949 95,175,214,189a,198a
1950 87,255,188a,200a
1951 91,186,187a,199a
1952 96,176,176i,206,189a,202a
1953 89,255,188a,200a
1954 152,208,255,260,271,188a,200a
1955 152,188,255,260,271,365a
1956 90,175,186a,198a
1957 94,256,188a,200a
1958 152,256,259,263,271,188a,200a
1959 91,256,188a,200a
1960 96,256,259,263,188a,200a
1961 88,256,188a,200a
1962 92,256,188a,200a
1963 96,256,188a,200a
1964 89,176,256,326a
1965 152,256,259,263,271,188a,200a
1966 152,176,256,259,263,271,326a
1967 162,176,256,259,263,269,326a
1968 95,175,186a,198a
1969 159,187,211,262,187a,199a
1970 152,188,256,259,262,271,331a
1971 96,257,260,188a,200a
1972 89,186,187a,199a
1973 93,215,189a,201a
1974 151,188,216,257,260,270,331a
1975 89,175,205,236,186a,196a
1976 95,257,188a,200a
1977 87,257,260,188a,200a
1978 152,257,271,188a,200a
1979 95,257,188a,200a
1980 88,186,257,331a
1981 92,189,257,331a
1982 96,188,212,257,260,366a
1983 89,213,257,336a
1984 94,202,214,224,263,350a
1985 86,199,188a,200a
1986 152,203,271,188a,200a
1987 95,199,188a,200a
1988 88,175,207,186a,204a
1989 92,199,226,337a
1990 96,195,226,337a
1991 88,200,259,262,188a,200a
1992 93,196,188a,200a
1993 85,200,188a,200a
1994 152,197,271,188a,200a
1995 94,201,228,337a
1996 87,176,176i,214,187a,197a
1997 91,215,189a,201a
1998 95,198,188a,200a
1999 88,176,205,186a,202a

30th October

1930 95,176,176i,208,189a,197a
1931 152,254,271,188a,200a
1932 152,176,254,263,271,326a
1933 157,211,189a,201a
1934 152,254,271,188a,200a
1935 175,212,186a,202a
1936 86,175,213,189a,198a
1937 162,230,246,187a,202a
1938 94,176,215,189a,199a
1939 87,255,188a,200a
1940 152,186,218,230,246,255,271, 296a
1941 96,175,207,189a,193a
1942 88,188,219,231,247,258,260, 187a,199a
1943 92,175,219,231,247,183a,195a
1944 85,255,188a,200a
1945 90,187,187a,199a

1946 94,255,188a,200a
1947 152,255,271,320a
1948 91,186,187a,199a
1949 95,175,214,189a,198a
1950 87,255,188a,200a
1951 152,255,271,188a,200a
1952 85,176,176i,206,189a,202a
1953 89,255,188a,200a
1954 152,208,255,260,271,188a,200a
1955 152,188,255,260,271,365a
1956 90,175,186a,198a
1957 95,256,188a,200a
1958 152,256,271,188a,200a
1959 91,256,188a,200a
1960 96,256,259,263,188a,200a
1961 88,256,188a,200a
1962 92,256,188a,200a
1963 85,256,188a,200a
1964 162,176,326a
1965 152,256,259,263,271,188a,200a
1966 86,177,256,263,326a
1967 162,176,256,259,263,269,326a
1968 96,175,186a,198a
1969 88,187,262,187a,199a
1970 152,256,259,262,271,188a,200a
1971 96,257,260,188a,200a
1972 89,186,187a,199a
1973 93,215,189a,201a
1974 151,188,216,257,260,270,331a
1975 90,175,205,236,186a,196a
1976 95,257,188a,200a
1977 87,257,260,188a,200a
1978 152,257,271,188a,200a
1979 96,257,188a,200a
1980 89,187,257,260,331a
1981 93,189,211,332a
1982 85,188,212,257,260,366a
1983 89,213,257,336a
1984 94,202,214,224,263,350a
1985 86,199,188a,200a
1986 152,203,271,183a,200a
1987 95,199,188a,200a
1988 88,175,250,187a,204a
1989 92,199,226,337a
1990 96,195,226,337a
1991 89,200,188a,200a
1992 94,227,190a,202a
1993 86,200,262,188a,200a
1994 152,197,271,188a,200a
1995 95,201,188a,200a
1996 87,176,176i,214,187a,198a
1997 91,215,189a,201a
1998 96,198,188a,200a
1999 88,176,205,186a,202a

31st October

1930 96,254,189a,197a
1931 152,254,259,263,271,188a,200a
1932 93,176,263,186a,198a
1933 157,211,189a,201a
1934 152,254,271,188a,200a
1935 93,175,212,186a,202a
1936 86,175,213,189a,198a
1937 91,176,255,187a,202a
1938 95,176,215,189a,199a
1939 87,255,188a,200a
1940 152,186,218,230,246,255,271, 296a
1941 96,175,207,189a,193a
1942 88,188,219,231,247,258,260, 187a,199a
1943 93,176,176i,183a,195a
1944 86,255,188a,200a
1945 90,187,187a,199a
1946 94,255,188a,200a
1947 152,255,271,320a
1948 91,186,187a,199a
1949 96,175,214,189a,198a
1950 88,255,188a,200a
1951 152,255,271,188a,200a
1952 85,176,176i,206,189a,202a
1953 89,255,188a,200a
1954 152,208,255,260,271,188a,200a
1955 152,188,255,271,365a
1956 91,175,256,326a
1957 95,256,188a,200a
1958 152,256,271,188a,200a
1959 92,256,263,188a,200a
1960 85,256,263,188a,200a
1961 89,256,188a,200a
1962 93,256,188a,200a
1963 85,256,188a,200a
1964 90,176,326a
1965 152,256,259,263,271,188a,200a
1966 87,177,256,326a
1967 91,176,234,256,326a
1968 96,175,186a,198a
1969 88,187,262,187a,199a
1970 152,256,259,262,271,188a,200a
1971 85,257,260,188a,200a
1972 90,187,219,235,187a,199a
1973 94,176,176i,215,189a,193a
1974 151,257,270,331a
1975 90,175,205,236,186a,196a
1976 95,257,188a,200a
1977 87,257,260,188a,200a
1978 152,257,271,188a,200a
1979 96,257,188a,200a
1980 89,187,257,260,331a
1981 93,189,211,332a
1982 85,188,212,257,260,366a
1983 90,176,176i,213,257,368a
1984 95,202,214,336a
1985 87,199,188a,200a
1986 152,203,271,188a,200a
1987 96,199,188a,200a
1988 88,175,250,187a,204a
1989 152,199,226,271,337a

1990 85,195,226,337a
1991 89,200,188a,200a
1992 227,190a,202a
1993 86,200,262,188a,200a
1994 152,197,271,188a,200a
1995 95,201,188a,200a
1996 88,176,176i,214,187a,198a
1997 152,215,271,336a
1998 96,198,188a,200a
1999 89,177,186a,202a

1st November

1930 96,254,259,263,189a,197a
1931 88,254,259,263,188a,200a
1932 93,176,176i,210,186a,198a
1933 157,211,189a,211a
1934 152,176,176i,254,271,326a
1935 166,230,246,259,262,186a,202a
1936 87,175,213,189a,198a
1937 91,176,176i,255,187a,202a
1938 95,176,176i,215,187a,199a
1939 87,177,216,188a,203a
1940 93,186,218,230,246,182a,194a
1941 85,175,207,189a,193a
1942 89,188,219,247,258,260,187a,
199a
1943 93,176,176i,183,195a
1944 86,255,188a,200a
1945 163,187,258,260,187a,199a
1946 95,255,260,188a,200a
1947 152,255,260,271,320a
1948 92,187,187a,199a
1949 96,175,214,189a,198a
1950 88,255,188a,200a
1951 93,176,176i,205,186a,198a
1952 86,177,206,189a,202a
1953 90,177,207,224,187a,198a
1954 152,255,271,188a,200a
1955 152,188,255,271,365a
1956 91,256,188a,200a
1957 96,256,188a,200a
1958 88,256,259,263,271,188a,200a
1959 92,256,263,188a,200a
1960 85,256,263,188a,200a
1961 89,256,188a,200a
1962 93,256,188a,200a
1963 86,256,188a,200a
1964 91,256,188a,200a
1965 152,256,271,188a,200a
1966 87,177,256,326a
1967 91,176,176i,234,256,326a
1968 96,175,186a,198a
1969 89,187,187a,199a
1970 152,256,271,188a,200a
1971 85,257,260,188a,200a
1972 90,187,219,235,257,187a,199a
1973 94,176,176i,215,189a,193a
1974 152,188,257,271,331a
1975 91,186,187a,199a
1976 96,257,187a,199a
1977 88,208,257,260,188a,200a
1978 152,257,271,188a,200a
1979 85,257,188a,200a
1980 89,187,257,260,331a
1981 93,189,211,332a
1982 86,188,257,331a
1983 90,176,176i,213,257,368a
1984 95,202,214,336a
1985 87,199,188a,200a
1986 152,203,271,188a,200a
1987 96,199,188a,200a
1988 89,175,250,187a,204a
1989 93,199,226,337a
1990 85,195a,226,337a
1991 162,176,176i,200,259,262,326a
1992 94,227,190a,202a
1993 87,200,262,188a,200a
1994 152,197,271,188a,200a
1995 95,201,188a,200a
1996 88,176,176i,214,187a,198a
1997 152,215,271,336a
1998 85,198,188a,200a
1999 89,177,205,186a,202a

2nd November

1930 96,254,259,263,189a,197a
1931 88,254,259,263,188a,200a
1932 94,176,176i,210,187a,197a
1933 86,211,189a,201a
1934 152,176,176i,271,326a
1935 166,230,246,259,262,186a,202a
1936 87,176,176i,213,189a,198a
1937 152,255,271,188a,200a
1938 96,176,176i,189a,199a
1939 88,177,216,188a,203a
1940 93,187,182a,194a
1941 85,175,207,189a,193a
1942 89,255,260,188a,200a
1943 94,176,176i,183a,195a
1944 87,255,188a,200a
1945 163,187,258,260,187a,199a
1946 95,255,260,188a,200a
1947 152,255,260,271,320a
1948 92,187,187a,199a
1949 85,175,214,189a,198a
1950 89,255,188a,200a
1951 93,176,176i,205,186a,198a
1952 86,177,206,189a,202a
1953 90,187,187a,199a
1954 152,255,271,188a,200a
1955 152,188,255,260,271,365a
1956 152,256,271,188a,200a
1957 96,256,188a,200a
1958 88,256,259,263,271,188a,200a
1959 93,213,256,263,336a
1960 85,256,263,188a,200a

1961 162,175,256,259,262,326a
1962 94,256,188a,200a
1963 86,256,188a,200a
1964 91,256,188a,200a
1965 95,208,189a,201a
1966 87,177,256,326a
1967 152,176,176i,234,256,259,265,
271,326a
1968 85,175,186a,198a
1969 89,187,256,325a
1970 152,256,271,188a,200a
1971 86,257,188a,200a
1972 163,187,270,187a,199a
1973 95,176,176i,215,260,189a,193a
1974 152,188,216,257,260,271,331a
1975 91,186,187a,199a
1976 96,257,188a,200a
1977 88,208,257,260,188a,200a
1978 93,209,257,336a
1979 85,257,188a,200a
1980 90,187,257,331a
1981 94,189,187a,199a
1982 86,188,257,331a
1983 91,213,257,336a
1984 96,214,202,259,263,336a
1985 88,199,188a,200a
1986 152,203,271,188a,200a
1987 96,199,188a,200a
1988 89,175,250,187a,193a
1989 93,199,226,337a
1990 86,195,226,337a
1991 162,176,176i,200,259,262,326a
1992 95,177,211,189a,196a
1993 87,200,262,188a,200a
1994 152,197,271,188a,200a
1995 96,201,188a,200a
1996 89,176,176i,214,187a,198a
1997 165,215,189a,201a
1998 85,177,239,188a,198a
1999 90,177,205,186a,202a

3rd November

1930 85,176,176i,208,263,189a,197a
1931 89,254,263,188a,200a
1932 94,177,210,187a,197a
1933 86,211,189a,201a
1934 152,176,176i,254,271,362a
1935 95,175,212,262,186a,202a
1936 88,228,254,259,263,189a,198a
1937 152,255,271,188a,200a
1938 96,176,176i,215,189a,199a
1939 88,177,216,188a,203a
1940 93,187,182a,194a
1941 86,189,182a,194a
1942 90,255,188a,200a
1943 94,176,176i,183a,195a
1944 87,255,188a,200a
1945 163,187,258,260,187a,199a
1946 95,255,260,188a,200a
1947 152,255,260,271,320a
1948 93,187,213,332a
1949 85,175,214,189a,198a
1950 89,255,188a,200a
1951 94,176,176i,205,186a,198a
1952 87,177,206,189a,202a
1953 163,187,258,260,187a,199a
1954 152,208,255,260,271,188a,200a
1955 152,188,255,260,271,365a
1956 152,256,271,188a,200a
1957 96,256,188a,200a
1958 88,256,259,263,271,188a,200a
1959 93,213,256,263,336a
1960 86,256,263,188a,200a
1961 162,175,256,259,262,326a
1962 94,256,188a,200a
1963 87,256,188a,200a
1964 152,256,271,188a,200a
1965 96,208,259,263,189a,201a
1966 88,177,256,263,326a
1967 152,176,176i,234,256,259,263,
271,326a
1968 85,175,186a,198a
1969 89,187,256,325a
1970 152,256,259,261,271,188a,200a
1971 86,257,188a,200a
1972 163,187,270,187a,199a
1973 95,176,176i,215,260,189a,193a
1974 152,188,216,257,260,271,331a
1975 92,257,188a,200a
1976 85,257,188a,200a
1977 152,257,260,271,320a
1978 93,209,257,336a
1979 86,257,188a,200a
1980 90,187,257,331a
1981 94,189,187a,199a
1982 87,257,188a,200a
1983 91,213,257,336a
1984 96,214,202,259,263,336a
1985 88,199,188a,200a
1986 152,203,271,188a,200a
1987 85,199,188a,200a
1988 90,175,207,187a,193a
1989 94,199,266,337a
1990 86,195,224,337a
1991 91,200,262,188a,200a
1992 95,177,211,189a,196a
1993 87,200,262,188a,200a
1994 92,197,271,188a,200a
1995 96,213,189a,201a
1996 89,176,176i,214,187a,198a
1997 165,215,189a,201a
1998 86,177,239,188a,198a
1999 90,177,205,186a,202a

4th November

1930 85,176,176i,208,263,189a,197a
1931 89,254,263,188a,200a
1932 95,177,210,187a,197a
1933 87,211,189a,201a
1934 152,254,271,188a,200a
1935 95,175,212,262,186a,202a
1936 88,228,254,259,263,189a,198a
1937 152,255,271,188a,200a
1938 96,176,176i,215,189a,199a
1939 89,177,206,188a,203a
1940 187,187a,194a
1941 86,189,182a,194a
1942 90,255,188a,200a
1943 167,176,176i,183a,195a
1944 88,255,188a,200a
1945 92,187,260,187a,199a
1946 96,255,260,188a,200a
1947 152,255,260,271,320a
1948 93,187,213,332a
1949 85,176,176i,247,189a,198a
1950 89,255,188a,200a
1951 94,176,176i,205,186a,198a
1952 87,177,206,189a,202a
1953 163,187,258,260,187a,199a
1954 152,208,255,260,271,188a,200a
1955 152,188,255,260,271,365a
1956 93,256,188a,200a
1957 85,256,188a,200a
1958 152,256,259,263,271,188a,200a
1959 94,256,263,188a,200a
1960 86,256,263,188a,200a
1961 90,175,256,262,326a
1962 95,256,188a,200a
1963 87,256,188a,200a
1964 152,256,271,188a,200a
1965 96,208,259,263,189a,201a
1966 88,177,256,263,326a
1967 93,176,176i,234,256,259,263, 326a
1968 86,175,186a,198a
1969 90,187,256,262,331a
1970 152,256,259,261,271,188a,200a
1971 159,257,258,260,188a,200a
1972 163,187,270,187a,199a
1973 95,176,176i,215,260,189a,193a
1974 88,188,216,257,260,331a
1975 92,257,188a,200a
1976 85,257,188a,200a
1977 152,257,260,271,320a
1978 93,209,257,336a
1979 86,210,189a,201a
1980 163,187,257,258,260,270,331a
1981 167,189,187a,199a
1982 87,257,188a,200a
1983 152,213,257,271,336a
1984 96,214,202,259,263,336a
1985 88,199,188a,200a
1986 152,203,216,271,336a
1987 157,205,189a,201a
1988 90,175,207,187a,193a
1989 152,200,226,259,263,271,337a
1990 87,195,226,337a
1991 91,200,188a,200a
1992 96,177,211,189a,196a
1993 88,200,259,262,188a,200a
1994 92,197,271,188a,200a
1995 85,201,213,263,336a
1996 89,176,176i,214,187a,198a
1997 94,217,190a,202a
1998 86,177,239,188a,198a
1999 91,177,205,186a,202a

5th November

1930 86,176,176i,208,263,189a,197a
1931 90,254,263,188a,200a
1932 95,177,210,187a,197a
1933 87,211,189a,201a
1934 152,254,271,188a,200a
1935 96,228,254,259,262,186a,202a
1936 89,176,176i,213,263,189a,198a
1937 93,176,176i,214,187a,202a
1938 85,176,176i,215,189a,199a
1939 89,177,216,188a,203a
1940 166,187,182a,194a
1941 86,189,182a,194a
1942 163,188,255,258,260,331a
1943 167,176,176i,183a,195a
1944 88,255,188a,200a
1945 92,187,260,187a,199a
1946 96,255,260,188a,200a
1947 161,255,258,260,320a
1948 94,187,187a,199a
1949 86,176,176i,247,189a,198a
1950 90,255,188a,200a
1951 95,176,176i,205,186a,198a
1952 87,177,206,189a,202a
1953 163,187,258,260,187a,199a
1954 96,208,255,260,188a,200a
1955 152,188,255,260,271,365a
1956 93,256,188a,200a
1957 85,256,188a,200a
1958 89,256,263,188a,200a
1959 94,256,263,188a,200a
1960 87,256,188a,200a
1961 91,187,256,262,331a
1962 152,256,271,188a,200a
1963 88,256,188a,200a
1964 152,256,271,188a,200a
1965 96,208,259,263,189a,201a
1966 89,177,263,326a
1967 93,176,176i,234,256,259,263, 326a
1968 86,175,186a,198a
1969 90,187,256,262,331a
1970 152,256,259,261,271,188a,200a
1971 159,213,258,260,189a,201a

1972 92,187,219,235,257,187a,199a
1973 96,176,176i,215,260,189a,193a
1974 88,188,216,257,260,331a
1975 175,205,186a,196a
1976 85,257,188a,200a
1977 152,257,260,271,320a
1978 94,209,257,336a
1979 86,210,189a,201a
1980 163,187,257,258,260,270,331a
1981 167,189,187a,199a
1982 88,257,188a,200a
1983 152,213,257,271,336a
1984 85,202,214,263,336a
1985 89,199,188a,200a
1986 152,203,216,271,336a
1987 86,205,189a,201a
1988 90,175,207,187a,193a
1989 94,200,226,259,262,263,273, 337a
1990 87,195,226,337a
1991 92,200,188a,200a
1992 96,177,211,189a,196a
1993 88,200,259,262,188a,200a
1994 152,197,271,188a,200a
1995 85,201,213,263,336a
1996 90,176,176i,214,187a,198a
1997 94,217,190a,202a
1998 87,177,216,188a,198a
1999 91,177,205,186a,202a

6th November

1930 86,176,176i,208,263,189a,197a
1931 90,254,263,188a,200a
1932 95,177,210,187a,197a
1933 87,211,189a,201a
1934 152,254,271,188a,200a
1935 96,228,254,259,262,186a,202a
1936 89,176,176i,213,263,189a,198a
1937 93,176,176i,214,187a,202a
1938 85,176,176i,215,189a,199a
1939 90,177,216,188a,203a
1940 95,187,182a,194a
1941 87,190,207,190a,193a
1942 163,188,255,258,260,331a
1943 96,176,176i,183a,195a
1944 88,255,188a,200a
1945 93,187,260,187a,199a
1946 157,255,258,260,188a,200a
1947 161,255,258,260,320a
1948 94,187,187a,199a
1949 86,176,176i,247,255,190a,198a
1950 90,255,188a,200a
1951 95,176,176i,205,186a,198a
1952 88,177,206,189a,202a
1953 92,187,255,260,331a
1954 96,208,255,260,188a,200a
1955 89,189,258,260,319a
1956 93,256,188a,200a
1957 86,256,188a,200a
1958 90,256,263,188a,200a
1959 94,256,263,188a,200a
1960 87,256,188a,200a
1961 91,187,256,262,331a
1962 152,256,271,188a,200a
1963 88,256,188a,200a
1964 93,176,176i,256,326a
1965 85,177,208,248,263,190a,201a
1966 89,177,263,326a
1967 166,176,176i,256,259,263,326a
1968 86,175,186a,198a
1969 163,187,211,256,262,311a
1970 152,256,259,261,271,188a,200a
1971 88,213,260,189a,201a
1972 92,187,219,235,257,187a,199a
1973 96,176,176i,215,190a,193a
1974 152,188,216,257,260,271,331a
1975 93,257,188a,200a
1976 86,257,188a,200a
1977 90,257,188a,200a
1978 94,209,257,336a
1979 87,210,189a,201a
1980 168,187,257,258,260,270,331a
1981 96,190,187a,199a
1982 88,257,188a,200a
1983 93,213,257,336a
1984 157,202,214,263,336a
1985 89,199,188a,200a
1986 152,203,271,188a,200a
1987 86,205,189a,201a
1988 91,187,187a,199a
1989 152,200,226,259,262,271,337a
1990 88,195,266,337a
1991 92,200,188a,200a
1992 96,177,211,189a,196a
1993 89,200,188a,200a
1994 152,197,271,188a,200a
1995 86,201,213,263,336a
1996 90,176,176i,214,187a,198a
1997 94,217,190a,202a
1998 87,177,216,188a,198a
1999 91,177,205,186a,202a

7th November

1930 86,176,176i,208,263,189a,197a
1931 91,254,188a,200a
1932 96,177,210,187a,197a
1933 88,177,211,190a,201a
1934 152,254,271,188a,200a
1935 85,175,212,186a,202a
1936 90,176,176i,263,186a,198a
1937 166,228,190a,202a
1938 86,177,215,189a,199a
1939 90,177,216,189a,203a
1940 95,187,182a,194a
1941 87,190,207,190a,193a
1942 163,208,255,260,188a,200a

1943 96,176,176i,183a,195a
1944 89,255,188a,200a
1945 93,187,260,187a,199a
1946 157,212,258,260,189a,201a
1947 152,221,255,271,185a,197a
1948 95,187,187a,199a
1949 87,176,176i,255,190a,198a
1950 91,255,188a,200a
1951 95,176,176i,205,186a,198a
1952 88,177,206,189a,202a
1953 152,187,255,260,271,331a
1954 152,208,255,260,271,188a,200a
1955 89,189,258,260,319a
1956 94,256,188a,200a
1957 86,256,188a,200a
1958 90,256,263,188a,200a
1959 95,256,188a,200a
1960 88,256,259,263,188a,200a
1961 92,256,262,188a,200a
1962 96,256,188a,200a
1963 89,256,188a,200a
1964 93,176,176i,326a
1965 85,177,208,248,263,190a,201a
1966 90,177,256,263,326a
1967 166,176,176i,256,259,263,326a
1968 87,175,186a,198a
1969 163,187,211,256,262,331a
1970 95,256,188a,200a
1971 88,213,260,189a,201a
1972 93,187,214,219,235,257,332a
1973 85,176,176i,215,190a,193a
1974 152,188,216,257,260,271,331a
1975 94,257,188a,200a
1976 86,257,188a,200a
1977 90,257,188a,200a
1978 95,209,257,336a
1979 87,210,189a,201a
1980 152,187,257,260,271,331a
1981 96,190,187a,199a
1982 89,257,188a,200a
1983 93,213,257,336a
1984 86,177,214,263,189a,202a
1985 90,199,188a,200a
1986 152,203,271,188a,200a
1987 87,205,189a,201a
1988 91,193,188a,200a
1989 152,200,226,259,262,271,337a
1990 88,195,226,337a
1991 92,200,188a,200a
1992 85,177,211,189a,196a
1993 89,200,188a,200a
1994 152,197,228,271,337a
1995 86,201,213,263,336a
1996 91,176,176i,214,187a,198a
1997 95,239,191a,203a
1998 88,177,239,188a,198a
1999 92,177,205,186a,202a

8th November

1930 87,176,176i,208,189a,197a
1931 91,176,176i,209,189a,201a
1932 96,177,210,187a,197a
1933 88,177,211,190a,201a
1934 152,254,271,188a,200a
1935 85,175,212,186a,202a
1936 90,176,176i,263,186a,198a
1937 166,228,190a,202a
1938 86,177,215,189a,199a
1939 91,177,216,189a,203a
1940 96,187,182a,194a
1941 88,175,207,190a,193a
1942 152,208,255,260,271,188a,200a
1943 96,176,176i,183a,195a
1944 89,255,188a,200a
1945 93,187,260,187a,199a
1946 86,255,188a,200a
1947 152,221,255,271,185a,197a
1948 95,187,187a,199a
1949 87,176,176i,255,190a,198a
1950 91,255,188a,200a
1951 96,177,205,186a,198a
1952 89,177,206,189a,202a
1953 93,187,255,260,331a
1954 152,208,255,260,271,188a,200a
1955 152,255,271,320a
1956 94,256,188a,200a
1957 86,256,188a,200a
1958 91,256,188a,200a
1959 95,256,188a,200a
1960 88,256,259,263,188a,200a
1961 92,256,262,188a,200a
1962 96,256,188a,200a
1963 89,256,188a,200a
1964 166,177,186a,198a
1965 86,177,208,248,263,190a,201a
1966 90,177,256,263,326a
1967 95,176,176i,256,326a
1968 87,176,176i,256,326a
1969 163,187,211,256,262,331a
1970 96,256,188a,200a
1971 88,213,260,189a,201a
1972 93,187,214,219,235,257,332a
1973 85,176,176i,215,190a,193a
1974 152,188,257,271,331a
1975 94,257,188a,200a
1976 87,257,188a,200a
1977 95,209,257,336a
1978 8,210,189a,201a
1979 88,210,189a,201a
1980 152,187,257,260,271,331a
1981 96,190,187a,199a
1982 89,257,188a,200a
1983 93,198,213,263,336a
1984 86,177,214,263,189a,202a
1985 90,199,188a,200a
1986 152,203,271,188a,200a
1987 87,205,189a,201a

1988 152,193,271,188a,200a
1989 96,200,226,259,262,263,337a
1990 89,195,226,337a
1991 93,200,188a,200a
1992 85,177,211,189a,196a
1993 90,200,262,188a,200a
1994 152,197,228,271,337a
1995 86,201,213,263,336a
1996 91,176,176i,214,187a,198a
1997 95,215,239,341a
1998 88,177,239,188a,198a
1999 92,177,205,186a,202a

9th November

1930 87,176,176i,208,189a,197a
1931 92,254,263,188a,200a
1932 85,177,210,187a,197a
1933 89,177,211,190a,201a
1934 152,254,271,188a,200a
1935 158,230,246,186a,202a
1936 90,176,176i,263,186a,198a
1937 166,228,190a,202a
1938 87,177,215,189a,199a
1939 91,177,216,189a,203a
1940 96,187,182a,194a
1941 88,175,207,190a,193a
1942 152,208,255,260,271,188a,200a
1943 85,176,176i,183a,195a
1944 90,255,188a,200a
1945 94,187,187a,199a
1946 86,255,188a,200a
1947 152,221,255,258,260,271,185a, 197a
1948 95,187,187a,199a
1949 87,176,176i,255,190a,198a
1950 152,255,271,188a,200a
1951 96,177,205,186a,198a
1952 89,177,206,189a,202a
1953 93,187,255,260,331a
1954 152,255,271,188a,200a
1955 152,255,271,320a
1956 95,256,188a,200a
1957 87,256,188a,200a
1958 91,256,188a,200a
1959 96,256,263,188a,200a
1960 88,256,259,263,188a,200a
1961 93,256,188a,200a
1962 152,256,271,188a,200a
1963 90,176,176i,256,326a
1964 166,177,186a,198a
1965 86,177,208,248,263,190a,201a
1966 91,177,256,326a
1967 95,176,176i,256,326a
1968 88,256,186a,198a
1969 152,187,256,262,271,331a
1970 96,256,188a,200a
1971 161,213,258,260,189a,201a
1972 93,187,214,219,235,257,332a
1973 86,176,176i,215,190a,193a
1974 152,188,257,271,331a
1975 95,257,188a,200a
1976 87,257,188a,200a
1977 95,209,257,336a
1978 96,209,257,336a
1979 88,210,189a,201a
1980 93,187,212,257,366a
1981 85,190,187a,199a
1982 90,257,188a,200a
1983 94,198,213,336a
1984 86,177,214,263,189a,202a
1985 91,187,199,331a
1986 152,203,271,188a,200a
1987 88,205,189a,201a
1988 152,193,271,188a,200a
1989 96,260,226,259,262,263,337a
1990 89,195,226,337a
1991 93,200,188a,200a
1992 86,177,211,189a,196a
1993 90,201,188a,200a
1994 152,197,271,188a,200a
1995 87,201,213,336a
1996 91,176,176i,214,187a,198a
1997 96,217,190a,202a
1998 88,177,239,188a,198a
1999 93,205,189a,201a

10th November

1930 88,208,259,263,184a,196a
1931 92,209,229,263,189a,201a
1932 85,177,210,187a,197a
1933 177,211,190a,201a
1934 152,254,271,188a,200a
1935 86,176,176i,213,187a,202a
1936 91,176,176i,263,189a,198a
1937 95,176,176i,255,187a,202a
1938 87,177,215,189a,199a
1939 92,177,216,189a,203a
1940 96,187,182a,194a
1941 88,175,207,190a,193a
1942 152,208,255,260,271,188a,200a
1943 85,176,176i,219,231,247,258, 260,183a,195a
1944 90,177,210,189a,200a
1945 94,187,187a,199a
1946 87,255,260,188a,200a
1947 152,221,255,258,260,271,185a, 197a
1948 96,176,176i,222,187a,201a
1949 88,176,176i,247,255,190a,198a
1950 152,255,271,188a,200a
1951 85,187,187a,199a
1952 89,177,206,189a,202a
1953 94,187,255,331a
1954 152,255,271,188a,200a
1955 152,189,255,260,271,365a
1956 95,256,188a,200a

1957 87,256,188a,200a
1958 152,256,259,263,271,188a,200a
1959 96,256,188a,200a
1960 89,256,263,188a,200a
1961 93,256,188a,200a
1962 152,256,271,188a,200a
1963 90,176,176i,256,326a
1964 166,177,186a,198a
1965 87,177,208,248,190a,201a
1966 91,177,256,326a
1967 96,176,176i,256,326a
1968 88,256,186a,198a
1969 152,187,256,262,271,331a
1970 85,256,188a,200a
1971 161,213,258,260,189a,201a
1972 94,187,219,235,257,187a,199a
1973 86,176,176i,215,190a,193a
1974 152,188,216,257,260,271,331a
1975 95,257,260,188a,200a
1976 87,257,188a,200a
1977 92,205,257,260,188a,200a
1978 96,209,257,336a
1979 161,210,189a,201a
1980 93,187,212,257,366a
1981 85,190,257,331a
1982 90,257,188a,200a
1983 94,198,213,336a
1984 87,202,214,336a
1985 91,199,188a,200a
1986 96,203,188a,200a
1987 88,205,189a,201a
1988 152,193,271,188a,201a
1989 152,200,226,259,263,271,337a
1990 89,195,226,337a
1991 94,200,227,337a
1992 86,177,211,189a,196a
1993 152,201,271,188a,200a
1994 152,197,271,188a,200a
1995 87,213,189a,201a
1996 152,198,271,188a,200a
1997 96,217,190a,202a
1998 89,177,239,188a,198a
1999 93,176,176i,205,187a,202a

11th November

1930 88,208,259,263,184a,196a
1931 165,209,263,189a,201a
1932 85,177,210,187a,197a
1933 89,177,211,190a,201a
1934 152,254,271,188a,200a
1935 87,176,176i,213,187a,202a
1936 91,176,176i,263,189a,198a
1937 95,176,176i,255,187a,202a
1938 88,177,215,189a,199a
1939 92,177,216,189a,203a
1940 85,187,182a,194a
1941 89,175,207,190a,193a
1942 152,208,255,260,271,188a,200a
1943 86,176,176i,219,231,247,183a, 195a
1944 90,177,210,189a,200a
1945 167,187,258,260,187a,199a
1946 87,255,260,188a,200a
1947 152,221,255,258,260,271,320a
1948 96,176,176i,222,187a,201a
1949 88,176,176i,247,255,190a,198a
1950 93,255,188a,200a
1951 85,187,187a,199a
1952 90,177,206,189a,202a
1953 94,187,255,331a
1954 152,208,255,260,271,188a,200a
1955 152,189,255,260,271,365a
1956 95,256,188a,200a
1957 88,256,188a,200a
1958 152,256,259,263,271,188a,200a
1959 85,256,188a,200a
1960 89,256,263,188a,200a
1961 152,256,271,188a,200a
1962 152,256,271,188a,200a
1963 90,176,176i,256,326a
1964 95,177,186a,198a
1965 87,177,208,248,190a,201a
1966 92,177,256,263,326a
1967 96,176,176i,256,326a
1968 88,256,186a,198a
1969 93,256,188a,200a
1970 85,256,188a,200a
1971 90,213,189a,201a
1972 94,187,219,235,257,187a,199a
1973 87,176,176i,215,190a,193a
1974 152,188,216,257,260,271,331a
1975 95,257,260,188a,200a
1976 88,257,188a,200a
1977 92,208,257,260,188a,200a
1978 157,209,257,336a
1979 161,210,189a,201a
1980 93,187,212,257,366a
1981 86,190,257,331a
1982 90,257,188a,200a
1983 95,198,213,336a
1984 87,202,214,336a
1985 92,199,271,188a,200a
1986 96,203,188a,200a
1987 88,205,189a,201a
1988 93,193,207,336a
1989 152,200,226,259,263,271,337a
1990 90,195,226,337a
1991 94,200,227,337a
1992 87,177,211,189a,196a
1993 152,201,271,188a,200a
1994 96,197,263,271,277,188a,200a
1995 88,213,263,189a,201a
1996 152,198,271,188a,200a
1997 85,217,190a,202a
1998 89,177,239,188a,198a
1999 93,176,176i,205,187a,202a

12th November

1930 89,176,176i,208,263,189a,197a
1931 165,209,263,189a,201a
1932 86,177,210,187a,197a
1933 90,177,211,190a,201a
1934 152,254,271,188a,200a
1935 87,176,176i,213,187a,202a
1936 152,254,259,263,271,186a,198a
1937 96,176,176i,255,187a,203a
1938 88,177,215,189a,199a
1939 165,216,189a,201a
1940 85,187,182a,194a
1941 89,176,176i,207,190a,193a
1942 152,255,271,188a,200a
1943 86,176,176i,219,231,247,183a, 195a
1944 91,177,210,189a,200a
1945 95,177,211,260,188a,197a
1946 88,255,260,188a,200a
1947 152,221,255,258,260,271,320a
1948 85,176,176i,222,187a,201a
1949 89,176,176i,247,190a,198a
1950 93,255,188a,200a
1951 86,187,187a,199a
1952 90,177,206,189a,202a
1953 152,255,271,188a,200a
1954 152,208,255,260,271,188a,200a
1955 152,189,255,260,271,365a
1956 96,256,188a,200a
1957 88,256,188a,200a
1958 93,212,256,263,336a
1959 85,256,188a,200a
1960 90,256,263,188a,200a
1961 152,256,259,262,271,188a,200a
1962 152,256,271,188a,200a
1963 91,256,188a,200a
1964 95,177,186a,198a
1965 88,228,248,259,263,190a,201a
1966 92,177,256,263,326a
1967 96,176,176i,256,326a
1968 89,256,186a,198a
1969 93,256,188a,200a
1970 86,256,188a,200a
1971 90,213,189a,201a
1972 167,187,187a,199a
1973 87,176,176i,215,190a,193a
1974 152,257,260,271,277,188a,200a
1975 96,257,260,188a,200a
1976 88,257,188a,200a
1977 165,208,257,258,260,336a
1978 157,209,257,336a
1979 161,210,189a,201a
1980 94,187,257,331a
1981 86,190,257,331a
1982 91,188,257,331a
1983 95,198,213,336a
1984 88,202,214,263,336a
1985 92,199,271,188a,200a
1986 152,203,271,188a,200a
1987 161,199,205,336a
1988 93,193,188a,200a
1989 86,200,226,259,262,263,337a
1990 90,195,226,337a
1991 94,200,277,337a
1992 87,177,211,189a,196a
1993 152,201,271,188a,200a
1994 96,197,263,271,177,188a,200a
1995 88,213,263,189a,201a
1996 93,176,176i,214,187a,198a
1997 85,217,190a,202a
1998 90,177,239,188a,198a
1999 94,176,176i,205,187a,202a

13th November

1930 89,176,176i,208,263,189a,197a
1931 94,209,229,263,189a,201a
1932 86,177,210,187a,197a
1933 90,177,211,190a,201a
1934 152,254,271,188a,200a
1935 87,176,176i,213,187a,202a
1936 152,254,259,263,271,186a,198a
1937 96,255,188a,200a
1938 161,217,255,189a,199a
1939 165,216,189a,201a
1940 158,187,182a,194a
1941 162,218,230,246,190a,193a
1942 152,255,271,188a,200a
1943 159,176,176i,258,260,183a,195a
1944 91,177,210,189a,200a
1945 95,177,211,260,188a,197a
1946 88,255,260,188a,200a
1947 152,221,255,258,260,271,320a
1948 85,176,176i,222,187a,201a
1949 89,176,176i,247,190a,198a
1950 94,255,188a,200a
1951 86,187,187a,199a
1952 91,189,187a,199a
1953 152,255,260,271,188a,200a
1954 88,255,260,277,313a
1955 152,255,260,271,320a
1956 96,256,188a,200a
1957 89,256,188a,200a
1958 93,212,256,263,336a
1959 85,256,188a,200a
1960 90,256,263,188a,200a
1961 152,256,259,262,271,188a,200a
1962 152,256,271,188a,200a
1963 91,256,188a,200a
1964 96,177,186a,198a
1965 88,228,248,259,263,190a,201a
1966 152,176,176i,256,259,263,271, 326a
1967 85,176,176i,256,326a
1968 89,256,186a,198a
1969 94,256,262,188a,200a
1970 86,256,188a,200a
1971 91,189,213,260,332a

1972 167,187,187a,199a
1973 88,176,176i,215,190a,193a
1974 152,257,260,271,277,188a,200a
1975 96,257,260,188a,200a
1976 89,257,188a,200a
1977 165,208,257,258,260,336a
1978 86,209,257,336a
1979 90,177,210,327a
1980 94,187,257,331a
1981 87,190,257,331a
1982 91,188,257,331a
1983 95,198,213,336a
1984 88,202,214,263,336a
1985 93,199,215,271,336a
1986 152,203,271,188a,200a
1987 161,199,205,336a
1988 94,193,226,337a
1989 86,200,226,259,262,263,337a
1990 91,195,226,337a
1991 95,200,188a,200a
1992 87,177,211,189a,196a
1993 152,201,271,188a,200a
1994 96,187,263,271,277,188a,200a
1995 88,213,263,189a,201a
1996 93,176,176i,214,187a,198a
1997 86,217,190a,202a
1998 90,177,239,188a,198a
1999 94,176,176i,205,187a,202a

14th November

1930 90,176,176i,208,263,189a,197a
1931 94,209,229,263,189a,201a
1932 87,177,186a,198a
1933 91,177,211,190a,201a
1934 152,254,271,188a,200a
1935 88,228,254,187a,202a
1936 152,254,259,263,271,186a
1937 96,177,214,188a,203a
1938 161,217,255,189a,199a
1939 94,177,216,189a,203a
1940 158,187,182a,194a
1941 162,218,230,246,190a,193a
1942 152,208,255,260,271,188a,200a
1943 159,176,176i,260,183a,195a
1944 92,255,188a,200a
1945 96,177,211,260,188a,197a
1946 89,255,258,260,320a
1947 165,213,258,260,321a
1948 85,176,176i,222,187a,201a
1949 162,176,176i,186a,198a
1950 94,255,188a,200a
1951 87,187,187a,199a
1952 91,189,187a,199a
1953 152,255,260,271,188a,200a
1954 88,255,260,277,313a
1955 152,255,260,271,320a
1956 85,256,188a,200a
1957 89,256,188a,200a
1958 94,256,263,188a,200a
1959 86,256,188a,200a
1960 90,256,263,188a,200a
1961 95,256,188a,200a
1962 152,256,271,188a,200a
1963 152,256,271,188a,200a
1964 96,177,186a,198a
1965 89,177,208,248,263,190a,202
1966 152,176,176i,256,259,263,271, 326a
1967 85,176,176i,256,326a
1968 90,176,176i,256,326a
1969 94,256,262,188a,200a
1970 87,256,188a,200a
1971 91,189,213,260,332a
1972 167,187,187a,199a
1973 88,176,176i,215,190a,193a
1974 152,257,260,271,277,188a,200a
1975 85,257,260,188a,200a
1976 89,257,188a,200a
1977 94,257,188a,200a
1978 86,209,257,336a
1979 90,177,210,327a
1980 167,187,257,258,260,331a
1981 87,190,257,331a
1982 152,257,271,188a,200a
1983 96,198,213,336a
1984 88,202,214,224,263,350a
1985 93,199,215,271,336a
1986 152,203,271,188a,200a
1987 90,199,205,336a
1988 94,193,226,337a
1989 152,200,226,259,262,271,337a
1990 91,195,226,337a
1991 95,200,188a,200a
1992 88,227,190a,202a
1993 152,201,271,188a,200a
1994 152,197,259,263,271,188a,200a
1995 161,213,263,189a,201a
1996 94,217,190a,202a
1997 86,217,190a,202a
1998 91,177,216,188a,198a
1999 95,239,191a,203a

15th November

1930 90,176,176i,208,263,189a,197a
1931 95,209,229,189a,201a
1932 87,177,186a,198a
1933 91,177,211,190a,201a
1934 96,212,254,188a,200a
1935 88,228,254,187a,202a
1936 93,213,189a,201a
1937 85,177,214,188a,203a
1938 90,177,215,189a,199a
1939 94,177,216,189a,203a
1940 158,187,182,194a
1941 91,176,176i,207,193a
1942 152,208,255,260,271,188a,200a

1943 88,176,176i,219,231,247,258, 260,183a,195a
1944 92,255,188a,200a
1945 96,177,211,260,188a,197a
1946 89,255,258,260,320a
1947 165,213,258,260,321a
1948 86,176,176i,214,187a,201a
1949 162,176,176i,186a,198a
1950 95,177,215,188a,202a
1951 87,187,187a,199a
1952 91,189,187a,199a
1953 96,255,260,188a,200a
1954 88,255,260,277,313a
1955 93,255,258,260,320a
1956 85,256,188a,200a
1957 90,256,188a,200a
1958 94,256,263,188a,200a
1959 86,256,188a,200a
1960 91,226,256,337a
1961 95,256,188a,200a
1962 88,256,188a,200a
1963 152,256,271,188a,200a
1964 96,177,186a,198a
1965 89,177,208,248,263,190a,202a
1966 152,176,176i,256,259,263,271, 326a
1967 158,176,176i,256,326a
1968 90,176,176i,256,326a
1969 95,256,262,188a,200a
1970 87,256,188a,200a
1971 91,189,213,260,332a
1972 96,187,219,235,257,187a,199a
1973 88,176,176i,215,190a,193a
1974 152,216,257,260,271,188a,200a
1975 85,257,260,188a,200a
1976 90,257,188a,200a
1977 94,257,188a,200a
1978 87,209,257,336a
1979 91,210,189a,201a
1980 167,187,257,258,260,331a
1981 88,190,257,331a
1982 152,257,271,188a,200a
1983 96,198,213,336a
1984 89,202,214,224,263,350a
1985 94,199,188a,200a
1986 152,203,271,188a,200a
1987 90,199,205,336a
1988 95,193,188a,200a
1989 152,200,226,259,262,271,337a
1990 92,195,226,337a
1991 96,200,188a,200a
1992 88,227,190a,202a
1993 152,201,271,188a,200a
1994 152,197,259,263,271,188a,200a
1995 161,213,263,189a,201a
1996 94,217,190a,202a
1997 87,217,190a,202a
1998 91,177,216,188a,198a
1999 95,239,191a,203a

16th November

1930 91,176,176i,208,189a,197a
1931 95,209,229,189a,201a
1932 87,177,186a,198a
1933 152,254,271,188a,200a
1934 96,212,254,188a,200a
1935 89,176,176i,213,187a,202a
1936 93,213,189a,201a
1937 85,177,214,188a,203a
1938 90,177,215,188a,199a
1939 94,177,216,189a,203a
1940 87,187,182a,194a
1941 91,176,176i,207,190a,193a
1942 96,208,255,260,188a,200a
1943 88,176,176i,219,231,247,258, 260,183a,195a
1944 93,177,210,190a,200a
1945 85,177,211,260,188a,197a
1946 90,255,188a,200a
1947 152,221,255,271,185a,197a
1948 86,176,176i,214,187a,201a
1949 91,176,176i,255,190a,198a
1950 95,177,215,188a,202a
1951 87,187,187a,199a
1952 92,177,206,190a,202a
1953 96,255,260,188a,200a
1954 152,208,255,260,271,188a,200a
1955 93,255,258,260,320a
1956 86,256,188a,200a
1957 90,256,188a,200a
1958 95,256,188a,200a
1959 87,256,188a,200a
1960 91,226,256,337a
1961 96,256,188a,200a
1962 88,256,188a,200a
1963 92,205,256,336a
1964 85,177,186a,198a
1965 89,177,208,248,263,190a,202a
1966 152,176,176i,256,259,263,271, 326a
1967 158,176,176i,256,326a
1968 91,190,256,331a
1969 95,256,262,188a,200a
1970 88,256,188a,200a
1971 92,213,260,189a,201a
1972 96,187,187a,199a
1973 89,176,176a,215,190a,193a
1974 152,216,257,260,271,188a,200a
1975 85,257,260,188a,200a
1976 90,257,188a,200a
1977 95,257,260,188a,200a
1978 87,209,257,336
1979 91,210,189a,201a
1980 96,187,257,260,331a
1981 88,190,187a,199a
1982 93,212,257,336a
1983 157,198,213,336a
1984 89,203,214,336a
1985 94,199,188a,200a

1986 152,203,271,188a,200a
1987 90,199,205,336a
1988 95,193,188a,200a
1989 88,200,226,259,262,263,337a
1990 92,195,226,337a
1991 96,200,188a,200a
1992 89,227,190a,202a
1993 152,201,271,188a,200a
1994 152,197,259,263,271,188a,200a
1995 90,213,263,189a,201a
1996 95,177,214,187a,198a
1997 87,217,190a,202a
1998 91,177,216,188a,198a
1999 95,239,191a,203a

17th November

1930 91,177,208,189a,197a
1931 95,209,229,189a,201a
1932 88,177,186a,198a
1933 152,254,271,188a,200a
1934 152,254,271,188a,200a
1935 89,176,176i,213,187a,202a
1936 94,176,176i,213,190a,199a
1937 86,177,214,188a,203a
1938 91,177,215,188a,199a
1939 95,177,216,189a,203a
1940 87,187,182a,194a
1941 152,254,271,188a,200a
1942 96,208,255,260,188a,200a
1943 88,176,176i,219,231,247,258,
260,183a,195a
1944 93,177,210,190a,200a
1945 85,177,211,260,188a,197a
1946 90,255,188a,200a
1947 152,221,255,271,185a,197a
1948 87,176,176i,214,187a,201a
1949 91,176,176i,255,190a,198a
1950 96,177,215,188a,202a
1951 88,187,187a,199a
1952 92,177,206,190a,202a
1953 152,255,260,271,188a,200a
1954 152,208,255,260,271,188a,200a
1955 93,255,188a,200a
1956 86,256,188a,200a
1957 90,256,188a,200a
1958 95,256,188a,200a
1959 87,256,188a,200a
1960 152,226,256,259,263,271,337a
1961 96,256,259,188a,200a
1962 152,256,271,188a,200a
1963 165,205,189a,201a
1964 85,177,186a,198a
1965 166,177,186a,198a
1966 152,176,176i,256,259,263,271,
326a
1967 158,176,176i,256,326a
1968 91,190,256,331a
1969 96,256,259,262,188a,200a
1970 88,256,188a,200a
1971 92,213,260,189a201a
1972 85,187,187a,199a
1973 89,176,176i,215,190a,193a
1974 152,257,271,188a,200a
1975 86,257,188a,200a
1976 90,257,188a,200a
1977 95,257,188a,200a
1978 87,209,257,336a
1979 91,210,189a,201a
1980 96,187,257,260,331a
1981 89,190,187a,199a
1982 93,212,257,336a
1983 157,198,213,336a
1984 90,203,214,336a
1985 95,199,205,336a
1986 152,203,271,188a,200a
1987 91,199,205,336a
1988 96,193,188a,200a
1989 88,200,226,259,262,263,337a
1990 92,195,226,337a
1991 96,200,188a,200a
1992 89,227,190a,202a
1993 152,227,201,271,337a
1994 152,197,259,263,271,188a,200a
1995 90,213,263,189a,201a
1996 95,177,214,187a,198a
1997 88,217,190a,202a
1998 92,198,188a,200a
1999 96,176,176i,205,187a,202a

18th November

1930 92,177,208,263,189a,197a
1931 96,209,229,263,189a,201a
1932 88,177,186a,198a
1933 93,176,176i,211,190a,201a
1934 152,254,271,188a,200a
1935 90,176,176i,213,187a,202a
1936 94,176,176i,213,190a,199a
1937 86,177,214,188a,203a
1938 91,177,215,188a,199a
1939 95,177,216,189a,203a
1940 88,187,182a,194a
1941 152,254,271,188a,200a
1942 152,208,255,260,271,188a,200a
1943 152,176,176i,219,231,247,258,
260,271,302a
1944 93,177,210,190a,200a
1945 86,177,211,188a,197a
1946 90,255,188a,200a
1947 152,221,255,271,185a,197a
1948 87,176,176i,214,187a,201a
1949 152,255,271,188a,200a
1950 96,177,215,188a,202a
1951 88,187,187a,199a
1952 93,177,206,190a,202a
1953 152,255,260,271,188a,200a
1954 152,255,271,188a,200a

1955 94,255,188a,200a
1956 86,256,188a,200a
1957 91,256,188a,200a
1958 95,256,288a,200a
1959 87,256,188a,200a
1960 152,226,256,259,263,271,337a
1961 85,256,188a,200a
1962 152,256,271,188a,200a
1963 165,205,189,201a
1964 158,177,186a,198a
1965 166,177,186a,198a
1966 152,176,176i,256,271,326a
1967 87,176,176i,256,326a
1968 152,190,256,271,331a
1969 96,256,259,262,188a,200a
1970 88,256,188a,200a
1971 165,213,258,260,272,189a,201a
1972 85,187,187a,199a
1973 90,176,176i,215,190a,193a
1974 152,257,271,188a,200a
1975 86,257,188a,200a
1976 91,257,188a,200a
1977 96,257,188a,200a
1978 88,209,257,336a
1979 152,257,271,188a,200a
1980 85,187,257,260,331a
1981 89,190,187a,199a
1982 93,212,257,336a
1983 86,199,213,336a
1984 90,203,214,336a
1985 95,199,205,336a
1986 152,203,271,188a,200a
1987 91,199,205,336a
1988 96,193,188a,200a
1989 89,200,226,263,337a
1990 93,209,226,340a
1991 85,200,188a,200a
1992 90,227,190a,202a
1993 152,227,201,271,337a
1994 152,197,259,263,271,188a,200a
1995 91,213,189a,201a
1996 96,177,214,187a,198a
1997 88,217,190a,202a
1998 92,216,189a,201a
1999 96,176,176i,205,187a,202a

19th November

1930 92,177,208,263,189a,197a
1931 96,209,229,263,189a,201a
1932 89,177,186a,198a
1933 93,176,176i,211,190a,202a
1934 152,254,271,188a,200a
1935 90,176,176i,213,187a,202a
1936 94,176,176i,213,190a,199a
1937 87,177,214,188a,203a
1938 91,177,215,188a,199a
1939 96,177,216,189a,203a
1940 88,187,182a,194a
1941 93,176,176i,207,190a,193a
1942 152,208,255,260,271,188a,200a
1943 152,177,219,231,247,258,260, 271,302a
1944 94,177,210,190a,200a
1945 86,177,211,188a,197a
1946 91,255,260,188a,200a
1947 152,221,255,258,260,271,185a, 197a
1948 88,176,176i,214,187a,201a
1949 152,255,271,188a,,200a
1950 85,177,215,188a,202a
1951 89,187,187a,199a
1952 93,177,206,190a,202a
1953 152,255,271,188a,200a
1954 152,255,271,188a,200a
1955 94,255,188a,200a
1956 87,177,248,256,187a,204a
1957 91,256,188a,200a
1958 96,256,259,263,188a,200a
1959 88,256,188a,200a
1960 93,226,256,263,337a
1961 85,256,188a,200a
1962 152,176,176i,256,271,326a
1963 94,205,189a,201a
1964 158,177,186a,198a
1965 91,177,207,248,190a,202a
1966 152,176,176i,256,271,326a
1967 87,176,176i,256,326a
1968 152,190,256,271,331a
1969 85,256,188a,200a
1970 89,256,188a,200a
1971 165,213,258,260,272,189a,201a
1972 86,187a,187a,199a
1973 90,176,176i,215,190a,193a
1974 152,216,257,260,271,188a,200a
1975 87,257,260,188a,200a
1976 91,257,188a,200a
1977 96,257,188a,200a
1978 88,209,257,336a
1979 152,257,271,188a,200a
1980 85,187,257,260,331a
1981 90,190,187a,199a
1982 94,212,257,336a
1983 86,199,213,336a
1984 91,203,214,336a
1985 95,199,205,336a
1986 152,203,271,188a,200a
1987 152,199,205,271,336a
1988 85,193,188a,200a
1989 89,200,226,263,337a
1990 93,209,226,340a
1991 85,200,188a,200a
1992 90,227,190a,202a
1993 152,201,271,188a,200a
1994 152,197,271,188a,200a
1995 91,213,189a,201a
1996 96,177,214,187a,198a
1997 88,217,190a,202a

1998 165,216,189a,201a
1999 85,176,176i,205,187a,202a

20th November

1930 92,177,208,263,189a,197a
1931 157,209,263,189a,201a
1932 89,177,186a,198a
1933 94,227,190a,202a
1934 152,254,271,188a,200a
1935 90,176,176i,213,187a,202a
1936 95,176,176i,213,190a,199a
1937 87,177,214,188a,203a
1938 92,255,188a,200a
1939 96,246,263,192a,204a
1940 89,187,182a,194a
1941 93,176,176i,207,190a,193a
1942 152,255,271,188a,200a
1943 90,177,219,231,247,183a,195a
1944 94,177,210,190a,200a
1945 87,177,211,260,188a,197a
1946 91,255,260,188a,200a
1947 152,221,255,258,260,271,185a, 197a
1948 88,176,176i,214,187a,201a
1949 93,176,176i,247,190a,198a
1950 85,177,215,188a,202a
1951 89,187,187a,199a
1952 94,223,190a,202a
1953 152,255,271,188a,200a
1954 152,208,255,260,271,188a,200a
1955 95,255,188a,200a
1956 87,177,248,256,187a,204a
1957 92,256,188a,200a
1958 96,256,259,263,188a,200a
1959 88,256,188a,200a
1960 93,226,256,263,337a,
1961 86,256,188a,200a
1962 152,176,176i,256,271,326a
1963 94,205,189a,201a
1964 87,177,186a,198a
1965 91,177,207,248,190a,202a
1966 96,176,176i,256,259,263,326a
1967 88,176,176i,256,326a,
1968 93,190,256,331a
1969 85,256,188a,200a
1970 89,256,188a,200a
1971 165,213,258,260,272,189a,201a
1972 86,187,187a,199a
1973 91,190,187a,199a
1974 152,216,257,260,271,188a,200a
1975 87,257,260,188a,200a
1976 92,257,188a,200a
1977 96,257,188a,200a
1978 161,209,257,336a
1979 93,176,176i,210,257,368a
1980 86,187,257,331a
1981 90,190a,187a,199a
1982 94,212,257,336a
1983 86,199,213,336a
1984 91,203,214,336a
1985 96,199,215,336a
1986 88,203,188a 200a
1987 152,199,205,271,336a
1988 85,193,188a,200a
1989 162,200,226,259,263,337a
1990 94,226,190a,202a
1991 86,200,188a,200a
1992 91,227,190a,202a
1993 152,201,271,188a,200a
1994 152,197,271,188a,200a
1995 91,213,189a,201a
1996 85,177,214,187a,198a
1997 89,217,190a,,202a
1998 165,216,189a,201a
1999 85,176,176i,205,187a,202a

21st November

1930 165,208,263,189a,201a
1931 157,209,263,189a,201a
1932 90,177,186a,198a
1933 94,227,190a,202a
1934 152,254,271,188a,200a
1935 91,176,176i,213,187a,202a
1936 95,177,213,190a,199a
1937 88,177,214,188a,203a
1938 92,255,188a,200a
1939 96,246,263,192a,204a
1940 89,187,255,296a
1941 166,218,230,246,190a,193a
1942 152,255,271,188a,200a
1943 90,177,219,231,247,183a,195a
1944 95,177,210,190a,200a
1945 87,177,211,260,188a,197a
1946 152,212,255,260,271,188a,200a
1947 152,221,255,258,260,271,185a, 197a
1948 88,176,176i,214,187a,201a
1949 93,176,176i,247,190a,198a
1950 85,177,215,189a,202a
1951 89,187,187a,199a
1952 94,223,190a,202a
1953 152,255,260,271,188a,200a
1954 152,208,255,260,271,188a,200a
1955 95,255,188a,200a
1956 88,177,248,256,187a,204a
1957 92,256,188a,200a
1958 157,212,256,263,336a
1959 89,256,188a,200a
1960 166,226,256,259,263,337a
1961 86,256,188a,200a
1962 152,176,176i,256,271,326a
1963 94,205,189a,201a
1964 87,177,186a,198a
1965 92,256,188a,200a
1966 96,176,176i,259,263,326a
1967 88,176,176i,256,326a

1968 93,190,256,331a
1969 85,256,188a,200a
1970 90,256,188a,200a
1971 94,213,189a,201a
1972 159,187,187a,199a
1973 91,190,187a,199a
1974 152,216,257,260,271,188a,200a
1975 87,257,260,188a,200a
1976 92,206,257,336a
1977 85,257,188a,200a
1978 161,209,257,336a
1979 176,176i,210,257,368a
1980 86,187,257,331a
1981 91,190,187a,199a
1982 95,212,257,336a
1983 87,199,213,260,336a
1984 92,203,224,337a
1985 96,199,215,336a
1986 88,203,188a,200a
1987 165,199,205,336a
1988 86,193,188a,200a
1989 162,200,226,259,263,337a
1990 94,226,190a,202a
1991 86,200,188a,200a
1992 91,227,190a,202a
1993 96,201,271,188a,200a
1994 88,187,263,271,277,188a,200a
1995 152,201,213,263,271,336a
1996 85,177,214,187a,198a
1997 89,217,190a,202a
1998 165,216,189a,201a
1999 86,176,176i,205,187a,202a

22nd November

1930 93,177,208,263,188a,197a
1931 157,209,263,189a,201a
1932 90,177,186a,198a
1933 95,176,229,190a,202a
1934 87,254,188a,200a
1935 91,176,176i,213,187a,202a
1936 108,213,189a,201a
1937 88,177,214,188a,203a
1938 93,177,215,188a,199a
1939 157,217,255,263,189a,204a
1940 101,187,182a,194a
1941 166,218,230,246,190a,193a
1942 86,255,188a,200a
1943 90,177,219,231,274,183a,195a
1944 107,177,210,190a,200a
1945 88,177,211,260,188a,197a
1946 152,212,255,260,271,188a,200a
1947 152,221,255,258,260,271,185a, 197a
1948 101,176,214,187a,201a
1949 93,177,247,190a,198a
1950 86,177,215,189a,202a
1951 90,187,187a,199a
1952 107,177,232,190a,203a
1953 152,255,260,271,188a,200a
1954 152,208,255,260,271,188a,200a
1955 95,255,188a,200a
1956 100,210,189a,201a
1957 93,211,256,336a
1958 157,212,256,263,336a
1959 89,256,188a,200a
1960 166,226,259,263,190a,202a
1961 87,256,188a,200a
1962 152,256,271,188a,200a
1963 95,205,189a,201a
1964 100,177,186a,198a
1965 92,256,188a,200a
1966 96,176,176i,256,259,263,326a
1967 88,176,176i,256,326a
1968 106,190,187a,199a
1969 98,177,211,188a,203a
1970 90,256,188a,200a
1971 94,213,189a,201a
1972 159,187,214,332a
1973 104,176,215,249,190a,193a
1974 96,260,257,277,188a,200a
1975 88,257,260,188a,200a
1976 153,206,272,189a,201a
1977 97,208,189a,201a
1978 161,209,257,336a
1979 94,176,176i,257,326a
1980 159,187,187a,199a
1981 103,190,211,332a
1982 95,212,189a,201a
1983 87,199,213,260,336a
1984 104,203,224,337a
1985 97,215,189a,201a
1986 152,203,271,188a,200a
1987 165,199,205,336a
1988 98,176,207,237,187a,193a
1989 162,226,259,263,190a,202a
1990 94,226,190a,202a
1991 87,200,188a,200a
1992 104,196,227,337a
1993 168,201,188a,200a
1994 88,197,263,271,277,188a,200a
1995 152,201,213,263,271,336a
1996 97,214,258,261,189a,201a
1997 102,215,217,261,340a
1998 94,216,189a,201a
1999 86,176,176i,205,187a,202a

23rd November

1930 106,177,208,263,188a,197a
1931 153,209,263,272,189a,201a
1932 102,177,186a,198a
1933 107,176,211,190a,202a
1934 99,176,212,189a,198a
1935 104,176,213,187a,202a
1936 108,213,189a,201a
1937 101,177,214,188a,203a
1938 153,215,272,189a,201a

1939 97,216,263,189a,201a
1940 162,187,182a,194a
1941 107,176,207,190a,193a
1942 99,176,260,183a,195a
1943 163,177,187,258,260,261,304a
1944 108,177,210,190a,200a
1945 100,177,211,260,188a,197a
1946 104,255,260,188a,200a
1947 153,213,221,255,258,260,
272,321a
1948 101,176,214,187a,201a
1949 166,222,190a,202a
1950 98,215,189a,201a
1951 102,187,187a,199a
1952 107,177,232,190a,203a
1953 160,255,260,188a,200a
1954 164,208,255,260,188a,200a
1955 108,176,210,189a,199a
1956 101,210,189a,201a
1957 153,211,272,189a,201a
1958 97,212,263,189a,201a
1959 101,213,189a,201a
1960 107,226,190a,202a
1961 99,256,188a,200a
1962 103,256,188a,200a
1963 153,205,272,189a,201a
1964 100,177,186a,198a
1965 153,207,263,272,189a,201a
1966 97,176,263,186a,198a
1967 101,176,186a,198a
1968 106,190,187a,199a
1969 98,177,211,188a,203a
1970 102,212,189a,201a
1971 153,213,258,260,272,189a,201a
1972 100,187,214,332a
1973 104,176,215,249,190a,193a
1974 168,216,257,260,336a
1975 100,176,205,249,260,187a,196a
1976 153,206,272,189a,201a
1977 98,177,249,257,188a,197a
1978 153,209,272,189a,201a
1979 106,176,210,327a
1980 159,187,187a,199a
1981 103,190,211,332a
1982 153,212,272,189a,201a
1983 153,213,258,260,272,189a,201a
1984 153,214,224,272,340a
1985 97,215,189a,201a
1986 101,203,216,336a
1987 153,225,237,272,189a,199a
1988 98,176,207,237,187a,193a
1989 103,226,190a,202a
1990 107,209,226,340a
1991 99,210,177,187a,200a
1992 104,196,227,337a
1993 168,201,188a,200a
1994 100,197,259,263,188a,200a
1995 153,213,263,272,278,189a,201a
1996 98,214,189a,201a
1997 102,215,217,261,340a
1998 153,216,272,189a,201a
1999 99,176,205,187a,202a

24th November

1930 106,177,208,263,188a,197a
1931 153,209,263,272,189a,201a
1932 103,177,186a,198a
1933 108,176,211,190a,202a
1934 100,176,227,189a,198a
1935 104,176,213,187a,202a
1936 97,213,189a,201a
1937 101,177,214,188a,203a
1938 153,215,272,189a,201a
1939 153,216,263,272,189a,201a
1940 162,187,182a,194a
1941 107,176,207,190a,193a
1942 99,176,260,183a,195a
1943 163,177,187,258,260,261,304a
1944 108,177,210,190a,200a
1945 101,211,258,260,185a,197a
1946 105,212,255,258,260,336a
1947 97,213,260,278,321a
1948 102,176,214,187a,201a
1949 166,222,190a,202a
1950 99,215,189a,201a
1951 163,187,258,260,187a,199a
1952 108,177,206,190a,203a
1953 160,255,260,188a,200a
1954 164,208,255,260,188a,200a
1955 108,176,210,189a,199a
1956 101,210,189a,201a
1957 106,211,189a,201a
1958 153,212,263,272,189a,201a
1959 102,213,189a,201a
1960 107,226,190a,202a
1961 99,256,188a,200a
1962 104,256,188a,200a
1963 153,205,272,189a,201a
1964 101,177,186a,198a
1965 153,207,263,272,189a,201a
1966 97,176,263,186a,198a
1967 101,176,186a,198a
1968 107,190,187a,199a
1969 99,177,211,188a,203a
1970 103,188,212,332a
1971 153,213,258,260,272,189a,201a
1972 100,187a,214,332a
1973 104,176,215,249,190a,193a
1974 168,216,257,260,336a
1975 101,221,249,258,260,187a,196a
1976 153,206,272,189a,201a
1977 98,177,249,257,188a,197a
1978 153,209,272,189a,201a
1979 107,176,210,327a
1980 100,188,257,331a
1981 104,190,211,332a
1982 153,212,272,189a,201a
1983 153,213,258,260,272,189a,201a

1984 153,214,224,272,340a
1985 97,215,189a,201a
1986 101,203,216,336a
1987 153,200,205,263,272,336a
1988 99,193,188a,200a
1989 103,226,190a,202a
1990 107,209,226,340a
1991 100,177,210,187a,200a
1992 105,227,190a,202a
1993 97,201,188a,200a
1994 101,197,228,259,263,188a,200a
1995 153,213,263,272,278,189a,201a
1996 98,214,189a,201a
1997 102,215,217,261,340a
1998 153,217,272,189a,198a
1999 99,176,205,187a,202a

25th November

1930 107,177,208,188a,197a
1931 153,209,272,189a,201a
1932 103,177,186a,198a
1933 108,176,211,190a,202a
1934 100,176,227,189a,198a
1935 104,176,213,187a,202a
1936 97,213,189a,201a
1937 102,177,214,188a,203a
1938 106,177,215,188a,199a
1939 153,216,263,272,189a,201a
1940 103,187,182a,194a
1941 107,176,207,190a,193a
1942 100,176,208,260,189a,200a
1943 104,177,219,247,258,260,183a, 195a
1945 101,211,258,260,185a,197a
1946 105,212,255,258,260,336a
1947 97,213,260,278,321a
1948 102,176,214,187a,201a
1949 107,177,232,190a,198a
1950 99,215,189a,201a
1951 163,187,258,260,187a,199a
1952 108,177,206,190a,203a
1953 101,255,260,188a,200a
1954 105,208,224,232,255,260,188a, 200a
1955 97,233,255,189a,199a
1956 102,177,210,327a
1957 106,211,189a,201a
1958 153,212,263,272,189a,201a
1959 102,256,188a,200a
1960 108,226,263,190a,202a
1961 100,256,188a,200a
1962 104,256,188a,200a
1963 153,205,272,189a,201a
1964 101,177,186a,198a
1965 166,228,190a,202a
1966 98,176,263,186a,198a
1967 162,176,186a,198a
1968 107,190,187a,199a
1969 99,177,211,188a,203a
1970 103,188,212,332a
1971 153,213,258,260,272,189a,201a
1972 101,214,189a,201a
1973 105,215,189a,201a
1974 97,216,220,236,257,260,336a
1975 101,205,221,249,258,260,189a, 201a
1976 153,206,272,189a,201a
1977 99,208,189a,201a
1978 153,209,272,189a,201a
1979 107,176,210,327a
1980 100,188,257,331a
1981 104,190,211,332a
1982 153,212,272,189a,201a
1983 101,213,258,260,272,189a,201a
1984 106,214,224,340a
1985 98,215,189a,201a
1986 102,203,216,336a
1987 153,200,205,263,272,336a
1988 99,207,189a,201a
1989 104,200,226,263,337a
1990 108,209,226,340a
1991 100,177,210,187a,200a
1992 105,227,190a,202a
1993 97,201,188a,200a
1994 101,197,228,259,263,188a,200a
1995 153,213,263,272,189a,201a
1996 99,214,189a,201a
1997 103,215,217,261,340a
1998 153,217,272,189a,198a
1999 100,176,205,187a,202a

26th November

1930 107,177,208,188a,197a
1931 153,209,272,189a,201a
1932 104,177,186a,198a
1933 97,176,211,190a,202a
1934 101,176,227,189a,198a
1935 105,213,189a,201a
1936 98,213,189a,201a
1937 102,177,214,188a,203a
1938 106,177,215,188a,199a
1939 153,216,263,272,189a,201a
1940 103,187,182a,194a
1941 108,176,207,190a,193a
1942 100,208,260,189a,201a
1943 104,177,219,231,247,258,260, 183a,195a
1944 97,210,189a,201a
1945 102,177,211,188a,197a
1946 106,255,188a,200a
1947 153,213,221,255,272,321a
1948 103,176,214,188a,201a
1949 107,177,232,190a,198a
1950 99,215,189a,201a
1951 163,187,258,260,187a,199a
1952 97,177,232,190a,203a

1953 101,255,260,188a,200a
1954 105,208,224,232,255,260,188a, 200a
1955 97,233,255,189a,199a
1956 102,177,210,263,327a
1957 103,210,189a,201a
1958 107,211,189a,201a
1959 103,256,188a,200a
1960 108,226,263,190a,202a
1961 100,256,188a,200a
1962 104,256,188a,200a
1963 97,205,189a,201a
1964 162,177,186a,198a
1965 166,228,190a,202a
1966 98,176,263,186a,198a
1967 162,176,186a,198a
1968 107,190,187a,199a
1969 100,177,211,188a,203a
1970 104,212,246,336a
1971 153,213,,258,272,189a,201a
1972 101,214,189a,201a
1973 105,215,189a,201a
1974 97,216,220,236,257,260,336a
1975 153,205,272,189a,201a
1976 153,206,272,189a,201a
1977 99,208,189a,201a
1978 153,209,272,189a,201a
1979 107,176,210,327a
1980 101,188,257,331a
1981 105,211,332a
1982 97,212,272,189a,201a
1983 101,213,258,260,272,189a,201a
1984 106,214,224,340a
1985 98,215,189a,201a
1986 102,204,216,259,263,336a
1987 153,200,205,272,336a
1988 100,207,189a,201a
1989 104,200,226,263,337a
1990 108,209,226,340a
1991 101,177,210,187a,200a
1992 106,227,190a,202a
1993 98,201,188a,200a
1994 102,197,259,263,188a,200a
1995 153,213,263,272,189a,201a
1996 99,214,189a,201a
1997 103,215,217,261,340a
1998 153,217,272,189a,198a
1999 100,239,191a,203a

27th November

1930 107,177,208,188a,197a
1931 153,209,272,189a,201a
1932 104,177,186a,198a
1933 97,176,211,190a,202a
1934 97,176,211,190a,202a
1935 101,176,227,189a,198a
1936 105,213,189a,201a
1937 98,213,189a,201a
1938 103,177,214,188a,203a
1939 107,177,215,188a,199a
1940 153,216,272,189a,201a
1941 104,188,263,296a
1942 108,176,207,190a,193a
1943 100,208,260,189a,201a
1944 153,177,219,231,247,258,260, 261,272,306a
1945 102,177,211,188a,197a
1946 106,255,188a,200a
1947 153,213,221,255,272,321a
1948 103,176,214,188a,202a
1949 108,177,247,190a,198a
1950 100,215,189a,201a
1951 104,187,260,187a,199a
1952 97,177,232,190a,203a
1953 101,255,260,188a,200a
1954 105,208,224,232,255,260,188a, 200a
1955 153,210,272,189a,201a
1956 103,210,189a,201a
1957 107,211,189a,201a
1958 153,212,272,189a,201a
1959 103,256,188a,200a
1960 108,226,263,190a,202a
1961 101,256,188a,200a
1962 153,216,272,189a,201a
1963 97,205,189a,201a
1964 162,177,186a,198a
1965 166,228,190a,202a
1966 98,176,263,186a,198a
1967 103,176,186a,198a
1968 108,190,187a,199a
1969 100,177,211,188a,203a
1970 104,212,246,336a
1971 153,213,258,260,272,189a,201a
1972 102,214,189a,201a
1973 106,176,215,249,190a,193a
1974 98,216,220,236,257,336a
1975 153,205,272,189a,201a
1976 153,206,272,189a,201a
1977 99,208,189a,201a
1978 153,209,272,189a,201a
1979 108,176,210,327a
1980 101,188,257,331a
1981 105,212,189a,201a
1982 97,212,272,189a,201a
1983 153,213,272,189a,201a
1984 107,214,224,340a
1985 99,215,189a,201a
1986 103,204,216,336a
1987 153,200,205,272,336a
1988 100,207,189a,201a
1989 104,200,226,263,337a
1990 108,209,226,340a
1991 101,177,210,187a,200a
1992 106,227,190a,202a
1993 98,201,188a,200a
1994 102,197,259,263,188a,200a
1995 153,213,272,189a,201a

1996 100,214,189a,201a
1997 104,215,217,340a
1998 153,216,272,189a,201a
1999 101,239,191a,203a

28th November

1930 108,177,208,263,188a,197a
1931 153,209,263,272,189a,201a
1932 153,177,210,272,327a
1933 97,176,211,190a,202a
1934 101,176,227,189a,198a
1935 106,176,213,187a,202a
1936 99,213,189a,201a
1937 103,177,214,188a,203a
1938 107,177,215,188a,199a
1939 153,216,272,189a,201a
1940 104,188,263,296a
1941 109,176,207,190a,193a
1942 101,208,258,260,189a,201a
1943 153,177,219,231,247,258,260,261,272,306a
1944 98,210,189a,201a
1945 102,177,211,188a,197a
1946 106,255,188a,200a
1947 153,213,221,255,258,260,272,321a
1948 104,255,188a,200a
1949 108,177,247,190a,198a
1950 100,215,189a,201a
1951 104,187,260,187a,199a
1952 97,177,232,190a,203a
1953 102,255,188a,200a
1954 106,224,232,255,188a,200a
1955 153,210,272,189a,201a
1956 104,210,256,263,336a
1957 107,211,189a,201a
1958 153,212,272,189a,201a
1959 104,256,188a,200a
1960 97,226,263,190a,202a
1961 101,256,188a,200a
1962 153,216,272,189a,201a
1963 153,205,272,189a,201a
1964 103,177,186a,198a
1965 107,177,207,190a,202a
1966 99,176,186a,198a
1967 103,176,186a,198a
1968 108,190,187a,199a
1969 100,177,211,188a,203a
1970 153,212,272,189a,201a
1971 97,213,258,260,272,189a,201a
1972 102,214,189a,201a
1973 106,176,215,249,190a,193a
1974 98,216,220,236,257,336a
1975 153,187,205,258,260,272,332a
1976 153,206,272,189a,201a
1977 100,208,189a,201a
1978 153,209,257,272,336a
1979 108,176,210,327a
1980 101,188,257,331a
1981 105,212,189a,201a
1982 153,212,272,189a,201a
1983 153,213,272,189a,201a
1984 107,214,224,340a
1985 99,215,189a,201a
1986 103,204,216,336a
1987 108,200,205,263,336a
1988 101,207,189a,201a
1989 153,208,226,263,272,340a
1990 97,209,226,340a
1991 102,177,210,187a,200a
1992 106,227,190a,202a
1993 98,201,188a,200a
1994 103,197,228,188a,200a
1995 153,213,228,272,340a
1996 100,214,189a,201a
1997 104,215,217,340a
1998 153,216,258,260,272,189a,201a
1999 101,239,191a,203a

29th November

1930 108,177,208,263,188a,197a
1931 153,209,263,272,189a,201a
1932 153,177,210,272,327a
1933 98,176,211,190a,202a
1994 102,176,186a,198a
1935 106,213,189a,201a
1936 99,213,189a,201a
1937 103,177,214,188a,203a
1938 107,177,215,188a,199a
1939 153,216,263,272,189a,201a
1940 105,188,255,263,296a
1941 109,176,207,190a,193a
1942 101,208,258,260,189a,201a
1943 106,177,219,231,247,258,261,183a,195a
1944 99,210,189a,201a
1945 103,188,260,187a,199a
1946 107,255,260,188a,200a
1947 153,213,221,255,258,260,272,321a
1948 104,255,188a,200a
1949 108,177,247,190a,198a
1950 100,215,189a,201a
1951 153,187,205,258,260,272,332a
1952 98,177,232,190a,203a
1953 102,255,188a,200a
1954 106,224,232,255,188a,200a
1955 153,210,272,189a,210a
1956 104,210,256,263,336a
1957 108,211,189a,201a
1958 153,212,263,272,189a,201a
1959 104,256,188a,200a
1960 97,226,263,190a,202a
1961 101,256,188a,200a
1962 106,177,227,188a,197a
1963 153,205,272,189a,201a

1964 103,177,186a,198a
1965 107,177,207,190a,202a
1966 99,176,186a,198a
1967 104,176,256,326a
1968 97,190,187a,199a
1969 101,177,211,188a,203a
1970 153,212,272,189a,201a
1971 97,213,189a,201a
1972 102,257,186a,198a
1973 106,176,215,249,190a,193a
1974 99,216,220,236,257,260,336a
1975 153,187,205,258,260,272,332a
1976 153,206,272,189a,201a
1977 100,208,189a,201a
1978 153,209,257,272,336a
1979 97,176,186a,198a
1980 102,188,257,331a
1981 106,212,189a,201a
1982 153,212,272,189a,201a
1983 153,187,213,258,260,272,332a
1984 107,214,224,340a
1985 99,215,189a,201a
1986 164,204,216,259,263,336a
1987 108,200,205,263,336a
1988 101,207,189a,201a
1989 153,208,226,263,272,340a
1990 97,209,226,340a
1991 102,210,189a,201a
1992 107,227,190a,202a
1993 99,201,188a,200a
1994 103,197,228,188a,200a
1995 153,213,228,263,272,340a
1996 100,214,189a,201a
1997 153,215,217,258,261,272,340a
1998 97,216,258,260,189a,201a
1999 102,239,191a,203a

30th November

1930 97,229,263,188a,197a
1931 101,209,263,278,189a,201a
1932 106,177,186a,198a
1933 98,176,211,190a,202a
1934 102,176,186a,198a
1935 107,213,189a,201a
1936 100,213,189a,201a
1937 104,177,214,188a,203a
1938 108,177,215,188a,199a
1939 153,216,263,272,189a,201a
1940 105,188,255,263,296a
1941 158,190,182a,194a
1943 106,177,219,231,247,258,261, 183a,195a
1944 99,210,189a,201a
1945 103,188,260,187a,199a
1946 107,255,260,188a,200a
1947 153,213,221,255,258,260,272, 321a
1948 153,214,272,18oa,201a
1949 97,177,232,247,190a,198a
1950 101,215,189a,201a
1951 153,187,205,258,260,272,332a
1952 98,177,232,190a,203a
1953 103,188,255,260,331a
1954 107,208,224,232,255,260,188a, 200a
1955 99,177,210,190a,200a
1956 104,210,256,263,336a
1957 108,211,189a,201a
1958 153,212,263,272,189a,201a
1959 105,213,256,336a
1960 158,226,259,263,190a,202a
1961 102,176,256,326a
1962 106,177,227,188a,197a
1963 99,205,189a,201a
1964 103,177,186a,198a
1965 108,177,207,190a,202a
1966 100,176,263,186a,198a
1967 104,176,256,326a
1968 97,190,187a,199a
1969 101,177,211,188a,203a
1970 153,212,272,189a,201a
1971 98,213,189a,201a
1972 103,188,257,331a
1973 107,176,215,249,190a,193a
1974 99,216,220,236,257,260,336a
1975 153,205,258,260,272,189a,201a
1976 97,206,189a,201a
1977 101,208,189a,201a
1978 153,209,272,189a,201a
1979 97,176,186a,198a
1980 102,188,257,331a
1981 106,212,189a,201a
1982 153,212,272,189a,201a
1983 153,187,213,258,260,272,332a
1984 108,214,224,340a
1985 100,215,189a,201a
1986 164,204,216,259,263,336a
1987 97,200,205,263,336a
1988 101,207,189a,201a
1989 166,208,226,263,273,190a,202a
1990 98,209,226,340a
1991 103,210,189a,201a
1992 107,227,190a,202a
1993 99,201,188a,200a
1994 164,197,259,263,188a,200a
1995 153,213,228,263,272,340a
1996 101,214,189a,201a
1997 153,215,217,258,261,272,340a
1998 97,216,258,260,189a,201a
1999 102,239,191a,203a

1st December

1930 97,229,263,188a,197a
1931 101,209,263,278,189a,201a
1932 106,177,186a,198a
1933 99,176,211,190a,202a

1934 103,176,212,189a,198a
1935 107,213,189a,201a
1936 100,213,189a,201a
1937 104,177,214,188a,203a
1938 108,177,215,188a,199a
1939 101,217,255,263,190a,204a
1940 166,188,255,259,263,296a
1941 158,190,182a,194a
1942 102,208,189a,201a
1943 106,177,219,231,247,258,261, 183a,195a
1944 99,210,189a,201a
1945 104,177,211,260,188a,197a
1946 108,255,260,188a,200a
1947 100,176,213,190a,198a
1948 153,214,272,189a,201a
1949 97,177,232,190a,198a
1950 101,215,189a,201a
1951 106,187,187a,199a
1952 99,177,232,190a,203a
1953 103,188,255,260,331a
1954 107,208,224,232,255,188a,200a
1955 100,177,247,190a,200a
1956 104,210,256,263,336a
1957 97,211,189a,201a
1958 101,212,263,189a,201a
1959 105,213,256,336a
1960 158,226,259,263,190a,202a
1961 102,177,215,327a
1962 106,177,227,188a,197a
1963 99,205,189a,201a
1964 104,178,234,256,326a
1965 108,177,207,190a,202a
1966 100,176,263,186a,198a
1967 105,176,186a,198a
1968 98,190,187a,199a
1969 102,177,211,188a,203a
1970 106,212,189a,201a
1971 98,213,189a,201a
1972 103,188,257,331a
1973 107,176,215,249,190a,193a
1974 160,216,257,260,336a
1975 153,205,258,260,272,189a,201a
1976 97,206,189a,201a
1977 101,178,249,257,188a,197a
1978 153,209,272,189a,201a
1979 158,176,186a,198a
1980 103,188,257,331a
1981 107,212,189a,201a
1982 153,212,272,189a,201a
1983 153,199,213,258,260,272,336a
1984 108,214,224,340a
1985 100,215,189a,201a
1986 105,204,216,259,263,336a
1987 97,200,205,263,336a
1988 102,177,206,237,263,188a,193a
1989 166,226,259,263,273,190a,202a
1990 98,209,226,340a
1991 103,210,189a,201a
1992 108,227,190a,202a
1993 160,201,188a,200a
1994 164,197,259,263,188a,200a
1995 97,213,228,263,340a
1996 101,214,189a,201a
1997 105,215,217,261,340a
1998 153,216,272,189a,201a
1999 102,239,191a,203a

2nd December

1930 97,229,263,188a,197a
1931 162,226,259,263,190a,202a
1932 107,177,186a,198a
1933 99,176,211,190a,202a
1934 103,176,212,189a,198a
1935 107,213,189a,201a
1936 101,177,214,190a,199a
1937 105,214,189a,201a
1938 97,217,255,188a,199a
1939 101,217,255,263,190a,204a
1940 166,188,255,259,263,296a
1941 158,190,182a,194a
1942 102,208,189a,201a
1943 167,177,258,260,261,183a, 195a
1944 100,178,210,190a,201a
1945 104,177,211,260,188a,197a
1946 108,255,260,188a,200a
1947 101,213,185a,197a
1948 106,222,190a,202a
1949 98,177,232,190a,198a
1950 102,215,189a,201a
1951 106,187,187a,199a
1952 99,177,232,190a,203a
1953 103,188,255,260,331a
1954 107,208,224,232,255,188a,200a
1955 100,177,247,190a,200a
1956 153,210,263,272,189a,201a
1957 97,178,211,225,190a,200a
1958 101,212,263,189a,201a
1959 106,256,188a,200a
1960 99,226,190a,202a
1961 103,215,189a,201a
1962 107,177,216,188a,197a
1963 100,205,189a,201a
1964 104,178,234,256,326a
1965 108,177,207,190a,202a
1966 101,176,263,186a,198a
1967 105,176,186a,198a
1968 98,190,187a,199a
1969 102,177,211,188a,203a
1970 106,212,189a,201a
1971 99,213,189a,201a
1972 104,257,188a,200a
1973 108,176,215,249,190a,193a
1974 160,216,260,189a,201a
1975 153,205,258,260,272,189a,201a
1976 97,206,189a,201a
1977 101,178,249,257,188a,197a

1978 153,209,272,189a,201a
1979 158,176,186a,198a
1980 103,188,257,331a
1981 107,212,189a,201a
1982 153,212,272,189a,201a
1983 153,199,213,258,260,272,336a
1984 97,224,190a,202a
1985 101,215,189a,201a
1986 105,204,216,259,263,336a
1987 153,200,205,263,272,336a
1988 102,177,206,237,263,188a,193a
1989 166,226,259,263,273,190a,202a
1990 99,226,190a,202a
1991 103,210,189a,201a
1992 108,227,190a,202a
1993 160,201,188a,200a
1994 153,197,212,263,272,336a
1995 97,213,228,263,340a
1996 102,214,189a,201a
1997 166,217,261,273,190a,202a
1998 153,216,272,189a,201a
1999 163,239,191a,203a

3rd December

1930 98,177,208,263,188a,197a
1931 162,226,259,263,190a,202a
1932 107,177,186a,198a
1933 99,176,211,190a,202a
1934 103,176,212,189a,198a
1935 108,213,189a,201a
1936 101,177,214,190a,199a
1937 105,214,189a,201a
1938 97,217,255,188a,199a
1939 102,176,216,263,190a,204a
1940 107,188,255,296a
1941 99,177,207,261,190a,193a
1942 103,208,260,189a,201a
1943 167,177,258,260,261,183a,195a
1944 100,178,210,190a,201a
1945 104,177,211,260,188a,197a
1946 108,255,260,188a,200a
1947 101,213,185a,195a
1948 106,222,190a,202a
1949 98,177,232,190a,198a
1950 102,215,189a,201a
1951 167,187,187a,199a
1952 100,177,206,190a,203a
1953 164,255,260,188a,200a
1954 168,208,255,188a,200a
1855 101,177,247,185a,197a
1956 153,210,263,272,189a,201a
1957 97,178,211,225,190a,200a
1958 153,212,263,272,189a,201a
1959 106,256,188a,200a
1960 99,226,190a,202a
1961 103,215,189a,201a
1962 107,177,216,188a,197a
1963 100,205,189a,201a
1964 105,178,234,256,186a,198a
1965 97,177,207,190a,202a
1966 101,176,263,186a,198a
1967 106,176,186a,198a
1968 98,190,187a,199a
1969 102,177,211,188a,203a
1970 107,178,212,249,188a,199a
1971 99,213,189a,201a
1972 104,257,188a,200a
1973 108,176,215,249,190a,193a
1974 101,216,258,260,189a,201a
1975 153,205,258,260,272,189a,201a
1976 153,206,272,189a,201a
1977 102,178,257,188a
1978 153,209,272,189a,201a
1979 99,176,186a,198a
1980 103,188,257,331a
1981 107,212,189a,201a
1982 153,212,272,189a,201a
1983 153,199,213,258,260,272,336a
1984 97,224,190a,202a
1985 101,215,189a,201a
1986 106,204,216,259,263,336a
1987 153,200,205,263,272,336a
1988 103,226,190a,202a
1989 107,226,190a,202a
1990 99,226,190a,202a
1991 104,210,189a,201a
1992 108,227,190a,202a
1993 101,201,212,336a
1994 153,197,212,263,272,336a
1995 158,213,228,259,263,340a
1996 102,214,189a,201a
1997 166,217,261,273,190a,202a
1998 153,216,258,260,272,189a,201a
1999 163,239,191a,203a

4th December

1930 98,177,208,263,188a,197a
1931 103,226,190a,202a
1932 108,177,186a,198a
1933 100,176,211,190a,202a
1934 104,254,188a,200a
1935 108,213,189a,201a
1936 101,177,214,190a,199a
1937 105,178,214,188a,203a
1938 98,177,215,188a,199a
1939 102,176,216,263,190a,204a
1940 107,188,255,296a
1941 99,177,207,261,190a,193a
1942 103,208,260,189a,201a
1943 108,177,219,231,247,258,260, 183a,195a
1944 101,178,220,190a,201a
1945 153,211,258,260,272,189a,201a
1946 97,255,258,260,188a,200a
1947 102,176,213,190a,198a
1948 106,222,190a,202a

1949 98,177,232,190a,198a
1950 103,189,215,332a
1951 167,187,187a,199a
1952 100,177,206,190a,203a
1953 164,255,260,188a,200a
1954 168,208,224,232,260,188a,204a
1955 101,177,247,185a,197a
1956 106,210,203,189a,201a
1957 98,178,211,225,190a,200a
1958 153,212,263,272,189a,201a
1959 107,213,189a,201a
1960 99,226,190a,202a
1961 103,215,189a,201a
1962 108,177,227,188a,197a
1963 100,205,189a,201a
1964 105,178,234,256,186a,198a
1965 97,177,207,190a,202a
1966 102,176,186a,198a
1967 106,176,186a,198a
1968 99,190,187a,199a
1969 103,188,187a,199a
1970 107,178,212,249,188a,199a
1971 100,213,189a,201a
1972 104,257,188a,200a
1973 108,176,215,249,190a,193a
1974 101,216,258,260,189a,201a
1975 153,205,272,189a,201a
1976 153,206,272,189a,201a
1977 102,208,189a,197a
1978 153,209,272,189a,201a
1979 99,176,186a,198a
1980 104,188,257,331a
1981 108,212,189a,201a
1982 101,212,272,189a,201a
1983 105,213,272,189a,201a
1984 97,224,190a,202a
1985 153,215,272,189a,201a
1986 106,204,216,259,263,336a
1987 153,205,272,189a,201a
1988 103,226,190a,202a
1989 107,226,190a,202a
1990 100,226,190a,202a
1991 104,210,189a,201a
1992 97,227,190a,202a
1993 101,201,212,336a
1994 106,197,228,263,337a
1995 158,213,228,259,263,340a
1996 102,214,189a,201a
1997 107,217,239,261,343a
1998 153,216,258,260,189a,201a
1999 104,239,191a,203a

5th December

1930 99,177,208,188a,197a
1931 103,226,190a,202a
1932 108,177,186a,198a
1933 100,176,211,190a,202a
1934 104,254,188a,200a
1935 97,213,189a,201a
1936 162,230,246,190a,199a
1937 166,228,190a,202a
1938 98,177,215,188a,199a
1939 103,176,216,190a,204a
1940 108,188,255,263,296a
1941 100,177,207,190a,193a
1942 104,208,260,189a,201a
1943 108,177,219,231,247,258,260,
183a,195a
1944 101,178,220,190a,201a
1945 153,211,258,260,272,189a,201a
1946 97,255,258,260,188a,200a
1947 102,176,213,190a,198a
1948 107,177,214,188a,202a
1949 99,177,232,190a,198a
1950 103,189,187a,199a
1951 108,187,187a,199a
1952 100,177,206,190a,203a
1953 105,255,260,188a,200a
1954 97,208,224,232,260,188a,204a
1955 102,177,247,190a,200a
1956 106,210,263,189a,201a
1957 98,178,211,225,190a,200a
1958 153,212,272,189a,201a
1959 107,213,189a,201a
1960 100,226,263,190a,202a
1961 104,215,189a,201a
1962 108,177,227,188a,197a
1963 101,177,227,248,190a,202a
1964 105,178,234,256,186a,198a
1965 158,234,256,190a,202a
1966 102,176,186a,198a
1967 107,176,186a,198a
1968 99,190,187a,199a
1969 103,187,211,332a
1970 108,178,212,249,188a,199a
1971 100,213,189a,201a
1972 105,214,257,336a
1973 97,176,215,249,190a,193a
1974 102,216,189a,201a
1975 153,205,272,189a,201a
1976 153,206,272,189a,201a
1977 103,208,189a,201a
1978 153.209.272.189a,201a
1979 100,176,186a,198a
1980 104,188,257,331a
1981 108,212,189a,201a
1982 101,212,272,189a,201a
1983 105,213,272,189a,201a
1984 158,224,190a,202a
1985 102,215,189a,201a
1986 107,204,216,336a
1987 153,205,272,189a,201a
1988 103,226,190a,202a
1989 108,226,263,190a,202a
1990 100,226,190a,202a
1991 153,210,272,189a,201a
1992 97,227,190a,202a
1993 101,201,212,336a

1994 106,197,228,263,337a
1995 158,213,259,263,340a
1996 103,217,190a,202a
1997 107,217,239,261,343a
1998 153,216,258,260,272,189a,201a
1999 104,239,191a,203a

6th December

1930 99,177,208,188a,197a
1931 104,226,263,190a,202a
1932 97,177,186a,198a
1933 101,176,211,191a,202a
1934 153,121,272,189a,201a
1935 97,213,189a,201a
1936 162,230,246,190a,199a
1937 166,228,190a,202a
1938 99,177,215,188a,199a
1939 103,176,216,190a,204a
1940 108,188,255,263,296a
1941 100,177,207,191a,193a
1942 104,208,260,189a,201a
1943 97,177,219,231,247,258,260,
261,183a,195a
1944 102,178,220,190a,201a
1945 153,211,272,189a,201a
1946 98,255,188a,200a
1947 103,176,213,190a,198a
1948 107,177,214,188a,202a
1949 99,177,232,191a,198a
1950 104,178,216,189a,202a
1951 108,187,187a,199a
1952 101,177,232,190a,203a
1953 105,207,260,189a,201a
1954 97,208,224,232,260,188a,204a
1955 102,177,247,190a,200a
1956 153,210,272,189a,201a
1957 99,178,211,190a,200a
1958 153,212,272,189a,201a
1959 108,213,189a,201a
1960 100,226,263,190a,202a
1961 104,215,189a,201a
1962 97,177,227,188a,197a
1963 101,227,234,256,190a,202a
1964 166,178,186a,198a
1965 158,234,256,190a,202a
1966 103,176,209,189a,199a
1967 107,177,186a,198a
1968 100,190,187a,199a
1969 104,211,189a,201a
1970 108,178,212,249,188a,199a
1971 101,213,189a,201a
1972 105,214,257,336a
1973 97,176,215,249,190a,193a
1974 102,216,189a,201a
1975 153,205,272,189a,201a
1976 99,206,189a,201a
1977 103,208,189a,201a
1978 153,209,272,189a,201a
1979 100,176,186a,198a
1980 153,188,211,272,332a
1981 97,212,189a,201a
1982 101,212,272,189a,201a
1983 106,213,189a,201a
1984 158,224,190a,202a
1985 102,215,189a,201a
1986 107,204,216,336a
1987 153,205,272,189a,201a
1988 104,193,226,263,337a
1989 108,226,263,190a,202a
1990 101,226,190a,202a
1991 153,210,272,189a,201a
1992 98,227,190a,202a
1993 102,201,212,336a
1994 107,197,188a,200a
1995 99,213,228,340a
1996 103,217,190a,202a
1997 108,217,190a,202a
1998 153,216,258,260,272,189a,201a
1999 104,203,239,338a

7th December

1930 160,208,263,184a,196a
1931 104,226,263,190a,202a
1932 97,177,186a,198a
1933 101,176,211,191a,202a
1934 153,212,272,189a,201a
1935 98,213,189a,201a
1936 103,177,214,190a,199a
1937 107,178,214,189a,203a
1938 99,177,215,188a,199a
1939 104,176,216,263,190a,204a
1940 108,188,255,263,296a
1941 100,177,207,191a,193a
1942 153,208,258,260,272,189a,201a
1943 97,177,219,231,247,258,260,
261,183a,195a
1944 102,178,220,190a,201a
1945 153,211,272,189a,201a
1946 98,255,188a,200a
1947 103,176,213,190a,198a
1948 108,177,214,188a,202a
1949 100,177,215,191a,198a
1950 104,178,216,189a,202a
1951 97,187,187a,199a
1952 101,177,232,190a,203a
1953 105,207,260,189a,201a
1954 98,224,232,188a,204a
1955 102,177,247,190a,200a
1956 153,210,272,189a,201a
1957 99,178,211,225,191a,200a
1958 153,212,256,263,272,336a
1959 108,213,189a,201a
1960 101,226,263,190a,202a
1961 153,215,272,189a,201a
1962 97,177,227,188a,197a
1963 162,178,227,328a

1964 166,178,186a,198a
1965 98,177,207,191a,202a
1966 103,176,209,189a,199a
1967 108,177,186a,198a
1968 100,190,187a,199a
1969 104,211,189a,201a
1970 97,256,188a,200a
1971 101,213,189a,201a
1972 106,257,199a,200a
1973 98,176,215,249,190a,193a
1974 102,216,189a,201a
1975 153,205,258,260,272,189a,201a
1976 99,206,189a,201a
1977 104,208,189a,201a
1978 153,209,272,189a,201a
1979 100,176,186a,198a
1980 153,188,211,272,332a
1981 97,212,189a,201a
1982 153,212,272,189a,201a
1983 106,199,213,336a
1984 99,224,190a,202a
1985 103,215,189a,201a
1986 168,204,216,250,259,263,370a
1987 153,205,263,272,189a,201a
1988 104,193,226,263,337a
1989 97,226,263,190a,202a
1990 101,226,190a,202a
1991 153,210,272,189a,201a
1992 98,227,190a,202a
1993 102,212,189a,201a
1994 107,197,188a,200a
1995 99,213,228,340a
1996 104,217,190a,202a
1997 108,217,190a,202a
1998 101,216,258,260,189a,201a
1999 105,205,239,341a

8th December

1930 160,208,263,184a,196a
1931 105,209,226,263,340a
1932 97,177,186a,198a
1933 101,176,211,191a,202a
1934 106,212,189a,201a
1935 98,213,189a,201a
1936 103,177,214,190a,199a
1937 107,178,214,189a,203a
1938 100,177,215,188a,199a
1939 104,176,216,263,190a,204a
1940 97,188,255,263,296a
1941 101,255,258,261,191a,193a
1942 153,208,258,260,272,189a,201a
1943 98,178,183a,195a
1944 102,178,220,190a,201a
1945 153,211,272,189a,201a
1946 99,255,260,188a,200a
1947 153,213,258,261,278,189a,201a
1948 108,177,214,188a,202a
1949 100,177,215,191a,198a
1950 105,216,189a,201a
1951 97,188,187a,199a
1952 102,177,232,190a,203a
1953 106,176,207,189a,199a
1954 98,224,232,188a,204a
1955 103,177,210,190a,200a
1956 107,178,210,225,188a,193a
1957 100,178,211,225,191a,200a
1958 153,212,256,263,272,336a
1959 97,213,256,263,336a
1960 101,226,263,190a,202a
1961 153,215,272,189a,201a
1962 98,177,227,188a,197a
1963 162,178,227,328a
1964 107,178,234,256,186a,198a
1965 99,177,207,191a,202a
1966 103,176,209,189a,199a
1967 108,177,186a,198a
1968 100,190,187a,199a
1969 153,211,272,189a,201a
1970 97,256,188a,200a
1971 102,213,189a,201a
1972 106,257,188a,200a
1973 98,176,215,249,191a,193a
1974 103,216,260,189a,201a
1975 153,205,258,260,272,189a,201a
1976 100,206,189a,201a
1977 104,208,189a,201a
1978 97,209,189a,201a
1979 101,176,186a,198a
1980 153,188,211,272,332a
1981 98,212,189a,201a
1982 153,212,272,189a,201a
1983 107,199,213,336a
1984 99,214,224,340a
1985 103,215,189a,201a
1986 168,204,216,250,259,263,390a
1987 153,205,263,272,189a,201a
1988 153,206,226,263,272,340a
1989 97,226,238,250,273,190a,202a
1990 162,226,190a,202a
1991 106,210,227,340a
1992 98,227,190a,202a
1993 103,212,189a,201a
1994 107,187,188a,200a
1995 100,213,228,263,340a
1996 104,217,190a,202a
1997 97,217,261,190a,202a
1998 101,216,258,260,189a,201a
1999 105,205,239,341a

9th December

1930 101,178,208,263,188a,197a
1931 105,209,226,263,340a
1932 98,177,186a,198a
1933 102,176,211,191a,202a
1934 106,212,189a,201a
1935 99,213,189a,201a

1936 103,177,214,190a,199a
1937 107,178,214,189a,203a
1938 100,177,215,188a,199a
1939 104,176,216,263,190a,204a
1940 97,188,255,263,296a
1941 101,255,258,261,191a,193a
1942 106,208,189a,201a
1943 98,178,183a,195a
1944 103,178,220,190a,201a
1945 153,211,258,260,272,189a,201a
1946 99,255,260,188a,200a
1947 153,213,272,189a,201a
1948 108,177,214,188a,202a
1949 101,177,232,191a,198a
1950 105,216,189a,201a
1951 98,188,187a,199a
1952 102,177,232,190a,203a
1953 106,176,207,189a,199a
1954 99,208,224,232,260,188a,204a
1955 103,177,210,190a,200a
1956 108,178,210,225,188a,193a
1957 100,178,211,225,191a,200a
1958 153,212,256,263,272,336a
1959 97,213,256,263,336a
1960 101,226,263,190a,202a
1961 106,215,189a,201a
1962 98,177,227,188a,197a
1963 103,227,234,256,190a,202a
1964 107,178,234,256,186a,198a
1965 99,177,207,191a,202a
1966 104,256,188a,200a
1967 108,177,186a,198a
1968 101,190,187a,199a
1969 153,211,272,189a,201a
1970 98,256,188a,200a
1971 102,213,189a,201a
1972 106,257,188a,200a
1973 159,215,258,260,189a,201a
1974 103,216,260,189a,201a
1975 153,205,258,260,189a,201a
1976 100,206,189a,201a
1977 104,208,189a,201a
1978 97,209,189a,201a
1979 101,176,186a,198a
1980 106,188,211,332a
1981 98,212,189a,201a
1982 153,212,272,189a,201a
1983 107,199,213,336a
1984 100,214,189a,201a
1985 104,199,215,336a
1986 97,204,216,259,263,336a
1987 101,205,263,189a,201a
1988 153,206,226,263,272,340a
1989 158,226,259,263,273,190a,202a
1990 162,226,190a,202a
1991 106,210,227,340a
1992 99,176,211,191a,196a
1993 103,212,189a,201a
1994 108,213,263,189a,201a
1995 100,213,228,263,340a
1996 105,214,217,340a
1997 97,217,261,190a,202a
1998 153,216,272,189a,201a
1999 106,239,191a,203a

10th December

1930 101,178,208,263,188a,197a
1931 166,226,259,263,190a,202a
1932 98,177,186a,198a
1933 102,176,211,191a,202a
1934 107,212,189a,201a
1935 99,213,189a,201a
1936 104,228,230,246,190a,202a
1937 108,178,214,189a,203a
1938 101,217,255,188a,199a
1939 105,176,216,263,190a,204a
1940 97,188,236,182a,194a
1941 102,177,207,261,191a,193a
1942 106,208,189a,201a
1943 159,178,183a,195a
1944 103,178,220,190a,201a
1945 153,211,258,260,272,189a,201a
1946 100,255,260,188a,200a
1947 153,213,272,189a,201a
1948 97,177,214,188a,202a
1949 101,177,232,191a,198a
1950 106,223,190a,202a
1951 98,188,187a,199a
1952 102,177,232,190a,203a
1953 107,176,207,260,189a,199a
1954 99,208,224,232,260,188a,204a
1955 104,255,188a,200a
1956 108,178,210,225,188a,193a
1957 100,178,211,225,191a,200a
1958 153,212,263,272,189a,201a
1959 97,213,256,263,336a
1960 102,177,214,191a,196a
1961 106,215,189a,201a
1962 99,177,216,188a,197a
1963 103,227,234,256,190a,202a
1964 107,178,234,256,186a,198a
1965 100,177,207,191a,202a
1966 104,256,188a,200a
1967 97,177,186a,198a
1968 101,191,187a,199a
1969 106,178,248,189a,203a
1970 98,256,188a,200a
1971 102,213,189a,201a
1972 107,257,188a,200a
1973 159,215,258,260,189a,201a
1974 164,216,257,260,336a
1975 153,205,258,260,272,189a,201a
1976 101,206,189a,201a
1977 105,208,189a,201a
1978 153,209,272,189a,201a
1979 162,176,186a,198a
1980 106,188,211,332a
1981 99,212,189a,201a

1982 153,212,258,260,272,189a,201a
1983 107,199,213,336a
1984 100,214,189a,201a
1985 104,199,215,336a
1986 97,216,263,189a,201a
1987 101,205,263,189a,201a
1988 166,226,259,263,190a,202a
1989 158,226,190a,202a
1990 103,226,190a,202a
1991 107,210,189a,201a
1992 99,176,211,191a,196a
1993 104,201,212,336a
1994 108,213,263,189a,201a
1995 100,213,228,263,340a
1996 105,214,217,340a
1997 158,217,261,190a,202a
1998 153,216,272,189a,201a
1999 106,239,191a,203a

11th December

1930 102,178,208,263,188a,197a
1931 166,226,259,263,190a,202a
1932 99,177,186a,198a
1933 103,176,211,191a,202a
1934 107,212,189a,201a
1935 100,213,189a,201a
1936 104,228,230,246,190a,202a
1937 108,178,214,189a,203a
1938 101,217,255,188a,199a
1939 105,176,216,263,190a,204a
1940 158,188,259,263,182a,194a
1941 102,177,207,261,191a,193a
1942 107,208,260,189a,201a
1943 159,178,183a,195a
1944 104,178,210,191a,201a
1945 153,211,258,260,272,189a,201a
1946 100,255,260,188a,200a
1947 153,213,258,261,272,189a,201a
1948 97,177,214,188a,202a
1949 101,177,232,191a,198a
1950 106,223,190a,202a
1951 98,188,187a,199a
1952 163,191,187a,199a
1953 107,207,260,189a,201a
1954 160,208,224,232,184a,196a
1955 104,255,188a,200a
1956 97,225,233,263,188a,193a
1957 101,178,211,225,191a,200a
1958 153,212,263,272,189a,201a
1959 98,213,256,263,336a
1960 102,177,214,191a,196a
1961 107,215,189a,201a
1962 99,177,216,188a,197a
1963 103,227,234,256,190a,202a
1964 108,178,234,256,186a,198a
1965 100,177,207,191a,202a
1966 105,209,189a,201a
1967 97,177,186a,198a
1968 102,191,187a,199a
1969 106,178,248,189a,203a
1970 99,256,188a,200a
1971 103,190,213,332a
1972 107,257,188a,200a
1973 100,215,260,189a,201a
1974 153,216,258,260,272,189a,201a
1975 153,205,258,260,272,189a,201a
1976 101,206,189a,201a
1977 106,208,189a,201a
1978 153,209,272,189a,201a
1979 162,176,186a,198a
1980 107,188,211,332a
1981 99,212,189a,201a
1982 104,212,257,336a
1983 108,199,213,336a
1984 100,214,189a,201a
1985 105,215,272,189a,201a
1986 97,216,263,189a,201a
1987 101,205,263,189a,201a
1988 166,226,259,263,190a,202a
1989 99,226,190a,202a
1990 103,226,190a,202a
1991 107,210,189a,201a
1992 100,176,211,191a,196a
1993 104,201,212,336a
1994 97,213,263,189a,201a
1995 101,213,228,263,340a
1996 166,217,190a,202a
1997 158,217,261,190a,202a
1998 153,216,272,189a,201a
1999 106,205,239,341a

12th December

1930 102,178,208,263,188a,197a
1931 166,226,259,263,190a,202a
1932 99,177,186a,198a
1933 103,177,254,191a,202a
1934 108,212,189a,201a
1935 100,213,189a,201a
1936 105,178,214,191a,199a
1937 97,178,214,189a,203a
1938 101,217,255,188a,200a
1939 106,176,216,263,190a,204a
1940 158,188,259,263,182a,194a
1941 102,177,207,261,191a,193a
1942 107,208,260,189a,201a
1943 159,178,183a,195a
1944 104,178,210,191a,201a
1945 153,211,258,260,272,189a,201a
1946 101,255,258,260,320a
1947 153,213,258,261,272,189a,201a
1948 98,177,214,188a,202a
1949 102,178,186a,198a
1950 107,178,216,189a,202a
1951 99,188,187a,199a
1952 163,191,187a,199a
1953 108,207,260,189a,201a

1954 160,208,224,232,260,184a,196a
1955 153,210,272,189a,201a
1956 97,225,233,263,188a,193a
1957 101,178,211,225,191a,200a
1958 153,212,263,272,189a,201a
1959 98,213,256,263,336a
1960 103,177,214,191a,196a
1961 107,215,189a,201a
1962 100,177,227,188a,197a
1963 104,227,234,256,190a,202a
1964 108,178,234,256,186a,198a
1965 101,177,207,191a,202a
1966 153,209,272,189a,201a
1967 98,177,186a,198a
1968 102,191,187a,199a
1969 107,178,248,189a,203a
1970 99,256,188a,200a
1971 103,190,213,332a
1972 108,257,188a,200a
1973 100,215,260,189a,201a
1974 153,216,258,260,272,189a,201a
1975 97,205,258,260,189a,201a
1976 101,206,189a,201a
1977 106,208,189a,201a
1978 153,209,272,189a,201a
1979 162,176,186a,198a
1980 107,188,211,332a
1981 100,202,189a,201a
1982 104,212,257,336a
1983 108,199,213,336a
1984 101,214,189a,201a
1985 153,215,272,189a,201a
1986 98,216,263,189a,201a
1987 153,205,263,272,189a,201a
1988 107,226,190a,202a
1989 99,226,190a,202a
1990 103,226,238,250,273,190a,202a
1991 107,210,189a,201a
1992 100,177,211,191a,196a
1993 153,212,272,189a,201a
1994 97,213,263,189a,201a
1995 101,213,228,238,250,259,263, 273,340a
1996 166,217,190a,202a
1997 98,217,239,261,343a
1998 103,216,189a,201a
1999 107,205,239,341a

13th December

1930 102,178,208,263,188a,197a
1931 107,226,246,190a,202a
1932 99,177,186a,198a
1933 104,177,211,191a,202a
1934 108,212,189a,201a
1935 101,213,189a,201a
1936 105,178,214,191a,199a
1937 97,178,214,189a,203a
1938 102,177,215,188a,200a
1939 106,176,216,263,190a,204a
1940 99,188,182a,194a
1941 103,177,207,261,191a,193a
1942 108,208,260,189a,201a
1943 100,178,183a,195a
1944 104,178,210,191a,201a
1945 97,211,258,260,189a,201a
1946 101,212,258,260,321a
1947 153,213,258,261,272,189a,201a
1948 98,177,214,188a,202a
1949 102,178,186a,198a
1950 107,178,216,189a,202a
1951 99,188,260,187a,199a
1952 104,177,206,191a,203a
1953 108,207,260,189a,201a
1954 101,208,224,232,260,188a,204a
1955 153,210,272,189a,201a
1956 97,225,233,188a,193a
1957 102,178,211,225,191a,200a
1958 153,212,263,272,189a,201a
1959 99,213,256,336a
1960 103,177,214,191a,196a
1961 108,215,189a,201a
1962 100,178,227,188a,197a
1963 104,227,234,256,190a,202a
1964 97,178,234,256,186a,198a
1965 101,177,207,191a,202a
1966 106,209,189a,201a
1967 98,177,186a,198a
1968 102,191,187a,199a
1969 107,178,248,189a,203a
1970 99,256,188a,200a
1971 104,213,189a,201a
1972 108,214,189a,201a
1973 101,215,258,260,189a,201a
1974 153,216,272,189a,201a
1975 97,205,258,260,189a,201a
1976 102,206,189a,201a
1977 107,208,189a,201a
1978 99,209,189a,201a
1979 103,177,210,327a
1980 108,188,211,332a
1981 100,212,189a,201a
1982 105,212,189a,201a
1983 97,199,213,336a
1984 101,214,189a,201a
1985 153,215,272,189a,201a
1986 98,216,263,189a,201a
1987 153,205,263,272,189a,201a
1988 107,226,190a,202a
1989 100,226,190a,202a
1990 104,226,238,250,273,190a,202a
1991 108,210,189a,201a
1992 101,177,211,191a,196a
1993 153,212,272,189a,201a
1994 98,213,263,189a,201a
1995 162,213,228,259,263,273,340a
1996 166,217,190a,202a
1997 99,217,239,260,343a

1998 103,216,189a,201a
1999 107,205,239,341a

14th December

1930 103,178,208,188a,197a
1931 107,226,246,190a,202a
1932 100,177,186a,198a
1933 104,177,211,191a,202a
1934 97,212,189a,201a
1935 101,213,189a,201a
1936 105,178,214,191a,199a
1937 158,230,246,189a,203a
1938 102,177,215,188a,200a
1939 107,177,216,190a,204a
1940 99,188,182a,194a
1941 103,177,207,261,191a,193a
1942 108,208,260,189a,201a
1943 100,178,183a,195a
1944 105,210,189a,201a
1945 97,211,258,260,189a,201a
1946 153,212,272,189a,201a
1947 153,213,258,261,272,189a,201a
1948 98,177,214,188a,202a
1949 103,178,232,191a,198a
1950 108,178,216,189a,202a
1951 100,188,260,187a,199a
1952 104,177,206,191a,203a
1953 97,207,258,260,189a,201a
1954 101,208,224,232,260,188a,204a
1955 153,210,272,189a,201a
1956 98,178,211,225,188a,193a
1957 102,178,211,225,191a,200a
1958 107,212,189a,201a
1959 153,213,272,189a,201a
1960 103,177,214,191a,196a
1961 108,215,189a,201a
1962 101,178,227,188a,197a
1963 105,227,234,256,190a,202a
1964 97,178,234,256,186a,198a
1965 102,177,186a,198a
1966 106,177,209,190a,199a
1967 98,177,186a,198a
1968 163,191,187a,199a
1969 108,178,211,189a,203a
1970 100,256,188a,200a
1971 104,213,189a,201a
1972 97,214,189a,201a
1973 101,215,258,260,189a,201a
1974 106,216,189a,201a
1975 98,178,205,249,188a,195a
1976 102,206,189a,201a
1977 107,208,189a,201a
1978 99,209,189a,201a
1979 103,177,210,327a
1980 108,188,211,332a
1981 101,212,189a,201a
1982 105,212,189a,201a
1983 97,199,213,336a
1984 102,214,189a,201a
1985 153,215,272,189a,201a
1986 99,216,189a,201a
1987 153,205,272,189a,201a
1988 108,226,238,250,259,263,190a, 202a
1989 100,226,190a,202a
1990 104,226,238,250,259,263,273, 190a,202a
1991 108,210,189a,201a
1992 101,177,211,191a,196a
1993 106,212,227,340a
1994 98,213,263,189a,201a
1995 162,213,228,259,263,273,340a
1996 107,217,190a,202a
1997 99,215,239,261,341a
1998 104,216,189a,201a
1999 108,205,239,341a

15th December

1930 103,178,208,188a,197a
1931 108,226,246,259,263,190a,202a
1932 100,177,186a,198a
1933 153,211,272,189a,201a
1934 97,212,189a,201a
1935 101,213,189a,201a
1936 166,228,190a,202a
1937 158,230,246,189a,203a
1938 103,177,215,188a,200a
1939 107,177,216,190a,204a
1940 100,188,263,182a,194a
1941 104,177,207,191a,193a
1942 97,178,208,189a,200a
1943 153,178,272,302a
1944 105,210,189a,201a
1945 153,211,272,189a,201a
1946 153,212,272,189a,201a
1947 153,213,261,272,189a,201a
1948 99,177,214,188a,202a
1949 103,178,232,191a,198a
1950 108,178,216,190a,203a
1951 100,188,260,187a,199a
1952 153,206,272,189a,201a
1953 97,207,258,260,189a,201a
1954 102,224,232,188a,204a
1955 106,177,247,190a,200a
1956 98,178,211,225,188a,193a
1957 103,178,211,191a,200a
1958 107,212,189a,201a
1959 153,213,272,189a,201a
1960 104,177,214,191a,196a
1961 97,215,189a,201a
1962 101,178,227,188a,197a
1963 105,227,234,256,190a,202a
1964 158,178,186a,198a
1965 102,177,186a,198a
1966 107,177,209,190a,199a
1967 99,177,186a,198a

1968 163,191,187a,199a
1969 108,178,211,189a,203a
1970 100,256,188a,200a
1971 104,213,189a,201a
1972 97,214,189a,201a
1973 102,215,189a,201a
1974 106,216,189a,201a
1975 98,178,205,249,188a,195a
1976 103,206,189a,201a
1977 107,208,189a,201a
1978 100,209,189a,201a
1979 104,177,210,327a
1980 108,188,211,332a
1981 101,212,189a,201a
1982 105,212,189a,201a
1983 97,199,213,336a
1984 102,214,189a,201a
1985 153,215,272,189a,201a
1986 99,216,189a,201a
1987 153,205,272,189a,201a
1988 108,226,238,250,259,263,190a, 202a
1989 101,226,190a,202a
1990 105,226,238,250,259,263,273, 190a,202a
1991 97,210,189a,201a
1992 102,177,211,191a,196a
1993 106,212,227,340a
1994 98,213,263,189a,201a
1995 162,213,228,259,263,273,340a
1996 107,217,190a,202a
1997 100,215,239,341a
1998 104,216,189a,201a
1999 108,205,239,341a

16th December

1930 104,178,208,263,188a,197a
1931 108,226,246,259,263,190a,202a
1932 101,177,186a,198a
1933 153,211,272,189a,201a
1934 98,177,212,190a,199a
1935 102,177,213,188a,203a
1936 166,228,190a,202a
1937 99,178,214,189a,203a
1938 103,177,215,188a,200a
1939 107,177,216,190a,204a
1940 100,188,263,182a,194a
1941 104,177,207,191a,193a
1942 97,178,208,190a,201a
1943 153,178,272,302a
1944 106,178,220,191a,201a
1945 153,211,272,189a,201a
1946 153,212,258,260,272,189a,201a
1947 153,213,258,261,272,189a,201a
1948 99,177,214,188a,202a
1949 104,178,215,191a,198a
1950 108,178,216,190a,203a
1951 100,188,260,187a,199a
1952 153,206,272,189a,201a
1953 98,207,189a,201a
1954 102,224,232,188a,204a
1955 106,224,190a,202a
1956 99,178,211,225,188a,193a
1957 103,178,211,191a,200a
1958 108,212,263,189a,201a
1959 153,213,263,272,189a,201a
1960 104,177,214,191a,196a
1961 97,215,189a,201a
1962 101,178,227,188a,197a
1963 105,227,234,256,190a,202a
1964 158,178,259,263,186a,198a
1965 103,177,207,191a,202a
1966 107,177,209,190a,199a
1967 99,177,186a,198a
1968 104,191,187a,199a
1969 97,178,211,189a,204a
1970 101,256,188a,200a
1971 153,213,272,189a,201a
1972 98,214,189a,201a
1973 102,215,189a,201a
1974 106,216,189a,201a
1975 98,178,205,249,188a,195a
1976 103,206,189a,201a
1977 108,208,189a,201a
1978 100,209,189a,201a
1979 104,177,210,327a
1980 97,188,211,332a
1981 102,191,212,332a
1982 106,212,224,340a
1983 98,199,213,336a
1984 103,214,189a,201a
1985 153,215,272,189a,201a
1986 99,216,189a,201a
1987 153,205,272,189a,201a
1988 108,226,238,250,259,263,190a, 202a
1989 101,226,190a,202a
1990 105,226,238,250,259,263,273, 190a,202a
1991 97,210,189a,201a
1992 102,177,211,191a,196a
1993 107,212,189a,201a
1994 99,213,189a,201a
1995 103,213,228,238,250,273,340a
1996 108,217,190a,202a
1997 100,215,239,341a
1998 104,216,189a,201a
1999 108,205,239,341a

17th December

1930 104,178,208,263,188a,197a
1931 97,226,246,259,263,190a,201a
1932 101,177,186a,198a
1933 106,177,254,191a,202a
1934 98,177,212,190a,199a
1935 102,177,213,188a,203a

1936 107,178,214,191a,199a
1937 99,178,214,189a,203a
1938 104,255,188a,200a
1939 108,246,263,192a,204a
1940 100,188,263,182a,194a
1941 153,207,258,261,272,189a,201a
1942 97,178,208,190a,201a
1943 153,178,272,302a
1944 106,178,220,191a,201a
1945 153,211,258,260,272,189a,201a
1946 103,177,212,188a,202a
1947 153,213,258,261,272,189a,201a
1948 100,177,214,188a,202a
1949 104,178,215,191a,198a
1950 97,178,216,190a,203a
1951 101,188,258,260,187a,199a
1952 106,177,232,191a,203a
1953 98,207,189a,201a
1954 102,224,232,188a,204a
1955 106,224,190a,202a
1956 99,178,211,225,188a,193a
1957 104,256,188a,200a
1958 108,212,263,189a,201a
1959 153,213,263,272,189a,201a
1960 153,214,272,189a,201a
1961 97,215,189a,201a
1962 102,178,186a,198a
1963 166,227,190a,202a
1964 99,177,186a,198a
1965 103,177,207,191a,202a
1966 107,177,209,190a,199a
1967 100,177,186a,198a
1968 104,191,187a,199a
1969 97,178,235,189a,204a
1970 101,256,188a,200a
1971 153,213,272,189a,201a
1972 98,214,189a,201a
1973 163,191,215,332a
1974 107,216,189a,201a
1975 99,178,205,249,188a,195a
1976 104,206,189a,201a
1977 108,208,189a,201a
1978 100,209,189a,201a
1979 153,177,210,272,327a
1980 97,188,211,332a
1981 102,191,212,332a
1982 106,212,224,340a
1983 98,199,213,336a
1984 103,214,189a,201a
1985 153,215,272,189a,201a
1986 160,216,259,263,189a,201a
1987 153,200,205,263,272,336a
1988 97,226,238,250,259,263,190a, 202a
1989 101,226,190a,202a
1990 105,226,238,250,259,263,273, 190a,202a
1991 98,210,189a,201a
1992 103,177,211,191a,196a
1993 107,212,189a,201a
1994 99,213,189a,201a
1995 103,213,228,238,250,273,340a
1996 108,214,217,340a
1997 101,215,239,258,261,341a
1998 153,216,272,189a,201a
1999 97,205,239,341a

18th December

1930 105,178,208,263,188a,197a
1931 97,226,246,259,263,190a,202a
1932 101,177,186a,198a
1933 106,177,254,191a,202a
1934 98,177,212,190a199a
1935 103,178,213,188a,203a
1936 107,178,214,191a,199a
1937 100,178,214,189a,203a
1938 104,255,188a,200a
1939 108,246,263,192a,204a
1940 101,188,263,182a,194a
1941 153,207,258,261,272,189a,201a
1942 98,178,208,190a,201a
1943 102,178,183a,195a
1944 107,178,220,191a,201a
1945 153,211,258,260,272,189a,201a
1946 104,255,188a,200a
1947 153,213,272,189a,201a
1948 100,177,214,188a,202a
1949 105,178,232,191a,198a
1950 97,178,216,190a,203a
1951 101,188,258,260,187a,199a
1952 106,177,232,191a,203a
1953 99,207,260,189a,201a
1954 103,208,224,232,250,188a,204a
1955 107,178,210,190a,200a
1956 100,178,211,225,188a,193a
1957 104,256,188a,200a
1958 97,212,263,189a,201a
1959 101,213,263,189a,201a
1960 153,214,272,189a,201a
1961 98,215,189a,201a
1962 102,178,186a,198a
1963 166,227,190a,202a
1964 99,177,186a,198a
1965 104,177,207,191a,202a
1966 108,177,209,190a,199a
1967 100,177,186a,198a
1968 105,191,187a,199a
1969 97,178,235,189a,204a
1970 102,256,188a,200a
1971 106,213,189a,201a
1972 98,214,189a,201a
1973 163,191,215,332a
1974 107,216,189a,201a
1975 99,178,205,249,195a
1976 104,206,189a,201a
1977 97,208,189a,201a
1978 101,209,189a,201a
1979 153,177,210,272,327a

1980 98,189,211,332a
1981 102,191,212,332a
1982 106,212,224,340a
1983 99,199,213,336a
1984 104,203,214,336a
1985 153,215,272,189a,201a
1986 160,216,259,263,189a,201a
1987 153,200,205,263,272,336a
1988 97,226,238,250,259,263,190a, 202a
1989 162,226,190a,202a
1990 166,226,263,276,190a,202a
1991 98,210,189a,201a
1992 103,177,211,191a,196a
1993 107,212,189a,201a
1994 100,213,263,189a,201a
1995 104,213,228,238,250,259,263, 273,340a
1996 97,214,217,261,340a
1997 101,215,239,258,261,341a
1998 153,216,272,189a,201a
1999 97,205,239,341a

19th December

1930 105,178,208,263,188a,197a
1931 97,226,246,259,263,190a,202a
1932 102,177,186a,198a
1933 107,229,191a,203a
1934 99,177,212,190a,199a
1935 103,178,213,188a,203a
1936 108,178,214,191a,199a
1937 100,178,214,189a,203a
1938 153,215,272,189a,201a
1939 97,217,255,263,190a,204a
1940 101,188,263,182a,194a
1941 106,177,207,261,191a,193a
1942 98,178,208,190a,201a
1943 102,178,183a,195a
1944 107,178,220,191a,201a
1945 153,211,258,260,272,189a,201a
1946 104,255,188a,200a
1947 153,213,272,189a,201a
1948 101,222,190a,202a
1949 105,178,232,191a,198a
1950 98,178,216,190a,203a
1951 102,188,187a,199a
1952 106,177,232,191a,203a
1953 99,207,260,189a,201a
1954 103,208,224,232,260,188a,204a
1955 107,178,210,190a,200a
1956 100,178,211,225,188a,193a
1957 105,211,189a,201a
1958 97,212,263,189a,201a
1959 101,213,263,189a,201a
1960 106,226,190a,202a
1961 98,215,189a,201a
1962 103,178,216,188a,197a
1963 107,227,234,256,190a,202a
1964 100,177,206,263,327a
1965 104,177,207,191a,202a
1966 108,177,209,190a,199a
1967 100,177,186a,198a
1968 105,191,187a,199a
1969 98,178,235,189a,204a
1970 102,256,188a,200a
1971 106,213,189a,201a
1972 99,214,189a,201a
1973 104,215,260,189a,201a
1974 108,216,189a,201a
1975 100,178,205,249,188a,195a
1976 105,206,189a,201a
1977 97,208,189a,201a
1978 101,209,189a,201a
1979 153,177,210,272,327a
1980 98,189,211,332a
1981 163,191,212,332a
1982 107,212,189a,201a
1983 99,199,213,336a
1984 104,203,214,336a
1985 97,215,189a,201a
1986 101,216,263,189a,201a
1987 153,205,263,272,189a,201a
1988 158,226,259,263,190a,202a
1989 162,226,190a,202a
1990 166,226,263,276,190a,202a
1991 99,210,189a,201a
1992 104,177,211,191a,196a
1993 108,212,189a,201a
1994 100,228,263,190a,202a
1995 104,213,228,238,250,259,263, 273,340a
1996 97,214,217,261,340a
1997 102,215,239,251,341a
1998 106,216,189a,201a
1999 98,205,341a

20th December

1930 106,226,263,190a,202a
1931 158,226,259,263,190a,202a
1932 102,177,186a,198a
1933 107,229,191a,203a
1934 99,177,212,190a,199a
1935 103,178,213,188a,203a
1936 108,178,214,191a,199a
1937 101,178,215,189a,203a
1938 153,215,272,189a,201a
1939 97,217,255,263,190a,204a
1940 162,188,259,263,182a,194a
1941 106,177,207,261,191a,193a
1942 99,178,183a,195a
1943 163,178,183a,195a
1944 108,178,210,191a,201a
1945 153,211,258,260,272,189a,201a
1946 104,255,188a,200a
1947 153,213,272,189a,201a
1948 101,222,261,190a,202a

1949 106,178,232,191a,198a
1950 98,178,216,190a,203a
1951 102,188,187a,199a
1952 167,232,191a,203a
1953 99,207,260,189a,201a
1954 164,208,255,260,188a,200a
1955 108,178,247,190a,200a
1956 101,211,189a,201a
1957 105,211,189a,201a
1958 97,212,263,189a,201a
1959 101,213,263,189a,201a
1960 106,226,190a,202a
1961 99,215,189a,201a
1962 103,178,216,188a,197a
1963 107,227,234,256,190a,202a
1964 100,177,206,263,327a
1965 153,207,272,189a,201a
1966 97,177,209,190a,199a
1967 101,177,186a,198a
1968 106,191,187a,199a
1969 98,178,235,189a,204a
1970 102,256,188a,200a
1971 107,213,189a,201a
1972 100,214,189a,201a
1973 104,215,260,189a,201a
1974 108,216,189a,201a
1975 100,178,205,249,188a,195a
1976 105,206,189a,201a
1977 98,208,189a,201a
1978 102,209,189a,201a
1979 166,177,210,327a
1980 99,189,211,332a
1981 163,191,212,332a
1982 107,212,189a,201a
1983 100,199,213,336a
1984 153,214,272,189a,201a
1985 97,215,189a,201a
1986 101,216,263,189a,201a
1987 153,205,263,272,189a,201a
1988 158,226,259,263,190a,202a
1989 103,226,190a,202a
1990 107,226,273,190a,202a
1991 99,210,189a,201a
1992 104,177,211,191a,196a
1993 108,212,227,340a
1994 100,228,263,190a,202a
1995 105,213,228,238,250,259,263, 273,340a
1996 158,214,217,261,340a
1997 102,215,239,251,341a
1998 106,216,189a,201a
1999 98,205,341a

21st December

1930 106,226,263,190a,202a
1931 158,226,259,263,190a,202a
1932 103,177,210,327a
1933 107,229,191a,203a
1934 100,177,212,190a,199a
1935 104,178,213,188a,203a
1936 108,178,214,191a,199a
1937 101,178,215,189a,203a
1938 153,215,272,189a,201a
1939 97,204,205,263,181a,193a
1940 162,189,206,259,263,297a
1941 107,177,207,261,191a,193a
1942 99,178,183a;195a
1943 163,178,183a,195a
1944 108,178,210,191a,201a
1945 101,211,258,260,321a
1946 153,212,272,189a,201a
1947 97,213,258,261,189a,201a
1948 162,214,222,260,190a,202a
1949 106,178,232,191a,198a
1950 98,178,216,190a,203a
1951 102,188,187a,199a
1952 167,232,191a,203a
1953 100,207,260,189a,201a
1954 164,208,255,260,188a,200a
1955 108,178,247,190a,200a
1956 101,211,189a,201a
1957 106,211,191a,200a
1958 98,212,263,189a,201a
1959 153,213,263,272,189a,201a
1960 107,177,214,191a,196a
1961 99,215,189a,201a
1962 103,178,216,188a,197a
1963 108,227,234,256,190a,202a
1964 101,177,206,263,327a
1965 153,207,272,189a,201a
1966 97,177,209,190a,199a
1967 101,177,186a,198a
1968 106,191,187a,199a
1969 99,178,212,189a,204a
1970 103,256,188a,200a
1971 107,213,189a,201a
1972 100,214,189a,201a
1973 104,215,260,189a,201a
1974 108,216,263,189a,201a
1975 101,221,249,188a,195a
1976 106,206,189a,201a
1977 153,208,272,189a,201a
1978 102,209,189a,201a
1979 166,177,210,327a
1980 99,189,211,332a
1981 104,191,212,332a
1982 108,212,189a,201a
1983 100,199,213,336a
1984 153,214,272,189a,201a
1985 97,215,189a,201a
1986 101,216,263,189a,201a
1987 153,205,225,263,272,340a
1988 99,226,238,250,190a,202a
1989 103,226,190a,202a
1990 107,226,273,190a,202a
1991 100,210,189a,201a
1992 104,177,211,191a,196a
1993 97,212,227,340a

1994 101,228,263,190a,202a
1995 105,213,228,238,250,259,263, 273,340a
1996 158,214,217,261,340a
1997 102,215,239,251,341a
1998 106,216,189a,201a
1999 99,205,239,341a

22nd December

1930 106,226,263,190a,202a
1931 99,226,190a,202a
1932 115,177,186a,198a
1933 120,177,211,191a,202a
1934 100,177,212,190a,199a
1935 104,178,213,188a,203a
1936 154,228,273,190a,202a
1937 114,230,246,189a,204a
1938 106,177,215,188a,200a
1939 153,205,217,255,263,272,190a, 204a
1940 154,189,273,182a,194a
1941 154,218,230,246,261,273,191a, 193a
1942 111,178,219,307a
1943 104,178,183a,195a
1944 120,178,210,191a,201a
1945 113,211,185a,197a
1946 117,177,212,188a,202a
1947 97,213,258,261,189a,201a
1948 114,214,222,261,190a,202a
1949 119,232,191a,203a
1950 111,223,190a,202a
1951 103,188,260,187a,199a
1952 120,177,206,191a,203a
1953 112,177,207,189a,200a
1954 164,255,188a,200a
1955 97,178,247,190a,200a
1956 114,178,248,189a,193a
1957 154,225,273,190a,202a
1958 110,256,259,263,190a,194a
1959 153,213,263,272,189a,201a
1960 119,226,190a,202a
1961 154,226,273,190a,202a
1962 116,256,188a,200a
1963 108,227,234,256,190a,202a
1964 154,177,259,263,273,186a,198a
1965 117,177,207,191a,202a
1966 109,177,209,190a,199a
1967 102,177,186a,198a
1968 167,191,187a,199a
1969 111,178,212,189a,204a
1970 115,256,188a,200a
1971 107,189a,201a
1972 112,214,189a,201a
1973 117,215,189a,201a
1974 109,220,190a,202a
1975 113,178,205,188a,195a
1976 154,221,273,190a,202a
1977 110,208,189a,201a
1978 114,177,257,188a,202a
1979 154,177,273,186a,198a
1980 112,189,211,332a
1981 116,191,187a,199a
1982 120,224,190a,202a
1983 113,199,213,336a
1984 118,177,214,250,191a,203a
1985 110,215,189a,201a
1986 114,216,263,189a,201a
1987 118,205,225,340a
1988 154,226,273,190a,202a
1989 154,226,273,190a,202a
1990 154,226,273,276,190a,202a
1991 112,227,190a,202a
1992 117,227,190a,202a
1993 109,227,190a,202a
1994 154,228,259,263,273,190a,202a
1995 154,228,273,190a,202a
1996 154,214,217,261,273,190a,202a
1997 163,239,258,261,191a,203a
1998 119,239,191a,203a
1999 99,205,239,341a

23rd December

1930 119,226,190a,202a
1931 154,226,273,190a,202a
1932 116,177,186a,198a
1933 120,177,211,191a,202a
1934 113,177,212,190a,199a
1935 117,178,213,188a,203a
1936 154,228,273,190a,202a
1937 114,230,246,189a,204a
1938 118,177,215,188a;200a
1939 110,230,246,259,263,190a,204a
1940 154,189,273,182a,194a
1941 154,218,230,246,273,191a;193a
1942 112,219,190a,202a
1943 116,178,183a,195a
1944 109,178,220,191a,201a
1945 113,211,185a,197a
1946 118,221,190a,202a
1947 110,177,213,261,190a,198a
1948 153,214,222,261,272,190a,202a
1949 119,232,191a,203a
1950 111,223,190a,202a
1951 115,188,187a,199a
1952 120,177,206,191a,203a
1953 113,177,207,189a,202a
1954 117,224,232,188a,204a
1955 109,224,190a,202a
1956 114,178,248,189a,193a
1957 154,225,273,190a,202a
1958 111,177,212,190a,194a
1959 115,213,189a,201a
1960 120,226,190a,202a
1961 154,226,273,190a,202a
1962 116,256,199a,200a

1963 154,227,273,190a,202a
1964 114,177,259,263,186a,198a
1965 118,177,207,191a,203a
1966 110,234,256,190a,199a
1967 114,177,186a,198a
1968 167,191,187a,199a
1969 111,178,212,189a,204a
1970 116,256,188a,200a
1971 120,213,189a,201a
1972 113,214,189a,201a
1973 117,215,189a,201a
1974 109,220,190a,202a
1975 114,178,205,188a,195a
1976 119,178,236,191a,201a
1977 111,208,189a,201a
1978 115,177,209,188a,202a
1979 119,177,186a,198a
1980 112,189,211,332a
1981 116,191,187a,199a
1982 109,224,190a,202a
1983 113,199,213,336a
1984 118,177,214,250,191a,203a
1985 110,215,189a,201a
1986 114,216,263,189a,201a
1987 119,225,190a,202a
1988 154,226,259,263,273,190a,202a
1989 154,226,273,190a,202a
1990 154,226,263,273,276,190a,202a
1991 113,227,190a,202a
1992 117,227,190a,202a
1993 109,227,190a,202a
1994 114,228,259,263,190a,202a
1995 154,228,273,190a,202a
1996 154,214,217,261,273,190a,202a
1997 163,239,258,261,191a,203a
1998 119,239,191a,203a
1999 100,239,191a,203a

24th December

1930 119,226,190a,202a
1931 154,226,273,190a,202a
1932 116,177,186a,198a
1933 109,177,254,191a,202a
1934 113,177,212,190a,199a
1935 117,178,213,188a,203a
1936 110,228,259,262,190a,202a
1937 115,178,215,189a,204a
1938 119,177,215,188a,200a
1939 111,177,205,190a,204a
1940 154,189,259,263,273,182a,194a
1941 154,218,230,246,273,191a,193a
1942 112,219,190a,202a
1943 116,178,183a,195a
1944 109,177,220,191a,201a
1945 114,177,220,189a,197a
1946 118,221,190a,202a
1947 110,177,213,261,190a,198a
1948 153,214,222,261,272,190a,202a
1949 120,178,255,191a,198a
1950 112,223,190a,202a
1951 116,188,187a,199a
1952 109,177,232,191a,203a
1953 113,177,207,189a,200a
1954 117,224,232,188a,204a
1955 109,255,188a,200a
1956 115,178,248,189a,193a
1957 119,178,248,191a,201a
1958 111,177,212,190a,194a
1959 115,213,189a,201a
1960 120,226,190a,202a
1961 154,226,273,190a,202a
1962 117,178,227,188a,197a
1963 154,227,273,190a,202a
1964 114,177,259,263,186a,198a
1965 118,177,207,191a,203a
1966 110,234,256,190a,199a
1967 115,177,186a,198a
1968 120,191,187a,199a
1969 112,178,235,189a,204a
1970 116,256,188a,200a
1971 120,213,189a,201a
1972 113,214,189a,201a
1973 118,177,220,191a,194a
1974 110,220,190a,202a
1975 114,178,205,188a,195a
1976 119,178,236,191a,201a
1977 111,208,189a,201a
1978 115,177,209,188a,202a
1979 120,177,186a,198a
1980 113,189,211,332a
1981 117,191,212,332a
1982 109,224,190a,202a
1983 114,199,213,336a
1984 188,177,214,250,191a,203a
1985 111,215,189a,201a
1986 115,216,189a,201a
1987 119,225,190a,202a
1988 154,226,259,263,273,190a,202a
1989 154,226,273,190a,202a
1990 154,226,263,273,276,190a,202a
1991 113,227,190a,202a
1992 118,227,190a,202a
1993 110,227,190a,202a
1994 114,228,259,263,190a,202a
1995 154,228,273,190a,202a
1996 154,214,217,261,273,190a,202a
1997 116,239,191a,203a
1998 120,177,216,190a,199a
1999 100,239,191a,203a

25th December

1930 120,226,263,190a,202a
1931 154,226,259,263,273,190a,202a
1932 117,177,210,327a
1933 109,177,254,191a,202a
1934 113,177,212,190a,199a

1935 117,178,213,188a,203a
1936 110,228,259,262,190a,202a
1937 115,178,215,189a,204a
1938 119,177,215,188a,200a
1939 111,177,205,191a,204a
1940 154,189,259,263,273,182a,194a
1941 154,218,230,246,261,273,191a, 193a
1942 113,219,190a,202a
1943 117,178,183a,195a
1944 110,177,220,191a,201a
1945 114,177,220,189a,197a
1946 118,221,190a,202a
1947 111,177,213,261,191a,198a
1948 153,222,272,190a,202a
1949 120,178,255,191a,198a
1950 112,223,190a,202a
1951 116,188,187a,199a
1952 109,177,232,191a,203a
1953 114,177,207,189a,200a
1954 154,224,232,273,190a,202a
1955 110,255,188a,200a
1956 115,178,248,189a,193a
1957 119,178,248,191a,201a
1958 111,177,212,190a,194a
1959 116,213,256,263,336a
1960 109,226,190a,202a
1961 154,226,273,190a,202a
1962 117,178,227,188a,197a
1963 154,227,273,190a,202a
1964 114,177,259,263,186a,198a
1965 119,234,191a,203a
1966 111,177,209,190a,199a
1967 154,178,273,186a,198a
1968 120,191,187a,199a
1969 112,178,235,189a,204a
1970 116,256,188a,200a
1971 109,213,189a,201a
1972 114,214,189a,201a
1973 118,177,220,191a,194a
1974 110,220,190a,202a
1975 115,178,205,188a,195a
1976 120,178,206,191a,201a
1977 112,208,189a,201a
1978 116,257,188a,200a
1979 120,177,186a,198a
1980 113,189,223,333a
1981 117,191,212,332a
1982 109,224,190a,202a
1983 114,199,213,336a
1984 119,224,190a,202a
1985 111,215,189a,201a
1986 115,216,189a,201a
1987 120,225,190a,202a
1988 154,226,259,263,273,190a,202a
1989 154,226,273,190a,202a
1990 154,226,263,273,276,190a,202a
1991 113,227,190a,202a
1992 118,227,190a,202a
1993 110,227,190a,202a
1994 114,228,259,263,190a,202a
1995 154,228,273,190a,202a
1996 154,217,273,190a,202a
1997 116,239,191a,203a
1998 120,177,216,190a,199a
1999 101,239,191a,203a

26th December

1930 120,226,263,190a,202a
1931 112,226,190a,202a
1932 117,177,210,327a
1933 110,177,254,191a,202a
1934 114,227,190a,202a
1935 154,228,273,190a,202a
1936 154,228,259,262,273,190a,202a
1937 115,178,215,189a,204a
1938 119,177,215,188a,200a
1939 112,177,205,191a,204a
1940 154,189,206,259,263,273,297a
1941 154,218,230,246,261,273, 191a,193a
1942 113,219,190a,202a
1943 117,178,183a,195a
1944 110,177,220,191a,201a
1945 115,189,187a,199a
1946 119,177,212,188a,202a
1947 111,177,213,261,191a,198a
1948 153,222,272,190a,202a
1949 120,178,255,191a,199a
1950 112,223,190a,202a
1951 117,188,187a,199a
1952 110,177,232,191a,203a
1953 114,177,207,189a,200a
1954 154,224,232,273,190a,202a
1955 110,255,188a,200a
1956 116,178,211,189a,193a
1957 120,178,211,191a,201a
1958 112,177,212,263,190a,194a
1959 116,213,256,263,336a
1960 109,226,190a,202a
1961 154,226,273,190a,202a
1962 117,178,227,188a,197a
1963 110,227,190a,202a
1964 154,177,273,186a,198a
1965 119,234,191a,203a
1966 111,177,209,190a,199a
1967 154,178,256,273,326a
1968 109,191,187a,199a
1969 113,178,235,189a,204a
1970 117,256,188a,200a
1971 109,213,189a,201a
1972 114,214,189a,201a
1973 118,177,220,191a,194a
1974 110,220,190a,202a
1975 115,178,205,188a,195a
1976 120,178,206,191a,201a
1977 112,208,189a,201a
1978 116,257,188a,200a

1979 109,177,186a,198a
1980 114,189,223,333a
1981 154,19,,223,273,333a
1982 110,213,224,340a
1983 115,199,213,336a
1984 119,224,190a,202a
1985 111,215,189a,201a
1986 164,204,216,259,263,336a
1987 120,225,190a,202a
1988 154,226,259,263,273,190a,202a
1989 154,226,273,190a,202a
1990 154,226,259,263,273,190a,202a
1991 114,227,190a,202a
1992 119,227,238,343a
1993 111,227,190a,202a
1994 154,228,273,190a,202a
1995 154,228,273,190a,202a
1996 154,217,273,190a,202a
1997 116,239,191a,203a
1998 109,177,216,190a,199a
1999 101,239,191a,203a

27th December

1930 120,226,263,190a,202a
1931 113,226,190a,202a
1932 118,177,186a,198a
1933 110,177,254,191a,202a
1934 114,227,190a,202a
1935 154,228,273,190a,202a
1936 154,228,259,262,273,190a,202a
1937 116,178,215,189a,204a
1938 120,177,215,188a,200a
1939 112,177,205,191a,204a
1940 154,189,206,259,263,273,297a
1941 154,218,230,246,261,273,191a, 193a
1942 113,219,190a,202a
1943 154,178,219,273,307a
1944 111,177,220,191a,201a
1945 115,189,187a,199a
1946 119,177,212,188a,202a
1947 111,178,213,261,191a,198a
1948 153,214,222,261,190a,202a
1949 109,178,232,191a,199a
1950 113,223,190a,202a
1951 117,188,187a,199a
1952 110,177,232,191a,203a
1953 114,177,207,189a,200a
1954 154,224,232,273,190a,202a
1955 111,255,188a,200a
1956 116,178,211,189a,193a
1957 120,178,211,191a,201a
1958 112,177,212,263,190a,194a
1959 165,213,263,189a,201a
1960 110,226,190a,202a
1961 114,178,226,276,328a
1962 154,227,273,190a,202a
1963 110,227,190a,202a
1964 154,177,273,186a,198a
1965 119,234,191a,203a
1966 112,177,209,190a,199a
1967 154,178,256,273,326a
1968 109,191,187a,199a
1969 113,178,235,189a,204a
1970 117,256,188a,200a
1971 110,213,261,189a,201a
1972 115,189,214,332a
1973 167,235,191a,203a
1974 111,220,190a,202a
1975 115,178,205,188a,195a
1976 120,178,206,191a,201a
1977 112,208,189a,201a
1978 117,209,189a,201a
1979 109,177,186a,198a
1980 114,189,223,333a
1981 154,191,223,273 333a
1982 110,213,224,340a
1983 115,199,213,336a
1984 120,224,190a,202a
1985 112,215,225,340a
1986 164,204,216,259,263,336a
1987 109,225,190a,202a
1988 154,226,259,263,273,190a,202a
1989 154,226,273,190a,202a,
1990 110,226,263,273,276,190a,202a
1991 114,227,190a,202a
1992 119,227,238,343a
1993 154,227,259,262,273,190a,202a
1994 154,228,273,190a,202a
1995 154,228,273,190a,202a
1996 154,214,217,261,273,190a,202a
1997 117,215,239,261,341a
1998 109,177,216,190a,199a
1999 102,239,191a,203a

28th December

1930 109,226,263,190a,202a
1931 113,226,190a,202a
1932 118,177,186a,198a
1933 110,229,191a,203a
1934 114,227,190a,202a
1935 119,178,213,188a,203a
1936 154,228,259,262,273,190a,202a
1937 116,178,215,189a,204a
1938 120,177,215,188a,200a
1939 161,217,255,191a,204a
1940 118,189,259,263,182a,194a
1941 110,191,261,182a,194a
1942 114,219,190a,202a
1943 154,178,219,273,307a
1944 111,177,220,191a,201a
1945 116,177,211,189a,196a
1946 120,177,212,188a,202a
1947 112,178,213,191a,198a
1948 153,214,222,261,272,190a,202a
1949 109,178,232,191a,199a

1950 113,223,190a,202a
1951 118,188,187a,199a
1952 159,223,247,191a,203a
1953 115,177,207,189a,200a
1954 119,224,232,188a,204a
1955 111,255,188a,200a
1956 116,178,211,189a,193a
1957 120,178,211,191a,201a
1958 113,177,212,263,190a,194a
1959 165,213,263,189a,201a
1960 110,226,190a,202a
1961 114,178,226,276,325a
1962 154,227,273,190a,202a
1963 154,227,273,190a,202a
1964 154,177,259,263,273,186a,198a
1965 120,177,207,191a,203a
1966 112,177,209,190a,199a
1967 154,178,256,273,326a
1968 109,191,187a,199a
1969 113,178,235,189a,204a
1970 154,218,256,337a
1971 110,213,261,189a,201a
1972 115,189,214,332a
1973 167,235,191a,203a
1974 111,220,190a,202a
1975 116,257,188a,200a
1976 109,178,236,191a,201a
1977 113,177,257,190a,197a
1978 117,209,189a,201a
1979 110,177,186a,198a
1980 114,189,223,333a
1981 154,191,223,273,333a
1982 111,213,224,340a
1983 115,199,213,336a
1984 120,224,190a,202a
1985 112,215,225,340a
1986 164,204,216,259,263,336a
1987 109,225,190a,202a
1988 114,226,263,273,276,190a,202a
1989 154,226,273,190a,202a
1990 110,226,263,273,276,190a,202a
1991 115,227,190a,202a
1992 119,227,238,343a
1993 154,227,259,262,273,190a,202a
1994 154,198,228,259,263,273,337a
1995 154,228,273,190a,202a,
1996 154,214,217,261,273,190a,202a
1997 117,215,239,261,341a
1998 110,177,216,190a,199a
1999 102,239,191a,203a

29th December

1930 109,226,263,190a,202a
1931 114,226,190a,202a
1932 119,177,186a,198a
1933 159,228,191a,203a
1934 115,227,190a,202a
1935 119,178,213,188a,203a
1936 154,228,259,262,273,190a,202a
1937 117,178,215,189a,204a
1938 109,177,215,188a,200a
1939 161,217,255,191a,204a
1940 154,189,218,263,273,276,298a
1941 110,191,261,182a,194a
1942 114,219,190a,202a
1943 167,178,183a,195a
1944 112,177,210,191a,201a
1945 116,177,211,189a,196a
1946 120,177,212,188a,202a
1947 154,261,273,185a,197a
1948 153,214,222,261,272,190a,202a
1949 110,178,232,255,191a,199a
1950 114,223,190a,202a
1951 118,188,187a,199a
1952 159,223,247,191a,203a
1953 115,177,207,189a,200a
1954 119,224,232,188a,204a
1955 112,255,188a,200a
1956 165,211,189a,201a
1957 157,211,189a,201a
1958 113,177,212,263,190a,194a
1959 118,213,226,263,340a
1960 110,226,190a,202a
1961 154,226,262,273,276,190a,201a
1962 119,178,227,188a,197a
1963 154,227,273,190a,202a
1964 154,177,259,263,273,186a,198a
1965 120,177,207,191a,203a
1966 113,177,209,190a,199a
1967 154,178,273,186a,198a
1968 110,191,187a,199a
1969 114,218,256,189a,204a
1970 154,218,256,337a
1971 159,213,258,261,189a,201a
1972 116,214,189a,201a
1973 120,178,249,191a,194a
1974 112,220,190a,202a
1975 116,257,188a,200a
1976 109,178,236,191a,201a
1977 113,177,257,190a,197a
1978 118,222,190a,202a
1979 110,177,186a,198a
1980 115,189,223,333a
1981 167,191,187a,199a
1982 111,213,224,340a
1983 116,199,213,336a
1984 109,224,190a,202a
1985 113,215,225,340a
1986 117,216,263,189a,201a
1987 110,225,190a,202a
1988 114,226,263,273,276,190a,202a
1989 154,226,273,190a,202a
1990 154,226,273,190a,202a
1991 115,227,190a,202a
1992 120,227,190a,202a
1993 154,227,259,262,273,190a,202a
1994 154,198,228,259,263,273,337a
1995 154,228,273,190a,202a

1996 154,214,217,261,273,190a,202a
1997 118,217,239,261,343a
1998 110,177,216,190a,199a
1999 103,239,191a,203a

30th December

1930 110,226,259,263,190a,202a
1931 114,226,190a,202a
1932 119,177,186a,198a
1933 159,229,191a,203a
1934 115,227,190a,202a
1935 120,178,213,188a,203a
1936 154,228,273,190a,202a
1937 117,178,215,189a,204a
1938 109,177,216,263,188a,200a
1939 114,177,205,191a,204a
1940 154,189,218,263,273,276,298a
1941 154,218,230,246,261,273,191a, 193a
1942 115,219,190a,202a
1943 167,178,183a,195a
1944 112,177,210,191a,201a
1945 116,177,211,190a,196a
1946 120,177,212,188a,202a
1947 154,261,273,185a,197a
1948 153,214,222,261,272,190a,202a
1949 110,178,232,255,191a,199a
1950 114,223,190a,202a
1951 119,188,187a,199a
1952 122,177,206,191a,203a
1953 116,255,188a,200a
1954 168,224,232,188a,204a
1955 112,255,188a,200a
1956 165,211,189a,201a
1957 157,211,189a,201a
1958 114,256,259,263,190a,194a
1959 118,213,226,263,340a
1960 154,226,273,190a,202a
1961 154,226,262,273,276,190a,202a
1962 119,178,227,188a,197a
1963 154,227,273,190a,202a
1964 154,177,206,259,263,273,327a
1965 109,177,207,191a,203a
1966 113,177,209,190a,199a
1967 154,178,273,186a,198a
1968 110,188,187a,199a
1969 114,218,256,189a,204a
1970 119,256,188a,200a
1971 159,213,258,261,189a,201a
1972 116,214,189a,201a
1973 120,178,249,191a,194a
1974 112,220,190a,202a
1975 117,178,205,188a,195a
1976 110,178,236,191a,201a
1977 114,177,257,190a,197a
1978 118,222,190a,202a
1979 111,177,186a,198a
1980 115,189,223,333a
1981 167,191,187a,199a
1982 112,213,224,340a
1983 116,199,213,336a
1984 109,224,190a,202a
1985 113,215,225,340a
1986 117,216,225,263,340a
1987 110,225,190a,202a
1988 154,226,273,190a,202a
1989 154,226,273,190a,202a
1990 154,226,273,190a,202a
1991 116,201,227,337a
1992 120,227,190a,202a
1993 154,227,259,262,273,190a,202a
1994 154,228,259,263,273,190a,202a
1995 154,228,273,190a,202a
1996 114,214,217,261,190a,202a
1997 118,217,239,261,343a
1998 111,177,216,190a,199a
1999 103,239,191a,203a

31st December

1930 110,226,259,263,190a,202a
1931 115,226,190a,202a
1932 120,177,186a,198a
1933 112,229,191a,203a
1934 116,227,190a,202a
1935 120,178,213,188a,203a
1936 154,228,273,190a,202a
1937 154,228,273,190a,202a
1938 109,177,216,263,188a,200a
1939 114,177,205,191a,204a
1940 154,189,273,182a,194a
1941 154,218,230,246,261,273,191a, 193a
1942 115,219,190a,202a
1943 120,178,183a,195a
1944 113,177,220,191a,201a
1945 117,177,211,190a,196a
1946 109,177,212,188a,202a
1947 114,178,213,261,191a,198a
1948 153,214,222,261,272,190a,202a
1949 110,178,232,255,191a,199a
1950 115,190,223,333a
1951 119,188,187a,199a
1952 112,177,206,191a,204a
1953 116,224,255,337a
1954 168,224,232,188a,204a
1955 154,255,273,320a
1956 154,225,273,190a,202a
1957 110,211,189a,201a
1958 114,256,259,263,190a,194a
1959 119,213,189a,201a
1960 154,226,273,190a,202a
1961 154,226,262,273,276,190a,202a
1962 120,178,227,188a,197a
1963 154,227,273,190a,202a
1964 154,177,206,259,263,273,327a
1965 109,177,207,191a,203a

1966 113,177,209,190a,199a
1967 154,178,217,273,328a
1968 111,188,187a,199a
1969 115,178,212,189a,204a
1970 119,256,188a,200a
1971 112,213,189a,201a
1972 117,214,189a,201a
1973 120,178,249,191a,194a
1974 113,220,190a,202a
1975 117,178,205,188a,195a
1976 110,178,236,191a,201a
1977 114,177,236,190a,197a
1978 119,177,209,188a,202a
1979 111,177,186a,198a
1980 116,189,187a,199a
1981 168,191,187a,199a
1982 112,213,224,340a
1983 117,199,213,336a
1984 109,224,190a,202a
1985 113,215,225,340a
1986 154,225,263,273,190a,202a
1987 110,225,190a,202a
1988 154,226,273,190a,202a
1989 154,226,273,190a,202a
1990 154,226,259,263,273,190a,202a
1991 116,201,227,337a
1992 109,227,190a,202a
1993 154,227,273,190a,202a
1994 154,228,259,263,273,190a,202a
1995 110,228,273,190a,202a
1996 114,214,217,261,190a,202a
1997 167,239,258,261,274,191a,203a
1998 111,177,216,190a,199a
1999 104,239,191a,203a

Sun/Moon Combinations

1. Sun in Aries/Moon in Aries ☉♈/☽♈
A forceful personality: energetic, independent, dominant, egotistical, intolerant of opposition and easily provoked. Perceptive. Has 'out of sight, out of mind' attitude.

1i. Sun in Aries/Moon in Aries with dominant Fire signs
Inclined to sado-masochism.

2. Sun in Aries/Moon in Taurus ☉♈/☽♉
A dogmatic type. Intellectually inclined and of a practical disposition; is likely to put ideas into effect.

3. Sun in Aries/Moon in Gemini ☉♈/☽♊
Has the need to be occupied constantly by a variety of things. Artistically gifted. Amusing.

4. Sun in Aries/Moon in Cancer ☉♈/☽♋
An energetic, egotistical domineering person with a powerful imagination and strong intuition. Tends to drain people. Cautious, shrewd, enterprising and strongly ambitious. A collector.

5. Sun in Aries/Moon in Leo ☉♈/☽♌
A forceful personality: self-confident, egotistical, energetic, enterprising, positive and ambitious. Has excellent organising ability. A cheerful extrovert who loves a grand occasion and enjoys flattery. Has an original turn of phrase. Very affectionate. Strongly intuitive.

6. Sun in Aries/Moon in Virgo ☉♈/☽♍
A studious type. Practical, analytical and highly critical. Inclined to science and music.

7. Sun in Aries/Moon in Libra ☉♈/☽♎
A strongly diplomatic person with a naturally charming disposition. Sociable, companionable, sensitive, observant and alert. Gives good advice. Receptive to all the Arts. Enjoys flattery.

8. Sun in Aries/Moon in Scorpio ☉♈/☽♏
A powerful personality: dogmatic, positive, aggressive, passionate and hard-working.

9. Sun in Aries/Moon in Sagittarius ☉♈/☽♐
A philanthropic nature. Generous, straightforward, quickly sympathetic and highly enthusiastic. A restless type with a sense of urgency — will apply energy and determination to any task while the mood lasts. Intuitive. Independent. Talkative.

10. Sun in Aries/Moon in Capricorn ☉♈/☽♑
A forceful personality: self-assertive, dominant, practical, energetic, ambitious, persistent. Will put full force into any business enterprise. A tendency to be moody. Appearance-conscious and enjoys flattery.

11. Sun in Aries/Moon in Aquarius ☉♈/☽♒
Eccentric and aggressive; strongly independent. Has original ideas; is imaginative, witty and artistic — can be effectively expressive and influential. Will give full weight to any enterprise.

12. Sun in Aries/Moon in Pisces ☉♈/☽♓
A restless, worrying type. A very kind, charitable person, sentimental but gently authoritative. Voluble. Artistic. Inclined to the Occult.

13. Sun in Taurus/Moon in Aries ☉♉/☽♈
Independent and enterprising. Has a strong will and great endurance. Determined to do well and usually achieves ambition by dint of energy, persistence and organisation. Fully expects the cooperation of others.

14. Sun in Taurus/Moon in Taurus ☉♉/☽♉
A very strong character: determined, persistent, positive, ambitious and optimistic. A cheerful, sensual, fun-loving person, companionable and sociable, but there is a reserved, secretive side. Musical and artistic.

15. Sun in Taurus/Moon in Gemini ☉♉/☽♊
Has good intellect and an excellent command of words. Inclined to the Arts.

16. Sun in Taurus/Moon in Cancer ☉♉/☽♋
Has a strong sense of economy; shrewd with money and property. Inclined to sensationalism.

17. Sun in Taurus/Moon in Leo ☉♉/☽♌
A self-confident, ostentatious, passionate, sensual person. Very sociable.

18. Sun in Taurus/Moon in Virgo ☉♉/☽♍
An adaptable person of diverse abilities. Good at developing other people's ideas and capable of taking on more than one project at a time. Ambition is usually realised by virtue of hard work, persistence and a seemingly indestructible determination. An analytical mind and a good critical ability.

19. Sun in Taurus/Moon in Libra ☉♉/☽♎
Friendly and charming. Musical and artistic.

20. Sun in Taurus/Moon in Scorpio ☉♉/☽♏
A self-reliant person, hard-working and determined.

21. Sun in Taurus/Moon in Sagittarius ☉♉/☽♐
Optimistic and over-ambitious: tends to overwork. A generous, sympathetic nature.

22. Sun in Taurus/Moon in Capricorn ☉♉/☽♑
Has strong organising ability: sets up ambitious plans and builds up financial resources.

23. Sun in Taurus/Moon in Aquarius ☉♉/☽♒
Sincere, purposeful, persistent and hard-working.

24. Sun in Taurus/Moon in Pisces ☉♉/☽♓
A kind and hospitable person who enjoys good living and harmonious surroundings. Very sociable.

25. Sun in Gemini/Moon in Aries ☉♊/☽♈
Strongly intellectual. Ambitious. Has artistic talent.

26. Sun in Gemini/Moon in Taurus ☉♊/☽♉
Mentally and physically restless. Artistic.

27. Sun in Gemini/Moon in Gemini ☉♊/☽♊
Strongly intellectual.

28. Sun in Gemini/Moon in Cancer ☉♊/☽♋
Highly sensitive and strongly imaginative. Has a good memory, stores knowledge and is able to converse on most subjects. Good at domestic economy. Has artistic talents.

29. Sun in Gemini/Moon in Leo ☉♊/☽♌
Has a self-confident, optimistic attitude and works hard but is never satisfied with efforts. Powerful imagination and emotions.

30. Sun in Gemini/Moon in Virgo ☉♊/☽♍
A studious, moody person.

31. Sun in Gemini/Moon in Libra ☉♊/☽♎
Strongly perceptive. Studious and artistic.

32. Sun in Gemini/Moon in Scorpio ☉♊/☽♏
Assertive and determined. A hard worker and a severe critic. Highly sensitive.

33. Sun in Gemini/Moon in Sagittarius ☉♊/☽♐
Intellectual and philosophical. Enthusiastic, friendly, kind and generous. Very restless; likes to be on the move.

34. Sun in Gemini/Moon in Capricorn ☉♊/☽♑
Calculating and methodical. Has a good memory.

35. Sun in Gemini/Moon in Aquarius ☉♊/☽♒
Mentally and physically active. Independent, inventive and original.

36. Sun in Gemini/Moon in Pisces ☉♊/☽♓
Restless, moody and never satisfied. Strongly receptive and has a yearning for knowledge. Inclined to music.

37. Sun in Cancer/Moon in Aries ☉♋/☽♈
Active, headstrong and rebellious. Independent and likes to be in charge; when under supervision becomes restless and discontented.

38. Sun in Cancer/Moon in Taurus ☉♋/☽♉
Practical, energetic, strongly imaginative and persevering. Inclined to property dealing.

39. Sun in Cancer/Moon in Gemini ☉♋/☽♊
Has a clever mind and a desire for knowledge. Physically restless and impatient. A very sensitive type — moody and artistic.

40. Sun in Cancer/Moon in Cancer ☉♋/☽♋
A very changeable personality. Shrewd with money and property. A traditionalist.

41. Sun in Cancer/Moon in Leo ☉♋/☽♌
Has powerful emotions. Demonstrative in love affairs.

42. Sun in Cancer/Moon in Virgo ☉♋/☽♍
Adaptable and cooperative. A hard worker but tends to worry about work. Inclined to a 'workaholic' state.

43. Sun in Cancer/Moon in Libra ☉♋/☽♎
Acutely observant and perceptive. Strongly sensuous. Needs a good home life to be contented.

44. Sun in Cancer/Moon in Scorpio ☉♋/☽♏
Hard-working and determined. Strong family ties but likely to make a complete break to an entirely new way of life.

45. Sun in Cancer/Moon in Sagittarius ☉♋/☽♐
A restless person who is always seeking out new areas and new ideas. Works quickly. Emotional and friendly.

46. Sun in Cancer/Moon in Capricorn ☉♋/☽♑
An ambitious, egotistical person with a strong sense of leadership. Believes in getting things ship-shape. Shrewd with money and property. Greatly influenced by family and likely to have emotional blockages.

47. Sun in Cancer/Moon in Aquarius ☉♋/☽♒
A very friendly person but prizes independence. Artistic. Inclined to the Occult.

48. Sun in Cancer/Moon in Pisces ☉♋/☽♓
Has a receptive mind and a love of knowledge; always interested in new things. Sociable. Likely to have psychic powers.

49. Sun in Leo/Moon in Aries ☉♌/☽♈
Independent, energetic, determined, persistent, positive and firm. Sometimes headstrong and quarrelsome but generally good-humoured.

50. Sun in Leo/Moon in Taurus ☉♌/☽♉
Determined and obstinate; puts heart and soul into everything. Sensual.

51. Sun in Leo/Moon in Gemini ☉♌/☽♊
Broadminded and knowledgeable. Likely to have gifted abilities.

52. Sun in Leo/Moon in Cancer ☉♌/☽♋
Very sociable, affectionate and strongly sensual. Highly sensitive and has a powerful family instinct.

53. Sun in Leo/Moon in Leo ☉♌/☽♌
Egotistical, resourceful and independent. Copes well with adversity and has definite potential for success. Generous and very sociable. Needs affection.

54. Sun in Leo/Moon in Virgo ☉♌/☽♍
A practical, resourceful person. Constantly aspires to better self. A worrier. Inclined to the Arts.

55. Sun in Leo/Moon in Libra ☉♌/☽♎
A very compassionate person. Gifted in the Arts.

56. Sun in Leo/Moon in Scorpio ☉♌/☽♏
A proud person.

57. Sun in Leo/Moon in Sagittarius ☉♌/☽♐
A strongly physical type who needs an energy outlet.

58. Sun in Leo/Moon in Capricorn ☉♌/☽♑
A strongly ambitious person. Success is achieved by dint of caution, determination and good organising ability.

59. Sun in Leo/Moon in Aquarius ☉♌/☽♒
Independent, intuitive and good-natured.

60. Sun in Leo/Moon in Pisces ☉♌/☽♓
Sympathetic; has a 'live and let live' attitude.

61. Sun in Virgo/Moon in Aries ☉♍/☽♈
Active, independent and egotistical. Perceptive, witty and prone to exaggeration. Enjoys arguments and controversy.

62. Sun in Virgo/Moon in Taurus ☉♍/☽♉
Persevering and hard-working. Always willing to listen and to help others.

63. Sun in Virgo/Moon in Gemini ☉♍/☽♊
Needs intellectual stimulus and a career in which the intellect and critical ability are more important than practical abilities. Friendly and hospitable with strong family ties.

64. Sun in Virgo/Moon in Cancer ☉♍/☽♋
Sensitive, perceptive and subtle. Quickly sees through people. Adaptable, hard-working and persevering. Strong family ties.

64i. Sun in Virgo/Moon in Cancer + dominant Mercury ☉♍/☽♋/☿
Has a very persuasive manner.

65. Sun in Virgo/Moon in Leo ☉♍/☽♌
A sensuous, warm person who delights in the grand occasion and enjoys love affairs.

66. Sun in Virgo/Moon in Virgo ☉♍/☽♍
A hard worker who deals admirably with anything requiring precision, accuracy and minute attention to detail. Strong family ties.

67. Sun in Virgo/Moon in Libra ☉♍/☽♎
Ambitious, well-read and knowledgeable. Clear-thinking but inclined to be impatient. Has artistic abilities.

68. Sun in Virgo/Moon in Scorpio ☉♍/☽♏
Has good judgement and critical ability.

69. Sun in Virgo/Moon in Sagittarius ☉♍/☽♐
An enthusiastic communicator; has a vast range of interests.

70. Sun in Virgo/Moon in Capricorn ☉♍/☽♑
Strongly independent. Has a retentive memory.

71. Sun in Virgo/Moon in Aquarius ☉♍/☽♒
An unconventional type with original ideas. Likely to be dependent on a select group of friends.

72. Sun in Virgo/Moon in Pisces ☉♍/☽♓
Enjoys working at anything unusual which involves detail. Prone to states of dissatisfaction and irritableness.

73. Sun in Libra/Moon in Aries ☉♎/☽♈
Has a clever mind. Generally quiet, easy-going and affectionate but can be aggressive, very determined and have a powerful influence over others. Athletic.

74. Sun in Libra/Moon in Taurus ☉♎/☽♉
Sociable and strongly sensuous. Inclined to music and the theatre.

75. Sun in Libra/Moon in Gemini ☉♎/☽♊
A versatile, adaptable, observant person with many interests; has great intellectual energy. Affectionate and faithful. Strong family ties.

76. Sun in Libra/Moon in Cancer ☉♎/☽♋
Very emotional and sensitive but hides real feelings.

77. Sun in Libra/Moon in Leo ☉♎/☽♌
A strongly sensuous person. Powerful emotions lead to intense love affairs.

78. Sun in Libra/Moon in Virgo ☉♎/☽♍
A charming, friendly, intuitive person.

79. Sun in Libra/Moon in Libra ☉♎/☽♎
A charming, affable, sensuous person with artistic abilities.

80. Sun in Libra/Moon in Scorpio ☉♎/☽♏
A very ambitious type, fully aware of own capabilities and with a set goal to aim for. Hard-working, energetic, aggressive and practical. A tough exterior hides a gentle, kind person.

81. Sun in Libra/Moon in Sagittarius ☉♎/☽♐
Imaginative, excitable, quick-witted and knowledgeable.

82. Sun in Libra/Moon in Capricorn ☉♎/☽♑
An ambitious person who should leave home early to avoid family influences. Inclined to music.

83. Sun in Libra/Moon in Aquarius ☉♎/☽♒
Has original ideas and a good memory.

84. Sun in Libra/Moon in Pisces ☉♎/☽♓
If interested enough to be involved in a project will work hard. Sociable.

85. Sun in Scorpio/Moon in Aries ☉♏/☽♈
A very strong personality; self-assertive, positive, courageous with a steely will-power. An independent type; practical, resourceful and coolly efficient. Loves a crisis and likes to put theory into practice to see if it works. Has strong likes and dislikes and is passionate about all things. Anger and jealousy can reach extremes but great self-control is exercised in public.

86. Sun in Scorpio/Moon in Taurus ☉♏/☽♉
Follows a planned course through life. Sociable and likes a good home life.

87. Sun in Scorpio/Moon in Gemini ☉♏/☽♊
Intellectually hard-working. Clever and shrewd.

88. Sun in Scorpio/Moon in Cancer ☉♏/☽♋
Practical, businesslike and positive with a good sense of economy. Becomes quickly emotionally involved with others.

89. Sun in Scorpio/Moon in Leo ☉♏/☽♌
A powerful and impressive personality; commanding, energetic, organising, ambitious and influential. Has a love of power and the grand occasion. Ostentatious, dramatic and arrogant. Has a romantic imagination and enjoys intensely passionate love affairs.

90. Sun in Scorpio/Moon in Virgo ☉♏/☽♍
Self-critical — anything short of perfection is not good enough. Proud and passionate.

91. Sun in Scorpio/Moon in Libra ☉♏/☽♎
Sociable, prophetic and psychic.

92. Sun in Scorpio/Moon in Scorpio ☉♏/☽♏
A strong personality; proud and independent, energetic and inquisitive.

93. Sun in Scorpio/Moon in Sagittarius ☉♏/☽♐
Very hard-working and tends to overdo things both physically and mentally. Has progressive ideas and is busy, enthusiastic and passionate about anything that is of personal interest. Likely to have an awesome temper.

94. Sun in Scorpio/Moon in Capricorn ☉♏/☽♑
Ambitious, shrewd, determined and persevering. Sensual.

95. Sun in Scorpio/Moon in Aquarius ☉♏/☽♒
Original and inventive and prefers to do things own way. Strong will-power and good concentration. Has pronounced likes and dislikes. A loyal friend and a steadfast enemy. Strong family ties.

96. Sun in Scorpio/Moon in Pisces ☉♏/☽♓
Ambitious. Has 'gift of the gab'. Kind, sympathetic and good with children. Inclined to the Occult.

97. Sun in Sagittarius/Moon in Aries ☉♐/☽♈
A loyal person with an impulsive, generous nature. Energetically active. Has a reforming, improving instinct and gets involved with causes, organisations, movements etc., of which could well be the originator. Rebellious and could be extremely aggressive.

98. Sun in Sagittarius/Moon in Taurus ☉♐/☽♉
A conscientious person; loyal, sympathetic and affectionate. Quickly perceptive, imaginative and sensuous. Inclined to music.

99. Sun in Sagittarius/Moon in Gemini ☉♐/☽♊
Quick actions and speech; excitable and generally over-active. Has good judgement and a good memory. Strong family ties.

100. Sun in Sagittarius/Moon in Cancer ☉♐/☽♋
Has powerful imagination and emotions verging on the sensational. Strongly sensuous and artistically gifted. Shrewd with money and property.

101. Sun in Sagittarius/Moon in Leo ☉♐/☽♌
A quick, alert mind and strong intuition. Likes the grand occasion; a passionate person and a compulsive flirt. Inclined to the theatre and politics.

102. Sun in Sagittarius/Moon in Virgo ☉♐/☽♍
Intelligent and articulate.

103. Sun in Sagittarius/Moon in Libra ☉♐/☽♎
An attractive personality. Ambitious, sensuous, artistic and very sociable.

104. Sun in Sagittarius/Moon in Scorpio ☉♐/☽♏
An energetic, hard-working, generous person. Independence, perseverance and endurance are strong qualities.

105. Sun in Sagittarius/Moon in Sagittarius ☉♐/☽♐
An independent, quick-thinking, quick-moving person. A rebellious nature but very sociable and generous.

106. Sun in Sagittarius/Moon in Capricorn ☉♐/☽♑
Ambitious with diverse abilities. Quick-witted. Given to speculative ventures. Has a liking for method and order. Musical. Sensual.

107. Sun in Sagittarius/Moon in Aquarius ☉♐/☽♒
Strongly intuitive. Has a deep interest in psychology, education and scientific research. Tends to overdo things.

108. Sun in Sagittarius/Moon in Pisces ☉♐/☽♓
A restless, anxious person. Very kind, with strong family ties, but has the urge to travel.

109. Sun in Capricorn/Moon in Aries ☉♑/☽♈
A forceful personality; likes to be boss. Independent, determined and ambitious and will work extremely hard to reap personal benefit.

110. Sun in Capricorn/Moon in Taurus ☉♑/☽♉
Practical and determined. Is ambitious for others and will encourage and inspire them to success.

111. Sun in Capricorn/Moon in Gemini ☉♑/☽♊
A deep-thinking person. Has a good memory.

112. Sun in Capricorn/Moon in Cancer ☉♑/☽♋
Very ambitious.

113. Sun in Capricorn/Moon in Leo ☉♑/☽♌
A forceful personality. Ambitious with a talent for speculation. Strong-willed and self-reliant.

114. Sun in Capricorn/Moon in Virgo ☉♑/☽♍
An analytical and logical mind. Method and order are of great importance.

115. Sun in Capricorn/Moon in Libra ☉♑/☽♎
Courteous, kind and dignified. Likes to be appreciated.

116. Sun in Capricorn/Moon in Scorpio ☉♑/☽♏
An independent person who delights in leadership. Positive, determined — a planner and controller. Inclined to materialism.

117. Sun in Capricorn/Moon in Sagittarius ☉♑/☽♐
A speculative mind. Inclined to religion.

118. Sun in Capricorn/Moon in Capricorn ☉♑/☽♑
Strongly independent. A persistent, determined worker.

119. Sun in Capricorn/Moon in Aquarius ☉♑/☽♒
Excellent organising abilities. Achievements are the result of planning and persistence. Perceptive and intuitive.

120. Sun in Capricorn/Moon in Pisces ☉♑/☽♓
A dark horse.

121. Sun in Aquarius/Moon in Aries ☉♒/☽♈
Likes to dominate any situation. Cannot tolerate supervision or opposition and will go to remarkable lengths to get own way. Perceptive and a good judge of character.

122. Sun in Aquarius/Moon in Taurus ☉♒/☽♉
Dislikes change and sees lifestyle and job as long-term. A dependable worker. A very friendly person.

123. Sun in Aquarius/Moon in Gemini ☉♒/☽♊
A studious, intellectual, hard-working person. Needs the opportunity to employ original ideas and talent for attention to detail. Likely to have many acquaintances but few intimate friends.

124. Sun in Aquarius/Moon in Cancer ☉♒/☽♋
Has great tenacity and a good sense of economy. Strong family ties.

125. Sun in Aquarius/Moon in Leo ☉♒/☽♌
A person of dignity and pride; enjoys flattery. Has a fertile imagination which should be given full rein.

126. Sun in Aquarius/Moon in Virgo ☉♒/☽♍
Intellectual, critical and precise.

127. Sun in Aquarius/Moon in Libra ☉♒/☽♎
A sensuous person who likes to make a success of relationships. Strong imagination, perception and intuition.

128. Sun in Aquarius/Moon in Scorpio ☉♒/☽♏
Self-reliant, hard-working, practical and positive.

129. Sun in Aquarius/Moon in Sagittarius ☉♒/☽♐
Physically and mentally alert. Strongly imaginative and sensuous.

130. Sun in Aquarius/Moon in Capricorn ☉♒/☽♑
Ambitious, serious, persevering and responsible. Shrewd and subtle. Takes adversity in stride. Has a good memory.

131. Sun in Aquarius/Moon in Aquarius ☉♒/☽♒
Self-reliant. Quick-witted with original ideas.

132. Sun in Aquarius/Moon in Pisces ☉♒/☽♓
Studious, imaginative and sensuous.

133. Sun in Pisces/Moon in Aries ☉♓/☽♈
Optimistic and positive. Full of ideas and loving detail.

134. Sun in Pisces/Moon in Taurus ☉♓/☽♉
A steady, conscientious worker. Artistic abilities. Strong family ties.

135. Sun in Pisces/Moon in Gemini ☉♓/☽♊
Quick-witted, anxious and restless.

136. Sun in Pisces/Moon in Cancer ☉♓/☽♋
Strong family ties, especially to the mother.

137. Sun in Pisces/Moon in Leo ☉♓/☽♌
Has a generous, warm disposition. Enjoys fine surroundings and has a considerable regard for appearances. Tends to take on more than can be coped with. Strong family ties.

138. Sun in Pisces/Moon in Virgo ☉♓/☽♍
An inspirational person of diverse abilities. Has a good memory. Inclined to opportunism.

139. Sun in Pisces/Moon in Libra ☉♓/☽♎
An inspirational person with a strong imagination. Sensuous with artistic gifts.

140. Sun in Pisces/Moon in Scorpio ☉♓/☽♏
Given to emotional extremes and often misunderstood.

141. Sun in Pisces/Moon in Sagittarius ☉♓/☽♐
Has a penetrating mind. Intellectual and voluble. Busy and hard-working, capable of doing two jobs at once. Is a person of great potential in social or artistic fields and chances should be taken as they arise. Likes changes — jobs, homes, travel — and enjoys the good things in life. Strong family ties.

142. Sun in Pisces/Moon in Capricorn ☉♓/☽♑
An economically-minded, practical type who likes to be involved in public affairs and to plan, organise and invest.

143. Sun in Pisces/Moon in Aquarius ☉♓/☽♒
Likes to be involved in public affairs. Has a good memory and a powerful imagination. Is sociablc but maintains a reserved attitude. Sensuous with musical and artistic abilities. Inclined to the Occult.

144. Sun in Pisces/Moon in Pisces ☉♓/☽♓
Likes to travel, make changes and try new ideas. Likely to be naturally psychic. Artistic.

Dominant Sun

145. Sun in Aries ☉♈
A powerful personality; egotistical, self-assertive, independent, dominating and can be ruthless. Restless, energetic, optimistic, enthusiastic with a great sense of fun. Has a direct approach and always wants quick results; time is precious. Rejects compromise. Hates to feel obligated. Full of initiative and enterprise. Has tremendous will-power. Quick-tempered; will not tolerate unfavourable situations, interference or advice. Takes difficulties in stride; never holds a grudge and forgets failures. Courageous and adventurous with an urge to explore and conquer. A freedom-lover, idealistic, satirical, passionate and violent. Impulsive and extravagant. Has a great need of love.

146. Sun in Taurus ☉♉
A strong, attractive personality. Has an instinctive need for security, comfort and contentment and is naturally materially resourceful. Dislikes changes. A practical type; a planner, determined, patient, persistent but has to be motivated to produce results. Is courageous, enduring, kindly, courteous and sympathetic. Has a keen sense of humour and is peace-loving but can erupt into furious, violent outbursts. Never malicious. Has an intense dislike of injustice. An affectionate, sensual, loyal person; has a tendency to be secretive. Very hospitable with a love of luxury.

147. Sun in Gemini ☉♊
Intelligent, articulate, witty, cunning and persuasive. A good storyteller. Highly-strung, restless, spontaneous, inquisitive and curious about life. An egocentric, complex, self-contradictory person. Likes to be the centre of attraction but is, at the same time, elusive and moody. Has a rebellious streak and dislikes advice. Tends to be materialistic and is businesslike when money is mentioned. Has an eye for good design.

148. Sun in Cancer ☉♋
Highly cmotional and self-pitying, verging on the unstable. A great sulker and worrier with inferiority feelings. Becomes progressively dependent

emotionally and has a draining effect on people. Can be easily swayed but is quick to see deception. Hates secrecy. Is highly sensitive and is easily hurt or offended but rarely shows it. Has an unforgiving nature and never forgets an injustice. Is impressed by the thoughtfulness of others. A sensationalist with a powerful imagination; always open to flattery, enjoys an audience and can go to extremes to attract attention. Strongly influenced by parents and likes to dwell on childhood memories. Enjoys the open air and outdoor life but is essentially a home and family type who dislikes leaving the security of the domestic scene in which he or she is strongly protective, dominating and resourceful. Patriotic and enjoys a good living.

149. Sun in Leo ☉♌

A powerful personality — magnanimous (generous, loyal, broadminded); dominant (a leader, authoritative, protective, confident, independent, decisive, strong-willed); dramatic (extrovert, revelling in personal glory, enthusiastic, reckless); dignified (easily hurt but will never show it, proud, diplomatic, a traditionalist, brave); intolerant (fixed opinions, dogmatic, conceited, suspicious); ambitious (a good intellect, hard-working, optimistic, strongly creative, a good organiser). Politically-minded with great potential in this field. Inclined to homosexuality.

150. Sun in Virgo ☉♍

A hard-working, practical type; methodical, conscientious, efficient, with meticulous attention to detail. Puts plans and ideas into effect. Financial security is important. Intelligent and highly-strung. Critical; analytical of self and others. Not easily taken advantage of — says NO and means it. Studious, patient, observant and caring; does not like to be influenced but tends to be interfering. A worrier and a hypochondriac but has great courage. Is socially charming and elegant but can be a depressing person to know intimately.

151. Sun in Libra ☉♎

Sociable, diplomatic, very charming and romantic. A naturally cooperative type and a consistent worker; can be led but will not be driven. Will become quarrelsome if meets with opposition to ideas. Likes to compare and criticise and tends to be curious about other people's business. Creative and strongly expressive. Inclined to politics.

152. Sun in Scorpio ☉♏

A powerful personality; magnetic and fascinating, ranging from fiery passion to ice-cold self-control. Aggressive, vengeful, jealous and capable of deliberate cruelty. Imaginative, secretive, manipulative and dangerous. Stubborn, determined, persistent; always likes to have the last word. Will not tolerate interference in affairs — will become hard and ruthless. Strongly prejudiced. Never forgets a slight. Sense of humour is often saving grace.

153. Sun in Sagittarius ☉♐

Has a strong urge to build on knowledge. Open-minded, rational and highly intelligent. Very restless; has a freedom impulse and a rebellious instinct. Gets things done for the underdog and the oppressed. Always ready to take a sporting chance. Enjoys hazards. An easy-going, play-boy type, careless of reputation but wary of exploitation. Independent, versatile, cheerful, optimistic, tactless and tends to exaggerate. Has a strong will-power and is sincere and loyal.

154. Sun in Capricorn ☉♑
A strongly ambitious person with definite goals in life. Will make careful and deliberate plans. Practical, thrifty, confident, hard-working, determined and persistent. Financial security is of great importance. Has an excellent memory. Patient, dutiful and loyal. Given to depressive moods.

155. Sun in Aquarius ☉♒
An attractive but complex personality. Unconventional, unpredictable and eccentric. Lives in world of own and is often misunderstood. Progressive and reforming, devoted to causes. Broadminded, knowledgeable and outspoken. Rebellious, tactless and unimpressed by wealth, rank or authority. Not easily deceived. Can be moody but has a good sense of humour.

156. Sun in Pisces ☉♓
Good-natured, undisciplined, unconventional and tends to depend on others to sort out problems. Has a remarkable ability to change personality with chameleon-like versatility. Hypocritical, indecisive and evasive; susceptible to drink, drugs and perversions. Emotional and impressionable, sensitive and sympathetic. Compassionate — a 'mothering' sort of person. Discreetly generous. Reaches extremes of elation and depression and has an explosive temper. A visionary; psychic, poetic and artistic.

Dominant Moon

157. Moon in Aries ☽♈
An unconventional, self-assertive person with a desire for power.

158. Moon in Taurus ☽♉
Strongly protective.

159. Moon in Gemini ☽♊
A very restless mentality in need of constant intellectual stimulation. Articulate. Likes to be fully occupied. Unpredictable; has remarkable changes of personality.

160. Moon in Cancer ☽♋
Hypersensitive and emotional with a powerful imagination. Will go to extremes to gain sympathy from others. Intuitive, protective, shrewd and tenacious. Has a good memory. Likely to suffer from indigestion and ulcers.

161. Moon in Leo ☽♌
Self-confident, cheerful, reliable and loyal — word is bond. A born organiser. Amusing and entertaining but can become overbearing. Has powerful emotions.

162. Moon in Virgo ☽♍
A hard worker and perfectionist. Has a studious, analytical mind, loving detail. Practical and meticulous; a worrying sort with a lot of nervous tension. Has a good memory. Inclined to health foods, etc..

163. Moon in Libra ☽♎
A sociable person, charming and diplomatic but has a changeable manner and can sometimes be very critical. Likes to be appreciated.

164. Moon in Scorpio ☽♏
A powerful personality; highly emotional and intense about all things, enjoying life to the full. Hard-working and determined. A dominant type, liable to manipulate others. Obstinate, moody, possessive and jealous.

165. Moon in Sagittarius ☽♐
A restless, physical, strongly independent person, quick-moving with a sense of urgency about everything. Optimistic, kind, cheerful and voluble. Strongly intuitive.

166. Moon in Capricorn ☽♑
A responsible, cautious person and an ambitious hard worker. Although reserved, does enjoy showing off sometimes.

167. Moon in Aquarius ☽♒
Has original ideas. Inclined to politics.

168. Moon in Pisces ☽♓
Highly imaginative, emotional, impressionable and self-indulgent. Tends to lapse into a fantasy world but has a remarkable ability to change personality with chameleon-like versatility. Restless and voluble. Seductive and poetic.

Dominant Mercury

169. Mercury in Aries ☿♈
Has a powerful imagination and is full of original, progressive ideas; a descriptive narrator. Needs intellectual stimulus. Trustworthy; word is bond.

170. Mercury in Taurus ☿♉
Hates to be contradicted and is angered when unable to understand something.

171. Mercury in Gemini ☿♊
Has a compulsive urge to communicate and will talk to anyone. Is a fluent, persistent talker, a good conversationalist, a highly imaginative storyteller and an accomplished bluffer. Restless, alert and quick-witted. Needs intellectual stimulus. Enjoys arguments and likes to glean information from others. Likely to make protracted telephone calls. A prolific correspondent.

172. Mercury in Cancer ☿♋
An emotional, highly imaginative person. Argumentative. A sympathetic confidante. Has an extraordinary memory.

172i. Mercury in Cancer + Sun in Gemini ☿♋/☉♊
Likely to have radio, television or record-player on virtually all the time.

173. Mercury in Leo ☿♌
Quick-witted and a good bluffer. Communicates well, especially with children. Prone to depressions.

174. Mercury in Virgo ☿♍
Quick-witted, articulate and a good conversationalist. Prone to psychosomatic troubles.

175. Mercury in Libra ☿♎
A sociable person liking friendly discussions. Needs intellectual stimulus. A sympathetic listener.

176. Mercury in Scorpio ☿♏
Once a decision is made will follow it right through. A subtle, cunning mind. Clever at repartee and good at knocking the nail on the head. Rarely fooled by anyone. Enjoys pressing home an advantage. Can be a disruptive influence. A tendency to be secretive and suspicious and prone to bouts of paranoia and depression. Inclined to the Occult.

176i. Mercury in Scorpio + Sun in Scorpio ☿♏/☉♏
Inclined to criminology.

177. Mercury in Sagittarius ☿♐
Versatile, restless, curious about everything and will talk to anyone to learn anything. Voluble, tends to exaggerate and loves to provoke an argument. Quick-witted — makes good, spontaneous decisions. Inclined to serious, deep and extensive study — a profound philosophical thinker. Has a lot of nervous tension and is prone to depression.

178. Mercury in Capricorn ☿♑
Has a mind like a computer — constructive, methodical and logical. Makes detailed plans and has definite goals in life. A great worrier and prone to depression.

179. Mercury in Aquarius ☿♒
An original, progressive thinker. Quick-witted, positive and obsessive; possibly eccentric. Well-informed and has a good memory.

180. Mercury in Pisces ☿♓
A powerfully imaginative person. Has a devious mind and is compulsively voluble. Values quiet moments. Has a deep feeling for music. Psychic.

180i. Dominant Mercury in Pisces + Sun in Pisces ☿♓/☉♓
A deep thinker who expounds at length.

Dominant Venus

181. Venus in Aries ♀♈
Falls in love quickly and violently. An overwhelmingly passionate and possessive lover, aggressively sexed with erotic compulsions. Will go to extremes to please loved one but is likely to be domineering in the home. Needs freedom in a relationship. Prefers courtship to marriage. A friendly, expansive, demonstrative type. Has a self-seeking attitude in relationships but is intensely loyal. Is imaginative, persuasive and often tactless and tends to get involved in unusual situations. A generous enemy. Clothes, possessions and lifestyle are individualistic and highly personal.

181a. Venus in Aries ♀♈
Social qualities: objective; impulsive; energetic; dominant; sensual.
Likely to enjoy: astronomy; athletics; badminton; bird-watching; boxing; chess; climbing; collecting; crosswords; football; golf; intimate relationships; languages; motoring; music; painting; photography; reading; restoration; sailing; shooting; squash; table-tennis; theatre; walking; woodcarving; writing.

182. Venus in Taurus ♀♉
A powerfully sensual lover; intense, possessive and jealous. There is a strong feminine impulse in both sexes. The financial position of the intended partner is of importance. A reliable, charming, warmly affectionate friend, loyal and generous of time and energy. Is a subtle manipulator. A generous host, artistic and sensuous with a natural gift for colour, dress and decoration, is at best in harmonious surroundings and in pleasant company.

182a. Venus in Taurus ♀♉
Social qualities: materialistic; sensational; receptive; possessive.
Likely to enjoy: acting; archaeology; astronomy; athletics; ballet; bird-

watching; bridge; climbing; collecting; cooking; cricket; embroidery; entertaining; family; fishing; food; gambling; gardening; golf; history; hockey; hunting; museums; music; opera; poetry; polo; reading; sculpture; shooting; skiing; squash; table-tennis; tennis; theatre; travel; walking.

183. Venus in Gemini ♀♊

An intellectual rapport is needed in marriage to ensure response, appreciation and support. Gregarious, cheerful, charming, flirtatious, a compulsive tease, loves gossip and avoids the dull and boring. Has a talent for getting people to do things for self. Loves flattery. Matures late and tends to be close to parents.

183a. Venus in Gemini ♀♊

Social qualities: communicative; adaptable; inquiring.
Likely to enjoy: astronomy; bird-watching; cinema; climbing; conversation; electronics; fishing; gardening; golf; jig-saws; languages; painting; railways; reading; riding; rowing; sailing; shooting; table-tennis; tennis; theatre; walking; writing.

184. Venus in Cancer ♀♋

Sensual and strongly protective. Highly emotional nature can give rise to misunderstanding. Family comes first. Has a strong desire for harmony. Likes luxury and comfort. An affectionate, generous, sympathetic, thoughtful, loyal friend. Maintains childhood friendships. Mixes easily. Is easily flattered and deeply hurt if ignored. Needs to have something or someone to care for. Good with children. Inclined to homosexuality.

184a. Venus in Cancer ♀♋

Social qualities: protective; instinctive; receptive.
Likely to enjoy: acting; animals; astronomy; athletics; bowls; bridge; carpentry; cinema; collecting; conversation; cooking; cricket; drawing; embroidery; entertaining; family; fishing; games; gardening; genealogy; golf; history; hunting; intimate relationships; languages; mathematics; music; photography; polo; reading; riding; rugby; sailing; skiing; squash; swimming; table-tennis; tennis; theatre; travel; walking; woodcarving; writing.

185. Venus in Leo ♀♌

Has powerful feelings. Needs a give-and-take partnership. A warm-hearted, friendly person. Tends to be interfering and will organise people, thinking that they would like to do same things as self. Is extravagant and offers generous hospitality to friend and stranger alike. Affectionate and cheerful. Has a strong sense of drama and likes to be the centre of attention; becomes depressed if ignored. Likes best those who are useful and reliable. Adores luxury and must have the best of everything. Good with children.

185a. Venus in Leo ♀♌

Social qualities: egotistical.
Likely to enjoy: acting; architecture; astronomy; athletics; camping; chess; collecting; dancing; family; fishing; flying; football; gambling; games; gardening; golf; history; intimate relationships; languages; model-making; music; painting; photography; railways; riding; rowing; rugby; sailing; shooting; singing; skiing; squash; tennis; theatre; travel; walking; woodcarving.

186. Venus in Virgo ♀♍
A very caring person; is always willing to help others. A perfectionist, has excellent taste and is always careful to get value for money. Inclined to homosexuality.

186a. Venus in Virgo ♀♍
Social qualities: critical; disciplined; communicative; independent.
Likely to enjoy: animals; athletics; bee-keeping; bowls; bridge; calligraphy; chess; cricket; crosswords; cycling; DIY; electronics; fishing; flying; games; gardening; golf; handicrafts; history; keep-fit; motoring; music; opera; painting; photography; quizzes; reading; shooting; skiing; squash; table-tennis; travel; walking.

187. Venus in Libra ♀♎
Needs a marriage of minds in a partnership and must have full give and take. Lack of harmony causes debility and animosity. The partner should have a strong personality. A charming person, sociable and easy to be with but expects full response to anything done for others. Makes a bad enemy. Loves luxury and is extravagant. Delights in attracting people and always creates a relaxing atmosphere; an excellent host. Should watch health, especially with regard to food and drink.

187a. Venus in Libra ♀♎
Social qualities: friendly.
Likely to enjoy: cultural activities — musical, artistic, creative; archery; athletics; bird-watching; bridge; climbing; fishing; flying; gardening; intimate relationships; languages; poetry; rugby; sailing; tennis; travel.

188. Venus in Scorpio ♀♏
A love-at-first-sight person. Intense, passionate, strongly sexual and erotic. Must never be deceived. Food and drink are emotional compensations. A very attractive personality; exciting and intense, enjoying everything. Likes good company but tends to be demanding of others. A good friend and a bad enemy.

188a. Venus in Scorpio ♀♏
Social qualities: sharing; sensual.
Likely to enjoy: archaeology; bird-watching; bowls; collecting; cricket; cycling; drinking; fishing; football; gambling; golf; intimate relationships; museums; the Occult; opera; reading; sailing; shooting; tennis; theatre; travel; walking.

189. Venus in Sagittarius ♀♐
An ardent, demonstrative lover. Needs intellectual rapport and freedom in a relationship. Cannot tolerate jealousy or possessiveness. Always interested in people's progress in life. A compulsive gossip but is a good, loyal friend.

189a. Venus in Sagittarius ♀♐
Social qualities: communicative; free.
Likely to enjoy: acting; animal breeding; camping; chess; climbing; collecting; cooking; DIY; embroidery; flying; football; gambling; history; intimate relationships; keep-fit; motoring; music; opera; photography; railways; reading; swimming; theatre; travel; walking; woodcarving.

190. Venus in Capricorn ♀♑
Flirtatious but faithful and protective in a relationship. Has a strong sense of duty. Has a compulsion to influence others in some way and can be interfering. Will never forget a slight. Makes a bitter enemy. A charming

guest and an excellent host. Has eccentric tastes. Inclined to social climbing.

190a. Venus in Capricorn ♀♑

Social qualities: responsible; self-sufficient.

Likely to enjoy: animals; ballet; bowls; climbing; collecting; crosswords; electronics; flying; gardening; genealogy; golf; history; music; preservation; reading; sailing; sculpture; skiing; walking.

191. Venus in Aquarius ♀♒

An attractive personality; friendly and unconventional. Has a caring nature and will do utmost to help any friend in need.

191a. Venus in Aquarius ♀♒

Social qualities: detached; unconventional.

Likely to enjoy: acting; athletics; beachcombing; bowls; chess; cooking; cricket; cycling; DIY; embroidery; entertaining; fishing; flying; football; gambling; gardening; golf; group activities; history; hunting; motoring; music; the Occult; photography; polo; preservation; reading; riding; rugby; sailing; shooting; singing; snooker; squash; swimming; table-tennis; tennis; travel; walking.

192. Venus in Pisces ♀♓

Is deeply emotional, needs a lot of affection and easily becomes involved in a relationship. Needs a partner with similar ideas to own. Very artistic and needs an expressive outlet in the arts. Gifted in music and painting. Likely to be psychic.

192a. Venus in Pisces ♀♓

Social qualities: sharing; excitable.

Likely to enjoy: acting; amateur radio; animals; archaeology; camping; canoeing; chess; cinema; collecting; cooking; cricket; cycling; drinking; entertaining; fishing; gardening; genealogy; golf; music; opera; painting; photography; poetry; polo; reading; rowing; sailing; shooting; skiing; squash; swimming; theatre; travel; zoos.

Dominant Mars

193. Mars in Aries ♂♈

A competitive, enterprising person. Enjoys a challenge and likes to explore untried ground in all spheres of personal interest. Needs to use initiative; likes to be in charge and prefers to control own career. Dislikes following in another's footsteps. Likes a busy atmosphere but dislikes routine. A natural worker; gets a lot done and has the capacity for getting a great deal out of others. Expects high standards. Must have freedom in work to be efficient and reliable; is likely to walk out of a job if ordered about. Courageous and daring. Has a lot of nervous, physical and mental energy. Indulges in considerable mental activity. Likely to have headaches and indigestion.

193a. Mars in Aries ♂♈

Career qualities: enterprising; competitive; unconventional; industrious; efficient. (Better suited to self-employment/freelancework.)

Suitable careers: actor; architect; builder; butcher; dentist; designer; doctor; explorer; faith healer; film director; fireman; historian; mechanical engineer; painter; philosopher; physiotherapist; property dealer; psychiatrist; psychologist; researcher; soldier; sportsman; surgeon; surveyor; writer.

194. Mars in Taurus ♂ ♉
A conscientious hard worker; determined, aggressive, persistent and loyal. Has a steely will-power and endurance. Ambitious and persevering. Believes in quality rather than quantity. Likes to work within a framework of rules and dislikes intensely to have a routine disrupted. Likes to be needed and to be approved of. Gives generous encouragement to others. Can be vengeful and have an uncontrollable temper.

194a. Mars in Taurus ♂ ♉
Career qualities: trustworthy; practical; artistic; patient; persevering. (Best when working alone within organisation.)
Suitable careers: accountant; actor; anthropologist; antique dealer; architect; art dealer; auctioneer; banker; beautician; builder; caterer; civil servant; craftsman; dancer; designer; economist; farmer; gardener; geologist; guardian; historian; hotelier; interviewer; musician; nurse; overseer; painter; photographer; physicist; property dealer; sculptor; singer; sportsman; surveyor; vet.

195. Mars in Gemini ♂ ♊
An inquiring type, impatient and restless. Has compulsion to communicate; an instinct for language, a flair for writing, energetically talkative. Busy and alert; is motivated by more than one thing at a time and is unlikely to miss opportunities. Hates to see others idle. Likes to travel and make new personal contacts. Has an erratic way of working but is hard-working if deeply interested in a project. Lives on nerves and is liable to panic; anything confusing will cause debility. Pressure of work can cause breakdowns. Needs plenty of sleep and a light diet.

195a. Mars in Gemini ♂ ♊
Career qualities: intellectual; inquiring. (Non-conformist; better suited to freelance work.)
Suitable careers: accountant; actor; advertising agent; architect; astronomer; broadcaster; chemist; computer operator; craftsman; diplomat; driver; electrical engineer; interpreter; interviewer; journalist; navigator; optician; psychologist; publisher; radiologist; reporter; retail trader; soldier; solicitor; teacher; writer; zoologist.

196. Mars in Cancer ♂ ♋
Ambitious, tenacious and financially shrewd. Will always finish what is begun. Has an excellent memory. Highly emotional nature causes indigestion and sometimes breakdowns.

196a. Mars in Cancer ♂ ♋
Career qualities: shrewd; constructive. (Best to work alone within framework.)
Suitable careers: actor; airman; anthropologist; antique dealer; archaeologist; architect; art dealer; carpenter; caterer; chemist; critic; curator; designer; diplomat; doctor; economist; editor; fisherman; gardener; historian; hotelier; housekeeper; journalist; mathematician; nanny; nurse; obstetrician; overseer; pathologist; philosopher; priest; property dealer; psychologist; researcher; sailor; soldier; solicitor; sportsman; surgeon; teacher; vet.; zoologist.

197. Mars in Leo ♂ ♌
Hard-working, enthusiastic, competitive and ambitious. An inspiring person; has a strong sense of purpose and becomes deeply involved in work. Likes to be boss. Has great organising ability, a talent for publicity

and the ability to put ideas into practice. Is very good at deputing work and giving clear, effective orders. Always gives of best and expects the same of others. A champion of good working conditions. Professional and responsible.

197a. Mars in Leo ♂ ♌

Career qualities: artistic; professional; leadership. (Work dominates life-style.)

Suitable careers: accountant; actor; airman; architect; art dealer; banker; dancer; dentist; economist; entertainer; film director; interviewer; journalist; musician; philosopher; photographer; politician; publisher; researcher; social worker; solicitor; sportsman; teacher; vet.

198. Mars in Virgo ♂ ♍

A dedicated, loyal hard worker who likes routine, facts, formulae, discipline, detail, precision and analysis. A perfectionist who becomes absorbed in work, giving willingly of time and energy to the point of fatigue. In caring for others is constantly active and rarely relaxing, extremely practical, systematic and diligent. Will not be taken advantage of, resents any lack of cooperation and expects everyone to pull their weight. Tendency to worry causes tension.

198a. Mars in Virgo ♂ ♍

Career qualities: analytical; enduring. (Job must offer security.)

Suitable careers: accountant; actor; airman; analyst; architect; astronomer; computer operator; craftsman; critic; dietician; economist; editor; engineer; farmer; interviewer; journalist; mathematician; nurse; optician; overseer; psychologist; reporter; retail trader; secretary; singer; social worker; solicitor; teacher; writer.

199. Mars in Libra ♂ ♎

When fully involved with a project, will apply the concentration and intense, sustained diligence of the perfectionist. Very sociable — needs a congenial atmosphere and contact with people. Has a strong sense of social duty and is deeply interested in anything to do with the human factor. Has leadership qualities for teamwork in social activities and public affairs. A generally patient, courteous, tactful person but can be quarrelsome.

199a. Mars in Libra ♂ ♎

Career qualities: friendly; caring. (Works best in partnership.)

Suitable careers: actor; antique dealer; architect; art dealer; astronomer; auctioneer; beautician; caterer; chemist; critic; designer; diplomat; musician; nurse; painter; photographer; physicist; poet; politician; researcher; singer; social worker; soldier; solicitor; sportsman; valuer; writer.

200. Mars in Scorpio ♂ ♏

An aggressive, dynamic, determined approach to work. Has a strong sense of purpose. Does nothing by half and goes all out to achieve success for self and others. Will work on something until finished and will expect immediate reaction from others. Has powerful energy and likes rapid progress but tends to sap endurance and stamina by over-working. Persistent, quick, accurately observant. Has a jealous nature. Inclined to sado-masochism.

200a. Mars in Scorpio ♂ ♏

Career qualities: commitment. (Work must be absorbing with scope for advancement.)

Suitable careers: analyst; archaeologist; beautician; builder; butcher; caterer; criminologist; critic; designer; detective; diplomat; doctor; explorer; faith healer; mechanical engineer; occultist; pathologist; researcher; sculptor; singer; soldier; sportsman; surgeon.

201. Mars in Sagittarius ♂ ♐
An ambitious person of great physical and mental energy with an adventurous, exploring spirit. An indefatigable hard worker who loves a challenge. Outspoken and questions everything. Must have freedom in work. A highly strung person liable to nervous breakdowns and can be dangerously aggressive.

201a. Mars in Sagittarius ♂ ♐
Career qualities: versatile; intellectual; cooperative; athletic. (Needs scope for positive expression.)
Suitable careers: advertising agent; animal breeder; banker; barrister; dancer; doctor; explorer; farmer; insurer; interpreter; mechanical engineer; musician; philosopher; politician; priest; psychiatrist; publisher; retail trader; soldier; sportsman; surgeon; teacher; vet.

202. Mars in Capricorn ♂ ♑
An ambitious person. A highly organised planner with a desire for power and authority. Has determination and self-discipline and will work hard for self-improvement. Likes routine work and has the persistence, concentration and endurance to do monotonous hard work. Is dutiful and responsible and never takes short cuts. Sticks to a decision and is very conscientious. Expects maximum effort from others.

202a. Mars in Capricorn ♂ ♑
Career qualities: patient; responsible; enduring; dutiful; methodical. (Needs a job which offers security.)
Suitable careers: accountant; airman; anthropologist; archaeologist; banker; barrister; builder; civil servant; dentist; diplomat; doctor; farmer; geologist; masseur; mechanical engineer; musician; osteopath; pathologist; photographer; plumber; politician; property dealer; radiologist; researcher; soldier.

203. Mars in Aquarius ♂ ♒
Finds it difficult to work with other people's ideas. Prefers to use originality and independence towards a definite objective and will work long hours with great determination and will-power. Has a strong sense of duty and is seemingly resistant to fatigue. Observant and has quick reactions. Is interested in freedom, reform, progress, social rights, humane factors and scientific matters. Dislikes anything underhand. Inclined to homosexuality.

203a. Mars in Aquarius ♂ ♒
Career qualities: intuitive; progressive; original; reformative. (Needs an exciting job with scope for advancement.)
Suitable careers: actor; airman; archaeologist; architect; astronomer; broadcaster; builder; dancer; economist; electrical engineer; explorer; faith healer; farmer; inventor; masseur; mechanical engineer; musician; photographer; pilot; psychologist; publisher; social worker; writer.

204. Mars in Pisces ♂ ♓
Is versatile and has artistic instincts and creative talent. Is likely to prefer to work alone. Has a genuine concern for those in need. Prone to emotional disturbances and stress.

204a. Mars in Pisces ♂ ♓
Career qualities: intuitive; creative; altruistic. (At best in creative work where there is no pressure.)
Suitable careers: actor; archaeologist; brewer; dancer; designer; explorer; medium; musician; occultist; painter; photographer; poet; priest; researcher; retail trader; sailor; writer.

Dominant Jupiter

205. Jupiter in Aries ♃ ♈
Ambitious and positive with a strongly personal attitude to life. Enjoys intellectual involvement and competitive physical activity. Enthusiastic and generous.

206. Jupiter in Taurus ♃ ♉
Has a strong sense of self-preservation and is a great believer in financial security; will accumulate and save money. Life centres on possessions.

207. Jupiter in Gemini ♃ ♊
An alert, clever mentality. Up-to-date with news and ideas. Constantly talking, arguing and debating. Versatile, artful, entertaining and persuasive.

208. Jupiter in Cancer ♃ ♋
Emotional, imaginative, intuitive.

209. Jupiter in Leo ♃ ♌
A good organiser with talent for putting ideas into practice. Has intellectual and artistic interests.

210. Jupiter in Virgo ♃ ♍
Ambitious, conscientious and highly efficient. Has constant desire to improve knowledge and progress.

211. Jupiter in Libra ♃ ♎
A champion of fair play and justice.

212. Jupiter in Scorpio ♃ ♏
A sensual person with deep feelings. Will overcome adversities and start anew with no trouble at all. Has analytical skill and strong will-power and will go to the root of any problem to sort it out. Tends to overdo things.

213. Jupiter in Sagittarius ♃ ♐
Superstitious.

214. Jupiter in Capricorn ♃ ♑
Likely to be a trend-setter.

215. Jupiter in Aquarius ♃ ♒
Egocentric. Is attracted to causes of the reformative, progressive type. Inclined to the Occult.

216. Jupiter in Pisces ♃ ♓
Should avoid drugs and alcohol.

Dominant Saturn

217. Saturn in Aries ♄ ♈
Self-reliant. Prone to headaches and depression. Inclined to sadism.

218. Saturn in Taurus ♄ ♉
Is a naturally kind person.

219. Saturn in Gemini ♄ ♊
Intellectual. Prone to depression and bouts of isolation.

220. Saturn in Cancer ♄ ♋
Will always see a job through to the finish. Has a strong mother influence. Inclined to homosexuality.

221. Saturn in Leo ♄ ♌
Self-assured, authoritative with excellent organising ability. Prone to bouts of hypochondria, and megalomania.

222. Saturn in Virgo ♄ ♍
A perfectionist who is a conscientious hard worker, devoted to duty. Prefers to work alone. Obsessed with detail and is demanding and critical of others.

223. Saturn in Libra ♄ ♎
A kind and conscientious person. Any lack of cooperation in others causes frustration, disappointment and depression.

224. Saturn in Scorpio ♄ ♏
Needs emotional outlets. Inclined to homosexuality.

225. Saturn in Sagittarius ♄ ♐
Intellectual and studious.

226. Saturn in Capricorn ♄ ♑
Practical and persevering. Gets as much as possible out of life.

227. Saturn in Aquarius ♄ ♒
Has a responsible attitude towards people but tends to have extreme opinions.

228. Saturn in Pisces ♄ ♓
Should leave home early.

Dominant Uranus

229. Uranus in Aries ♅ ♈
Is always firmly convinced that self is right and is determined to have own way at any cost. Will not tolerate opposition.

230. Uranus in Taurus ♅ ♉
Has very strong independence, determination and will-power. Will make sudden changes irrespective of effect on others. Restless.

231. Uranus in Gemini ♅ ♊
An unconventional person with an original, inquisitive, inventive mind and persuasive manner. Will not let anything stand in way of chance to make progress.

232. Uranus in Cancer ♅ ♋
Eccentric.

233. Uranus in Leo ♅ ♌
Egotistical and individualistic. Freedom is of great importance.

234. Uranus in Virgo ♅ ♍
Intellectual. Eccentric ideas about health. Likely to be attracted to computers.

235. Uranus in Libra ♅ ♎
A sociable, charming person but too independent, self-willed and restless to keep relationships on an even keel.

236. Uranus in Scorpio ♅♏
Strongly emotional.

237. Uranus in Sagittarius ♅♐
Inclined to research. Prone to depression.

238. Uranus to Capricorn ♅♑
Strongly ambitious.

239. Uranus in Aquarius ♅♒
An original, inventive mind. Strong-willed and independent, intensely disliking any form of restriction.

240. Uranus in Pisces ♅♓
A strongly intuitive person. Fluctuating emotions cause inner tension. Inclined to the Occult.

Dominant Neptune

241. Neptune in Aries ♆♈
Highly imaginative and can be disruptive. Prone to headaches.

242. Neptune in Taurus ♆♉
Likely to be careless about possessions. Should avoid drink.

243. Neptune in Gemini ♆♊
Full of curiosity and loves to gossip.

244. Neptune in Cancer ♆♋
Sentimental.

245. Neptune in Leo. ♆♌
Egotistical.

246. Neptune in Virgo ♆♍
Hypercritical, analytical and discriminating. Is a worrier prone to stomach disorders. Easily offended. Likely to be psychic.

247. Neptune in Libra ♆♎
Attracted to drugs.

247i. Neptune in Libra + Sun in Libra ♆♎/☉♎
Easily attracted to people, drugs, opting out.

248. Neptune in Scorpio ♆♏
A subtle manipulator, sensitive, perceptive and highly sexed.

249. Neptune in Sagittarius ♆♐
Prone to mental disorders.

250. Neptune in Capricorn ♆♑
Has a liking for intrigue and schemes. A strong practical drive can turn dreams into reality.

251. Neptune in Aquarius. ♆♒
Independent and philanthropic.

252. Neptune in Pisces ♆♓
Inspirational, spiritual and mystical.

Dominant Pluto

253. Pluto in Gemini ♇♊
A restless, scientific mind full of inventive ideas.

254. Pluto in Cancer ♇ ♋
Easily takes offence and gives vent to petty arguments and complaints.

255. Pluto in Leo ♇ ♌
An authoritative type with a love of power. Has creative talent and dramatic self-expression. Inclined to sadism.

256. Pluto in Virgo ♇ ♍
Inquisitive and analytical. Given to food fads. Inclined to psychosomatic troubles.

257. Pluto in Libra ♇ ♎
Has a good business head. Inclined to homosexuality.

Dominant Fire/Air Signs

258. Five or more planets in Fire/Air signs
Very active, always restless. Becomes intensely involved in work and tends to overdo things to the point of exhaustion.

259. Five or more planets in Earth/Water signs
Life centres on finance, security and possessions.

Lack of Water, Earth, Fire or Air Signs

260. No Earth signs
Neglects health.

261. No Water signs
A career type.

262. No Fire signs
Subject to acute tension and psychosomatic complaints.

263. No Air signs
Easily provoked.

Five or More Planets in One Sign (also used with dominant Sun signs)

264. Five or more planets in Aries
Has quick enthusiasm, unnerving directness and great courage. Likes to dominate a situation. Tends to overdo things. Prone to nervous troubles, severe headaches, depression, indigestion, neuralgia, sunstroke, toothache, claustrophobia. Should eat: raw tomatoes, beetroot, celery, apples, lemons, grapefruit.

265. Five or more planets in Taurus
Self-centred but warmly hospitable, loyal and generous to favourites. Inclination to self-indulgence in food, drink and sex can cause health problems. Should always keep occupied and not succumb to laziness. Prone to jaundice, melancholia, throat and ear troubles, kidney and liver complaints, wens, rheumatism, headaches, lumbar and womb troubles. Should eat: spinach, celery, radishes, strawberries.

266. Five or more planets in Gemini
Clever with words. An opportunist. A great worrier. Health is likely to break down under strain. Needs light diet, plenty of sleep and fresh air. Prone to bronchial complaints, nervous troubles (asthma, eczema), rheumatism, exhaustion. Should eat: turnips, brussels sprouts, cauliflower, kale, watercress, pineapple, lettuce.

267. Five or more planets in Cancer
Emotional and of a nervous disposition. Powerfully protective. Dominates the domestic scene. Health gives way under strain. Health fluctuates; should have careful diet and plenty of fresh air and exercise. Emotional nature and imagination can cause health breakdowns. Prone to varicose veins, haemorrhoids, dropsy, dental and eye troubles, breast and stomach troubles, coughs and indigestion. Should eat: cabbage, prunes, onions, sesame seeds.

268. Five or more planets in Leo
A very strong ego. Emotional discord, wounded vanity, lack of love, praise or harmonious surroundings can cause health breakdowns. Depression will debilitate the system. Should slow up in middle age and should keep an eye on the blood condition. Prone to nervous troubles, neuralgia, heart strain, eye troubles, back troubles. Should eat: plums, peas, oranges, wheat, bran, oats, cocoa.

269. Five or more planets in Virgo
Analytical — likes to cover every point of a situation. Critical, practical and conscientious. Needs congenial surroundings; change of scene always stimulates. Plenty of fresh air and careful diet (possibly vegetarian). Should try to avoid drugs. Prone to skin infections, nervous troubles, headaches, ulcers, indigestion, pneumonia, colds, coughs, bronchial, stomach and bowel troubles. Should eat: asparagus, figs, lemons, dates, raw tomatoes, beetroot, celery, apples, grapefruit.

270. Five or more planets in Libra
A compulsive flirt. Quickly sympathetic and caring. Should watch intake of food and drink. Needs exercise. Inharmonious situations can cause health problems. When below par in any way best remedy is rest and careful diet. Prone to digestive problems, jaundice, troubles with the back, kidneys, bladder and sometimes the nerves. Eye troubles. Should eat spinach, celery, radishes, strawberries.

271. Five or more planets in Scorpio
Secretive, subtle and fascinating. When ill, is totally ill and desires all remedies however drastic. Sexual frustration can lead to violence. Prone to boils, ulcers, abscesses, varicose veins, kidney, liver and bladder troubles, haemorrhoids, nose, dental and eye troubles. Headaches, blood pressure. Tendency to genital troubles. Should eat: oranges, chives, raisins, leeks, egg yolks, rye bread, cabbage, prunes, onions, sesame seeds.

272. Five or more planets in Sagittarius
Unconventional, free and rebellious. Should keep off drink. Is highly strung and needs mental and physical exercise but should take care not to overdo it. Problems can cause weight increase. Prone to hair, nail and skin troubles, headaches, sciatica, rheumatism, fevers, troubles with heart, lungs, nerves, lumbar region and thighs. Likely to suffer from claustrophobia. Should eat: parsnips, cucumbers, rice, horseradish, barley, asparagus.

273. Five or more planets in Capricorn
Self-disciplined, ambitious, persistent and diplomatic. Should keep the system regular and avoid alcohol. Worry and suppressed emotions cause digestive upsets and skin rashes. A change of air is beneficial to any form of discontent but, at such times, should keep in company of others and not be alone. Prone to anaemia, deafness, chilblains, varicose veins, rheu-

matism, haemorrhoids, dental and eye troubles, boils, ulcers, abscesses. Should eat: cabbage, prunes, onions, sesame seeds, oranges, chives, raisins, leeks, egg yolk, rye bread.

274. Five or more planets in Aquarius
Unpredictable, unconventional, humanitarian. Tends to loneliness, despondency and depression — needs friendship, plenty of warmth, light, fresh air and exercise. Tendency to sexual perversions and sudden nervous breakdowns. Prone to dropsy, catarrh, diarrhoea, jaundice, cramps, nerves and troubles with ankles and eyes. Should eat: pomegranates, spinach, celery, radishes, strawberries.

275. Five or more planets in Pisces
Secretive, hypocritical and indecisive. Sympathetic and very kind. Likely to suffer from emotional disturbances and deep-rooted neuroses. Should avoid alcohol and drugs. Needs plenty of fresh air, exercise and warmth. Prone to low blood pressure, fevers, haemorrhages, anaemia, gastric troubles, boils, ulcers, rheumatism, foot and bowel troubles, inflammation of the eyes. Should eat: raw green leafy vegetables, raw root vegetables, raisins, dates, cereals.

Seven or More Planets in Earth, Water, Fire or Air Signs

276. Seven or more planets in Earth signs
Practical and tenacious.

277. Seven or more planets in Water signs
Highly emotional and strongly intuitive.

278. Seven or more planets in Fire signs
Fanatical.

279. Seven or more planets in Air signs
Intellectual and communicative. An opportunist.

Amalgamated Dominant Signs

280a. Aries/Taurus ♈/♉
Social qualities: impulsive; energetic; dominant.
Likely to enjoy: astronomy; athletics; bird-watching; climbing; collecting; golf; music; reading; shooting; squash; table-tennis; theatre; walking.
Career qualities: enterprising; competitive; unconventional; trustworthy; practical; persevering; industrious; efficient.
Suitable careers: actor; architect; builder; designer; historian; painter; property dealer; surveyor; sportsman.

281a. Aries/Gemini ♈/♊
Social qualities: impulsive; energetic; adaptable.
Likely to enjoy: astronomy; bird-watching; cinema; climbing; golf; languages; painting; reading; sailing; shooting; table-tennis; theatre; walking; writing.
Career qualities: enterprising; competitive; unconventional; inquiring; industrious; efficient.
Suitable careers: actor; architect; doctor; engineer; psychologist; soldier; writer.

282a. Aries/Cancer ♈/♋
Social qualities: impulsive; energetic; dominant; instinctive.
Likely to enjoy: astronomy; athletics; cinema; collecting; golf; intimate

relationships; language; music; photography; reading; sailing; squash; table-tennis; theatre; walking; woodcarving; writing.
Career qualities: enterprising; competitive; unconventional; constructive; industrious; efficient.
Suitable careers: actor; architect; designer; doctor; historian; philosopher; property dealer; psychologist; researcher; soldier; sportsman; surgeon.

283a. Aries/Leo ♈/♌
Social qualities: energetic; egotistical.
Likely to enjoy: astronomy; athletics; chess; collecting; football; intimate relationships; languages; music; painting; sailing; shooting; squash; theatre; woodcarving; walking.
Career qualities: enterprising; competitive; unconventional; leadership; professional; principled; industrious; efficient.
Suitable careers: actor; architect; dentist; film director; philosopher; researcher; sportsman.

284a. Aries/Virgo ♈/♍
Social qualities: impulsive; energetic; dominant; critical.
Likely to enjoy: athletics; chess; crosswords; golf; motoring; music; painting; photography; reading; shooting; squash; table-tennis; walking.
Career qualities: enterprising; competitive; unconventional; analytical; industrious; efficient.
Suitable careers: actor; architect; doctor; engineer; psychologist; surgeon; writer.

285a. Aries/Libra ♈/♎
Social qualities: impulsive; energetic; dominant; friendly.
Likely to enjoy: athletics; bird-watching; climbing; intimate relationships; languages; sailing.
Career qualities: enterprising; competitive; unconventional; industrious; friendly; efficient.
Suitable careers: actor; architect; designer; painter; researcher; soldier; sportsman; writer.

286a. Aries/Scorpio ♈/♏
Social qualities: impulsive; energetic; dominant.
Likely to enjoy: bird-watching; collecting; football; golf; intimate relationships; reading; sailing; shooting; theatre; walking.
Career qualities: enterprising; competitive; unconventional; committed; industrious; efficient.
Suitable careers: builder; butcher; designer; doctor; explorer; faith healer; fireman; mechanical engineer; physiotherapist; policeman; psychologist; researcher; soldier; sportsman; surgeon.

287a. Aries/Sagittarius ♈/♐
Social qualities: impulsive; energetic; dominant.
Likely to enjoy: chess; collecting; football; intimate relationships; motoring; music; photography; reading; theatre; walking; woodcarving.
Career qualities: enterprising; competitive; unconventional; ambitious; versatile; industrious; efficient; cooperative; athletic.
Suitable careers: doctor; explorer; mechanical engineer; philosopher; psychiatrist; soldier; sportsman; surgeon.

288a. Aries/Capricorn ♈/♑
Social qualities: energetic; dominant; responsible.

Likely to enjoy: crosswords; golf; intimate relationships; walking.
Career qualities: enterprising; competitive; dutiful; methodical; industrious; efficient.
Suitable careers: builder; dentist; doctor; engineer; explorer; property dealer; researcher; soldier.

289a. Aries/Aquarius ♈/♒
Social qualities: impulsive; energetic; dominant; unconventional.
Likely to enjoy: athletics; chess; golf; group activities; motoring; music; photography; reading; sailing; shooting; squash; table-tennis; walking.
Career qualities: enterprising; competitive; unconventional; progressive; original; reformative; industrious; efficient.
Suitable careers: actor, architect; builder; engineer; explorer; faith healer; psychologist; writer.

290a. Aries/Pisces ♈/♓
Social qualities: impulsive; energetic; dominant; excitable.
Likely to enjoy: chess; cinema; collecting; golf; music; painting; photography; reading; sailing; shooting; squash; theatre.
Career qualities: enterprising; competitive; altruistic; imaginative; industrious; efficient.
Suitable careers: actor; designer; doctor; explorer; painter; policeman; psychiatrist; psychologist; researcher; soldier; writer.

291a. Taurus/Gemini ♉/♊
Social qualities: adaptable.
Likely to enjoy: astronomy; bird-watching; climbing; fishing; gardening; golf; reading; table-tennis; tennis; theatre; travel; walking.
Career qualities: trustworthy; practical; persevering; inquiring.
Suitable careers: accountant; actor; architect; craftsman; interviewer; scientist.

292a. Taurus/Cancer ♉/♋
Social qualities: adaptable; instinctive.
Likely to enjoy: acting; astronomy; athletics; bridge; collecting; cooking; cricket; embroidery; entertaining; family; fishing; gardening; golf; hunting; music; polo; reading; skiing; squash; table-tennis; theatre; travel; walking.
Career qualities: trustworthy; practical; persevering; shrewd; constructive; economical.
Suitable careers: actor; anthropologist; antique dealer; architect; art dealer; caterer; designer; economist; gardener; historian; hotelier; nurse; overseer; property dealer; scientist; sportsman; vet.

293a. Taurus/Leo ♉/♌
Social qualities: adaptable; egotistical.
Likely to enjoy: acting; astronomy; athletics; collecting; family; gambling; gardening; golf; music; shooting; skiing; squash; tennis; theatre; travel; walking.
Career qualities: trustworthy; practical; artistic; leadership; professional; persevering.
Suitable careers: accountant; actor; architect; art dealer; banker; dancer; economist; interviewer; musician; organiser; photographer; sportsman; vet.

294a. Taurus/Virgo ♉/♍
Social qualities: critical.
Likely to enjoy: athletics; bridge; cricket; fishing; gardening; golf; music; opera; reading; shooting; skiing; squash; table-tennis; travel; walking.
Career qualities: trustworthy; practical; persevering; analytical.
Suitable careers: accountant; actor; architect; craftsman; doctor; economist; farmer; interviewer; nurse; overseer; scientist; singer.

295a. Taurus/Libra ♉/♎
Social qualities: friendly.
Likely to enjoy: athletics; bird-watching; bridge; climbing; fishing; gardening; poetry; tennis; travel.
Career qualities: trustworthy; practical; persevering; friendly.
Suitable careers: actor; antique dealer; architect; art dealer; auctioneer; beautician; caterer; designer; musician; nurse; painter; photographer; physicist; singer; sportsman.

296a. Taurus/Scorpio ♉/♏
Social qualities: sensational.
Likely to enjoy: archaeology; bird-watching; collecting; cricket; gambling; golf; museums; opera; reading; shooting; tennis; theatre; travel; walking.
Career qualities: trustworthy; practical; committed.
Suitable careers: beautician; builder; caterer; designer; historian; physicist; sculptor; singer; sportsman.

297a. Taurus/Sagittarius ♉/♐
Social qualities: reckless.
Likely to enjoy: acting; bridge; climbing; collecting; cooking; embroidery; gambling; music, opera; reading; travel; theatre; walking.
Career qualities: trustworthy; practical; persevering; ambitious; versatile; cooperative; athletic.
Suitable careers: banker; dancer; farmer; musician; sportsman; vet.

298a. Taurus/Capricorn ♉/♑
Social qualities: responsible.
Likely to enjoy: ballet; climbing; collecting; gardening; golf; music; reading; sculpture; skiing; walking.
Career qualities: trustworthy; practical; patient; persevering; dutiful; methodical.
Suitable careers: accountant; anthropologist; banker; builder; civil servant; farmer; geologist; musician; photographer; property dealer;

299a. Taurus/Aquarius ♉/♒
Social qualities: unconventional.
Likely to enjoy: acting; archaeology; athletics; cooking; cricket; embroidery; entertaining; fishing; gambling; gardening; golf; group activities; hunting; music; polo; reading; shooting; squash; table-tennis; tennis; travel; walking.
Career qualities: trustworthy; practical; persevering; progressive; original; reformative.
Suitable careers: actor; architect; builder; dancer; economist; farmer; musician; photographer; scientist; vet.

300a. Taurus/Pisces ♉/♓
Social qualities: unselfish; excitable.

Likely to enjoy: archaeology; cooking; dramatics; entertaining; fishing; golf; music; painting; poetry; reading; shooting; skiing; squash; theatre; travel.
Career qualities: trustworthy; persevering; practical; altruistic; imaginative.
Suitable careers: actor; dancer; designer; musician; painter; photographer; vet.

301a. Gemini/Cancer ♊/♋
Social qualities: adaptable; instinctive.
Likely to enjoy: astronomy; cinema; conversation; fishing; gardening; golf; languages; reading; riding; sailing; table-tennis; tennis; theatre; walking; writing.
Career qualities: inquiring; constructive; shrewd.
Suitable careers: actor; architect; chemist; diplomat; doctor; journalist; psychologist; soldier; solicitor; teacher; zoologist.

302a. Gemini/Leo ♊/♌
Social qualities: adaptable; egotistical.
Likely to enjoy: astronomy; fishing; gardening; golf; languages; painting; railways; riding; rowing; sailing; shooting; tennis; theatre; travel; walking.
Career qualities: inquiring; leadership; professional.
Suitable careers: accountant; actor; architect; interviewer; journalist; priest; publisher; solicitor; teacher.

303a. Gemini/Virgo ♊/♍
Social qualities: adaptable; communicative; critical.
Likely to enjoy: electronics; fishing; gardening; golf; painting; reading; shooting; table-tennis; travel; walking.
Career qualities: inquiring; analytical.
Suitable careers: accountant; architect; astronomer; computer operator; craftsman; doctor; engineer; interviewer; journalist; optician; psychologist; reporter; retail trader; secretary; solicitor; teacher; writer.

304a. Gemini/Libra ♊/♎
Social qualities: adaptable; friendly.
Likely to enjoy: bird-watching; climbing; fishing; gardening; languages; sailing; tennis; travel.
Career qualities: inquiring; friendly.
Suitable careers: actor; architect; astronomer; diplomat; soldier; solicitor; writer.

305a. Gemini/Scorpio ♊/♏
Social qualities: adaptable.
Likely to enjoy: bird-watching; fishing; golf; reading; sailing; shooting; tennis; theatre; travel; walking.
Career qualities: inquiring; committed.
Suitable careers: diplomat; doctor; engineer; psychologist; scientist; soldier; solicitor.

306a. Gemini/Sagittarius ♊/♐
Social qualities: communicative; adaptable; reckless.
Likely to enjoy: climbing; railways; reading; travel; walking.
Career qualities: inquiring; ambitious; versatile; cooperative; athletic.
Suitable careers: advertising agent; doctor; engineer; interpreter; publisher; retail trader; soldier; solicitor; teacher.

307a. Gemini/Capricorn ♊/♑
Social qualities: adaptable; responsible.
Likely to enjoy: climbing; electronics; gardening; golf; sailing; walking.
Career qualities: inquiring; methodical; dutiful.
Suitable careers: accountant; diplomat; doctor; engineer; radiologist; soldier; solicitor.

308a. Gemini/Aquarius ♊/♒
Social qualities: adaptable; unconventional.
Likely to enjoy: fishing; gardening; golf; group activities; reading; riding; sailing; shooting; table-tennis; tennis; travel; walking.
Career qualities: inquiring; progressive; original; reformative.
Suitable careers: actor; architect; astronomer; broadcaster; chemist; electrical engineer; psychologist; publisher; writer.

309a. Gemini/Pisces ♊/♓
Social qualities: adaptable; unselfish; excitable.
Likely to enjoy: amateur radio; cinema; fishing; gardening; golf; painting; reading; rowing; sailing; shooting; theatre; travel.
Career qualities: inquiring; altruistic; imaginative.
Suitable careers: actor; chemist; doctor; psychologist; retail trader; soldier; writer.

310a. Cancer/Leo ♋/♌
Social qualities: instinctive; egotistical.
Likely to enjoy: acting; astronomy; athletics; collecting; family; fishing; games; gardening; golf; history; languages; music; photography; riding; rugby; sailing; skiing; squash; tennis; theatre; travel; walking; woodcarving.
Career qualities: shrewd; constructive; leadership; professional.
Suitable careers: actor; airman; architect; art dealer; economist; journalist; philosopher; researcher; solicitor; sportsman; teacher; vet.

311a. Cancer/Virgo ♋/♍
Social qualities: instinctive; critical.
Likely to enjoy: animals; athletics; bowls; bridge; cricket; fishing; games; gardening; golf; history; music; photography; reading; skiing; squash; table-tennis; travel; walking.
Career qualities: shrewd; constructive; analytical.
Suitable careers: actor; airman; architect; critic; doctor; economist; editor; journalist; nurse; overseer; psychologist; scientist; solicitor; surgeon; teacher.

312a. Cancer/Libra ♋/♎
Social qualities: instinctive; friendly.
Likely to enjoy: athletics; bridge; fishing; gardening; intimate relationships; languages; rugby; sailing; tennis; travel.
Career qualities: shrewd; constructive; friendly.
Suitable career: actor; antique dealer; architect; art dealer; caterer; critic; designer; diplomat; nurse; researcher; soldier; solicitor; sportsman.

313a. Cancer/Scorpio ♋/♏
Social qualities: instinctive.
Likely to enjoy: bowls; collecting; cricket; fishing; golf; intimate relationships; reading; sailing; tennis; theatre; travel; walking.
Career qualities: shrewd; constructive; committed.
Suitable careers: archaeologist; astronomer; caterer; critic; designer; doc-

tor; diplomat; pathologist; psychologist; researcher; soldier; solicitor; surgeon; writer.

314a. Cancer/Sagittarius ♋/♐
Social qualities: instinctive; reckless.
Likely to enjoy: bridge; collecting; cooking; embroidery; history; intimate relationships; music; photography; reading; swimming; theatre; travel; woodcarving; walking.
Career qualities: shrewd; constructive; ambitious; versatile; cooperative; athletic.
Suitable careers: doctor; philosopher; priest; soldier; solicitor; sportsman; surgeon; teacher; vet.

315a. Cancer/Capricorn ♋/♑
Social qualities: instinctive; responsible.
Likely to enjoy: animals; bowls; collecting; gardening; genealogy; golf; history; music; reading; sailing; skiing; walking.
Career qualities: shrewd; constructive; dutiful.
Suitable careers: airman; anthropologist; archaeologist; dentist; diplomat; doctor; pathologist; property dealer; researcher; scientist; soldier; solicitor; statistician.

316a. Cancer/Aquarius ♋/♒
Social qualities: instinctive; unconventional.
Likely to enjoy: athletics; bowls; cooking; cricket; embroidery; entertaining; fishing; gardening; golf; group activities; history; hunting; music; photography; polo; reading; riding; rugby; sailing; squash; table-tennis; tennis; travel; walking.
Career qualities: shrewd; constructive; progressive; original; reformative.
Suitable careers: actor; airman; archaeologist; architect; chemist; economist; psychologist; vet.

317a. Cancer/Pisces ♋/♓
Social qualities: instinctive; unselfish; excitable.
Likely to enjoy: animals; cinema; cooking; entertaining; fishing; genealogy; golf; music; photography; polo; reading; sailing; skiing; squash; swimming; theatre; travel.
Career qualities: shrewd; constructive; altruistic; imaginative.
Suitable careers: actor; archaeologist; doctor; fashion designer; priest; psychologist; researcher; sailor; soldier; vet.

318a. Leo/Virgo ♌/♍
Social qualities: critical, egotistical.
Likely to enjoy: athletics; chess; fishing; flying; games; golf; history; music; painting; photography; shooting; skiing; squash; travel; walking.
Career qualities: analytical; leadership; professional.
Suitable careers: accountant; actor; airman; architect; economist; interviewer; journalist; social worker; solicitor; teacher.

319a. Leo/Libra ♌/♎
Social qualities: egotistical; friendly.
Likely to enjoy: athletics; fishing; flying; gardening; intimate relationships; languages; music; rugby; sailing; tennis; travel.
Career qualities: friendly; leadership; professional.
Suitable careers: actor; architect; art dealer; musician; photographer; politician; researcher; social worker; solicitor; sportsman.

320a. Leo/Scorpio ♌/♏
Social qualities: egotistical.
Likely to enjoy: collecting; fishing; football; gambling; golf; intimate relationships; sailing; shooting; tennis; theatre; travel.
Career qualities: leadership; professional; committed.
Suitable careers: researcher; solicitor; sportsman.

321a. Leo/Sagittarius ♌/♐
Social qualities: egotistical; reckless.
Likely to enjoy: acting; camping; chess; collecting; flying; football; gambling; history; intimate relationships; music; photography; railways; theatre; travel; walking; woodcarving.
Career qualities: leadership; professional; cooperative; ambitious; versatile; athletic.
Suitable careers: banker; dancer; musician; philosopher; politician; publisher; solicitor; teacher; vet.

322a. Leo/Capricorn ♌/♑
Social qualities: egotistical; responsible.
Likely to enjoy: collecting; flying; gardening; history; music; sailing; skiing; walking.
Career qualities: leadership; professional; dutiful; methodical.
Suitable careers: accountant; airman; banker; musician; photographer; politician; researcher; solicitor.

323a. Leo/Aquarius ♌/♒
Social qualities: egotistical; unconventional.
Likely to enjoy: acting; athletics; chess; fishing; flying; gambling; gardening; group activities; history; music; photography; riding; rugby; sailing; shooting; singing; squash; tennis; travel; walking.
Career qualities: leadership; professional; progressive; original; reformative.
Suitable careers: actor; airman; architect; dancer; economist; musician; photographer; publisher; social worker; vet.

324a. Leo/Pisces ♌/♓
Social qualities: unselfish; excitable.
Likely to enjoy: camping; chess; collecting; fishing; gardening; golf; history; music; painting; photography; rowing; sailing; shooting; skiing; squash; theatre; travel.
Career qualities: leadership; creative; professional; altruistic; imaginative.
Suitable careers: actor; dancer; musician; photographer; researcher; social worker; vet.

325a. Virgo/Libra ♍/♎
Social qualities: critical; friendly.
Likely to enjoy: athletics, bridge; fishing; flying; gardening; travel.
Career qualities: analytical; friendly.
Suitable careers: actor; architect; astronomer; critic; nurse; singer; social worker; solicitor; writer.

326a. Virgo/Scorpio ♍/♏
Social qualities: critical.
Likely to enjoy: bowls; cricket; cycling; fishing; golf; opera; reading; shooting; travel; walking.
Career qualities: analytical; committed.

Suitable careers: analyst; critic; doctor; engineer; psychologist; singer; solicitor.

327a. Virgo/Sagittarius ♍/♐
Social qualities: critical; reckless; independent.
Likely to enjoy: bridge; chess; DIY; flying; history; keep-fit; motoring; music; opera; painting; photography; reading; travel; walking.
Career qualities: analytical; ambitious; versatile; cooperative.
Suitable career: doctor; engineer; farmer; retail trader; solicitor; surgeon; teacher.

328a. Virgo/Capricorn ♍/♑
Social qualities: critical; responsible; independent.
Likely to enjoy: animals; bowls; crosswords; electronics; flying; gardening; golf; history; music; reading; skiing; walking.
Career qualities: analytical; enduring; dutiful; methodical.
Suitable careers: accountant; airmen; doctor; engineer; farmer; scientist; solicitor; statistician.

329a. Virgo/Aquarius ♍/♒
Social qualities: critical; unconventional.
Likely to enjoy: athletics; bowls; chess; cricket; cycling; DIY; fishing; flying; gardening; golf; group activities; history; motoring; music; photography; reading; shooting; squash; table-tennis; travel; walking.
Career qualities: analytical; progressive; original; reformative.
Suitable careers: actor; airman; architect; astronomer; economist; engineer; farmer; psychologist; social worker; writer.

330a. Virgo/Pisces ♍/♓
Social qualities: critical; unselfish; excitable.
Likely to enjoy: animals; chess; cricket; cycling; fishing; gardening; golf; history; music; opera; painting; photography; reading; shooting; skiing; squash; travel.
Career qualities: analytical; altruistic; imaginative.
Suitable careers: actor; doctor; psychologist; social worker; writer.

331a. Libra/Scorpio ♎/♏
Social qualities: friendly.
Likely to enjoy: bird-watching; fishing; intimate relationships; sailing; tennis; travel.
Career qualities: friendly; committed.
Suitable careers: beautician; caterer; critic; designer; diplomat; physicist; researcher; singer; soldier; solicitor; sportsman.

332a. Libra/Sagittarius ♎/♐
Social qualities: friendly; reckless.
Likely to enjoy: bridge; climbing; flying; intimate relationships; travel.
Career qualities: friendly; ambitious; versatile; cooperative; athletic.
Suitable careers: musician; politician; soldier; solicitor; sportsman.

333a. Libra/Capricorn ♎/♑
Social qualities: friendly; responsible.
Likely to enjoy: climbing; flying; gardening; sailing.
Career qualities: friendly; dutiful; methodical.
Suitable careers: diplomat; musician; photographer; politician; scientist; soldier; solicitor.

334a. Libra/Aquarius ♎/♒
Social qualities: friendly; unconventional.
Likely to enjoy: athletics; fishing; flying; gardening; rugby; sailing; tennis; travel.
Career qualities: friendly; progressive; original; reformative.
Suitable careers: actor; astronomer; musician; photographer; physicist; social worker; teacher; writer.

335a. Libra/Pisces ♎/♓
Social qualities: friendly; unselfish; excitable.
Likely to enjoy: fishing; gardening; poetry; sailing; travel.
Career qualities: friendly; altruistic; imaginative.
Suitable careers: actor; fashion designer; musician; painter; photographer; priest; researcher; social worker; soldier; solicitor; writer.

336a. Scorpio/Sagittarius ♏/♐
Social qualities: reckless.
Likely to enjoy: collecting; football; gambling; intimate relationships; opera; reading; theatre; travel; walking.
Career qualities: committed; ambitious; versatile; cooperative; athletic.
Suitable careers: doctor; explorer; insurer; mechanical engineer; soldier; solicitor; sportsman; surgeon.

337a. Scorpio/Capricorn ♏/♑
Social qualities: responsible.
Likely to enjoy: bowls; collecting; golf; reading; sailing; walking.
Career qualities: committed; dutiful; methodical.
Suitable careers: archaeologist; builder; diplomat; doctor; engineer; masseur; pathologist; researcher; scientist; soldier; solicitor.

338a. Scorpio/Aquarius ♏/♒
Social qualities: unconventional.
Likely to enjoy: archaeology; bowls; cricket; cycling; fishing; gambling; golf; group activities; the Occult; reading; sailing; shooting; tennis; travel; walking.
Career qualities: committed; progressive; original; reformative.
Suitable careers: archaeologist; builder; engineer; explorer; faith healer; occultist; psychologist; scientist.

339a. Scorpio/Pisces ♏/♓
Social qualities: sharing; excitable.
Likely to enjoy: archaeology; collecting; cricket; cycling; drinking; fishing; golf; opera; reading; sailing; shooting; theatre; travel.
Career qualities: committed; altruistic; imaginative.
Suitable careers: archaeologist; designer; doctor; explorer; occultist; policeman; psychologist; researcher; soldier; solicitor.

340a. Sagittarius/Capricorn ♐/♑
Social qualities: independent; responsible.
Likely to enjoy: climbing; collecting; flying; history; music; reading.
Career qualities: ambitious; versatile; dutiful; methodical; cooperative; athletic.
Suitable career: banker; barrister; doctor; engineer; explorer; farmer; musician; politician; soldier.

341a. Sagittarius/Aquarius ♐/♒
Social qualities: unconventional; reckless.
Likely to enjoy: acting; chess; cooking; DIY; embroidery; football; flying;

gambling; golf; history; motoring; music; photography; reading; travel; walking.
Career qualities: ambitious; versatile; progressive; original; reformative; cooperative.
Suitable careers: animal care; dancer; doctor; explorer; farmer; musician; publisher; vet.

342a. Sagittarius/Pisces ♐/♓
Social qualities: unselfish; excitable; reckless.
Likely to enjoy: acting; camping; chess; collecting; cooking; history; music; opera; photography; readings; swimming; theatre; travel.
Career qualities: ambitious; versatile; athletic; altruistic; imaginative; cooperative.
Suitable careers: dancer; doctor; explorer; musician; priest; psychiatrist; retail trader; soldier; vet.

343a. Capricorn/Aquarius ♑/♒
Social qualities: responsible; unconventional.
Likely to enjoy: bowls; flying; gardening; golf; group activities; history; music; preservation; reading; sailing.
Career qualities: dutiful; methodical; progressive; original; reformative.
Suitable careers: airman; archaeologist; builder; engineer; explorer; farmer; masseur; musician; photographer; scientist; statistician.

344a. Capricorn/Pisces ♑/♓
Social qualities: responsible; unselfish; excitable.
Likely to enjoy: animals; collecting; gardening; genealogy; golf; history; music; reading; sailing; skiing.
Career qualities: dutiful; methodical; altruistic; imaginative.
Suitable careers: archaeologist; doctor; explorer; musician; photographer; researcher; soldier.

345a. Aquarius/Pisces ♒/♓
Social qualities: unconventional; unselfish; excitable.
Likely to enjoy: acting; archaeology; chess; cooking; cricket; cycling; entertaining; fishing; gardening; golf; group activities; history; music; photography; polo; reading; sailing; shooting; snooker; squash; travel.
Career qualities: intuitive; progressive; original; reformative; altruistic; imaginative.
Suitable careers: actor; archaeologist; chemist; dancer; explorer; musician; occultist; photographer; psychologist; social worker; vet.; writer.

346a. Aquarius/Sagittarius/Libra ♒/♐/♎
Social qualities: friendly; unconventional; reckless.
Likely to enjoy: acting; athletics; bridge; chess; cooking; DIY; embroidery; fishing; flying; gambling; gardening; group activities; history; motoring; music; photography; reading; rugby; tennis; travel; walking.
Career qualities: reformative; cooperative; athletic; friendly; ambitious; versatile; progressive; original.
Suitable careers: astronomer; builder; dancer; designer; engineer; explorer; farmer; musician; photographer; politician; publisher; social worker; soldier; solicitor; sportsman; vet.

347a. Sagittarius/Gemini/Capricorn ♐/♊/♑
Social qualities: communicative; adaptable; independent; responsible.
Likely to enjoy: climbing; collecting; electronics; flying; gardening; golf; history; music; railways; reading; sailing; theatre; travel; walking.

Career qualities: intellectual; ambitious; versatile; athletic; dutiful; methodical; cooperative.
Suitable career: accountant; advertising agent; banker; diplomat; doctor; engineer; explorer; farmer; interpreter; politician; publisher; radiologist; retail trader; soldier; solicitor; teacher.

348a. Capricorn/Pisces/Gemini ♑/♓/♊
Social qualities: adaptable; responsible; unselfish; excitable.
Likely to enjoy: amateur radio; animals; cinema; collecting; electronics; fishing; gardening; genealogy; golf; history; music; painting; reading; rowing; sailing; shooting; skiing; theatre; travel.
Career qualities: inquiring; dutiful; methodical; altruistic; imaginative.
Suitable careers: actor; archaeologist; diplomat; doctor; engineer; explorer; psychologist; radiologist; researcher; retail trader; social worker; soldier; solicitor; writer;

349a. Capricorn/Aquarius/Pisces ♑/♒/♓
Social qualities: responsible; unconventional; unselfish; excitable.
Likely to enjoy: acting; animals; bowls; chess; collecting; cooking; cricket; cycling; entertaining; fishing; gardening; genealogy; golf; group activities; history; music; photography; polo; preservation; reading; sailing; shooting; skiing; snooker; squash; travel.
Career qualities: dutiful; methodical; intuitive; progressive; original; reformative; altruistic; imaginative.
Suitable careers: airman; archaeologist; builder; dancer; doctor; engineer; explorer; farmer; masseur; musician; occultist; photographer; psychologist; researcher; scientist; social worker; soldier; vet.

350a. Capricorn/Sagittarius/Scorpio ♑/♐/♏
Social qualities: independent; responsible.
Likely to enjoy: bowls; collecting; flying; gambling; golf; history; music; opera; reading; theatre; travel; walking.
Career qualities: committed; ambitious; versatile; dutiful; methodical; cooperative.
Suitable careers: archaeologist; banker; builder; diplomat; doctor; engineer; explorer; farmer; insurer; masseur; pathologist; politician; researcher; scientist; soldier; solicitor; sportsman; surgeon.

351a. Gemini/Aries/Sagittarius ♊/♈/♐
Social qualities: impulsive; energetic; dominant; communicative; adaptable.
Likely to enjoy: astronomy; bird-watching; chess; cinema; collecting; golf; languages; painting; photography; railways; reading; sailing; shooting; table-tennis; travel; walking; writing; woodcarving.
Career qualities: enterprising; competitive; industrious; unconventional; efficient; ambitious; intellectual; versatile; cooperative; athletic.
Suitable careers: actor; advertising agent; architect; doctor; engineer; explorer; interpreter; philosopher; psychiatrist; psychologist; publisher; retail trader; soldier; solicitor; sportsman; surgeon; teacher; writer.

352a. Pisces/Sagittarius/Libra ♓/♐/♎
Social qualities: friendly; unselfish; excitable.
Likely to enjoy: acting; bridge; camping; chess; collecting; cooking; fishing; flying; gardening; history; music; opera; photography; reading; sailing; swimming; theatre; travel.
Career qualities: ambitious; versatile; altruistic; imaginative; cooperative.

Suitable careers: actor; dancer; designer; doctor; explorer; musician; painter; politician; priest; psychiatrist; researcher; retail trader; social worker; soldier; solicitor; sportsman; writer.

353a. Aries/Gemini/Capricorn ♈/♊/♑

Social qualities: responsible; energetic; impulsive; communicative; adaptable.
Likely to enjoy: astronomy; bird-watching; collecting; crosswords; electronics; gardening; golf; languages; music; painting; reading; sailing; shooting; table-tennis; theatre; walking; writing.
Career qualities: enterprising; competitive; industrious; efficient; intellectual; committed; responsible; enduring; dutiful; methodical.
Suitable careers: accountant; actor; architect; builder; diplomat; doctor; engineer; explorer; property dealer; psychologist; radiologist; researcher; soldier; solicitor; writer.

354a. Gemini/Cancer/Leo ♊/♋/♌

Social qualities: receptive; communicative; adaptable; instinctive; egotistical.
Likely to enjoy: astronomy; athletics; collecting; conversation; family; fishing; gardening; golf; history; languages; music; painting; photography; railways; reading; riding; rugby; sailing; shooting; skiing; squash; table-tennis; tennis; travel; walking; writing; woodcarving.
Career qualities: committed; caring; creative; constructive; professional; leadership.
Suitable careers: accountant; actor; airman; architect; art dealer; chemist; diplomat; doctor; economist; interviewer; journalist; philosopher; psychologist; researcher; soldier; solicitor; sportsman; teacher; vet.; zoologist.

355a. Aries/Cancer/Leo ♈/♋/♌

Social qualities: impulsive; energetic; receptive; instinctive; egotistical.
Likely to enjoy: astronomy; athletics; chess; collecting; family; fishing; gardening; golf; history; intimate relationships; languages; music; painting; photography; reading; riding; rugby; sailing; shooting; skiing; squash; table-tennis; tennis; theatre; travel; walking; writing; woodcarving.
Career qualities: professional; competitive; enterprising; unconventional; artistic; caring; shrewd; constructive; leadership.
Suitable careers: actor; airman; architect; art dealer; dentist; designer; doctor; economist; journalist; philosopher; property dealer; psychologist; researcher; soldier; solicitor; sportsman; surgeon; vet.

356a. Gemini/Sagittarius/Libra ♊/♐/♎

Social qualities: communicative; friendly; adaptable; independent; reckless.
Likely to enjoy: bird-watching; bridge; climbing; fishing; flying; gardening; languages; railway; reading; sailing; tennis: theatre; travel; walking.
Career qualities: caring; friendly; intellectual; committed; ambitious; versatile.
Suitable careers: actor; advertising agent; architect; astronomer; diplomat; doctor; engineer; interpreter; musician; politician; publisher; retail trader; soldier; solicitor; sportsman; teacher; writer.

357a. Gemini/Leo/Sagittarius ♊/♌/♐

Social qualities: communicative; adaptable; independent; egotistical.
Likely to enjoy: astronomy; camping; chess; collecting; fishing; flying;

gambling; gardening; golf; history; languages; music; painting; photography; railways; reading; riding; rowing; sailing; shooting; tennis; theatre; travel; walking; woodcarving.
Career qualities: versatile; committed; leadership; professional; ambitious.
Suitable careers: accountant; actor; advertising agent; architect; banker; dancer; doctor; engineer; interpreter; journalist; musician; philosopher; politician; publisher; retail trader; soldier; sportsman; teacher; vet.

358a. Leo/Taurus/Cancer ♌/♉/♋
Social qualities: sensational; instinctive; egotistical.
Likely to enjoy: acting; astronomy; athletics; bridge; collecting; cooking; cricket; embroidery; entertaining; family; fishing; games; gardening; golf; history; hunting; languages; music; photography; polo; reading; riding; rugby; sailing; shooting; skiing; squash; table-tennis; tennis; theatre; travel; walking; woodcarving.
Career qualities: professional; trustworthy; practical; artistic; patient; persevering; caring; shrewd; constructive; leadership.
Suitable careers: actor; airman; anthropologist; antique dealer; architect; art dealer; banker; caterer; dancer; designer; economist; gardener; historian; hotelier; interviewer; journalist; musician; overseer; philosopher; photographer; property dealer; researcher; scientist; sportsman; vet.

359a. Libra/Cancer/Sagittarius ♎/♋/♐
Social qualities: receptive; communicative; independent; reckless.
Likely to enjoy: athletics; bridge; collecting; cooking; embroidery; fishing; flying; gardening; history; intimate relationships; languages; music; photography; reading; rugby; sailing; swimming; tennis; theatre; travel; walking; woodcarving.
Career qualities: versatile; friendly; ambitious; shrewd; athletic.
Suitable careers: actor; antique dealer; architect; caterer; critic; designer; diplomat; doctor; musician; nurse; philosopher; politician; priest; researcher; scientist; soldier; solicitor; sportsman; teacher; vet.

360a. Cancer/Virgo/Leo ♋/♍/♌
Social qualities: receptive; communicative; egotistical.
Likely to enjoy: animals; astronomy; athletics; bowls; bridge; chess; collecting; cricket; family; fishing; flying; games; gardening; golf; history; languages; music; painting; photography; riding; rugby; sailing; shooting; skiing; squash; table-tennis; tennis; theatre; travel; walking; woodcarving.
Career qualities: enduring; analytical; caring; shrewd; constructive; leadership; professional.
Suitable career: accountant; actor; airman; architect; art dealer; critic; doctor; economist; editor; journalist; nurse; overseer; philosopher; psychologist; researcher; scientist; social worker; solicitor; sportsman; surgeon; teacher; vet.

361a. Leo/Virgo/Scorpio ♌/♍/♏
Social qualities: communicative; egotistical; critical; disciplined; independent.
Likely to enjoy: athletics; bowls; chess; cricket; cycling; fishing; flying; games; gardening; golf; history; music; opera; painting; photography; shooting; skiing; squash; tennis; theatre; travel; walking.
Career qualities: artistic; caring; leadership; professional; analytical; enduring.

Suitable careers: actor; airman; analyst; architect; critic; doctor; engineer; psychologist; researcher; singer; social worker; solicitor; sportsman; surgeon.

362a. Leo/Gemini/Libra ♌/♊/♎

Social qualities: communicative; adaptable; egotistical; friendly.
Likely to enjoy: astronomy; athletics; bird-watching; climbing; fishing; flying; gardening; golf; languages; painting; railways; riding; rowing; rugby; sailing; shooting; tennis; theatre; travel; walking.
Career qualities: artistic; intellectual; committed; caring; leadership; professional; principled; friendly.
Suitable careers: accountant; actor; architect; astronomer; diplomat; interviewer; journalist; musician; photographer; politician; researcher; social worker; soldier; sportsman; writer.

363a. Leo/Libra/Virgo ♌/♎/♍

Social qualities: friendly; communicative; egotistical; critical; disciplined; independent.
Likely to enjoy: athletics; bridge; chess; fishing; flying; games; gardening; golf; history; languages; music; painting; photography; rugby; sailing; shooting; skiing; squash; tennis; travel.
Career qualities: artistic; caring; analytical; professional; enduring; friendly; leadership.
Suitable careers: accountant; actor; airman; architect; critic; economist; journalist; musician; nurse; photographer; politician; researcher; singer; social worker; solicitor; sportsman; writer.

364a. Libra/Virgo/Scorpio ♎/♍/♏

Social qualities: communicative; critical; disciplined; friendly; sharing.
Likely to enjoy: athletics; bird-watching; bowls; bridge; cricket; cycling; fishing; flying; gardening; golf; opera; shooting; tennis; travel.
Career qualities: committed; caring; analytical; enduring; friendly.
Suitable careers: actor; analyst; architect; astronomer; beautician; caterer; critic; designer; diplomat; doctor; engineer; nurse; physicist; psychologist; researcher; singer; social worker; soldier; solicitor; sportsman; writer.

365a. Leo/Scorpio/Libra ♌/♏/♎

Social qualities: friendly; sharing; egotistical.
Likely to enjoy: athletics; bird-watching; fishing; flying; gardening; golf; intimate relationships; languages; rugby; sailing; shooting; tennis; theatre; travel; walking.
Career qualities: committed; shrewd; leadership; professional; friendly.
Suitable careers: actor; architect; beautician; caterer; critic; designer; diplomat; musician; photographer; physicist; politician; researcher; singer; social worker; soldier; solicitor; sportsman.

366a. Sagittarius/Libra/Scorpio ♐/♎/♏

Social qualities: communicative; independent; friendly; sharing; reckless.
Likely to enjoy: bird-watching; bridge; fishing; flying; gambling; intimate relationships; opera; reading; tennis; theatre; travel; walking.
Career qualities: committed; caring; friendly; athletic; ambitious; versatile.
Suitable careers: beautician; caterer; critic; designer; diplomat; doctor; engineer; explorer; insurer; musician; physicist; politician; researcher; singer; soldier; solicitor; sportsman.

367a. Sagittarius/Libra/Virgo ♐/♎/♍
Social qualities: communicative; materialistic; independent; friendly; reckless.
Likely to enjoy: athletics; bird-watching; bridge; chess; DIY; fishing; flying; gardening; history; motoring; music; opera; photography; travel.
Career qualities: athletic; shrewd; analytical, ambitious; enduring; friendly; versatile.
Suitable careers: actor; architect; astronomer; critic; doctor; engineer; farmer; musician; nurse; politician; retail trader; singer; social worker; soldier; solicitor; sportsman; teacher; writer.

368a. Sagittarius/Virgo/Scorpio ♐/♍/♏
Social qualities: communicative; critical; sharing.
Likely to enjoy: bowls; bridge; chess; cricket; cycling; DIY; fishing; flying; golf; history; motoring; music; opera; photography; reading; shooting; theatre; travel; walking.
Career qualities: committed; analytical; enduring; ambitious; versatile.
Suitable careers: analyst; critic; doctor; engineer; explorer; farmer; insurer; psychologist; retail trader; singer; soldier; solicitor; sportsman; teacher.

369a. Scorpio/Capricorn/Libra ♏/♑/♎
Social qualities: friendly; responsible; sharing.
Likely to enjoy: bird-watching; bowls; flying; gardening; golf; reading; sailing; tennis; travel.
Career qualities: committed; responsible; enduring; friendly; dutiful; methodical.
Suitable careers: archaeologist; beautician; builder; caterer; critic; designer; diplomat; engineer; explorer; masseur; pathologist; photographer; physicist; politician; researcher; singer; soldier; solicitor; sportsman.

370a. Sagittarius/Pisces/Scorpio ♐/♓/♏
Social qualities: communicative; sharing; excitable; reckless.
Likely to enjoy: acting; archaeology; camping; collecting; cooking; cricket; cycling; fishing; gambling; golf; history; music; opera; photography; reading; shooting; swimming; theatre; travel; walking.
Career qualities: altruistic; committed; imaginative; ambitious; versatile; athletic; intuitive.
Suitable careers: archaeologist; dancer; designer; doctor; engineer; explorer; insurer; musician; occultist; policeman; priest; psychologist; researcher; retail trader; soldier; solicitor; sportsman; vet.

BIRTHDATES